The History of The Decline and Fall of the Roman Empire by Edward Gibbon

Volume IV (of VI)

For decades, perhaps centuries, the standard work of reference on Roman History has been courtesy of Edward Gibbon. In its original printing it was a best-seller and a publishing sensation. History was brought to the masses in vivid detail.

Within its massive six volumes Gibbon put into context the entire sweep of this huge and complex Empire. We visit its far-flung regions, its most charismatic characters as we travel through centuries of its existence and its eternal influence on Western and, most probably, World culture.

Considering the times and the resources at his disposal it quite incredible what Gibbon has been able to put together, to distil, to formulate and precisely plot in this most seducing of histories.

Index of Contents
CHAPTER XXXIX - Gothic Kingdom of Italy
CHAPTER XL - Reign of Justinian
CHAPTER XLI - Conquests of Justinian, Charact Of Balisarius
CHAPTER XLII - State of The Barbaric World
CHAPTER XLIII - Last Victory and Death of Belisarius, Death of Justinian
CHAPTER XLIV - Idea of the Roman Jurisprudence
CHAPTER XLV - State of Italy Under the Lombards
CHAPTER XLVI - Troubles in Persia
CHAPTER XLVII - Ecclesiastical Discord
CHAPTER XLVIII - Succession and Characters of the Greek Emperors
Edward Gibbon – A Short Biography
Edward Gibbon – A Concise Bibliography

CHAPTER XXXIX

GOTHIC KINGDOM OF ITALY

PART I

ZENO AND ANASTASIUS, EMPERORS OF THE EAST—BIRTH, EDUCATION, AND FIRST EXPLOITS OF THEODORIC THE OSTROGOTH—HIS INVASION AND CONQUEST OF ITALY—THE GOTHIC KINGDOM OF ITALY—STATE OF THE WEST—MILITARY AND CIVIL GOVERNMENT—THE SENATOR BOETHIUS—LAST ACTS AND DEATH OF THEODORIC

After the fall of the Roman empire in the West, an interval of fifty years, till the memorable reign of Justinian, is faintly marked by the obscure names and imperfect annals of Zeno, Anastasius, and Justin, who successively ascended to the throne of Constantinople. During the same period, Italy revived and flourished under the government of a Gothic king, who might have deserved a statue among the best and bravest of the ancient Romans.

Theodoric the Ostrogoth, the fourteenth in lineal descent of the royal line of the Amali, [1] was born in the neighborhood of Vienna [2] two years after the death of Attila. [2/1] A recent victory had restored the independence of the Ostrogoths; and the three brothers, Walamir, Theodemir, and Widimir, who ruled that warlike nation with united counsels, had separately pitched their habitations in the fertile though desolate province of Pannonia. The Huns still threatened their revolted subjects, but their hasty attack was repelled by the single forces of Walamir, and the news of his victory reached the distant camp of his brother in the same auspicious moment that the favorite concubine of Theodemir was delivered of a son and heir. In the eighth year of his age, Theodoric was reluctantly yielded by his father to the public interest, as the pledge of an alliance which Leo, emperor of the East, had consented to purchase by an annual subsidy of three hundred pounds of gold. The royal hostage was educated at Constantinople with care and tenderness. His body was formed to all the exercises of war, his mind was expanded by the habits of liberal conversation; he frequented the schools of the most skilful masters; but he disdained or neglected the arts of Greece, and so ignorant did he always remain of the first elements of science, that a rude mark was contrived to represent the signature of the illiterate king of Italy. [3] As soon as he had attained the age of eighteen, he was restored to the wishes of the Ostrogoths, whom the emperor aspired to gain by liberality and confidence. Walamir had fallen in battle; the youngest of the brothers, Widimir, had led away into Italy and Gaul an army of Barbarians, and the whole nation acknowledged for their king the father of Theodoric. His ferocious subjects admired the strength and stature of their young prince; [4] and he soon convinced them that he had not degenerated from the valor of his ancestors. At the head of six thousand volunteers, he secretly left the camp in quest of adventures, descended the Danube as far as Singidunum, or Belgrade, and soon returned to his father with the spoils of a Sarmatian king whom he had vanquished and slain. Such triumphs, however, were productive only of fame, and the invincible Ostrogoths were reduced to extreme distress by the want of clothing and food. They unanimously resolved to desert their Pannonian encampments, and boldly to advance into the warm and wealthy neighborhood of the Byzantine court, which already maintained in pride and luxury so many bands of confederate Goths. After proving, by some acts of hostility, that they could be dangerous, or at least troublesome, enemies, the Ostrogoths sold at a high price their reconciliation and fidelity, accepted a donative of lands and money, and were intrusted with the defence of the Lower Danube, under the command of Theodoric, who succeeded after his father's death to the hereditary throne of the Amali. [5]

[Footnote 1: Jornandes (de Rebus Geticis, c. 13, 14, p. 629, 630, edit. Grot.) has drawn the pedigree of Theodoric from Gapt, one of the Anses or Demigods, who lived about the time of Domitian. Cassiodorus, the first who celebrates the royal race of the Amali, (Viriar. viii. 5, ix. 25, x. 2, xi. 1,) reckons the grandson of Theodoric as the xviith in descent. Peringsciold (the Swedish commentator of Cochloeus, Vit. Theodoric. p. 271, &c., Stockholm, 1699) labors to connect this genealogy with the legends or traditions of his native country. Note: Amala was a name of hereditary sanctity and honor among the Visigoths. It enters into the names of Amalaberga, Amala suintha, (swinther means strength,) Amalafred, Amalarich. In the poem of the Nibelungen written three hundred years later, the Ostrogoths are called the Amilungen. According to Wachter it means, unstained, from the privative a, and malo a stain. It is pure Sanscrit, Amala, immaculatus. Schlegel. Indische Bibliothek, 1. p. 233—M.]

[Footnote 2: More correctly on the banks of the Lake Pelso, (Nieusiedler-see,) near Carnuntum, almost on the same spot where Marcus Antoninus composed his meditations, Jornandes, c. 52, p. 659. Severin. Pannonia Illustrata, p. 22. Cellarius, Geograph. Antiq. (tom. i. p. 350.)]

[Footnote 2/1: The date of Theodoric's birth is not accurately determined. We can hardly err, observes Manso, in placing it between the years 453 and 455, Manso, Geschichte des Ost Gothischen Reichs, p. 14—M.]

[Footnote 3: The four first letters of his name were inscribed on a gold plate, and when it was fixed on the paper, the king drew his pen through the intervals (Anonym. Valesian. ad calcem Amm. Marcellin p. 722.) This authentic fact, with the testimony of Procopius, or at least of the contemporary Goths, (Gothic. 1. i. c. 2, p. 311,) far outweighs the vague praises of Ennodius (Sirmond Opera, tom. i. p. 1596) and Theophanes, (Chronograph. p. 112.) Note: Le Beau and his Commentator, M. St. Martin, support, though with no very satisfactory evidence, the opposite opinion. But Lord Mahon (Life of Belisarius, p. 19) urges the much stronger argument, the Byzantine education of Theodroic—M.]

[Footnote 4: Statura est quae resignet proceritate regnantem, (Ennodius, p. 1614.) The bishop of Pavia (I mean the ecclesiastic who wished to be a bishop) then proceeds to celebrate the complexion, eyes, hands, &c, of his sovereign.]

[Footnote 5: The state of the Ostrogoths, and the first years of Theodoric, are found in Jornandes, (c. 52—56, p. 689—696) and Malchus, (Excerpt. Legat. p. 78—80,) who erroneously styles him the son of Walamir.]

A hero, descended from a race of kings, must have despised the base Isaurian who was invested with the Roman purple, without any endowment of mind or body, without any advantages of royal birth, or superior qualifications. After the failure of the Theodosian life, the choice of Pulcheria and of the senate might be justified in some measure by the characters of Martin and Leo, but the latter of these princes confirmed and dishonored his reign by the perfidious murder of Aspar and his sons, who too rigorously exacted the debt of gratitude and obedience. The inheritance of Leo and of the East was peaceably devolved on his infant grandson, the son of his daughter Ariadne; and her Isaurian husband, the fortunate Trascalisseus, exchanged that barbarous sound for the Grecian appellation of Zeno. After the decease of the elder Leo, he approached with unnatural respect the throne of his son, humbly received, as a gift, the second rank in the empire, and soon excited the public suspicion on the sudden and premature death of his young colleague, whose life could no longer promote the success of his ambition. But the palace of Constantinople was ruled by female influence, and agitated by female passions: and Verina, the widow of Leo, claiming his empire as her own, pronounced a sentence of deposition against the worthless and ungrateful servant on whom she alone had bestowed the sceptre of the East. [6] As soon as she sounded a revolt in the ears of Zeno, he fled with precipitation into the mountains of Isauria, and her brother Basiliscus, already infamous by his African expedition, [7] was unanimously proclaimed by the servile senate. But the reign of the usurper was short and turbulent. Basiliscus presumed to assassinate the lover of his sister; he dared to offend the lover of his wife, the vain and insolent Harmatius, who, in the midst of Asiatic luxury, affected the dress, the demeanor, and the surname of Achilles. [8] By the conspiracy of the malecontents, Zeno was recalled from exile; the armies, the capital, the person, of Basiliscus, were betrayed; and his whole family was condemned to the long agony of cold and hunger by the inhuman conqueror, who wanted courage to encounter or to forgive his enemies. [8/1] The haughty spirit of Verina was still incapable of submission or repose. She provoked the enmity of a favorite general, embraced his cause as soon as he was disgraced, created a new emperor in Syria and Egypt, [8/2] raised an army of seventy thousand men, and persisted to the last moment of her life in a fruitless rebellion, which, according to the fashion of the age, had been predicted by Christian hermits and Pagan magicians. While the East was afflicted by the passions of

Verina, her daughter Ariadne was distinguished by the female virtues of mildness and fidelity; she followed her husband in his exile, and after his restoration, she implored his clemency in favor of her mother. On the decease of Zeno, Ariadne, the daughter, the mother, and the widow of an emperor, gave her hand and the Imperial title to Anastasius, an aged domestic of the palace, who survived his elevation above twenty-seven years, and whose character is attested by the acclamation of the people, "Reign as you have lived!" [9] [9/1]

[Footnote 6: Theophanes (p. 111) inserts a copy of her sacred letters to the provinces. Such female pretensions would have astonished the slaves of the first Caesars.]

[Footnote 7: Vol. iii. p. 504—508.]

[Footnote 8: Suidas, tom. i. p. 332, 333, edit. Kuster.]

[Footnote 8/1: Joannes Lydus accuses Zeno of timidity, or, rather, of cowardice; he purchased an ignominious peace from the enemies of the empire, whom he dared not meet in battle; and employed his whole time at home in confiscations and executions. Lydus, de Magist. iii. 45, p. 230—M.]

[Footnote 8/2: Named Illus—M.]

[Footnote 9: The contemporary histories of Malchus and Candidus are lost; but some extracts or fragments have been saved by Photius, (lxxviii. lxxix. p. 100—102,) Constantine Porphyrogenitus, (Excerpt. Leg. p. 78—97,) and in various articles of the Lexicon of Suidas. The Chronicles of Marcellinus (Imago Historiae) are originals for the reigns of Zeno and Anastasius; and I must acknowledge, almost for the last time, my obligations to the large and accurate collections of Tillemont, (Hist. des Emp. tom. vi. p. 472—652).]

[Footnote 9/1: The Panegyric of Procopius of Gaza, (edited by Villoison in his Anecdota Graeca, and reprinted in the new edition of the Byzantine historians by Niebuhr, in the same vol. with Dexippus and Eunapius, viii. p. 488 516,) was unknown to Gibbon. It is vague and pedantic, and contains few facts. The same criticism will apply to the poetical panegyric of Priscian edited from the Ms. of Bobbio by Ang. Mai. Priscian, the gram marian, Niebuhr argues from this work, must have been born in the African, not in either of the Asiatic Caesareas. Pref. p. xi—M.]

Whatever fear of affection could bestow, was profusely lavished by Zeno on the king of the Ostrogoths; the rank of patrician and consul, the command of the Palatine troops, an equestrian statue, a treasure in gold and silver of many thousand pounds, the name of son, and the promise of a rich and honorable wife. As long as Theodoric condescended to serve, he supported with courage and fidelity the cause of his benefactor; his rapid march contributed to the restoration of Zeno; and in the second revolt, the Walamirs, as they were called, pursued and pressed the Asiatic rebels, till they left an easy victory to the Imperial troops. [10] But the faithful servant was suddenly converted into a formidable enemy, who spread the flames of war from Constantinople to the Adriatic; many flourishing cities were reduced to ashes, and the agriculture of Thrace was almost extirpated by the wanton cruelty of the Goths, who deprived their captive peasants of the right hand that guided the plough. [11] On such occasions, Theodoric sustained the loud and specious reproach of disloyalty, of ingratitude, and of insatiate avarice, which could be only excused by the hard necessity of his situation. He reigned, not as the monarch, but as the minister of a ferocious people, whose spirit was unbroken by slavery, and impatient of real or imaginary insults. Their poverty was incurable; since the most liberal donatives were soon dissipated in wasteful luxury, and the most fertile estates became barren in their hands; they despised, but they envied, the laborious provincials; and when their subsistence had failed, the Ostrogoths embraced the familiar resources of war and rapine. It had been the wish of Theodoric (such at least was his declaration) to lead a peaceful, obscure, obedient life on the confines of Scythia, till the Byzantine court, by splendid and fallacious promises, seduced him to attack a confederate tribe of Goths, who had been engaged in the party of Basiliscus. He marched from his station in Maesia, on the solemn assurance that before he reached Adrianople, he should meet a plentiful convoy of provisions, and a reenforcement of eight thousand horse and thirty thousand foot, while the legions of Asia were encamped at Heraclea to second his operations. These measures were disappointed by mutual jealousy. As he advanced into Thrace, the son of Theodemir found an inhospitable solitude, and his Gothic followers, with a heavy train of horses, of mules, and of wagons, were betrayed by their guides among the rocks and precipices of Mount Sondis, where he was assaulted by the arms and invectives of Theodoric the son of Triarius. From a neighboring height, his artful rival harangued the camp of the Walamirs, and branded their leader with the opprobrious names of child, of madman, of perjured traitor, the enemy of his blood and nation. "Are you ignorant," exclaimed the son of Triarius, "that it is the constant policy of the Romans to destroy the Goths by each other's swords? Are you insensible that the victor in this unnatural contest will be exposed, and justly exposed, to their implacable revenge? Where are those warriors, my kinsmen and thy own, whose widows now lament that their lives were sacrificed to thy rash ambition? Where is the wealth which thy soldiers possessed when they were first allured from their native homes to enlist under thy standard? Each of them was then master of three or four horses; they now follow thee on foot, like slaves, through the deserts of Thrace; those men who were tempted by the hope of measuring gold with a bushel, those brave men who are as free and as noble as thyself." A language so well suited to the temper of the Goths excited clamor and discontent; and the son of Theodemir, apprehensive of being left alone, was compelled to embrace his brethren, and to imitate the example of Roman perfidy. [12] [12/1]

[Footnote 10: In ipsis congressionis tuae foribus cessit invasor, cum profugo per te sceptra redderentur de salute dubitanti. Ennodius then proceeds (p. 1596, 1597, tom. i. Sirmond.) to transport his hero (on a flying dragon?) into Aethiopia, beyond the tropic of Cancer. The evidence of the Valesian Fragment, (p. 717,) Liberatus, (Brev. Eutych. c. 25 p. 118,) and Theophanes, (p. 112,) is more sober and rational.]

[Footnote 11: This cruel practice is specially imputed to the Triarian Goths, less barbarous, as it should seem, than the Walamirs; but the son of Theodemir is charged with the ruin of many Roman cities, (Malchus, Excerpt. Leg. p. 95.)]

[Footnote 12: Jornandes (c. 56, 57, p. 696) displays the services of Theodoric, confesses his rewards, but dissembles his revolt, of which such curious details have been preserved by Malchus, (Excerpt. Legat. p. 78—97.) Marcellinus, a domestic of Justinian, under whose ivth consulship (A.D. 534) he composed his Chronicle, (Scaliger, Thesaurus Temporum, P. ii, p. 34—57,) betrays his prejudice and passion: in Graeciam debacchantem ...Zenonis munificentia pene pacatus...beneficiis nunquam satiatus, &c.]

[Footnote 12/1: Gibbon has omitted much of the complicated intrigues of the Byzantine court with the two Theodorics. The weak emperor attempted to play them one against the other, and was himself in turn insulted, and the empire ravaged, by both. The details of the successive alliance and revolt, of hostility and of union, between the two Gothic chieftains, to dictate terms to the emperor, may be found in Malchus—M.]

In every state of his fortune, the prudence and firmness of Theodoric were equally conspicuous; whether he threatened Constantinople at the head of the confederate Goths, or retreated with a faithful band to the mountains and sea-coast of Epirus. At length the accidental death of the son of Triarius [13] destroyed the balance which the Romans had been so anxious to preserve, the whole nation acknowledged the supremacy of the Amali, and the Byzantine court subscribed an ignominious and oppressive treaty. [14] The senate had already declared, that it was necessary to choose a party among the Goths, since the public was unequal to the support of their united forces; a subsidy of two thousand pounds of gold, with the ample pay of thirteen thousand men, were required for the least considerable of their armies; [15] and the Isaurians, who guarded not the empire but the emperor, enjoyed, besides the privilege of rapine, an annual pension of five thousand pounds. The sagacious mind of Theodoric soon perceived that he was odious to the Romans, and suspected by the Barbarians: he understood the popular murmur, that his subjects were exposed in their frozen huts to intolerable hardships, while their king was dissolved in the luxury of Greece, and he prevented the painful alternative of encountering the Goths, as the champion, or of leading them to the field, as the enemy, of Zeno. Embracing an enterprise worthy of his courage and ambition, Theodoric addressed the emperor in the following words: "Although your servant is maintained in affluence by your liberality, graciously listen to the wishes of my heart! Italy, the inheritance of your predecessors, and Rome itself, the head and mistress of the world, now fluctuate under the violence and oppression of Odoacer the mercenary. Direct me, with my national troops, to march against the tyrant. If I fall, you will be relieved from an expensive and troublesome friend: if, with the divine permission, I succeed, I shall govern in your name, and to your glory, the Roman senate, and the part of the republic delivered from slavery by my victorious arms." The proposal of Theodoric was accepted, and perhaps had been suggested, by the Byzantine court. But the forms of the commission, or grant, appear to have been expressed with a prudent ambiguity, which might be explained by the event; and it was left doubtful, whether the conqueror of Italy should reign as the lieutenant, the vassal, or the ally, of the emperor of the East. [16

[Footnote 13: As he was riding in his own camp, an unruly horse threw him against the point of a spear which hung before a tent, or was fixed on a wagon, (Marcellin. in Chron. Evagrius, l. iii. c. 25.)]

[Footnote 14: See Malchus (p. 91) and Evagrius, (l. iii. c. 35.)]

[Footnote 15: Malchus, p. 85. In a single action, which was decided by the skill and discipline of Sabinian, Theodoric could lose 5000 men.]

[Footnote 16: Jornandes (c. 57, p. 696, 697) has abridged the great history of Cassiodorus. See, compare, and reconcile Procopius, (Gothic. l. i. c. i.,) the Valesian Fragment, (p. 718,) Theophanes, (p. 113,) and Marcellinus, (in Chron.)]

The reputation both of the leader and of the war diffused a universal ardor; the Walamirs were multiplied by the Gothic swarms already engaged in the service, or seated in the provinces, of the empire; and each bold Barbarian, who had heard of the wealth and beauty of Italy, was impatient to seek, through the most perilous adventures, the possession of such enchanting objects. The march of Theodoric must be considered as the emigration of an entire people; the wives and children of the Goths, their aged parents, and most precious effects, were carefully transported; and some idea may be formed of the heavy baggage that now followed the camp, by the loss of two thousand wagons, which had been sustained in a single action in the war of Epirus. For their subsistence, the Goths depended on the magazines of corn which was ground in portable mills by the hands of their women; on the milk and flesh of their flocks and herds; on the casual produce of the chase, and upon the contributions which they might impose on all who should presume to dispute the passage, or to refuse their friendly assistance. Notwithstanding these precautions, they were exposed to the danger, and almost to the distress, of famine, in a march of seven hundred miles, which had been undertaken in the depth of a rigorous winter. Since the fall of the Roman power, Dacia and Pannonia no longer exhibited the rich prospect of populous cities, well-cultivated fields, and convenient highways: the reign of barbarism and desolation was restored, and the tribes of Bulgarians, Gepidae, and Sarmatians, who had occupied the vacant province, were prompted by their native fierceness, or the solicitations of Odoacer, to resist the progress of his enemy. In many obscure though bloody battles, Theodoric fought and vanquished; till at length, surmounting every obstacle by skilful conduct and persevering courage, he descended from the Julian Alps, and displayed his invincible banners on the confines of Italy. [17]

[Footnote 17: Theodoric's march is supplied and illustrated by Ennodius, (p. 1598—1602,) when the bombast of the oration is translated into the language of common sense.]

Odoacer, a rival not unworthy of his arms, had already occupied the advantageous and well-known post of the River Sontius, near the ruins of Aquileia, at the head of a powerful host, whose independent kings [18] or leaders disdained the duties of subordination and the prudence of delays. No sooner had Theodoric gained a short repose and refreshment to his wearied cavalry, than he boldly attacked the fortifications of the enemy; the Ostrogoths showed more ardor to acquire, than the mercenaries to defend, the lands of Italy; and the reward of the first victory was the possession of the Venetian province as far as the walls of Verona. In the neighborhood of that city, on the steep banks of the rapid Adige, he was opposed by a new army, reenforced in its numbers, and not impaired in its courage: the contest was more obstinate, but the event was still more decisive; Odoacer fled to Ravenna, Theodoric advanced to Milan, and the vanquished troops saluted their conqueror with loud acclamations of respect and fidelity. But their want either of constancy or of faith soon exposed him to the most imminent danger; his vanguard, with several Gothic counts, which had been rashly intrusted to a deserter, was betrayed and destroyed near Faenza by his double treachery; Odoacer again appeared master of the field, and the invader, strongly intrenched in his camp of Pavia, was reduced to solicit the aid of a kindred nation, the Visigoths of Gaul. In the course of this History, the most voracious appetite for war will be abundantly satiated; nor can I much lament that our dark and imperfect materials do not afford a more ample narrative of the distress of Italy, and of the fierce conflict, which was finally decided by the abilities, experience, and valor of the Gothic king. Immediately before the battle of Verona, he visited the tent of his mother [19] and sister, and requested, that on a day, the most illustrious festival of his life, they would adorn him with the rich garments which they had worked with their own hands. "Our glory," said he, "is mutual and inseparable. You are known to the world as the mother of Theodoric; and it becomes me to prove, that I am the genuine offspring of those heroes from whom I claim my descent." The wife or concubine of Theodemir was inspired with the spirit of the German matrons, who esteemed their sons' honor far above their safety; and it is reported, that in a desperate action, when Theodoric himself was hurried along by the torrent of a flying crowd, she boldly met them at the entrance of the camp, and, by her generous reproaches, drove them back on the swords of the enemy. [20]

[Footnote 18: Tot reges, &c., (Ennodius, p. 1602.) We must recollect how much the royal title was multiplied and degraded, and that the mercenaries of Italy were the fragments of many tribes and nations.]

[Footnote 19: See Ennodius, p. 1603, 1604. Since the orator, in the king's presence, could mention and praise his mother, we may conclude that the magnanimity of Theodoric was not hurt by the vulgar reproaches of concubine and bastard. Note: Gibbon here assumes that the mother of Theodoric was the concubine of Theodemir, which he leaves doubtful in the text—M.]

[Footnote 20: This anecdote is related on the modern but respectable authority of Sigonius, (Op. tom. i. p. 580. De Occident. Impl. l. xv.:) his words are curious: "Would you return?" &c. She presented and almost displayed the original recess. Note: The authority of Sigonius would scarcely have weighed with Gibboa except for an indecent anecdote. I have a recollection of a similar story in some of the Italian wars—M.]

From the Alps to the extremity of Calabria, Theodoric reigned by the right of conquest; the Vandal ambassadors surrendered the Island of Sicily, as a lawful appendage of his kingdom; and he was accepted as the deliverer of Rome by the senate and people, who had shut their gates against the flying usurper. [21] Ravenna alone, secure in the fortifications of art and nature, still sustained a siege of almost three years; and the daring sallies of Odoacer carried slaughter and dismay into the Gothic camp. At length, destitute of provisions and hopeless of relief, that unfortunate monarch yielded to the groans of his subjects and the clamors of his soldiers. A treaty of peace was negotiated by the bishop of Ravenna; the Ostrogoths were admitted into the city, and the hostile kings consented, under the sanction of an oath, to rule with equal and undivided authority the provinces of Italy. The event of such an agreement may be easily foreseen. After some days had been devoted to the semblance of joy and friendship, Odoacer, in the midst of a solemn banquet, was stabbed by the hand, or at least by the command, of his rival. Secret and effectual orders had been previously despatched; the faithless and rapacious mercenaries, at the same moment, and without resistance, were universally massacred; and the royalty of Theodoric was proclaimed by the Goths, with the tardy, reluctant, ambiguous consent of the emperor of the East. The design of a conspiracy was imputed, according to the usual forms, to the prostrate tyrant; but his innocence, and the guilt of his conqueror, [22] are sufficiently proved by the advantageous treaty which force would not sincerely have granted, nor weakness have rashly infringed. The jealousy of power, and the mischiefs of discord, may suggest a more decent apology, and a sentence less rigorous may be pronounced against a crime which was necessary to introduce into Italy a generation of public felicity. The living author of this felicity was audaciously praised in his own presence by sacred and profane orators; [23] but history (in his time she was mute and inglorious) has not left any just representation of the events which displayed, or of the defects which clouded, the virtues of Theodoric. [24] One record of his fame, the volume of public epistles composed by Cassiodorus in the royal name, is still extant, and has obtained more implicit credit than it seems to deserve. [25] They exhibit the forms, rather than the substance, of his government; and we should vainly search for the pure and spontaneous sentiments of the Barbarian amidst the declamation and learning of a sophist, the wishes of a Roman senator, the precedents of office, and the vague professions, which, in every court, and on every occasion, compose the language of discreet ministers. The reputation of Theodoric may repose with more confidence on the visible peace and prosperity of a reign of thirty-three years; the unanimous esteem of his own times, and the memory of his wisdom and courage, his justice and humanity, which was deeply impressed on the minds of the Goths and Italians.

[Footnote 21: Hist. Miscell. l. xv., a Roman history from Janus to the ixth century, an Epitome of Eutropius, Paulus Diaconus, and Theophanes which Muratori has published from a Ms. in the Ambrosian library, (Script. Rerum Italicarum, tom. i. p. 100.)]

[Footnote 22: Procopius (Gothic. l. i. c. i.) approves himself an impartial sceptic. Cassiodorus (in Chron.) and Ennodius (p. 1604) are loyal and credulous, and the testimony of the Valesian Fragment (p. 718) may justify their belief. Marcellinus spits the venom of a Greek subject—*perjuriis illectus, interfectusque est,* (in Chron.)]

[Footnote 23: The sonorous and servile oration of Ennodius was pronounced at Milan or Ravenna in the years 507 or 508, (Sirmond, tom. i. p. 615.) Two or three years afterwards, the orator was rewarded with the bishopric of Pavia, which he held till his death in the year 521. (Dupin, Bibliot. Eccles. tom. v. p. 11-14. See Saxii Onomasticon, tom. ii. p. 12.)]

[Footnote 24: Our best materials are occasional hints from Procopius and the Valesian Fragment, which was discovered by Sirmond, and is published at the end of Ammianus Marcellinus. The author's name is unknown, and his style is barbarous; but in his various facts he exhibits the knowledge, without the passions, of a contemporary. The president Montesquieu had formed the plan of a history of Theodoric, which at a distance might appear a rich and interesting subject.]

[Footnote 25: The best edition of the Variarum Libri xii. is that of Joh. Garretius, (Rotomagi, 1679, in Opp. Cassiodor. 2 vols. in fol.;) but they deserved and required such an editor as the Marquis Scipio Maffei, who thought of publishing them at Verona. The Barbara Eleganza (as it is ingeniously named by Tiraboschi) is never simple, and seldom perspicuous]

The partition of the lands of Italy, of which Theodoric assigned the third part to his soldiers, is honorably arraigned as the sole injustice of his life. [25/1] And even this act may be fairly justified by the example of Odoacer, the rights of conquest, the true interest of the Italians, and the sacred duty of subsisting a whole people, who, on the faith of his promises, had transported themselves into a distant land. [26] Under the reign of Theodoric, and in the happy climate of Italy, the Goths soon multiplied to a formidable host of two hundred thousand men, [27] and the whole amount of their families may be computed by the ordinary addition of women and children. Their invasion of property, a part of which must have been already vacant, was disguised by the generous but improper name of hospitality; these unwelcome guests were irregularly dispersed over the face of Italy, and the lot of each Barbarian was adequate to his birth and office, the number of his followers, and the rustic wealth which he possessed in slaves and cattle. The distinction of noble and plebeian were acknowledged; [28] but the lands of every freeman were exempt from taxes, [28/1] and he enjoyed the inestimable privilege of being subject only to the laws of his country. [29] Fashion, and even convenience, soon persuaded the conquerors to assume the more elegant dress of the natives, but they still persisted in the use of their mother-tongue; and their contempt for the Latin schools was applauded by Theodoric himself, who gratified their prejudices, or his own, by declaring, that the child who had trembled at a rod, would never dare to look upon a sword. [30] Distress might sometimes provoke the indigent Roman to assume the ferocious manners which were insensibly relinquished by the rich and luxurious Barbarian; [31] but these mutual conversions were not encouraged by the policy of a monarch who perpetuated the separation of the Italians and Goths; reserving the former for the arts of peace, and the latter for the service of war. To accomplish this design, he studied to protect his industrious subjects, and to moderate the violence, without enervating the valor, of his soldiers, who were maintained for the public defence. They held their lands and benefices as a military stipend: at the sound of the trumpet, they were prepared to march under the conduct of their provincial officers; and the whole extent of Italy was distributed into the several quarters of a well-regulated camp. The service of the palace and of the frontiers was performed by choice or by rotation; and each extraordinary fatigue was recompensed by an increase of pay and occasional donatives. Theodoric had convinced his brave companions, that empire must be acquired and defended by the same arts. After his example, they strove to excel in the use, not only of the lance and sword, the instruments of their victories, but of the missile weapons, which they were too much inclined to neglect; and the lively image of war was displayed in the daily exercise and annual reviews of the Gothic cavalry. A firm though gentle discipline imposed the habits of modesty, obedience, and temperance; and the Goths were instructed to spare the people, to reverence the laws, to understand the duties of civil society, and to disclaim the barbarous license of judicial combat and private revenge. [32]

[Footnote 25/1: Compare Gibbon, ch. xxxvi. vol. iii. p. 459, &c—Manso observes that this division was conducted not in a violent and irregular, but in a legal and orderly, manner. The Barbarian, who could not show a title of grant from the officers of Theodoric appointed for the purpose, or a prescriptive right of thirty years, in case he had obtained the property before the Ostrogothic conquest, was ejected from the estate. He conceives that estates too small to bear division paid a third of their produce—Geschichte des Os Gothischen Reiches, p. 82—M.]

[Footnote 26: Procopius, Gothic, l. i. c. i. Variarum, ii. Maffei (Verona Illustrata, P. i. p. 228) exaggerates the injustice of the Goths, whom he hated as an Italian noble. The plebeian Muratori crouches under their oppression.]

[Footnote 27: Procopius, Goth. l. iii. c. 421. Ennodius describes (p. 1612, 1613) the military arts and increasing numbers of the Goths.]

[Footnote 28: When Theodoric gave his sister to the king of the Vandals she sailed for Africa with a guard of 1000 noble Goths, each of whom was attended by five armed followers, (Procop. Vandal. l. i. c. 8.) The Gothic nobility must have been as numerous as brave.]

[Footnote 28/1: Manso (p. 100) quotes two passages from Cassiodorus to show that the Goths were not exempt from the fiscal claims—Cassiodor, i. 19, iv. 14—M.]

[Footnote 29: See the acknowledgment of Gothic liberty, (Var. v. 30.)]

[Footnote 30: Procopius, Goth. l. i. c. 2. The Roman boys learnt the language (Var. viii. 21) of the Goths. Their general ignorance is not destroyed by the exceptions of Amalasuntha, a female, who might study without shame, or of Theodatus, whose learning provoked the indignation and contempt of his countrymen.]

[Footnote 31: A saying of Theodoric was founded on experience: "Romanus miser imitatur Gothum; ut utilis (dives) Gothus imitatur Romanum." (See the Fragment and Notes of Valesius, p. 719.)]

[Footnote 32: The view of the military establishment of the Goths in Italy is collected from the Epistles of Cassiodorus (Var. i. 24, 40; iii. 3, 24, 48; iv. 13, 14; v. 26, 27; viii. 3, 4, 25.) They are illustrated by the learned Mascou, (Hist. of the Germans, l. xi. 40—44, Annotation xiv.) Note: Compare Manso, Geschichte des Ost Gothischen Reiches, p. 114—M.]

PART II

Among the Barbarians of the West, the victory of Theodoric had spread a general alarm. But as soon as it appeared that he was satisfied with conquest and desirous of peace, terror was changed into respect, and they submitted to a powerful mediation, which was uniformly employed for the best purposes of reconciling their quarrels and civilizing their manners. [33] The ambassadors who resorted to Ravenna from the most distant countries of Europe, admired his wisdom, magnificence, [34] and courtesy; and if he sometimes accepted either slaves or arms, white horses or strange animals, the gift of a sun-dial, a water-clock, or a musician, admonished even the princes of Gaul of the superior art and industry of his Italian subjects. His domestic alliances, [35] a wife, two daughters, a sister, and a niece, united the family of Theodoric with the kings of the Franks, the Burgundians, the Visigoths, the Vandals, and the Thuringians, and contributed to maintain the harmony, or at least the balance, of the great republic of the West. [36] It is difficult in the dark forests of Germany and Poland to pursue the emigrations of the Heruli, a fierce people who disdained the use of armor, and who condemned their widows and aged parents not to survive the loss of their husbands, or the decay of their strength. [37] The king of these savage warriors solicited the friendship of Theodoric, and was elevated to the rank of his son, according to the barbaric rites of a military adoption. [38] From the shores of the Baltic, the Aestians or Livonians laid their offerings of native amber [39] at the feet of a prince, whose fame had excited them to undertake an unknown and dangerous journey of fifteen hundred miles. With the country [40] from whence the Gothic nation derived their origin, he maintained a frequent and friendly correspondence: the Italians were clothed in the rich sables [41] of Sweden; and one of its sovereigns, after a voluntary or reluctant abdication, found a hospitable retreat in the palace of Ravenna. He had reigned over one of the thirteen populous tribes who cultivated a small portion of the great island or peninsula of Scandinavia, to which the vague appellation of Thule has been sometimes applied. That northern region was peopled, or had been explored, as high as the sixty-eighth degree of latitude, where the natives of the polar circle enjoy and lose the presence of the sun at each summer and winter solstice during an equal period of forty days. [42] The long night of his absence or death was the mournful season of distress and anxiety, till the messengers, who had been sent to the mountain tops, descried the first rays of returning light, and proclaimed to the plain below the festival of his resurrection. [43]

[Footnote 33: See the clearness and vigor of his negotiations in Ennodius, (p. 1607,) and Cassiodorus, (Var. iii. 1, 2, 3, 4; iv. 13; v. 43, 44,) who gives the different styles of friendship, counsel expostulation, &c.]

[Footnote 34: Even of his table (Var. vi. 9) and palace, (vii. 5.) The admiration of strangers is represented as the most rational motive to justify these vain expenses, and to stimulate the diligence of the officers to whom these provinces were intrusted.]

[Footnote 35: See the public and private alliances of the Gothic monarch, with the Burgundians, (Var. i. 45, 46,) with the Franks, (ii. 40,) with the Thuringians, (iv. 1,) and with the Vandals, (v. 1;) each of these epistles affords some curious knowledge of the policy and manners of the Barbarians.]

[Footnote 36: His political system may be observed in Cassiodorus, (Var. iv. l ix. l,) Jornandes, (c. 58, p. 698, 699,) and the Valesian Fragment, (p. 720, 721.) Peace, honorable peace, was the constant aim of Theodoric.]

[Footnote 37: The curious reader may contemplate the Heruli of Procopius, (Goth. l. ii. c. 14,) and the patient reader may plunge into the dark and minute researches of M. de Buat, (Hist. des Peuples Anciens, tom. ix. p. 348—396. Note: Compare Manso, Ost Gothische Reich. Beylage, vi. Malte-Brun brings them from Scandinavia: their names, the only remains of their language, are Gothic. "They fought almost naked, like the Icelandic Berserkirs their bravery was like madness: few in number, they were mostly of royal blood. What ferocity, what unrestrained license, sullied their victories! The Goth respects the church, the priests, the senate; the Heruli mangle all in a general massacre: there is no pity for age, no refuge for chastity. Among themselves there is the same ferocity: the sick and the aged are put to death. at their own request, during a solemn festival; the widow ends her days by hanging herself upon the tree which shadows her husband's tomb. All these circumstances, so striking to a mind familiar with Scandinavian history, lead us to discover among the Heruli not so much a nation as a confederacy of princes and nobles, bound by an oath to live and die together with their arms in their hands. Their name, sometimes written Heruli or Eruli. sometimes Aeruli, signified, according to an ancient author, (Isid. Hispal. in gloss. p. 24, ad calc. Lex. Philolog. Martini, II,) nobles, and appears to correspond better with the Scandinavian word iarl or earl, than with any of those numerous derivations proposed by etymologists." Malte-Brun, vol. i. p. 400, (edit. 1831.) Of all the Barbarians who threw themselves on the ruins of the Roman empire, it is most difficult to trace the origin of the Heruli. They seem never to have been very powerful as a nation, and branches of them are found in countries very remote from each other. In my opinion they belong to the Gothic race, and have a close affinity with the Scyrri or Hirri. They were, possibly, a division of that nation. They are often mingled and confounded with the Alani. Though brave and formidable. they were never numerous. nor did they found any state—St. Martin, vol. vi. p. 375—M. Schafarck considers them descendants of the Hirri. of which Heruli is a diminutive,—Slawische Alter thinner—M. 1845.]

[Footnote 38: Variarum, iv. 2. The spirit and forms of this martial institution are noticed by Cassiodorus; but he seems to have only translated the sentiments of the Gothic king into the language of Roman eloquence.]

[Footnote 39: Cassiodorus, who quotes Tacitus to the Aestians, the unlettered savages of the Baltic, (Var. v. 2,) describes the amber for which their shores have ever been famous, as the gum of a tree, hardened by the sun, and purified and wafted by the waves. When that singular substance is analyzed by the chemists, it yields a vegetable oil and a mineral acid.]

[Footnote 40: Scanzia, or Thule, is described by Jornandes (c. 3, p. 610—613) and Procopius, (Goth. l. ii. c. 15.) Neither the Goth nor the Greek had visited the country: both had conversed with the natives in their exile at Ravenna or Constantinople.]

[Footnote 41: Sapherinas pelles. In the time of Jornandes they inhabited Suethans, the proper Sweden; but that beautiful race of animals has gradually been driven into the eastern parts of Siberia. See Buffon, (Hist. Nat. tom. xiii. p. 309—313, quarto edition;) Pennant, (System of Quadrupeds, vol. i. p. 322—328;) Gmelin, (Hist. Gen des. Voyages, tom. xviii. p. 257, 258;) and Levesque, (Hist. de Russie, tom. v. p. 165, 166, 514, 515.)]

[Footnote 42: In the system or romance of Mr. Bailly, (Lettres sur les Sciences et sur l'Atlantide, tom. i. p. 249—256, tom. ii. p. 114—139,) the phoenix of the Edda, and the annual death and revival of Adonis and Osiris, are the allegorical symbols of the absence and return of the sun in the Arctic regions. This ingenious writer is a worthy disciple of the great Buffon; nor is it easy for the coldest reason to withstand the magic of their philosophy.]

[Footnote 43: Says Procopius. At present a rude Manicheism (generous enough) prevails among the Samoyedes in Greenland and in Lapland, (Hist. des Voyages, tom. xviii. p. 508, 509, tom. xix. p. 105, 106, 527, 528;) yet, according to Orotius Samojutae coelum atque astra adorant, numina haud aliis iniquiora, (de Rebus Belgicis, l. iv. p. 338, folio edition) a sentence which Tacitus would not have disowned.]

The life of Theodoric represents the rare and meritorious example of a Barbarian, who sheathed his sword in the pride of victory and the vigor of his age. A reign of three and thirty years was consecrated to the duties of civil government, and the hostilities, in which he was sometimes involved, were speedily terminated by the conduct of his lieutenants, the discipline of his troops, the arms of his allies, and even by the terror of his name. He reduced, under a strong and regular government, the unprofitable countries of Rhaetia, Noricum, Dalmatia, and Pannonia, from the source of the Danube and the territory of the Bavarians, [44] to the petty kingdom erected by the Gepidae on the ruins of Sirmium. His prudence could not safely intrust the bulwark of Italy to such feeble and turbulent neighbors; and his justice might claim the lands which they oppressed, either as a part of his kingdom, or as the inheritance of his father. The greatness of a servant, who was named perfidious because he was successful, awakened the jealousy of the emperor Anastasius; and a war was kindled on the Dacian frontier, by the protection which the Gothic king, in the vicissitude of human affairs, had granted to one of the descendants of Attila. Sabinian, a general illustrious by his own and father's merit, advanced at the head of ten thousand Romans; and the provisions and arms, which filled a long train of wagons, were distributed to the fiercest of the Bulgarian tribes. But in the fields of Margus, the eastern powers were defeated by the inferior forces of the Goths and Huns; the flower and even the hope of the Roman armies was irretrievably destroyed; and such was the temperance with which Theodoric had inspired his victorious troops, that, as their leader had not given the signal of pillage, the rich spoils of the enemy lay untouched at their feet. [45] Exasperated by this disgrace, the Byzantine court despatched two hundred ships and eight thousand men to plunder the sea-coast of Calabria and Apulia: they assaulted the ancient city of Tarentum, interrupted the trade and agriculture of a happy country, and sailed back to the Hellespont, proud of their piratical victory over a people whom they still presumed to consider as their Roman brethren. [46] Their retreat was possibly hastened by the activity of Theodoric; Italy was covered by a fleet of a thousand light vessels, [47] which he constructed with incredible despatch; and his firm moderation was soon rewarded by a solid and honorable peace. He maintained, with a powerful hand, the balance of the West, till it was at length overthrown by the ambition of Clovis; and although unable to assist his rash and unfortunate kinsman, the king of the Visigoths, he saved the remains of his family and people, and checked the Franks in the midst of their victorious career. I am not desirous to prolong or repeat [48] this narrative of military events, the least interesting of the reign of Theodoric; and shall be content to add, that the Alemanni were protected, [49] that an inroad of the Burgundians was severely chastised, and that the conquest of Arles and Marseilles opened a free communication with the Visigoths, who revered him as their national protector, and as the guardian of his grandchild, the infant son of Alaric. Under this respectable character, the king of Italy restored the praetorian praefecture of the Gauls, reformed some abuses in the civil government of Spain, and accepted the annual tribute and apparent submission of its military governor, who wisely refused to trust his person in the palace of Ravenna. [50] The Gothic sovereignty was established from Sicily to the Danube, from Sirmium or Belgrade to the Atlantic Ocean; and the Greeks themselves have acknowledged that Theodoric reigned over the fairest portion of the Western empire. [51]

[Footnote 44: See the Hist. des Peuples Anciens, &c., tom. ix. p. 255—273, 396—501. The count de Buat was French minister at the court of Bavaria: a liberal curiosity prompted his inquiries into the antiquities of the country, and that curiosity was the germ of twelve respectable volumes.]

[Footnote 45: See the Gothic transactions on the Danube and the Illyricum, in Jornandes, (c. 58, p. 699;) Ennodius, (p. 1607-1610;) Marcellmus (in Chron. p. 44, 47, 48;) and Cassiodorus, in (in Chron and Var. iii. 29 50, iv. 13, vii. 4 24, viii. 9, 10, 11, 21, ix. 8, 9.)]

[Footnote 46: I cannot forbear transcribing the liberal and classic style of Count Marcellinus: Romanus comes domesticorum, et Rusticus comes scholariorum cum centum armatis navibus, totidemque dromonibus, octo millia militum armatorum secum ferentibus, ad devastanda Italiae littora processerunt, ut usque ad Tarentum antiquissimam civitatem aggressi sunt; remensoque mari in honestam victoriam quam piratico ausu Romani ex Romanis rapuerunt, Anastasio Caesari reportarunt, (in Chron. p. 48.) See Variar. i. 16, ii. 38.]

[Footnote 47: See the royal orders and instructions, (Var. iv. 15, v. 16—20.) These armed boats should be still smaller than the thousand vessels of Agamemnon at the siege of Troy. (Manso, p. 121.)]

[Footnote 48: Vol. iii. p. 581—585.]

[Footnote 49: Ennodius (p. 1610) and Cassiodorus, in the royal name, (Var. ii 41,) record his salutary protection of the Alemanni.]

[Footnote 50: The Gothic transactions in Gaul and Spain are represented with some perplexity in Cassiodorus, (Var. iii. 32, 38, 41, 43, 44, v. 39.) Jornandes, (c. 58, p. 698, 699,) and Procopius, (Goth. l. i. c. 12.) I will neither hear nor reconcile the long and contradictory arguments of the Abbe Dubos and the Count de Buat, about the wars of Burgundy.]

[Footnote 51: Theophanes, p. 113.]

The union of the Goths and Romans might have fixed for ages the transient happiness of Italy; and the first of nations, a new people of free subjects and enlightened soldiers, might have gradually arisen from the mutual emulation of their respective virtues. But the sublime merit of guiding or seconding such a revolution was not reserved for the reign of Theodoric: he wanted either the genius or the opportunities of a legislator; [52] and while he indulged the Goths in the enjoyment of rude liberty, he servilely copied the institutions, and even the abuses, of the political system which had been framed by Constantine and his successors. From a tender regard to the expiring prejudices of Rome, the Barbarian declined the name, the purple, and the diadem, of the emperors; but he assumed, under the hereditary title of king, the whole substance and plenitude of Imperial prerogative. [53] His addresses to the eastern throne were respectful and ambiguous: he celebrated, in pompous style, the harmony of the two republics, applauded his own government as the perfect similitude of a sole and undivided empire, and claimed above the kings of the earth the same preeminence which he modestly allowed to the person or rank of Anastasius. The alliance of the East and West was annually declared by the unanimous choice of two consuls; but it should seem that the Italian candidate who was named by Theodoric accepted a formal confirmation from the sovereign of Constantinople. [54] The Gothic palace of Ravenna reflected the image of the court of Theodosius or Valentinian. The Praetorian praefect, the praefect of Rome, the quaestor, the master of the offices, with the public and patrimonial treasurers, [54/1] whose functions are painted in gaudy colors by the rhetoric of Cassiodorus, still continued to act as the ministers of state. And the subordinate care of justice and the revenue was delegated to seven consulars, three correctors, and five presidents, who governed the fifteen regions of Italy according to the principles, and even the forms, of Roman jurisprudence; [55] The violence of the conquerors was abated or eluded by the slow artifice of judicial proceedings; the civil administration, with its honors and emoluments, was confined to the Italians; and the people still preserved their dress and language, their laws and customs, their personal freedom, and two thirds of their landed property. [55/1] It had been the object of Augustus to conceal the introduction of monarchy; it was the policy of Theodoric to disguise the reign of a Barbarian. [56] If his subjects were sometimes awakened from this pleasing vision of a Roman government, they derived more substantial comfort from the character of a Gothic prince, who had penetration to discern, and firmness to pursue, his own and the public interest. Theodoric loved the virtues which he possessed, and the talents of which he was destitute. Liberius was promoted to the office of Praetorian praefect for his unshaken fidelity to the unfortunate cause of Odoacer. The ministers of Theodoric, Cassiodorus, [57] and Boethius, have reflected on his reign the lustre of their genius and learning. More prudent or more fortunate than his colleague, Cassiodorus preserved his own esteem without forfeiting the royal favor; and after passing thirty years in the honors of the world, he was blessed with an equal term of repose in the devout and studious solitude of Squillace. [57/1]

[Footnote 52: Procopius affirms that no laws whatsoever were promulgated by Theodoric and the succeeding kings of Italy, (Goth. l. ii. c. 6.) He must mean in the Gothic language. A Latin edict of Theodoric is still extant, in one hundred and fifty-four articles. Note: See Manso, 92. Savigny, vol. ii. p. 164, et seq—M.]

[Footnote 53: The image of Theodoric is engraved on his coins: his modest successors were satisfied with adding their own name to the head of the reigning emperor, (Muratori, Antiquitat. Italiae Medii Aevi, tom. ii. dissert. xxvii. p. 577—579. Giannone, Istoria Civile di Napoli tom. i. p. 166.)]

[Footnote 54: The alliance of the emperor and the king of Italy are represented by Cassiodorus (Var. i. l, ii. 1, 2, 3, vi. l) and Procopius, (Goth. l. ii. c. 6, l. iii. c. 21,) who celebrate the friendship of Anastasius and Theodoric; but the figurative style of compliment was interpreted in a very different sense at Constantinople and Ravenna.]

[Footnote 54/1: All causes between Roman and Roman were judged by the old Roman courts. The comes Gothorum judged between Goth and Goth; between Goths and Romans, (without considering which was the plaintiff.) the comes Gothorum, with a Roman jurist as his assessor, making a kind of mixed jurisdiction, but with a natural predominance to the side of the Goth Savigny, vol. i. p. 290—M.]

[Footnote 55: To the xvii. provinces of the Notitia, Paul Warnefrid the deacon (De Reb. Longobard. l. ii. c. 14—22) has subjoined an xviiith, the Apennine, (Muratori, Script. Rerum Italicarum, tom. i. p. 431—443.) But of these Sardinia and Corsica were possessed by the Vandals, and the two Rhaetias, as well as the Cottian Alps, seem to have been abandoned to a military government. The state of the four provinces that now form the kingdom of Naples is labored by Giannone (tom. i. p. 172, 178) with patriotic diligence.]

[Footnote 55/1: Manso enumerates and develops at some length the following sources of the royal revenue of Theodoric: 1. A domain, either by succession to that of Odoacer, or a part of the third of the lands was reserved for the royal patrimony. 1. Regalia, including mines, unclaimed estates, treasure-trove, and confiscations. 3. Land tax. 4. Aurarium, like the Chrysargyrum, a tax on certain branches of trade. 5. Grant of Monopolies. 6. Siliquaticum, a small tax on the sale of all kinds of commodities. 7. Portoria, customs Manso, 96, 111. Savigny (i. 285) supposes that in many cases the property remained in the original owner, who paid his tertia, a third of the produce to the crown, vol. i. p. 285—M.]

[Footnote 56: See the Gothic history of Procopius, (l. i. c. 1, l. ii. c. 6,) the Epistles of Cassiodorus, passim, but especially the vth and vith books, which contain the formulae, or patents of offices,) and the Civil History of Giannone, (tom. i. l. ii. iii.) The Gothic counts, which he places in every Italian city, are annihilated, however, by Maffei, (Verona Illustrata, P. i. l. viii. p. 227; for those of Syracuse and Naples (Var vi. 22, 23) were special and temporary commissions.]

[Footnote 57: Two Italians of the name of Cassiodorus, the father (Var. i. 24, 40) and the son, (ix. 24, 25,) were successively employed in the administration of Theodoric. The son was born in the year 479: his various epistles as quaestor, master of the offices, and Praetorian praefect, extend from 509 to 539, and he lived as a monk about thirty years, (Tiraboschi Storia della Letteratura Italiana, tom. iii. p. 7—24. Fabricius, Bibliot. Lat. Med. Aevi, tom. i. p. 357, 358, edit. Mansi.)]

[Footnote 57/1: Cassiodorus was of an ancient and honorable family; his grandfather had distinguished himself in the defence of Sicily against the ravages of Genseric; his father held a high rank at the court of Valentinian III., enjoyed the friendship of Aetius, and was one of the ambassadors sent to arrest the progress of Attila. Cassiodorus himself was first the treasurer of the private expenditure to Odoacer, afterwards "count of the sacred largesses." Yielding with the rest of the Romans to the dominion of Theodoric, he was instrumental in the peaceable submission of Sicily; was successively governor of his native provinces of Bruttium and Lucania, quaestor, magister, palatii, Praetorian praefect, patrician, consul, and private secretary, and, in fact, first minister of the king. He was five times Praetorian praefect under different sovereigns, the last time in the reign of Vitiges. This is the theory of Manso, which is not unencumbered with difficulties. M. Buat had supposed that it was the father of Cassiodorus who held the office first named. Compare Manso, p. 85, &c., and Beylage, vii. It certainly appears improbable that Cassiodorus should have been count of the sacred largesses at twenty years old—M.]

As the patron of the republic, it was the interest and duty of the Gothic king to cultivate the affections of the senate [58] and people. The nobles of Rome were flattered by sonorous epithets and formal professions of respect, which had been more justly applied to the merit and authority of their ancestors. The people enjoyed, without fear or danger, the three blessings of a capital, order, plenty, and public amusements. A visible diminution of their numbers may be found even in the measure of liberality; [59] yet Apulia, Calabria, and Sicily, poured their tribute of corn into the granaries of Rome an allowance of bread and meat was distributed to the indigent citizens; and every office was deemed honorable which was consecrated to the care of their health and happiness. The public games, such as the Greek ambassador might politely applaud, exhibited a faint and feeble copy of the magnificence of the Caesars: yet the musical, the gymnastic, and the pantomime arts, had not totally sunk in oblivion; the wild beasts of Africa still exercised in the amphitheatre the courage and dexterity of the hunters; and the indulgent Goth either patiently tolerated or gently restrained the blue and green factions, whose contests so often filled the circus with clamor and even with blood. [60] In the seventh year of his peaceful reign, Theodoric visited the old capital of the world; the senate and people advanced in solemn procession to salute a second Trajan, a new Valentinian; and he nobly supported that character by the assurance of a just and legal government, [61] in a discourse which he was not afraid to pronounce in public, and to inscribe on a tablet of brass. Rome, in this august ceremony, shot a last ray of declining glory; and a saint, the spectator of this pompous scene, could only hope, in his pious fancy, that it was excelled by the celestial splendor of the new Jerusalem. [62] During a residence of six months, the fame, the person, and the courteous demeanor of the Gothic king, excited the admiration of the Romans, and he contemplated, with equal curiosity and surprise, the monuments that remained of their ancient greatness. He imprinted the footsteps of a conqueror on the Capitoline hill, and frankly confessed that each day he viewed with fresh wonder the forum of Trajan and his lofty column. The theatre of Pompey appeared, even in its decay, as a huge mountain artificially hollowed, and polished, and adorned by human industry; and he vaguely computed, that a river of gold must have been drained to erect the colossal amphitheatre of Titus. [63] From the mouths of fourteen aqueducts, a pure and copious stream was diffused into every part of the city; among these the Claudian water, which arose at the distance of thirty-eight miles in the Sabine mountains, was conveyed along a gentle though constant declivity of solid arches, till it descended on the summit of the Aventine hill. The long and spacious vaults which had been constructed for the purpose of common sewers, subsisted, after twelve centuries, in their pristine strength; and these subterraneous channels have been preferred to all the visible wonders of Rome. [64] The Gothic kings, so injuriously accused of the ruin of antiquity, were anxious to preserve the monuments of the nation whom they had subdued. [65] The royal edicts were framed to prevent the abuses, the neglect, or the depredations of the citizens themselves; and a professed architect, the annual sum of two hundred pounds of gold, twenty-five thousand tiles, and the receipt of customs from the Lucrine port, were assigned for the ordinary repairs of the walls and public edifices. A similar care was extended to the statues of metal or marble of men or animals. The spirit of the horses, which have given a modern name to the Quirinal, was applauded by the Barbarians; [66] the brazen elephants of the Via sacra were diligently restored; [67] the famous heifer of Myron deceived the cattle, as they were driven through the forum of peace; [68] and an officer was created to protect those works of rat, which Theodoric considered as the noblest ornament of his kingdom.

[Footnote 58: See his regard for the senate in Cochlaeus, (Vit. Theod. viii. p. 72—80.)]

[Footnote 59: No more than 120,000 modii, or four thousand quarters, (Anonym. Valesian. p. 721, and Var. i. 35, vi. 18, xi. 5, 39.)]

[Footnote 60: See his regard and indulgence for the spectacles of the circus, the amphitheatre, and the theatre, in the Chronicle and Epistles of Cassiodorus, (Var. i. 20, 27, 30, 31, 32, iii. 51, iv. 51, illustrated by the xivth Annotation of Mascou's History), who has contrived to sprinkle the subject with ostentatious, though agreeable, learning.]

[Footnote 61: Anonym. Vales. p. 721. Marius Aventicensis in Chron. In the scale of public and personal merit, the Gothic conqueror is at least as much above Valentinian, as he may seem inferior to Trajan.]

[Footnote 62: Vit. Fulgentii in Baron. Annal. Eccles. A.D. 500, No. 10.]

[Footnote 63: Cassiodorus describes in his pompous style the Forum of Trajan (Var. vii. 6,) the theatre of Marcellus, (iv. 51,) and the amphitheatre of Titus, (v. 42;) and his descriptions are not unworthy of the reader's perusal. According to the modern prices, the Abbe Barthelemy computes that the brick work and masonry of the Coliseum would now cost twenty millions of French livres, (Mem. de l'Academie des Inscriptions, tom. xxviii. p. 585, 586.) How small a part of that stupendous fabric!]

[Footnote 64: For the aqueducts and cloacae, see Strabo, (l. v. p. 360;) Pliny, (Hist. Natur. xxxvi. 24; Cassiodorus, Var. iii. 30, 31, vi. 6;) Procopius, (Goth. l. i. c. 19;) and Nardini, (Roma Antica, p. 514—522.) How such works could be executed by a king of Rome, is yet a problem. Note: See Niebuhr, vol. i. p. 402. These stupendous works are among the most striking confirmations of Niebuhr's views of the early Roman history; at least they appear to justify his strong sentence—"These works and the building of the Capitol attest with unquestionable evidence that this Rome of the later kings was the chief city of a great state."—Page 110—M.]

[Footnote 65: For the Gothic care of the buildings and statues, see Cassiodorus (Var. i. 21, 25, ii. 34, iv. 30, vii. 6, 13, 15) and the Valesian Fragment, (p. 721.)]

[Footnote 66: Var. vii. 15. These horses of Monte Cavallo had been transported from Alexandria to the baths of Constantine, (Nardini, p. 188.) Their sculpture is disdained by the Abbe Dubos, (Reflexions sur la Poesie et sur la Peinture, tom. i. section 39,) and admired by Winkelman, (Hist. de l'Art, tom. ii. p. 159.)]

[Footnote 67: Var. x. 10. They were probably a fragment of some triumphal car, (Cuper de Elephantis, ii. 10.)]

[Footnote 68: Procopius (Goth. l. iv. c. 21) relates a foolish story of Myron's cow, which is celebrated by the false with of thirty-six Greek epigrams, (Antholog. l. iv. p. 302—306, edit. Hen. Steph.; Auson. Epigram. xiii—lxviii.)]

PART III

After the example of the last emperors, Theodoric preferred the residence of Ravenna, where he cultivated an orchard with his own hands. [69] As often as the peace of his kingdom was threatened (for it was never invaded) by the Barbarians, he removed his court to Verona [70] on the northern frontier, and the image of his palace, still extant on a coin, represents the oldest and most authentic model of Gothic architecture. These two capitals, as well as Pavia, Spoleto, Naples, and the rest of the Italian cities, acquired under his reign the useful or splendid decorations of churches, aqueducts, baths, porticos, and palaces. [71] But the happiness of the subject was more truly conspicuous in the busy scene of labor and luxury, in the rapid increase and bold enjoyment of national wealth. From the shades of Tibur and Praeneste, the Roman senators still retired in the winter season to the warm sun, and salubrious springs of Baiae; and their villas, which advanced on solid moles into the Bay of Naples, commanded the various prospect of the sky, the earth, and the water. On the eastern side of the Adriatic, a new Campania was formed in the fair and fruitful province of Istria, which communicated with the palace of Ravenna by an easy navigation of one hundred miles. The rich productions of Lucania and the adjacent provinces were exchanged at the Marcilian fountain, in a populous fair annually dedicated to trade, intemperance, and superstition. In the solitude of Comum, which had once been animated by the mild genius of Pliny, a transparent basin above sixty miles in length still reflected the rural seats which encompassed the margin of the Larian lake; and the gradual ascent of the hills was covered by a triple plantation of olives, of vines, and of chestnut trees. [72] Agriculture revived under the shadow of peace, and the number of husbandmen was multiplied by the redemption of captives. [73] The iron mines of Dalmatia, a gold mine in Bruttium, were carefully explored, and the Pomptine marshes, as well as those of Spoleto, were drained and cultivated by private undertakers, whose distant reward must depend on the continuance of the public prosperity. [74] Whenever the seasons were less propitious, the doubtful precautions of forming magazines of corn, fixing the price, and prohibiting the exportation, attested at least the benevolence of the state; but such was the extraordinary plenty which an industrious people produced from a grateful soil, that a gallon of wine was sometimes sold in Italy for less than three farthings, and a quarter of wheat at about five shillings and sixpence. [75] A country possessed of so many valuable objects of exchange soon attracted the merchants of the world, whose beneficial traffic was encouraged and protected by the liberal spirit of Theodoric. The free intercourse of the provinces by land and water was restored and extended; the city gates were never shut either by day or by night; and the common saying, that a purse of gold might be safely left in the fields, was expressive of the conscious security of the inhabitants.

[Footnote 69: See an epigram of Ennodius (ii. 3, p. 1893, 1894) on this garden and the royal gardener.]

[Footnote 70: His affection for that city is proved by the epithet of "Verona tua," and the legend of the hero; under the barbarous name of Dietrich of Bern, (Peringsciold and Cochloeum, p. 240,) Maffei traces him with knowledge and pleasure in his native country, (l. ix. p. 230—236.)]

[Footnote 71: See Maffei, (Verona Illustrata, Part i. p. 231, 232, 308, &c.) His amputes Gothic architecture, like the corruption of language, writing &c., not to the Barbarians, but to the Italians themselves. Compare his sentiments with those of Tiraboschi, (tom. iii. p. 61.) Note: Mr. Hallam (vol. iii. p. 432) observes that "the image of Theodoric's palace" is represented in Maffei, not from a coin, but from a seal. Compare D'Agincourt (Storia dell'arte, Italian Transl., Arcitecttura, Plate xvii. No. 2, and Pittura, Plate xvi. No. 15,) where there is likewise an engraving from a mosaic in the church of St. Apollinaris in Ravenna, representing a building ascribed to Theodoric in that city. Neither of these, as Mr. Hallam justly observes, in the least approximates to what is called the Gothic style. They are evidently the degenerate Roman architecture, and more resemble the early attempts of our architects to get back from our national Gothic into a classical Greek style. One of them calls to mind Inigo Jones inner quadrangle in St. John's College Oxford. Compare Hallam and D'Agincon vol. i. p. 140—145—M]

[Footnote 72: The villas, climate, and landscape of Baiae, (Var. ix. 6; see Cluver Italia Antiq. l. iv. c. 2, p. 1119, &c.,) Istria, (Var. xii. 22, 26,) and Comum, (Var. xi. 14; compare with Pliny's two villas, ix. 7,) are agreeably painted in the Epistles of Cassiodorus.]

[Footnote 73: In Liguria numerosa agricolarum progenies, (Ennodius, p. 1678, 1679, 1680.) St. Epiphanius of Pavia redeemed by prayer or ransom 6000 captives from the Burgundians of Lyons and Savoy. Such deeds are the best of miracles.]

[Footnote 74: The political economy of Theodoric (see Anonym. Vales. p. 721, and Cassiodorus, in Chron.) may be distinctly traced under the following heads: iron mine, (Var. iii. 23;) gold mine, (ix. 3;) Pomptine marshes, (ii. 32, 33;) Spoleto, (ii. 21;) corn, (i. 34, x. 27, 28, xi. 11, 12;) trade, (vi. 7, vii. 9, 23;) fair of Leucothoe or St. Cyprian in Lucania, (viii. 33;) plenty, (xii. 4;) the cursus, or public post, (i. 29, ii. 31, iv. 47, v. 5, vi 6, vii. 33;) the Flaminian way, (xii. 18.) Note: The inscription commemorative of the draining of the Pomptine marshes may be found in many works; in Gruter, Inscript. Ant. Heidelberg, p. 152, No. 8. With variations, in Nicolai De' bonificamenti delle terre Pontine, p. 103. In Sartorius, in his prize essay on the reign of Theodoric, and Manse Beylage, xi—M.]

[Footnote 75: LX modii tritici in solidum ipsius tempore fuerunt, et vinum xxx amphoras in solidum, (Fragment. Vales.) Corn was distributed from the granaries at xv or xxv modii for a piece of gold, and the price was still moderate.]

A difference of religion is always pernicious, and often fatal, to the harmony of the prince and people: the Gothic conqueror had been educated in the profession of Arianism, and Italy was devoutly attached to the Nicene faith. But the persuasion of Theodoric was not infected by zeal; and he piously adhered to the heresy of his fathers, without condescending to balance the subtile arguments of theological metaphysics. Satisfied with the private toleration of his Arian sectaries, he justly conceived himself to be the guardian of the public worship, and his external reverence for a superstition which he despised, may have nourished in his mind the salutary indifference of a statesman or philosopher. The Catholics of his dominions acknowledged, perhaps with reluctance, the peace of the church; their clergy, according to the degrees of rank or merit, were honorably entertained in the palace of Theodoric; he esteemed the living sanctity of Caesarius [76] and Epiphanius, [77] the orthodox bishops of Arles and Pavia; and presented a decent offering on the tomb of St. Peter, without any scrupulous inquiry into the creed of the apostle. [78] His favorite Goths, and even his mother, were permitted to retain or embrace the Athanasian faith, and his long reign could not afford the example of an Italian Catholic, who, either from choice or compulsion, had deviated into the religion of the conqueror. [79] The people, and the Barbarians themselves, were edified by the pomp and order of religious worship; the magistrates were instructed to defend the just immunities of ecclesiastical persons and possessions; the bishops held their synods, the metropolitans exercised their jurisdiction, and the privileges of sanctuary were maintained or moderated according to the spirit of the Roman jurisprudence. [80] With the protection, Theodoric assumed the legal supremacy, of the church; and his firm administration restored or extended some useful prerogatives which had been neglected by the feeble emperors of the West. He was not ignorant of the dignity and importance of the Roman pontiff, to whom the venerable name of Pope was now appropriated. The peace or the revolt of Italy might depend on the character of a wealthy and popular bishop, who claimed such ample dominion both in heaven and earth; who had been declared in a numerous synod to be pure from all sin, and exempt from all judgment. [81] When the chair of St. Peter was disputed by Symmachus and Laurence, they appeared at his summons before the tribunal of an Arian monarch, and he confirmed the election of the most worthy or the most obsequious candidate. At the end of his life, in a moment of jealousy and resentment, he prevented the choice of the Romans, by nominating a pope in the palace of Ravenna. The danger and furious contests of a schism were mildly restrained, and the last decree of the senate was enacted to extinguish, if it were possible, the scandalous venality of the papal elections. [82]

[Footnote 76: See the life of St. Caesarius in Baronius, (A.D. 508, No. 12, 13, 14.) The king presented him with 300 gold solidi, and a discus of silver of the weight of sixty pounds.]

[Footnote 77: Ennodius in Vit. St. Epiphanii, in Sirmond, Op. tom. i. p. 1672—1690. Theodoric bestowed some important favors on this bishop, whom he used as a counsellor in peace and war.]

[Footnote 78: Devotissimus ac si Catholicus, (Anonym. Vales. p. 720;) yet his offering was no more than two silver candlesticks (cerostrata) of the weight of seventy pounds, far inferior to the gold and gems of Constantinople and France, (Anastasius in Vit. Pont. in Hormisda, p. 34, edit. Paris.)]

[Footnote 79: The tolerating system of his reign (Ennodius, p. 1612. Anonym. Vales. p. 719. Procop. Goth. l. i. c. 1, l. ii. c. 6) may be studied in the Epistles of Cassiodorous, under the following heads: bishops, (Var. i. 9, vii. 15, 24, xi. 23;) immunities, (i. 26, ii. 29, 30;) church lands (iv. 17, 20;) sanctuaries, (ii. 11, iii. 47;) church plate, (xii. 20;) discipline, (iv. 44;) which prove, at the same time, that he was the head of the church as well as of the state. Note: He recommended the same toleration to the emperor Justin—M.]

[Footnote 80: We may reject a foolish tale of his beheading a Catholic deacon who turned Arian, (Theodor. Lector. No. 17.) Why is Theodoric surnamed After? From Vafer? (Vales. ad loc.) A light conjecture.]

[Footnote 81: Ennodius, p. 1621, 1622, 1636, 1638. His libel was approved and registered (synodaliter) by a Roman council, (Baronius, A.D. 503, No. 6, Franciscus Pagi in Breviar. Pont. Rom. tom. i. p. 242.)]

[Footnote 82: See Cassiodorus, (Var. viii. 15, ix. 15, 16,) Anastasius, (in Symmacho, p. 31,) and the xviith Annotation of Mascou. Baronius, Pagi, and most of the Catholic doctors, confess, with an angry growl, this Gothic usurpation.]

I have descanted with pleasure on the fortunate condition of Italy; but our fancy must not hastily conceive that the golden age of the poets, a race of men without vice or misery, was realized under the Gothic conquest. The fair prospect was sometimes overcast with clouds; the wisdom of Theodoric might be deceived, his power might be resisted and the declining age of the monarch was sullied with popular hatred and patrician blood. In the first insolence of victory, he had been tempted to deprive the whole party of Odoacer of the civil and even the natural rights of society; [83] a tax unseasonably imposed after the calamities of war, would have crushed the rising agriculture of Liguria; a rigid preemption of corn, which was intended for the public relief, must have aggravated the distress of Campania. These dangerous projects were defeated by the virtue and eloquence of Epiphanius and Boethius, who, in the presence of Theodoric himself, successfully pleaded the cause of the people: [84] but if the royal ear was open to the voice of truth, a saint and a philosopher are not always to be found at the ear of kings.

The privileges of rank, or office, or favor, were too frequently abused by Italian fraud and Gothic violence, and the avarice of the king's nephew was publicly exposed, at first by the usurpation, and afterwards by the restitution of the estates which he had unjustly extorted from his Tuscan neighbors. Two hundred thousand Barbarians, formidable even to their master, were seated in the heart of Italy; they indignantly supported the restraints of peace and discipline; the disorders of their march were always felt and sometimes compensated; and where it was dangerous to punish, it might be prudent to dissemble, the sallies of their native fierceness. When the indulgence of Theodoric had remitted two thirds of the Ligurian tribute, he condescended to explain the difficulties of his situation, and to lament the heavy though inevitable burdens which he imposed on his subjects for their own defence. [85] These ungrateful subjects could never be cordially reconciled to the origin, the religion, or even the virtues of the Gothic conqueror; past calamities were forgotten, and the sense or suspicion of injuries was rendered still more exquisite by the present felicity of the times.

[Footnote 83: He disabled them—alicentia testandi; and all Italy mourned—lamentabili justitio. I wish to believe, that these penalties were enacted against the rebels who had violated their oath of allegiance; but the testimony of Ennodius (p. 1675-1678) is the more weighty, as he lived and died under the reign of Theodoric.]

[Footnote 84: Ennodius, in Vit. Epiphan. p. 1589, 1690. Boethius de Consolatione Philosphiae, l. i. pros. iv. p. 45, 46, 47. Respect, but weigh the passions of the saint and the senator; and fortify and alleviate their complaints by the various hints of Cassiodorus, (ii. 8, iv. 36, viii. 5.)]

[Footnote 85: Immanium expensarum pondus...pro ipsorum salute, &c.; yet these are no more than words.]

Even the religious toleration which Theodoric had the glory of introducing into the Christian world, was painful and offensive to the orthodox zeal of the Italians. They respected the armed heresy of the Goths; but their pious rage was safely pointed against the rich and defenceless Jews, who had formed their establishments at Naples, Rome, Ravenna, Milan, and Genoa, for the benefit of trade, and under the sanction of the laws. [86] Their persons were insulted, their effects were pillaged, and their synagogues were burned by the mad populace of Ravenna and Rome, inflamed, as it should seem, by the most frivolous or extravagant pretences. The government which could neglect, would have deserved such an outrage. A legal inquiry was instantly directed; and as the authors of the tumult had escaped in the crowd, the whole community was condemned to repair the damage; and the obstinate bigots, who refused their contributions, were whipped through the streets by the hand of the executioner. [8611] This simple act of justice exasperated the discontent of the Catholics, who applauded the merit and patience of these holy confessors. Three hundred pulpits deplored the persecution of the church; and if the chapel of St. Stephen at Verona was demolished by the command of Theodoric, it is probable that some miracle hostile to his name and dignity had been performed on that sacred theatre. At the close of a glorious life, the king of Italy discovered that he had excited the hatred of a people whose happiness he had so assiduously labored to promote; and his mind was soured by indignation, jealousy, and the bitterness of unrequited love. The Gothic conqueror condescended to disarm the unwarlike natives of Italy, interdicting all weapons of offence, and excepting only a small knife for domestic use. The deliverer of Rome was accused of conspiring with the vilest informers against the lives of senators whom he suspected of a secret and treasonable correspondence with the Byzantine court. [87] After the death of Anastasius, the diadem had been placed on the head of a feeble old man; but the powers of government were assumed by his nephew Justinian, who already meditated the extirpation of heresy, and the conquest of Italy and Africa. A rigorous law, which was published at Constantinople, to reduce the Arians by the dread of punishment within the pale of the church, awakened the just resentment of Theodoric, who claimed for his distressed brethren of the East the same indulgence which he had so long granted to the Catholics of his dominions. [87/1] At his stern command, the Roman pontiff, with four illustrious senators, embarked on an embassy, of which he must have alike dreaded the failure or the success. The singular veneration shown to the first pope who had visited Constantinople was punished as a crime by his jealous monarch; the artful or peremptory refusal of the Byzantine court might excuse an equal, and would provoke a larger, measure of retaliation; and a mandate was prepared in Italy, to prohibit, after a stated day, the exercise of the Catholic worship. By the bigotry of his subjects and enemies, the most tolerant of princes was driven to the brink of persecution; and the life of Theodoric was too long, since he lived to condemn the virtue of Boethius and Symmachus. [88]

[Footnote 86: The Jews were settled at Naples, (Procopius, Goth. l. i. c. 8,) at Genoa, (Var. ii. 28, iv. 33,) Milan, (v. 37,) Rome, (iv. 43.) See likewise Basnage, Hist. des Juifs, tom. viii. c. 7, p. 254.]

[Footnote 8611: See History of the Jews vol. iii. p. 217—M.]

[Footnote 87: Rex avidus communis exitii, &c., (Boethius, l. i. p. 59:) rex colum Romanis tendebat, (Anonym. Vales. p. 723.) These are hard words: they speak the passions of the Italians and those (I fear) of Theodoric himself.]

[Footnote 87/1: Gibbon should not have omitted the golden words of Theodoric in a letter which he addressed to Justin: That to pretend to a dominion over the conscience is to usurp the prerogative of God; that by the nature of things the power of sovereigns is confined to external government; that they have no right of punishment but over those who disturb the public peace, of which they are the guardians; that the most dangerous heresy is that of a sovereign who separates from himself a part of his subjects because they believe not according to his belief. Compare Le Beau, vol viii. p. 68—M]

[Footnote 88: I have labored to extract a rational narrative from the dark, concise, and various hints of the Valesian Fragment, (p. 722, 723, 724,) Theophanes, (p. 145,) Anastasius, (in Johanne, p. 35,) and the Hist Miscella, (p. 103, edit. Muratori.) A gentle pressure and paraphrase of their words is no violence. Consult likewise Muratori (Annali d' Italia, tom. iv. p. 471-478,) with the Annals and Breviary (tom. i. p. 259—263) of the two Pagis, the uncle and the nephew.]

The senator Boethius [89] is the last of the Romans whom Cato or Tully could have acknowledged for their countryman. As a wealthy orphan, he inherited the patrimony and honors of the Anician family, a name ambitiously assumed by the kings and emperors of the age; and the appellation of Manlius asserted his genuine or fabulous descent from a race of consuls and dictators, who had repulsed the Gauls from the Capitol, and sacrificed their sons to the discipline of the republic. In the youth of Boethius the studies of Rome were not totally abandoned; a Virgil [90] is now extant, corrected by the hand of a consul; and the professors of grammar, rhetoric, and jurisprudence, were maintained in their privileges and pensions by the liberality of the Goths. But the erudition of the Latin language was insufficient to satiate his ardent curiosity: and Boethius is said to have employed eighteen laborious years in the schools of Athens, [91] which were supported by the zeal, the learning, and the diligence of Proclus and his disciples. The reason and piety of their Roman pupil were fortunately saved from the contagion of mystery and magic, which polluted the groves of the academy; but he imbibed the spirit, and imitated the method, of his dead and living masters, who attempted to reconcile the strong and subtile sense of Aristotle with the devout contemplation and sublime fancy of Plato. After his return to Rome, and his marriage with the daughter of his friend, the patrician Symmachus, Boethius still continued, in a palace of ivory and marble, to prosecute the same studies. [92] The church was edified by his profound defence of the orthodox creed against the Arian, the Eutychian, and the Nestorian heresies; and the Catholic unity was explained or exposed in a formal treatise by the indifference of three distinct though consubstantial persons. For the benefit of his Latin readers, his genius submitted to teach the first elements of the arts and sciences of Greece. The geometry of Euclid, the music of Pythagoras, the arithmetic of Nicomachus, the mechanics of Archimedes, the astronomy of Ptolemy, the theology of Plato, and the logic of Aristotle, with the commentary of Porphyry, were translated and illustrated by the indefatigable pen of the Roman senator. And he alone was esteemed capable of describing the wonders of art, a sun-dial, a water-clock, or a sphere which represented the motions of the planets. From these abstruse speculations, Boethius stooped, or, to speak more truly, he rose to the social duties of public and private life: the indigent were relieved by his liberality; and his eloquence, which flattery might compare to the voice of Demosthenes or Cicero, was uniformly exerted in the cause of innocence and humanity. Such conspicuous merit was felt and rewarded by a discerning prince: the dignity of Boethius was adorned with the titles of consul and patrician, and his talents were usefully employed in the important station of master of the offices. Notwithstanding the equal claims of the East and West, his two sons were created, in their tender youth, the consuls of the same year. [93] On the memorable day of their inauguration, they proceeded in solemn pomp from their palace to the forum amidst the applause of the senate and people; and their joyful father, the true consul of Rome, after pronouncing an oration in the praise of his royal benefactor, distributed a triumphal largess in the games of the circus. Prosperous in his fame and fortunes, in his public honors and private alliances, in the cultivation of science and the consciousness of virtue, Boethius might have been styled happy, if that precarious epithet could be safely applied before the last term of the life of man.

[Footnote 89: Le Clerc has composed a critical and philosophical life of Anicius Manlius Severinus Boetius, (Bibliot. Choisie, tom. xvi. p. 168—275;) and both Tiraboschi (tom. iii.) and Fabricius (Bibliot Latin.) may be usefully consulted. The date of his birth may be placed about the year 470, and his death in 524, in a premature old age, (Consol. Phil. Metrica. i. p. 5.)]

[Footnote 90: For the age and value of this Ms., now in the Medicean library at Florence, see the Cenotaphia Pisana (p. 430-447) of Cardinal Noris.]

[Footnote 91: The Athenian studies of Boethius are doubtful, (Baronius, A.D. 510, No. 3, from a spurious tract, De Disciplina Scholarum,) and the term of eighteen years is doubtless too long: but the simple fact of a visit to Athens is justified by much internal evidence, (Brucker, Hist. Crit. Philosoph. tom. iii. p. 524—527,) and by an expression (though vague and ambiguous) of his friend Cassiodorus, (Var. i. 45,) "longe positas Athenas introisti."]

[Footnote 92: Bibliothecae comptos ebore ac vitro parietes, &c., (Consol. Phil. l. i. pros. v. p. 74.) The Epistles of Ennodius (vi. 6, vii. 13, viii. 1 31, 37, 40) and Cassiodorus (Var. i. 39, iv. 6, ix. 21) afford many proofs of the high reputation which he enjoyed in his own times. It is true, that the bishop of Pavia wanted to purchase of him an old house at Milan, and praise might be tendered and accepted in part of payment. Note: Gibbon translated vitro, marble; under the impression, no doubt that glass was unknown—M.]

[Footnote 93: Pagi, Muratori, &c., are agreed that Boethius himself was consul in the year 510, his two sons in 522, and in 487, perhaps, his father. A desire of ascribing the last of these consulships to the philosopher had perplexed the chronology of his life. In his honors, alliances, children, he celebrates his own felicity—his past felicity, (p. 109 110)]

A philosopher, liberal of his wealth and parsimonious of his time, might be insensible to the common allurements of ambition, the thirst of gold and employment. And some credit may be due to the asseveration of Boethius, that he had reluctantly obeyed the divine Plato, who enjoins every virtuous citizen to rescue the state from the usurpation of vice and ignorance. For the integrity of his public conduct he appeals to the memory of his country. His authority had restrained the pride and oppression of the royal officers, and his eloquence had delivered Paulianus from the dogs of the palace. He had always pitied, and often relieved, the distress of the provincials, whose fortunes were exhausted by public and private rapine; and Boethius alone had courage to oppose the tyranny of the Barbarians, elated by conquest, excited by avarice, and, as he complains, encouraged by impunity. In these honorable contests his spirit soared above the consideration of danger, and perhaps of prudence; and we may learn from the example of Cato, that a character of pure and inflexible virtue is the most apt to be misled by prejudice, to be heated by enthusiasm, and to confound private enmities with public justice. The disciple of Plato might exaggerate the infirmities of nature, and the imperfections of society; and the mildest form of a Gothic kingdom, even the weight of allegiance and gratitude, must be insupportable to the free spirit of a Roman patriot. But the favor and fidelity of Boethius declined in just proportion with the public happiness; and an unworthy colleague was imposed to divide and control the power of the master of the offices. In the last gloomy season of Theodoric, he indignantly felt that he was a slave; but as his master had only power over his life, he stood without arms and without fear against the face of an angry Barbarian, who had been provoked to believe that the safety of the senate was incompatible with his own. The senator Albinus was accused and already convicted on the presumption of hoping, as it was said, the liberty of Rome. "If Albinus be criminal," exclaimed the orator, "the senate and myself are all guilty of the same crime. If we are innocent, Albinus is equally entitled to the protection of the laws." These laws might not have punished the simple and barren wish of an unattainable blessing; but they would have shown less indulgence to the rash confession of Boethius, that, had he known of a conspiracy, the tyrant never should. [94] The advocate of Albinus was soon involved in the danger and perhaps the guilt of his client; their signature (which they denied as a forgery) was affixed to the original address, inviting the emperor to deliver Italy from the Goths; and three witnesses of honorable rank, perhaps of infamous reputation, attested the treasonable designs of the Roman patrician. [95] Yet his innocence must be presumed, since he was deprived by Theodoric of the means of justification, and rigorously confined in the tower of Pavia, while the senate, at the distance of five hundred miles, pronounced a sentence of confiscation and death against the most illustrious of its members. At the command of the Barbarians, the occult science of a philosopher was stigmatized with the names of sacrilege and magic. [96] A devout and dutiful attachment to the senate was condemned as criminal by the trembling voices of the senators themselves; and their ingratitude deserved the wish or prediction of Boethius, that, after him, none should be found guilty of the same offence. [97]

[Footnote 94: Si ego scissem tu nescisses. Beothius adopts this answer (l. i. pros. 4, p. 53) of Julius Canus, whose philosophic death is described by Seneca, (De Tranquillitate Animi, c. 14.)]

[Footnote 95: The characters of his two delators, Basilius (Var. ii. 10, 11, iv. 22) and Opilio, (v. 41, viii. 16,) are illustrated, not much to their honor, in the Epistles of Cassiodorus, which likewise mention Decoratus, (v. 31,) the worthless colleague of Beothius, (l. iii. pros. 4, p. 193.)]

[Footnote 96: A severe inquiry was instituted into the crime of magic, (Var. iv 22, 23, ix. 18;) and it was believed that many necromancers had escaped by making their jailers mad: for mad I should read drunk.]

[Footnote 97: Boethius had composed his own Apology, (p. 53,) perhaps more interesting than his Consolation. We must be content with the general view of his honors, principles, persecution, &c., (l. i. pros. 4, p. 42—62,) which may be compared with the short and weighty words of the Valesian Fragment, (p. 723.) An anonymous writer (Sinner, Catalog. Mss. Bibliot. Bern. tom. i. p. 287) charges him home with honorable and patriotic treason.]

While Boethius, oppressed with fetters, expected each moment the sentence or the stroke of death, he composed, in the tower of Pavia, the Consolation of Philosophy; a golden volume not unworthy of the leisure of Plato or Tully, but which claims incomparable merit from the barbarism of the times and the situation of the author. The celestial guide, whom he had so long invoked at Rome and Athens, now condescended to illumine his dungeon, to revive his courage, and to pour into his wounds her salutary balm. She taught him to compare his long prosperity and his recent distress, and to conceive new hopes from the inconstancy of fortune. Reason had informed him of the precarious condition of her gifts; experience had satisfied him of their real value; he had enjoyed them without guilt; he might resign them without a sigh, and calmly disdain the impotent malice of his enemies, who had left him happiness, since they had left him virtue. From the earth, Boethius ascended to heaven in search of the Supreme Good; explored the metaphysical labyrinth of chance and destiny, of prescience and free will, of time and eternity; and generously attempted to reconcile the perfect attributes of the Deity with the apparent disorders of his moral and physical government. Such topics of consolation so obvious, so vague, or so abstruse, are ineffectual to subdue the feelings of human nature. Yet the sense of misfortune may be diverted by the labor of thought; and the sage who could artfully combine in the same work the various riches of philosophy, poetry, and eloquence, must already have possessed the intrepid calmness which he affected to seek. Suspense, the worst of evils, was at length determined by the ministers of death, who executed, and perhaps exceeded, the inhuman mandate of Theodoric. A strong cord was fastened round the head of Boethius, and forcibly tightened, till his eyes almost started from their sockets; and some mercy may be discovered in the milder torture of beating him with clubs till he expired. [98] But his genius survived to diffuse a ray of knowledge over the darkest ages of the Latin world; the writings of the philosopher were translated by the most glorious of the English kings, [99] and the third emperor of the name of Otho removed to a more honorable tomb the bones of a Catholic saint, who, from his Arian persecutors, had acquired the honors of martyrdom, and the fame of miracles. [100] In the last hours of Boethius, he derived some comfort from the safety of his two sons, of his wife, and of his father-in-law, the venerable Symmachus. But the grief of Symmachus was indiscreet, and perhaps disrespectful: he had presumed to lament, he might dare to revenge, the death of an injured friend. He was dragged in chains from Rome to the palace of Ravenna; and the suspicions of Theodoric could only be appeased by the blood of an innocent and aged senator. [101]

[Footnote 98: He was executed in Agro Calventiano, (Calvenzano, between Marignano and Pavia,) Anonym. Vales. p. 723, by order of Eusebius, count of Ticinum or Pavia. This place of confinement is styled the baptistery, an edifice and name peculiar to cathedrals. It is claimed by the perpetual tradition of the church of Pavia. The tower of Boethius subsisted till the year 1584, and the draught is yet preserved, (Tiraboschi, tom. iii. p. 47, 48.)]

[Footnote 99: See the Biographia Britannica, Alfred, tom. i. p. 80, 2d edition. The work is still more honorable if performed under the learned eye of Alfred by his foreign and domestic doctors. For the reputation of Boethius in the middle ages, consult Brucker, (Hist. Crit. Philosoph. tom. iii. p. 565, 566.)]

[Footnote 100: The inscription on his new tomb was composed by the preceptor of Otho III., the learned Pope Silvester II., who, like Boethius himself, was styled a magician by the ignorance of the times. The Catholic martyr had carried his head in his hands a considerable way, (Baronius, A.D. 526, No. 17, 18;) and yet on a similar tale, a lady of my acquaintance once observed, "La distance n'y fait rien; il n'y a que lo remier pas qui coute." Note: Madame du Deffand. This witticism referred to the miracle of St. Denis—G.]

[Footnote 101: Boethius applauds the virtues of his father-in-law, (l. i. pros. 4, p. 59, l. ii. pros. 4, p. 118.) Procopius, (Goth. l. i. c. i.,) the Valesian Fragment, (p. 724,) and the Historia Miscella, (l. xv. p. 105,) agree in praising the superior innocence or sanctity of Symmachus; and in the estimation of the legend, the guilt of his murder is equal to the imprisonment of a pope.]

Humanity will be disposed to encourage any report which testifies the jurisdiction of conscience and the remorse of kings; and philosophy is not ignorant that the most horrid spectres are sometimes created by the powers of a disordered fancy, and the weakness of a distempered body. After a life of virtue and glory, Theodoric was now descending with shame and guilt into the grave; his mind was humbled by the contrast of the past, and justly alarmed by the invisible terrors of futurity. One evening, as it is related, when the head of a large fish was served on the royal table, [102] he suddenly exclaimed, that he beheld the angry countenance of Symmachus, his eyes glaring fury and revenge, and his mouth armed with long sharp teeth, which threatened to devour him. The monarch instantly retired to his chamber, and, as he lay, trembling with aguish cold, under a weight of bed-clothes, he expressed, in broken murmurs to his physician Elpidius, his deep repentance for the murders of Boethius and Symmachus. [103] His malady increased, and after a dysentery which continued three days, he expired in the palace of Ravenna, in the thirty-third, or, if we compute from the invasion of Italy, in the thirty-seventh year of his reign. Conscious of his approaching end, he divided his treasures and provinces between his two grandsons, and fixed the Rhone as their common boundary. [104] Amalaric was restored to the throne of Spain. Italy, with all the conquests of the Ostrogoths, was bequeathed to Athalaric; whose age did not exceed ten years, but who was cherished as the last male offspring of the line of Amali, by the short-lived marriage of his mother Amalasuntha with a royal fugitive of the same blood. [105] In the presence of the dying monarch, the Gothic chiefs and Italian magistrates mutually engaged their faith and loyalty to the young prince, and to his guardian mother; and received, in the same awful moment, his last salutary advice, to maintain the laws, to love the senate and people of Rome, and to cultivate with decent reverence the friendship of the emperor. [106] The monument of Theodoric was erected by his daughter Amalasuntha, in a conspicuous situation, which commanded the city of Ravenna, the harbor, and the adjacent coast. A chapel of a circular form, thirty feet in diameter, is crowned by a dome of one entire piece of granite: from the centre of the dome four columns arose, which supported, in a vase of porphyry, the remains of the Gothic king, surrounded by the brazen statues of the twelve apostles. [107]

His spirit, after some previous expiation, might have been permitted to mingle with the benefactors of mankind, if an Italian hermit had not been witness, in a vision, to the damnation of Theodoric, [108] whose soul was plunged, by the ministers of divine vengeance, into the volcano of Lipari, one of the flaming mouths of the infernal world. [109]

[Footnote 102: In the fanciful eloquence of Cassiodorus, the variety of sea and river fish are an evidence of extensive dominion; and those of the Rhine, of Sicily, and of the Danube, were served on the table of Theodoric, (Var. xii. 14.) The monstrous turbot of Domitian (Juvenal Satir. iii. 39) had been caught on the shores of the Adriatic.]

[Footnote 103: Procopius, Goth. l. i. c. 1. But he might have informed us, whether he had received this curious anecdote from common report or from the mouth of the royal physician.]

[Footnote 104: Procopius, Goth. l. i. c. 1, 2, 12, 13. This partition had been directed by Theodoric, though it was not executed till after his death, Regni hereditatem superstes reliquit, (Isidor. Chron. p. 721, edit. Grot.)]

[Footnote 105: Berimund, the third in descent from Hermanric, king of the Ostrogoths, had retired into Spain, where he lived and died in obscurity, (Jornandes, c. 33, p. 202, edit. Muratori.) See the discovery, nuptials, and death of his grandson Eutharic, (c. 58, p. 220.) His Roman games might render him popular, (Cassiodor. in Chron.,) but Eutharic was asper in religione, (Anonym. Vales. p. 723.)]

[Footnote 106: See the counsels of Theodoric, and the professions of his successor, in Procopius, (Goth. l. i. c. 1, 2,) Jornandes, (c. 59, p. 220, 221,) and Cassiodorus, (Var. viii. 1—7.) These epistles are the triumph of his ministerial eloquence.]

[Footnote 107: Anonym. Vales. p. 724. Agnellus de Vitis. Pont. Raven. in Muratori Script. Rerum Ital. tom. ii. P. i. p. 67. Alberti Descrittione d' Italia, p. 311. Note: The Mausoleum of Theodoric, now Sante Maria della Rotonda, is engraved in D'Agincourt, Histoire de l'Art, p xviii. of the Architectural Prints—M]

[Footnote 108: This legend is related by Gregory I., (Dialog. iv. 36,) and approved by Baronius, (A.D. 526, No. 28;) and both the pope and cardinal are grave doctors, sufficient to establish a probable opinion.]

[Footnote 109: Theodoric himself, or rather Cassiodorus, had described in tragic strains the volcanos of Lipari (Cluver. Sicilia, p. 406—410) and Vesuvius, (v 50.)]

CHAPTER XL

REIGN OF JUSTINIAN

PART I

ELEVATION OF JUSTIN THE LEDER—REIGN OF JUSTINIAN—I. THE EMPRESS THEODORA—II. FACTIONS OF THE CIRCUS, AND SEDITION OF CONSTANTINOPLE—III. TRADE AND MANUFACTURE OF SILK— IV. FINANCES AND TAXES—V. EDIFICES OF JUSTINIAN—CHURCH OF ST. SOPHIA—FORTIFICATIONS AND

FRONTIERS OF THE EASTERN EMPIRE—ABOLITION OF THE SCHOOLS OF ATHENS, AND THE CONSULSHIP OF ROME.

The emperor Justinian was born [1] near the ruins of Sardica, (the modern Sophia,) of an obscure race [2] of Barbarians, [3] the inhabitants of a wild and desolate country, to which the names of Dardania, of Dacia, and of Bulgaria, have been successively applied. His elevation was prepared by the adventurous spirit of his uncle Justin, who, with two other peasants of the same village, deserted, for the profession of arms, the more useful employment of husbandmen or shepherds. [4] On foot, with a scanty provision of biscuit in their knapsacks, the three youths followed the high road of Constantinople, and were soon enrolled, for their strength and stature, among the guards of the emperor Leo. Under the two succeeding reigns, the fortunate peasant emerged to wealth and honors; and his escape from some dangers which threatened his life was afterwards ascribed to the guardian angel who watches over the fate of kings. His long and laudable service in the Isaurian and Persian wars would not have preserved from oblivion the name of Justin; yet they might warrant the military promotion, which in the course of fifty years he gradually obtained; the rank of tribune, of count, and of general; the dignity of senator, and the command of the guards, who obeyed him as their chief, at the important crisis when the emperor Anastasius was removed from the world. The powerful kinsmen whom he had raised and enriched were excluded from the throne; and the eunuch Amantius, who reigned in the palace, had secretly resolved to fix the diadem on the head of the most obsequious of his creatures. A liberal donative, to conciliate the suffrage of the guards, was intrusted for that purpose in the hands of their commander. But these weighty arguments were treacherously employed by Justin in his own favor; and as no competitor presumed to appear, the Dacian peasant was invested with the purple by the unanimous consent of the soldiers, who knew him to be brave and gentle, of the clergy and people, who believed him to be orthodox, and of the provincials, who yielded a blind and implicit submission to the will of the capital. The elder Justin, as he is distinguished from another emperor of the same family and name, ascended the Byzantine throne at the age of sixty-eight years; and, had he been left to his own guidance, every moment of a nine years' reign must have exposed to his subjects the impropriety of their choice. His ignorance was similar to that of Theodoric; and it is remarkable that in an age not destitute of learning, two contemporary monarchs had never been instructed in the knowledge of the alphabet. [411] But the genius of Justin was far inferior to that of the Gothic king: the experience of a soldier had not qualified him for the government of an empire; and though personally brave, the consciousness of his own weakness was naturally attended with doubt, distrust, and political apprehension. But the official business of the state was diligently and faithfully transacted by the quaestor Proclus; [5] and the aged emperor adopted the talents and ambition of his nephew Justinian, an aspiring youth, whom his uncle had drawn from the rustic solitude of Dacia, and educated at Constantinople, as the heir of his private fortune, and at length of the Eastern empire.

[Footnote 1: There is some difficulty in the date of his birth (Ludewig in Vit. Justiniani, p. 125;) none in the place—the district Bederiana—the village Tauresium, which he afterwards decorated with his name and splendor, (D'Anville, Hist. de l'Acad. &c., tom. xxxi. p. 287—292.)]

[Footnote 2: The names of these Dardanian peasants are Gothic, and almost English: Justinian is a translation of uprauda, (upright;) his father Sabatius (in Graeco-barbarous language stipes) was styled in his village Istock, (Stock;) his mother Bigleniza was softened into Vigilantia.]

[Footnote 3: Ludewig (p. 127—135) attempts to justify the Anician name of Justinian and Theodora, and to connect them with a family from which the house of Austria has been derived.]

[Footnote 4: See the anecdotes of Procopius, (c. 6,) with the notes of N. Alemannus. The satirist would not have sunk, in the vague and decent appellation of Zonaras. Yet why are those names disgraceful?—and what German baron would not be proud to descend from the Eumaeus of the Odyssey! Note: It is whimsical enough that, in our own days, we should have, even in jest, a claimant to lineal descent from the godlike swineherd not in the person of a German baron, but in that of a professor of the Ionian University. Constantine Koliades, or some malicious wit under this name, has written a tall folio to prove Ulysses to be Homer, and himself the descendant, the heir (?), of the Eumaeus of the Odyssey—M]

[Footnote 4/1: St. Martin questions the fact in both cases. The ignorance of Justin rests on the secret history of Procopius, vol. viii. p. 8. St. Martin's notes on Le Beau—M]

[Footnote 5: His virtues are praised by Procopius, (Persic. l. i. c. 11.) The quaestor Proclus was the friend of Justinian, and the enemy of every other adoption.]

Since the eunuch Amantius had been defrauded of his money, it became necessary to deprive him of his life. The task was easily accomplished by the charge of a real or fictitious conspiracy; and the judges were informed, as an accumulation of guilt, that he was secretly addicted to the Manichaean heresy. [6] Amantius lost his head; three of his companions, the first domestics of the palace, were punished either with death or exile; and their unfortunate candidate for the purple was cast into a deep dungeon, overwhelmed with stones, and ignominiously thrown, without burial, into the sea. The ruin of Vitalian was a work of more difficulty and danger. That Gothic chief had rendered himself popular by the civil war which he boldly waged against Anastasius for the defence of the orthodox faith, and after the conclusion of an advantageous treaty, he still remained in the neighborhood of Constantinople at the head of a formidable and victorious army of Barbarians. By the frail security of oaths, he was tempted to relinquish this advantageous situation, and to trust his person within the walls of a city, whose inhabitants, particularly the blue faction, were artfully incensed against him by the remembrance even of his pious hostilities. The emperor and his nephew embraced him as the faithful and worthy champion of the church and state; and gratefully adorned their favorite with the titles of consul and general; but in the seventh month of his consulship, Vitalian was stabbed with seventeen wounds at the royal banquet; [7] and Justinian, who inherited the spoil, was accused as the assassin of a spiritual brother, to whom he had recently pledged his faith in the participation of the Christian mysteries. [8] After the fall of his rival, he was promoted, without any claim of military service, to the office of master-general of the Eastern armies, whom it was his duty to lead into the field against the public enemy. But, in the pursuit of fame, Justinian might have lost his present dominion over the age and weakness of his uncle; and instead of acquiring by Scythian or Persian trophies the applause of his countrymen, [9] the prudent warrior solicited their favor in the churches, the circus, and the senate, of Constantinople. The Catholics were attached to the nephew of Justin, who, between the Nestorian and Eutychian heresies, trod the narrow path of inflexible and intolerant orthodoxy. [10] In the first days of the new reign, he prompted and gratified the popular enthusiasm against the memory of the deceased emperor. After a schism of thirty-four years, he reconciled the proud and angry spirit of the Roman pontiff, and spread among the Latins a favorable report of his pious respect for the apostolic see. The thrones of the East were filled with Catholic bishops, devoted to his interest, the clergy and the monks were gained by his liberality, and the people were taught to pray for their future sovereign, the hope and pillar of the true religion. The magnificence of Justinian was displayed in the superior pomp of his public spectacles, an object not less sacred and important in the eyes of the multitude than the creed of Nice or Chalcedon: the expense of his consulship was esteemed at two hundred and twenty-eight thousand pieces of gold; twenty lions, and thirty leopards, were produced at the same time in the amphitheatre, and a numerous train of horses, with their rich trappings, was bestowed as an extraordinary gift on the victorious charioteers of the circus. While he indulged the people of Constantinople, and received the addresses of foreign kings, the nephew of Justin assiduously cultivated the friendship of the senate. That venerable name seemed to qualify its members to declare the sense of the nation, and to regulate the succession of the Imperial throne: the feeble Anastasius had permitted the vigor of government to degenerate into the form or substance of an aristocracy; and the military officers who had obtained the senatorial rank were followed by their domestic guards, a band of veterans, whose arms or acclamations might fix in a tumultuous moment the diadem of the East. The treasures of the state were lavished to procure the voices of the senators, and their unanimous wish, that he would be pleased to adopt Justinian for his colleague, was communicated to the emperor. But this request, which too clearly admonished him of his approaching end, was unwelcome to the jealous temper of an aged monarch, desirous to retain the power which he was incapable of exercising; and Justin, holding his purple with both his hands, advised them to prefer, since an election was so profitable, some older candidate. Not withstanding this reproach, the senate proceeded to decorate Justinian with the royal epithet of nobilissimus; and their decree was ratified by the affection or the fears of his uncle. After some time the languor of mind and body, to which he was reduced by an incurable wound in his thigh, indispensably required the aid of a guardian. He summoned the patriarch and senators; and in their presence solemnly placed the diadem on the head of his nephew, who was conducted from the palace to the circus, and saluted by the loud and joyful applause of the people. The life of Justin was prolonged about four months; but from the instant of this ceremony, he was considered as dead to the empire, which acknowledged Justinian, in the forty-fifth year of his age, for the lawful sovereign of the East. [11]

[Footnote 6: Manichaean signifies Eutychian. Hear the furious acclamations of Constantinople and Tyre, the former no more than six days after the decease of Anastasius. They produced, the latter applauded, the eunuch's death, (Baronius, A.D. 518, P. ii. No. 15. Fleury, Hist Eccles. tom. vii. p. 200, 205, from the Councils, tom. v. p. 182, 207.)]

[Footnote 7: His power, character, and intentions, are perfectly explained by the court de Buat, (tom. ix. p. 54—81.) He was great-grandson of Aspar, hereditary prince in the Lesser Scythia, and count of the Gothic foederati of Thrace. The Bessi, whom he could influence, are the minor Goths of Jornandes, (c. 51.)]

[Footnote 8: Justiniani patricii factione dicitur interfectus fuisse, (Victor Tu nunensis, Chron. in Thesaur. Temp. Scaliger, P. ii. p. 7.) Procopius (Anecdot. c. 7) styles him a tyrant, but acknowledges something which is well explained by Alemannus.]

[Footnote 9: In his earliest youth (plane adolescens) he had passed some time as a hostage with Theodoric. For this curious fact, Alemannus (ad Procop. Anecdot. c. 9, p. 34, of the first edition) quotes a Ms. history of Justinian, by his preceptor Theophilus. Ludewig (p. 143) wishes to make him a soldier.]

[Footnote 10: The ecclesiastical history of Justinian will be shown hereafter. See Baronius, A.D. 518—521, and the copious article Justinianas in the index to the viith volume of his Annals.]

[Footnote 11: The reign of the elder Justin may be found in the three Chronicles of Marcellinus, Victor, and John Malala, (tom. ii. p. 130—150,) the last of whom (in spite of Hody, Prolegom. No. 14, 39, edit. Oxon.) lived soon after Justinian, (Jortin's Remarks, &c., vol. iv p. 383:) in the Ecclesiastical History of Evagrius, (l. iv. c. 1, 2, 3, 9,) and the Excerpta of Theodorus Lector, (No. 37,) and in Cedrenus, (p. 362—366,) and Zonaras, (l. xiv. p. 58—61,) who may pass for an original. Note: Dindorf, in his preface to the *new edition of Malala, p. vi., concurs with this opinion of Gibbon, which was also that of Reiske, as to the age of the chronicler—M.]*

From his elevation to his death, Justinian governed the Roman empire thirty-eight years, seven months, and thirteen days.

The events of his reign, which excite our curious attention by their number, variety, and importance, are diligently related by the secretary of Belisarius, a rhetorician, whom eloquence had promoted to the rank of senator and praefect of Constantinople. According to the vicissitudes of courage or servitude, of favor or disgrace, Procopius [12] successively composed the history, the panegyric, and the satire of his own times. The eight books of the Persian, Vandalic, and Gothic wars, [13] which are continued in the five books of Agathias, deserve our esteem as a laborious and successful imitation of the Attic, or at least of the Asiatic, writers of ancient Greece. His facts are collected from the personal experience and free conversation of a soldier, a statesman, and a traveller; his style continually aspires, and often attains, to the merit of strength and elegance; his reflections, more especially in the speeches, which he too frequently inserts, contain a rich fund of political knowledge; and the historian, excited by the generous ambition of pleasing and instructing posterity, appears to disdain the prejudices of the people, and the flattery of courts. The writings of Procopius [14] were read and applauded by his contemporaries: [15] but, although he respectfully laid them at the foot of the throne, the pride of Justinian must have been wounded by the praise of a hero, who perpetually eclipses the glory of his inactive sovereign. The conscious dignity of independence was subdued by the hopes and fears of a slave; and the secretary of Belisarius labored for pardon and reward in the six books of the Imperial edifices. He had dexterously chosen a subject of apparent splendor, in which he could loudly celebrate the genius, the magnificence, and the piety of a prince, who, both as a conqueror and legislator, had surpassed the puerile virtues of Themistocles and Cyrus. [16] Disappointment might urge the flatterer to secret revenge; and the first glance of favor might again tempt him to suspend and suppress a libel, [17] in which the Roman Cyrus is degraded into an odious and contemptible tyrant, in which both the emperor and his consort Theodora are seriously represented as two daemons, who had assumed a human form for the destruction of mankind. [18] Such base inconsistency must doubtless sully the reputation, and detract from the credit, of Procopius: yet, after the venom of his malignity has been suffered to exhale, the residue of the anecdotes, even the most disgraceful facts, some of which had been tenderly hinted in his public history, are established by their internal evidence, or the authentic monuments of the times. [19] [19/1] From these various materials, I shall now proceed to describe the reign of Justinian, which will deserve and occupy an ample space. The present chapter will explain the elevation and character of Theodora, the factions of the circus, and the peaceful administration of the sovereign of the East. In the three succeeding chapters, I shall relate the wars of Justinian, which achieved the conquest of Africa and Italy; and I shall follow the victories of Belisarius and Narses, without disguising the vanity of their triumphs, or the hostile virtue of the Persian and Gothic heroes. The series of this and the following volume will embrace the jurisprudence and theology of the emperor; the controversies and sects which still divide the Oriental church; the reformation of the Roman law which is obeyed or respected by the nations of modern Europe.

[Footnote 12: See the characters of Procopius and Agathias in La Mothe le Vayer, (tom. viii. p. 144—174,) Vossius, (de Historicis Graecis, l. ii. c. 22,) and Fabricius, (Bibliot. Graec. l. v. c. 5, tom. vi. p. 248—278.) Their religion, an honorable problem, betrays occasional conformity, with a secret attachment to Paganism and Philosophy.]

[Footnote 13: In the seven first books, two Persic, two Vandalic, and three Gothic, Procopius has borrowed from Appian the division of provinces and wars: the viiith book, though it bears the name of Gothic, is a miscellaneous and general supplement down to the spring of the year 553, from whence it is continued by Agathias till 559, (Pagi, Critica, A.D. 579, No. 5.)]

[Footnote 14: The literary fate of Procopius has been somewhat unlucky.

1. His book de Bello Gothico were stolen by Leonard Aretin, and published (Fulginii, 1470, Venet. 1471, apud Janson. Mattaire, Annal Typograph. tom. i. edit. posterior, p. 290, 304, 279, 299,) in his own name, (see Vossius de Hist. Lat. l. iii. c. 5, and the feeble defence of the Venice Giornale de Letterati, tom. xix. p. 207.)

2. His works were mutilated by the first Latin translators, Christopher Persona, (Giornale, tom. xix. p. 340—348,) and Raphael de Volaterra, (Huet, de Claris Interpretibus, p. 166,) who did not even consult the Ms. of the Vatican library, of which they were praefects, (Aleman. in Praefat Anecdot.) 3. The Greek text was not printed till 1607, by Hoeschelius of Augsburg, (Dictionnaire de Bayle, tom. ii. p. 782.)

4. The Paris edition was imperfectly executed by Claude Maltret, a Jesuit of Toulouse, (in 1663,) far distant from the Louvre press and the Vatican Ms., from which, however, he obtained some supplements. His promised commentaries, &c., have never appeared. The Agathias of Leyden (1594) has been wisely reprinted by the Paris editor, with the Latin version of Bonaventura Vulcanius, a learned interpreter, (Huet, p. 176.)

Note: Procopius forms a part of the new Byzantine collection under the superintendence of Dindorf—M.]

[Footnote 15: Agathias in Praefat. p. 7, 8, l. iv. p. 137. Evagrius, l. iv. c. 12. See likewise Photius, cod. lxiii. p. 65.]

[Footnote 16: Says, he, Praefat. ad l. de Edificiis is no more than a pun! In these five books, Procopius affects a Christian as well as a courtly style.]

[Footnote 17: Procopius discloses himself, (Praefat. ad Anecdot. c. 1, 2, 5,) and the anecdotes are reckoned as the ninth book by Suidas, (tom. iii. p. 186, edit. Kuster.) The silence of Evagrius is a poor objection. Baronius (A.D. 548, No. 24) regrets the loss of this secret history: it was then in the Vatican library, in his own custody, and was first published sixteen years after his death, with the learned, but partial notes of Nicholas Alemannus, (Lugd. 1623.)]

[Footnote 18: Justinian an ass—the perfect likeness of Domitian—Anecdot. c. 8—Theodora's lovers driven from her bed by rival daemons—her marriage foretold with a great daemon—a monk saw the prince of the daemons, instead of Justinian, on the throne—the servants who watched beheld a face without features, a body walking without a head, &c., &c. Procopius declares his own and his friends' belief in these diabolical stories, (c. 12.)]

[Footnote 19: Montesquieu (Considerations sur la Grandeur et la Decadence des Romains, c. xx.) gives credit to these anecdotes, as connected, 1. with the weakness of the empire, and, 2. with the instability of Justinian's laws.]

[Footnote 19/1: *The Anecdota of Procopius, compared with the former works of the same author, appear to me the basest and most disgraceful work in literature. The wars, which he has described in the former volumes as glorious or necessary, are become unprofitable and wanton massacres; the buildings which he celebrated, as raised to the immortal honor of the great emperor, and his admirable queen, either as magnificent embellishments of the city, or useful fortifications for the defence of the frontier, are become works of vain prodigality and useless ostentation. I doubt whether Gibbon has made sufficient allowance for the "malignity" of the Anecdota; at all events, the extreme and disgusting profligacy of Theodora's early life rests entirely on this viratent libel—M.*]

I. In the exercise of supreme power, the first act of Justinian was to divide it with the woman whom he loved, the famous Theodora, [20] whose strange elevation cannot be applauded as the triumph of female virtue. Under the reign of Anastasius, the care of the wild beasts maintained by the green faction at Constantinople was intrusted to Acacius, a native of the Isle of Cyprus, who, from his employment, was surnamed the master of the bears. This honorable office was given after his death to another candidate, notwithstanding the diligence of his widow, who had already provided a husband and a successor. Acacius had left three daughters, Comito, [21] Theodora, and Anastasia, the eldest of whom did not then exceed the age of seven years. On a solemn festival, these helpless orphans were sent by their distressed and indignant mother, in the garb of suppliants, into the midst of the theatre: the green faction received them with contempt, the blues with compassion; and this difference, which sunk deep into the mind of Theodora, was felt long afterwards in the administration of the empire. As they improved in age and beauty, the three sisters were successively devoted to the public and private pleasures of the Byzantine people: and Theodora, after following Comito on the stage, in the dress of a slave, with a stool on her head, was at length permitted to exercise her independent talents. She neither danced, nor sung, nor played on the flute; her skill was confined to the pantomime arts; she excelled in buffoon characters, and as often as the comedian swelled her cheeks, and complained with a ridiculous tone and gesture of the blows that were inflicted, the whole theatre of Constantinople resounded with laughter and applause. The beauty of Theodora [22] was the subject of more flattering praise, and the source of more exquisite delight. Her features were delicate and regular; her complexion, though somewhat pale, was tinged with a natural color; every sensation was instantly expressed by the vivacity of her eyes; her easy motions displayed the graces of a small but elegant figure; and either love or adulation might proclaim, that painting and poetry were incapable of delineating the matchless excellence of her form. But this form was degraded by the facility with which it was exposed to the public eye, and prostituted to licentious desire. Her venal charms were abandoned to a promiscuous crowd of citizens and strangers of every rank, and of every profession: the fortunate lover who had been promised a night of enjoyment, was often driven from her bed by a stronger or more wealthy favorite; and when she passed through the streets, her presence was avoided by all who wished to escape either the scandal or the temptation. The satirical historian has not blushed [23] to describe the naked scenes which Theodora was not ashamed to exhibit in the theatre. [24] After exhausting the arts of sensual pleasure, [25] she most ungratefully murmured against the parsimony of Nature; [26] but her murmurs, her pleasures, and her arts, must be veiled in the obscurity of a learned language. After reigning for some time, the delight and contempt of the capital, she condescended to accompany Ecebolus, a native of Tyre, who had obtained the government of the African Pentapolis. But this union was frail and transient; Ecebolus soon rejected an expensive or faithless concubine; she was reduced at Alexandria to extreme distress; and in her laborious return to Constantinople, every city of the East admired and enjoyed the fair Cyprian, whose merit appeared to justify her descent from the peculiar island of Venus. The vague commerce of Theodora, and the most detestable precautions, preserved her from the danger which she feared; yet once, and once only, she became a mother. The infant was saved and educated in Arabia, by his father, who imparted to him on his death-bed, that he was the son of an empress. Filled with ambitious hopes, the unsuspecting youth immediately hastened to the palace of Constantinople, and was admitted to the presence of his mother. As he was never more seen, even after the decease of Theodora, she deserves the foul imputation of extinguishing with his life a secret so offensive to her Imperial virtue. [26/1]

[Footnote 20: For the life and manners of the empress Theodora see the Anecdotes; more especially c. 1—5, 9, 10—15, 16, 17, with the learned notes of Alemannus—a reference which is always implied.]

[Footnote 21: Comito was afterwards married to Sittas, duke of Armenia, the father, perhaps, at least she might be the mother, of the empress Sophia. Two nephews of Theodora may be the sons of Anastasia, (Aleman. p. 30, 31.)]

[Footnote 22: Her statute was raised at Constantinople, on a porphyry column. See Procopius, (de Edif. l. i. c. 11,) who gives her portrait in the Anecdotes, (c. 10.) Aleman. (p. 47) produces one from a Mosaic at Ravenna, loaded with pearls and jewels, and yet handsome.]

[Footnote 23: A fragment of the Anecdotes, (c. 9,) somewhat too naked, was suppressed by Alemannus, though extant in the Vatican Ms.; nor has the defect been supplied in the Paris or Venice editions. La Mothe le Vayer (tom. viii. p. 155) gave the first hint of this curious and genuine passage, (Jortin's Remarks, vol. iv. p. 366,) which he had received from Rome, and it has been since published in the Menagiana (tom. iii. p. 254—259) with a Latin version.]

[Footnote 24: After the mention of a narrow girdle, (as none could appear stark naked in the theatre,) Procopius thus proceeds. I have heard that a learned prelate, now deceased, was fond of quoting this passage in conversation.]

[Footnote 25: Theodora surpassed the Crispa of Ausonius, (Epigram lxxi.,) who imitated the capitalis luxus of the females of Nola. See Quintilian Institut. viii. 6, and Torrentius ad Horat. Sermon. l. i. sat. 2, v. 101. At a memorable supper, thirty slaves waited round the table ten young men feasted with Theodora. Her charity was universal. Et lassata viris, necdum satiata, recessit.]

[Footnote 26: She wished for a fourth altar, on which she might pour libations to the god of love.]

[Footnote 26/1: Gibbon should have remembered the axiom which he quotes in another piece, scelera ostendi oportet dum puniantur abscondi flagitia—M.]

In the most abject state of her fortune, and reputation, some vision, either of sleep or of fancy, had whispered to Theodora the pleasing assurance that she was destined to become the spouse of a potent monarch. Conscious of her approaching greatness, she returned from Paphlagonia to Constantinople; assumed, like a skilful actress, a more decent character; relieved her poverty by the laudable industry of spinning wool; and affected a life of chastity and solitude in a small house, which she afterwards changed into a magnificent temple. [27] Her beauty, assisted by art or accident, soon attracted, captivated, and fixed, the patrician Justinian, who already reigned with absolute sway under the name of his uncle. Perhaps she contrived to enhance the value of a gift which she had so often lavished on the meanest of mankind; perhaps she inflamed, at first by modest delays, and at last by sensual allurements, the desires of a lover, who, from nature or devotion, was addicted to long vigils and abstemious diet. When his first transports had subsided, she still maintained the same ascendant over his mind, by the more solid merit of temper and understanding. Justinian delighted to ennoble and enrich the object of his affection; the treasures of the East were poured at her feet, and the nephew of Justin was determined, perhaps by religious scruples, to bestow on his concubine the sacred and legal character of a wife. But the laws of Rome expressly prohibited the marriage of a senator with any female who had been dishonored by a servile origin or theatrical profession: the empress Lupicina, or Euphemia, a Barbarian of rustic manners, but of irreproachable virtue, refused to accept a prostitute for her niece; and even Vigilantia, the superstitious mother of Justinian, though she acknowledged the wit and beauty of Theodora, was seriously apprehensive, lest the levity and arrogance of that artful paramour might corrupt the piety and happiness of her son. These obstacles were removed by the inflexible constancy of Justinian. He patiently expected the death of the empress; he despised the tears of his mother, who soon sunk under the weight of her affliction; and a law was promulgated in the name of the emperor Justin, which abolished the rigid jurisprudence of antiquity. A glorious repentance (the words of the edict) was left open for the unhappy females who had prostituted their persons on the theatre, and they were permitted to contract a legal union with the most illustrious of the Romans. [28] This indulgence was speedily followed by the solemn nuptials of Justinian and Theodora; her dignity was gradually exalted with that of her lover, and, as soon as Justin had invested his nephew with the purple, the patriarch of Constantinople placed the diadem on the heads of the emperor and empress of the East. But the usual honors which the severity of Roman manners had allowed to the wives of princes, could not satisfy either the ambition of Theodora or the fondness of Justinian. He seated her on the throne as an equal and independent colleague in the sovereignty of the empire, and an oath of allegiance was imposed on the governors of the provinces in the joint names of Justinian and Theodora. [29] The Eastern world fell prostrate before the genius and fortune of the daughter of Acacius. The prostitute who, in the presence of innumerable spectators, had polluted the theatre of Constantinople, was adored as a queen in the same city, by grave magistrates, orthodox bishops, victorious generals, and captive monarchs. [30]

[Footnote 27: Anonym. de Antiquitat. C. P. l. iii. 132, in Banduri Imperium Orient. tom. i. p. 48. Ludewig (p. 154) argues sensibly that Theodora would not have immortalized a brothel: but I apply this fact to her second and chaster residence at Constantinople.]

[Footnote 28: See the old law in Justinian's Code, (l. v. tit. v. leg. 7, tit. xxvii. leg. 1,) under the years 336 and 454. The new edict (about the year 521 or 522, Aleman. p. 38, 96) very awkwardly repeals no more than the clause of mulieres scenicoe, libertinae, tabernariae. See the novels 89 and 117, and a Greek rescript from Justinian to the bishops, (Aleman. p. 41.)]

[Footnote 29: I swear by the Father, &c., by the Virgin Mary, by the four Gospels, quae in manibus teneo, and by the Holy Archangels Michael and Gabriel, puram conscientiam germanumque servitium me servaturum, sacratissimis DDNN. Justiniano et Theodorae conjugi ejus, (Novell. viii. tit. 3.) Would the oath have been binding in favor of the widow? Communes tituli et triumphi, &c., (Aleman. p. 47, 48.)]

[Footnote 30: "Let greatness own her, and she's mean no more," &c. Without Warburton's critical telescope, I should never have seen, in this general picture of triumphant vice, any personal allusion to Theodora.]

PART II

Those who believe that the female mind is totally depraved by the loss of chastity, will eagerly listen to all the invectives of private envy, or popular resentment which have dissembled the virtues of Theodora, exaggerated her vices, and condemned with rigor the venal or voluntary sins of the youthful harlot. From a motive of shame, or contempt, she often declined the servile homage of the multitude, escaped from the odious light of the capital, and passed the greatest part of the year in the palaces and gardens which were pleasantly seated on the sea-coast of the Propontis and the Bosphorus. Her private hours were devoted to the prudent as well as grateful care of her beauty, the luxury of the bath and table, and the long slumber of the evening and the morning. Her secret apartments were occupied by the favorite women and eunuchs, whose interests and passions she indulged at the expense of justice; the most illustrious person ages of the state were crowded into a dark and sultry antechamber, and when at last, after tedious attendance, they were admitted to kiss the feet of Theodora, they experienced, as her humor might suggest, the silent arrogance of an empress, or the capricious levity of a comedian. Her rapacious avarice to accumulate an immense treasure, may be excused by the apprehension of her husband's death, which could leave no alternative between ruin and the throne; and fear as well as ambition might exasperate Theodora against two generals, who, during the malady of the emperor, had rashly declared that they were not disposed to acquiesce in the choice of the capital. But the reproach of cruelty, so repugnant even to her softer vices, has left an indelible stain on the memory of Theodora. Her numerous spies observed, and zealously reported, every action, or word, or look, injurious to their royal mistress. Whomsoever they accused were cast into her peculiar prisons, [31] inaccessible to the inquiries of justice; and it was rumored, that the torture of the rack, or scourge, had been inflicted in the presence of the female tyrant, insensible to the voice of prayer or of pity. [32] Some of these unhappy victims perished in deep, unwholesome dungeons, while others were permitted, after the loss of their limbs, their reason, or their fortunes, to appear in the world, the living monuments of her vengeance, which was commonly extended to the children of those whom she had suspected or injured. The senator or bishop, whose death or exile Theodora had pronounced, was delivered to a trusty messenger, and his diligence was quickened by a menace from her own mouth. "If you fail in the execution of my commands, I swear by Him who liveth forever, that your skin shall be flayed from your body." [33]

[Footnote 31: Her prisons, a labyrinth, a Tartarus, (Anecdot. c. 4,) were under the palace. Darkness is propitious to cruelty, but it is likewise favorable to calumny and fiction.]

[Footnote 32: A more jocular whipping was inflicted on Saturninus, for presuming to say that his wife, a favorite of the empress, had not been found. (Anecdot. c. 17.)]

[Footnote 33: Per viventem in saecula excoriari te faciam. Anastasius de Vitis Pont. Roman. in Vigilio, p. 40.]

If the creed of Theodora had not been tainted with heresy, her exemplary devotion might have atoned, in the opinion of her contemporaries, for pride, avarice, and cruelty. But, if she employed her influence to assuage the intolerant fury of the emperor, the present age will allow some merit to her religion, and much indulgence to her speculative errors. [34] The name of Theodora was introduced, with equal honor, in all the pious and charitable foundations of Justinian; and the most benevolent institution of his reign may be ascribed to the sympathy of the empress for her less fortunate sisters, who had been seduced or compelled to embrace the trade of prostitution. A palace, on the Asiatic side of the Bosphorus, was converted into a stately and spacious monastery, and a liberal maintenance was assigned to five hundred women, who had been collected from the streets and brothels of Constantinople. In this safe and holy retreat, they were devoted to perpetual confinement; and the despair of some, who threw themselves headlong into the sea, was lost in the gratitude of the penitents, who had been delivered from sin and misery by their generous benefactress. [35] The prudence of Theodora is celebrated by Justinian himself; and his laws are attributed to the sage counsels of his most reverend wife whom he had received as the gift of the Deity. [36] Her courage was displayed amidst the tumult of the people and the terrors of the court. Her chastity, from the moment of her union with Justinian, is founded on the silence of her implacable enemies; and although the daughter of Acacius might be satiated with love, yet some applause is due to the firmness of a mind which could sacrifice pleasure and habit to the stronger sense either of duty or interest. The wishes and prayers of Theodora could never obtain the blessing of a lawful son, and she buried an infant daughter, the sole offspring of her marriage. [37] Notwithstanding this disappointment, her dominion was permanent and absolute; she preserved, by art or merit, the affections of Justinian; and their seeming dissensions were always fatal to the courtiers who believed them to be sincere. Perhaps her health had been impaired by the licentiousness of her youth; but it was always delicate, and she was directed by her physicians to use the Pythian warm baths. In this journey, the empress was followed by the Praetorian praefect, the great treasurer, several counts and patricians, and a splendid train of four thousand attendants: the highways were repaired at her approach; a palace was erected for her reception; and as she passed through Bithynia, she distributed liberal alms to the churches, the monasteries, and the hospitals, that they might implore Heaven for the restoration of her health. [38] At length, in the twenty-fourth year of her marriage, and the twenty-second of her reign, she was consumed by a cancer; [39] and the irreparable loss was deplored by her husband, who, in the room of a theatrical prostitute, might have selected the purest and most noble virgin of the East. [40]

[Footnote 34: Ludewig, p. 161—166. I give him credit for the charitable attempt, although he hath not much charity in his temper.]

[Footnote 35: Compare the anecdotes (c. 17) with the Edifices (l. i. c. 9)—how differently may the same fact be stated! John Malala (tom. ii. p. 174, 175) observes, that on this, or a similar occasion, she released and clothed the girls whom she had purchased from the stews at five aurei apiece.]

[Footnote 36: Novel. viii. 1. An allusion to Theodora. Her enemies read the name Daemonodora, (Aleman. p. 66.)]

[Footnote 37: St. Sabas refused to pray for a son of Theodora, lest he should prove a heretic worse than Anastasius himself, (Cyril in Vit. St. Sabae, apud Aleman. p. 70, 109.)]

[Footnote 38: See John Malala, tom. ii. p. 174. Theophanes, p. 158. Procopius de Edific. l. v. c. 3.]

[Footnote 39: Theodora Chalcedonensis synodi inimica canceris plaga toto corpore perfusa vitam prodigiose finivit, (Victor Tununensis in Chron.) On such occasions, an orthodox mind is steeled against pity. Alemannus (p. 12, 13) understands of Theophanes as civil language, which does not imply either piety or repentance; yet two years after her death, St. Theodora is celebrated by Paul Silentiarius, (in proem. v. 58—62.)]

[Footnote 40: As she persecuted the popes, and rejected a council, Baronius exhausts the names of Eve, Dalila, Herodias, &c.; after which he has recourse to his infernal dictionary: civis inferni—alumna daemonum—satanico agitata spiritu-oestro percita diabolico, &c., &c., (A.D. 548, No. 24.)]

II. A material difference may be observed in the games of antiquity: the most eminent of the Greeks were actors, the Romans were merely spectators. The Olympic stadium was open to wealth, merit, and ambition; and if the candidates could depend on their personal skill and activity, they might pursue the footsteps of Diomede and Menelaus, and conduct their own horses in the rapid career. [41] Ten, twenty, forty chariots were allowed to start at the same instant; a crown of leaves was the reward of the victor; and his fame, with that of his family and country, was chanted in lyric strains more durable than monuments of brass and marble. But a senator, or even a citizen, conscious of his dignity, would have blushed to expose his person, or his horses, in the circus of Rome. The games were exhibited at the expense of the republic, the magistrates, or the emperors: but the reins were abandoned to servile hands; and if the profits of a favorite charioteer sometimes exceeded those of an advocate, they must be considered as the effects of popular extravagance, and the high wages of a disgraceful profession. The race, in its first institution, was a simple contest of two chariots, whose drivers were distinguished by white and red liveries: two additional colors, a light green, and a caerulean blue, were afterwards introduced; and as the races were repeated twenty-five times, one hundred chariots contributed in the same day to the pomp of the circus. The four factions soon acquired a legal establishment, and a mysterious origin, and their fanciful colors were derived from the various appearances of nature in the four seasons of the year; the red dogstar of summer, the snows of winter, the deep shades of autumn, and the cheerful verdure of the spring. [42] Another interpretation preferred the elements to the seasons, and the struggle of the green and blue was supposed to represent the conflict of the earth and sea. Their respective victories announced either a plentiful harvest or a prosperous navigation, and the hostility of the husbandmen and mariners was somewhat less absurd than the blind ardor of the Roman people, who devoted their lives and fortunes to the color which they had espoused. Such folly was disdained and indulged by the wisest princes; but the names of Caligula, Nero, Vitellius, Verus, Commodus, Caracalla, and Elagabalus, were enrolled in the blue or green factions of the circus; they frequented their stables, applauded their favorites, chastised their antagonists, and deserved the esteem of the populace, by the natural or affected imitation of their manners. The bloody and tumultuous contest continued to disturb the public festivity, till the last age of the spectacles of Rome; and Theodoric, from a motive of justice or affection, interposed his authority to protect the greens against the violence of a consul and a patrician, who were passionately addicted to the blue faction of the circus. [43]

[Footnote 41: Read and feel the xxiid book of the Iliad, a living picture of manners, passions, and the whole form and spirit of the chariot race West's Dissertation on the Olympic Games (sect. xii—xvii.) affords much curious and authentic information.]

[Footnote 42: The four colors, albati, russati, prasini, veneti, represent the four seasons, according to Cassiodorus, (Var. iii. 51,) who lavishes much wit and eloquence on this theatrical mystery. Of these colors, the three first may be fairly translated white, red, and green. Venetus is explained by coeruleus, a word various and vague: it is properly the sky reflected in the sea; but custom and convenience may allow blue as an equivalent, (Robert. Stephan. sub voce. Spence's Polymetis, p. 228.)]

[Footnote 43: See Onuphrius Panvinius de Ludis Circensibus, l. i. c. 10, 11; the xviith Annotation on Mascou's History of the Germans; and Aleman ad c. vii.]

Constantinople adopted the follies, though not the virtues, of ancient Rome; and the same factions which had agitated the circus, raged with redoubled fury in the hippodrome. Under the reign of Anastasius, this popular frenzy was inflamed by religious zeal; and the greens, who had treacherously concealed stones and daggers under baskets of fruit, massacred, at a solemn festival, three thousand of their blue adversaries. [44] From this capital, the pestilence was diffused into the provinces and cities of the East, and the sportive distinction of two colors produced two strong and irreconcilable factions, which shook the foundations of a feeble government. [45] The popular dissensions, founded on the most serious interest, or holy pretence, have scarcely equalled the obstinacy of this wanton discord, which invaded the peace of families, divided friends and brothers, and tempted the female sex, though seldom seen in the circus, to espouse the inclinations of their lovers, or to contradict the wishes of their husbands. Every law, either human or divine, was trampled under foot, and as long as the party was successful, its deluded followers appeared careless of private distress or public calamity. The license, without the freedom, of democracy, was revived at Antioch and Constantinople, and the support of a faction became necessary to every candidate for civil or ecclesiastical honors. A secret attachment to the family or sect of Anastasius was imputed to the greens; the blues were zealously devoted to the cause of orthodoxy and Justinian, [46] and their grateful patron protected, above five years, the disorders of a faction, whose seasonable tumults overawed the palace, the senate, and the capitals of the East. Insolent with royal favor, the blues affected to strike terror by a peculiar and Barbaric dress, the long hair of the Huns, their close sleeves and ample garments, a lofty step, and a sonorous voice. In the day they concealed their two-edged poniards, but in the night they boldly assembled in arms, and in numerous bands, prepared for every act of violence and rapine. Their adversaries of the green faction, or even inoffensive citizens, were stripped and often murdered by these nocturnal robbers, and it became dangerous to wear any gold buttons or girdles, or to appear at a late hour in the streets of a peaceful capital. A daring spirit, rising with impunity, proceeded to violate the safeguard of private houses; and fire was employed to facilitate the attack, or to conceal the crimes of these factious rioters. No place was safe or sacred from their depredations; to gratify either avarice or revenge, they profusely spilt the blood of the innocent; churches and altars were polluted by atrocious murders; and it was the boast of the assassins, that their dexterity could always inflict a mortal wound with a single stroke of their dagger. The dissolute youth of Constantinople adopted the blue livery of disorder; the laws were silent, and the bonds of society were relaxed: creditors were compelled to resign their obligations; judges to reverse their sentence; masters to enfranchise their slaves; fathers to supply the extravagance of their children; noble matrons were prostituted to the lust of their servants; beautiful boys were torn from the arms of their parents; and wives, unless they preferred a voluntary death, were ravished in the presence of their husbands. [47] The despair of the greens, who were persecuted by their enemies, and deserted by the magistrates, assumed the privilege of defence, perhaps of retaliation; but those who survived the combat were dragged to execution, and the unhappy fugitives, escaping to woods and caverns, preyed without mercy on the society from whence they were expelled. Those ministers of justice who had courage to punish the crimes, and to brave the resentment, of the blues, became the victims of their indiscreet zeal; a praefect of Constantinople fled for refuge to the holy sepulchre, a count of the East was ignominiously whipped, and a governor of Cilicia was hanged, by the order of Theodora, on the tomb of two assassins whom he had condemned for the murder of his groom, and a daring attack upon his own life. [48] An aspiring candidate may be tempted to build his greatness on the public confusion, but it is the interest as well as duty of a sovereign to maintain the authority of the laws. The first edict of Justinian, which was often repeated, and sometimes executed, announced his firm resolution to support the innocent, and to chastise the guilty, of every denomination and color. Yet the balance of justice was still inclined in favor of the blue faction, by the secret affection, the habits, and the fears of the emperor; his equity, after an apparent struggle, submitted, without reluctance, to the implacable passions of Theodora, and the empress never forgot, or forgave, the injuries of the comedian. At the accession of the younger Justin, the proclamation of equal and rigorous justice indirectly condemned the partiality of the former reign. "Ye blues, Justinian is no more! ye greens, he is still alive!" [49]

[Footnote 44: Marcellin. in Chron. p. 47. Instead of the vulgar word venata he uses the more exquisite terms of coerulea and coerealis. Baronius (A.D. 501, No. 4, 5, 6) is satisfied that the blues were orthodox; but Tillemont is angry at the supposition, and will not allow any martyrs in a playhouse, (Hist. des Emp. tom. vi. p. 554.)]

[Footnote 45: See Procopius, (Persic. l. i. c. 24.) In describing the vices of the factions and of the government, the public, is not more favorable than the secret, historian. Aleman. (p. 26) has quoted a fine passage from Gregory Nazianzen, which proves the inveteracy of the evil.]

[Footnote 46: The partiality of Justinian for the blues (Anecdot. c. 7) is attested by Evagrius, (Hist. Eccles. l. iv. c. 32,) John Malala, (tom ii p. 138, 139,) especially for Antioch; and Theophanes, (p. 142.)]

[Footnote 47: A wife, (says Procopius,) who was seized and almost ravished by a blue-coat, threw herself into the Bosphorus. The bishops of the second Syria (Aleman. p. 26) deplore a similar suicide, the guilt or glory of female chastity, and name the heroine.]

[Footnote 48: The doubtful credit of Procopius (Anecdot. c. 17) is supported by the less partial Evagrius, who confirms the fact, and specifies the names. The tragic fate of the praefect of Constantinople is related by John Malala, (tom. ii. p. 139.)]

[Footnote 49: See John Malala, (tom. ii. p. 147;) yet he owns that Justinian was attached to the blues. The seeming discord of the emperor and Theodora is, perhaps, viewed with too much jealousy and refinement by Procopius, (Anecdot. c. 10.) See Aleman. Praefat. p. 6.]

A sedition, which almost laid Constantinople in ashes, was excited by the mutual hatred and momentary reconciliation of the two factions. In the fifth year of his reign, Justinian celebrated the festival of the ides of January; the games were incessantly disturbed by the clamorous discontent of the greens: till the twenty-second race, the emperor maintained his silent gravity; at length, yielding to his impatience, he condescended to hold, in abrupt sentences, and by the voice of a crier, the most singular dialogue [50] that ever passed between a prince and his subjects. Their first complaints were respectful and modest; they accused the subordinate ministers of oppression, and proclaimed their wishes for the long life and victory of the emperor. "Be patient and attentive, ye insolent railers!" exclaimed Justinian; "be mute, ye Jews, Samaritans, and Manichaeans!" The greens still attempted to awaken his compassion. "We are poor, we are innocent, we are injured, we dare not pass through the streets: a general persecution is exercised against our name and color. Let us die, O emperor! but let us die by your command, and for your service!" But the repetition of partial and passionate invectives degraded, in their eyes, the majesty of the purple; they renounced allegiance to the prince who refused justice to his people; lamented that the father of Justinian had been born; and branded his son with the opprobrious names of a homicide, an ass, and a perjured tyrant. "Do you despise your lives?" cried the indignant monarch: the blues rose up with fury from their seats; their hostile clamors thundered in the hippodrome; and their adversaries, deserting the unequal contest spread terror and despair through the streets of Constantinople. At this dangerous moment, seven notorious assassins of both factions, who had been condemned by the praefect, were carried round the city, and afterwards transported to the place of execution in the suburb of Pera. Four were immediately beheaded; a fifth was hanged: but when the same punishment was inflicted on the remaining two, the rope broke, they fell alive to the ground, the populace applauded their escape, and the monks of St. Conon, issuing from the neighboring convent, conveyed them in a boat to the sanctuary of the church. [51] As one of these criminals was of the blue, and the other of the green livery, the two factions were equally provoked by the cruelty of their oppressor, or the ingratitude of their patron; and a short truce was concluded till they had delivered their prisoners and satisfied their revenge. The palace of the praefect, who withstood the seditious torrent, was instantly burnt, his officers and guards were massacred, the prisons were forced open, and freedom was restored to those who could only use it for the public destruction. A military force, which had been despatched to the aid of the civil magistrate, was fiercely encountered by an armed multitude, whose numbers and boldness continually increased; and the Heruli, the wildest Barbarians in the service of the empire, overturned the priests and their relics, which, from a pious motive, had been rashly interposed to separate the bloody conflict. The tumult was exasperated by this sacrilege, the people fought with enthusiasm in the cause of God; the women, from the roofs and windows, showered stones on the heads of the soldiers, who darted fire brands against the houses; and the various flames, which had been kindled by the hands of citizens and strangers, spread without control over the face of the city. The conflagration involved the cathedral of St. Sophia, the baths of Zeuxippus, a part of the palace, from the first entrance to the altar of Mars, and the long portico from the palace to the forum of Constantine: a large hospital, with the sick patients, was consumed; many churches and stately edifices were destroyed and an immense treasure of gold and silver was either melted or lost. From such scenes of horror and distress, the wise and wealthy citizens escaped over the Bosphorus to the Asiatic side; and during five days Constantinople was abandoned to the factions, whose watchword, Nika, vanquish! has given a name to this memorable sedition. [52]

[Footnote 50: This dialogue, which Theophanes has preserved, exhibits the popular language, as well as the manners, of Constantinople, in the vith century. Their Greek is mingled with many strange and barbarous words, for which Ducange cannot always find a meaning or etymology.]

[Footnote 51: See this church and monastery in Ducange, C. P. Christiana, l. iv p 182.]

[Footnote 52: The history of the Nika sedition is extracted from Marcellinus, (in Chron.,) Procopius, (Persic. l. i. c. 26,) John Malala, (tom. ii. p. 213—218,) Chron. Paschal., (p. 336—340,) Theophanes, (Chronograph. p. 154—158) and Zonaras, (l. xiv. p. 61—63.)]

As long as the factions were divided, the triumphant blues, and desponding greens, appeared to behold with the same indifference the disorders of the state. They agreed to censure the corrupt management of justice and the finance; and the two responsible ministers, the artful Tribonian, and the rapacious John of Cappadocia, were loudly arraigned as the authors of the public misery. The peaceful murmurs of the people would have been disregarded: they were heard with respect when the city was in flames; the quaestor, and the praefect, were instantly removed, and their offices were filled by two senators of blameless integrity. After this popular concession, Justinian proceeded to the hippodrome to confess his own errors, and to accept the repentance of his grateful subjects; but they distrusted his assurances, though solemnly pronounced in the presence of the holy Gospels; and the emperor, alarmed by their distrust, retreated with precipitation to the strong fortress of the palace. The obstinacy of the tumult was now imputed to a secret and ambitious conspiracy, and a suspicion was entertained, that the insurgents, more especially the green faction, had been supplied with arms and money by Hypatius and Pompey, two patricians, who could neither forget with honor, nor remember with safety, that they were the nephews of the emperor Anastasius. Capriciously trusted, disgraced, and pardoned, by the jealous levity of the monarch, they had appeared as loyal servants before the throne; and, during five days of the tumult, they were detained as important hostages; till at length, the fears of Justinian prevailing over his prudence, he viewed the two brothers in the light of spies, perhaps of assassins, and sternly commanded them to depart from the palace. After a fruitless representation, that obedience might lead to involuntary treason, they retired to their houses, and in the morning of the sixth day, Hypatius was surrounded and seized by the people, who, regardless of his virtuous resistance, and the tears of his wife, transported their favorite to the forum of Constantine, and instead of a diadem, placed a rich collar on his head. If the usurper, who afterwards pleaded the merit of his delay, had complied with the advice of his senate, and urged the fury of the multitude, their first irresistible effort might have oppressed or expelled his trembling competitor. The Byzantine palace enjoyed a free communication with the sea; vessels lay ready at the garden stairs; and a secret resolution was already formed, to convey the emperor with his family and treasures to a safe retreat, at some distance from the capital.

Justinian was lost, if the prostitute whom he raised from the theatre had not renounced the timidity, as well as the virtues, of her sex. In the midst of a council, where Belisarius was present, Theodora alone displayed the spirit of a hero; and she alone, without apprehending his future hatred, could save the emperor from the imminent danger, and his unworthy fears. "If flight," said the consort of Justinian, "were the only means of safety, yet I should disdain to fly. Death is the condition of our birth; but they who have reigned should never survive the loss of dignity and dominion. I implore Heaven, that I may never be seen, not a day, without my diadem and purple; that I may no longer behold the light, when I cease to be saluted with the name of queen. If you resolve, O Caesar! to fly, you have treasures; behold the sea, you have ships; but tremble lest the desire of life should expose you to wretched exile and ignominious death. For my own part, I adhere to the maxim of antiquity, that the throne is a glorious sepulchre." The firmness of a woman restored the courage to deliberate and act, and courage soon discovers the resources of the most desperate situation. It was an easy and a decisive measure to revive the animosity of the factions; the blues were astonished at their own guilt and folly, that a trifling injury should provoke them to conspire with their implacable enemies against a gracious and liberal benefactor; they again proclaimed the majesty of Justinian; and the greens, with their upstart emperor, were left alone in the hippodrome. The fidelity of the guards was doubtful; but the military force of Justinian consisted in three thousand veterans, who had been trained to valor and discipline in the Persian and Illyrian wars.

Under the command of Belisarius and Mundus, they silently marched in two divisions from the palace, forced their obscure way through narrow passages, expiring flames, and falling edifices, and burst open at the same moment the two opposite gates of the hippodrome. In this narrow space, the disorderly and affrighted crowd was incapable of resisting on either side a firm and regular attack; the blues signalized the fury of their repentance; and it is computed, that above thirty thousand persons were slain in the merciless and promiscuous carnage of the day. Hypatius was dragged from his throne, and conducted, with his brother Pompey, to the feet of the emperor: they implored his clemency; but their crime was manifest, their innocence uncertain, and Justinian had been too much terrified to forgive. The next morning the two nephews of Anastasius, with eighteen illustrious accomplices, of patrician or consular rank, were privately executed by the soldiers; their bodies were thrown into the sea, their palaces razed, and their fortunes confiscated. The hippodrome itself was condemned, during several years, to a mournful silence: with the restoration of the games, the same disorders revived; and the blue and green factions continued to afflict the reign of Justinian, and to disturb the tranquility of the Eastern empire. [53]

[Footnote 53: *Marcellinus says in general terms, innumeris populis in circotrucidatis. Procopius numbers 30,000 victims: and the 35,000 of Theophanes are swelled to 40,000 by the more recent Zonaras. Such is the usual progress of exaggeration.*]

III. That empire, after Rome was barbarous, still embraced the nations whom she had conquered beyond the Adriatic, and as far as the frontiers of Aethiopia and Persia. Justinian reigned over sixty-four provinces, and nine hundred and thirty-five cities; [54] his dominions were blessed by nature with the advantages of soil, situation, and climate: and the improvements of human art had been perpetually diffused along the coast of the Mediterranean and the banks of the Nile from ancient Troy to the Egyptian Thebes. Abraham [55] had been relieved by the well-known plenty of Egypt; the same country, a small and populous tract, was still capable of exporting, each year, two hundred and sixty thousand quarters of wheat for the use of Constantinople; [56] and the capital of Justinian was supplied with the manufactures of Sidon, fifteen centuries after they had been celebrated in the poems of Homer. [57] The annual powers of vegetation, instead of being exhausted by two thousand harvests, were renewed and invigorated by skilful husbandry, rich manure, and seasonable repose. The breed of domestic animals was infinitely multiplied. Plantations, buildings, and the instruments of labor and luxury, which are more durable than the term of human life, were accumulated by the care of successive generations. Tradition preserved, and experience simplified, the humble practice of the arts: society was enriched by the division of labor and the facility of exchange; and every Roman was lodged, clothed, and subsisted, by the industry of a thousand hands. The invention of the loom and distaff has been piously ascribed to the gods. In every age, a variety of animal and vegetable productions, hair, skins, wool, flax, cotton, and at length silk, have been skilfully manufactured to hide or adorn the human body; they were stained with an infusion of permanent colors; and the pencil was successfully employed to improve the labors of the loom. In the choice of those colors [58] which imitate the beauties of nature, the freedom of taste and fashion was indulged; but the deep purple [59] which the Phoenicians extracted from a shell-fish, was restrained to the sacred person and palace of the emperor; and the penalties of treason were denounced against the ambitious subjects who dared to usurp the prerogative of the throne. [60]

[Footnote 54: Hierocles, a contemporary of Justinian, composed his (Itineraria, p. 631,) review of the eastern provinces and cities, before the year 535, (Wesseling, in Praefat. and Not. ad p. 623, &c.)]

[Footnote 55: See the Book of Genesis (xii. 10) and the administration of Joseph. The annals of the Greeks and Hebrews agree in the early arts and plenty of Egypt: but this antiquity supposes a long series of improvement; and Warburton, who is almost stifled by the Hebrew calls aloud for the Samaritan, Chronology, (Divine Legation, vol. iii. p. 29, &c.) Note: The recent extraordinary discoveries in Egyptian antiquities strongly confirm the high notion of the early Egyptian civilization, and imperatively demand a longer period for their development. As to the common Hebrew chronology, as far as such a subject is capable of demonstration, it appears to me to have been framed, with a particular view, by the Jews of Tiberias. It was not the chronology of the Samaritans, not that of the LXX., not that of Josephus, not that of St. Paul—M.]

[Footnote 56: Eight millions of Roman modii, besides a contribution of 80,000 aurei for the expenses of water-carriage, from which the subject was graciously excused. See the 13th Edict of Justinian: the numbers are checked and verified by the agreement of the Greek and Latin texts.]

[Footnote 57: Homer's Iliad, vi. 289. These veils, were the work of the Sidonian women. But this passage is more honorable to the manufactures than to the navigation of Phoenicia, from whence they had been imported to Troy in Phrygian bottoms.]

[Footnote 58: See in Ovid (de Arte Amandi, iii. 269, &c.) a poetical list of twelve colors borrowed from flowers, the elements, &c. But it is almost impossible to discriminate by words all the nice and various shades both of art and nature.]

[Footnote 59: By the discovery of cochineal, &c., we far surpass the colors of antiquity. Their royal purple had a strong smell, and a dark cast as deep as bull's blood—obscuritas rubens, (says Cassiodorus, Var. 1, 2,) nigredo saguinea. The president Goguet (Origine des Loix et des Arts, part ii. l. ii. c. 2, p. 184—215) will amuse and satisfy the reader. I doubt whether his book, especially in England, is as well known as it deserves to be.]

[Footnote 60: Historical proofs of this jealousy have been occasionally introduced, and many more might have been added; but the arbitrary acts of despotism were justified by the sober and general declarations of law, (Codex Theodosian. l. x. tit. 21, leg. 3. Codex Justinian. l. xi. tit. 8, leg. 5.) An inglorious permission, and necessary restriction, was applied to the mince, the female dancers, (Cod. Theodos. l. xv. tit. 7, leg. 11.)]

PART III

I need not explain that silk [61] is originally spun from the bowels of a caterpillar, and that it composes the golden tomb, from whence a worm emerges in the form of a butterfly. Till the reign of Justinian, the silk-worm who feed on the leaves of the white mulberry-tree were confined to China; those of the pine, the oak, and the ash, were common in the forests both of Asia and Europe; but as their education is more difficult, and their produce more uncertain, they were generally neglected, except in the little island of Ceos, near the coast of Attica. A thin gauze was procured from their webs, and this Cean manufacture, the invention of a woman, for female use, was long admired both in the East and at Rome. Whatever suspicions may be raised by the garments of the Medes and Assyrians, Virgil is the most ancient writer, who expressly mentions the soft wool which was combed from the trees of the Seres or Chinese; [62] and this natural error, less marvellous than the truth, was slowly corrected by the knowledge of a valuable insect, the first artificer of the luxury of nations. That rare and elegant luxury was censured, in the reign of Tiberius, by the gravest of the Romans; and Pliny, in affected though forcible language, has condemned the thirst of gain, which explores the last confines of the earth, for the pernicious purpose of exposing to the public eye naked draperies and transparent matrons. [63] [63/1] A dress which showed the turn of the limbs, and color of the skin, might gratify vanity, or provoke desire; the silks which had been closely woven in China were sometimes unravelled by the Phoenician women, and the precious materials were multiplied by a looser texture, and the intermixture of linen threads. [64] Two hundred years after the age of Pliny, the use of pure, or even of mixed silks, was confined to the female sex, till the opulent citizens of Rome and the provinces were insensibly familiarized with the example of Elagabalus, the first who, by this effeminate habit, had sullied the dignity of an emperor and a man. Aurelian complained, that a pound of silk was sold at Rome for twelve ounces of gold; but the supply increased with the demand, and the price diminished with the supply. If accident or monopoly sometimes raised the value even above the standard of Aurelian, the manufacturers of Tyre and Berytus were sometimes compelled, by the operation of the same causes, to content themselves with a ninth part of that extravagant rate. [65] A law was thought necessary to discriminate the dress of comedians from that of senators; and of the silk exported from its native country the far greater part was consumed by the subjects of Justinian. They were still more intimately acquainted with a shell-fish of the Mediterranean, surnamed the silk-worm of the sea: the fine wool or hair by which the mother-of-pearl affixes itself to the rock is now manufactured for curiosity rather than use; and a robe obtained from the same singular materials was the gift of the Roman emperor to the satraps of Armenia. [66]

[Footnote 61: In the history of insects (far more wonderful than Ovid's Metamorphoses) the silk-worm holds a conspicuous place. The bombyx of the Isle of Ceos, as described by Pliny, (Hist. Natur. xi. 26, 27, with the notes of the two learned Jesuits, Hardouin and Brotier,) may be illustrated by a similar species in China, (Memoires sur les Chinois, tom. ii. p. 575—598;) but our silk-worm, as well as the white mulberry-tree, were unknown to Theophrastus and Pliny.]

[Footnote 62: Georgic. ii. 121. Serica quando venerint in usum planissime non acio: suspicor tamen in Julii Caesaris aevo, nam ante non invenio, says Justus Lipsius, (Excursus i. ad Tacit. Annal. ii. 32.) See Dion Cassius, (l. xliii. p. 358, edit. Reimar,) and Pausanius, (l. vi. p. 519,) the first who describes, however strangely, the Seric insect.]

[Footnote 63: Tam longinquo orbe petitur, ut in publico matrona transluceat...ut denudet foeminas vestis, (Plin. vi. 20, xi. 21.) Varro and Publius Syrus had already played on the Toga vitrea, ventus texilis, and nebula linen, (Horat. Sermon. i. 2, 101, with the notes of Torrentius and Dacier.)]

[Footnote 63/1: Gibbon must have written transparent draperies and naked matrons. Through sometimes affected, he is never inaccurate—M.]

[Footnote 64: On the texture, colors, names, and use of the silk, half silk, and liuen garments of antiquity, see the profound, diffuse, and obscure researches of the great Salmasius, (in Hist. August. p. 127, 309, 310, 339, 341, 342, 344, 388—391, 395, 513,) who was ignorant of the most common trades of Dijon or Leyden.]

[Footnote 65: Flavius Vopiscus in Aurelian. c. 45, in Hist. August. p. 224. See Salmasius ad Hist. Aug. p. 392, and Plinian. Exercitat. in Solinum, p. 694, 695. The Anecdotes of Procopius (c. 25) state a partial and imperfect rate of the price of silk in the time of Justinian.]

[Footnote 66: Procopius de Edit. l. iii. c. 1. These pinnes de mer are found near Smyrna, Sicily, Corsica, and Minorca; and a pair of gloves of their silk was presented to Pope Benedict XIV.]

A valuable merchandise of small bulk is capable of defraying the expense of land-carriage; and the caravans traversed the whole latitude of Asia in two hundred and forty-three days from the Chinese Ocean to the sea-coast of Syria. Silk was immediately delivered to the Romans by the Persian merchants, [67] who frequented the fairs of Armenia and Nisibis; but this trade, which in the intervals of truce was oppressed by avarice and jealousy, was totally interrupted by the long wars of the rival monarchies. The great king might proudly number Sogdiana, and even Serica, among the provinces of his empire; but his real dominion was bounded by the Oxus and his useful intercourse with the Sogdoites, beyond the river, depended on the pleasure of their conquerors, the white Huns, and the Turks, who successively reigned over that industrious people. Yet the most savage dominion has not extirpated the seeds of agriculture and commerce, in a region which is celebrated as one of the four gardens of Asia; the cities of Samarcand and Bochara are advantageously seated for the exchange of its various productions; and their merchants purchased from the Chinese, [68] the raw or manufactured silk which they transported into Persia for the use of the Roman empire. In the vain capital of China, the Sogdian caravans were entertained as the suppliant embassies of tributary kingdoms, and if they returned in safety, the bold adventure was rewarded with exorbitant gain. But the difficult and perilous march from Samarcand to the first town of Shensi, could not be performed in less than sixty, eighty, or one hundred days: as soon as they had passed the Jaxartes they entered the desert; and the wandering hordes, unless they are restrained by armies and garrisons, have always considered the citizen and the traveller as the objects of lawful rapine. To escape the Tartar robbers, and the tyrants of Persia, the silk caravans explored a more southern road; they traversed the mountains of Thibet, descended the streams of the Ganges or the Indus, and patiently expected, in the ports of Guzerat and Malabar, the annual fleets of the West. [69] But the dangers of the desert were found less intolerable than toil, hunger, and the loss of time; the attempt was seldom renewed, and the only European who has passed that unfrequented way, applauds his own diligence, that, in nine months after his departure from Pekin, he reached the mouth of the Indus. The ocean, however, was open to the free communication of mankind. From the great river to the tropic of Cancer, the provinces of China were subdued and civilized by the emperors of the North; they were filled about the time of the Christian aera with cities and men, mulberry-trees and their precious inhabitants; and if the Chinese, with the knowledge of the compass, had possessed the genius of the Greeks or Phoenicians, they might have spread their discoveries over the southern hemisphere. I am not qualified to examine, and I am not disposed to believe, their distant voyages to the Persian Gulf, or the Cape of Good Hope; but their ancestors might equal the labors and success of the present race, and the sphere of their navigation might extend from the Isles of Japan to the Straits of Malacca, the pillars, if we may apply that name, of an Oriental Hercules. [70] Without losing sight of land, they might sail along the coast to the extreme promontory of Achin, which is annually visited by ten or twelve ships laden with the productions, the manufactures, and even the artificers of China; the Island of Sumatra and the opposite peninsula are faintly delineated [71] as the regions of gold and silver; and the trading cities named in the geography of Ptolemy may indicate, that this wealth was not solely derived from the mines. The direct interval between Sumatra and Ceylon is about three hundred leagues: the Chinese and Indian navigators were conducted by the flight of birds and periodical winds; and the ocean might be securely traversed in square-built ships, which, instead of iron, were sewed together with the strong thread of the cocoanut. Ceylon, Serendib, or Taprobana, was divided between two hostile princes; one of whom possessed the mountains, the elephants, and the luminous carbuncle, and the other enjoyed the more solid riches of domestic industry, foreign trade, and the capacious harbor of Trinquemale, which received and dismissed the fleets of the East and West. In this hospitable isle, at an equal distance (as it was computed) from their respective countries, the silk merchants of China, who had collected in their voyages aloes, cloves, nutmeg, and sandal wood, maintained a free and beneficial commerce with the inhabitants of the Persian Gulf. The subjects of the great king exalted, without a rival, his power and magnificence: and the Roman, who confounded their vanity by comparing his paltry coin with a gold medal of the emperor Anastasius, had sailed to Ceylon, in an Aethiopian ship, as a simple passenger. [72]

[Footnote 67: Procopius, Persic. l. i. c. 20, l. ii. c. 25; Gothic. l. iv. c. 17. Menander in Excerpt. Legat. p. 107. Of the Parthian or Persian empire, Isidore of Charax (in Stathmis Parthicis, p. 7, 8, in Hudson, Geograph. Minor. tom. ii.) has marked the roads, and Ammianus Marcellinus (l. xxiii. c. 6, p. 400) has enumerated the provinces. Note: See St. Martin, Mem. sur l'Armenie, vol. ii. p. 41—M.]

[Footnote 68: The blind admiration of the Jesuits confounds the different periods of the Chinese history. They are more critically distinguished by M. de Guignes, (Hist. des Huns, tom. i. part i. in the Tables, part ii. in the Geography. Memoires de l'Academie des Inscriptions, tom. xxxii. xxxvi. xlii. xliii.,) who discovers the gradual progress of the truth of the annals and the extent of the monarchy, till the Christian aera. He has searched, with a curious eye, the connections of the Chinese with the nations of the West; but these connections are slight, casual, and obscure; nor did the Romans entertain a suspicion that the Seres or Sinae possessed an empire not inferior to their own. Note: An abstract of the various opinions of the learned modern writers, Gosselin, Mannert, Lelewel, Malte-Brun, Heeren, and La Treille, on the Serica and the Thinae of the ancients, may be found in the new edition of Malte-Brun, vol. vi. p. 368, 382—M.]

[Footnote 69: The roads from China to Persia and Hindostan may be investigated in the relations of Hackluyt and Thevenot, the ambassadors of Sharokh, Anthony Jenkinson, the Pere Greuber, &c. See likewise Hanway's Travels, vol. i. p. 345—357. A communication through Thibet has been lately explored by the English sovereigns of Bengal.]

[Footnote 70: For the Chinese navigation to Malacca and Achin, perhaps to Ceylon, see Renaudot, (on the two Mahometan Travellers, p. 8—11, 13—17, 141—157;) Dampier, (vol. ii. p. 136;) the Hist. Philosophique des deux Indes, (tom. i. p. 98,) and Hist. Generale des Voyages, (tom. vi. p. 201.)]

[Footnote 71: The knowledge, or rather ignorance, of Strabo, Pliny, Ptolemy, Arrian, Marcian, &c., of the countries eastward of Cape Comorin, is finely illustrated by D'Anville, (Antiquite Geographique de l'Inde, especially p. 161—198.) Our geography of India is improved by commerce and conquest; and has been illustrated by the excellent maps and memoirs of Major Rennel. If he extends the sphere of his inquiries with the same critical knowledge and sagacity, he will succeed, and may surpass, the first of modern geographers.]

[Footnote 72: The Taprobane of Pliny, (vi. 24,) Solinus, (c. 53,) and Salmas. Plinianae Exercitat., (p. 781, 782,) and most of the ancients, who often confound the islands of Ceylon and Sumatra, is more clearly described by Cosmas Indicopleustes; yet even the Christian topographer has exaggerated its dimensions. His information on the Indian and Chinese trade is rare and curious, (l. ii. p. 138, l. xi. p. 337, 338, edit. Montfaucon.)]

As silk became of indispensable use, the emperor Justinian saw with concern that the Persians had occupied by land and sea the monopoly of this important supply, and that the wealth of his subjects was continually drained by a nation of enemies and idolaters. An active government would have restored the trade of Egypt and the navigation of the Red Sea, which had decayed with the prosperity of the empire; and the Roman vessels might have sailed, for the purchase of silk, to the ports of Ceylon, of Malacca, or even of China. Justinian embraced a more humble expedient, and solicited the aid of his Christian allies, the Aethiopians of Abyssinia, who had recently acquired the arts of navigation, the spirit of trade, and the seaport of Adulis, [73] [73/1] still decorated with the trophies of a Grecian conqueror. Along the African coast, they penetrated to the equator in search of gold, emeralds, and aromatics; but they wisely declined an unequal competition, in which they must be always prevented by the vicinity of the Persians to the markets of India; and the emperor submitted to the disappointment, till his wishes were gratified by an unexpected event. The gospel had been preached to the Indians: a bishop already governed the Christians of St. Thomas on the pepper-coast of Malabar; a church was planted in Ceylon, and the missionaries pursued the footsteps of commerce to the extremities of Asia. [74] Two Persian monks had long resided in China, perhaps in the royal city of Nankin, the seat of a monarch addicted to foreign superstitions, and who actually received an embassy from the Isle of Ceylon. Amidst their pious occupations, they viewed with a curious eye the common dress of the Chinese, the manufactures of silk, and the myriads of silk-worms, whose education (either on trees or in houses) had once been considered as the labor of queens. [75] They soon discovered that it was impracticable to transport the short-lived insect, but that in the eggs a numerous progeny might be preserved and multiplied in a distant climate. Religion or interest had more power over the Persian monks than the love of their country: after a long journey, they arrived at Constantinople, imparted their project to the emperor, and were liberally encouraged by the gifts and promises of Justinian. To the historians of that prince, a campaign at the foot of Mount Caucasus has seemed more deserving of a minute relation than the labors of these missionaries of commerce, who again entered China, deceived a jealous people by concealing the eggs of the silk-worm in a hollow cane, and returned in triumph with the spoils of the

East. Under their direction, the eggs were hatched at the proper season by the artificial heat of dung; the worms were fed with mulberry leaves; they lived and labored in a foreign climate; a sufficient number of butterflies was saved to propagate the race, and trees were planted to supply the nourishment of the rising generations. Experience and reflection corrected the errors of a new attempt, and the Sogdoite ambassadors acknowledged, in the succeeding reign, that the Romans were not inferior to the natives of China in the education of the insects, and the manufactures of silk, [76] in which both China and Constantinople have been surpassed by the industry of modern Europe. I am not insensible of the benefits of elegant luxury; yet I reflect with some pain, that if the importers of silk had introduced the art of printing, already practised by the Chinese, the comedies of Menander and the entire decads of Livy would have been perpetuated in the editions of the sixth century.

A larger view of the globe might at least have promoted the improvement of speculative science, but the Christian geography was forcibly extracted from texts of Scripture, and the study of nature was the surest symptom of an unbelieving mind. The orthodox faith confined the habitable world to one temperate zone, and represented the earth as an oblong surface, four hundred days' journey in length, two hundred in breadth, encompassed by the ocean, and covered by the solid crystal of the firmament. [77]

[Footnote 73: See Procopius, Persic. (l. ii. c. 20.) Cosmas affords some interesting knowledge of the port and inscription of Adulis, (Topograph. Christ. l. ii. p. 138, 140—143,) and of the trade of the Axumites along the African coast of Barbaria or Zingi, (p. 138, 139,) and as far as Taprobane, (l. xi. p. 339.)]

[Footnote 73/1: Mr. Salt obtained information of considerable ruins of an ancient town near Zulla, called Azoole, which answers to the position of Adulis. Mr. Salt was prevented by illness, Mr. Stuart, whom he sent, by the jealousy of the natives, from investigating these ruins: of their existence there seems no doubt. Salt's 2d Journey, p. 452—M.]

[Footnote 74: See the Christian missions in India, in Cosmas, (l. iii. p. 178, 179, l. xi. p. 337,) and consult Asseman. Bibliot. Orient. (tom. iv. p. 413—548.)]

[Footnote 75: The invention, manufacture, and general use of silk in China, may be seen in Duhalde, (Description Generale de la Chine, tom. ii. p. 165, 205—223.) The province of Chekian is the most renowned both for quantity and quality.]

[Footnote 76: Procopius, (l. viii. Gothic. iv. c. 17. Theophanes Byzant. apud Phot. Cod. lxxxiv. p. 38. Zonaras, tom. ii. l. xiv. p. 69. Pagi tom. ii. p. 602) assigns to the year 552 this memorable importation. Menander (in Excerpt. Legat. p. 107) mentions the admiration of the Sogdoites; and Theophylact Simocatta (l. vii. c. 9) darkly represents the two rival kingdoms in (China) the country of silk.]

[Footnote 77: Cosmas, surnamed Indicopleustes, or the Indian navigator, performed his voyage about the year 522, and composed at Alexandria, between 535, and 547, Christian Topography, (Montfaucon, Praefat. c. i.,) in which he refutes the impious opinion, that the earth is a globe; and Photius had read this work, (Cod. xxxvi. p. 9, 10,) which displays the prejudices of a monk, with the knowledge of a merchant; the most valuable part has been given in French and in Greek by Melchisedec Thevenot, (Relations Curieuses, part i.,) and the whole is since published in a splendid edition by Pere Montfaucon, (Nova Collectio Patrum, Paris, 1707, 2 vols. in fol., tom. ii. p. 113—346.) But the editor, a theologian, might blush at not discovering the Nestorian heresy of Cosmas, which has been detected by La Croz (Christianisme des Indes, tom. i. p. 40—56.)]

IV. The subjects of Justinian were dissatisfied with the times, and with the government. Europe was overrun by the Barbarians, and Asia by the monks: the poverty of the West discouraged the trade and manufactures of the East: the produce of labor was consumed by the unprofitable servants of the church, the state, and the army; and a rapid decrease was felt in the fixed and circulating capitals which constitute the national wealth. The public distress had been alleviated by the economy of Anastasius, and that prudent emperor accumulated an immense treasure, while he delivered his people from the most odious or oppressive taxes. [77/1] Their gratitude universally applauded the abolition of the gold of affliction, a personal tribute on the industry of the poor, [78] but more intolerable, as it should seem, in the form than in the substance, since the flourishing city of Edessa paid only one hundred and forty pounds of gold, which was collected in four years from ten thousand artificers. [79] Yet such was the parsimony which supported this liberal disposition, that, in a reign of twenty-seven years, Anastasius saved, from his annual revenue, the enormous sum of thirteen millions sterling, or three hundred and twenty thousand pounds of gold. [80] His example was neglected, and his treasure was abused, by the nephew of Justin. The riches of Justinian were speedily exhausted by alms and buildings, by ambitious wars, and ignominious treaties. His revenues were found inadequate to his expenses. Every art was tried to extort from the people the gold and silver which he scattered with a lavish hand from Persia to France: [81] his reign was marked by the vicissitudes or rather by the combat, of rapaciousness and avarice, of splendor and poverty; he lived with the reputation of hidden treasures, [82] and bequeathed to his successor the payment of his debts. [83] Such a character has been justly accused by the voice of the people and of posterity: but public discontent is credulous; private malice is bold; and a lover of truth will peruse with a suspicious eye the instructive anecdotes of Procopius. The secret historian represents only the vices of Justinian, and those vices are darkened by his malevolent pencil. Ambiguous actions are imputed to the worst motives; error is confounded with guilt, accident with design, and laws with abuses; the partial injustice of a moment is dexterously applied as the general maxim of a reign of thirty-two years; the emperor alone is made responsible for the faults of his officers, the disorders of the times, and the corruption of his subjects; and even the calamities of nature, plagues, earthquakes, and inundations, are imputed to the prince of the daemons, who had mischievously assumed the form of Justinian. [84]

[Footnote 77/1: See the character of Anastasius in Joannes Lydus de Magistratibus, iii. c. 45, 46, p. 230—232. His economy is there said to have degenerated into parsimony. He is accused of having taken away the levying of taxes and payment of the troops from the municipal authorities, (the decurionate) in the Eastern cities, and intrusted it to an extortionate officer named Mannus. But he admits that the imperial revenue was enormously increased by this measure. A statue of iron had been erected to Anastasius in the Hippodrome, on which appeared one morning this pasquinade. This epigram is also found in the Anthology. Jacobs, vol. iv. p. 114 with some better readings. This iron statue meetly do we place To thee, world-wasting king, than brass more base; For all the death, the penury, famine, woe, That from thy wide-destroying avarice flow, This fell Charybdis, Scylla, near to thee, This fierce devouring Anastasius, see; And tremble, Scylla! on thee, too, his greed, Coining thy brazen deity, may feed. But Lydus, with no uncommon inconsistency in such writers, proceeds to paint the character of Anastasius as endowed with almost every virtue, not excepting the utmost liberality. He was only prevented by death from relieving his subjects altogether from the capitation tax, which he greatly diminished—M.]

[Footnote 78: Evagrius (l. ii. c. 39, 40) is minute and grateful, but angry with Zosimus for calumniating the great Constantine. In collecting all the bonds and records of the tax, the humanity of Anastasius was diligent and artful: fathers were sometimes compelled to prostitute their daughters, (Zosim. Hist. l. ii. c. 38, p. 165, 166, Lipsiae, 1784.) Timotheus of Gaza chose such an event for the subject of a tragedy,

(Suidas, tom. iii. p. 475,) which contributed to the abolition of the tax, (Cedrenus, p. 35,)—a happy instance (if it be true) of the use of the theatre.]

[Footnote 79: See Josua Stylites, in the Bibliotheca Orientalis of Asseman, (tom. p. 268.) This capitation tax is slightly mentioned in the Chronicle of Edessa.]

[Footnote 80: Procopius (Anecdot. c. 19) fixes this sum from the report of the treasurers themselves. Tiberias had vicies ter millies; but far different was his empire from that of Anastasius.]

[Footnote 81: Evagrius, (l. iv. c. 30,) in the next generation, was moderate and well informed; and Zonaras, (l. xiv. c. 61,) in the xiith century, had read with care, and thought without prejudice; yet their colors are almost as black as those of the anecdotes.]

[Footnote 82: Procopius (Anecdot. c. 30) relates the idle conjectures of the times. The death of Justinian, says the secret historian, will expose his wealth or poverty.]

[Footnote 83: See Corippus de Laudibus Justini Aug. l. ii. 260, &c., 384, &c "Plurima sunt vivo nimium neglecta parenti, Unde tot exhaustus contraxit debita fiscus." Centenaries of gold were brought by strong men into the Hippodrome, "Debita persolvit, genitoris cauta recepit."]

[Footnote 84: The Anecdotes (c. 11—14, 18, 20—30) supply many facts and more complaints. Note: The work of Lydus de Magistratibus (published by Hase at Paris, 1812, and reprinted in the new edition of the Byzantine Historians,) was written during the reign of Justinian. This work of Lydus throws no great light on the earlier history of the Roman magistracy, but gives some curious details of the changes and retrenchments in the offices of state, which took place at this time. The personal history of the author, with the account of his early and rapid advancement, and the emoluments of the posts which he successively held, with the bitter disappointment which he expresses, at finding himself, at the height of his ambition, in an unpaid place, is an excellent illustration of this statement. Gibbon has before, c. iv. n. 45, and c. xvii. n. 112, traced the progress of a Roman citizen to the highest honors of the state under the empire; the steps by which Lydus reached his humbler eminence may likewise throw light on the civil service at this period. He was first received into the office of the Praetorian praefect; became a notary in that office, and made in one year 1000 golden solidi, and that without extortion. His place and the influence of his relatives obtained him a wife with 400 pounds of gold for her dowry. He became chief chartularius, with an annual stipend of twenty-four solidi, and considerable emoluments for all the various services which he performed. He rose to an Augustalis, and finally to the dignity of Corniculus, the highest, and at one time the most lucrative office in the department. But the Praetorian praefect had gradually been deprived of his powers and his honors. He lost the superintendence of the supply and manufacture of arms; the uncontrolled charge of the public posts; the levying of the troops; the command of the army in war when the emperors ceased nominally to command in person, but really through the Praetorian praefect; that of the household troops, which fell to the magister aulae. At length the office was so completely stripped of its power, as to be virtually abolished, (see de Magist. l. iii. c. 40, p. 220, &c.) This diminution of the office of the praefect destroyed the emoluments of his subordinate officers, and Lydus not only drew no revenue from his dignity, but expended upon it all the gains of his former services. Lydus gravely refers this calamitous, and, as he considers it, fatal degradation of the Praetorian office to the alteration in the style of the official documents from Latin to Greek; and refers to a prophecy of a certain Fonteius, which connected the ruin of the Roman empire with its abandonment of its language. Lydus chiefly owed his promotion to his knowledge of Latin!—M.]

After this precaution, I shall briefly relate the anecdotes of avarice and rapine under the following heads: I. Justinian was so profuse that he could not be liberal. The civil and military officers, when they were admitted into the service of the palace, obtained an humble rank and a moderate stipend; they ascended by seniority to a station of affluence and repose; the annual pensions, of which the most honorable class was abolished by Justinian, amounted to four hundred thousand pounds; and this domestic economy was deplored by the venal or indigent courtiers as the last outrage on the majesty of the empire. The posts, the salaries of physicians, and the nocturnal illuminations, were objects of more general concern; and the cities might justly complain, that he usurped the municipal revenues which had been appropriated to these useful institutions. Even the soldiers were injured; and such was the decay of military spirit, that they were injured with impunity. The emperor refused, at the return of each fifth year, the customary donative of five pieces of gold, reduced his veterans to beg their bread, and suffered unpaid armies to melt away in the wars of Italy and Persia. II. The humanity of his predecessors had always remitted, in some auspicious circumstance of their reign, the arrears of the public tribute, and they dexterously assumed the merit of resigning those claims which it was impracticable to enforce. "Justinian, in the space of thirty-two years, has never granted a similar indulgence; and many of his subjects have renounced the possession of those lands whose value is insufficient to satisfy the demands of the treasury. To the cities which had suffered by hostile inroads Anastasius promised a general exemption of seven years: the provinces of Justinian have been ravaged by the Persians and Arabs, the Huns and Sclavonians; but his vain and ridiculous dispensation of a single year has been confined to those places which were actually taken by the enemy." Such is the language of the secret historian, who expressly denies that any indulgence was granted to Palestine after the revolt of the Samaritans; a false and odious charge, confuted by the authentic record which attests a relief of thirteen centenaries of gold (fifty-two thousand pounds) obtained for that desolate province by the intercession of St. Sabas. [85] III. Procopius has not condescended to explain the system of taxation, which fell like a hail-storm upon the land, like a devouring pestilence on its inhabitants: but we should become the accomplices of his malignity, if we imputed to Justinian alone the ancient though rigorous principle, that a whole district should be condemned to sustain the partial loss of the persons or property of individuals. The Annona, or supply of corn for the use of the army and capital, was a grievous and arbitrary exaction, which exceeded, perhaps in a tenfold proportion, the ability of the farmer; and his distress was aggravated by the partial injustice of weights and measures, and the expense and labor of distant carriage. In a time of scarcity, an extraordinary requisition was made to the adjacent provinces of Thrace, Bithynia, and Phrygia: but the proprietors, after a wearisome journey and perilous navigation, received so inadequate a compensation, that they would have chosen the alternative of delivering both the corn and price at the doors of their granaries. These precautions might indicate a tender solicitude for the welfare of the capital; yet Constantinople did not escape the rapacious despotism of Justinian. Till his reign, the Straits of the Bosphorus and Hellespont were open to the freedom of trade, and nothing was prohibited except the exportation of arms for the service of the Barbarians. At each of these gates of the city, a praetor was stationed, the minister of Imperial avarice; heavy customs were imposed on the vessels and their merchandise; the oppression was retaliated on the helpless consumer; the poor were afflicted by the artificial scarcity, and exorbitant price of the market; and a people, accustomed to depend on the liberality of their prince, might sometimes complain of the deficiency of water and bread. [86] The aerial tribute, without a name, a law, or a definite object, was an annual gift of one hundred and twenty thousand pounds, which the emperor accepted from his Praetorian praefect; and the means of payment were abandoned to the discretion of that powerful magistrate.

IV. Even such a tax was less intolerable than the privilege of monopolies, [86/1] which checked the fair competition of industry, and, for the sake of a small and dishonest gain, imposed an arbitrary burden on the wants and luxury of the subject. "As soon" (I transcribe the Anecdotes) "as the exclusive sale of silk was usurped by the Imperial treasurer, a whole people, the manufacturers of Tyre and Berytus, was reduced to extreme misery, and either perished with hunger, or fled to the hostile dominions of Persia." A province might suffer by the decay of its manufactures, but in this example of silk, Procopius has partially overlooked the inestimable and lasting benefit which the empire received from the curiosity of Justinian. His addition of one seventh to the ordinary price of copper money may be interpreted with the same candor; and the alteration, which might be wise, appears to have been innocent; since he neither alloyed the purity, nor enhanced the value, of the gold coin, [87] the legal measure of public and private payments. V. The ample jurisdiction required by the farmers of the revenue to accomplish their engagements might be placed in an odious light, as if they had purchased from the emperor the lives and fortunes of their fellow-citizens. And a more direct sale of honors and offices was transacted in the palace, with the permission, or at least with the connivance, of Justinian and Theodora. The claims of merit, even those of favor, were disregarded, and it was almost reasonable to expect, that the bold adventurer, who had undertaken the trade of a magistrate, should find a rich compensation for infamy, labor, danger, the debts which he had contracted, and the heavy interest which he paid. A sense of the disgrace and mischief of this venal practice, at length awakened the slumbering virtue of Justinian; and he attempted, by the sanction of oaths [88] and penalties, to guard the integrity of his government: but at the end of a year of perjury, his rigorous edict was suspended, and corruption licentiously abused her triumph over the impotence of the laws. VI. The testament of Eulalius, count of the domestics, declared the emperor his sole heir, on condition, however, that he should discharge his debts and legacies, allow to his three daughters a decent maintenance, and bestow each of them in marriage, with a portion of ten pounds of gold. But the splendid fortune of Eulalius had been consumed by fire, and the inventory of his goods did not exceed the trifling sum of five hundred and sixty-four pieces of gold. A similar instance, in Grecian history, admonished the emperor of the honorable part prescribed for his imitation. He checked the selfish murmurs of the treasury, applauded the confidence of his friend, discharged the legacies and debts, educated the three virgins under the eye of the empress Theodora, and doubled the marriage portion which had satisfied the tenderness of their father. [89] The humanity of a prince (for princes cannot be generous) is entitled to some praise; yet even in this act of virtue we may discover the inveterate custom of supplanting the legal or natural heirs, which Procopius imputes to the reign of Justinian. His charge is supported by eminent names and scandalous examples; neither widows nor orphans were spared; and the art of soliciting, or extorting, or supposing testaments, was beneficially practised by the agents of the palace. This base and mischievous tyranny invades the security of private life; and the monarch who has indulged an appetite for gain, will soon be tempted to anticipate the moment of succession, to interpret wealth as an evidence of guilt, and to proceed, from the claim of inheritance, to the power of confiscation. VII. Among the forms of rapine, a philosopher may be permitted to name the conversion of Pagan or heretical riches to the use of the faithful; but in the time of Justinian this holy plunder was condemned by the sectaries alone, who became the victims of his orthodox avarice. [90]

[Footnote 85: One to Scythopolis, capital of the second Palestine, and twelve for the rest of the province. Aleman. (p. 59) honestly produces this fact from a Ms. life of St. Sabas, by his disciple Cyril, in the Vatican Library, and since published by Cotelerius.]

[Footnote 86: John Malala (tom. ii. p. 232) mentions the want of bread, and Zonaras (l. xiv. p. 63) the leaden pipes, which Justinian, or his servants, stole from the aqueducts.]

[Footnote 86/1: Hullman (Geschichte des Byzantinischen Handels. p. 15) shows that the despotism of the government was aggravated by the unchecked rapenity of the officers. This state monopoly, even of corn, wine, and oil, was to force at the time of the first crusade—M.]

[Footnote 87: For an aureus, one sixth of an ounce of gold, instead of 210, he gave no more than 180 folles, or ounces of copper. A disproportion of the mint, below the market price, must have soon produced a scarcity of small money. In England twelve pence in copper would sell for no more than seven pence, (Smith's Inquiry into the Wealth of Nations, vol. i. p. 49.) For Justinian's gold coin, see Evagrius, (l. iv. c. 30.)]

[Footnote 88: The oath is conceived in the most formidable words, (Novell. viii. tit. 3.) The defaulters imprecate on themselves, quicquid haben: telorum armamentaria coeli: the part of Judas, the leprosy of Gieza, the tremor of Cain, &c., besides all temporal pains.]

[Footnote 89: A similar or more generous act of friendship is related by Lucian of Eudamidas of Corinth, (in Toxare, c. 22, 23, tom. ii. p. 530,) and the story has produced an ingenious, though feeble, comedy of Fontenelle.]

[Footnote 90: John Malala, tom. ii. p. 101, 102, 103.]

PART IV

Dishonor might be ultimately reflected on the character of Justinian; but much of the guilt, and still more of the profit, was intercepted by the ministers, who were seldom promoted for their virtues, and not always selected for their talents. [91] The merits of Tribonian the quaestor will hereafter be weighed in the reformation of the Roman law; but the economy of the East was subordinate to the Praetorian praefect, and Procopius has justified his anecdotes by the portrait which he exposes in his public history, of the notorious vices of John of Cappadocia. [92]

[92/1] His knowledge was not borrowed from the schools, [93] and his style was scarcely legible; but he excelled in the powers of native genius, to suggest the wisest counsels, and to find expedients in the most desperate situations. The corruption of his heart was equal to the vigor of his understanding. Although he was suspected of magic and Pagan superstition, he appeared insensible to the fear of God or the reproaches of man; and his aspiring fortune was raised on the death of thousands, the poverty of millions, the ruins of cities, and the desolation of provinces. From the dawn of light to the moment of dinner, he assiduously labored to enrich his master and himself at the expense of the Roman world; the remainder of the day was spent in sensual and obscene pleasures, [93/1] and the silent hours of the night were interrupted by the perpetual dread of the justice of an assassin. His abilities, perhaps his vices, recommended him to the lasting friendship of Justinian: the emperor yielded with reluctance to the fury of the people; his victory was displayed by the immediate restoration of their enemy; and they felt above ten years, under his oppressive administration, that he was stimulated by revenge, rather than instructed by misfortune. Their murmurs served only to fortify the resolution of Justinian; but the resentment of Theodora, disdained a power before which every knee was bent, and attempted to sow the seeds of discord between the emperor and his beloved consort. Even Theodora herself was constrained to dissemble, to wait a favorable moment, and, by an artful conspiracy, to render John of Cappadocia the accomplice of his own destruction. [93/2] At a time when Belisarius, unless he had been a hero, must have shown himself a rebel, his wife Antonina, who enjoyed the secret confidence of the empress, communicated his feigned discontent to Euphemia, the daughter of the praefect; the credulous virgin imparted to her father the dangerous project, and John, who might have known the value of oaths and promises, was tempted to accept a nocturnal, and almost treasonable, interview with the wife of Belisarius. An ambuscade of guards and eunuchs had been posted by the command of Theodora; they rushed with drawn swords to seize or to punish the guilty minister: he was saved by the fidelity of his attendants; but instead of appealing to a gracious sovereign, who had privately warned him of his danger, he pusillanimously fled to the sanctuary of the church. The favorite of Justinian was sacrificed to conjugal tenderness or domestic tranquility; the conversion of a praefect into a priest extinguished his ambitious hopes: but the friendship of the emperor alleviated his disgrace, and he retained in the mild exile of Cyzicus an ample portion of his riches. Such imperfect revenge could not satisfy the unrelenting hatred of Theodora; the murder of his old enemy, the bishop of Cyzicus, afforded a decent pretence; and John of Cappadocia, whose actions had deserved a thousand deaths, was at last condemned for a crime of which he was innocent. A great minister, who had been invested with the honors of consul and patrician, was ignominiously scourged like the vilest of malefactors; a tattered cloak was the sole remnant of his fortunes; he was transported in a bark to the place of his banishment at Antinopolis in Upper Egypt, and the praefect of the East begged his bread through the cities which had trembled at his name. During an exile of seven years, his life was protracted and threatened by the ingenious cruelty of Theodora; and when her death permitted the emperor to recall a servant whom he had abandoned with regret, the ambition of John of Cappadocia was reduced to the humble duties of the sacerdotal profession. His successors convinced the subjects of Justinian, that the arts of oppression might still be improved by experience and industry; the frauds of a Syrian banker were introduced into the administration of the finances; and the example of the praefect was diligently copied by the quaestor, the public and private treasurer, the governors of provinces, and the principal magistrates of the Eastern empire. [94]

[Footnote 91: One of these, Anatolius, perished in an earthquake—doubtless a judgment! The complaints and clamors of the people in Agathias (l. v. p. 146, 147) are almost an echo of the anecdote. The aliena pecunia reddenda of Corippus (l. ii. 381, &c.,) is not very honorable to Justinian's memory.]

[Footnote 92: See the history and character of John of Cappadocia in Procopius. (Persic, l. i. c. 35, 25, l. ii. c. 30. Vandal. l. i. c. 13. Anecdot. c. 2, 17, 22.) The agreement of the history and anecdotes is a mortal wound to the reputation of the praefct.]

[Footnote 92/1: This view, particularly of the cruelty of John of Cappadocia, is confirmed by the testimony of Joannes Lydus, who was in the office of the praefect, and eye-witness of the tortures inflicted by his command on the miserable debtors, or supposed debtors, of the state. He mentions one horrible instance of a respectable old man, with whom he was personally acquainted, who, being suspected of possessing money, was hung up by the hands till he was dead. Lydus de Magist. lib. iii. c. 57, p. 254—M.]

[Footnote 93: A forcible expression.]

[Footnote 93/1: Joannes Lydus is diffuse on this subject, lib. iii. c. 65, p. 268. But the indignant virtue of Lydus seems greatly stimulated by the loss of his official fees, which he ascribes to the innovations of the minister—M.]

[Footnote 93/2: According to Lydus, Theodora disclosed the crimes and unpopularity of the minister to Justinian, but the emperor had not the courage to remove, and was unable to replace, a servant, under whom his finances seemed to prosper. He attributes the sedition and conflagration to the popular

resentment against the tyranny of John, lib. iii. c 70, p. 278. Unfortunately there is a large gap in his work just at this period—M.]

[Footnote 94: The chronology of Procopius is loose and obscure; but with the aid of Pagi I can discern that John was appointed Praetorian praefect of the East in the year 530—that he was removed in January, 532—restored before June, 533—banished in 541—and recalled between June, 548, and April 1, 549. Aleman. (p. 96, 97) gives the list of his ten successors—a rapid series in a part of a single reign. Note: Lydus gives a high character of Phocas, his successor tom. iii. c. 78 p. 288—M.]

V. The edifices of Justinian were cemented with the blood and treasure of his people; but those stately structures appeared to announce the prosperity of the empire, and actually displayed the skill of their architects. Both the theory and practice of the arts which depend on mathematical science and mechanical power, were cultivated under the patronage of the emperors; the fame of Archimedes was rivalled by Proclus and Anthemius; and if their miracles had been related by intelligent spectators, they might now enlarge the speculations, instead of exciting the distrust, of philosophers. A tradition has prevailed, that the Roman fleet was reduced to ashes in the port of Syracuse, by the burning-glasses of Archimedes; [95] and it is asserted, that a similar expedient was employed by Proclus to destroy the Gothic vessels in the harbor of Constantinople, and to protect his benefactor Anastasius against the bold enterprise of Vitalian. [96] A machine was fixed on the walls of the city, consisting of a hexagon mirror of polished brass, with many smaller and movable polygons to receive and reflect the rays of the meridian sun; and a consuming flame was darted, to the distance, perhaps of two hundred feet. [97] The truth of these two extraordinary facts is invalidated by the silence of the most authentic historians; and the use of burning-glasses was never adopted in the attack or defence of places. [98] Yet the admirable experiments of a French philosopher [99] have demonstrated the possibility of such a mirror; and, since it is possible, I am more disposed to attribute the art to the greatest mathematicians of antiquity, than to give the merit of the fiction to the idle fancy of a monk or a sophist. According to another story, Proclus applied sulphur to the destruction of the Gothic fleet; [100] in a modern imagination, the name of sulphur is instantly connected with the suspicion of gunpowder, and that suspicion is propagated by the secret arts of his disciple Anthemius. [101] A citizen of Tralles in Asia had five sons, who were all distinguished in their respective professions by merit and success. Olympius excelled in the knowledge and practice of the Roman jurisprudence. Dioscorus and Alexander became learned physicians; but the skill of the former was exercised for the benefit of his fellow-citizens, while his more ambitious brother acquired wealth and reputation at Rome. The fame of Metrodorus the grammarian, and of Anthemius the mathematician and architect, reached the ears of the emperor Justinian, who invited them to Constantinople; and while the one instructed the rising generation in the schools of eloquence, the other filled the capital and provinces with more lasting monuments of his art. In a trifling dispute relative to the walls or windows of their contiguous houses, he had been vanquished by the eloquence of his neighbor Zeno; but the orator was defeated in his turn by the master of mechanics, whose malicious, though harmless, stratagems are darkly represented by the ignorance of Agathias. In a lower room, Anthemius arranged several vessels or caldrons of water, each of them covered by the wide bottom of a leathern tube, which rose to a narrow top, and was artificially conveyed among the joists and rafters of the adjacent building. A fire was kindled beneath the caldron; the steam of the boiling water ascended through the tubes; the house was shaken by the efforts of imprisoned air, and its trembling inhabitants might wonder that the city was unconscious of the earthquake which they had felt. At another time, the friends of Zeno, as they sat at table, were dazzled by the intolerable light which flashed in their eyes from the reflecting mirrors of Anthemius; they were astonished by the noise which he produced from the collision of certain minute and sonorous particles; and the orator declared in tragic style to the senate, that a mere mortal must yield to the power of an antagonist, who shook the earth with the trident of Neptune, and imitated the thunder and lightning of Jove himself. The genius of Anthemius, and his colleague Isidore the Milesian, was excited and employed by a prince, whose taste for architecture had degenerated into a mischievous and costly passion. His favorite architects submitted their designs and difficulties to Justinian, and discreetly confessed how much their laborious meditations were surpassed by the intuitive knowledge of celestial inspiration of an emperor, whose views were always directed to the benefit of his people, the glory of his reign, and the salvation of his soul. [102]

[Footnote 95: This conflagration is hinted by Lucian (in Hippia, c. 2) and Galen, (l. iii. de Temperamentis, tom. i. p. 81, edit. Basil.) in the second century. A thousand years afterwards, it is positively affirmed by Zonaras, (l. ix. p. 424,) on the faith of Dion Cassius, Tzetzes, (Chiliad ii. 119, &c.,) Eustathius, (ad Iliad. E. p. 338,) and the scholiast of Lucian. See Fabricius, (Bibliot. Graec. l. iii. c. 22, tom. ii. p. 551, 552,) to whom I am more or less indebted for several of these quotations.]

[Footnote 96: Zonaras (l. xi. c. p. 55) affirms the fact, without quoting any evidence.]

[Footnote 97: Tzetzes describes the artifice of these burning-glasses, which he had read, perhaps, with no learned eyes, in a mathematical treatise of Anthemius. That treatise has been lately published, translated, and illustrated, by M. Dupuys, a scholar and a mathematician, (Memoires de l'Academie des Inscriptions, tom xlii p. 392—451.)]

[Footnote 98: In the siege of Syracuse, by the silence of Polybius, Plutarch, Livy; in the siege of Constantinople, by that of Marcellinus and all the contemporaries of the vith century.]

[Footnote 99: Without any previous knowledge of Tzetzes or Anthemius, the immortal Buffon imagined and executed a set of burning-glasses, with which he could inflame planks at the distance of 200 feet, (Supplement a l'Hist. Naturelle, tom. i. 399—483, quarto edition.) What miracles would not his genius have performed for the public service, with royal expense, and in the strong sun of Constantinople or Syracuse?]

[Footnote 100: John Malala (tom. ii. p. 120—124) relates the fact; but he seems to confound the names or persons of Proclus and Marinus.]

[Footnote 101: Agathias, l. v. p. 149—152. The merit of Anthemius as an architect is loudly praised by Procopius (de Edif. l. i. c. 1) and Paulus Silentiarius, (part i. 134, &c.)]

[Footnote 102: See Procopius, (de Edificiis, l. i. c. 1, 2, l. ii. c. 3.) He relates a coincidence of dreams, which supposes some fraud in Justinian or his architect. They both saw, in a vision, the same plan for stopping an inundation at Dara. A stone quarry near Jerusalem was revealed to the emperor, (l. v. c. 6:) an angel was tricked into the perpetual custody of St. Sophia, (Anonym. de Antiq. C. P. l. iv. p. 70.)]

The principal church, which was dedicated by the founder of Constantinople to St. Sophia, or the eternal wisdom, had been twice destroyed by fire; after the exile of John Chrysostom, and during the Nika of the blue and green factions. No sooner did the tumult subside, than the Christian populace deplored their sacrilegious rashness; but they might have rejoiced in the calamity, had they foreseen the glory of the new temple, which at the end of forty days was strenuously undertaken by the piety of Justinian. [103] The ruins were cleared away, a more spacious plan was described, and as it required the consent of some proprietors of ground, they obtained the most exorbitant terms from the eager desires and timorous conscience of the monarch. Anthemius formed the design, and his genius directed the hands of ten thousand workmen, whose payment in pieces of fine silver was never delayed beyond the evening. The emperor himself, clad in a linen tunic, surveyed each day their rapid progress, and encouraged their diligence by his familiarity, his zeal, and his rewards. The new Cathedral of St. Sophia was consecrated by the patriarch, five years, eleven months, and ten days from the first foundation; and in the midst of the solemn festival Justinian exclaimed with devout vanity, "Glory be to God, who hath thought me worthy to accomplish so great a work; I have vanquished thee, O Solomon!" [104] But the pride of the Roman Solomon, before twenty years had elapsed, was humbled by an earthquake, which overthrew the eastern part of the dome. Its splendor was again restored by the perseverance of the same prince; and in the thirty-sixth year of his reign, Justinian celebrated the second dedication of a temple which remains, after twelve centuries, a stately monument of his fame. The architecture of St. Sophia, which is now converted into the principal mosch, has been imitated by the Turkish sultans, and that venerable pile continues to excite the fond admiration of the Greeks, and the more rational curiosity of European travellers. The eye of the spectator is disappointed by an irregular prospect of half-domes and shelving roofs: the western front, the principal approach, is destitute of simplicity and magnificence; and the scale of dimensions has been much surpassed by several of the Latin cathedrals. But the architect who first erected and aerial cupola, is entitled to the praise of bold design and skilful execution. The dome of St. Sophia, illuminated by four-and-twenty windows, is formed with so small a curve, that the depth is equal only to one sixth of its diameter; the measure of that diameter is one hundred and fifteen feet, and the lofty centre, where a crescent has supplanted the cross, rises to the perpendicular height of one hundred and eighty feet above the pavement. The circle which encompasses the dome, lightly reposes on four strong arches, and their weight is firmly supported by four massy piles, whose strength is assisted, on the northern and southern sides, by four columns of Egyptian granite.

A Greek cross, inscribed in a quadrangle, represents the form of the edifice; the exact breadth is two hundred and forty-three feet, and two hundred and sixty-nine may be assigned for the extreme length from the sanctuary in the east, to the nine western doors, which open into the vestibule, and from thence into the narthex or exterior portico. That portico was the humble station of the penitents. The nave or body of the church was filled by the congregation of the faithful; but the two sexes were prudently distinguished, and the upper and lower galleries were allotted for the more private devotion of the women. Beyond the northern and southern piles, a balustrade, terminated on either side by the thrones of the emperor and the patriarch, divided the nave from the choir; and the space, as far as the steps of the altar, was occupied by the clergy and singers. The altar itself, a name which insensibly became familiar to Christian ears, was placed in the eastern recess, artificially built in the form of a demi-cylinder; and this sanctuary communicated by several doors with the sacristy, the vestry, the baptistery, and the contiguous buildings, subservient either to the pomp of worship, or the private use of the ecclesiastical ministers. The memory of past calamities inspired Justinian with a wise resolution, that no wood, except for the doors, should be admitted into the new edifice; and the choice of the materials was applied to the strength, the lightness, or the splendor of the respective parts. The solid piles which contained the cupola were composed of huge blocks of freestone, hewn into squares and triangles, fortified by circles of iron, and firmly cemented by the infusion of lead and quicklime: but the weight of the cupola was diminished by the levity of its substance, which consists either of pumice-stone that floats in the water, or of bricks from the Isle of Rhodes, five times less ponderous than the ordinary sort. The whole frame of the edifice was constructed of brick; but those base materials were concealed by a crust of marble; and the inside of St. Sophia, the cupola, the two larger, and the six smaller, semi-domes, the walls, the hundred columns, and the pavement, delight even the eyes of Barbarians, with a rich and variegated picture. A poet, [105] who beheld the primitive lustre of St. Sophia, enumerates the colors, the shades, and the spots of ten or twelve marbles, jaspers, and porphyries, which nature had profusely diversified, and which were blended and contrasted as it were by a skilful painter. The triumph of Christ was adorned with the last spoils of Paganism, but the greater part of these costly stones was extracted from the quarries of Asia Minor, the isles and continent of Greece, Egypt, Africa, and Gaul. Eight columns of porphyry, which Aurelian had placed in the temple of the sun, were offered by the piety of a Roman matron; eight others of green marble were presented by the ambitious zeal of the magistrates of Ephesus: both are admirable by their size and beauty, but every order of architecture disclaims their fantastic capital. A variety of ornaments and figures was curiously expressed in mosaic; and the images of Christ, of the Virgin, of saints, and of angels, which have been defaced by Turkish fanaticism, were dangerously exposed to the superstition of the Greeks. According to the sanctity of each object, the precious metals were distributed in thin leaves or in solid masses. The balustrade of the choir, the capitals of the pillars, the ornaments of the doors and galleries, were of gilt bronze; the spectator was dazzled by the glittering aspect of the cupola; the sanctuary contained forty thousand pounds weight of silver; and the holy vases and vestments of the altar were of the purest gold, enriched with inestimable gems. Before the structure of the church had arisen two cubits above the ground, forty-five thousand two hundred pounds were already consumed; and the whole expense amounted to three hundred and twenty thousand: each reader, according to the measure of his belief, may estimate their value either in gold or silver; but the sum of one million sterling is the result of the lowest computation. A magnificent temple is a laudable monument of national taste and religion; and the enthusiast who entered the dome of St. Sophia might be tempted to suppose that it was the residence, or even the workmanship, of the Deity. Yet how dull is the artifice, how insignificant is the labor, if it be compared with the formation of the vilest insect that crawls upon the surface of the temple!

[Footnote 103: Among the crowd of ancients and moderns who have celebrated the edifice of St. Sophia, I shall distinguish and follow, 1. Four original spectators and historians: Procopius, (de Edific. l. i. c. 1,) Agathias, (l. v. p. 152, 153,) Paul Silentiarius, (in a poem of 1026 hexameters, and calcem Annae Commen. Alexiad.,) and Evagrius, (l. iv. c. 31.) 2. Two legendary Greeks of a later period: George Codinus, (de Origin. C. P. p. 64-74,) and the anonymous writer of Banduri, (Imp. Orient. tom. i. l. iv. p. 65—80.)3. The great Byzantine antiquarian. Ducange, (Comment. ad Paul Silentiar. p. 525—598, and C. P. Christ. l. iii. p. 5—78.) 4. Two French travellers—the one, Peter Gyllius, (de Topograph. C. P. l. ii. c. 3, 4,) in the xvith; the other, Grelot, (Voyage de C. P. p. 95—164, Paris, 1680, in 4to:) he has given plans, prospects, and inside views of St. Sophia; and his plans, though on a smaller scale, appear more correct than those of Ducange. I have adopted and reduced the measures of Grelot: but as no Christian can now ascend the dome, the height is borrowed from Evagrius, compared with Gyllius, Greaves, and the Oriental Geographer.]

[Footnote 104: Solomon's temple was surrounded with courts, porticos, &c.; but the proper structure of the house of God was no more (if we take the Egyptian or Hebrew cubic at 22 inches) than 55 feet in height, 36 2/3 in breadth, and 110 in length—a small parish church, says Prideaux, (Connection, vol. i. p. 144, folio;) but few sanctuaries could be valued at four or five millions sterling! Note: Hist of Jews, vol i p 257—M]

[Footnote 105: Paul Silentiarius, in dark and poetic language, describes the various stones and marbles that were employed in the edifice of St. Sophia, (P. ii. p. 129, 133, &c., &c.:)

1. The Carystian—pale, with iron veins.

2. *The Phrygian*—of two sorts, both of a rosy hue; the one with a white shade, the other purple, with silver flowers.

3. *The Porphyry of Egypt*—with small stars.

4. *The green marble of Laconia.*

5. *The Carian*—from Mount Iassis, with oblique veins, white and red. 6. *The Lydian*—pale, with a red flower.

7. *The African, or Mauritanian*—of a gold or saffron hue. 8. *The Celtic*—black, with white veins.

9. *The Bosphoric*—white, with black edges. Besides the Proconnesian which formed the pavement; the Thessalian, Molossian, &c., which are less distinctly painted.]

So minute a description of an edifice which time has respected, may attest the truth, and excuse the relation, of the innumerable works, both in the capital and provinces, which Justinian constructed on a smaller scale and less durable foundations. [106] In Constantinople alone and the adjacent suburbs, he dedicated twenty-five churches to the honor of Christ, the Virgin, and the saints: most of these churches were decorated with marble and gold; and their various situation was skilfully chosen in a populous square, or a pleasant grove; on the margin of the sea-shore, or on some lofty eminence which overlooked the continents of Europe and Asia. The church of the Holy Apostles at Constantinople, and that of St. John at Ephesus, appear to have been framed on the same model: their domes aspired to imitate the cupolas of St. Sophia; but the altar was more judiciously placed under the centre of the dome, at the junction of four stately porticos, which more accurately expressed the figure of the Greek cross. The Virgin of Jerusalem might exult in the temple erected by her Imperial votary on a most ungrateful spot, which afforded neither ground nor materials to the architect. A level was formed by raising part of a deep valley to the height of the mountain. The stones of a neighboring quarry were hewn into regular forms; each block was fixed on a peculiar carriage, drawn by forty of the strongest oxen, and the roads were widened for the passage of such enormous weights. Lebanon furnished her loftiest cedars for the timbers of the church; and the seasonable discovery of a vein of red marble supplied its beautiful columns, two of which, the supporters of the exterior portico, were esteemed the largest in the world. The pious munificence of the emperor was diffused over the Holy Land; and if reason should condemn the monasteries of both sexes which were built or restored by Justinian, yet charity must applaud the wells which he sunk, and the hospitals which he founded, for the relief of the weary pilgrims. The schismatical temper of Egypt was ill entitled to the royal bounty; but in Syria and Africa, some remedies were applied to the disasters of wars and earthquakes, and both Carthage and Antioch, emerging from their ruins, might revere the name of their gracious benefactor. [107] Almost every saint in the calendar acquired the honors of a temple; almost every city of the empire obtained the solid advantages of bridges, hospitals, and aqueducts; but the severe liberality of the monarch disdained to indulge his subjects in the popular luxury of baths and theatres. While Justinian labored for the public service, he was not unmindful of his own dignity and ease. The Byzantine palace, which had been damaged by the conflagration, was restored with new magnificence; and some notion may be conceived of the whole edifice, by the vestibule or hall, which, from the doors perhaps, or the roof, was surnamed chalce, or the brazen. The dome of a spacious quadrangle was supported by massy pillars; the pavement and walls were incrusted with many-colored marbles—the emerald green of Laconia, the fiery red, and the white Phrygian stone, intersected with veins of a sea-green hue: the mosaic paintings of the dome and sides represented the glories of the African and Italian triumphs. On the Asiatic shore of the

Propontis, at a small distance to the east of Chalcedon, the costly palace and gardens of Heraeum [108] were prepared for the summer residence of Justinian, and more especially of Theodora. The poets of the age have celebrated the rare alliance of nature and art, the harmony of the nymphs of the groves, the fountains, and the waves: yet the crowd of attendants who followed the court complained of their inconvenient lodgings, [109] and the nymphs were too often alarmed by the famous Porphyrio, a whale of ten cubits in breadth, and thirty in length, who was stranded at the mouth of the River Sangaris, after he had infested more than half a century the seas of Constantinople. [110]

[Footnote 106: The six books of the Edifices of Procopius are thus distributed the first is confined to Constantinople: the second includes Mesopotamia and Syria the third, Armenia and the Euxine; the fourth, Europe; the fifth, Asia Minor and Palestine; the sixth, Egypt and Africa. Italy is forgot by the emperor or the historian, who published this work of adulation before the date (A.D. 555) of its final conquest.]

[Footnote 107: Justinian once gave forty-five centenaries of gold (180,000 L.) for the repairs of Antioch after the earthquake, (John Malala, tom. ii p 146—149.)]

[Footnote 108: For the Heraeum, the palace of Theodora, see Gyllius, (de Bosphoro Thracio, l. iii. c. xi.,) Aleman. (Not. ad. Anec. p. 80, 81, who quotes several epigrams of the Anthology,) and Ducange, (C. P. Christ. l. iv. c. 13, p. 175, 176.)]

[Footnote 109: Compare, in the Edifices, (l. i. c. 11,) and in the Anecdotes, (c. 8, 15.) the different styles of adulation and malevolence: stripped of the paint, or cleansed from the dirt, the object appears to be the same.]

[Footnote 110: Procopius, l. viii. 29; most probably a stranger and wanderer, as the Mediterranean does not breed whales. Balaenae quoque in nostra maria penetrant, (Plin. Hist. Natur. ix. 2.) Between the polar circle and the tropic, the cetaceous animals of the ocean grow to the length of 50, 80, or 100 feet, (Hist. des Voyages, tom. xv. p. 289. Pennant's British Zoology, vol. iii. p. 35.)]

The fortifications of Europe and Asia were multiplied by Justinian; but the repetition of those timid and fruitless precautions exposes, to a philosophic eye, the debility of the empire. [111] From Belgrade to the Euxine, from the conflux of the Save to the mouth of the Danube, a chain of above fourscore fortified places was extended along the banks of the great river. Single watch-towers were changed into spacious citadels; vacant walls, which the engineers contracted or enlarged according to the nature of the ground, were filled with colonies or garrisons; a strong fortress defended the ruins of Trajan's bridge, [112] and several military stations affected to spread beyond the Danube the pride of the Roman name. But that name was divested of its terrors; the Barbarians, in their annual inroads, passed, and contemptuously repassed, before these useless bulwarks; and the inhabitants of the frontier, instead of reposing under the shadow of the general defence, were compelled to guard, with incessant vigilance, their separate habitations. The solitude of ancient cities, was replenished; the new foundations of Justinian acquired, perhaps too hastily, the epithets of impregnable and populous; and the auspicious place of his own nativity attracted the grateful reverence of the vainest of princes. Under the name of Justiniana prima, the obscure village of Tauresium became the seat of an archbishop and a praefect, whose jurisdiction extended over seven warlike provinces of Illyricum; [113] and the corrupt appellation of Giustendil still indicates, about twenty miles to the south of Sophia, the residence of a Turkish sanjak. [114] For the use of the emperor's countryman, a cathedral, a place, and an aqueduct, were speedily constructed; the public and private edifices were adapted to the greatness of a royal city; and the strength of the walls resisted, during the lifetime of Justinian, the unskilful assaults of the Huns and Sclavonians. Their progress was sometimes retarded, and their hopes of rapine were disappointed, by the innumerable castles which, in the provinces of Dacia, Epirus, Thessaly, Macedonia, and Thrace, appeared to cover the whole face of the country. Six hundred of these forts were built or repaired by the emperor; but it seems reasonable to believe, that the far greater part consisted only of a stone or brick tower, in the midst of a square or circular area, which was surrounded by a wall and ditch, and afforded in a moment of danger some protection to the peasants and cattle of the neighboring villages. [115] Yet these military works, which exhausted the public treasure, could not remove the just apprehensions of Justinian and his European subjects. The warm baths of Anchialus in Thrace were rendered as safe as they were salutary; but the rich pastures of Thessalonica were foraged by the Scythian cavalry; the delicious vale of Tempe, three hundred miles from the Danube, was continually alarmed by the sound of war; [116] and no unfortified spot, however distant or solitary, could securely enjoy the blessings of peace. The Straits of Thermopylae, which seemed to protect, but which had so often betrayed, the safety of Greece, were diligently strengthened by the labors of Justinian. From the edge of the sea-shore, through the forests and valleys, and as far as the summit of the Thessalian mountains, a strong wall was continued, which occupied every practicable entrance. Instead of a hasty crowd of peasants, a garrison of two thousand soldiers was stationed along the rampart; granaries of corn and reservoirs of water were provided for their use; and by a precaution that inspired the cowardice which it foresaw, convenient fortresses were erected for their retreat. The walls of Corinth, overthrown by an earthquake, and the mouldering bulwarks of Athens and Plataea, were carefully restored; the Barbarians were discouraged by the prospect of successive and painful sieges: and the naked cities of Peloponnesus were covered by the fortifications of the Isthmus of Corinth. At the extremity of Europe, another peninsula, the Thracian Chersonesus, runs three days' journey into the sea, to form, with the adjacent shores of Asia, the Straits of the Hellespont. The intervals between eleven populous towns were filled by lofty woods, fair pastures, and arable lands; and the isthmus, of thirty seven stadia or furlongs, had been fortified by a Spartan general nine hundred years before the reign of Justinian. [117] In an age of freedom and valor, the slightest rampart may prevent a surprise; and Procopius appears insensible of the superiority of ancient times, while he praises the solid construction and double parapet of a wall, whose long arms stretched on either side into the sea; but whose strength was deemed insufficient to guard the Chersonesus, if each city, and particularly Gallipoli and Sestus, had not been secured by their peculiar fortifications. The long wall, as it was emphatically styled, was a work as disgraceful in the object, as it was respectable in the execution. The riches of a capital diffuse themselves over the neighboring country, and the territory of Constantinople a paradise of nature, was adorned with the luxurious gardens and villas of the senators and opulent citizens. But their wealth served only to attract the bold and rapacious Barbarians; the noblest of the Romans, in the bosom of peaceful indolence, were led away into Scythian captivity, and their sovereign might view from his palace the hostile flames which were insolently spread to the gates of the Imperial city. At the distance only of forty miles, Anastasius was constrained to establish a last frontier; his long wall, of sixty miles from the Propontis to the Euxine, proclaimed the impotence of his arms; and as the danger became more imminent, new fortifications were added by the indefatigable prudence of Justinian. [118]

[Footnote 111: Montesquieu observes, (tom. iii. p. 503, Considerations sur la Grandeur et la Decadence des Romains, c. xx.,) that Justinian's empire was like France in the time of the Norman inroads—never so weak as when every village was fortified.]

[Footnote 112: Procopius affirms (l. iv. c. 6) that the Danube was stopped by the ruins of the bridge. Had Apollodorus, the architect, left a description of his own work, the fabulous wonders of Dion Cassius (l lxviii. p. 1129) would have been corrected by the genuine picture Trajan's bridge consisted of twenty or

twenty-two stone piles with wooden arches; the river is shallow, the current gentle, and the whole interval no more than 443 (Reimer ad Dion. from Marsigli) or 5l7 toises, (D'Anville, Geographie Ancienne, tom. i. p. 305.)]

[Footnote 113: Of the two Dacias, Mediterranea and Ripensis, Dardania, Pravalitana, the second Maesia, and the second Macedonia. See Justinian (Novell. xi.,) who speaks of his castles beyond the Danube, and on omines semper bellicis sudoribus inhaerentes.]

[Footnote 114: See D'Anville, (Memoires de l'Academie, &c., tom. xxxi p. 280, 299,) Rycaut, (Present State of the Turkish Empire, p. 97, 316,) Max sigli, (Stato Militare del Imperio Ottomano, p. 130.) The sanjak of Giustendil is one of the twenty under the beglerbeg of Rurselis, and his district maintains 48 zaims and 588 timariots.]

[Footnote 115: These fortifications may be compared to the castles in Mingrelia (Chardin, Voyages en Perse, tom. i. p. 60, 131)—a natural picture.]

[Footnote 116: The valley of Tempe is situate along the River Peneus, between the hills of Ossa and Olympus: it is only five miles long, and in some places no more than 120 feet in breadth. Its verdant beauties are elegantly described by Pliny, (Hist. Natur. l. iv. 15,) and more diffusely by Aelian, (Hist. Var. l. iii. c. i.)]

[Footnote 117: Xenophon Hellenic. l. iii. c. 2. After a long and tedious conversation with the Byzantine declaimers, how refreshing is the truth, the simplicity, the elegance of an Attic writer!]

[Footnote 118: See the long wall in Evagarius, (l. iv. c. 38.) This whole article is drawn from the fourth book of the Edifices, except Anchialus, (l. iii. c. 7.)]

Asia Minor, after the submission of the Isaurians, [119] remained without enemies and without fortifications. Those bold savages, who had disdained to be the subjects of Gallienus, persisted two hundred and thirty years in a life of independence and rapine. The most successful princes respected the strength of the mountains and the despair of the natives; their fierce spirit was sometimes soothed with gifts, and sometimes restrained by terror; and a military count, with three legions, fixed his permanent and ignominious station in the heart of the Roman provinces. [120] But no sooner was the vigilance of power relaxed or diverted, than the light-armed squadrons descended from the hills, and invaded the peaceful plenty of Asia. Although the Isaurians were not remarkable for stature or bravery, want rendered them bold, and experience made them skilful in the exercise of predatory war. They advanced with secrecy and speed to the attack of villages and defenceless towns; their flying parties have sometimes touched the Hellespont, the Euxine, and the gates of Tarsus, Antioch, or Damascus; [121] and the spoil was lodged in their inaccessible mountains, before the Roman troops had received their orders, or the distant province had computed its loss. The guilt of rebellion and robbery excluded them from the rights of national enemies; and the magistrates were instructed, by an edict, that the trial or punishment of an Isaurian, even on the festival of Easter, was a meritorious act of justice and piety. [122] If the captives were condemned to domestic slavery, they maintained, with their sword or dagger, the private quarrel of their masters; and it was found expedient for the public tranquillity to prohibit the service of such dangerous retainers. When their countryman Tarcalissaeus or Zeno ascended the throne, he invited a faithful and formidable band of Isaurians, who insulted the court and city, and were rewarded by an annual tribute of five thousand pounds of gold. But the hopes of fortune depopulated the mountains, luxury enervated the hardiness of their minds and bodies, and in proportion as they mixed with mankind, they became less qualified for the enjoyment of poor and solitary freedom. After the death of Zeno, his successor Anastasius suppressed their pensions, exposed their persons to the revenge of the people, banished them from Constantinople, and prepared to sustain a war, which left only the alternative of victory or servitude. A brother of the last emperor usurped the title of Augustus; his cause was powerfully supported by the arms, the treasures, and the magazines, collected by Zeno; and the native Isaurians must have formed the smallest portion of the hundred and fifty thousand Barbarians under his standard, which was sanctified, for the first time, by the presence of a fighting bishop. Their disorderly numbers were vanquished in the plains of Phrygia by the valor and discipline of the Goths; but a war of six years almost exhausted the courage of the emperor. [123] The Isaurians retired to their mountains; their fortresses were successively besieged and ruined; their communication with the sea was intercepted; the bravest of their leaders died in arms; the surviving chiefs, before their execution, were dragged in chains through the hippodrome; a colony of their youth was transplanted into Thrace, and the remnant of the people submitted to the Roman government. Yet some generations elapsed before their minds were reduced to the level of slavery. The populous villages of Mount Taurus were filled with horsemen and archers: they resisted the imposition of tributes, but they recruited the armies of Justinian; and his civil magistrates, the proconsul of Cappadocia, the count of Isauria, and the praetors of Lycaonia and Pisidia, were invested with military power to restrain the licentious practice of rapes and assassinations. [124]

[Footnote 119: Turn back to vol. i. p. 328. In the course of this History, I have sometimes mentioned, and much oftener slighted, the hasty inroads of the Isaurians, which were not attended with any consequences.]

[Footnote 120: Trebellius Pollio in Hist. August. p. 107, who lived under Diocletian, or Constantine. See likewise Pancirolus ad Notit. Imp. Orient c. 115, 141. See Cod. Theodos. l. ix. tit. 35, leg. 37, with a copious collective Annotation of Godefroy, tom. iii. p. 256, 257.]

[Footnote 121: See the full and wide extent of their inroads in Philostorgius (Hist. Eccles. l. xi. c. 8,) with Godefroy's learned Dissertations.]

[Footnote 122: Cod. Justinian. l. ix. tit. 12, leg. 10. The punishments are severs—a fine of a hundred pounds of gold, degradation, and even death. The public peace might afford a pretence, but Zeno was desirous of monopolizing the valor and service of the Isaurians.]

[Footnote 123: The Isaurian war and the triumph of Anastasius are briefly and darkly represented by John Malala, (tom. ii. p. 106, 107,) Evagrius, (l. iii. c. 35,) Theophanes, (p. 118—120,) and the Chronicle of Marcellinus.]

[Footnote 124: Fortes ea regio (says Justinian) viros habet, nec in ullo differt ab Isauria, though Procopius (Persic. l. i. c. 18) marks an essential difference between their military character; yet in former times the Lycaonians and Pisidians had defended their liberty against the great king, Xenophon. (Anabasis, l. iii. c. 2.) Justinian introduces some false and ridiculous erudition of the ancient empire of the Pisidians, and of Lycaon, who, after visiting Rome, (long before Aeenas,) gave a name and people to Lycaoni, (Novell. 24, 25, 27, 30.)]

PART V

If we extend our view from the tropic to the mouth of the Tanais, we may observe, on one hand, the precautions of Justinian to curb the savages of Aethiopia, [125] and on the other, the long walls which he constructed in Crimaea for the protection of his friendly Goths, a colony of three thousand shepherds and warriors. [126] From that peninsula to Trebizond, the eastern curve of the Euxine was secured by forts, by alliance, or by religion; and the possession of Lazica, the Colchos of ancient, the Mingrelia of modern, geography, soon became the object of an important war. Trebizond, in after-times the seat of a romantic empire, was indebted to the liberality of Justinian for a church, an aqueduct, and a castle, whose ditches are hewn in the solid rock. From that maritime city, frontier line of five hundred miles may be drawn to the fortress of Circesium, the last Roman station on the Euphrates. [127] Above Trebizond immediately, and five days' journey to the south, the country rises into dark forests and craggy mountains, as savage though not so lofty as the Alps and the Pyrenees. In this rigorous climate, [128] where the snows seldom melt, the fruits are tardy and tasteless, even honey is poisonous: the most industrious tillage would be confined to some pleasant valleys; and the pastoral tribes obtained a scanty sustenance from the flesh and milk of their cattle. The Chalybians [129] derived their name and temper from the iron quality of the soil; and, since the days of Cyrus, they might produce, under the various appellations of Cha daeans and Zanians, an uninterrupted prescription of war and rapine. Under the reign of Justinian, they acknowledged the god and the emperor of the Romans, and seven fortresses were built in the most accessible passages, to exclude the ambition of the Persian monarch. [130] The principal source of the Euphrates descends from the Chalybian mountains, and seems to flow towards the west and the Euxine: bending to the south-west, the river passes under the walls of Satala and Melitene, (which were restored by Justinian as the bulwarks of the Lesser Armenia,) and gradually approaches the Mediterranean Sea; till at length, repelled by Mount Taurus, [131] the Euphrates inclines its long and flexible course to the south-east and the Gulf of Persia. Among the Roman cities beyond the Euphrates, we distinguish two recent foundations, which were named from Theodosius, and the relics of the martyrs; and two capitals, Amida and Edessa, which are celebrated in the history of every age. Their strength was proportioned by Justinian to the danger of their situation. A ditch and palisade might be sufficient to resist the artless force of the cavalry of Scythia; but more elaborate works were required to sustain a regular siege against the arms and treasures of the great king. His skilful engineers understood the methods of conducting deep mines, and of raising platforms to the level of the rampart: he shook the strongest battlements with his military engines, and sometimes advanced to the assault with a line of movable turrets on the backs of elephants. In the great cities of the East, the disadvantage of space, perhaps of position, was compensated by the zeal of the people, who seconded the garrison in the defence of their country and religion; and the fabulous promise of the Son of God, that Edessa should never be taken, filled the citizens with valiant confidence, and chilled the besiegers with doubt and dismay. [132] The subordinate towns of Armenia and Mesopotamia were diligently strengthened, and the posts which appeared to have any command of ground or water were occupied by numerous forts, substantially built of stone, or more hastily erected with the obvious materials of earth and brick. The eye of Justinian investigated every spot; and his cruel precautions might attract the war into some lonely vale, whose peaceful natives, connected by trade and marriage, were ignorant of national discord and the quarrels of princes. Westward of the Euphrates, a sandy desert extends above six hundred miles to the Red Sea. Nature had interposed a vacant solitude between the ambition of two rival empires; the Arabians, till Mahomet arose, were formidable only as robbers; and in the proud security of peace the fortifications of Syria were neglected on the most vulnerable side.

[Footnote 125: See Procopius, Persic. l. i. c. 19. The altar of national concern, of annual sacrifice and oaths, which Diocletian had created in the Isla of Elephantine, was demolished by Justinian with less policy than]

[Footnote 126: Procopius de Edificiis, l. iii. c. 7. Hist. l. viii. c. 3, 4. These unambitious Goths had refused to follow the standard of Theodoric. As late as the xvth and xvith century, the name and nation might be discovered between Caffa and the Straits of Azoph, (D'Anville, Memoires de l'academie, tom. xxx. p. 240.) They well deserved the curiosity of Busbequius, (p. 321-326;) but seem to have vanished in the more recent account of the Missions du Levant, (tom. i.,) Tott, Peysonnnel, &c.]

[Footnote 127: For the geography and architecture of this Armenian border, see the Persian Wars and Edifices (l. ii. c. 4-7, l. iii. c. 2—7) of Procopius.]

[Footnote 128: The country is described by Tournefort, (Voyage au Levant, tom. iii. lettre xvii. xviii.) That skilful botanist soon discovered the plant that infects the honey, (Plin. xxi. 44, 45:) he observes, that the soldiers of Lucullus might indeed be astonished at the cold, since, even in the plain of Erzerum, snow sometimes falls in June, and the harvest is seldom finished before September. The hills of Armenia are below the fortieth degree of latitude; but in the mountainous country which I inhabit, it is well known that an ascent of some hours carries the traveller from the climate of Languedoc to that of Norway; and a general theory has been introduced, that, under the line, an elevation of 2400 toises is equivalent to the cold of the polar circle, (Remond, Observations sur les Voyages de Coxe dans la Suisse, tom. ii. p. 104.)]

[Footnote 129: The identity or proximity of the Chalybians, or Chaldaeana may be investigated in Strabo, (l. xii. p. 825, 826,) Cellarius, (Geograph. Antiq. tom. ii. p. 202—204,) and Freret, (Mem. de Academie, tom. iv. p. 594) Xenophon supposes, in his romance, (Cyropaed l. iii.,) the same Barbarians, against whom he had fought in his retreat, (Anabasis, l. iv.)]

[Footnote 130: Procopius, Persic. l. i. c. 15. De Edific. l. iii. c. 6.]

[Footnote 131: Ni Taurus obstet in nostra maria venturus, (Pomponius Mela, iii. 8.) Pliny, a poet as well as a naturalist, (v. 20,) personifies the river and mountain, and describes their combat. See the course of the Tigris and Euphrates in the excellent treatise of D'Anville.]

[Footnote 132: Procopius (Persic. l. ii. c. 12) tells the story with the tone, half sceptical, half superstitious, of Herodotus. The promise was not in the primitive lie of Eusebius, but dates at least from the year 400; and a third lie, the Veronica, was soon raised on the two former, (Evagrius, l. iv. c. 27.) As Edessa has been taken, Tillemont must disclaim the promise, (Mem. Eccles. tom. i. p. 362, 383, 617.)]

But the national enmity, at least the effects of that enmity, had been suspended by a truce, which continued above fourscore years. An ambassador from the emperor Zeno accompanied the rash and unfortunate Perozes, [132/1] in his expedition against the Nepthalites, [132/2] or white Huns, whose conquests had been stretched from the Caspian to the heart of India, whose throne was enriched with emeralds, [133] and whose cavalry was supported by a line of two thousand elephants. [134] The Persians [134/1] were twice circumvented, in a situation which made valor useless and flight impossible; and the double victory of the Huns was achieved by military stratagem. They dismissed their royal captive after he had submitted to adore the majesty of a Barbarian; and the humiliation was poorly evaded by the casuistical subtlety of the Magi, who instructed Perozes to direct his attention to the rising sun. [134/2] The indignant successor of Cyrus forgot his danger and his gratitude; he renewed the attack with headstrong fury, and lost both his army and his life. [135] The death of Perozes abandoned Persia to her foreign and domestic enemies; [135/1] and twelve years of confusion elapsed before his son Cabades, or Kobad, could embrace any designs of ambition or revenge. The unkind parsimony of Anastasius was the motive or pretence of a Roman war; [136] the Huns and Arabs marched under the Persian standard, and the fortifications of Armenia and Mesopotamia were, at that time, in a ruinous or imperfect condition. The emperor returned his thanks to the governor and people of Martyropolis for the prompt surrender of a city which could not be successfully defended, and the conflagration of Theodosiopolis might justify the conduct of their prudent neighbors. Amida sustained a long and destructive siege: at the end of three months the loss of fifty thousand of the soldiers of Cabades was not balanced by any prospect of success, and it was in vain that the Magi deduced a flattering prediction from the indecency of the women [136/1] on the ramparts, who had revealed their most secret charms to the eyes of the assailants. At length, in a silent night, they ascended the most accessible tower, which was guarded only by some monks, oppressed, after the duties of a festival, with sleep and wine. Scaling-ladders were applied at the dawn of day; the presence of Cabades, his stern command, and his drawn sword, compelled the Persians to vanquish; and before it was sheathed, fourscore thousand of the inhabitants had expiated the blood of their companions. After the siege of Amida, the war continued three years, and the unhappy frontier tasted the full measure of its calamities. The gold of Anastasius was offered too late, the number of his troops was defeated by the number of their generals; the country was stripped of its inhabitants, and both the living and the dead were abandoned to the wild beasts of the desert. The resistance of Edessa, and the deficiency of spoil, inclined the mind of Cabades to peace: he sold his conquests for an exorbitant price; and the same line, though marked with slaughter and devastation, still separated the two empires. To avert the repetition of the same evils, Anastasius resolved to found a new colony, so strong, that it should defy the power of the Persian, so far advanced towards Assyria, that its stationary troops might defend the province by the menace or operation of offensive war. For this purpose, the town of Dara, [137] fourteen miles from Nisibis, and four days' journey from the Tigris, was peopled and adorned; the hasty works of Anastasius were improved by the perseverance of Justinian; and, without insisting on places less important, the fortifications of Dara may represent the military architecture of the age. The city was surrounded with two walls, and the interval between them, of fifty paces, afforded a retreat to the cattle of the besieged. The inner wall was a monument of strength and beauty: it measured sixty feet from the ground, and the height of the towers was one hundred feet; the loopholes, from whence an enemy might be annoyed with missile weapons, were small, but numerous; the soldiers were planted along the rampart, under the shelter of double galleries, and a third platform, spacious and secure, was raised on the summit of the towers. The exterior wall appears to have been less lofty, but more solid; and each tower was protected by a quadrangular bulwark. A hard, rocky soil resisted the tools of the miners, and on the south-east, where the ground was more tractable, their approach was retarded by a new work, which advanced in the shape of a half-moon. The double and treble ditches were filled with a stream of water; and in the management of the river, the most skilful labor was employed to supply the inhabitants, to distress the besiegers, and to prevent the mischiefs of a natural or artificial inundation. Dara continued more than sixty years to fulfil the wishes of its founders, and to provoke the jealousy of the Persians, who incessantly complained, that this impregnable fortress had been constructed in manifest violation of the treaty of peace between the two empires. [137/1]

[Footnote 132/1: Firouz the Conqueror—unfortunately so named. See St. Martin, vol. vi. p. 439—M.]

[Footnote 132/2: Rather Hepthalites—M.]

[Footnote 133: They were purchased from the merchants of Adulis who traded to India, (Cosmas, Topograph. Christ. l. xi. p. 339;) yet, in the estimate of precious stones, the Scythian emerald was the first, the Bactrian the second, the Aethiopian only the third, (Hill's Theophrastus, p. 61, &c., 92.) The production, mines, &c., of emeralds, are involved in darkness; and it is doubtful whether we possess any of the twelve sorts known to the ancients, (Goguet, Origine des Loix, &c., part ii. l. ii. c. 2, art. 3.) In this war the Huns got, or at least Perozes lost, the finest pearl in the world, of which Procopius relates a ridiculous fable.]

[Footnote 134: The Indo-Scythae continued to reign from the time of Augustus (Dionys. Perieget. 1088, with the Commentary of Eustathius, in Hudson, Geograph. Minor. tom. iv.) to that of the elder Justin, (Cosmas, Topograph. Christ. l. xi. p. 338, 339.) On their origin and conquests, see D'Anville, (sur l'Inde, p. 18, 45, &c., 69, 85, 89.) In the second century they were masters of Larice or Guzerat.]

[Footnote 134/1: According to the Persian historians, he was misled by guides who used he old stratagem of Zopyrus. Malcolm, vol. i. p. 101—M.]

[Footnote 134/2: In the Ms. Chronicle of Tabary, it is said that the Moubedan Mobed, or Grand Pontiff, opposed with all his influence the violation of the treaty. St. Martin, vol. vii. p. 254—M.]

[Footnote 135: See the fate of Phirouz, or Perozes, and its consequences, in Procopius, (Persic. l. i. c. 3—6,) who may be compared with the fragments of Oriental history, (D'Herbelot, Bibliot. Orient. p. 351, and Texeira, History of Persia, translated or abridged by Stephens, l. i. c. 32, p. 132—138.) The chronology is ably ascertained by Asseman. (Bibliot. Orient. tom. iii. p. 396—427.)]

[Footnote 135/1: When Firoze advanced, Khoosh-Nuaz (the king of the Huns) presented on the point of a lance the treaty to which he had sworn, and exhorted him yet to desist before he destroyed his fame forever. Malcolm, vol. i. p. 103—M.]

[Footnote 136: The Persian war, under the reigns of Anastasius and Justin, may be collected from Procopius, (Persic. l. i. c. 7, 8, 9,) Theophanes, (in Chronograph. p. 124—127,) Evagrius, (l. iii. c. 37,) Marcellinus, (in Chron. p. 47,) and Josue Stylites, (apud Asseman. tom. i. p. 272—281.)]

[Footnote 136/1: Gibbon should have written "some prostitutes." Proc Pers. vol. 1 p. 7—M.]

[Footnote 137: The description of Dara is amply and correctly given by Procopius, (Persic. l. i. c. 10, l. ii. c. 13. De Edific. l. ii. c. 1, 2, 3, l. iii. c. 5.) See the situation in D'Anville, (l'Euphrate et le Tigre, p. 53, 54, 55,) though he seems to double the interval between Dara and Nisibis.]

[Footnote 137/1: The situation (of Dara) does not appear to give it strength, as it must have been commanded on three sides by the mountains, but opening on the south towards the plains of Mesopotamia. The foundation of the walls and towers, built of large hewn stone, may be traced across the valley, and over a number of low rocky hills which branch out from the foot of Mount Masius. The circumference I conceive to be nearly two miles and a half; and a small stream, which flows through the middle of the place, has induced several Koordish and Armenian families to fix their residence within the ruins. Besides the walls and towers, the remains of many other buildings attest the former grandeur of Dara; a considerable part of the space within the walls is arched and vaulted underneath, and in one place we perceived a large cavern, supported by four ponderous columns, somewhat resembling the great cistern of Constantinople. In the centre of the village are the ruins of a palace (probably that mentioned by Procopius) or church, one hundred paces in length, and sixty in breadth. The foundations, which are quite entire, consist of a prodigious number of subterraneous vaulted chambers, entered by a narrow passage forty paces in length. The gate is still standing; a considerable part of the wall has bid defiance to time, &c. M Donald Kinneir's Journey, p. 438—M]

Between the Euxine and the Caspian, the countries of Colchos, Iberia, and Albania, are intersected in every direction by the branches of Mount Caucasus; and the two principal gates, or passes, from north to south, have been frequently confounded in the geography both of the ancients and moderns. The name of Caspian or Albanian gates is properly applied to Derbend, [138] which occupies a short declivity between the mountains and the sea: the city, if we give credit to local tradition, had been founded by the Greeks; and this dangerous entrance was fortified by the kings of Persia with a mole, double walls, and doors of iron. The Iberian gates [139] [139/1] are formed by a narrow passage of six miles in Mount Caucasus, which opens from the northern side of Iberia, or Georgia, into the plain that reaches to the Tanais and the Volga. A fortress, designed by Alexander perhaps, or one of his successors, to command that important pass, had descended by right of conquest or inheritance to a prince of the Huns, who offered it for a moderate price to the emperor; but while Anastasius paused, while he timorously computed the cost and the distance, a more vigilant rival interposed, and Cabades forcibly occupied the Straits of Caucasus. The Albanian and Iberian gates excluded the horsemen of Scythia from the shortest and most practicable roads, and the whole front of the mountains was covered by the rampart of Gog and Magog, the long wall which has excited the curiosity of an Arabian caliph [140] and a Russian conqueror. [141] According to a recent description, huge stones, seven feet thick, and twenty-one feet in length or height, are artificially joined without iron or cement, to compose a wall, which runs above three hundred miles from the shores of Derbend, over the hills, and through the valleys of Daghestan and Georgia.

Without a vision, such a work might be undertaken by the policy of Cabades; without a miracle, it might be accomplished by his son, so formidable to the Romans, under the name of Chosroes; so dear to the Orientals, under the appellation of Nushirwan. The Persian monarch held in his hand the keys both of peace and war; but he stipulated, in every treaty, that Justinian should contribute to the expense of a common barrier, which equally protected the two empires from the inroads of the Scythians. [142]

[Footnote 138: For the city and pass of Derbend, see D'Herbelot, (Bibliot. Orient. p. 157, 291, 807,) Petit de la Croix. (Hist. de Gengiscan, l. iv. c. 9,) Histoire Genealogique des Tatars, (tom. i. p. 120,) Olearius, (Voyage en Perse, p. 1039—1041,) and Corneille le Bruyn, (Voyages, tom. i. p. 146, 147:) his view may be compared with the plan of Olearius, who judges the wall to be of shells and gravel hardened by time.]

[Footnote 139: Procopius, though with some confusion, always denominates them Caspian, (Persic. l. i. c. 10.) The pass is now styled Tatar-topa, the Tartar-gates, (D'Anville, Geographie Ancienne, tom. ii. p. 119, 120.)]

[Footnote 139/1: Malte-Brun. tom. viii. p. 12, makes three passes: 1. The central, which leads from Mosdok to Teflis. 2. The Albanian, more inland than the Derbend Pass. 3. The Derbend—the Caspian Gates. But the narrative of Col. Monteith, in the Journal of the Geographical Society of London. vol. iii. p. i. p. 39, clearly shows that there are but two passes between the Black Sea and the Caspian; the central, the Caucasian, or, as Col. Monteith calls it, the Caspian Gates, and the pass of Derbend, though it is practicable to turn this position (of Derbend) by a road a few miles distant through the mountains, p. 40—M.]

[Footnote 140: The imaginary rampart of Gog and Magog, which was seriously explored and believed by a caliph of the ninth century, appears to be derived from the gates of Mount Caucasus, and a vague *report of the wall of China, (Geograph. Nubiensis, p. 267-270. Memoires de l'Academie, tom. xxxi. p. 210—219.)]*

[Footnote 141: *See a learned dissertation of Baier, de muro Caucaseo, in Comment. Acad. Petropol. ann. 1726, tom. i. p. 425-463; but it is destitute of a map or plan. When the czar Peter I. became master of Derbend in the year 1722, the measure of the wall was found to be 3285 Russian orgyioe, or fathom, each of seven feet English; in the whole somewhat more than four miles in length.*]

[Footnote 142: *See the fortifications and treaties of Chosroes, or Nushirwan, in Procopius (Persic. l. i. c. 16, 22, l. ii.) and D'Herbelot, (p. 682.)]*

VII. Justinian suppressed the schools of Athens and the consulship of Rome, which had given so many sages and heroes to mankind. Both these institutions had long since degenerated from their primitive glory; yet some reproach may be justly inflicted on the avarice and jealousy of a prince, by whose hand such venerable ruins were destroyed.

Athens, after her Persian triumphs, adopted the philosophy of Ionia and the rhetoric of Sicily; and these studies became the patrimony of a city, whose inhabitants, about thirty thousand males, condensed, within the period of a single life, the genius of ages and millions. Our sense of the dignity of human nature is exalted by the simple recollection, that Isocrates [143] was the companion of Plato and Xenophon; that he assisted, perhaps with the historian Thucydides, at the first representation of the Oedipus of Sophocles and the Iphigenia of Euripides; and that his pupils Aeschines and Demosthenes contended for the crown of patriotism in the presence of Aristotle, the master of Theophrastus, who taught at Athens with the founders of the Stoic and Epicurean sects. [144] The ingenuous youth of Attica enjoyed the benefits of their domestic education, which was communicated without envy to the rival cities. Two thousand disciples heard the lessons of Theophrastus; [145] the schools of rhetoric must have been still more populous than those of philosophy; and a rapid succession of students diffused the fame of their teachers as far as the utmost limits of the Grecian language and name. Those limits were enlarged by the victories of Alexander; the arts of Athens survived her freedom and dominion; and the Greek colonies which the Macedonians planted in Egypt, and scattered over Asia, undertook long and frequent pilgrimages to worship the Muses in their favorite temple on the banks of the Ilissus. The Latin conquerors respectfully listened to the instructions of their subjects and captives; the names of Cicero and Horace were enrolled in the schools of Athens; and after the perfect settlement of the Roman empire, the natives of Italy, of Africa, and of Britain, conversed in the groves of the academy with their fellow-students of the East. The studies of philosophy and eloquence are congenial to a popular state, which encourages the freedom of inquiry, and submits only to the force of persuasion. In the republics of Greece and Rome, the art of speaking was the powerful engine of patriotism or ambition; and the schools of rhetoric poured forth a colony of statesmen and legislators. When the liberty of public debate was suppressed, the orator, in the honorable profession of an advocate, might plead the cause of innocence and justice; he might abuse his talents in the more profitable trade of panegyric; and the same precepts continued to dictate the fanciful declamations of the sophist, and the chaster beauties of historical composition. The systems which professed to unfold the nature of God, of man, and of the universe, entertained the curiosity of the philosophic student; and according to the temper of his mind, he might doubt with the Sceptics, or decide with the Stoics, sublimely speculate with Plato, or severely argue with Aristotle. The pride of the adverse sects had fixed an unattainable term of moral happiness and perfection; but the race was glorious and salutary; the disciples of Zeno, and even those of Epicurus, were taught both to act and to suffer; and the death of Petronius was not less effectual than that of Seneca, to humble a tyrant by the discovery of his impotence. The light of science could not indeed be confined within the walls of Athens. Her incomparable writers address themselves to the human race; the living masters emigrated to Italy and Asia; Berytus, in later times, was devoted to the study of the law; astronomy and physic were cultivated in the musaeum of Alexandria; but the Attic schools of rhetoric and philosophy maintained their superior reputation from the Peloponnesian war to the reign of Justinian. Athens, though situate in a barren soil, possessed a pure air, a free navigation, and the monuments of ancient art. That sacred retirement was seldom disturbed by the business of trade or government; and the last of the Athenians were distinguished by their lively wit, the purity of their taste and language, their social manners, and some traces, at least in discourse, of the magnanimity of their fathers. In the suburbs of the city, the academy of the Platonists, the lycaeum of the Peripatetics, the portico of the Stoics, and the garden of the Epicureans, were planted with trees and decorated with statues; and the philosophers, instead of being immured in a cloister, delivered their instructions in spacious and pleasant walks, which, at different hours, were consecrated to the exercises of the mind and body. The genius of the founders still lived in those venerable seats; the ambition of succeeding to the masters of human reason excited a generous emulation; and the merit of the candidates was determined, on each vacancy, by the free voices of an enlightened people. The Athenian professors were paid by their disciples: according to their mutual wants and abilities, the price appears to have varied; and Isocrates himself, who derides the avarice of the sophists, required, in his school of rhetoric, about thirty pounds from each of his hundred pupils. The wages of industry are just and honorable, yet the same Isocrates shed tears at the first receipt of a stipend: the Stoic might blush when he was hired to preach the contempt of money; and I should be sorry to discover that Aristotle or Plato so far degenerated from the example of Socrates, as to exchange knowledge for gold. But some property of lands and houses was settled by the permission of the laws, and the legacies of deceased friends, on the philosophic chairs of Athens. Epicurus bequeathed to his disciples the gardens which he had purchased for eighty minae or two hundred and fifty pounds, with a fund sufficient for their frugal subsistence and monthly festivals; [146] and the patrimony of Plato afforded an annual rent, which, in eight centuries, was gradually increased from three to one thousand pieces of gold. [147] The schools of Athens were protected by the wisest and most virtuous of the Roman princes. The library, which Hadrian founded, was placed in a portico adorned with pictures, statues, and a roof of alabaster, and supported by one hundred columns of Phrygian marble. The public salaries were assigned by the generous spirit of the Antonines; and each professor of politics, of rhetoric, of the Platonic, the Peripatetic, the Stoic, and the Epicurean philosophy, received an annual stipend of ten thousand drachmae, or more than three hundred pounds sterling. [148] After the death of Marcus, these liberal donations, and the privileges attached to the thrones of science, were abolished and revived, diminished and enlarged; but some vestige of royal bounty may be found under the successors of Constantine; and their arbitrary choice of an unworthy candidate might tempt the philosophers of Athens to regret the days of independence and poverty. [149] It is remarkable, that the impartial favor of the Antonines was bestowed on the four adverse sects of philosophy, which they considered as equally useful, or at least, as equally innocent. Socrates had formerly been the glory and the reproach of his country; and the first lessons of Epicurus so strangely scandalized the pious ears of the Athenians, that by his exile, and that of his antagonists, they silenced all vain disputes concerning the nature of the gods. But in the ensuing year they recalled the hasty decree, restored the liberty of the schools, and were convinced by the experience of ages, that the moral character of philosophers is not affected by the diversity of their theological speculations. [150]

[Footnote 143: The life of Isocrates extends from Olymp. lxxxvi. 1. to cx. 3, (ante Christ. 436—438.) See Dionys. Halicarn. tom. ii. p. 149, 150, edit. Hudson. Plutarch (sive anonymus) in Vit. X. Oratorum, p. 1538—1543, edit. H. Steph. Phot. cod. cclix. p. 1453.]

[Footnote 144: The schools of Athens are copiously though concisely represented in the Fortuna Attica of Meursius, (c. viii. p. 59—73, in tom. i. Opp.) For the state and arts of the city, see the first book of Pausanias, and a small tract of Dicaearchus, in the second volume of Hudson's Geographers, who wrote about Olymp. cxvii. (Dodwell's Dissertia sect. 4.)]

[Footnote 145: Diogen Laert. de Vit. Philosoph. l. v. segm. 37, p. 289.]

[Footnote 146: See the Testament of Epicurus in Diogen. Laert. l. x. segm. 16—20, p. 611, 612. A single epistle (ad Familiares, xiii. l.) displays the injustice of the Areopagus, the fidelity of the Epicureans, the dexterous politeness of Cicero, and the mixture of contempt and esteem with which the Roman senators considered the philosophy and philosophers of Greece.]

[Footnote 147: Damascius, in Vit. Isidor. apud Photium, cod. ccxlii. p. 1054.]

[Footnote 148: See Lucian (in Eunuch. tom. ii. p. 350—359, edit. Reitz,) Philostratus (in Vit. Sophist. l. ii. c. 2,) and Dion Cassius, or Xiphilin, (lxxi. p. 1195,) with their editors Du Soul, Olearius, and Reimar, and, above all, Salmasius, (ad Hist. August. p. 72.) A judicious philosopher (Smith's Wealth of Nations, vol. ii. p. 340—374) prefers the free contributions of the students to a fixed stipend for the professor.]

[Footnote 149: Brucker, Hist. Crit. Philosoph. tom. ii. p. 310, &c.]

[Footnote 150: The birth of Epicurus is fixed to the year 342 before Christ, (Bayle,) Olympiad cix. 3; and he opened his school at Athens, Olmp. cxviii. 3, 306 years before the same aera. This intolerant law (Athenaeus, l. xiii. p. 610. Diogen. Laertius, l. v. s. 38. p. 290. Julius Pollux, ix. 5) was enacted in the same or the succeeding year, (Sigonius, Opp. tom. v. p. 62. Menagius ad Diogen. Laert. p. 204. Corsini, Fasti Attici, tom. iv. p. 67, 68.) Theophrastus chief of the Peripatetics, and disciple of Aristotle, was involved in the same exile.]

The Gothic arms were less fatal to the schools of Athens than the establishment of a new religion, whose ministers superseded the exercise of reason, resolved every question by an article of faith, and condemned the infidel or sceptic to eternal flames. In many a volume of laborious controversy, they exposed the weakness of the understanding and the corruption of the heart, insulted human nature in the sages of antiquity, and proscribed the spirit of philosophical inquiry, so repugnant to the doctrine, or at least to the temper, of an humble believer. The surviving sects of the Platonists, whom Plato would have blushed to acknowledge, extravagantly mingled a sublime theory with the practice of superstition and magic; and as they remained alone in the midst of a Christian world, they indulged a secret rancor against the government of the church and state, whose severity was still suspended over their heads. About a century after the reign of Julian, [151] Proclus [152] was permitted to teach in the philosophic chair of the academy; and such was his industry, that he frequently, in the same day, pronounced five lessons, and composed seven hundred lines. His sagacious mind explored the deepest questions of morals and metaphysics, and he ventured to urge eighteen arguments against the Christian doctrine of the creation of the world. But in the intervals of study, he personally conversed with Pan, Aesculapius, and Minerva, in whose mysteries he was secretly initiated, and whose prostrate statues he adored; in the devout persuasion that the philosopher, who is a citizen of the universe, should be the priest of its various deities. An eclipse of the sun announced his approaching end; and his life, with that of his scholar Isidore, [153] compiled by two of their most learned disciples, exhibits a deplorable picture of the second childhood of human reason. Yet the golden chain, as it was fondly styled, of the Platonic succession, continued forty-four years from the death of Proclus to the edict of Justinian, [154] which imposed a perpetual silence on the schools of Athens, and excited the grief and indignation of the few remaining votaries of Grecian science and superstition. Seven friends and philosophers, Diogenes and Hermias, Eulalius and Priscian, Damascius, Isidore, and Simplicius, who dissented from the religion of their sovereign, embraced the resolution of seeking in a foreign land the freedom which was denied in their native country. They had heard, and they credulously believed, that the republic of Plato was realized in the despotic government of Persia, and that a patriot king reigned ever the happiest and most virtuous of nations. They were soon astonished by the natural discovery, that Persia resembled the other countries of the globe; that Chosroes, who affected the name of a philosopher, was vain, cruel, and ambitious; that bigotry, and a spirit of intolerance, prevailed among the Magi; that the nobles were haughty, the courtiers servile, and the magistrates unjust; that the guilty sometimes escaped, and that the innocent were often oppressed. The disappointment of the philosophers provoked them to overlook the real virtues of the Persians; and they were scandalized, more deeply perhaps than became their profession, with the plurality of wives and concubines, the incestuous marriages, and the custom of exposing dead bodies to the dogs and vultures, instead of hiding them in the earth, or consuming them with fire. Their repentance was expressed by a precipitate return, and they loudly declared that they had rather die on the borders of the empire, than enjoy the wealth and favor of the Barbarian. From this journey, however, they derived a benefit which reflects the purest lustre on the character of Chosroes. He required, that the seven sages who had visited the court of Persia should be exempted from the penal laws which Justinian enacted against his Pagan subjects; and this privilege, expressly stipulated in a treaty of peace, was guarded by the vigilance of a powerful mediator. [155] Simplicius and his companions ended their lives in peace and obscurity; and as they left no disciples, they terminate the long list of Grecian philosophers, who may be justly praised, notwithstanding their defects, as the wisest and most virtuous of their contemporaries. The writings of Simplicius are now extant. His physical and metaphysical commentaries on Aristotle have passed away with the fashion of the times; but his moral interpretation of Epictetus is preserved in the library of nations, as a classic book, most excellently adapted to direct the will, to purify the heart, and to confirm the understanding, by a just confidence in the nature both of God and man.

[Footnote 151: This is no fanciful aera: the Pagans reckoned their calamities from the reign of their hero. Proclus, whose nativity is marked by his horoscope, (A.D. 412, February 8, at C. P.,) died 124 years, A.D. 485, (Marin. in Vita Procli, c. 36.)]

[Footnote 152: The life of Proclus, by Marinus, was published by Fabricius (Hamburg, 1700, et ad calcem Bibliot. Latin. Lond. 1703.) See Saidas, (tom. iii. p. 185, 186,) Fabricius, (Bibliot. Graec. l. v. c. 26 p. 449—552,) and Brucker, (Hist. Crit. Philosoph. tom. ii. p. 319—326)]

[Footnote 153: The life of Isidore was composed by Damascius, (apud Photium, sod. ccxlii. p. 1028—1076.) See the last age of the Pagan philosophers, in Brucker, (tom. ii. p. 341—351.)]

[Footnote 154: The suppression of the schools of Athens is recorded by John Malala, (tom. ii. p. 187, sub Decio Cos. Sol.,) and an anonymous Chronicle in the Vatican library, (apud Aleman. p. 106.)]

[Footnote 155: Agathias (l. ii. p. 69, 70, 71) relates this curious story Chosroes ascended the throne in the year 531, and made his first peace with the Romans in the beginning of 533—a date most compatible with his young fame and the old age of Isidore, (Asseman. Bibliot. Orient. tom. iii. p. 404. Pagi, tom. ii. p. 543, 550.)]

About the same time that Pythagoras first invented the appellation of philosopher, liberty and the consulship were founded at Rome by the elder Brutus. The revolutions of the consular office, which may be viewed in the successive lights of a substance, a shadow, and a name, have been occasionally mentioned in the present History. The first magistrates of the republic had been chosen by the people, to exercise, in the senate and in the camp, the powers of peace and war, which were afterwards translated to the emperors. But the tradition of ancient dignity was long revered by the Romans and Barbarians. A Gothic historian applauds the consulship of Theodoric as the height of all temporal glory and greatness; [156] the king of Italy himself congratulated those annual favorites of fortune who, without the cares, enjoyed the splendor of the throne; and at the end of a thousand years, two consuls were created by the sovereigns of Rome and Constantinople, for the sole purpose of giving a date to the year, and a festival to the people. But the expenses of this festival, in which the wealthy and the vain aspired to surpass their predecessors, insensibly arose to the enormous sum of fourscore thousand pounds; the wisest senators declined a useless honor, which involved the certain ruin of their families, and to this reluctance I should impute the frequent chasms in the last age of the consular Fasti. The predecessors of Justinian had assisted from the public treasures the dignity of the less opulent candidates; the avarice of that prince preferred the cheaper and more convenient method of advice and regulation. [157] Seven processions or spectacles were the number to which his edict confined the horse and chariot races, the athletic sports, the music, and pantomimes of the theatre, and the hunting of wild beasts; and small pieces of silver were discreetly substituted to the gold medals, which had always excited tumult and drunkenness, when they were scattered with a profuse hand among the populace. Notwithstanding these precautions, and his own example, the succession of consuls finally ceased in the thirteenth year of Justinian, whose despotic temper might be gratified by the silent extinction of a title which admonished the Romans of their ancient freedom. [158] Yet the annual consulship still lived in the minds of the people; they fondly expected its speedy restoration; they applauded the gracious condescension of successive princes, by whom it was assumed in the first year of their reign; and three centuries elapsed, after the death of Justinian, before that obsolete dignity, which had been suppressed by custom, could be abolished by law. [159] The imperfect mode of distinguishing each year by the name of a magistrate, was usefully supplied by the date of a permanent aera: the creation of the world, according to the Septuagint version, was adopted by the Greeks; [160] and the Latins, since the age of Charlemagne, have computed their time from the birth of Christ. [161]

[Footnote 156: Cassiodor. Variarum Epist. vi. 1. Jornandes, c. 57, p. 696, dit. Grot. Quod summum bonum primumque in mundo decus dicitur.]

[Footnote 157: See the regulations of Justinian, (Novell. cv.,) dated at Constantinople, July 5, and addressed to Strategius, treasurer of the empire.]

[Footnote 158: Procopius, in Anecdot. c. 26. Aleman. p. 106. In the xviiith year after the consulship of Basilius, according to the reckoning of Marcellinus, Victor, Marius, &c., the secret history was composed, and, in the eyes of Procopius, the consulship was finally abolished.]

[Footnote 159: By Leo, the philosopher, (Novell. xciv. A.D. 886-911.) See Pagi (Dissertat. Hypatica, p. 325—362) and Ducange, (Gloss, Graec p. 1635, 1636.) Even the title was vilified: consulatus codicilli.. vilescunt, says the emperor himself.]

[Footnote 160: According to Julius Africanus, &c., the world was created the first of September, 5508 years, three months, and twenty-five days before the birth of Christ. (See Pezron, Antiquite des Tems defendue, p. 20—28.) And this aera has been used by the Greeks, the Oriental Christians, and even by the

Russians, till the reign of Peter I The period, however arbitrary, is clear and convenient. Of the 7296 years which are supposed to elapse since the creation, we shall find 3000 of ignorance and darkness; 2000 either fabulous or doubtful; 1000 of ancient history, commencing with the Persian empire, and the Republics of Rome and Athens; 1000 from the fall of the Roman empire in the West to the discovery of America; and the remaining 296 will almost complete three centuries of the modern state of Europe and mankind. I regret this chronology, so far preferable to our double and perplexed method of counting backwards and forwards the years before and after the Christian era.]

[Footnote 161: The aera of the world has prevailed in the East since the vith general council, (A.D. 681.) In the West, the Christian aera was first invented in the vith century: it was propagated in the viiith by the authority and writings of venerable Bede; but it was not till the xth that the use became legal and popular. See l'Art de Veriner les Dates, Dissert. Preliminaire, p. iii. xii. Dictionnaire Diplomatique, tom. i. p. 329—337; the works of a laborious society of Benedictine monks.]

CHAPTER XLI

CONQUESTS OF JUSTINIAN, CHARACTER OF BALISARIUS

PART I

CONQUESTS OF JUSTINIAN IN THE WEST—CHARACTER AND FIRST CAMPAIGNS OF BELISARIUS—HE INVADES AND SUBDUES THE VANDAL KINGDOM OF AFRICA—HIS TRIUMPH—THE GOTHIC WARD—HE RECOVERS SICILY, NAPLES, AND ROME—SIEGE OF ROME BY THE GOTHS—THEIR RETREAT AND LOSSES—SURRENDER OF RAVENNA—GLORY OF BELISARIUS—HIS DOMESTIC SHAME AND MISFORTUNES

When Justinian ascended the throne, about fifty years after the fall of the Western empire, the kingdoms of the Goths and Vandals had obtained a solid, and, as it might seem, a legal establishment both in Europe and Africa. The titles, which Roman victory had inscribed, were erased with equal justice by the sword of the Barbarians; and their successful rapine derived a more venerable sanction from time, from treaties, and from the oaths of fidelity, already repeated by a second or third generation of obedient subjects. Experience and Christianity had refuted the superstitious hope, that Rome was founded by the gods to reign forever over the nations of the earth. But the proud claim of perpetual and indefeasible dominion, which her soldiers could no longer maintain, was firmly asserted by her statesmen and lawyers, whose opinions have been sometimes revived and propagated in the modern schools of jurisprudence. After Rome herself had been stripped of the Imperial purple, the princes of Constantinople assumed the sole and sacred sceptre of the monarchy; demanded, as their rightful inheritance, the provinces which had been subdued by the consuls, or possessed by the Caesars; and feebly aspired to deliver their faithful subjects of the West from the usurpation of heretics and Barbarians. The execution of this splendid design was in some degree reserved for Justinian. During the five first years of his reign, he reluctantly waged a costly and unprofitable war against the Persians; till his pride submitted to his ambition, and he purchased at the price of four hundred and forty thousand pounds sterling, the benefit of a precarious truce, which, in the language of both nations, was dignified with the appellation of the endless peace. The safety of the East enabled the emperor to employ his forces against the Vandals; and the internal state of Africa afforded an honorable motive, and promised a powerful support, to the Roman arms. [1]

[Footnote 1: The complete series of the Vandal war is related by Procopius in a regular and elegant narrative, (l. i. c. 9—25, l. ii. c. 1—13,) and happy would be my lot, could I always tread in the footsteps of such a guide. From the entire and diligent perusal of the Greek text, I have a right to pronounce that the Latin and French versions of Grotius and Cousin may not be implicitly trusted; yet the president Cousin has been often praised, and Hugo Grotius was the first scholar of a learned age.]

According to the testament of the founder, the African kingdom had lineally descended to Hilderic, the eldest of the Vandal princes. A mild disposition inclined the son of a tyrant, the grandson of a conqueror, to prefer the counsels of clemency and peace; and his accession was marked by the salutary edict, which restored two hundred bishops to their churches, and allowed the free profession of the Athanasian creed. [2] But the Catholics accepted, with cold and transient gratitude, a favor so inadequate to their pretensions, and the virtues of Hilderic offended the prejudices of his countrymen. The Arian clergy presumed to insinuate that he had renounced the faith, and the soldiers more loudly complained that he had degenerated from the courage, of his ancestors. His ambassadors were suspected of a secret and disgraceful negotiation in the Byzantine court; and his general, the Achilles, [3] as he was named, of the Vandals, lost a battle against the naked and disorderly Moors. The public discontent was exasperated by Gelimer, whose age, descent, and military fame, gave him an apparent title to the succession: he assumed, with the consent of the nation, the reins of government; and his unfortunate sovereign sunk without a struggle from the throne to a dungeon, where he was strictly guarded with a faithful counsellor, and his unpopular nephew the Achilles of the Vandals. But the indulgence which Hilderic had shown to his Catholic subjects had powerfully recommended him to the favor of Justinian, who, for the benefit of his own sect, could acknowledge the use and justice of religious toleration: their alliance, while the nephew of Justin remained in a private station, was cemented by the mutual exchange of gifts and letters; and the emperor Justinian asserted the cause of royalty and friendship. In two successive embassies, he admonished the usurper to repent of his treason, or to abstain, at least, from any further violence which might provoke the displeasure of God and of the Romans; to reverence the laws of kindred and succession, and to suffer an infirm old man peaceably to end his days, either on the throne of Carthage or in the palace of Constantinople. The passions, or even the prudence, of Gelimer compelled him to reject these requests, which were urged in the haughty tone of menace and command; and he justified his ambition in a language rarely spoken in the Byzantine court, by alleging the right of a free people to remove or punish their chief magistrate, who had failed in the execution of the kingly office.

After this fruitless expostulation, the captive monarch was more rigorously treated, his nephew was deprived of his eyes, and the cruel Vandal, confident in his strength and distance, derided the vain threats and slow preparations of the emperor of the East. Justinian resolved to deliver or revenge his friend, Gelimer to maintain his usurpation; and the war was preceded, according to the practice of civilized nations, by the most solemn protestations, that each party was sincerely desirous of peace.

[Footnote 2: See Ruinart, Hist. Persecut. Vandal. c. xii. p. 589. His best evidence is drawn from the life of St. Fulgentius, composed by one of his disciples, transcribed in a great measure in the annals of Baronius, and printed in several great collections, (Catalog. Bibliot. Bunavianae, tom. i. vol. ii. p. 1258.)]

[Footnote 3: For what quality of the mind or body? For speed, or beauty, or valor?—In what language did the Vandals read Homer?—Did he speak German?—The Latins had four versions, (Fabric. tom. i. l. ii. c. 8, p. 297:) yet, in spite of the praises of Seneca, (Consol. c. 26,) they appear to have been more successful in *imitating than in translating the Greek poets. But the name of Achilles might be famous and popular even among the illiterate Barbarians.]*

The report of an African war was grateful only to the vain and idle populace of Constantinople, whose poverty exempted them from tribute, and whose cowardice was seldom exposed to military service. But the wiser citizens, who judged of the future by the past, revolved in their memory the immense loss, both of men and money, which the empire had sustained in the expedition of Basiliscus. The troops, which, after five laborious campaigns, had been recalled from the Persian frontier, dreaded the sea, the climate, and the arms of an unknown enemy. The ministers of the finances computed, as far as they might compute, the demands of an African war; the taxes which must be found and levied to supply those insatiate demands; and the danger, lest their own lives, or at least their lucrative employments, should be made responsible for the deficiency of the supply. Inspired by such selfish motives, (for we may not suspect him of any zeal for the public good,) John of Cappadocia ventured to oppose in full council the inclinations of his master. He confessed, that a victory of such importance could not be too dearly purchased; but he represented in a grave discourse the certain difficulties and the uncertain event. "You undertake," said the praefect, "to besiege Carthage: by land, the distance is not less than one hundred and forty days' journey; on the sea, a whole year [4] must elapse before you can receive any intelligence from your fleet. If Africa should be reduced, it cannot be preserved without the additional conquest of Sicily and Italy. Success will impose the obligations of new labors; a single misfortune will attract the Barbarians into the heart of your exhausted empire." Justinian felt the weight of this salutary advice; he was confounded by the unwonted freedom of an obsequious servant; and the design of the war would perhaps have been relinquished, if his courage had not been revived by a voice which silenced the doubts of profane reason. "I have seen a vision," cried an artful or fanatic bishop of the East. "It is the will of Heaven, O emperor! that you should not abandon your holy enterprise for the deliverance of the African church. The God of battles will march before your standard, and disperse your enemies, who are the enemies of his Son." The emperor, might be tempted, and his counsellors were constrained, to give credit to this seasonable revelation: but they derived more rational hope from the revolt, which the adherents of Hilderic or Athanasius had already excited on the borders of the Vandal monarchy. Pudentius, an African subject, had privately signified his loyal intentions, and a small military aid restored the province of Tripoli to the obedience of the Romans. The government of Sardinia had been intrusted to Godas, a valiant Barbarian he suspended the payment of tribute, disclaimed his allegiance to the usurper, and gave audience to the emissaries of Justinian, who found him master of that fruitful island, at the head of his guards, and proudly invested with the ensigns of royalty. The forces of the Vandals were diminished by discord and suspicion; the Roman armies were animated by the spirit of Belisarius; one of those heroic names which are familiar to every age and to every nation.

[Footnote 4: A year—absurd exaggeration! The conquest of Africa may be dated A. D 533, September 14. It is celebrated by Justinian in the preface to his Institutes, which were published November 21 of the same year. Including the voyage and return, such a computation might be truly applied to our Indian empire.]

The Africanus of new Rome was born, and perhaps educated, among the Thracian peasants, [5] without any of those advantages which had formed the virtues of the elder and younger Scipio; a noble origin, liberal studies, and the emulation of a free state.

The silence of a loquacious secretary may be admitted, to prove that the youth of Belisarius could not afford any subject of praise: he served, most assuredly with valor and reputation, among the private guards of Justinian; and when his patron became emperor, the domestic was promoted to military command. After a bold inroad into Persarmenia, in which his glory was shared by a colleague, and his progress was checked by an enemy, Belisarius repaired to the important station of Dara, where he first accepted the service of Procopius, the faithful companion, and diligent historian, of his exploits. [6] The Mirranes of Persia advanced, with forty thousand of her best troops, to raze the fortifications of Dara; and signified the day and the hour on which the citizens should prepare a bath for his refreshment, after the toils of victory. He encountered an adversary equal to himself, by the new title of General of the East; his superior in the science of war, but much inferior in the number and quality of his troops, which amounted only to twenty-five thousand Romans and strangers, relaxed in their discipline, and humbled by recent disasters. As the level plain of Dara refused all shelter to stratagem and ambush, Belisarius protected his front with a deep trench, which was prolonged at first in perpendicular, and afterwards in parallel, lines, to cover the wings of cavalry advantageously posted to command the flanks and rear of the enemy. When the Roman centre was shaken, their well-timed and rapid charge decided the conflict: the standard of Persia fell; the immortals fled; the infantry threw away their bucklers, and eight thousand of the vanquished were left on the field of battle. In the next campaign, Syria was invaded on the side of the desert; and Belisarius, with twenty thousand men, hastened from Dara to the relief of the province. During the whole summer, the designs of the enemy were baffled by his skilful dispositions: he pressed their retreat, occupied each night their camp of the preceding day, and would have secured a bloodless victory, if he could have resisted the impatience of his own troops. Their valiant promise was faintly supported in the hour of battle; the right wing was exposed by the treacherous or cowardly desertion of the Christian Arabs; the Huns, a veteran band of eight hundred warriors, were oppressed by superior numbers; the flight of the Isaurians was intercepted; but the Roman infantry stood firm on the left; for Belisarius himself, dismounting from his horse, showed them that intrepid despair was their only safety. [611] They turned their backs to the Euphrates, and their faces to the enemy: innumerable arrows glanced without effect from the compact and shelving order of their bucklers; an impenetrable line of pikes was opposed to the repeated assaults of the Persian cavalry; and after a resistance of many hours, the remaining troops were skilfully embarked under the shadow of the night. The Persian commander retired with disorder and disgrace, to answer a strict account of the lives of so many soldiers, which he had consumed in a barren victory. But the fame of Belisarius was not sullied by a defeat, in which he alone had saved his army from the consequences of their own rashness: the approach of peace relieved him from the guard of the eastern frontier, and his conduct in the sedition of Constantinople amply discharged his obligations to the emperor. When the African war became the topic of popular discourse and secret deliberation, each of the Roman generals was apprehensive, rather than ambitious, of the dangerous honor; but as soon as Justinian had declared his preference of superior merit, their envy was rekindled by the unanimous applause which was given to the choice of Belisarius. The temper of the Byzantine court may encourage a suspicion, that the hero was darkly assisted by the intrigues of his wife, the fair and subtle Antonina, who alternately enjoyed the confidence, and incurred the hatred, of the empress Theodora.

The birth of Antonina was ignoble; she descended from a family of charioteers; and her chastity has been stained with the foulest reproach. Yet she reigned with long and absolute power over the mind of her illustrious husband; and if Antonina disdained the merit of conjugal fidelity, she expressed a manly friendship to Belisarius, whom she accompanied with undaunted resolution in all the hardships and dangers of a military life. [7]

[Footnote 5: (Procop. Vandal. l. i. c. 11.) Aleman, (Not. ad Anecdot. p. 5,) an Italian, could easily reject the German vanity of Giphanius and Velserus, who wished to claim the hero; but his Germania, a metropolis of Thrace, I cannot find in any civil or ecclesiastical lists of the provinces and cities. Note: M. von Hammer (in a review of Lord Mahon's Life of Belisarius in the Vienna Jahrbucher) shows that the name of

Belisarius is a Sclavonic word, Beli-tzar, the White Prince, and that the place of his birth was a village of Illvria, which still bears the name of Germany—M.]

[Footnote 6: The two first Persian campaigns of Belisarius are fairly and copiously related by his secretary, (Persic. l. i. c. 12—18.)]

[Footnote 611: The battle was fought on Easter Sunday, April 19, not at the end of the summer. The date is supplied from John Malala by Lord Mabon p. 47—M.]

[Footnote 7: See the birth and character of Antonina, in the Anecdotes, c. l. and the notes of Alemannus, p. 3.]

The preparations for the African war were not unworthy of the last contest between Rome and Carthage. The pride and flower of the army consisted of the guards of Belisarius, who, according to the pernicious indulgence of the times, devoted themselves, by a particular oath of fidelity, to the service of their patrons. Their strength and stature, for which they had been curiously selected, the goodness of their horses and armor, and the assiduous practice of all the exercises of war, enabled them to act whatever their courage might prompt; and their courage was exalted by the social honor of their rank, and the personal ambition of favor and fortune. Four hundred of the bravest of the Heruli marched under the banner of the faithful and active Pharas; their untractable valor was more highly prized than the tame submission of the Greeks and Syrians; and of such importance was it deemed to procure a reenforcement of six hundred Massagetae, or Huns, that they were allured by fraud and deceit to engage in a naval expedition. Five thousand horse and ten thousand foot were embarked at Constantinople, for the conquest of Africa; but the infantry, for the most part levied in Thrace and Isauria, yielded to the more prevailing use and reputation of the cavalry; and the Scythian bow was the weapon on which the armies of Rome were now reduced to place their principal dependence. From a laudable desire to assert the dignity of his theme, Procopius defends the soldiers of his own time against the morose critics, who confined that respectable name to the heavy-armed warriors of antiquity, and maliciously observed, that the word archer is introduced by Homer [8] as a term of contempt. "Such contempt might perhaps be due to the naked youths who appeared on foot in the fields of Troy, and lurking behind a tombstone, or the shield of a friend, drew the bow-string to their breast, [9] and dismissed a feeble and lifeless arrow. But our archers (pursues the historian) are mounted on horses, which they manage with admirable skill; their head and shoulders are protected by a casque or buckler; they wear greaves of iron on their legs, and their bodies are guarded by a coat of mail. On their right side hangs a quiver, a sword on their left, and their hand is accustomed to wield a lance or javelin in closer combat. Their bows are strong and weighty; they shoot in every possible direction, advancing, retreating, to the front, to the rear, or to either flank; and as they are taught to draw the bow-string not to the breast, but to the right ear, firm indeed must be the armor that can resist the rapid violence of their shaft." Five hundred transports, navigated by twenty thousand mariners of Egypt, Cilicia, and Ionia, were collected in the harbor of Constantinople. The smallest of these vessels may be computed at thirty, the largest at five hundred, tons; and the fair average will supply an allowance, liberal, but not profuse, of about one hundred thousand tons, [10] for the reception of thirty-five thousand soldiers and sailors, of five thousand horses, of arms, engines, and military stores, and of a sufficient stock of water and provisions for a voyage, perhaps, of three months. The proud galleys, which in former ages swept the Mediterranean with so many hundred oars, had long since disappeared; and the fleet of Justinian was escorted only by ninety-two light brigantines, covered from the missile weapons of the enemy, and rowed by two thousand of the brave and robust youth of Constantinople. Twenty-two generals are named, most of whom were afterwards distinguished in the wars of Africa and Italy: but the supreme command, both by land and sea, was delegated to Belisarius alone, with a boundless power of acting according to his discretion, as if the emperor himself were present. The separation of the naval and military professions is at once the effect and the cause of the modern improvements in the science of navigation and maritime war. [Footnote 8: See the preface of Procopius. The enemies of archery might quote the reproaches of Diomede (Iliad. Delta. 385, &c.) and the permittere vulnera ventis of Lucan, (viii. 384:) yet the Romans could not despise the arrows of the Parthians; and in the siege of Troy, Pandarus, Paris, and Teucer, pierced those haughty warriors who insulted them as women or children.]

[Footnote 9: (Iliad. Delta. 123.) How concise—how just—how beautiful is the whole picture! I see the attitudes of the archer—I hear the twanging of the bow.]

[Footnote 10: The text appears to allow for the largest vessels 50,000 medimni, or 3000 tons, (since the medimnus weighed 160 Roman, or 120 avoirdupois, pounds.) I have given a more rational interpretation, by supposing that the Attic style of Procopius conceals the legal and popular modius, a sixth part of the medimnus, (Hooper's Ancient Measures, p. 152, &c.) A contrary and indeed a stranger mistake has crept into an oration of Dinarchus, (contra Demosthenem, in Reiske Orator. Graec tom iv. P. ii. p. 34.) By reducing the number of ships from 500 to 50, and translating by mines, or pounds, Cousin has generously allowed 500 tons for the whole of the Imperial fleet! Did he never think?]

In the seventh year of the reign of Justinian, and about the time of the summer solstice, the whole fleet of six hundred ships was ranged in martial pomp before the gardens of the palace. The patriarch pronounced his benediction, the emperor signified his last commands, the general's trumpet gave the signal of departure, and every heart, according to its fears or wishes, explored, with anxious curiosity, the omens of misfortune and success. The first halt was made at Perinthus or Heraclea, where Belisarius waited five days to receive some Thracian horses, a military gift of his sovereign. From thence the fleet pursued their course through the midst of the Propontis; but as they struggled to pass the Straits of the Hellespont, an unfavorable wind detained them four days at Abydus, where the general exhibited a memorable lesson of firmness and severity. Two of the Huns, who in a drunken quarrel had slain one of their fellow-soldiers, were instantly shown to the army suspended on a lofty gibbet. The national dignity was resented by their countrymen, who disclaimed the servile laws of the empire, and asserted the free privilege of Scythia, where a small fine was allowed to expiate the hasty sallies of intemperance and anger. Their complaints were specious, their clamors were loud, and the Romans were not averse to the example of disorder and impunity. But the rising sedition was appeased by the authority and eloquence of the general: and he represented to the assembled troops the obligation of justice, the importance of discipline, the rewards of piety and virtue, and the unpardonable guilt of murder, which, in his apprehension, was aggravated rather than excused by the vice of intoxication. [11] In the navigation from the Hellespont to Peloponnesus, which the Greeks, after the siege of Troy, had performed in four days, [12] the fleet of Belisarius was guided in their course by his master-galley, conspicuous in the day by the redness of the sails, and in the night by the torches blazing from the mast head. It was the duty of the pilots, as they steered between the islands, and turned the Capes of Malea and Taenarium, to preserve the just order and regular intervals of such a multitude of ships: as the wind was fair and moderate, their labors were not unsuccessful, and the troops were safely disembarked at Methone on the Messenian coast, to repose themselves for a while after the fatigues of the sea. In this place they experienced how avarice, invested with authority, may sport with the lives of thousands which are bravely exposed for the public service. According to military practice, the bread or biscuit of the Romans was twice prepared in the oven, and the diminution of one fourth was cheerfully allowed for the loss of weight. To gain this miserable profit, and to save the expense of wood, the praefect John of Cappadocia had given orders that the flour should be slightly baked by the same fire which warmed the baths of

Constantinople; and when the sacks were opened, a soft and mouldy paste was distributed to the army. Such unwholesome food, assisted by the heat of the climate and season, soon produced an epidemical disease, which swept away five hundred soldiers. Their health was restored by the diligence of Belisarius, who provided fresh bread at Methone, and boldly expressed his just and humane indignation the emperor heard his complaint; the general was praised but the minister was not punished. From the port of Methone, the pilots steered along the western coast of Peloponnesus, as far as the Isle of Zacynthus, or Zante, before they undertook the voyage (in their eyes a most arduous voyage) of one hundred leagues over the Ionian Sea. As the fleet was surprised by a calm, sixteen days were consumed in the slow navigation; and even the general would have suffered the intolerable hardship of thirst, if the ingenuity of Antonina had not preserved the water in glass bottles, which she buried deep in the sand in a part of the ship impervious to the rays of the sun. At length the harbor of Caucana, [13] on the southern side of Sicily, afforded a secure and hospitable shelter. The Gothic officers who governed the island in the name of the daughter and grandson of Theodoric, obeyed their imprudent orders, to receive the troops of Justinian like friends and allies: provisions were liberally supplied, the cavalry was remounted, [14] and Procopius soon returned from Syracuse with correct information of the state and designs of the Vandals. His intelligence determined Belisarius to hasten his operations, and his wise impatience was seconded by the winds. The fleet lost sight of Sicily, passed before the Isle of Malta, discovered the capes of Africa, ran along the coast with a strong gale from the north-east, and finally cast anchor at the promontory of Caput Vada, about five days' journey to the south of Carthage. [15]

[Footnote 11: I have read of a Greek legislator, who inflicted a double penalty on the crimes committed in a state of intoxication; but it seems agreed that this was rather a political than a moral law.]

[Footnote 12: Or even in three days, since they anchored the first evening in the neighboring isle of Tenedos: the second day they sailed to Lesbon the third to the promontory of Euboea, and on the fourth they reached Argos, (Homer, Odyss. P. 130—183. Wood's Essay on Homer, p. 40—46.) A pirate sailed from the Hellespont to the seaport of Sparta in three days, (Xenophon. Hellen. l. ii. c. l.)]

[Footnote 13: Caucana, near Camarina, is at least 50 miles (350 or 400 stadia) from Syracuse, (Cluver. Sicilia Antiqua, p. 191.) Note: Lord Mahon. (Life of Belisarius, p.88) suggests some valid reasons for reading Catana, the ancient name of Catania—M.]

[Footnote 14: Procopius, Gothic. l. i. c. 3. Tibi tollit hinnitum apta quadrigis equa, in the Sicilian pastures of Grosphus, (Horat. Carm. ii. 16.) Acragas.... magnanimum quondam generator equorum, (Virg. Aeneid. iii. 704.) Thero's horses, whose victories are immortalized by Pindar, were bred in this country.]

[Footnote 15: The Caput Vada of Procopius (where Justinian afterwards founded a city—De Edific.l. vi. c. 6) is the promontory of Ammon in Strabo, the Brachodes of Ptolemy, the Capaudia of the moderns, a long narrow slip that runs into the sea, (Shaw's Travels, p. 111.)]

If Gelimer had been informed of the approach of the enemy, he must have delayed the conquest of Sardinia for the immediate defence of his person and kingdom. A detachment of five thousand soldiers, and one hundred and twenty galleys, would have joined the remaining forces of the Vandals; and the descendant of Genseric might have surprised and oppressed a fleet of deep laden transports, incapable of action, and of light brigantines that seemed only qualified for flight. Belisarius had secretly trembled when he overheard his soldiers, in the passage, emboldening each other to confess their apprehensions: if they were once on shore, they hoped to maintain the honor of their arms; but if they should be attacked at sea, they did not blush to acknowledge that they wanted courage to contend at the same time with the winds, the waves, and the Barbarians. [16] The knowledge of their sentiments decided Belisarius to seize the first opportunity of landing them on the coast of Africa; and he prudently rejected, in a council of war, the proposal of sailing with the fleet and army into the port of Carthage. [16/1] Three months after their departure from Constantinople, the men and horses, the arms and military stores, were safely disembarked, and five soldiers were left as a guard on board each of the ships, which were disposed in the form of a semicircle. The remainder of the troops occupied a camp on the sea-shore, which they fortified, according to ancient discipline, with a ditch and rampart; and the discovery of a source of fresh water, while it allayed the thirst, excited the superstitious confidence, of the Romans. The next morning, some of the neighboring gardens were pillaged; and Belisarius, after chastising the offenders, embraced the slight occasion, but the decisive moment, of inculcating the maxims of justice, moderation, and genuine policy. "When I first accepted the commission of subduing Africa, I depended much less," said the general, "on the numbers, or even the bravery of my troops, than on the friendly disposition of the natives, and their immortal hatred to the Vandals. You alone can deprive me of this hope; if you continue to extort by rapine what might be purchased for a little money, such acts of violence will reconcile these implacable enemies, and unite them in a just and holy league against the invaders of their country." These exhortations were enforced by a rigid discipline, of which the soldiers themselves soon felt and praised the salutary effects. The inhabitants, instead of deserting their houses, or hiding their corn, supplied the Romans with a fair and liberal market: the civil officers of the province continued to exercise their functions in the name of Justinian: and the clergy, from motives of conscience and interest, assiduously labored to promote the cause of a Catholic emperor. The small town of Sullecte, [17] one day's journey from the camp, had the honor of being foremost to open her gates, and to resume her ancient allegiance: the larger cities of Leptis and Adrumetum imitated the example of loyalty as soon as Belisarius appeared; and he advanced without opposition as far as Grasse, a palace of the Vandal kings, at the distance of fifty miles from Carthage. The weary Romans indulged themselves in the refreshment of shady groves, cool fountains, and delicious fruits; and the preference which Procopius allows to these gardens over any that he had seen, either in the East or West, may be ascribed either to the taste, or the fatigue, or the historian. In three generations, prosperity and a warm climate had dissolved the hardy virtue of the Vandals, who insensibly became the most luxurious of mankind. In their villas and gardens, which might deserve the Persian name of Paradise, [18] they enjoyed a cool and elegant repose; and, after the daily use of the bath, the Barbarians were seated at a table profusely spread with the delicacies of the land and sea. Their silken robes loosely flowing, after the fashion of the Medes, were embroidered with gold; love and hunting were the labors of their life, and their vacant hours were amused by pantomimes, chariot-races, and the music and dances of the theatre.

[Footnote 16: A centurion of Mark Antony expressed, though in a more manly train, the same dislike to the sea and to naval combats, (Plutarch in Antonio, p. 1730, edit. Hen. Steph.)]

[Footnote 16/1: Rather into the present Lake of Tunis. Lord Mahon, p. 92—M.]

[Footnote 17: Sullecte is perhaps the Turris Hannibalis, an old building, now as large as the Tower of London. The march of Belisarius to Leptis. Adrumetum, &c., is illustrated by the campaign of Caesar, (Hirtius, de Bello Africano, with the Analyse of Guichardt,) and Shaw's Travels (p. 105—113) in the same country.]

[Footnote 18: The paradises, a name and fashion adopted from Persia, may be represented by the royal garden of Ispahan, (Voyage d'Olearius, p. 774.) See, in the Greek romances, their most perfect model, (Longus. Pastoral. l. iv. p. 99—101 Achilles Tatius. l. i. p. 22, 23.)]

In a march of ten or twelve days, the vigilance of Belisarius was constantly awake and active against his unseen enemies, by whom, in every place, and at every hour, he might be suddenly attacked. An officer of confidence and merit, John the Armenian, led the vanguard of three hundred horse; six hundred Massagetae covered at a certain distance the left flank; and the whole fleet, steering along the coast, seldom lost sight of the army, which moved each day about twelve miles, and lodged in the evening in strong camps, or in friendly towns. The near approach of the Romans to Carthage filled the mind of Gelimer with anxiety and terror. He prudently wished to protract the war till his brother, with his veteran troops, should return from the conquest of Sardinia; and he now lamented the rash policy of his ancestors, who, by destroying the fortifications of Africa, had left him only the dangerous resource of risking a battle in the neighborhood of his capital. The Vandal conquerors, from their original number of fifty thousand, were multiplied, without including their women and children, to one hundred and sixty thousand fighting men: [18/1] and such forces, animated with valor and union, might have crushed, at their first landing, the feeble and exhausted bands of the Roman general. But the friends of the captive king were more inclined to accept the invitations, than to resist the progress, of Belisarius; and many a proud Barbarian disguised his aversion to war under the more specious name of his hatred to the usurper. Yet the authority and promises of Gelimer collected a formidable army, and his plans were concerted with some degree of military skill. An order was despatched to his brother Ammatas, to collect all the forces of Carthage, and to encounter the van of the Roman army at the distance of ten miles from the city: his nephew Gibamund, with two thousand horse, was destined to attack their left, when the monarch himself, who silently followed, should charge their rear, in a situation which excluded them from the aid or even the view of their fleet. But the rashness of Ammatas was fatal to himself and his country. He anticipated the hour of the attack, outstripped his tardy followers, and was pierced with a mortal wound, after he had slain with his own hand twelve of his boldest antagonists. His Vandals fled to Carthage; the highway, almost ten miles, was strewed with dead bodies; and it seemed incredible that such multitudes could be slaughtered by the swords of three hundred Romans. The nephew of Gelimer was defeated, after a slight combat, by the six hundred Massagetae: they did not equal the third part of his numbers; but each Scythian was fired by the example of his chief, who gloriously exercised the privilege of his family, by riding, foremost and alone, to shoot the first arrow against the enemy. In the mean while, Gelimer himself, ignorant of the event, and misguided by the windings of the hills, inadvertently passed the Roman army, and reached the scene of action where Ammatas had fallen. He wept the fate of his brother and of Carthage, charged with irresistible fury the advancing squadrons, and might have pursued, and perhaps decided, the victory, if he had not wasted those inestimable moments in the discharge of a vain, though pious, duty to the dead. While his spirit was broken by this mournful office, he heard the trumpet of Belisarius, who, leaving Antonina and his infantry in the camp, pressed forwards with his guards and the remainder of the cavalry to rally his flying troops, and to restore the fortune of the day. Much room could not be found, in this disorderly battle, for the talents of a general; but the king fled before the hero; and the Vandals, accustomed only to a Moorish enemy, were incapable of withstanding the arms and discipline of the Romans. Gelimer retired with hasty steps towards the desert of Numidia: but he had soon the consolation of learning that his private orders for the execution of Hilderic and his captive friends had been faithfully obeyed. The tyrant's revenge was useful only to his enemies. The death of a lawful prince excited the compassion of his people; his life might have perplexed the victorious Romans; and the lieutenant of Justinian, by a crime of which he was innocent, was relieved from the painful alternative of forfeiting his honor or relinquishing his conquests.

[Footnote 18/1: 80,000. Hist. Arc. c. 18. Gibbon has been misled by the translation. See Lord ov. p. 99—M.]

PART II

As soon as the tumult had subsided, the several parts of the army informed each other of the accidents of the day; and Belisarius pitched his camp on the field of victory, to which the tenth mile-stone from Carthage had applied the Latin appellation of Decimus. From a wise suspicion of the stratagems and resources of the Vandals, he marched the next day in order of battle, halted in the evening before the gates of Carthage, and allowed a night of repose, that he might not, in darkness and disorder, expose the city to the license of the soldiers, or the soldiers themselves to the secret ambush of the city. But as the fears of Belisarius were the result of calm and intrepid reason, he was soon satisfied that he might confide, without danger, in the peaceful and friendly aspect of the capital. Carthage blazed with innumerable torches, the signals of the public joy; the chain was removed that guarded the entrance of the port; the gates were thrown open, and the people, with acclamations of gratitude, hailed and invited their Roman deliverers. The defeat of the Vandals, and the freedom of Africa, were announced to the city on the eve of St. Cyprian, when the churches were already adorned and illuminated for the festival of the martyr whom three centuries of superstition had almost raised to a local deity. The Arians, conscious that their reign had expired, resigned the temple to the Catholics, who rescued their saint from profane hands, performed the holy rites, and loudly proclaimed the creed of Athanasius and Justinian. One awful hour reversed the fortunes of the contending parties. The suppliant Vandals, who had so lately indulged the vices of conquerors, sought an humble refuge in the sanctuary of the church; while the merchants of the East were delivered from the deepest dungeon of the palace by their affrighted keeper, who implored the protection of his captives, and showed them, through an aperture in the wall, the sails of the Roman fleet. After their separation from the army, the naval commanders had proceeded with slow caution along the coast till they reached the Hermaean promontory, and obtained the first intelligence of the victory of Belisarius. Faithful to his instructions, they would have cast anchor about twenty miles from Carthage, if the more skilful seamen had not represented the perils of the shore, and the signs of an impending tempest. Still ignorant of the revolution, they declined, however, the rash attempt of forcing the chain of the port; and the adjacent harbor and suburb of Mandracium were insulted only by the rapine of a private officer, who disobeyed and deserted his leaders. But the Imperial fleet, advancing with a fair wind, steered through the narrow entrance of the Goletta, and occupied, in the deep and capacious lake of Tunis, a secure station about five miles from the capital. [19] No sooner was Belisarius informed of their arrival, than he despatched orders that the greatest part of the mariners should be immediately landed to join the triumph, and to swell the apparent numbers, of the Romans. Before he allowed them to enter the gates of Carthage, he exhorted them, in a discourse worthy of himself and the occasion, not to disgrace the glory of their arms; and to remember that the Vandals had been the tyrants, but that they were the deliverers, of the Africans, who must now be respected as the voluntary and affectionate subjects of their common sovereign. The Romans marched through the streets in close ranks prepared for battle if an enemy had appeared: the strict order maintained by the general imprinted on their minds the duty of obedience; and in an age in which custom and impunity almost sanctified the abuse of conquest, the genius of one man repressed the passions of a victorious army. The voice of menace and complaint was silent; the trade of Carthage was not interrupted; while Africa changed her master and her government, the shops continued open and busy; and the soldiers, after sufficient guards had been posted, modestly departed to the houses which were allotted for their reception. Belisarius fixed his residence in the palace; seated himself on the throne of Genseric; accepted and distributed the Barbaric spoil; granted their lives to the suppliant Vandals; and labored to repair the damage which the suburb of Mandracium had sustained in the preceding night. At supper he entertained his principal officers with the form and magnificence of a royal banquet. [20] The victor was respectfully served by the captive officers of the household; and in the moments of festivity, when the impartial spectators applauded the fortune and merit of Belisarius, his envious flatterers secretly shed their venom on every word and gesture which might alarm the suspicions of a jealous monarch. One day was given to these pompous scenes, which may not be despised as useless, if they attracted the popular veneration; but the active mind of Belisarius, which in the pride of victory could suppose a defeat, had already resolved that the Roman empire in Africa should not depend on the chance of arms, or the favor of the people. The fortifications of Carthage [20/1] had alone been exempted from the general proscription; but in the reign of ninety-five years they were suffered to decay by the thoughtless and indolent Vandals. A wiser conqueror restored, with incredible despatch, the walls and ditches of the city. His liberality encouraged the workmen; the soldiers, the mariners, and the citizens, vied with each other in the salutary labor; and Gelimer, who had feared to trust his person in an open town, beheld with astonishment and despair, the rising strength of an impregnable fortress.

[Footnote 19: The neighborhood of Carthage, the sea, the land, and the rivers, are changed almost as much as the works of man. The isthmus, or neck of the city, is now confounded with the continent; the harbor is a dry plain; and the lake, or stagnum, no more than a morass, with six or seven feet water in the mid-channel. See D'Anville, (Geographie Ancienne, tom. iii. p. 82,) Shaw, (Travels, p. 77—84,) Marmol, (Description de l'Afrique, tom. ii. p. 465,) and Thuanus, (lviii. 12, tom. iii. p. 334.)]

[Footnote 20: From Delphi, the name of Delphicum was given, both in Greek and Latin, to a tripod; and by an easy analogy, the same appellation was extended at Rome, Constantinople, and Carthage, to the royal banquetting room, (Procopius, Vandal. l. i. c. 21. Ducange, Gloss, Graec. p. 277., ad Alexiad. p. 412.)]

[Footnote 20/1: And a few others. Procopius states in his work De Edi Sciis. l. vi. vol i. p. 5—M]

That unfortunate monarch, after the loss of his capital, applied himself to collect the remains of an army scattered, rather than destroyed, by the preceding battle; and the hopes of pillage attracted some Moorish bands to the standard of Gelimer. He encamped in the fields of Bulla, four days' journey from Carthage; insulted the capital, which he deprived of the use of an aqueduct; proposed a high reward for the head of every Roman; affected to spare the persons and property of his African subjects, and secretly negotiated with the Arian sectaries and the confederate Huns. Under these circumstances, the conquest of Sardinia served only to aggravate his distress: he reflected, with the deepest anguish, that he had wasted, in that useless enterprise, five thousand of his bravest troops; and he read, with grief and shame, the victorious letters of his brother Zano, [20/2] who expressed a sanguine confidence that the king, after the example of their ancestors, had already chastised the rashness of the Roman invader. "Alas! my brother," replied Gelimer, "Heaven has declared against our unhappy nation. While you have subdued Sardinia, we have lost Africa. No sooner did Belisarius appear with a handful of soldiers, than courage and prosperity deserted the cause of the Vandals. Your nephew Gibamund, your brother Ammatas, have been betrayed to death by the cowardice of their followers. Our horses, our ships, Carthage itself, and all Africa, are in the power of the enemy. Yet the Vandals still prefer an ignominious repose, at the expense of their wives and children, their wealth and liberty. Nothing now remains, except the fields of Bulla, and the hope of your valor. Abandon Sardinia; fly to our relief; restore our empire, or perish by our side." On the receipt of this epistle, Zano imparted his grief to the principal Vandals; but the intelligence was prudently concealed from the natives of the island. The troops embarked in one hundred and twenty galleys at the port of Caghari, cast anchor the third day on the confines of Mauritania, and hastily pursued their march to join the royal standard in the camp of Bulla.

Mournful was the interview: the two brothers embraced; they wept in silence; no questions were asked of the Sardinian victory; no inquiries were made of the African misfortunes: they saw before their eyes the whole extent of their calamities; and the absence of their wives and children afforded a melancholy proof that either death or captivity had been their lot. The languid spirit of the Vandals was at length awakened and united by the entreaties of their king, the example of Zano, and the instant danger which threatened their monarchy and religion. The military strength of the nation advanced to battle; and such was the rapid increase, that before their army reached Tricameron, about twenty miles from Carthage, they might boast, perhaps with some exaggeration, that they surpassed, in a tenfold proportion, the diminutive powers of the Romans. But these powers were under the command of Belisarius; and, as he was conscious of their superior merit, he permitted the Barbarians to surprise him at an unseasonable hour. The Romans were instantly under arms; a rivulet covered their front; the cavalry formed the first line, which Belisarius supported in the centre, at the head of five hundred guards; the infantry, at some distance, was posted in the second line; and the vigilance of the general watched the separate station and ambiguous faith of the Massagetae, who secretly reserved their aid for the conquerors. The historian has inserted, and the reader may easily supply, the speeches [21] of the commanders, who, by arguments the most apposite to their situation, inculcated the importance of victory, and the contempt of life. Zano, with the troops which had followed him to the conquest of Sardinia, was placed in the centre; and the throne of Genseric might have stood, if the multitude of Vandals had imitated their intrepid resolution. Casting away their lances and missile weapons, they drew their swords, and expected the charge: the Roman cavalry thrice passed the rivulet; they were thrice repulsed; and the conflict was firmly maintained, till Zano fell, and the standard of Belisarius was displayed. Gelimer retreated to his camp; the Huns joined the pursuit; and the victors despoiled the bodies of the slain. Yet no more than fifty Romans, and eight hundred Vandals were found on the field of battle; so inconsiderable was the carnage of a day, which extinguished a nation, and transferred the empire of Africa. In the evening Belisarius led his infantry to the attack of the camp; and the pusillanimous flight of Gelimer exposed the vanity of his recent declarations, that to the vanquished, death was a relief, life a burden, and infamy the only object of terror. His departure was secret; but as soon as the Vandals discovered that their king had deserted them, they hastily dispersed, anxious only for their personal safety, and careless of every object that is dear or valuable to mankind. The Romans entered the camp without resistance; and the wildest scenes of disorder were veiled in the darkness and confusion of the night. Every Barbarian who met their swords was inhumanly massacred; their widows and daughters, as rich heirs, or beautiful concubines, were embraced by the licentious soldiers; and avarice itself was almost satiated with the treasures of gold and silver, the accumulated fruits of conquest or economy in a long period of prosperity and peace. In this frantic search, the troops, even of Belisarius, forgot their caution and respect. Intoxicated with lust and rapine, they explored, in small parties, or alone, the adjacent fields, the woods, the rocks, and the caverns, that might possibly conceal any desirable prize: laden with booty, they deserted their ranks, and wandered without a guide, on the high road to Carthage; and if the flying enemies had dared to return, very few of the conquerors would have escaped. Deeply sensible of the disgrace and danger, Belisarius passed an apprehensive night on the field of victory: at the dawn of day, he planted his standard on a hill, recalled his guardians and veterans, and gradually restored the modesty and obedience of the camp. It was equally the concern of the Roman general to subdue the hostile, and to save the prostrate, Barbarian; and the suppliant Vandals, who could be found only in churches, were protected by his authority, disarmed, and separately confined, that they might neither disturb the public peace, nor become the victims of popular revenge. After despatching a light detachment to tread the footsteps of Gelimer, he advanced, with his whole army, about ten days' march, as far as Hippo Regius, which no longer possessed the relics of St. Augustin. [22] The season, and the certain intelligence that the Vandal had fled to an inaccessible country of the Moors, determined Belisarius to relinquish the vain pursuit, and to fix his winter quarters at Carthage. From thence he despatched his principal lieutenant, to inform the emperor, that in the space of three months he had achieved the conquest of Africa.

[Footnote 20/2: Gibbon had forgotten that the bearer of the "victorious letters of his brother" had sailed into the port of Carthage; and that the letters had fallen into the hands of the Romans. Proc. Vandal. l. i. c. 23—M.]

[Footnote 21: These orations always express the sense of the times, and sometimes of the actors. I have condensed that sense, and thrown away declamation.]

[Footnote 22: The relics of St. Augustin were carried by the African bishops to their Sardinian exile, (A.D. 500;) and it was believed, in the viiith century, that Liutprand, king of the Lombards, transported them (A.D. 721) from Sardinia to Pavia. In the year 1695, the Augustan friars of that city found a brick arch, marble coffin, silver case, silk wrapper, bones, blood, &c., and perhaps an inscription of Agostino in Gothic letters. But this useful discovery has been disputed by reason and jealousy, (Baronius, Annal. A.D. 725, No. 2-9. Tillemont, Mem. Eccles. tom. xiii. p. 944. Montfaucon, Diarium Ital. p. 26-30. Muratori, Antiq. Ital. Medii Aevi, tom. v. dissert. lviii. p. 9, who had composed a separate treatise before the decree of the bishop of Pavia, and Pope Benedict XIII.)]

Belisarius spoke the language of truth. The surviving Vandals yielded, without resistance, their arms and their freedom; the neighborhood of Carthage submitted to his presence; and the more distant provinces were successively subdued by the report of his victory. Tripoli was confirmed in her voluntary allegiance; Sardinia and Corsica surrendered to an officer, who carried, instead of a sword, the head of the valiant Zano; and the Isles of Majorca, Minorca, and Yvica consented to remain an humble appendage of the African kingdom. Caesarea, a royal city, which in looser geography may be confounded with the modern Algiers, was situate thirty days' march to the westward of Carthage: by land, the road was infested by the Moors; but the sea was open, and the Romans were now masters of the sea. An active and discreet tribune sailed as far as the Straits, where he occupied Septem or Ceuta, [23] which rises opposite to Gibraltar on the African coast; that remote place was afterwards adorned and fortified by Justinian; and he seems to have indulged the vain ambition of extending his empire to the columns of Hercules. He received the messengers of victory at the time when he was preparing to publish the Pandects of the Roman laws; and the devout or jealous emperor celebrated the divine goodness, and confessed, in silence, the merit of his successful general. [24] Impatient to abolish the temporal and spiritual tyranny of the Vandals, he proceeded, without delay, to the full establishment of the Catholic church. Her jurisdiction, wealth, and immunites, perhaps the most essential part of episcopal religion, were restored and amplified with a liberal hand; the Arian worship was suppressed; the Donatist meetings were proscribed; [25] and the synod of Carthage, by the voice of two hundred and seventeen bishops, [26] applauded the just measure of pious retaliation. On such an occasion, it may not be presumed, that many orthodox prelates were absent; but the comparative smallness of their number, which in ancient councils had been twice or even thrice multiplied, most clearly indicates the decay both of the church and state. While Justinian approved himself the defender of the faith, he entertained an ambitious hope, that his victorious lieutenant would speedily enlarge the narrow limits of his dominion to the space which they occupied before the invasion of the Moors and Vandals; and Belisarius was instructed to establish five dukes or commanders in the convenient stations of Tripoli, Leptis, Cirta, Caesarea, and Sardinia, and to compute the military force of palatines or borderers that might be sufficient for the defence of Africa. The kingdom of the Vandals was not unworthy of the presence of a Praetorian praefect; and four consulars, three presidents, were appointed to administer the seven provinces under his civil jurisdiction. The number of their subordinate officers, clerks, messengers, or assistants, was minutely expressed; three hundred and ninety-six for the praefect himself, fifty for each of his vicegerents; and the rigid definition of their fees and salaries was more effectual to confirm the right than to prevent the abuse. These magistrates might be oppressive, but they were not idle; and the subtile questions of justice and revenue were infinitely propagated under the new government, which professed to revive the freedom and equity of the Roman republic. The conqueror was solicitous to extract a prompt and plentiful supply from his African subjects; and he allowed them to claim, even in the third degree, and from the collateral line, the houses and lands of which their families had been unjustly despoiled by the Vandals. After the departure of Belisarius, who acted by a high and special commission, no ordinary provision was made for a master-general of the forces; but the office of Praetorian praefect was intrusted to a soldier; the civil and military powers were united, according to the practice of Justinian, in the chief governor; and the representative of the emperor in Africa, as well as in Italy, was soon distinguished by the appellation of Exarch. [27]

[Footnote 23: The expression of Procopius (de Edific. l. vi. c. 7.) Ceuta, which has been defaced by the Portuguese, flourished in nobles and palaces, in agriculture and manufactures, under the more prosperous reign of the Arabs, (l'Afrique de Marmai, tom. ii. p. 236.)]

[Footnote 24: See the second and third preambles to the Digest, or Pandects, promulgated A.D. 533, December 16. To the titles of Vandalicus and Africanus, Justinian, or rather Belisarius, had acquired a just claim; Gothicus was premature, and Francicus false, and offensive to a great nation.]

[Footnote 25: See the original acts in Baronius, (A.D. 535, No. 21—54.) The emperor applauds his own clemency to the heretics, cum sufficiat eis vivere.]

[Footnote 26: Dupin (Geograph. Sacra Africana, p. lix. ad Optat. Milav.) observes and bewails this episcopal decay. In the more prosperous age of the church, he had noticed 690 bishoprics; but however minute were the dioceses, it is not probable that they all existed at the same time.]

[Footnote 27: The African laws of Justinian are illustrated by his German biographer, (Cod. l. i. tit. 27. Novell. 36, 37, 131. Vit. Justinian, p. 349—377.)]

Yet the conquest of Africa was imperfect till her former sovereign was delivered, either alive or dead, into the hands of the Romans. Doubtful of the event, Gelimer had given secret orders that a part of his treasure should be transported to Spain, where he hoped to find a secure refuge at the court of the king of the Visigoths. But these intentions were disappointed by accident, treachery, and the indefatigable pursuit of his enemies, who intercepted his flight from the sea-shore, and chased the unfortunate monarch, with some faithful followers, to the inaccessible mountain of Papua, [28] in the inland country of Numidia. He was immediately besieged by Pharas, an officer whose truth and sobriety were the more applauded, as such qualities could seldom be found among the Heruli, the most corrupt of the Barbarian tribes. To his vigilance Belisarius had intrusted this important charge and, after a bold attempt to scale the mountain, in which he lost a hundred and ten soldiers, Pharas expected, during a winter siege, the operation of distress and famine on the mind of the Vandal king. From the softest habits of pleasure, from the unbounded command of industry and wealth, he was reduced to share the poverty of the Moors, [29] supportable only to themselves by their ignorance of a happier condition. In their rude hovels, of mud and hurdles, which confined the smoke and excluded the light, they promiscuously slept on the ground, perhaps on a sheep-skin, with their wives, their children, and their cattle. Sordid and scanty were their garments; the use of bread and wine was unknown; and their oaten or barley cakes, imperfectly baked in the ashes, were devoured almost in a crude state, by the hungry savages. The health of Gelimer must have sunk under these strange and unwonted hardships, from whatsoever cause they had been endured; but his actual misery was imbittered by the recollection of past greatness, the daily insolence of his protectors, and the just apprehension, that the light and venal Moors might be tempted to betray the rights of hospitality. The knowledge of his situation dictated the humane and friendly epistle of Pharas. "Like yourself," said the chief of the Heruli, "I am an illiterate Barbarian, but I speak the language of plain sense and an honest heart. Why will you persist in hopeless obstinacy? Why will you ruin yourself, your family, and nation? The love of freedom and abhorrence of slavery? Alas! my dearest Gelimer, are you not already the worst of slaves, the slave of the vile nation of the Moors? Would it not be preferable to sustain at Constantinople a life of poverty and servitude, rather than to reign the undoubted monarch of the mountain of Papua? Do you think it a disgrace to be the subject of Justinian? Belisarius is his subject; and we ourselves, whose birth is not inferior to your own, are not ashamed of our obedience to the Roman emperor. That generous prince will grant you a rich inheritance of lands, a place in the senate, and the dignity of patrician: such are his gracious intentions, and you may depend with full assurance on the word of Belisarius. So long as Heaven has condemned us to suffer, patience is a virtue; but if we reject the proffered deliverance, it degenerates into blind and stupid despair." "I am not insensible" replied the king of the Vandals, "how kind and rational is your advice. But I cannot persuade myself to become the slave of an unjust enemy, who has deserved my implacable hatred. Him I had never injured either by word or deed: yet he has sent against me, I know not from whence, a certain Belisarius, who has cast me headlong from the throne into his abyss of misery. Justinian is a man; he is a prince; does he not dread for himself a similar reverse of fortune? I can write no more: my grief oppresses me. Send me, I beseech you, my dear Pharas, send me, a lyre, [30] a sponge, and a loaf of bread." From the Vandal messenger, Pharas was informed of the motives of this singular request. It was long since the king of Africa had tasted bread; a defluxion had fallen on his eyes, the effect of fatigue or incessant weeping; and he wished to solace the melancholy hours, by singing to the lyre the sad story of his own misfortunes. The humanity of Pharas was moved; he sent the three extraordinary gifts; but even his humanity prompted him to redouble the vigilance of his guard, that he might sooner compel his prisoner to embrace a resolution advantageous to the Romans, but salutary to himself. The obstinacy of Gelimer at length yielded to reason and necessity; the solemn assurances of safety and honorable treatment were ratified in the emperor's name, by the ambassador of Belisarius; and the king of the Vandals descended from the mountain. The first public interview was in one of the suburbs of Carthage; and when the royal captive accosted his conqueror, he burst into a fit of laughter. The crowd might naturally believe, that extreme grief had deprived Gelimer of his senses: but in this mournful state, unseasonable mirth insinuated to more intelligent observers, that the vain and transitory scenes of human greatness are unworthy of a serious thought. [31]

[Footnote 28: *Mount Papua is placed by D'Anville (tom. iii. p. 92, and Tabul. Imp. Rom. Occident.) near Hippo Regius and the sea; yet this situation ill agrees with the long pursuit beyond Hippo, and the words of Procopius, (l. ii.c.4,). Note: Compare Lord Mahon, 120. conceive Gibbon to be right—M.*]

[Footnote 29: *Shaw (Travels, p. 220) most accurately represents the manners of the Bedoweens and Kabyles, the last of whom, by their language, are the remnant of the Moors; yet how changed—how civilized are these modern savages!—provisions are plenty among them and bread is common.*]

[Footnote 30: *By Procopius it is styled a lyre; perhaps harp would have been more national. The instruments of music are thus distinguished by Venantius Fortunatus:— Romanusque lyra tibi plaudat, Barbarus harpa.*]

[Footnote 31: Herodotus elegantly describes the strange effects of grief in another royal captive, Psammetichus of Egypt, who wept at the lesser and was silent at the greatest of his calamities, (l. iii. c. 14.) In the interview of Paulus Aemilius and Perses, Belisarius might study his part; but it is probable that he never read either Livy or Plutarch; and it is certain that his generosity did not need a tutor.]

Their contempt was soon justified by a new example of a vulgar truth; that flattery adheres to power, and envy to superior merit. The chiefs of the Roman army presumed to think themselves the rivals of a hero. Their private despatches maliciously affirmed, that the conqueror of Africa, strong in his reputation and the public love, conspired to seat himself on the throne of the Vandals. Justinian listened with too patient an ear; and his silence was the result of jealousy rather than of confidence. An honorable alternative, of remaining in the province, or of returning to the capital, was indeed submitted to the discretion of Belisarius; but he wisely concluded, from intercepted letters and the knowledge of his sovereign's temper, that he must either resign his head, erect his standard, or confound his enemies by his presence and submission. Innocence and courage decided his choice; his guards, captives, and treasures, were diligently embarked; and so prosperous was the navigation, that his arrival at Constantinople preceded any certain account of his departure from the port of Carthage. Such unsuspecting loyalty removed the apprehensions of Justinian; envy was silenced and inflamed by the public gratitude; and the third Africanus obtained the honors of a triumph, a ceremony which the city of Constantine had never seen, and which ancient Rome, since the reign of Tiberius, had reserved for the auspicious arms of the Caesars. [32] From the palace of Belisarius, the procession was conducted through the principal streets to the hippodrome; and this memorable day seemed to avenge the injuries of Genseric, and to expiate the shame of the Romans. The wealth of nations was displayed, the trophies of martial or effeminate luxury; rich armor, golden thrones, and the chariots of state which had been used by the Vandal queen; the massy furniture of the royal banquet, the splendor of precious stones, the elegant forms of statues and vases, the more substantial treasure of gold, and the holy vessels of the Jewish temple, which after their long peregrination were respectfully deposited in the Christian church of Jerusalem. A long train of the noblest Vandals reluctantly exposed their lofty stature and manly countenance. Gelimer slowly advanced: he was clad in a purple robe, and still maintained the majesty of a king. Not a tear escaped from his eyes, not a sigh was heard; but his pride or piety derived some secret consolation from the words of Solomon, [33] which he repeatedly pronounced, Vanity! vanity! all is vanity! Instead of ascending a triumphal car drawn by four horses or elephants, the modest conqueror marched on foot at the head of his brave companions; his prudence might decline an honor too conspicuous for a subject; and his magnanimity might justly disdain what had been so often sullied by the vilest of tyrants. The glorious procession entered the gate of the hippodrome; was saluted by the acclamations of the senate and people; and halted before the throne where Justinian and Theodora were seated to receive homage of the captive monarch and the victorious hero. They both performed the customary adoration; and falling prostrate on the ground, respectfully touched the footstool of a prince who had not unsheathed his sword, and of a prostitute who had danced on the theatre; some gentle violence was used to bend the stubborn spirit of the grandson of Genseric; and however trained to servitude, the genius of Belisarius must have secretly rebelled. He was immediately declared consul for the ensuing year, and the day of his inauguration resembled the pomp of a second triumph: his curule chair was borne aloft on the shoulders of captive Vandals; and the spoils of war, gold cups, and rich girdles, were profusely scattered among the populace. [Footnote 32: After the title of imperator had lost the old military sense, and the Roman auspices were abolished by Christianity, (see La Bleterie, Mem. de l'Academie, tom. xxi. p. 302—332,) a triumph might be given with less inconsistency to a private general.]

[Footnote 33: If the Ecclesiastes be truly a work of Solomon, and not, like Prior's poem, a pious and moral composition of more recent times, in his name, and on the subject of his repentance. The latter is the opinion of the learned and free-spirited Grotius, (Opp. Theolog. tom. i. p. 258;) and indeed the Ecclesiastes and Proverbs display a larger compass of thought and experience than seem to belong either to a Jew or a king. Note: Rosenmuller, arguing from the difference of style from that of the greater part of the book of Proverbs, and from its nearer approximation to the Aramaic dialect than any book of the Old Testament, assigns the Ecclesiastes to some period between Nehemiah and Alexander the Great Schol. in Vet. Test. ix. Proemium ad Eccles. p. 19—M.]

PART III

Although Theodatus descended from a race of heroes, he was ignorant of the art, and averse to the dangers, of war. Although he had studied the writings of Plato and Tully, philosophy was incapable of purifying his mind from the basest passions, avarice and fear. He had purchased a sceptre by ingratitude and murder: at the first menace of an enemy, he degraded his own majesty and that of a nation, which already disdained their unworthy sovereign. Astonished by the recent example of Gelimer, he saw himself dragged in chains through the streets of Constantinople: the terrors which Belisarius inspired were heightened by the eloquence of Peter, the Byzantine ambassador; and that bold and subtle advocate persuaded him to sign a treaty, too ignominious to become the foundation of a lasting peace. It was stipulated, that in the acclamations of the Roman people, the name of the emperor should be always proclaimed before that of the Gothic king; and that as often as the statue of Theodatus was erected in brass on marble, the divine image of Justinian should be placed on its right hand. Instead of conferring, the king of Italy was reduced to solicit, the honors of the senate; and the consent of the emperor was made indispensable before he could execute, against a priest or senator, the sentence either of death or confiscation. The feeble monarch resigned the possession of Sicily; offered, as the annual mark of his dependence, a crown of gold of the weight of three hundred pounds; and promised to supply, at the requisition of his sovereign, three thousand Gothic auxiliaries, for the service of the empire. Satisfied with these extraordinary concessions, the successful agent of Justinian hastened his journey to Constantinople; but no sooner had he reached the Alban villa, [60] than he was recalled by the anxiety of Theodatus; and the dialogue which passed between the king and the ambassador deserves to be represented in its original simplicity. "Are you of opinion that the emperor will ratify this treaty? Perhaps. If he refuses, what consequence will ensue? War. Will such a war, be just or reasonable? Most assuredly: every to his character. What is your meaning? You are a philosopher—Justinian is emperor of the Romans: it would all become the disciple of Plato to shed the blood of thousands in his private quarrel: the successor of Augustus should vindicate his rights, and recover by arms the ancient provinces of his empire." This reasoning might not convince, but it was sufficient to alarm and subdue the weakness of Theodatus; and he soon descended to his last offer, that for the poor equivalent of a pension of forty-eight thousand pounds sterling, he would resign the kingdom of the Goths and Italians, and spend the remainder of his days in the innocent pleasures of philosophy and agriculture.

Both treaties were intrusted to the hands of the ambassador, on the frail security of an oath not to produce the second till the first had been positively rejected. The event may be easily foreseen: Justinian required and accepted the abdication of the Gothic king. His indefatigable agent returned from Constantinople to Ravenna, with ample instructions; and a fair epistle, which praised the wisdom and generosity of the royal philosopher, granted his pension, with the assurance of such honors as a subject and a Catholic might enjoy; and wisely referred the final execution of the treaty to the presence and authority of Belisarius. But in the interval of suspense, two Roman generals, who had entered the province of Dalmatia, were defeated and slain by the Gothic troops. From blind and abject despair, Theodatus capriciously rose to groundless and fatal presumption, [61] and dared to receive, with menace and contempt, the ambassador of Justinian; who claimed his promise, solicited the allegiance of his subjects, and boldly asserted the inviolable privilege of his own character. The march of Belisarius dispelled this visionary pride; and as the first campaign [62] was employed in the reduction of Sicily, the invasion of Italy is applied by Procopius to the second year of the Gothic war. [63]

[Footnote 60: The ancient Alba was ruined in the first age of Rome. On the same spot, or at least in the neighborhood, successively arose. 1. The villa of Pompey, &c.; 2. A camp of the Praetorian cohorts; 3. The modern episcopal city of Albanum or Albano. (Procop. Goth. l. ii. c. 4 Oluver. Ital. Antiq tom. ii. p. 914.)]

[Footnote 61: A Sibylline oracle was ready to pronounce—Africa capta munitus cum nato peribit; a sentence of portentous ambiguity, (Gothic. l. i. c. 7,) which has been published in unknown characters by Opsopaeus, an editor of the oracles. The Pere Maltret has promised a commentary; but all his promises have been vain and fruitless.]

[Footnote 62: In his chronology, imitated, in some degree, from Thucydides, Procopius begins each spring the years of Justinian and of the Gothic war; and his first aera coincides with the first of April, 535, and not 536, according to the Annals of Baronius, (Pagi, Crit. tom. ii. p. 555, who is followed by Muratori and the editors of Sigonius.) Yet, in some passages, we are at a loss to reconcile the dates of Procopius with himself, and with the Chronicle of Marcellinus.]

[Footnote 63: The series of the first Gothic war is represented by Procopius (l. i. c. 5—29, l. ii. c. l—30, l. iii. c. l) till the captivity of Vitigas. With the aid of Sigonius (Opp. tom. i. de Imp. Occident. l. xvii. xviii.) and Muratori, (Annali d'Itaia, tom. v.,) I have gleaned some few additional facts.]

After Belisarius had left sufficient garrisons in Palermo and Syracuse, he embarked his troops at Messina, and landed them, without resistance, on the opposite shores of Rhegium. A Gothic prince, who had married the daughter of Theodatus, was stationed with an army to guard the entrance of Italy; but he imitated, without scruple, the example of a sovereign faithless to his public and private duties. The perfidious Ebermor deserted with his followers to the Roman camp, and was dismissed to enjoy the servile honors of the Byzantine court. [64] From Rhegium to Naples, the fleet and army of Belisarius, almost always in view of each other, advanced near three hundred miles along the sea-coast. The people of Bruttium, Lucania, and Campania, who abhorred the name and religion of the Goths, embraced the specious excuse, that their ruined walls were incapable of defence: the soldiers paid a just equivalent for a plentiful market; and curiosity alone interrupted the peaceful occupations of the husbandman or artificer. Naples, which has swelled to a great and populous capital, long cherished the language and manners of a Grecian colony; [65] and the choice of Virgil had ennobled this elegant retreat, which attracted the lovers of repose and study, elegant retreat, which attracted the lovers of repose and study, from the noise, the smoke, and the laborious opulence of Rome. [66] As soon as the place was invested by sea and land, Belisarius gave audience to the deputies of the people, who exhorted him to disregard a conquest unworthy of his arms, to seek the Gothic king in a field of battle, and, after his victory, to claim, as the sovereign of Rome, the allegiance of the dependent cities. "When I treat with my enemies," replied the Roman chief, with a haughty smile, "I am more accustomed to give than to receive counsel; but I hold in one hand inevitable ruin, and in the other peace and freedom, such as Sicily now enjoys." The impatience of delay urged him to grant the most liberal terms; his honor secured their performance: but Naples was divided into two factions; and the Greek democracy was inflamed by their orators, who, with much spirit and some truth, represented to the multitude that the Goths would punish their defection, and that Belisarius himself must esteem their loyalty and valor. Their deliberations, however, were not perfectly free: the city was commanded by eight hundred Barbarians, whose wives and children were detained at Ravenna as the pledge of their fidelity; and even the Jews, who were rich and numerous, resisted, with desperate enthusiasm, the intolerant laws of Justinian. In a much later period, the circumference of Naples [67] measured only two thousand three hundred and sixty three paces: [68] the fortifications were defended by precipices or the sea; when the aqueducts were intercepted, a supply of water might be drawn from wells and fountains; and the stock of provisions was sufficient to consume the patience of the besiegers. At the end of twenty days, that of Belisarius was almost exhausted, and he had reconciled himself to the disgrace of abandoning the siege, that he might march, before the winter season, against Rome and the Gothic king. But his anxiety was relieved by the bold curiosity of an Isaurian, who explored the dry channel of an aqueduct, and secretly reported, that a passage might be perforated to introduce a file of armed soldiers into the heart of the city. When the work had been silently executed, the humane general risked the discovery of his secret by a last and fruitless admonition of the impending danger. In the darkness of the night, four hundred Romans entered the aqueduct, raised themselves by a rope, which they fastened to an olive-tree, into the house or garden of a solitary matron, sounded their trumpets, surprised the sentinels, and gave admittance to their companions, who on all sides scaled the walls, and burst open the gates of the city. Every crime which is punished by social justice was practised as the rights of war; the Huns were distinguished by cruelty and sacrilege, and Belisarius alone appeared in the streets and churches of Naples to moderate the calamities which he predicted. "The gold and silver," he repeatedly exclaimed, "are the just rewards of your valor. But spare the inhabitants; they are Christians, they are suppliants, they are now your fellow-subjects. Restore the children to their parents, the wives to their husbands; and show them by you, generosity of what friends they have obstinately deprived themselves." The city was saved by the virtue and authority of its conqueror; [69] and when the Neapolitans returned to their houses, they found some consolation in the secret enjoyment of their hidden treasures. The Barbarian garrison enlisted in the service of the emperor; Apulia and Calabria, delivered from the odious presence of the Goths, acknowledged his dominion; and the tusks of the Calydonian boar, which were still shown at Beneventum, are curiously described by the historian of Belisarius. [70]

[Footnote 64: Jornandes, de Rebus Geticis, c. 60, p. 702, edit. Grot., and tom. i. p. 221. Muratori, de Success, Regn. p. 241.]

[Footnote 65: Nero (says Tacitus, Annal. xv. 35) Neapolim quasi Graecam urbem delegit. One hundred and fifty years afterwards, in the time of Septimius Severus, the Hellenism of the Neapolitans is praised by Philostratus. (Icon. l. i. p. 763, edit. Olear.)]

[Footnote 66: The otium of Naples is praised by the Roman poets, by Virgil, Horace, Silius Italicus, and Statius, (Cluver. Ital. Ant. l. iv. p. 1149, 1150.) In an elegant epistles, (Sylv. l. iii. 5, p. 94—98, edit. Markland,) Statius undertakes the difficult task of drawing his wife from the pleasures of Rome to that calm retreat.]

[Footnote 67: This measure was taken by Roger I., after the conquest of Naples, (A.D. 1139,) which he made the capital of his new kingdom, (Giannone, Istoria Civile, tom. ii. p. 169.) That city, the third in Christian Europe, is now at least twelve miles in circumference, (Jul. Caesar. Capaccii Hist. Neapol. l. i. p. 47,) and contains more inhabitants (350,000) in a given space, than any other spot in the known world.]

[Footnote 68: Not geometrical, but common, paces or steps, of 22 French inches, (D' Anville, Mesures Itineraires, p. 7, 8.) The 2363 do not take an English mile.]

[Footnote 69: Belisarius was reproved by Pope Silverius for the massacre. He repeopled Naples, and imported colonies of African captives into Sicily, Calabria, and Apulia, (Hist. Miscell. l. xvi. in Muratori, tom. i. p. 106, 107.)]

[Footnote 70: Beneventum was built by Diomede, the nephew of Meleager (Cluver. tom. ii. p. 1195, 1196.) The Calydonian hunt is a picture of savage life, (Ovid, Metamorph. l. viii.) Thirty or forty heroes were leagued against a hog: the brutes (not the hog) quarrelled with lady for the head.]

The faithful soldiers and citizens of Naples had expected their deliverance from a prince, who remained the inactive and almost indifferent spectator of their ruin. Theodatus secured his person within the walls of Rome, whilst his cavalry advanced forty miles on the Appian way, and encamped in the Pomptine marshes; which, by a canal of nineteen miles in length, had been recently drained and converted into excellent pastures. [71] But the principal forces of the Goths were dispersed in Dalmatia, Venetia, and Gaul; and the feeble mind of their king was confounded by the unsuccessful event of a divination, which seemed to presage the downfall of his empire. [72] The most abject slaves have arraigned the guilt or weakness of an unfortunate master. The character of Theodatus was rigorously scrutinized by a free and idle camp of Barbarians, conscious of their privilege and power: he was declared unworthy of his race, his nation, and his throne; and their general Vitiges, whose valor had been signalized in the Illyrian war, was raised with unanimous applause on the bucklers of his companions. On the first rumor, the abdicated monarch fled from the justice of his country; but he was pursued by private revenge. A Goth, whom he had injured in his love, overtook Theodatus on the Flaminian way, and, regardless of his unmanly cries, slaughtered him, as he lay, prostrate on the ground, like a victim (says the historian) at the foot of the altar. The choice of the people is the best and purest title to reign over them; yet such is the prejudice of every age, that Vitiges impatiently wished to return to Ravenna, where he might seize, with the reluctant hand of the daughter of Amalasontha, some faint shadow of hereditary right. A national council was immediately held, and the new monarch reconciled the impatient spirit of the Barbarians to a measure of disgrace, which the misconduct of his predecessor rendered wise and indispensable. The Goths consented to retreat in the presence of a victorious enemy; to delay till the next spring the operations of offensive war; to summon their scattered forces; to relinquish their distant possessions, and to trust even Rome itself to the faith of its inhabitants. Leuderis, an ancient warrior, was left in the capital with four thousand soldiers; a feeble garrison, which might have seconded the zeal, though it was incapable of opposing the wishes, of the Romans. But a momentary enthusiasm of religion and patriotism was kindled in their minds. They furiously exclaimed, that the apostolic throne should no longer be profaned by the triumph or toleration of Arianism; that the tombs of the Caesars should no longer be trampled by the savages of the North; and, without reflecting, that Italy must sink into a province of Constantinople, they fondly hailed the restoration of a Roman emperor as a new aera of freedom and prosperity. The deputies of the pope and clergy, of the senate and people, invited the lieutenant of Justinian to accept their voluntary allegiance, and to enter the city, whose gates would be thrown open for his reception. As soon as Belisarius had fortified his new conquests, Naples and Cumae, he advanced about twenty miles to the banks of the Vulturnus, contemplated the decayed grandeur of Capua, and halted at the separation of the Latin and Appian ways. The work of the censor, after the incessant use of nine centuries, still preserved its primaeval beauty, and not a flaw could be discovered in the large polished stones, of which that solid, though narrow road, was so firmly compacted. [73] Belisarius, however, preferred the Latin way, which, at a distance from the sea and the marshes, skirted in a space of one hundred and twenty miles along the foot of the mountains. His enemies had disappeared: when he made his entrance through the Asinarian gate, the garrison departed without molestation along the Flaminian way; and the city, after sixty years' servitude, was delivered from the yoke of the Barbarians. Leuderis alone, from a motive of pride or discontent, refused to accompany the fugitives; and the Gothic chief, himself a trophy of the victory, was sent with the keys of Rome to the throne of the emperor Justinian. [74]

[Footnote 71: The Decennovium is strangely confounded by Cluverius (tom. ii. p. 1007) with the River Ufens. It was in truth a canal of nineteen miles, from Forum Appii to Terracina, on which Horace embarked in the night. The Decennovium, which is mentioned by Lucan, Dion Cassius, and Cassiodorus, has been sufficiently ruined, restored, and obliterated, (D'Anville, Anayse de l'Italie, p. 185, &c.)]

[Footnote 72: A Jew, gratified his contempt and hatred for all the Christians, by enclosing three bands, each of ten hogs, and discriminated by the names of Goths, Greeks, and Romans. Of the first, almost all were found dead; almost all the second were alive: of the third, half died, and the rest lost their bristles. No unsuitable emblem of the event]

[Footnote 73: Bergier (Hist. des Grands Chemins des Romains, tom. i. p. 221-228, 440-444) examines the structure and materials, while D'Anville (Analyse d'Italie, p. 200—123) defines the geographical line.]

[Footnote 74: Of the first recovery of Rome, the year (536) is certain, from the series of events, rather than from the corrupt, or interpolated, text of Procopius. The month (December) is ascertained by Evagrius, (l. iv. v. 19;) and the day (the tenth) may be admitted on the slight evidence of Nicephorus Callistus, (l. xvii. c. 13.) For this accurate chronology, we are indebted to the diligence and judgment of Pagi, (tom, ii. p. 659, 560.) Note: Compare Maltret's note, in the edition of Dindorf the ninth is the day, according to his reading,—M.]

The first days, which coincided with the old Saturnalia, were devoted to mutual congratulation and the public joy; and the Catholics prepared to celebrate, without a rival, the approaching festival of the nativity of Christ. In the familiar conversation of a hero, the Romans acquired some notion of the virtues which history ascribed to their ancestors; they were edified by the apparent respect of Belisarius for the successor of St. Peter, and his rigid discipline secured in the midst of war the blessings of tranquillity and justice. They applauded the rapid success of his arms, which overran the adjacent country, as far as Narni, Perusia, and Spoleto; but they trembled, the senate, the clergy, and the unwarlike people, as soon as they understood that he had resolved, and would speedily be reduced, to sustain a siege against the powers of the Gothic monarchy. The designs of Vitiges were executed, during the winter season, with diligence and effect. From their rustic habitations, from their distant garrisons, the Goths assembled at Ravenna for the defence of their country; and such were their numbers, that, after an army had been detached for the relief of Dalmatia, one hundred and fifty thousand fighting men marched under the royal standard. According to the degrees of rank or merit, the Gothic king distributed arms and horses, rich gifts, and liberal promises; he moved along the Flaminian way, declined the useless sieges of Perusia and Spoleto, respected he impregnable rock of Narni, and arrived within two miles of Rome at the foot of the Milvian bridge. The narrow passage was fortified with a tower, and Belisarius had computed the value of the twenty days which must be lost in the construction of another bridge. But the consternation of the soldiers of the tower, who either fled or deserted, disappointed his hopes, and betrayed his person into the most imminent danger. At the head of one thousand horse, the Roman general sallied from the Flaminian gate to mark the ground of an advantageous position, and to survey the camp of the Barbarians; but while he still believed them on the other side of the Tyber, he was suddenly encompassed and assaulted by their numerous squadrons. The fate of Italy depended on his life; and the deserters pointed to the conspicuous horse a bay, [75] with a white face, which he rode on that memorable day. "Aim at the bay horse," was the universal cry. Every bow was bent, every javelin was directed, against that fatal object, and the command was repeated and obeyed by thousands who were ignorant of its real motive. The bolder Barbarians advanced to the more honorable combat of swords and spears; and the praise of an enemy has graced the fall of Visandus, the standard-bearer, [76] who maintained his foremost station, till he was pierced with thirteen wounds, perhaps by the hand of Belisarius himself. The Roman general was strong, active, and dexterous; on every side he discharged his weighty and mortal strokes: his faithful guards imitated his valor, and defended his person; and the Goths, after the loss of a thousand men, fled before the arms of a hero. They were rashly pursued to their camp; and the Romans, oppressed by multitudes, made a gradual, and at length a precipitate retreat to the gates of the city: the gates were shut against the fugitives; and the public terror was increased, by the report that Belisarius was slain. His countenance was indeed disfigured by sweat, dust, and blood; his voice was hoarse, his strength was almost exhausted; but his unconquerable spirit still remained; he imparted that spirit to his desponding companions; and their last desperate charge was felt by the flying Barbarians, as if a new army, vigorous and entire, had been poured from the city. The Flaminian gate was thrown open to a real triumph; but it was not before Belisarius had visited every post, and provided for the public safety, that he could be persuaded, by his wife and friends, to taste the needful refreshments of food and sleep. In the more improved state of the art of war, a general is seldom required, or even permitted to display the personal prowess of a soldier; and the example of Belisarius may be added to the rare examples of Henry IV., of Pyrrhus, and of Alexander.

[Footnote 75: A horse of a bay or red color was styled by the Greeks, balan by the Barbarians, and spadix by the Romans. Honesti spadices, says Virgil, (Georgic. l. iii. 72, with the Observations of Martin and Heyne.) It signifies a branch of the palm-tree, whose name is synonymous to red, (Aulus Gellius, ii. 26.)]

[Footnote 76: I interpret it, not as a proper, name, but an office, standard-bearer, from bandum, (vexillum,) a Barbaric word adopted by the Greeks and Romans, (Paul Diacon. l. i. c. 20, p. 760. Grot. Nomina Hethica, p. 575. Ducange, Gloss. Latin. tom. i. p. 539, 540.)]

After this first and unsuccessful trial of their enemies, the whole army of the Goths passed the Tyber, and formed the siege of the city, which continued above a year, till their final departure. Whatever fancy may conceive, the severe compass of the geographer defines the circumference of Rome within a line of twelve miles and three hundred and forty-five paces; and that circumference, except in the Vatican, has invariably been the same from the triumph of Aurelian to the peaceful but obscure reign of the modern popes. [77] But in the day of her greatness, the space within her walls was crowded with habitations and inhabitants; and the populous suburbs, that stretched along the public roads, were darted like so many rays from one common centre. Adversity swept away these extraneous ornaments, and left naked and desolate a considerable part even of the seven hills. Yet Rome in its present state could send into the field about thirty thousand males of a military age; [78] and, notwithstanding the want of discipline and exercise, the far greater part, inured to the hardships of poverty, might be capable of bearing arms for the defence of their country and religion. The prudence of Belisarius did not neglect this important resource. His soldiers were relieved by the zeal and diligence of the people, who watched while they slept, and labored while they reposed: he accepted the voluntary service of the bravest and most indigent of the Roman youth; and the companies of townsmen sometimes represented, in a vacant post, the presence of the troops which had been drawn away to more essential duties. But his just confidence was placed in the veterans who had fought under his banner in the Persian and African wars; and although that gallant band was reduced to five thousand men, he undertook, with such contemptible numbers, to defend a circle of twelve miles, against an army of one hundred and fifty thousand

Barbarians. In the walls of Rome, which Belisarius constructed or restored, the materials of ancient architecture may be discerned; [79] and the whole fortification was completed, except in a chasm still extant between the Pincian and Flaminian gates, which the prejudices of the Goths and Romans left under the effectual guard of St. Peter the apostle. [80]

[Footnote 77: M. D'Anville has given, in the Memoirs of the Academy for the year 1756, (tom. xxx. p. 198—236,) a plan of Rome on a smaller scale, but far more accurate than that which he had delineated in 1738 for Rollin's history. Experience had improved his knowledge and instead of Rossi's topography, he used the new and excellent map of Nolli. Pliny's old measure of thirteen must be reduced to eight miles. It is easier to alter a text, than to remove hills or buildings. Note: Compare Gibbon, ch. xi. note 43, and xxxi. 67, and ch. lxxi. "It is quite clear," observes Sir J. Hobhouse, "that all these measurements differ, (in the first and second it is 21, in the text 12 and 345 paces, in the last 10,) yet it is equally clear that the historian avers that they are all the same." The present extent, 12 3/4 nearly agrees with the second statement of Gibbon. Sir. J. Hobhouse also observes that the walls were enlarged by Constantine; but there can be no doubt that the circuit has been much changed. Illust. of Ch. Harold, p. 180—M.]

[Footnote 78: In the year 1709, Labat (Voyages en Italie, tom. iii. p. 218) reckoned 138,568 Christian souls, besides 8000 or 10,000 Jews—without souls? In the year 1763, the numbers exceeded 160,000.]

[Footnote 79: The accurate eye of Nardini (Roma Antica, l. i. c. viii. p. 31) could distinguish the tumultuarie opere di Belisario.]

[Footnote 80: The fissure and leaning in the upper part of the wall, which Procopius observed, (Goth. l. i. c. 13,) is visible to the present hour, (Douat. Roma Vetus, l. i. c. 17, p. 53, 54.)]

The battlements or bastions were shaped in sharp angles a ditch, broad and deep, protected the foot of the rampart; and the archers on the rampart were assisted by military engines; the balistri, a powerful cross-bow, which darted short but massy arrows; the onagri, or wild asses, which, on the principle of a sling, threw stones and bullets of an enormous size. [81] A chain was drawn across the Tyber; the arches of the aqueducts were made impervious, and the mole or sepulchre of Hadrian [82] was converted, for the first time, to the uses of a citadel. That venerable structure, which contained the ashes of the Antonines, was a circular turret rising from a quadrangular basis; it was covered with the white marble of Paros, and decorated by the statues of gods and heroes; and the lover of the arts must read with a sigh, that the works of Praxiteles or Lysippus were torn from their lofty pedestals, and hurled into the ditch on the heads of the besiegers. [83] To each of his lieutenants Belisarius assigned the defence of a gate, with the wise and peremptory instruction, that, whatever might be the alarm, they should steadily adhere to their respective posts, and trust their general for the safety of Rome. The formidable host of the Goths was insufficient to embrace the ample measure of the city, of the fourteen gates, seven only were invested from the Proenestine to the Flaminian way; and Vitiges divided his troops into six camps, each of which was fortified with a ditch and rampart. On the Tuscan side of the river, a seventh encampment was formed in the field or circus of the Vatican, for the important purpose of commanding the Milvian bridge and the course of the Tyber; but they approached with devotion the adjacent church of St. Peter; and the threshold of the holy apostles was respected during the siege by a Christian enemy. In the ages of victory, as often as the senate decreed some distant conquest, the consul denounced hostilities, by unbarring, in solemn pomp, the gates of the temple of Janus. [84] Domestic war now rendered the admonition superfluous, and the ceremony was superseded by the establishment of a new religion. But the brazen temple of Janus was left standing in the forum; of a size sufficient only to contain the statue of the god, five cubits in height, of a human form, but with two faces directed to the east and west. The double gates were likewise of brass; and a fruitless effort to turn them on their rusty hinges revealed the scandalous secret that some Romans were still attached to the superstition of their ancestors.

[Footnote 81: Lipsius (Opp. tom. iii. Poliorcet, l. iii.) was ignorant of this clear and conspicuous passage of Procopius, (Goth. l. i. c. 21.) The engine was named the wild ass, a calcitrando, (Hen. Steph. Thesaur. Linguae Graec. tom. ii. p. 1340, 1341, tom. iii. p. 877.) I have seen an ingenious model, contrived and executed by General Melville, which imitates or surpasses the art of antiquity.]

[Footnote 82: The description of this mausoleum, or mole, in Procopius, (l. i. c. 25.) is the first and best. The height above the walls. On Nolli's great plan, the sides measure 260 English feet. Note: Donatus and Nardini suppose that Hadrian's tomb was fortified by Honorius; it was united to the wall by men of old, (Procop in loc.) Gibbon has mistaken the breadth for the height above the walls Hobhouse, Illust. of Childe Harold, p. 302—M.]

[Footnote 83: Praxiteles excelled in Fauns, and that of Athens was his own masterpiece. Rome now contains about thirty of the same character. When the ditch of St. Angelo was cleansed under Urban VIII., the workmen found the sleeping Faun of the Barberini palace; but a leg, a thigh, and the right arm, had been broken from that beautiful statue, (Winkelman, Hist. de l'Art, tom. ii. p. 52, 53, tom iii. p. 265.)]

[Footnote 84: Procopius has given the best description of the temple of Janus a national deity of Latium, (Heyne, Excurs. v. ad l. vii. Aeneid.) It was once a gate in the primitive city of Romulus and Numa, (Nardini, p. 13, 256, 329.) Virgil has described the ancient rite like a poet and an antiquarian.]

Eighteen days were employed by the besiegers, to provide all the instruments of attack which antiquity had invented. Fascines were prepared to fill the ditches, scaling-ladders to ascend the walls. The largest trees of the forest supplied the timbers of four battering-rams: their heads were armed with iron; they were suspended by ropes, and each of them was worked by the labor of fifty men. The lofty wooden turrets moved on wheels or rollers, and formed a spacious platform of the level of the rampart. On the morning of the nineteenth day, a general attack was made from the Praenestine gate to the Vatican: seven Gothic columns, with their military engines, advanced to the assault; and the Romans, who lined the ramparts, listened with doubt and anxiety to the cheerful assurances of their commander. As soon as the enemy approached the ditch, Belisarius himself drew the first arrow; and such was his strength and dexterity, that he transfixed the foremost of the Barbarian leaders.

As shout of applause and victory was reechoed along the wall. He drew a second arrow, and the stroke was followed with the same success and the same acclamation. The Roman general then gave the word, that the archers should aim at the teams of oxen; they were instantly covered with mortal wounds; the towers which they drew remained useless and immovable, and a single moment disconcerted the laborious projects of the king of the Goths. After this disappointment, Vitiges still continued, or feigned to continue, the assault of the Salarian gate, that he might divert the attention of his adversary, while his principal forces more strenuously attacked the Praenestine gate and the sepulchre of Hadrian, at the distance of three miles from each other. Near the former, the double walls of the Vivarium [85] were low or broken; the fortifications of the latter were feebly guarded: the vigor of the Goths was excited by the hope of victory and spoil; and if a single post had given way, the Romans, and Rome itself, were irrecoverably lost. This perilous day was the most glorious in the life of Belisarius. Amidst tumult and dismay, the whole plan of the attack and defence was distinctly present to his mind; he observed the changes of each instant, weighed every possible advantage, transported his person to the scenes of danger, and communicated his spirit in calm and decisive orders. The contest was fiercely maintained from the morning to the evening; the Goths were repulsed on all sides; and each Roman might boast that he had vanquished thirty Barbarians, if the strange disproportion of numbers were not counterbalanced by the merit of one man. Thirty thousand Goths, according to the confession of their own chiefs, perished in this bloody action; and the multitude of the wounded was equal to that of the slain. When they advanced to the assault, their close disorder suffered not a javelin to fall without effect; and as they retired, the populace of the city joined the pursuit, and slaughtered, with impunity, the backs of their flying enemies. Belisarius instantly sallied from the gates; and while the soldiers chanted his name and victory, the hostile engines of war were reduced to ashes. Such was the loss and consternation of the Goths, that, from this day, the siege of Rome degenerated into a tedious and indolent blockade; and they were incessantly harassed by the Roman general, who, in frequent skirmishes, destroyed above five thousand of their bravest troops. Their cavalry was unpractised in the use of the bow; their archers served on foot; and this divided force was incapable of contending with their adversaries, whose lances and arrows, at a distance, or at hand, were alike formidable. The consummate skill of Belisarius embraced the favorable opportunities; and as he chose the ground and the moment, as he pressed the charge or sounded the retreat, [86] the squadrons which he detached were seldom unsuccessful. These partial advantages diffused an impatient ardor among the soldiers and people, who began to feel the hardships of a siege, and to disregard the dangers of a general engagement. Each plebeian conceived himself to be a hero, and the infantry, who, since the decay of discipline, were rejected from the line of battle, aspired to the ancient honors of the Roman legion. Belisarius praised the spirit of his troops, condemned their presumption, yielded to their clamors, and prepared the remedies of a defeat, the possibility of which he alone had courage to suspect. In the quarter of the Vatican, the Romans prevailed; and if the irreparable moments had not been wasted in the pillage of the camp, they might have occupied the Milvian bridge, and charged in the rear of the Gothic host. On the other side of the Tyber, Belisarius advanced from the Pincian and Salarian gates. But his army, four thousand soldiers perhaps, was lost in a spacious plain; they were encompassed and oppressed by fresh multitudes, who continually relieved the broken ranks of the Barbarians. The valiant leaders of the infantry were unskilled to conquer; they died: the retreat (a hasty retreat) was covered by the prudence of the general, and the victors started back with affright from the formidable aspect of an armed rampart. The reputation of Belisarius was unsullied by a defeat; and the vain confidence of the Goths was not less serviceable to his designs than the repentance and modesty of the Roman troops.

[Footnote 85: Vivarium was an angle in the new wall enclosed for wild beasts, (Procopius, Goth. l. i. c. 23.) The spot is still visible in Nardini (l iv. c. 2, p. 159, 160,) and Nolli's great plan of Rome.]

[Footnote 86: For the Roman trumpet, and its various notes, consult Lipsius de Militia Romana, (Opp. tom. iii. l. iv. Dialog. x. p. 125-129.) A mode of distinguishing the charge by the horse-trumpet of solid brass, and the retreat by the foot-trumpet of leather and light wood, was recommended by Procopius, and adopted by Belisarius.]

PART IV

From the moment that Belisarius had determined to sustain a siege, his assiduous care provided Rome against the danger of famine, more dreadful than the Gothic arms. An extraordinary supply of corn was imported from Sicily: the harvests of Campania and Tuscany were forcibly swept for the use of the city; and the rights of private property were infringed by the strong plea of the public safety. It might easily be foreseen that the enemy would intercept the aqueducts; and the cessation of the water-mills was the first inconvenience, which was speedily removed by mooring large vessels, and fixing mill-stones in the current of the river. The stream was soon embarrassed by the trunks of trees, and polluted with dead bodies; yet so effectual were the precautions of the Roman general, that the waters of the Tyber still continued to give motion to the mills and drink to the inhabitants: the more distant quarters were supplied from domestic wells; and a besieged city might support, without impatience, the privation of her public baths. A large portion of Rome, from the Praenestine gate to the church of St. Paul, was never invested by the Goths; their excursions were restrained by the activity of the Moorish troops: the navigation of the Tyber, and the Latin, Appian, and Ostian ways, were left free and unmolested for the introduction of corn and cattle, or the retreat of the inhabitants, who sought refuge in Campania or Sicily. Anxious to relieve himself from a useless and devouring multitude, Belisarius issued his peremptory orders for the instant departure of the women, the children, and slaves; required his soldiers to dismiss their male and female attendants, and regulated their allowance that one moiety should be given in provisions, and the other in money. His foresight was justified by the increase of the public distress, as soon as the Goths had occupied two important posts in the neighborhood of Rome. By the loss of the port, or, as it is now called, the city of Porto, he was deprived of the country on the right of the Tyber, and the best communication with the sea; and he reflected, with grief and anger, that three hundred men, could he have spared such a feeble band, might have defended its impregnable works. Seven miles from the capital, between the Appian and the Latin ways, two principal aqueducts crossing, and again crossing each other: enclosed within their solid and lofty arches a fortified space, [87] where Vitiges established a camp of seven thousand Goths to intercept the convoy of Sicily and Campania. The granaries of Rome were insensibly exhausted, the adjacent country had been wasted with fire and sword; such scanty supplies as might yet be obtained by hasty excursions were the reward of valor, and the purchase of wealth: the forage of the horses, and the bread of the soldiers, never failed: but in the last months of the siege, the people were exposed to the miseries of scarcity, unwholesome food, [88] and contagious disorders. Belisarius saw and pitied their sufferings; but he had foreseen, and he watched the decay of their loyalty, and the progress of their discontent. Adversity had awakened the Romans from the dreams of grandeur and freedom, and taught them the humiliating lesson, that it was of small moment to their real happiness, whether the name of their master was derived from the Gothic or the Latin language. The lieutenant of Justinian listened to their just complaints, but he rejected with disdain the idea of flight or capitulation; repressed their clamorous impatience for battle; amused them with the prospect of a sure and speedy relief; and secured himself and the city from the effects of their despair or treachery. Twice in each month he changed the station of the officers to whom the custody of the gates was committed: the various precautions of patroles, watch words, lights, and music, were repeatedly employed to discover whatever passed on the ramparts; out-guards were posted beyond the ditch, and the trusty vigilance of dogs supplied the more doubtful fidelity of mankind. A letter was intercepted, which assured the king of the Goths that the Asinarian gate, adjoining to the Lateran church, should be secretly opened to his troops. On the proof or suspicion of treason, several senators were banished, and the pope Sylverius was summoned to attend the representative of his sovereign, at his head-quarters in the Pincian palace. [89] The ecclesiastics, who followed their bishop, were detained in the first or second apartment, [90] and he alone was admitted to the presence of Belisarius. The conqueror of Rome and Carthage was modestly seated at the feet of Antonina, who reclined on a stately couch: the general was silent, but the voice of reproach and menace issued from the mouth of his imperious wife. Accused by credible witnesses, and the evidence of his own subscription, the successor of St. Peter was despoiled of his pontifical ornaments, clad in the mean habit of a monk, and embarked, without delay, for a distant exile in the East. [90/1] At the emperor's command, the clergy of Rome proceeded to the choice of a new bishop; and after a solemn invocation of the Holy Ghost, elected the deacon Vigilius, who had purchased the papal throne by a bribe of two hundred pounds of gold. The profit, and consequently the guilt, of this simony, was imputed to Belisarius: but the hero obeyed the orders of his wife; Antonina served the passions of the empress; and Theodora lavished her treasures, in the vain hope of obtaining a pontiff hostile or indifferent to the council of Chalcedon. [91]

[Footnote 87: Procopius (Goth. l. ii. c. 3) has forgot to name these aqueducts nor can such a double intersection, at such a distance from Rome, be clearly ascertained from the writings of Frontinus, Fabretti, and Eschinard, de Aquis and de Agro Romano, or from the local maps of Lameti and Cingolani. Seven or eight miles from the city, (50 stadia,) on the road to Albano, between the Latin and Appian ways, I discern the remains of an aqueduct, (probably the Septimian,) a series (630 paces) of arches twenty-five feet high.]

[Footnote 88: They made sausages of mule's flesh; unwholesome, if the animals had died of the plague. Otherwise, the famous Bologna sausages are said to be made of ass flesh, (Voyages de Labat, tom. ii. p. 218.)]

[Footnote 89: The name of the palace, the hill, and the adjoining gate, were all derived from the senator Pincius. Some recent vestiges of temples and churches are now smoothed in the garden of the Minims of the Trinita del Monte, (Nardini, l. iv. c. 7, p. 196. Eschinard, p. 209, 210, the old plan of Buffalino, and the great plan of Nolli.) Belisarius had fixed his station between the Pincian and Salarian gates, (Procop. Goth. l. i. c. 15.)]

[Footnote 90: From the mention of the primum et secundum velum, it should seem that Belisarius, even in a siege, represented the emperor, and maintained the proud ceremonial of the Byzantine palace.]

[Footnote 90/1: De Beau, as a good Catholic, makes the Pope the victim of a dark intrigue. Lord Mahon, (p. 225.) with whom I concur, summed up against him—M.]

[Footnote 91: Of this act of sacrilege, Procopius (Goth. l. i. c. 25) is a dry and reluctant witness. The narratives of Liberatus (Breviarium, c. 22) and Anastasius (de Vit. Pont. p. 39) are characteristic, but passionate. Hear the execrations of Cardinal Baronius, (A.D. 536, No. 123 A.D. 538, No. 4—20:) portentum, facinus omni execratione dignum.]

The epistle of Belisarius to the emperor announced his victory, his danger, and his resolution. "According to your commands, we have entered the dominions of the Goths, and reduced to your obedience Sicily, Campania, and the city of Rome; but the loss of these conquests will be more disgraceful than their acquisition was glorious. Hitherto we have successfully fought against the multitudes of the Barbarians, but their multitudes may finally prevail. Victory is the gift of Providence, but the reputation of kings and generals depends on the success or the failure of their designs. Permit me to speak with freedom: if you wish that we should live, send us subsistence; if you desire that we should conquer, send us arms, horses, and men. The Romans have received us as friends and deliverers: but in our present distress, they will be either betrayed by their confidence, or we shall be oppressed by their treachery and hatred. For myself, my life is consecrated to your service: it is yours to reflect, whether my death in this situation will contribute to the glory and prosperity of your reign." Perhaps that reign would have been equally prosperous if the peaceful master of the East had abstained from the conquest of Africa and Italy: but as Justinian was ambitious of fame, he made some efforts (they were feeble and languid) to support and rescue his victorious general. A reenforcement of sixteen hundred Sclavonians and Huns was led by Martin and Valerian; and as they reposed during the winter season in the harbors of Greece, the strength of the men and horses was not impaired by the fatigues of a sea-voyage; and they distinguished their valor in the first sally against the besiegers. About the time of the summer solstice, Euthalius landed at Terracina with large sums of money for the payment of the troops: he cautiously proceeded along the Appian way, and this convoy entered Rome through the gate Capena, [92] while Belisarius, on the other side, diverted the attention of the Goths by a vigorous and successful skirmish. These seasonable aids, the use and reputation of which were dexterously managed by the Roman general, revived the courage, or at least the hopes, of the soldiers and people. The historian Procopius was despatched with an important commission to collect the troops and provisions which Campania could furnish, or Constantinople had sent; and the secretary of Belisarius was soon followed by Antonina herself, [93] who boldly traversed the posts of the enemy, and returned with the Oriental succors to the relief of her husband and the besieged city. A fleet of three thousand Isaurians cast anchor in the Bay of Naples and afterwards at Ostia. Above two thousand horse, of whom a part were Thracians, landed at Tarentum; and, after the junction of five hundred soldiers of Campania, and a train of wagons laden with wine and flour, they directed their march on the Appian way, from Capua to the neighborhood of Rome. The forces that arrived by land and sea were united at the mouth of the Tyber. Antonina convened a council of war: it was resolved to surmount, with sails and oars, the adverse stream of the river; and the Goths were apprehensive of disturbing, by any rash hostilities, the negotiation to which Belisarius had craftily listened. They credulously believed that they saw no more than the vanguard of a fleet and army, which already covered the Ionian Sea and the plains of Campania; and the illusion was supported by the haughty language of the Roman general, when he gave audience to the ambassadors of Vitiges. After a specious discourse to vindicate the justice of his cause, they declared, that, for the sake of peace, they were disposed to renounce the possession of Sicily. "The emperor is not less generous," replied his lieutenant, with a disdainful smile, "in return for a gift which you no longer possess: he presents you with an ancient province of the empire; he resigns to the Goths the sovereignty of the British island." Belisarius rejected with equal firmness and contempt the offer of a tribute; but he allowed the Gothic ambassadors to seek their fate from the mouth of Justinian himself; and consented, with seeming reluctance, to a truce of three months, from the winter solstice to the equinox of spring. Prudence might not safely trust either the oaths or hostages of the Barbarians, and the conscious superiority of the Roman chief was expressed in the distribution of his troops. As soon as fear or hunger compelled the Goths to evacuate Alba, Porto, and Centumcellae, their place was instantly supplied; the garrisons of Narni, Spoleto, and Perusia, were reenforced, and the seven camps of the besiegers were gradually encompassed with the calamities of a siege. The prayers and pilgrimage of Datius, bishop of Milan, were not without effect; and he obtained one thousand Thracians and Isaurians, to assist the revolt of Liguria against her Arian tyrant. At the same time, John the Sanguinary, [94] the nephew of Vitalian, was detached with two thousand chosen horse, first to Alba, on the Fucine Lake, and afterwards to the frontiers of Picenum, on the Hadriatic Sea. "In the province," said Belisarius, "the Goths have deposited their families and treasures, without a guard or the suspicion of danger. Doubtless they will violate the truce: let them feel your presence, before they hear of your motions. Spare the Italians; suffer not any fortified places to remain hostile in your rear; and faithfully reserve the spoil for an equal and common partition. It would not be reasonable," he added with a laugh, "that whilst we are toiling to the destruction of the drones, our more fortunate brethren should rifle and enjoy the honey."

[Footnote 92: The old Capena was removed by Aurelian to, or near, the modern gate of St. Sebastian, (see Nolli's plan.) That memorable spot has been consecrated by the Egerian grove, the memory of Numa two umphal arches, the sepulchres of the Scipios, Metelli, &c.]

[Footnote 93: The expression of Procopius has an invidious cast, (Goth. l. ii. c. 4.) Yet he is speaking of a woman.]

[Footnote 94: Anastasius (p. 40) has preserved this epithet of Sanguinarius which might do honor to a tiger.]

The whole nation of the Ostrogoths had been assembled for the attack, and was almost entirely consumed in the siege of Rome. If any credit be due to an intelligent spectator, one third at least of their enormous host was destroyed, in frequent and bloody combats under the walls of the city. The bad fame and pernicious qualities of the summer air might already be imputed to the decay of agriculture and population; and the evils of famine and pestilence were aggravated by their own licentiousness, and the unfriendly disposition of the country. While Vitiges struggled with his fortune, while he hesitated between shame and ruin, his retreat was hastened by domestic alarms. The king of the Goths was informed by trembling messengers, that John the Sanguinary spread the devastations of war from the Apennine to the Hadriatic; that the rich spoils and innumerable captives of Picenum were lodged in the fortifications of Rimini; and that this formidable chief had defeated his uncle, insulted his capital, and seduced, by secret correspondence, the fidelity of his wife, the imperious daughter of Amalasontha. Yet, before he retired, Vitiges made a last effort, either to storm or to surprise the city. A secret passage was discovered in one of the aqueducts; two citizens of the Vatican were tempted by bribes to intoxicate the guards of the Aurelian gate; an attack was meditated on the walls beyond the Tyber, in a place which was not fortified with towers; and the Barbarians advanced, with torches and scaling-ladders, to the assault of the Pincian gate. But every attempt was defeated by the intrepid vigilance of Belisarius and his band of veterans, who, in the most perilous moments, did not regret the absence of their companions; and the Goths, alike destitute of hope and subsistence, clamorously urged their departure before the truce should expire, and the Roman cavalry should again be united. One year and nine days after the commencement of the siege, an army, so lately strong and triumphant, burnt their tents, and tumultuously repassed the Milvian bridge. They repassed not with impunity: their thronging multitudes, oppressed in a narrow passage, were driven headlong into the Tyber, by their own fears and the pursuit of the enemy; and the Roman general, sallying from the Pincian gate, inflicted a severe and disgraceful wound on their retreat. The slow length of a sickly and desponding host was heavily dragged along the Flaminian way; from whence the Barbarians were sometimes compelled to deviate, lest they should encounter the hostile garrisons that guarded the high road to Rimini and Ravenna. Yet so powerful was this flying army, that Vitiges spared ten thousand men for the defence of the cities which he was most solicitous to preserve, and detached his nephew Uraias, with an adequate force, for the chastisement of rebellious Milan. At the head of his principal army, he besieged Rimini, only thirty-three miles distant from the Gothic capital. A feeble rampart, and a shallow ditch, were maintained by the skill and valor of John the Sanguinary, who shared the danger and fatigue of the meanest soldier, and emulated, on a theatre less illustrious, the military virtues of his great commander. The towers and battering-engines of the Barbarians were rendered useless; their attacks were repulsed; and the tedious blockade, which reduced the garrison to the last extremity of hunger, afforded time for the union and march of the Roman forces. A fleet, which had surprised Ancona, sailed along the coast of the Hadriatic, to the relief of the besieged city. The eunuch Narses landed in Picenum with two thousand Heruli and five thousand of the bravest troops of the East. The rock of the Apennine was forced; ten thousand veterans moved round the foot of the mountains, under the command of Belisarius himself; and a new army, whose encampment blazed with innumerable lights, appeared to advance along the Flaminian way. Overwhelmed with astonishment and despair, the Goths abandoned the siege of Rimini, their tents, their standards, and their leaders; and Vitiges, who gave or followed the example of flight, never halted till he found a shelter within the walls and morasses of Ravenna. To these walls, and to some fortresses destitute of any mutual support, the Gothic monarchy was now reduced. The provinces of Italy had embraced the party of the emperor and his army, gradually recruited to the number of twenty thousand men, must have achieved an easy and rapid conquest, if their invincible powers had not been weakened by the discord of the Roman chiefs. Before the end of the siege, an act of blood, ambiguous and indiscreet, sullied the fair fame of Belisarius. Presidius, a loyal Italian, as he fled from Ravenna to Rome, was rudely stopped by Constantine, the military governor of Spoleto, and despoiled, even in a church, of two daggers richly inlaid with gold and precious stones. As soon as the public danger had subsided, Presidius complained of the loss and injury: his complaint was heard, but the order of restitution was disobeyed by the pride and avarice of the offender. Exasperated by the delay, Presidius boldly arrested the general's horse as he passed through the forum; and, with the spirit of a citizen, demanded the common benefit of the Roman laws. The honor of Belisarius was engaged; he summoned a council; claimed the obedience of his subordinate officer; and was provoked, by an insolent reply, to call hastily for the presence of his guards. Constantine, viewing their entrance as the signal of death, drew his sword, and rushed on the general, who nimbly eluded the stroke, and was protected by his friends; while the desperate assassin was disarmed, dragged into a neighboring chamber, and executed, or rather murdered, by the guards, at the arbitrary command of Belisarius. [95] In this hasty act of violence, the guilt of Constantine was no longer remembered; the despair and death of that valiant officer were secretly imputed to the revenge of Antonina; and each of his colleagues, conscious of the same rapine, was apprehensive of the same fate. The fear of a common enemy suspended the effects of their envy and discontent; but in the confidence of approaching victory, they instigated a powerful rival to oppose the conqueror of Rome and Africa. From the domestic service of the palace, and the administration of the private revenue, Narses the eunuch was suddenly exalted to the head of an army; and the spirit of a hero, who afterwards equalled the merit and glory of Belisarius, served only to perplex the operations of the Gothic war. To his prudent counsels, the relief of Rimini was ascribed by the leaders of the discontented faction, who exhorted Narses to assume an independent and separate command. The epistle of Justinian had indeed enjoined his obedience to the general; but the dangerous exception, "as far as may be advantageous to the public service," reserved some freedom of judgment to the discreet favorite, who had so lately departed from the sacred and familiar conversation of his sovereign. In the exercise of this doubtful right, the eunuch perpetually dissented from the opinions of Belisarius; and, after yielding with reluctance to the siege of Urbino, he deserted his colleague in the night, and marched away to the conquest of the Aemilian province. The fierce and formidable bands of the Heruli were attached to the person of Narses; [96] ten thousand Romans and confederates were persuaded to march under his banners; every malecontent embraced the fair opportunity of revenging his private or imaginary wrongs; and the remaining troops of Belisarius were divided and dispersed from the garrisons of Sicily to the shores of the Hadriatic. His skill and perseverance overcame every obstacle: Urbino was taken, the sieges of Faesulae Orvieto, and Auximum, were undertaken and vigorously prosecuted; and the eunuch Narses was at length recalled to the domestic cares of the palace. All dissensions were healed, and all opposition was subdued, by the temperate authority of the Roman general, to whom his enemies could not refuse their esteem; and Belisarius inculcated the salutary lesson that the forces of the state should compose one body, and be animated by one soul. But in the interval of discord, the Goths were permitted to breathe; an important season was lost, Milan was destroyed, and the northern provinces of Italy were afflicted by an inundation of the Franks.

[Footnote 95: This transaction is related in the public history (Goth. l. ii. c. 8) with candor or caution; in the Anecdotes (c. 7) with malevolence or freedom; but Marcellinus, or rather his continuator, (in Chron.,) casts a shade of premeditated assassination over the death of Constantine. He had performed good service at Rome and Spoleto, (Procop. Goth l. i. c. 7, 14;) but Alemannus confounds him with a Constantianus comes stabuli.]

[Footnote 96: They refused to serve after his departure; sold their captives and cattle to the Goths; and swore never to fight against them. Procopius introduces a curious digression on the manners and adventures of this wandering nation, a part of whom finally emigrated to Thule or Scandinavia. (Goth. l. ii. c. 14, 15.)]

When Justinian first meditated the conquest of Italy, he sent ambassadors to the kings of the Franks, and adjured them, by the common ties of alliance and religion, to join in the holy enterprise against the Arians. The Goths, as their want were more urgent, employed a more effectual mode of persuasion, and vainly strove, by the gift of lands and money, to purchase the friendship, or at least the neutrality, of a light and perfidious nation. [97] But the arms of Belisarius, and the revolt of the Italians, had no sooner shaken the Gothic monarchy, than Theodebert of Austrasia, the most powerful and warlike of the Merovingian kings, was persuaded to succor their distress by an indirect and seasonable aid. Without expecting the consent of their sovereign, the thousand Burgundians, his recent subjects, descended from the Alps, and joined the troops which Vitiges had sent to chastise the revolt of Milan. After an obstinate siege, the capital of Liguria was reduced by famine; but no capitulation could be obtained, except for the safe retreat of the Roman garrison. Datius, the orthodox bishop, who had seduced his countrymen to rebellion [98] and ruin, escaped to the luxury and honors of the Byzantine court; [99] but the clergy, perhaps the Arian clergy, were slaughtered at the foot of their own altars by the defenders of the Catholic faith. Three hundred thousand males were reported to be slain; [100] the female sex, and the more precious spoil, was resigned to the Burgundians; and the houses, or at least the walls, of Milan, were levelled with the ground. The Goths, in their last moments, were revenged by the destruction of a city, second only to Rome in size and opulence, in the splendor of its buildings, or the number of its inhabitants; and Belisarius sympathized alone in the fate of his deserted and devoted friends. Encouraged by this successful inroad, Theodebert himself, in the ensuing spring, invaded the plains of Italy with an army of one hundred thousand Barbarians. [101] The king, and some chosen followers, were mounted on horseback, and armed with lances; the infantry, without bows or spears, were satisfied with a shield, a sword, and a double-edged battle-axe, which, in their hands, became a deadly and unerring weapon. Italy trembled at the march of the Franks; and both the Gothic prince and the Roman general, alike ignorant of their designs, solicited, with hope and terror, the friendship of these dangerous allies. Till he had secured the passage of the Po on the bridge of Pavia, the grandson of Clovis dissembled his intentions, which he at length declared, by assaulting, almost at the same instant, the hostile camps of the Romans and Goths. Instead of uniting their arms, they fled with equal precipitation; and the fertile, though desolate provinces of Liguria and Aemilia, were abandoned to a licentious host of Barbarians, whose rage was not mitigated by any thoughts of settlement or conquest. Among the cities which they ruined, Genoa, not yet constructed of marble, is particularly enumerated; and the deaths of thousands, according to the regular practice of war, appear to have excited less horror than some idolatrous sacrifices of women and children, which were performed with impunity in the camp of the most Christian king. If it were not a melancholy truth, that the first and most cruel sufferings must be the lot of the innocent and helpless, history might exult in the misery of the conquerors, who, in the midst of riches, were left destitute of bread or wine, reduced to drink the waters of the Po, and to feed on the flesh of distempered cattle. The dysentery swept away one third of their army; and the clamors of his subjects, who were impatient to pass the Alps, disposed Theodebert to listen with respect to the mild exhortations of Belisarius. The memory of this inglorious and destructive warfare was perpetuated on the medals of Gaul; and Justinian, without unsheathing his sword, assumed the title of conqueror of the Franks. The Merovingian prince was offended by the vanity of the emperor; he affected to pity the fallen fortunes of the Goths; and his insidious offer of a federal union was fortified by the promise or menace of descending from the Alps at the head of five hundred thousand men. His plans of conquest were boundless, and perhaps chimerical. The king of Austrasia threatened to chastise Justinian, and to march to the gates of Constantinople: [102] he was overthrown and slain [103] by a wild bull, [104] as he hunted in the Belgic or German forests. [Footnote 97: This national reproach of perfidy (Procop. Goth. l. ii. c. 25) offends the ear of La Mothe le Vayer, (tom. viii. p. 163—165,) who criticizes, as if he had not read, the Greek historian.]

[Footnote 98: Baronius applauds his treason, and justifies the Catholic bishops—qui ne sub heretico principe degant omnem lapidem movent—a useful caution. The more rational Muratori (Annali d'Italia, tom. v. p. 54) hints at the guilt of perjury, and blames at least the imprudence of Datius.]

[Footnote 99: St. Datius was more successful against devils than against Barbarians. He travelled with a numerons retinue, and occupied at Corinth a large house. (Baronius, A.D. 538, No. 89, A.D. 539, No. 20.)]

[Footnote 100: (Compare Procopius, Goth. l. ii. c. 7, 21.) Yet such population is incredible; and the second or third city of Italy need not repine if we only decimate the numbers of the present text Both Milan and Genoa revived in less than thirty years, (Paul Diacon de Gestis Langobard. l. ii. c. 38.) Note: Procopius says distinctly that Milan was the second city of the West. Which did Gibbon suppose could compete with it, Ravenna or Naples; the next page he calls it the second—M.]

[Footnote 101: Besides Procopius, perhaps too Roman, see the Chronicles of Marius and Marcellinus, Jornandes, (in Success. Regn. in Muratori, tom. i. p. 241,) and Gregory of Tours, (l. iii. c. 32, in tom. ii. of the Historians of France.) Gregory supposes a defeat of Belisarius, who, in Aimoin, (de Gestis Franc. l. ii. c. 23, in tom. iii. p. 59,) is slain by the Franks.]

[Footnote 102: Agathias, l. i. p. 14, 15. Could he have seduced or subdued the Gepidae or Lombards of Pannonia, the Greek historian is confident that he must have been destroyed in Thrace.]

[Footnote 103: The king pointed his spear—the bull overturned a tree on his head—he expired the same day. Such is the story of Agathias; but the original historians of France (tom. ii. p. 202, 403, 558, 667) impute his death to a fever.]

[Footnote 104: Without losing myself in a labyrinth of species and names—the aurochs, urus, bisons, bubalus, bonasus, buffalo, &c., (Buffon. Hist. Nat. tom. xi., and Supplement, tom. iii. vi.,) it is certain, that in the sixth century a large wild species of horned cattle was hunted in the great forests of the Vosges in Lorraine, and the Ardennes, (Greg. Turon. tom. ii. l. x. c. 10, p. 369.)]

PART V

As soon as Belisarius was delivered from his foreign and domestic enemies, he seriously applied his forces to the final reduction of Italy. In the siege of Osimo, the general was nearly transpierced with an arrow, if the mortal stroke had not been intercepted by one of his guards, who lost, in that pious office, the use of his hand. The Goths of Osimo, [104/1] four thousand warriors, with those of Faesulae and the Cottian Alps, were among the last who maintained their independence; and their gallant resistance, which almost tired the patience, deserved the esteem, of the conqueror. His prudence refused to subscribe the safe conduct which they asked, to join their brethren of Ravenna; but they saved, by an honorable capitulation, one moiety at least of their wealth, with the free alternative of retiring peaceably to their estates, or enlisting to serve the emperor in his Persian wars. The multitudes which yet adhered to the standard of Vitiges far surpassed the number of the Roman troops; but neither prayers nor defiance, nor the extreme danger of his most faithful subjects, could tempt the Gothic king beyond the fortifications of Ravenna. These fortifications were, indeed, impregnable to the assaults of art or violence; and when Belisarius invested the capital, he was soon convinced that famine only could tame the stubborn spirit of the Barbarians. The sea, the land, and the channels of the Po, were guarded by the vigilance of the Roman general; and his morality extended the rights of war to the practice of poisoning the waters, [105] and secretly firing the granaries [106] of a besieged city. [107] While he pressed the blockade of Ravenna, he was surprised by the arrival of two ambassadors from Constantinople, with a treaty of peace, which Justinian had imprudently signed, without deigning to consult the author of his victory. By this disgraceful and precarious agreement, Italy and the Gothic treasure were divided, and the provinces beyond the Po were left with the regal title to the successor of Theodoric. The ambassadors were eager to accomplish their salutary commission; the captive Vitiges accepted, with transport, the unexpected offer of a crown; honor was less prevalent among the Goths, than the want and appetite of food; and the Roman chiefs, who murmured at the continuance of the war, professed implicit submission to the commands of the emperor. If Belisarius had possessed only the courage of a soldier, the laurel would have been snatched from his hand by timid and envious counsels; but in this decisive moment, he resolved, with the magnanimity of a statesman, to sustain alone the danger and merit of generous disobedience. Each of his officers gave a written opinion that the siege of Ravenna was impracticable and hopeless: the general then rejected the treaty of partition, and declared his own resolution of leading Vitiges in chains to the feet of Justinian. The Goths retired with doubt and dismay: this peremptory refusal deprived them of the only signature which they could trust, and filled their minds with a just apprehension, that a sagacious enemy had discovered the full extent of their deplorable state. They compared the fame and fortune of Belisarius with the weakness of their ill-fated king; and the comparison suggested an extraordinary project, to which Vitiges, with apparent resignation, was compelled to acquiesce. Partition would ruin the strength, exile would disgrace the honor, of the nation; but they offered their arms, their treasures, and the fortifications of Ravenna, if Belisarius would disclaim the authority of a master, accept the choice of the Goths, and assume, as he had deserved, the kingdom of Italy. If the false lustre of a diadem could have tempted the loyalty of a faithful subject, his prudence must have foreseen the inconstancy of the Barbarians, and his rational ambition would prefer the safe and honorable station of a Roman general. Even the patience and seeming satisfaction with which he entertained a proposal of treason, might be susceptible of a malignant interpretation. But the lieutenant of Justinian was conscious of his own rectitude; he entered into a dark and crooked path, as it might lead to the voluntary submission of the Goths; and his dexterous policy persuaded them that he was disposed to comply with their wishes, without engaging an oath or a promise for the performance of a treaty which he secretly abhorred. The day of the surrender of Ravenna was stipulated by the Gothic ambassadors: a fleet, laden with provisions, sailed as a welcome guest into the deepest recess of the harbor: the gates were opened to the fancied king of Italy; and Belisarius, without meeting an enemy, triumphantly marched through the streets of an impregnable city. [108] The Romans were astonished by their success; the multitudes of tall and robust Barbarians were confounded by the image of their own patience and the masculine females, spitting in the faces of their sons and husbands, most bitterly reproached them for betraying their dominion and freedom to these pygmies of the south, contemptible in their numbers, diminutive in their stature. Before the Goths could recover from the first surprise, and claim the accomplishment of their doubtful hopes, the victor established his power in Ravenna, beyond the danger of repentance and revolt.

[Footnote 104/1: Auximum, p. 175—M.]

[Footnote 105: In the siege of Auximum, he first labored to demolish an old aqueduct, and then cast into the stream, 1. dead bodies; 2. mischievous herbs; and 3. quicklime. (says Procopius, l. ii. c. 27) Yet both words are used as synonymous in Galen, Dioscorides, and Lucian, (Hen. Steph. Thesaur. Ling. Graec. tom. iii. p. 748.)]

[Footnote 106: The Goths suspected Mathasuintha as an accomplice in the mischief, which perhaps was occasioned by accidental lightning.]

[Footnote 107: In strict philosophy, a limitation of the rights of war seems to imply nonsense and contradiction. Grotius himself is lost in an idle distinction between the jus naturae and the jus gentium, between poison and infection. He balances in one scale the passages of Homer (Odyss. A 259, &c.) and Florus, (l. ii. c. 20, No. 7, ult.;) and in the other, the examples of Solon (Pausanias, l. x. c. 37) and Belisarius. See his great work De Jure Belli et Pacis, (l. iii. c. 4, s. 15, 16, 17, and in Barbeyrac's version, tom. ii. p. 257, &c.) Yet I can understand the benefit and validity of an agreement, tacit or express, mutually to abstain from certain modes of hostility. See the Amphictyonic oath in Aeschines, de falsa Legatione.]

[Footnote 108: Ravenna was taken, not in the year 540, but in the latter end of 539; and Pagi (tom. ii. p. 569) is rectified by Muratori. (Annali d'Italia, tom. v. p. 62,) who proves from an original act on papyrus, (Antiquit. Italiae Medii Aevi, tom. ii. dissert. xxxii. p. 999—1007,) Maffei, (Istoria Diplomat. p. 155-160,) that before the third of January, 540, peace and free correspondence were restored between Ravenna and Faenza.] Vitiges, who perhaps had attempted to escape, was honorably guarded in his palace; [109] the flower of the Gothic youth was selected for the service of the emperor; the remainder of the people was dismissed to their peaceful habitations in the southern provinces; and a colony of Italians was invited to replenish the depopulated city. The submission of the capital was imitated in the towns and villages of Italy, which had not been subdued, or even visited, by the Romans; and the independent Goths, who remained in arms at Pavia and Verona, were ambitious only to become the subjects of Belisarius. But his inflexible loyalty rejected, except as the substitute of Justinian, their oaths of allegiance; and he was not offended by the reproach of their deputies, that he rather chose to be a slave than a king.

[Footnote 109: He was seized by John the Sanguinary, but an oath or sacrament was pledged for his safety in the Basilica Julii, (Hist. Miscell. l. xvii. in Muratori, tom. i. p. 107.) Anastasius (in Vit. Pont. p. 40) gives a dark but probable account. Montfaucon is quoted by Mascou (Hist. of the Germans, xii. 21) for a votive shield representing the captivity of Vitiges and now in the collection of Signor Landi at Rome.]

After the second victory of Belisarius, envy again whispered, Justinian listened, and the hero was recalled. "The remnant of the Gothic war was no longer worthy of his presence: a gracious sovereign was impatient to reward his services, and to consult his wisdom; and he alone was capable of defending the East against the innumerable armies of Persia." Belisarius understood the suspicion, accepted the excuse, embarked at Ravenna his spoils and trophies; and proved, by his ready obedience, that such an abrupt removal from the government of Italy was not less unjust than it might have been indiscreet. The emperor received with honorable courtesy both Vitiges and his more noble consort; and as the king of the Goths conformed to the Athanasian faith, he obtained, with a rich inheritance of land in Asia, the rank of senator and patrician. [110] Every spectator admired, without peril, the strength and stature of the young Barbarians: they adored the majesty of the throne, and promised to shed their blood in the service of their benefactor. Justinian deposited in the Byzantine palace the treasures of the Gothic monarchy. A flattering senate was sometime admitted to gaze on the magnificent spectacle; but it was enviously secluded from the public view: and the conqueror of Italy renounced, without a murmur, perhaps without a sigh, the well-earned honors of a second triumph. His glory was indeed exalted above all external pomp; and the faint and hollow praises of the court were supplied, even in a servile age, by the respect and admiration of his country. Whenever he appeared in the streets and public places of Constantinople, Belisarius attracted and satisfied the eyes of the people. His lofty stature and majestic countenance fulfilled their expectations of a hero; the meanest of his fellow-citizens were emboldened by his gentle and gracious demeanor; and the martial train which attended his footsteps left his person more accessible than in a day of battle. Seven thousand horsemen, matchless for beauty and valor, were maintained in the service, and at the private expense, of the general. [111] Their prowess was always conspicuous in single combats, or in the foremost ranks; and both parties confessed that in the siege of Rome, the guards of Belisarius had alone vanquished the Barbarian host. Their numbers were continually augmented by the bravest and most faithful of the enemy; and his fortunate captives, the Vandals, the Moors, and the Goths, emulated the attachment of his domestic followers. By the union of liberality and justice, he acquired the love of the soldiers, without alienating the affections of the people. The sick and wounded were relieved with medicines and money; and still more efficaciously, by the healing visits and smiles of their commander. The loss of a weapon or a horse was instantly repaired, and each deed of valor was rewarded by the rich and honorable gifts of a bracelet or a collar, which were rendered more precious by the judgment of Belisarius. He was endeared to the husbandmen by the peace and plenty which they enjoyed under the shadow of his standard. Instead of being injured, the country was enriched by the march of the Roman armies; and such was the rigid discipline of their camp, that not an apple was gathered from the tree, not a path could be traced in the fields of corn. Belisarius was chaste and sober. In the license of a military life, none could boast that they had seen him intoxicated with wine: the most beautiful captives of Gothic or Vandal race were offered to his embraces; but he turned aside from their charms, and the husband of Antonina was never suspected of violating the laws of conjugal fidelity. The spectator and historian of his exploits has observed, that amidst the perils of war, he was daring without rashness, prudent without fear, slow or rapid according to the exigencies of the moment; that in the deepest distress he was animated by real or apparent hope, but that he was modest and humble in the most prosperous fortune. By these virtues, he equalled or excelled the ancient masters of the military art. Victory, by sea and land, attended his arms. He subdued Africa, Italy, and the adjacent islands; led away captives the successors of Genseric and Theodoric; filled Constantinople with the spoils of their palaces; and in the space of six years recovered half the provinces of the Western empire. In his fame and merit, in wealth and power, he remained without a rival, the first of the Roman subjects; the voice of envy could only magnify his dangerous importance; and the emperor might applaud his own discerning spirit, which had discovered and raised the genius of Belisarius.

[Footnote 110: Vitiges lived two years at Constantinople, and imperatoris in affectu convictus (or conjunctus) rebus excessit humanis. His widow Mathasuenta, the wife and mother of the patricians, the elder and younger Germanus, united the streams of Anician and Amali blood, (Jornandes, c. 60, p. 221, in Muratori, tom. i.)]

[Footnote 111: Procopius, Goth. l. iii. c. 1. Aimoin, a French monk of the xith century, who had obtained, and has disfigured, some authentic information of Belisarius, mentions, in his name, 12,000, pueri or slaves—quos propriis alimus stipendiis—besides 18,000 soldiers, (Historians of France, tom. iii. De Gestis Franc. l. ii. c. 6, p. 48.)]

It was the custom of the Roman triumphs, that a slave should be placed behind the chariot to remind the conqueror of the instability of fortune, and the infirmities of human nature. Procopius, in his

Anecdotes, has assumed that servile and ungrateful office. The generous reader may cast away the libel, but the evidence of facts will adhere to his memory; and he will reluctantly confess, that the fame, and even the virtue, of Belisarius, were polluted by the lust and cruelty of his wife; and that hero deserved an appellation which may not drop from the pen of the decent historian. The mother of Antonina [112] was a theatrical prostitute, and both her father and grandfather exercised, at Thessalonica and Constantinople, the vile, though lucrative, profession of charioteers. In the various situations of their fortune she became the companion, the enemy, the servant, and the favorite of the empress Theodora: these loose and ambitious females had been connected by similar pleasures; they were separated by the jealousy of vice, and at length reconciled by the partnership of guilt. Before her marriage with Belisarius, Antonina had one husband and many lovers: Photius, the son of her former nuptials, was of an age to distinguish himself at the siege of Naples; and it was not till the autumn of her age and beauty [113] that she indulged a scandalous attachment to a Thracian youth. Theodosius had been educated in the Eunomian heresy; the African voyage was consecrated by the baptism and auspicious name of the first soldier who embarked; and the proselyte was adopted into the family of his spiritual parents, [114] Belisarius and Antonina. Before they touched the shores of Africa, this holy kindred degenerated into sensual love: and as Antonina soon overleaped the bounds of modesty and caution, the Roman general was alone ignorant of his own dishonor. During their residence at Carthage, he surprised the two lovers in a subterraneous chamber, solitary, warm, and almost naked. Anger flashed from his eyes. "With the help of this young man," said the unblushing Antonina, "I was secreting our most precious effects from the knowledge of Justinian." The youth resumed his garments, and the pious husband consented to disbelieve the evidence of his own senses. From this pleasing and perhaps voluntary delusion, Belisarius was awakened at Syracuse, by the officious information of Macedonia; and that female attendant, after requiring an oath for her security, produced two chamberlains, who, like herself, had often beheld the adulteries of Antonina. A hasty flight into Asia saved Theodosius from the justice of an injured husband, who had signified to one of his guards the order of his death; but the tears of Antonina, and her artful seductions, assured the credulous hero of her innocence: and he stooped, against his faith and judgment, to abandon those imprudent friends, who had presumed to accuse or doubt the chastity of his wife. The revenge of a guilty woman is implacable and bloody: the unfortunate Macedonia, with the two witnesses, were secretly arrested by the minister of her cruelty; their tongues were cut out, their bodies were hacked into small pieces, and their remains were cast into the Sea of Syracuse. A rash though judicious saying of Constantine, "I would sooner have punished the adulteress than the boy," was deeply remembered by Antonina; and two years afterwards, when despair had armed that officer against his general, her sanguinary advice decided and hastened his execution. Even the indignation of Photius was not forgiven by his mother; the exile of her son prepared the recall of her lover; and Theodosius condescended to accept the pressing and humble invitation of the conqueror of Italy. In the absolute direction of his household, and in the important commissions of peace and war, [115] the favorite youth most rapidly acquired a fortune of four hundred thousand pounds sterling; and after their return to Constantinople, the passion of Antonina, at least, continued ardent and unabated. But fear, devotion, and lassitude perhaps, inspired Theodosius with more serious thoughts. He dreaded the busy scandal of the capital, and the indiscreet fondness of the wife of Belisarius; escaped from her embraces, and retiring to Ephesus, shaved his head, and took refuge in the sanctuary of a monastic life. The despair of the new Ariadne could scarcely have been excused by the death of her husband. She wept, she tore her hair, she filled the palace with her cries; "she had lost the dearest of friends, a tender, a faithful, a laborious friend!" But her warm entreaties, fortified by the prayers of Belisarius, were insufficient to draw the holy monk from the solitude of Ephesus. It was not till the general moved forward for the Persian war, that Theodosius could be tempted to return to Constantinople; and the short interval before the departure of Antonina herself was boldly devoted to love and pleasure.

[Footnote 112: The diligence of Alemannus could add but little to the four first and most curious chapters of the Anecdotes. Of these strange Anecdotes, a part may be true, because probable—and a part true, because improbable. Procopius must have known the former, and the latter he could scarcely invent. Note: The malice of court scandal is proverbially inventive; and of such scandal the "Anecdota" may be an embellished record—M.]

[Footnote 113: Procopius intimates (Anecdot. c. 4) that when Belisarius returned to Italy, (A.D. 543,) Antonina was sixty years of age. A forced, but more polite construction, which refers that date to the moment when he was writing, (A.D. 559,) would be compatible with the manhood of Photius, (Gothic. l. i. c. 10) in 536.]

[Footnote 114: Gompare the Vandalic War (l. i. c. 12) with the Anecdotes (c. i.) and Alemannus, (p. 2, 3.) This mode of baptismal adoption was revived by Leo the philosopher.]

[Footnote 115: In November, 537, Photius arrested the pope, (Liberat. Brev. c. 22. Pagi, tom. ii. p. 562) About the end of 539, Belisarius sent Theodosius on an important and lucrative commission to Ravenna, (Goth. l. ii. c. 18.)]

A philosopher may pity and forgive the infirmities of female nature, from which he receives no real injury: but contemptible is the husband who feels, and yet endures, his own infamy in that of his wife. Antonina pursued her son with implacable hatred; and the gallant Photius [116] was exposed to her secret persecutions in the camp beyond the Tigris. Enraged by his own wrongs, and by the dishonor of his blood, he cast away in his turn the sentiments of nature, and revealed to Belisarius the turpitude of a woman who had violated all the duties of a mother and a wife. From the surprise and indignation of the Roman general, his former credulity appears to have been sincere: he embraced the knees of the son of Antonina, adjured him to remember his obligations rather than his birth, and confirmed at the altar their holy vows of revenge and mutual defence. The dominion of Antonina was impaired by absence; and when she met her husband, on his return from the Persian confines, Belisarius, in his first and transient emotions, confined her person, and threatened her life. Photius was more resolved to punish, and less prompt to pardon: he flew to Ephesus; extorted from a trusty eunuch of his another the full confession of her guilt; arrested Theodosius and his treasures in the church of St. John the Apostle, and concealed his captives, whose execution was only delayed, in a secure and sequestered fortress of Cilicia. Such a daring outrage against public justice could not pass with impunity; and the cause of Antonina was espoused by the empress, whose favor she had deserved by the recent services of the disgrace of a praefect, and the exile and murder of a pope. At the end of the campaign, Belisarius was recalled; he complied, as usual, with the Imperial mandate. His mind was not prepared for rebellion: his obedience, however adverse to the dictates of honor, was consonant to the wishes of his heart; and when he embraced his wife, at the command, and perhaps in the presence, of the empress, the tender husband was disposed to forgive or to be forgiven. The bounty of Theodora reserved for her companion a more precious favor. "I have found," she said, "my dearest patrician, a pearl of inestimable value; it has not yet been viewed by any mortal eye; but the sight and the possession of this jewel are destined for my friend." [116/1] As soon as the curiosity and impatience of Antonina were kindled, the door of a bed-chamber was thrown open, and she beheld her lover, whom the diligence of the eunuchs had discovered in his secret prison. Her silent wonder burst into passionate exclamations of gratitude and joy, and she named Theodora her queen, her benefactress, and her savior. The monk of Ephesus was nourished in the palace with luxury and ambition; but instead of assuming, as he was promised, the command of the Roman armies, Theodosius expired in the first fatigues of an amorous interview. [116/2] The grief of Antonina could only be assuaged by the sufferings of her son. A youth of consular rank, and a sickly constitution, was punished, without a trial, like a malefactor and a slave: yet such was the constancy of his mind, that Photius sustained the tortures of the scourge and the rack, [116/3] without violating the faith which he had sworn to Belisarius. After this fruitless cruelty, the son of Antonina, while his mother feasted with the empress, was buried in her subterraneous prisons, which admitted not the distinction of night and day. He twice escaped to the most venerable sanctuaries of Constantinople, the churches of St. Sophia, and of the Virgin: but his tyrants were insensible of religion as of pity; and the helpless youth, amidst the clamors of the clergy and people, was twice dragged from the altar to the dungeon. His third attempt was more successful. At the end of three years, the prophet Zachariah, or some mortal friend, indicated the means of an escape: he eluded the spies and guards of the empress, reached the holy sepulchre of Jerusalem, embraced the profession of a monk; and the abbot Photius was employed, after the death of Justinian, to reconcile and regulate the churches of Egypt. The son of Antonina suffered all that an enemy can inflict: her patient husband imposed on himself the more exquisite misery of violating his promise and deserting his friend.

[Footnote 116: Theophanes (Chronograph. p. 204) styles him Photinus, the son-in-law of Belisarius; and he is copied by the Historia Miscella and Anastasius.]

[Footnote 116/1: This and much of the private scandal in the "Anecdota" is liable to serious doubt. Who reported all these private conversations, and how did they reach the ears of Procopius?—M.]

[Footnote 116/2: This is a strange misrepresentation—he died of a dysentery; nor does it appear that it was immediately after this scene. Antonina proposed to raise him to the generalship of the army. Procop. Anecd. p. 14. The sudden change from the abstemious diet of a monk to the luxury of the court is a much more probable cause of his death—M.]

[Footnote 116/3: The expression of Procopius does not appear to me to mean this kind of torture. Ibid—M.]

In the succeeding campaign, Belisarius was again sent against the Persians: he saved the East, but he offended Theodora, and perhaps the emperor himself. The malady of Justinian had countenanced the rumor of his death; and the Roman general, on the supposition of that probable event spoke the free language of a citizen and a soldier. His colleague Buzes, who concurred in the same sentiments, lost his rank, his liberty, and his health, by the persecution of the empress: but the disgrace of Belisarius was alleviated by the dignity of his own character, and the influence of his wife, who might wish to humble, but could not desire to ruin, the partner of her fortunes. Even his removal was colored by the assurance, that the sinking state of Italy would be retrieved by the single presence of its conqueror.

But no sooner had he returned, alone and defenceless, than a hostile commission was sent to the East, to seize his treasures and criminate his actions; the guards and veterans, who followed his private banner, were distributed among the chiefs of the army, and even the eunuchs presumed to cast lots for the partition of his martial domestics. When he passed with a small and sordid retinue through the streets of Constantinople, his forlorn appearance excited the amazement and compassion of the people. Justinian and Theodora received him with cold ingratitude; the servile crowd, with insolence and contempt; and in the evening he retired with trembling steps to his deserted palace. An indisposition, feigned or real, had confined Antonina to her apartment; and she walked disdainfully silent in the adjacent portico, while Belisarius threw himself on his bed, and expected, in an agony of grief and terror, the death which he had so often braved under the walls of Rome. Long after sunset a messenger was announced from the empress: he opened, with anxious curiosity, the letter which contained the sentence of his fate. "You cannot be ignorant how much you have deserved my displeasure. I am not insensible of the services of Antonina. To her merits and intercession I have granted your life, and permit you to retain a part of your treasures, which might be justly forfeited to the state. Let your gratitude, where it is due, be displayed, not in words, but in your future behavior." I know not how to believe or to relate the transports with which the hero is said to have received this ignominious pardon. He fell prostrate before his wife, he kissed the feet of his savior, and he devoutly promised to live the grateful and submissive slave of Antonina. A fine of one hundred and twenty thousand pounds sterling was levied on the fortunes of Belisarius; and with the office of count, or master of the royal stables, he accepted the conduct of the Italian war. At his departure from Constantinople, his friends, and even the public, were persuaded that as soon as he regained his freedom, he would renounce his dissimulation, and that his wife, Theodora, and perhaps the emperor himself, would be sacrificed to the just revenge of a virtuous rebel. Their hopes were deceived; and the unconquerable patience and loyalty of Belisarius appear either below or above the character of a man. [117]

[Footnote 117: The continuator of the Chronicle of Marcellinus gives, in a few decent words, the substance of the Anecdotes: Belisarius de Oriente evocatus, in offensam periculumque incurrens grave, et invidiae subeacens rursus remittitur in Italiam, (p. 54.)]

CHAPTER XLII

STATE OF THE BARBARIC WORLD

PART I

STATE OF THE BARBARIC WORLD—ESTABLISHMENT OF THE LOMBARDS ON THE DANUBE—TRIBES AND INROADS OF THE SCLAVONIANS—ORIGIN, EMPIRE, AND EMBASSIES OF THE TURKS—THE FLIGHT OF THE AVARS—CHOSROES I, OR NUSHIRVAN, KING OF PERSIA—HIS PROSPEROUS REIGN AND WARS WITH THE ROMANS—THE COLCHIAN OR LAZIC WAR—THE AETHIOPIANS

Our estimate of personal merit, is relative to the common faculties of mankind. The aspiring efforts of genius, or virtue, either in active or speculative life, are measured, not so much by their real elevation, as by the height to which they ascend above the level of their age and country; and the same stature, which in a people of giants would pass unnoticed, must appear conspicuous in a race of pygmies. Leonidas, and his three hundred companions, devoted their lives at Thermopylae; but the education of the infant, the boy, and the man, had prepared, and almost insured, this memorable sacrifice; and each Spartan would approve, rather than admire, an act of duty, of which himself and eight thousand of his fellow-citizens were equally capable. [1] The great Pompey might inscribe on his trophies, that he had defeated in battle two millions of enemies, and reduced fifteen hundred cities from the Lake Maeotis to the Red Sea: [2] but the fortune of Rome flew before his eagles; the nations were oppressed by their own fears, and the invincible legions which he commanded, had been formed by the habits of conquest and the discipline of ages. In this view, the character of Belisarius may be deservedly placed above the heroes of the ancient republics. His imperfections flowed from the contagion of the times; his virtues were his own, the free gift of nature or reflection; he raised himself without a master or a rival; and so inadequate were the arms committed to his hand, that his sole advantage was derived from the pride and presumption of his adversaries. Under his command, the subjects of Justinian often deserved to be called Romans: but the unwarlike appellation of Greeks was imposed as a term of reproach by the haughty Goths; who affected to blush, that they must dispute the kingdom of Italy with a nation of tragedians pantomimes, and pirates. [3] The climate of Asia has indeed been found less congenial than that of Europe to military spirit: those populous countries were enervated by luxury, despotism, and superstition; and the monks were more expensive and more numerous than the soldiers of the East. The regular force of the empire had once amounted to six hundred and forty-five thousand men: it was reduced, in the time of Justinian, to one hundred and fifty thousand; and this number, large as it may seem, was thinly scattered over the sea and land; in Spain and Italy, in Africa and Egypt, on the banks of the Danube, the coast of the Euxine, and the frontiers of Persia. The citizen was exhausted, yet the soldier was unpaid; his poverty was mischievously soothed by the privilege of rapine and indolence; and the tardy payments were detained and intercepted by the fraud of those agents who usurp, without courage or danger, the emoluments of war. Public and private distress recruited the armies of the state; but in the field, and still more in the presence of the enemy, their numbers were always defective. The want of national spirit was supplied by the precarious faith and disorderly service of Barbarian mercenaries.

Even military honor, which has often survived the loss of virtue and freedom, was almost totally extinct. The generals, who were multiplied beyond the example of former times, labored only to prevent the success, or to sully the reputation of their colleagues; and they had been taught by experience, that if merit sometimes provoked the jealousy, error, or even guilt, would obtain the indulgence, of a gracious emperor. [4] In such an age, the triumphs of Belisarius, and afterwards of Narses, shine with incomparable lustre; but they are encompassed with the darkest shades of disgrace and calamity. While the lieutenant of Justinian subdued the kingdoms of the Goths and Vandals, the emperor, [5] timid, though ambitious, balanced the forces of the Barbarians, fomented their divisions by flattery and falsehood, and invited by his patience and liberality the repetition of injuries. [6] The keys of Carthage, Rome, and Ravenna, were presented to their conqueror, while Antioch was destroyed by the Persians, and Justinian trembled for the safety of Constantinople.

[Footnote 1: *It will be a pleasure, not a task, to read Herodotus, (l. vii. c. 104, 134, p. 550, 615.) The conversation of Xerxes and Demaratus at Thermopylae is one of the most interesting and moral scenes in history. It was the torture of the royal Spartan to behold, with anguish and remorse, the virtue of his country.*]

[Footnote 2: *See this proud inscription in Pliny, (Hist. Natur. vii. 27.) Few men have more exquisitely tasted of glory and disgrace; nor could Juvenal (Satir. x.) produce a more striking example of the vicissitudes of fortune, and the vanity of human wishes.*]

[Footnote 3: *This last epithet of Procopius is too nobly translated by pirates; naval thieves is the proper word; strippers of garments, either for injury or insult, (Demosthenes contra Conon Reiske, Orator, Graec. tom. ii. p. 1264.)*]

[Footnote 4: *See the third and fourth books of the Gothic War: the writer of the Anecdotes cannot aggravate these abuses.*]

[Footnote 5: *Agathias, l. v. p. 157, 158. He confines this weakness of the emperor and the empire to the old age of Justinian; but alas! he was never young.*]

[Footnote 6: *This mischievous policy, which Procopius (Anecdot. c. 19) imputes to the emperor, is revealed in his epistle to a Scythian prince, who was capable of understanding it.*]

Even the Gothic victories of Belisarius were prejudicial to the state, since they abolished the important barrier of the Upper Danube, which had been so faithfully guarded by Theodoric and his daughter. For the defence of Italy, the Goths evacuated Pannonia and Noricum, which they left in a peaceful and flourishing condition: the sovereignty was claimed by the emperor of the Romans; the actual possession was abandoned to the boldness of the first invader. On the opposite banks of the Danube, the plains of Upper Hungary and the Transylvanian hills were possessed, since the death of Attila, by the tribes of the Gepidae, who respected the Gothic arms, and despised, not indeed the gold of the Romans, but the secret motive of their annual subsidies. The vacant fortifications of the river were instantly occupied by these Barbarians; their standards were planted on the walls of Sirmium and Belgrade; and the ironical tone of their apology aggravated this insult on the majesty of the empire. "So extensive, O Caesar, are your dominions, so numerous are your cities, that you are continually seeking for nations to whom, either in peace or in war, you may relinquish these useless possessions. The Gepidae are your brave and faithful allies; and if they have anticipated your gifts, they have shown a just confidence in your bounty." Their presumption was excused by the mode of revenge which Justinian embraced. Instead of asserting the rights of a sovereign for the protection of his subjects, the emperor invited a strange people to invade and possess the Roman provinces between the Danube and the Alps and the ambition of the Gepidae was checked by the rising power and fame of the Lombards. [7] This corrupt appellation has been diffused in the thirteenth century by the merchants and bankers, the Italian posterity of these savage warriors: but the original name of Langobards is expressive only of the peculiar length and fashion of their beards. I am not disposed either to question or to justify their Scandinavian origin; [8] nor to pursue the migrations of the Lombards through unknown regions and marvellous adventures. About the time of Augustus and Trajan, a ray of historic light breaks on the darkness of their antiquities, and they are discovered, for the first time, between the Elbe and the Oder. Fierce, beyond the example of the Germans, they delighted to propagate the tremendous belief, that their heads were formed like the heads of dogs, and that they drank the blood of their enemies, whom they vanquished in battle. The smallness of their numbers was recruited by the adoption of their bravest slaves; and alone, amidst their powerful neighbors, they defended by arms their high-spirited independence. In the tempests of the north, which overwhelmed so many names and nations, this little bark of the Lombards still floated on the surface: they gradually descended towards the south and the Danube, and, at the end of four hundred years, they again appear with their ancient valor and renown. Their manners were not less ferocious. The assassination of a royal guest was executed in the presence, and by the command, of the king's daughter, who had been provoked by some words of insult, and disappointed by his diminutive stature; and a tribute, the price of blood, was imposed on the Lombards, by his brother the king of the Heruli. Adversity revived a sense of moderation and justice, and the insolence of conquest was chastised by the signal defeat and irreparable dispersion of the Heruli, who were seated in the southern provinces of Poland. [9] The victories of the Lombards recommended them to the friendship of the emperors; and at the solicitations of Justinian, they passed the Danube, to reduce, according to their treaty, the cities of Noricum and the fortresses of Pannonia. But the spirit of rapine soon tempted them beyond these ample limits; they wandered along the coast of the Hadriatic as far as Dyrrachium, and presumed, with familiar rudeness to enter the towns and houses of their Roman allies, and to seize the captives who had escaped from their audacious hands. These acts of hostility, the sallies, as it might be pretended, of some loose adventurers, were disowned by the nation, and excused by the emperor; but the arms of the Lombards were more seriously engaged by a contest of thirty years, which was terminated only by the extirpation of the Gepidae. The hostile nations often pleaded their cause before the throne of Constantinople; and the crafty Justinian, to whom the Barbarians were almost equally odious, pronounced a partial and ambiguous sentence, and dexterously protracted the war by slow and ineffectual succors. Their strength was formidable, since the Lombards, who sent into the field several myriads of soldiers, still claimed, as the weaker side, the protection of the Romans. Their spirit was intrepid; yet such is the uncertainty of courage, that the two armies were suddenly struck with a panic; they fled from each other, and the rival kings remained with their guards in the midst of an empty plain. A short truce was obtained; but their mutual resentment again kindled; and the remembrance of their shame rendered the next encounter more desperate and bloody Forty thousand of the Barbarians perished in the decisive battle, which broke the power of the Gepidae, transferred the fears and wishes of Justinian, and first displayed the character of Alboin, the youthful prince of the Lombards, and the future conqueror of Italy. [10]

[Footnote 7: Gens Germana feritate ferocior, says Velleius Paterculus of the Lombards, (ii. 106.) Langobardos paucitas nobilitat. Plurimis ac valentissimis nationibus cincti non per obsequium, sed praeliis et perilitando, tuti sunt, (Tacit. de Moribus German. c. 40.) See likewise Strabo, (l. viii. p. 446.) The best geographers place them beyond the Elbe, in the bishopric of Magdeburgh and the middle march of Brandenburgh; and their situation will agree with the patriotic remark of the count de Hertzberg, that most of the Barbarian conquerors issued from the same countries which still produce the armies of Prussia. Note: See Malte Brun, vol. i. p 402—M]

[Footnote 8: The Scandinavian origin of the Goths and Lombards, as stated by Paul Warnefrid, surnamed the deacon, is attacked by Cluverius, (Germania, Antiq. l. iii. c. 26, p. 102, &c.,) a native of Prussia, and defended by Grotius, (Prolegom. ad Hist. Goth. p. 28, &c.,) the Swedish Ambassador.]

[Footnote 9: Two facts in the narrative of Paul Diaconus (l. i. c. 20) are expressive of national manners: 1. Dum ad tabulam luderet—while he played at draughts. 2. Camporum viridantia lina. The cultivation of flax supposes property, commerce, agriculture, and manufactures]

[Footnote 10: I have used, without undertaking to reconcile, the facts in Procopius, (Goth. l. ii. c. 14, l. iii. c. 33, 34, l. iv. c. 18, 25,) Paul Diaconus, (de Gestis Langobard, l. i. c. 1-23, in Muratori, Script. Rerum Italicarum, tom. i. p. 405-419,) and Jornandes, (de Success. Regnorum, p. 242.) The patient reader may draw some light from Mascou (Hist. of the Germans, and Annotat. xxiii.) and De Buat, (Hist. des Peuples, &c., tom. ix. x. xi.)]

The wild people who dwelt or wandered in the plains of Russia, Lithuania, and Poland, might be reduced, in the age of Justinian, under the two great families of the Bulgarians [11] and the Sclavonians. According to the Greek writers, the former, who touched the Euxine and the Lake Maeotis, derived from the Huns their name or descent; and it is needless to renew the simple and well-known picture of Tartar manners. They were bold and dexterous archers, who drank the milk, and feasted on the flesh, of their fleet and indefatigable horses; whose flocks and herds followed, or rather guided, the motions of their roving camps; to whose inroads no country was remote or impervious, and who were practised in flight, though incapable of fear. The nation was divided into two powerful and hostile tribes, who pursued each other with fraternal hatred. They eagerly disputed the friendship, or rather the gifts, of the emperor; and the distinctions which nature had fixed between the faithful dog and the rapacious wolf was applied by an ambassador who received only verbal instructions from the mouth of his illiterate prince. [12] The Bulgarians, of whatsoever species, were equally attracted by Roman wealth: they assumed a vague dominion over the Sclavonian name, and their rapid marches could only be stopped by the Baltic Sea, or the extreme cold and poverty of the north. But the same race of Sclavonians appears to have maintained, in every age, the possession of the same countries. Their numerous tribes, however distant or adverse, used one common language, (it was harsh and irregular,) and where known by the resemblance of their form, which deviated from the swarthy Tartar, and approached without attaining the lofty stature and fair complexion of the German. Four thousand six hundred villages [13] were scattered over the provinces of Russia and Poland, and their huts were hastily built of rough timber, in a country deficient both in stone and iron. Erected, or rather concealed, in the depth of forests, on the banks of rivers, or the edges of morasses, we may not perhaps, without flattery, compare them to the architecture of the beaver; which they resembled in a double issue, to the land and water, for the escape of the savage inhabitant, an animal less cleanly, less diligent, and less social, than that marvellous quadruped. The fertility of the soil, rather than the labor of the natives, supplied the rustic plenty of the Sclavonians. Their sheep and horned cattle were large and numerous, and the fields which they sowed with millet or panic [14] afforded, in place of bread, a coarse and less nutritive food. The incessant rapine of their neighbors compelled them to bury this treasure in the earth; but on the appearance of a stranger, it was freely imparted by a people, whose unfavorable character is qualified by the epithets of chaste, patient, and hospitable. As their supreme god, they adored an invisible master of the thunder. The rivers and the nymphs obtained their subordinate honors, and the popular worship was expressed in vows and sacrifice. The Sclavonians disdained to obey a despot, a prince, or even a magistrate; but their experience was too narrow, their passions too headstrong, to compose a system of equal law or general defence. Some voluntary respect was yielded to age and valor; but each tribe or village existed as a separate republic, and all must be persuaded where none could be compelled. They fought on foot, almost naked, and except an unwieldy shield, without any defensive armor; their weapons of offence were a bow, a quiver of small poisoned arrows, and a long rope, which they dexterously threw from a distance, and entangled their enemy in a running noose. In the field, the Sclavonian infantry was dangerous by their speed, agility, and hardiness: they swam, they dived, they remained under water, drawing their breath through a hollow cane; and a river or lake was often the scene of their unsuspected ambuscade. But these were the achievements of spies or stragglers; the military art was unknown to the Sclavonians; their name was obscure, and their conquests were inglorious. [15]

[Footnote 11: I adopt the appellation of Bulgarians from Ennodius, (in Panegyr. Theodorici, Opp. Sirmond, tom. i. p. 1598, 1599,) Jornandes, (de Rebus Geticis, c. 5, p. 194, et de Regn. Successione, p. 242,) Theophanes, (p. 185,) and the Chronicles of Cassiodorus and Marcellinus. The name of Huns is too vague; the tribes of the Cutturgurians and Utturgurians are too minute and too harsh. Note: The Bulgarians are first mentioned among the writers of the West in the Panegyric on Theodoric by Ennodius, Bishop of Pavia. Though they perhaps took part in the conquests of the Huns, they did not advance to the Danube till after the dismemberment of that monarchy on the death of Attila. But the Bulgarians are mentioned much earlier by the Armenian writers. Above 600 years before Christ, a tribe of Bulgarians, driven from their native possessions beyond the Caspian, occupied a part of Armenia, north of the Araxes. They were of the Finnish race; part of the nation, in the fifth century, moved westward, and reached the modern Bulgaria; part remained along the Volga, which is called Etel, Etil, or Athil, in all the Tartar languages, but from the Bulgarians, the Volga. The power of the eastern Bulgarians was broken by Batou, son of Tchingiz Khan; that of the western will appear in the course of the history. From St. Martin, vol. vii p. 141. Malte-Brun, on the contrary, conceives that the Bulgarians took their name from the river. According to the Byzantine historians they were a branch of the Ougres, (Thunmann, Hist. of the People to the East of Europe,) but they have more resemblance to the Turks. Their first country, Great Bulgaria, was washed by the Volga. Some remains of their capital are still shown near Kasan. They afterwards dwelt in Kuban, and finally on the Danube, where they subdued (about the year 500) the Slavo-Servians established on the Lower Danube. Conquered in their turn by the Avars, they freed themselves from that yoke in 635; their empire then comprised the Cutturgurians, the remains of the Huns established on the Palus Maeotis. The Danubian Bulgaria, a dismemberment of this vast state, was long formidable to the Byzantine empire. Malte-Brun, Prec. de Geog Univ. vol. i. p. 419—M. —According to Shafarik, the Danubian Bulgaria was peopled by a Slavo Bulgarian race. The Slavish population was conquered by the Bulgarian (of Uralian and Finnish descent,) and incorporated with them. This mingled race are the Bulgarians bordering on the Byzantine empire. Shafarik, ii 152, et seq—M. 1845]

[Footnote 12: Procopius, (Goth. l. iv. c. 19.) His verbal message (he owns him self an illiterate Barbarian) is delivered as an epistle. The style is savage, figurative, and original.]

[Footnote 13: This sum is the result of a particular list, in a curious Ms. fragment of the year 550, found in the library of Milan. The obscure geography of the times provokes and exercises the patience of the count de Buat, (tom. xi. p. 69—189.) The French minister often loses himself in a wilderness which requires a Saxon and Polish guide.]

[Footnote 14: Panicum, milium. See Columella, l. ii. c. 9, p. 430, edit. Gesner. Plin. Hist. Natur. xviii. 24, 25. The Samaritans made a pap of millet, mingled with mare's milk or blood. In the wealth of modern husbandry, our millet feeds poultry, and not heroes. See the dictionaries of Bomare and Miller.]

[Footnote 15: For the name and nation, the situation and manners, of the Sclavonians, see the original evidence of the vith century, in Procopius, (Goth. l. l. c. 26, l. iii. c. 14,) and the emperor Mauritius or Maurice (Stratagemat. l. ii. c. 5, apud Mascon Annotat. xxxi.) The stratagems of Maurice have been printed only, as I understand, at the end of Scheffer's edition of Arrian's Tactics, at Upsal, 1664, (Fabric. Bibliot. Graec. l. iv. c. 8, tom. iii. p. 278,) a scarce, and hitherto, to me, an inaccessible book.]

I have marked the faint and general outline of the Sclavonians and Bulgarians, without attempting to define their intermediate boundaries, which were not accurately known or respected by the Barbarians themselves. Their importance was measured by their vicinity to the empire; and the level country of Moldavia and Wallachia was occupied by the Antes, [16] a Sclavonian tribe, which swelled the titles of Justinian with an epithet of conquest. [17] Against the Antes he erected the fortifications of the Lower Danube; and labored to secure the alliance of a people seated in the direct channel of northern inundation, an interval of two hundred miles between the mountains of Transylvania and the Euxine Sea. But the Antes wanted power and inclination to stem the fury of the torrent; and the light-armed Sclavonians, from a hundred tribes, pursued with almost equal speed the footsteps of the Bulgarian horse. The payment of one piece of gold for each soldier procured a safe and easy retreat through the country of the Gepidae, who commanded the passage of the Upper Danube. [18] The hopes or fears of the Barbarians; their intense union or discord; the accident of a frozen or shallow stream; the prospect of harvest or vintage; the prosperity or distress of the Romans; were the causes which produced the uniform repetition of annual visits, [19] tedious in the narrative, and destructive in the event. The same year, and possibly the same month, in which Ravenna surrendered, was marked by an invasion of the Huns or Bulgarians, so dreadful, that it almost effaced the memory of their past inroads. They spread from the suburbs of Constantinople to the Ionian Gulf, destroyed thirty-two cities or castles, erased Potidaea, which Athens had built, and Philip had besieged, and repassed the Danube, dragging at their horses' heels one hundred and twenty thousand of the subjects of Justinian. In a subsequent inroad they pierced the wall of the Thracian Chersonesus, extirpated the habitations and the inhabitants, boldly traversed the Hellespont, and returned to their companions, laden with the spoils of Asia. Another party, which seemed a multitude in the eyes of the Romans, penetrated, without opposition, from the Straits of Thermopylae to the Isthmus of Corinth; and the last ruin of Greece has appeared an object too minute for the attention of history. The works which the emperor raised for the protection, but at the expense of his subjects, served only to disclose the weakness of some neglected part; and the walls, which by flattery had been deemed impregnable, were either deserted by the garrison, or scaled by the

Barbarians. Three thousand Sclavonians, who insolently divided themselves into two bands, discovered the weakness and misery of a triumphant reign. They passed the Danube and the Hebrus, vanquished the Roman generals who dared to oppose their progress, and plundered, with impunity, the cities of Illyricum and Thrace, each of which had arms and numbers to overwhelm their contemptible assailants. Whatever praise the boldness of the Sclavonians may deserve, it is sullied by the wanton and deliberate cruelty which they are accused of exercising on their prisoners. Without distinction of rank, or age, or sex, the captives were impaled or flayed alive, or suspended between four posts, and beaten with clubs till they expired, or enclosed in some spacious building, and left to perish in the flames with the spoil and cattle which might impede the march of these savage victors. [20] Perhaps a more impartial narrative would reduce the number, and qualify the nature, of these horrid acts; and they might sometimes be excused by the cruel laws of retaliation. In the siege of Topirus, [21] whose obstinate defence had enraged the Sclavonians, they massacred fifteen thousand males; but they spared the women and children; the most valuable captives were always reserved for labor or ransom; the servitude was not rigorous, and the terms of their deliverance were speedy and moderate. But the subject, or the historian of Justinian, exhaled his just indignation in the language of complaint and reproach; and Procopius has confidently affirmed, that in a reign of thirty-two years, each annual inroad of the Barbarians consumed two hundred thousand of the inhabitants of the Roman empire. The entire population of Turkish Europe, which nearly corresponds with the provinces of Justinian, would perhaps be incapable of supplying six millions of persons, the result of this incredible estimate. [22]

[Footnote 16: Antes eorum fortissimi.... Taysis qui rapidus et vorticosus in Histri fluenta furens devolvitur, (Jornandes, c. 5, p. 194, edit. Murator. Procopius, Goth. l. iii. c. 14, et de Edific. l iv. c. 7.) Yet the same Procopius mentions the Goths and Huns as neighbors to the Danube, (de Edific. l. v. c. 1.)]

[Footnote 17: The national title of Anticus, in the laws and inscriptions of Justinian, was adopted by his successors, and is justified by the pious Ludewig (in Vit. Justinian. p. 515.) It had strangely puzzled the civilians of the middle age.]

[Footnote 18: Procopius, Goth. l. iv. c. 25.]

[Footnote 19: An inroad of the Huns is connected, by Procopius, with a comet perhaps that of 531, (Persic. l. ii. c. 4.) Agathias (l. v. p. 154, 155) borrows from his predecessors some early facts.]

[Footnote 20: The cruelties of the Sclavonians are related or magnified by Procopius, (Goth. l. iii. c. 29, 38.) For their mild and liberal behavior to their prisoners, we may appeal to the authority, somewhat more recent of the emperor Maurice, (Stratagem. l. ii. c. 5.)]

[Footnote 21: Topirus was situate near Philippi in Thrace, or Macedonia, opposite to the Isle of Thasos, twelve days' journey from Constantinople (Cellarius, tom. i. p. 676, 846.)]

[Footnote 22: According to the malevolent testimony of the Anecdotes, (c. 18,) these inroads had reduced the provinces south of the Danube to the state of a Scythian wilderness.]

In the midst of these obscure calamities, Europe felt the shock of revolution, which first revealed to the world the name and nation of the Turks. [22/1] Like Romulus, the founder [22/2] of that martial people was suckled by a she-wolf, who afterwards made him the father of a numerous progeny; and the representation of that animal in the banners of the Turks preserved the memory, or rather suggested the idea, of a fable, which was invented, without any mutual intercourse, by the shepherds of Latium and those of Scythia. At the equal distance of two thousand miles from the Caspian, the Icy, the Chinese, and the Bengal Seas, a ridge of mountains is conspicuous, the centre, and perhaps the summit, of Asia; which, in the language of different nations, has been styled Imaus, and Caf, [23] and Altai, and the Golden Mountains, [23/1] and the Girdle of the Earth. The sides of the hills were productive of minerals; and the iron forges, [24] for the purpose of war, were exercised by the Turks, the most despised portion of the slaves of the great khan of the Geougen. But their servitude could only last till a leader, bold and eloquent, should arise to persuade his countrymen that the same arms which they forged for their masters, might become, in their own hands, the instruments of freedom and victory. They sallied from the mountains; [25] a sceptre was the reward of his advice; and the annual ceremony, in which a piece of iron was heated in the fire, and a smith's hammer [25/1] was successively handled by the prince and his nobles, recorded for ages the humble profession and rational pride of the Turkish nation. Bertezena, [25/2] their first leader, signalized their valor and his own in successful combats against the neighboring tribes; but when he presumed to ask in marriage the daughter of the great khan, the insolent demand of a slave and a mechanic was contemptuously rejected. The disgrace was expiated by a more noble alliance with a princess of China; and the decisive battle which almost extirpated the nation of the Geougen, established in Tartary the new and more powerful empire of the Turks. [25/3] They reigned over the north; but they confessed the vanity of conquest, by their faithful attachment to the mountain of their fathers. The royal encampment seldom lost sight of Mount Altai, from whence the River Irtish descends to water the rich pastures of the Calmucks, [26] which nourish the largest sheep and oxen in the world. The soil is fruitful, and the climate mild and temperate: the happy region was ignorant of earthquake and pestilence; the emperor's throne was turned towards the East, and a golden wolf on the top of a spear seemed to guard the entrance of his tent. One of the successors of Bertezena was tempted by the luxury and superstition of China; but his design of building cities and temples was defeated by the simple wisdom of a Barbarian counsellor. "The Turks," he said, "are not equal in number to one hundredth part of the inhabitants of China. If we balance their power, and elude their armies, it is because we wander without any fixed habitations in the exercise of war and hunting. Are we strong? we advance and conquer: are we feeble? we retire and are concealed. Should the Turks confine themselves within the walls of cities, the loss of a battle would be the destruction of their empire. The bonzes preach only patience, humility, and the renunciation of the world. Such, O king! is not the religion of heroes." They entertained, with less reluctance, the doctrines of Zoroaster; but the greatest part of the nation acquiesced, without inquiry, in the opinions, or rather in the practice, of their ancestors. The honors of sacrifice were reserved for the supreme deity; they acknowledged, in rude hymns, their obligations to the air, the fire, the water, and the earth; and their priests derived some profit from the art of divination. Their unwritten laws were rigorous and impartial: theft was punished with a tenfold restitution; adultery, treason, and murder, with death; and no chastisement could be inflicted too severe for the rare and inexpiable guilt of cowardice. As the subject nations marched under the standard of the Turks, their cavalry, both men and horses, were proudly computed by millions; one of their effective armies consisted of four hundred thousand soldiers, and in less than fifty years they were connected in peace and war with the Romans, the Persians, and the Chinese. In their northern limits, some vestige may be discovered of the form and situation of Kamptchatka, of a people of hunters and fishermen, whose sledges were drawn by dogs, and whose habitations were buried in the earth. The Turks were ignorant of astronomy; but the observation taken by some learned Chinese, with a gnomon of eight feet, fixes the royal camp in the latitude of forty-nine degrees, and marks their extreme progress within three, or at least ten degrees, of the polar circle. [27] Among their southern conquests the most splendid was that of the Nephthalites, or white Huns, a polite and warlike people, who possessed the commercial cities of Bochara and Samarcand, who had vanquished the Persian monarch, and carried their victorious arms along the banks, and perhaps to the mouth, of the Indus. On the side of the West, the Turkish cavalry advanced to the Lake Maeotis. They passed that lake on the ice. The khan who dwelt at the foot of Mount Altai issued his commands for the siege of Bosphorus, [28] a city the voluntary subject of Rome, and whose princes had formerly been the friends of Athens. [29] To the east, the Turks invaded China, as often as the vigor of the government was relaxed: and I am taught to read in the history of the times, that they mowed down their patient enemies like hemp or grass; and that the mandarins applauded the wisdom of an emperor who repulsed these Barbarians with golden lances. This extent of savage empire compelled the Turkish monarch to establish three subordinate princes of his own blood, who soon forgot their gratitude and allegiance. The conquerors were enervated by luxury, which is always fatal except to an industrious people; the policy of China solicited the vanquished nations to resume their independence and the power of the Turks was limited to a period of two hundred years. The revival of their name and dominion in the southern countries of Asia are the events of a later age; and the dynasties, which succeeded to their native realms, may sleep in oblivion; since their history bears no relation to the decline and fall of the Roman empire. [30]

[Footnote 22/1: It must be remembered that the name of Turks is extended to a whole family of the Asiatic races, and not confined to the Assena, or Turks of the Altai—M.]

[Footnote 22/2: Assena (the wolf) was the name of this chief. Klaproth, Tabl. Hist. de l'Asie p. 114—M.]

[Footnote 23: From Caf to Caf; which a more rational geography would interpret, from Imaus, perhaps, to Mount Atlas. According to the religious philosophy of the Mahometans, the basis of Mount Caf is an emerald, whose reflection produces the azure of the sky. The mountain is endowed with a sensitive action in its roots or nerves; and their vibration, at the command of God, is the cause of earthquakes. (D'Herbelot, p. 230, 231.)]

[Footnote 23/1: Altai, i. e. Altun Tagh, the Golden Mountain. Von Hammer Osman Geschichte, vol. i. p. 2—M.]

[Footnote 24: The Siberian iron is the best and most plentiful in the world; and in the southern parts, above sixty mines are now worked by the industry of the Russians, (Strahlenberg, Hist. of Siberia, p. 342, 387. Voyage en Siberie, par l'Abbe Chappe d'Auteroche, p. 603—608, edit in 12mo. Amsterdam. 1770.) The Turks offered iron for sale; yet the Roman ambassadors, with strange obstinacy, persisted in believing that it was all a trick, and that their country produced none, (Menander in Excerpt. Leg. p. 152.)]

[Footnote 25: Of Irgana-kon, (Abulghazi Khan, Hist. Genealogique des Tatars, P ii. c. 5, p. 71—77, c. 15, p. 155.) The tradition of the Moguls, of the 450 years which they passed in the mountains, agrees with the Chinese periods of the history of the Huns and Turks, (De Guignes, tom. i. part ii. p. 376,) and the twenty generations, from their restoration to Zingis.]

[Footnote 25/1: The Mongol Temugin is also, though erroneously, explained by Rubruquis, a smith. Schmidt, p 876—M.]

[Footnote 25/2: There appears the same confusion here. Bertezena (Berte-Scheno) is claimed as the founder of the Mongol race. The name means the gray (blauliche) wolf. In fact, the same tradition of the origin from a wolf seems common to the Mongols and the Turks. The Mongol Berte-Scheno, of the very curious Mongol History, published and translated by M. Schmidt of Petersburg, is brought from Thibet. M. Schmidt considers this tradition of the Thibetane descent of the royal race of the Mongols to be much earlier than their conversion to Lamaism, yet it seems very suspicious. See Klaproth, Tabl. de l'Asie, p.

159. The Turkish Bertezena is called Thou-men by Klaproth, p. 115. In 552, Thou-men took the title of Kha-Khan, and was called Il Khan—M.]

[Footnote 25/3: Great Bucharia is called Turkistan: see Hammer, 2. It includes all the last steppes at the foot of the Altai. The name is the same with that of the Turan of Persian poetic legend—M.]

[Footnote 26: The country of the Turks, now of the Calmucks, is well described in the Genealogical History, p. 521—562. The curious notes of the French translator are enlarged and digested in the second volume of the English version.]

[Footnote 27: Visdelou, p. 141, 151. The fact, though it strictly belongs to a subordinate and successive tribe, may be introduced here.]

[Footnote 28: Procopius, Persic. l. i. c. 12, l. ii. c. 3. Peyssonel, Observations sur les Peuples Barbares, p. 99, 100, defines the distance between Caffa and the old Bosphorus at xvi. long Tartar leagues.]

[Footnote 29: See, in a Memoire of M. de Boze, (Mem. de l'Academie des Inscriptions, tom. vi. p. 549—565,) the ancient kings and medals of the Cimmerian Bosphorus; and the gratitude of Athens, in the Oration of Demosthenes against Leptines, (in Reiske, Orator. Graec. tom. i. p. 466, 187.)]

[Footnote 30: For the origin and revolutions of the first Turkish empire, the Chinese details are borrowed from De Guignes (Hist. des Huns, tom. P. ii. p. 367—462) and Visdelou, (Supplement a la Bibliotheque Orient. d'Herbelot, p. 82—114.) The Greek or Roman hints are gathered in Menander (p. 108—164) and Theophylact Simocatta, (l. vii. c. 7, 8.)]

PART II

In the rapid career of conquest, the Turks attacked and subdued the nation of the Ogors or Varchonites [30/1] on the banks of the River Til, which derived the epithet of Black from its dark water or gloomy forests. [31] The khan of the Ogors was slain with three hundred thousand of his subjects, and their bodies were scattered over the space of four days' journey: their surviving countrymen acknowledged the strength and mercy of the Turks; and a small portion, about twenty thousand warriors, preferred exile to servitude. They followed the well-known road of the Volga, cherished the error of the nations who confounded them with the Avars, and spread the terror of that false though famous appellation, which had not, however, saved its lawful proprietors from the yoke of the Turks. [32] After a long and victorious march, the new Avars arrived at the foot of Mount Caucasus, in the country of the Alani [33] and Circassians, where they first heard of the splendor and weakness of the Roman empire. They humbly requested their confederate, the prince of the Alani, to lead them to this source of riches; and their ambassador, with the permission of the governor of Lazica, was transported by the Euxine Sea to Constantinople. The whole city was poured forth to behold with curiosity and terror the aspect of a strange people: their long hair, which hung in tresses down their backs, was gracefully bound with ribbons, but the rest of their habit appeared to imitate the fashion of the Huns. When they were admitted to the audience of Justinian, Candish, the first of the ambassadors, addressed the Roman emperor in these terms: "You see before you, O mighty prince, the representatives of the strongest and most populous of nations, the invincible, the irresistible Avars. We are willing to devote ourselves to your service: we are able to vanquish and destroy all the enemies who now disturb your repose. But we expect, as the price of our alliance, as the reward of our valor, precious gifts, annual subsidies, and fruitful possessions." At the time of this embassy, Justinian had reigned above thirty, he had lived above seventy-five years: his mind, as well as his body, was feeble and languid; and the conqueror of Africa and Italy, careless of the permanent interest of his people, aspired only to end his days in the bosom even of inglorious peace. In a studied oration, he imparted to the senate his resolution to dissemble the insult, and to purchase the friendship of the Avars; and the whole senate, like the mandarins of China, applauded the incomparable wisdom and foresight of their sovereign. The instruments of luxury were immediately prepared to captivate the Barbarians; silken garments, soft and splendid beds, and chains and collars incrusted with gold. The ambassadors, content with such liberal reception, departed from Constantinople, and Valentin, one of the emperor's guards, was sent with a similar character to their camp at the foot of Mount Caucasus. As their destruction or their success must be alike advantageous to the empire, he persuaded them to invade the enemies of Rome; and they were easily tempted, by gifts and promises, to gratify their ruling inclinations. These fugitives, who fled before the Turkish arms, passed the Tanais and Borysthenes, and boldly advanced into the heart of Poland and Germany, violating the law of nations, and abusing the rights of victory. Before ten years had elapsed, their camps were seated on the Danube and the Elbe, many Bulgarian and Sclavonian names were obliterated from the earth, and the remainder of their tribes are found, as tributaries and vassals, under the standard of the Avars. The chagan, the peculiar title of their king, still affected to cultivate the friendship of the emperor; and Justinian entertained some thoughts of fixing them in Pannonia, to balance the prevailing power of the Lombards. But the virtue or treachery of an Avar betrayed the secret enmity and ambitious designs of their countrymen; and they loudly complained of the timid, though jealous policy, of detaining their ambassadors, and denying the arms which they had been allowed to purchase in the capital of the empire. [34]

[Footnote 30/1: The Ogors or Varchonites, from Var. a river, (obviously connected with the name Avar,) must not be confounded with the Uigours, the eastern Turks, (v. Hammer, Osmanische Geschichte, vol. i. p. 3,) who speak a language the parent of the more modern Turkish dialects. Compare Klaproth, page 121. They are the ancestors of the Usbeck Turks. These Ogors were of the same Finnish race with the Huns; and the 20,000 families which fled towards the west, after the Turkish invasion, were of the same race with those which remained to the east of the Volga, the true Avars of Theophy fact—M.]

[Footnote 31: The River Til, or Tula, according to the geography of De Guignes, (tom. i. part ii. p. lviii. and 352,) is a small, though grateful, stream of the desert, that falls into the Orhon, Selinga, &c. See Bell, Journey from Petersburg to Pekin, (vol. ii. p. 124;) yet his own description of the Keat, down which he sailed into the Oby, represents the name and attributes of the black river, (p. 139.) Note: M. Klaproth, (Tableaux Historiques de l'Asie, p. 274) supposes this river to be an eastern affluent of the Volga, the Kama, which, from the color of its waters, might be called black. M. Abel Remusat (Recherchea sur les Langues Tartares, vol. i. p. 320) and M. St. Martin (vol. ix. p. 373) consider it the Volga, which is called Atel or Etel by all the Turkish tribes. It is called Attilas by Menander, and Ettilia by the monk Ruysbreek (1253.) See Klaproth, Tabl. Hist. p. 247. This geography is much more clear and simple than that adopted by Gibbon from De Guignes, or suggested from Bell—M.]

[Footnote 32: Theophylact, l. vii. c. 7, 8. And yet his true Avars are invisible even to the eyes of M. de Guignes; and what can be more illustrious than the false? The right of the fugitive Ogors to that national appellation is confessed by the Turks themselves, (Menander, p. 108.)]

[Footnote 33: The Alani are still found in the Genealogical History of the Tartars, (p. 617,) and in D'Anville's maps. They opposed the march of the generals of Zingis round the Caspian Sea, and were overthrown in a great battle, (Hist. de Gengiscan, l. iv. c. 9, p. 447.)]

[Footnote 34: The embassies and first conquests of the Avars may be read in Menander, (Excerpt. Legat. p. 99, 100, 101, 154, 155,) Theophanes, (p. 196,) the Historia Miscella, (l. xvi. p. 109,) and Gregory of Tours, (L iv. c. 23, 29, in the Historians of France, tom. ii. p. 214, 217.)]

Perhaps the apparent change in the dispositions of the emperors may be ascribed to the embassy which was received from the conquerors of the Avars. [35] The immense distance which eluded their arms could not extinguish their resentment: the Turkish ambassadors pursued the footsteps of the vanquished to the Jaik, the Volga, Mount Caucasus, the Euxine and Constantinople, and at length appeared before the successor of Constantine, to request that he would not espouse the cause of rebels and fugitives. Even commerce had some share in this remarkable negotiation: and the Sogdoites, who were now the tributaries of the Turks, embraced the fair occasion of opening, by the north of the Caspian, a new road for the importation of Chinese silk into the Roman empire. The Persian, who preferred the navigation of Ceylon, had stopped the caravans of Bochara and Samarcand: their silk was contemptuously burnt: some Turkish ambassadors died in Persia, with a suspicion of poison; and the great khan permitted his faithful vassal Maniach, the prince of the Sogdoites, to propose, at the Byzantine court, a treaty of alliance against their common enemies. Their splendid apparel and rich presents, the fruit of Oriental luxury, distinguished Maniach and his colleagues from the rude savages of the North: their letters, in the Scythian character and language, announced a people who had attained the rudiments of science: [36] they enumerated the conquests, they offered the friendship and military aid of the Turks; and their sincerity was attested by direful imprecations (if they were guilty of falsehood) against their own head, and the head of Disabul their master. The Greek prince entertained with hospitable regard the ambassadors of a remote and powerful monarch: the sight of silk-worms and looms disappointed the hopes of the Sogdoites; the emperor renounced, or seemed to renounce, the fugitive Avars, but he accepted the alliance of the Turks; and the ratification of the treaty was carried by a Roman minister to the foot of Mount Altai. Under the successors of Justinian, the friendship of the two nations was cultivated by frequent and cordial intercourse; the most favored vassals were permitted to imitate the example of the great khan, and one hundred and six Turks, who, on various occasions, had visited Constantinople, departed at the same time for their native country. The duration and length of the journey from the Byzantine court to Mount Altai are not specified: it might have been difficult to mark a road through the nameless deserts, the mountains, rivers, and morasses of Tartary; but a curious account has been preserved of the reception of the Roman ambassadors at the royal camp. After they had been purified with fire and incense, according to a rite still practised under the sons of Zingis, [36/1] they were introduced to the presence of Disabul. In a valley of the Golden Mountain, they found the great khan in his tent, seated in a chair with wheels, to which a horse might be occasionally harnessed. As soon as they had delivered their presents, which were received by the proper officers, they exposed, in a florid oration, the wishes of the Roman emperor, that victory might attend the arms of the Turks, that their reign might be long and prosperous, and that a strict alliance, without envy or deceit, might forever be maintained between the two most powerful nations of the earth. The answer of Disabul corresponded with these friendly professions, and the ambassadors were seated by his side, at a banquet which lasted the greatest part of the day: the tent was surrounded with silk hangings, and a Tartar liquor was served on the table, which possessed at least the intoxicating qualities of wine. The entertainment of the succeeding day was more sumptuous; the silk hangings of the second tent were embroidered in various figures; and the royal seat, the cups, and the vases, were of gold. A third pavilion was supported by columns of gilt wood; a bed of pure and massy gold was raised on four peacocks of the same metal: and before the entrance of the tent, dishes, basins, and statues of solid silver, and admirable art, were ostentatiously piled in wagons, the monuments of valor rather than of industry. When Disabul led his armies against the frontiers of Persia, his Roman allies followed many days the march of the Turkish camp, nor were they dismissed till they had enjoyed their precedency over the envoy of the great king, whose loud and intemperate clamors interrupted the silence of the royal banquet. The power and ambition of Chosroes cemented the union of the Turks and Romans, who touched his dominions on either side: but those distant nations, regardless of each other, consulted the dictates of interest, without recollecting the obligations of oaths and treaties. While the successor of Disabul celebrated his father's obsequies, he was saluted by the ambassadors of the emperor Tiberius, who proposed an invasion of Persia, and sustained, with firmness, the angry and perhaps the just reproaches of that haughty Barbarian. "You see my ten fingers," said the great khan, and he applied them to his mouth. "You Romans speak with as many tongues, but they are tongues of deceit and perjury. To me you hold one language, to my subjects another; and the nations are successively deluded by your perfidious eloquence. You precipitate your allies into war and danger, you enjoy their labors, and you neglect your benefactors. Hasten your return, inform your master that a Turk is incapable of uttering or forgiving falsehood, and that he shall speedily meet the punishment which he deserves. While he solicits my friendship with flattering and hollow words, he is sunk to a confederate of my fugitive Varchonites. If I condescend to march against those contemptible slaves, they will tremble at the sound of our whips; they will be trampled, like a nest of ants, under the feet of my innumerable cavalry. I am not ignorant of the road which they have followed to invade your empire; nor can I be deceived by the vain pretence, that Mount Caucasus is the impregnable barrier of the Romans. I know the course of the Niester, the Danube, and the Hebrus; the most warlike nations have yielded to the arms of the Turks; and from the rising to the setting sun, the earth is my inheritance." Notwithstanding this menace, a sense of mutual advantage soon renewed the alliance of the Turks and Romans: but the pride of the great khan survived his resentment; and when he announced an important conquest to his friend the emperor Maurice, he styled himself the master of the seven races, and the lord of the seven climates of the world. [37]

[Footnote 35: Theophanes, (Chron. p. 204,) and the Hist. Miscella, (l. xvi. p. 110,) as understood by De Guignes, (tom. i. part ii. p. 354,) appear to speak of a Turkish embassy to Justinian himself; but that of Maniach, in the fourth year of his successor Justin, is positively the first that reached Constantinople, (Menander p. 108.)]

[Footnote 36: The Russians have found characters, rude hieroglyphics, on the Irtish and Yenisei, on medals, tombs, idols, rocks, obelisks, &c., (Strahlenberg, Hist. of Siberia, p. 324, 346, 406, 429.) Dr. Hyde (de Religione Veterum Persarum, p. 521, &c.) has given two alphabets of Thibet and of the Eygours. I have long harbored a suspicion, that all the Scythian, and some, perhaps much, of the Indian science, was derived from the Greeks of Bactriana. Note: Modern discoveries give no confirmation to this suspicion. The character of Indian science, as well as of their literature and mythology, indicates an original source. Grecian art may have occasionally found its way into India. One or two of the sculptures in Col. Tod's account of the Jain temples, if correct, show a finer outline, and purer sense of beauty, than appears native to India, where the monstrous always predominated over simple nature—M.]

[Footnote 36/1: This rite is so curious, that I have subjoined the description of it:— When these (the exorcisers, the Shamans) approached Zemarchus, they took all our baggage and placed it in the centre. Then, kindling a fire with branches of frankincense, lowly murmuring certain barbarous words in the Scythian language, beating on a kind of bell (a gong) and a drum, they passed over the baggage the leaves of the frankincense, crackling with the fire, and at the same time themselves becoming frantic, *and violently leaping about, seemed to exorcise the evil spirits. Having thus as they thought, averted all evil, they led Zemarchus himself through the fire. Menander, in Niebuhr's Bryant. Hist. p. 381. Compare Carpini's Travels. The princes of the race of Zingis Khan condescended to receive the ambassadors of the king of France, at the end of the 13th century without their submitting to this humiliating rite. See Correspondence published by Abel Remusat, Nouv. Mem. de l'Acad des Inscrip. vol. vii. On the embassy of Zemarchus, compare Klaproth, Tableaux de l'Asie p. 116—M.]*

[Footnote 37: All the details of these Turkish and Roman embassies, so curious in the history of human manners, are drawn from the extracts of Menander, (p. 106—110, 151—154, 161-164,) in which we often regret the want of order and connection.]

Disputes have often arisen between the sovereigns of Asia for the title of king of the world; while the contest has proved that it could not belong to either of the competitors. The kingdom of the Turks was bounded by the Oxus or Gihon; and Touran was separated by that great river from the rival monarchy of Iran, or Persia, which in a smaller compass contained perhaps a larger measure of power and population. The Persians, who alternately invaded and repulsed the Turks and the Romans, were still ruled by the house of Sassan, which ascended the throne three hundred years before the accession of Justinian. His contemporary, Cabades, or Kobad, had been successful in war against the emperor Anastasius; but the reign of that prince was distracted by civil and religious troubles. A prisoner in the hands of his subjects, an exile among the enemies of Persia, he recovered his liberty by prostituting the honor of his wife, and regained his kingdom with the dangerous and mercenary aid of the Barbarians, who had slain his father. His nobles were suspicious that Kobad never forgave the authors of his expulsion, or even those of his restoration. The people was deluded and inflamed by the fanaticism of Mazdak, [38] who asserted the community of women, [39] and the equality of mankind, whilst he appropriated the richest lands and most beautiful females to the use of his sectaries. The view of these disorders, which had been fomented by his laws and example, [40] imbittered the declining age of the Persian monarch; and his fears were increased by the consciousness of his design to reverse the natural and customary order of succession, in favor of his third and most favored son, so famous under the names of Chosroes and Nushirvan. To render the youth more illustrious in the eyes of the nations, Kobad was desirous that he should be adopted by the emperor Justin: [40/1] the hope of peace inclined the Byzantine court to accept this singular proposal; and Chosroes might have acquired a specious claim to the inheritance of his Roman parent. But the future mischief was diverted by the advice of the quaestor Proclus: a difficulty was started, whether the adoption should be performed as a civil or military rite; [41] the treaty was abruptly dissolved; and the sense of this indignity sunk deep into the mind of Chosroes, who had already advanced to the Tigris on his road to Constantinople. His father did not long survive the disappointment of his wishes: the testament of their deceased sovereign was read in the assembly of the nobles; and a powerful faction, prepared for the event, and regardless of the priority of age, exalted Chosroes to the throne of Persia. He filled that throne during a prosperous period of forty-eight years; [42] and the Justice of Nushirvan is celebrated as the theme of immortal praise by the nations of the East.

[Footnote 38: See D'Herbelot, (Bibliot. Orient. p. 568, 929;) Hyde, (de Religione Vet. Persarum, c. 21, p. 290, 291;) Pocock, (Specimen Hist. Arab. p. 70, 71;) Eutychius, (Annal. tom. ii. p. 176;) Texeira, (in Stevens, Hist. of Persia, l. i. c. 34.) Note: Mazdak was an Archimagus, born, according to Mirkhond, (translated by De Sacy, p. 353, and Malcolm, vol. i. p. 104,) at Istakhar or Persepolis, according to an inedited and anonymous history, (the Modjmal-alte-warikh in the Royal Library at Paris, quoted by St. Martin, vol. vii. p. 322) at Wischapour in Chorasan: his father's name was Bamdadam. He announces himself as a reformer of Zoroastrianism, and carried the doctrine of the two principles to a much grater

height. He preached the absolute indifference of human action, perfect equality of rank, community of property and of women, marriages between the nearest kindred; he interdicted the use of animal food, proscribed the killing of animals for food, enforced a vegetable diet. See St. Martin, vol. vii. p. 322. Malcolm, vol. i. p. 104. Mirkhond translated by De Sacy. It is remarkable that the doctrine of Mazdak spread into the West. Two inscriptions found in Cyrene, in 1823, and explained by M. Gesenius, and by M. Hamaker of Leyden, prove clearly that his doctrines had been eagerly embraced by the remains of the ancient Gnostics; and Mazdak was enrolled with Thoth, Saturn, Zoroaster, Pythagoras, Epicurus, John, and Christ, as the teachers of true Gnostic wisdom. See St. Martin, vol. vii. p. 338. Gesenius de Inscriptione Phoenicio-Graeca in Cyrenaica nuper reperta, Halle, 1825. Hamaker, Lettre a M. Raoul Rochette, Leyden, 1825—M.]

[Footnote 39: The fame of the new law for the community of women was soon propagated in Syria (Asseman. Bibliot. Orient. tom. iii. p. 402) and Greece, (Procop. Persic. l. i. c. 5.)]

[Footnote 40: He offered his own wife and sister to the prophet; but the prayers of Nushirvan saved his mother, and the indignant monarch never forgave the humiliation to which his filial piety had stooped: pedes tuos deosculatus (said he to Mazdak,) cujus foetor adhuc nares occupat, (Pocock, Specimen Hist. Arab. p. 71.)]

[Footnote 40/1: St. Martin questions this adoption: he urges its improbability; and supposes that Procopius, perverting some popular traditions, or the remembrance of some fruitless negotiations which took place at that time, has mistaken, for a treaty of adoption some treaty of guaranty or protection for the purpose of insuring the crown, after the death of Kobad, to his favorite son Chosroes, vol. viii. p. 32. Yet the Greek historians seem unanimous as to the proposal: the Persians might be expected to maintain silence on such a subject—M.]

[Footnote 41: Procopius, Persic. l. i. c. 11. Was not Proclus over-wise? Was not the danger imaginary?— The excuse, at least, was injurious to a nation not ignorant of letters. Whether any mode of adoption was practised in Persia, I much doubt.]

[Footnote 42: From Procopius and Agathias, Pagi (tom. ii. p. 543, 626) has proved that Chosroes Nushirvan ascended the throne in the fifth year of Justinian, (A.D. 531, April 1—A.D. 532, April 1.) But the true chronology, which harmonizes with the Greeks and Orientals, is ascertained by John Malala, (tom. ii. 211.) Cabades, or Kobad, after a reign of forty-three years and two months, sickened the 8th, and died the 13th of September, A.D. 531, aged eighty-two years. According to the annals of Eutychius, Nushirvan reigned forty seven years and six months; and his death must consequently be placed in March, A.D. 579.]

But the justice of kings is understood by themselves, and even by their subjects, with an ample indulgence for the gratification of passion and interest. The virtue of Chosroes was that of a conqueror, who, in the measures of peace and war, is excited by ambition, and restrained by prudence; who confounds the greatness with the happiness of a nation, and calmly devotes the lives of thousands to the fame, or even the amusement, of a single man. In his domestic administration, the just Nushirvan would merit in our feelings the appellation of a tyrant. His two elder brothers had been deprived of their fair expectations of the diadem: their future life, between the supreme rank and the condition of subjects, was anxious to themselves and formidable to their master: fear as well as revenge might tempt them to rebel: the slightest evidence of a conspiracy satisfied the author of their wrongs; and the repose of Chosroes was secured by the death of these unhappy princes, with their families and adherents. One guiltless youth was saved and dismissed by the compassion of a veteran general; and this act of humanity, which was revealed by his son, overbalanced the merit of reducing twelve nations to the obedience of Persia. The zeal and prudence of Mebodes had fixed the diadem on the head of Chosroes himself; but he delayed to attend the royal summons, till he had performed the duties of a military review: he was instantly commanded to repair to the iron tripod, which stood before the gate of the palace, [43] where it was death to relieve or approach the victim; and Mebodes languished several days before his sentence was pronounced, by the inflexible pride and calm ingratitude of the son of Kobad. But the people, more especially in the East, is disposed to forgive, and even to applaud, the cruelty which strikes at the loftiest heads; at the slaves of ambition, whose voluntary choice has exposed them to live in the smiles, and to perish by the frown, of a capricious monarch. In the execution of the laws which he had no temptation to violate; in the punishment of crimes which attacked his own dignity, as well as the happiness of individuals; Nushirvan, or Chosroes, deserved the appellation of just. His government was firm, rigorous, and impartial. It was the first labor of his reign to abolish the dangerous theory of common or equal possessions: the lands and women which the sectaries of Mazdak has usurped were restored to their lawful owners; and the temperate [43/1] chastisement of the fanatics or impostors confirmed the domestic rights of society. Instead of listening with blind confidence to a favorite minister, he established four viziers over the four great provinces of his empire, Assyria, Media, Persia, and Bactriana. In the choice of judges, praefects, and counsellors, he strove to remove the mask which is always worn in the presence of kings: he wished to substitute the natural order of talents for the accidental distinctions of birth and fortune; he professed, in specious language, his intention to prefer those men who carried the poor in their bosoms, and to banish corruption from the seat of justice, as dogs were excluded from the temples of the Magi. The code of laws of the first Artaxerxes was revived and published as the rule of the magistrates; but the assurance of speedy punishment was the best security of their virtue. Their behavior was inspected by a thousand eyes, their words were overheard by a thousand ears, the secret or public agents of the throne; and the provinces, from the Indian to the Arabian confines, were enlightened by the frequent visits of a sovereign, who affected to emulate his celestial brother in his rapid and salutary career. Education and agriculture he viewed as the two objects most deserving of his care. In every city of Persia orphans, and the children of the poor, were maintained and instructed at the public expense; the daughters were given in marriage to the richest citizens of their own rank, and the sons, according to their different talents, were employed in mechanic trades, or promoted to more honorable service. The deserted villages were relieved by his bounty; to the peasants and farmers who were found incapable of cultivating their lands, he distributed cattle, seed, and the instruments of husbandry; and the rare and inestimable treasure of fresh water was parsimoniously managed, and skilfully dispersed over the arid territory of Persia. [44] The prosperity of that kingdom was the effect and evidence of his virtues; his vices are those of Oriental despotism; but in the long competition between Chosroes and Justinian, the advantage both of merit and fortune is almost always on the side of the Barbarian. [45]

[Footnote 43: Procopius, Persic. l. i. c. 23. Brisson, de Regn. Pers. p. 494. The gate of the palace of Ispahan is, or was, the fatal scene of disgrace or death, (Chardin, Voyage en Perse, tom. iv. p. 312, 313.)]

[Footnote 43/1: This is a strange term. Nushirvan employed a stratagem similar to that of Jehu, 2 Kings, x. 18—28, to separate the followers of Mazdak from the rest of his subjects, and with a body of his troops cut them all in pieces. The Greek writers concur with the Persian in this representation of Nushirvan's temperate conduct. Theophanes, p. 146. Mirkhond. p. 362. Eutychius, Ann. vol. ii. p. 179. Abulfeda, in an unedited part, consulted by St. Martin as well as in a passage formerly cited. Le Beau vol. viii. p. 38. Malcolm vol I p. 109—M.]

[Footnote 44: In Persia, the prince of the waters is an officer of state. The number of wells and subterraneous channels is much diminished, and with it the fertility of the soil: 400 wells have been recently lost near Tauris, and 42,000 were once reckoned in the province of Khorasan (Chardin, tom. iii. p. 99, 100. Tavernier, tom. i. p. 416.)]

[Footnote 45: The character and government of Nushirvan is represented some times in the words of D'Herbelot, (Bibliot. Orient. p. 680, &c., from Khondemir,) Eutychius, (Annal. tom. ii. p. 179, 180,—very rich,) Abulpharagius, (Dynast. vii. p. 94, 95,—very poor,) Tarikh Schikard, (p. 144—150,) Texeira, (in Stevens, l. i. c. 35,) Asseman, (Bibliot Orient. tom. iii. p. 404-410,) and the Abbe Fourmont, (Hist. de l'Acad. des Inscriptions, tom. vii. p. 325—334,) who has translated a spurious or genuine testament of Nushirvan.]

To the praise of justice Nushirvan united the reputation of knowledge; and the seven Greek philosophers, who visited his court, were invited and deceived by the strange assurance, that a disciple of Plato was seated on the Persian throne. Did they expect, that a prince, strenuously exercised in the toils of war and government, should agitate, with dexterity like their own, the abstruse and profound questions which amused the leisure of the schools of Athens? Could they hope that the precepts of philosophy should direct the life, and control the passions, of a despot, whose infancy had been taught to consider his absolute and fluctuating will as the only rule of moral obligation? [46] The studies of Chosroes were ostentatious and superficial: but his example awakened the curiosity of an ingenious people, and the light of science was diffused over the dominions of Persia. [47] At Gondi Sapor, in the neighborhood of the royal city of Susa, an academy of physic was founded, which insensibly became a liberal school of poetry, philosophy, and rhetoric. [48] The annals of the monarchy [49] were composed; and while recent and authentic history might afford some useful lessons both to the prince and people, the darkness of the first ages was embellished by the giants, the dragons, and the fabulous heroes of Oriental romance. [50] Every learned or confident stranger was enriched by the bounty, and flattered by the conversation, of the monarch: he nobly rewarded a Greek physician, [51] by the deliverance of three thousand, captives; and the sophists, who contended for his favor, were exasperated by the wealth and insolence of Uranius, their more successful rival. Nushirvan believed, or at least respected, the religion of the Magi; and some traces of persecution may be discovered in his reign. [52] Yet he allowed himself freely to compare the tenets of the various sects; and the theological disputes, in which he frequently presided, diminished the authority of the priest, and enlightened the minds of the people. At his command, the most celebrated writers of Greece and India were translated into the Persian language; a smooth and elegant idiom, recommended by Mahomet to the use of paradise; though it is branded with the epithets of savage and unmusical, by the ignorance and presumption of Agathias. [53] Yet the Greek historian might reasonably wonder that it should be found possible to execute an entire version of Plato and Aristotle in a foreign dialect, which had not been framed to express the spirit of freedom and the subtilties of philosophic disquisition. And, if the reason of the Stagyrite might be equally dark, or equally intelligible in every tongue, the dramatic art and verbal argumentation of the disciple of Socrates, [54] appear to be indissolubly mingled with the grace and perfection of his Attic style. In the search of universal knowledge, Nushirvan was informed, that the moral and political fables of Pilpay, an ancient Brachman, were preserved with jealous reverence among the treasures of the kings of India. The physician Perozes was secretly despatched to the banks of the Ganges, with instructions to procure, at any price, the communication of this valuable work. His dexterity obtained a transcript, his learned diligence accomplished the translation; and the fables of Pilpay [55] were read and admired in the assembly of Nushirvan and his nobles. The Indian original, and the Persian copy, have long since disappeared; but this venerable monument has been saved by the curiosity of the Arabian caliphs, revived in the modern Persic, the Turkish, the Syriac, the Hebrew, and the Greek idioms, and transfused through successive versions into the modern languages of Europe. In their present form, the peculiar character, the manners and religion of the Hindoos, are completely obliterated; and the intrinsic merit of the fables of Pilpay is far inferior to the concise elegance of Phaedrus, and the native graces of La Fontaine. Fifteen moral and political sentences are illustrated in a series of apologues: but the composition is intricate, the narrative prolix, and the precept obvious and barren. Yet the Brachman may assume the merit of inventing a pleasing fiction, which adorns the nakedness of truth, and alleviates, perhaps, to a royal ear, the harshness of instruction. With a similar design, to admonish kings that they are strong only in the strength of their subjects, the same Indians invented the game of chess, which was likewise introduced into Persia under the reign of Nushirvan. [56]

[Footnote 46: A thousand years before his birth, the judges of Persia had given a solemn opinion, (Herodot. l. iii. c. 31, p. 210, edit. Wesseling.) Nor had this constitutional maxim been neglected as a useless and barren theory.]

[Footnote 47: On the literary state of Persia, the Greek versions, philosophers, sophists, the learning or ignorance of Chosroes, Agathias (l. ii. c. 66—71) displays much information and strong prejudices.]

[Footnote 48: Asseman. Bibliot. Orient. tom. iv. p. DCCXLV. vi. vii.]

[Footnote 49: The Shah Nameh, or Book of Kings, is perhaps the original record of history which was translated into Greek by the interpreter Sergius, (Agathias, l. v. p. 141,) preserved after the Mahometan conquest, and versified in the year 994, by the national poet Ferdoussi. See D'Anquetil (Mem. de l'Academie, tom. xxxi. p. 379) and Sir William Jones, (Hist. of Nadir Shah, p. 161.)]

[Footnote 50: In the fifth century, the name of Restom, or Rostam, a hero who equalled the strength of twelve elephants, was familiar to the Armenians, (Moses Chorenensis, Hist. Armen. l. ii. c. 7, p. 96, edit. Whiston.) In the beginning of the seventh, the Persian Romance of Rostam and Isfendiar was applauded at Mecca, (Sale's Koran, c. xxxi. p. 335.) Yet this exposition of ludicrum novae historiae is not given by Maracci, (Refutat. Alcoran. p. 544—548.)]

[Footnote 51: Procop. (Goth. l. iv. c. 10.) Kobad had a favorite Greek physician, Stephen of Edessa, (Persic. l. ii. c. 26.) The practice was ancient; and Herodotus relates the adventures of Democedes of Crotona, (l. iii p. 125—137.)]

[Footnote 52: See Pagi, tom. ii. p. 626. In one of the treaties an honorable article was inserted for the toleration and burial of the Catholics, (Menander, in Excerpt. Legat. p. 142.) Nushizad, a son of Nushirvan, was a Christian, a rebel, and—a martyr? (D'Herbelot, p. 681.)]

[Footnote 53: On the Persian language, and its three dialects, consult D'Anquetil (p. 339—343) and Jones, (p. 153—185:) is the character which Agathias (l. ii. p. 66) ascribes to an idiom renowned in the East for poetical softness.]

[Footnote 54: Agathias specifies the Gorgias, Phaedon, Parmenides, and Timaeus. Renaudot (Fabricius, Bibliot. Graec. tom. xii. p. 246—261) does not mention this Barbaric version of Aristotle.]

[Footnote 55: Of these fables, I have seen three copies in three different languages: 1. In Greek, translated by Simeon Seth (A.D. 1100) from the Arabic, and published by Starck at Berlin in 1697, in 12mo. 2. In Latin, a version from the Greek Sapientia Indorum, inserted by Pere Poussin at the end of his edition of Pachymer, (p. 547—620, edit. Roman.) 3. In French, from the Turkish, dedicated, in 1540, to Sultan Soliman Contes et Fables Indiennes de Bidpai et de Lokman, par Mm. Galland et Cardonne, Paris, 1778, 3 vols. in 12mo. Mr. Warton (History of English Poetry, vol. i. p. 129—131) takes a larger scope. Note: The oldest Indian collection extant is the Pancha-tantra, (the five collections,) analyzed by Mr. Wilson in the Transactions of the Royal Asiat. Soc. It was translated into Persian by Barsuyah, the physician of Nushirvan, under the name of the Fables of Bidpai, (Vidyapriya, the Friend of Knowledge, or, as the Oriental writers understand it, the Friend of Medicine.) It was translated into Arabic by Abdolla Ibn Mokaffa, under the name of Kalila and Dimnah. From the Arabic it passed into the European languages. Compare Wilson, in Trans. As. Soc. i. 52. dohlen, das alte Indien, ii. p. 386. Silvestre de Sacy, Memoire sur Kalila vs Dimnah—M.]

[Footnote 56: See the Historia Shahiludii of Dr. Hyde, (Syntagm. Dissertat. tom. ii. p. 61—69.)]

PART III

The son of Kobad found his kingdom involved in a war with the successor of Constantine; and the anxiety of his domestic situation inclined him to grant the suspension of arms, which Justinian was impatient to purchase. Chosroes saw the Roman ambassadors at his feet. He accepted eleven thousand pounds of gold, as the price of an endless or indefinite peace: [57] some mutual exchanges were regulated; the Persian assumed the guard of the gates of Caucasus, and the demolition of Dara was suspended, on condition that it should never be made the residence of the general of the East. This interval of repose had been solicited, and was diligently improved, by the ambition of the emperor: his African conquests were the first fruits of the Persian treaty; and the avarice of Chosroes was soothed by a large portion of the spoils of Carthage, which his ambassadors required in a tone of pleasantry and under the color of friendship. [58] But the trophies of Belisarius disturbed the slumbers of the great king; and he heard with astonishment, envy, and fear, that Sicily, Italy, and Rome itself, had been reduced, in three rapid campaigns, to the obedience of Justinian. Unpractised in the art of violating treaties, he secretly excited his bold and subtle vassal Almondar. That prince of the Saracens, who resided at Hira, [59] had not been included in the general peace, and still waged an obscure war against his rival Arethas, the chief of the tribe of Gassan, and confederate of the empire. The subject of their dispute was an extensive sheep-walk in the desert to the south of Palmyra. An immemorial tribute for the license of pasture appeared to attest the rights of Almondar, while the Gassanite appealed to the Latin name of strata, a paved road, as an unquestionable evidence of the sovereignty and labors of the Romans. [60] The two monarchs supported the cause of their respective vassals; and the Persian Arab, without expecting the event of a slow and doubtful arbitration, enriched his flying camp with the spoil and captives of Syria. Instead of repelling the arms, Justinian attempted to seduce the fidelity of Almondar, while he called from the extremities of the earth the nations of Aethiopia and Scythia to invade the dominions of his rival. But the aid of such allies was distant and precarious, and the discovery of this hostile correspondence justified the complaints of the Goths and Armenians, who implored, almost at the same time, the protection of Chosroes. The descendants of Arsaces, who were still numerous in Armenia, had been provoked to assert the last relics of national freedom and hereditary rank; and the ambassadors of Vitiges had secretly traversed the empire to expose the instant, and almost inevitable, danger of the kingdom of Italy. Their representations were uniform, weighty, and effectual. "We stand before your throne, the advocates of your interest as well as of our own. The ambitious and faithless Justinian aspires to be the sole master of the world. Since the endless peace, which betrayed the common freedom of mankind, that prince, your ally in words, your enemy in actions, has alike insulted his friends and foes, and has filled the earth with blood and confusion. Has he not violated the privileges of Armenia, the independence of Colchos, and the wild liberty of the Tzanian mountains? Has he not usurped, with equal avidity, the city of Bosphorus on the frozen Maeotis, and the vale of palm-trees on the shores of the Red Sea? The Moors, the Vandals, the Goths, have been successively oppressed, and each nation has calmly remained the spectator of their neighbor's ruin. Embrace, O king! the favorable moment; the East is left without defence, while the armies of Justinian and his renowned general are detained in the distant regions of the West. If you hesitate or delay, Belisarius and his victorious troops will soon return from the Tyber to the Tigris, and Persia may enjoy the wretched consolation of being the last devoured." [61] By such arguments, Chosroes was easily persuaded to imitate the example which he condemned: but the Persian, ambitious of military fame, disdained the inactive warfare of a rival, who issued his sanguinary commands from the secure station of the Byzantine palace. [Footnote 57: The endless peace (Procopius, Persic. l. i. c. 21) was concluded or ratified in the vith year, and iiid consulship, of Justinian, (A.D. 533, between January 1 and April 1. Pagi, tom. ii. p. 550.) Marcellinus, in his Chronicle, uses the style of Medes and Persians.]

[Footnote 58: Procopius, Persic. l. i. c. 26.]

[Footnote 59: Almondar, king of Hira, was deposed by Kobad, and restored by Nushirvan. His mother, from her beauty, was surnamed Celestial Water, an appellation which became hereditary, and was extended for a more noble cause (liberality in famine) to the Arab princes of Syria, (Pocock, Specimen Hist. Arab. p. 69, 70.)]

[Footnote 60: Procopius, Persic. l. ii. c. 1. We are ignorant of the origin and object of this strata, a paved road of ten days' journey from Auranitis to Babylonia. (See a Latin note in Delisle's Map Imp. Orient.) Wesseling and D'Anville are silent.]

[Footnote 61: I have blended, in a short speech, the two orations of the Arsacides of Armenia and the Gothic ambassadors. Procopius, in his public history, feels, and makes us feel, that Justinian was the true author of the war, (Persic. l. ii. c. 2, 3.)]

Whatever might be the provocations of Chosroes, he abused the confidence of treaties; and the just reproaches of dissimulation and falsehood could only be concealed by the lustre of his victories. [62] The Persian army, which had been assembled in the plains of Babylon, prudently declined the strong cities of Mesopotamia, and followed the western bank of the Euphrates, till the small, though populous, town of Dura [62/1] presumed to arrest the progress of the great king. The gates of Dura, by treachery and surprise, were burst open; and as soon as Chosroes had stained his cimeter with the blood of the inhabitants, he dismissed the ambassador of Justinian to inform his master in what place he had left the enemy of the Romans. The conqueror still affected the praise of humanity and justice; and as he beheld a noble matron with her infant rudely dragged along the ground, he sighed, he wept, and implored the divine justice to punish the author of these calamities. Yet the herd of twelve thousand captives was ransomed for two hundred pounds of gold; the neighboring bishop of Sergiopolis pledged his faith for the payment: and in the subsequent year the unfeeling avarice of Chosroes exacted the penalty of an obligation which it was generous to contract and impossible to discharge. He advanced into the heart of Syria: but a feeble enemy, who vanished at his approach, disappointed him of the honor of victory; and as he could not hope to establish his dominion, the Persian king displayed in this inroad the mean and rapacious vices of a robber. Hierapolis, Berrhaea or Aleppo, Apamea and Chalcis, were successively besieged: they redeemed their safety by a ransom of gold or silver, proportioned to their respective strength and opulence; and their new master enforced, without observing, the terms of capitulation.

Educated in the religion of the Magi, he exercised, without remorse, the lucrative trade of sacrilege; and, after stripping of its gold and gems a piece of the true cross, he generously restored the naked relic to the devotion of the Christians of Apamea. No more than fourteen years had elapsed since Antioch was ruined by an earthquake; [62/2] but the queen of the East, the new Theopolis, had been raised from the ground by the liberality of Justinian; and the increasing greatness of the buildings and the people already erased the memory of this recent disaster. On one side, the city was defended by the mountain, on the other by the River Orontes; but the most accessible part was commanded by a superior eminence: the proper remedies were rejected, from the despicable fear of discovering its weakness to the enemy; and Germanus, the emperor's nephew, refused to trust his person and dignity within the walls of a besieged city. The people of Antioch had inherited the vain and satirical genius of their ancestors: they were elated by a sudden reenforcement of six thousand soldiers; they disdained the offers of an easy capitulation and their intemperate clamors insulted from the ramparts the majesty of the great king. Under his eye the Persian myriads mounted with scaling-ladders to the assault; the Roman mercenaries fled through the opposite gate of Daphne; and the generous assistance of the youth of Antioch served only to aggravate the miseries of their country. As Chosroes, attended by the ambassadors of Justinian, was descending from the mountain, he affected, in a plaintive voice, to deplore the obstinacy and ruin of that unhappy people; but the slaughter still raged with unrelenting fury; and the city, at the command of a Barbarian, was delivered to the flames. The cathedral of Antioch was indeed preserved by the avarice, not the piety, of the conqueror: a more honorable exemption was granted to the church of St. Julian, and the quarter of the town where the ambassadors resided; some distant streets were saved by the shifting of the wind, and the walls still subsisted to protect, and soon to betray, their new inhabitants. Fanaticism had defaced the ornaments of Daphne, but Chosroes breathed a purer air amidst her groves and fountains; and some idolaters in his train might sacrifice with impunity to the nymphs of that elegant retreat. Eighteen miles below Antioch, the River Orontes falls into the Mediterranean. The haughty Persian visited the term of his conquests; and, after bathing alone in the sea, he offered a solemn sacrifice of thanksgiving to the sun, or rather to the Creator of the sun, whom the Magi adored. If this act of superstition offended the prejudices of the Syrians, they were pleased by the courteous and even eager attention with which he assisted at the games of the circus; and as Chosroes had heard that the blue faction was espoused by the emperor, his peremptory command secured the victory of the green charioteer. From the discipline of his camp the people derived more solid consolation; and they interceded in vain for the life of a soldier who had too faithfully copied the rapine of the just Nushirvan. At length, fatigued, though unsatiated, with the spoil of Syria, [62/3] he slowly moved to the Euphrates, formed a temporary bridge in the neighborhood of Barbalissus, and defined the space of three days for the entire passage of his numerous host. After his return, he founded, at the distance of one day's journey from the palace of Ctesiphon, a new city, which perpetuated the joint names of Chosroes and of Antioch. The Syrian captives recognized the form and situation of their native abodes: baths and a stately circus were constructed for their use; and a colony of musicians and charioteers revived in Assyria the pleasures of a Greek capital. By the munificence of the royal founder, a liberal allowance was assigned to these fortunate exiles; and they enjoyed the singular privilege of bestowing freedom on the slaves whom they acknowledged as their kinsmen. Palestine, and the holy wealth of Jerusalem, were the next objects that attracted the ambition, or rather the avarice, of Chosroes. Constantinople, and the palace of the Caesars, no longer appeared impregnable or remote; and his aspiring fancy already covered Asia Minor with the troops, and the Black Sea with the navies, of Persia.

[Footnote 62: The invasion of Syria, the ruin of Antioch, &c., are related in a full and regular series by Procopius, (Persic. l. ii. c. 5—14.) Small collateral aid can be drawn from the Orientals: yet not they, but D'Herbelot himself, (p. 680,) should blush when he blames them for making Justinian and Nushirvan

contemporaries. On the geography of the seat of war, D'Anville (l'Euphrate et le Tigre) is sufficient and satisfactory.]

[Footnote 62/1: It is Sura in Procopius. Is it a misprint in Gibbon?—M.]

[Footnote 62/2: Joannes Lydus attributes the easy capture of Antioch to the want of fortifications which had not been restored since the earthquake, l. iii. c. 54. p. 246—M.]

[Footnote 62/3: Lydus asserts that he carried away all the statues, pictures, and marbles which adorned the city, l. iii. c. 54, p. 246—M.]

These hopes might have been realized, if the conqueror of Italy had not been seasonably recalled to the defence of the East. [63] While Chosroes pursued his ambitious designs on the coast of the Euxine, Belisarius, at the head of an army without pay or discipline, encamped beyond the Euphrates, within six miles of Nisibis. He meditated, by a skilful operation, to draw the Persians from their impregnable citadel, and improving his advantage in the field, either to intercept their retreat, or perhaps to enter the gates with the flying Barbarians. He advanced one day's journey on the territories of Persia, reduced the fortress of Sisaurane, and sent the governor, with eight hundred chosen horsemen, to serve the emperor in his Italian wars. He detached Arethas and his Arabs, supported by twelve hundred Romans, to pass the Tigris, and to ravage the harvests of Assyria, a fruitful province, long exempt from the calamities of war. But the plans of Belisarius were disconcerted by the untractable spirit of Arethas, who neither returned to the camp, nor sent any intelligence of his motions. The Roman general was fixed in anxious expectation to the same spot; the time of action elapsed, the ardent sun of Mesopotamia inflamed with fevers the blood of his European soldiers; and the stationary troops and officers of Syria affected to tremble for the safety of their defenceless cities. Yet this diversion had already succeeded in forcing Chosroes to return with loss and precipitation; and if the skill of Belisarius had been seconded by discipline and valor, his success might have satisfied the sanguine wishes of the public, who required at his hands the conquest of Ctesiphon, and the deliverance of the captives of Antioch. At the end of the campaign, he was recalled to Constantinople by an ungrateful court, but the dangers of the ensuing spring restored his confidence and command; and the hero, almost alone, was despatched, with the speed of post-horses, to repel, by his name and presence, the invasion of Syria. He found the Roman generals, among whom was a nephew of Justinian, imprisoned by their fears in the fortifications of Hierapolis. But instead of listening to their timid counsels, Belisarius commanded them to follow him to Europus, where he had resolved to collect his forces, and to execute whatever God should inspire him to achieve against the enemy. His firm attitude on the banks of the Euphrates restrained Chosroes from advancing towards Palestine; and he received with art and dignity the ambassadors, or rather spies, of the Persian monarch. The plain between Hierapolis and the river was covered with the squadrons of cavalry, six thousand hunters, tall and robust, who pursued their game without the apprehension of an enemy. On the opposite bank the ambassadors descried a thousand Armenian horse, who appeared to guard the passage of the Euphrates. The tent of Belisarius was of the coarsest linen, the simple equipage of a warrior who disdained the luxury of the East. Around his tent, the nations who marched under his standard were arranged with skilful confusion. The Thracians and Illyrians were posted in the front, the Heruli and Goths in the centre; the prospect was closed by the Moors and Vandals, and their loose array seemed to multiply their numbers. Their dress was light and active; one soldier carried a whip, another a sword, a third a bow, a fourth, perhaps, a battle axe, and the whole picture exhibited the intrepidity of the troops and the vigilance of the general. Chosroes was deluded by the address, and awed by the genius, of the lieutenant of Justinian. Conscious of the merit, and ignorant of the force, of his antagonist, he dreaded a decisive battle in a distant country, from whence not a Persian might return to relate the melancholy tale. The great king hastened to repass the Euphrates; and Belisarius pressed his retreat, by affecting to oppose a measure so salutary to the empire, and which could scarcely have been prevented by an army of a hundred thousand men. Envy might suggest to ignorance and pride, that the public enemy had been suffered to escape: but the African and Gothic triumphs are less glorious than this safe and bloodless victory, in which neither fortune, nor the valor of the soldiers, can subtract any part of the general's renown. The second removal of Belisarius from the Persian to the Italian war revealed the extent of his personal merit, which had corrected or supplied the want of discipline and courage. Fifteen generals, without concert or skill, led through the mountains of Armenia an army of thirty thousand Romans, inattentive to their signals, their ranks, and their ensigns. Four thousand Persians, intrenched in the camp of Dubis, vanquished, almost without a combat, this disorderly multitude; their useless arms were scattered along the road, and their horses sunk under the fatigue of their rapid flight. But the Arabs of the Roman party prevailed over their brethren; the Armenians returned to their allegiance; the cities of Dara and Edessa resisted a sudden assault and a regular siege, and the calamities of war were suspended by those of pestilence. A tacit or formal agreement between the two sovereigns protected the tranquillity of the Eastern frontier; and the arms of Chosroes were confined to the Colchian or Lazic war, which has been too minutely described by the historians of the times. [64]

[Footnote 63: In the public history of Procopius, (Persic. l. ii. c. 16, 18, 19, 20, 21, 24, 25, 26, 27, 28;) and, with some slight exceptions, we may reasonably shut our ears against the malevolent whisper of the Anecdotes, (c. 2, 3, with the Notes, as usual, of Alemannus.)]

[Footnote 64: The Lazic war, the contest of Rome and Persia on the Phasis, is tediously spun through many a page of Procopius (Persic. l. ii. c. 15, 17, 28, 29, 30.) Gothic. (l. iv. c. 7—16) and Agathias, (l. ii. iii. and iv. p. 55—132, 141.)]

The extreme length of the Euxine Sea [65] from Constantinople to the mouth of the Phasis, may be computed as a voyage of nine days, and a measure of seven hundred miles. From the Iberian Caucasus, the most lofty and craggy mountains of Asia, that river descends with such oblique vehemence, that in a short space it is traversed by one hundred and twenty bridges. Nor does the stream become placid and navigable, till it reaches the town of Sarapana, five days' journey from the Cyrus, which flows from the same hills, but in a contrary direction to the Caspian Lake. The proximity of these rivers has suggested the practice, or at least the idea, of wafting the precious merchandise of India down the Oxus, over the Caspian, up the Cyrus, and with the current of the Phasis into the Euxine and Mediterranean Seas. As it successively collects the streams of the plain of Colchos, the Phasis moves with diminished speed, though accumulated weight. At the mouth it is sixty fathom deep, and half a league broad, but a small woody island is interposed in the midst of the channel; the water, so soon as it has deposited an earthy or metallic sediment, floats on the surface of the waves, and is no longer susceptible of corruption. In a course of one hundred miles, forty of which are navigable for large vessels, the Phasis divides the celebrated region of Colchos, [66] or Mingrelia, [67] which, on three sides, is fortified by the Iberian and Armenian mountains, and whose maritime coast extends about two hundred miles from the neighborhood of Trebizond to Dioscurias and the confines of Circassia. Both the soil and climate are relaxed by excessive moisture: twenty-eight rivers, besides the Phasis and his dependent streams, convey their waters to the sea; and the hollowness of the ground appears to indicate the subterraneous channels between the Euxine and the Caspian. In the fields where wheat or barley is sown, the earth is too soft to sustain the action of the plough; but the gom, a small grain, not unlike the millet or coriander seed, supplies the ordinary food of the people; and the use of bread is confined to the prince and his nobles. Yet the vintage is more plentiful than the harvest; and the bulk of the stems, as well as the quality of the wine, display the unassisted powers of nature. The same powers continually tend to overshadow the face of the country with thick forests; the timber of the hills, and the flax of the plains, contribute to the abundance of naval stores; the wild and tame animals, the horse, the ox, and the hog, are remarkably prolific, and the name of the pheasant is expressive of his native habitation on the banks of the Phasis. The gold mines to the south of Trebizond, which are still worked with sufficient profit, were a subject of national dispute between Justinian and Chosroes; and it is not unreasonable to believe, that a vein of precious metal may be equally diffused through the circle of the hills, although these secret treasures are neglected by the laziness, or concealed by the prudence, of the Mingrelians. The waters, impregnated with particles of gold, are carefully strained through sheep-skins or fleeces; but this expedient, the groundwork perhaps of a marvellous fable, affords a faint image of the wealth extracted from a virgin earth by the power and industry of ancient kings. Their silver palaces and golden chambers surpass our belief; but the fame of their riches is said to have excited the enterprising avarice of the Argonauts. [68] Tradition has affirmed, with some color of reason, that Egypt planted on the Phasis a learned and polite colony, [69] which manufactured linen, built navies, and invented geographical maps. The ingenuity of the moderns has peopled, with flourishing cities and nations, the isthmus between the Euxine and the Caspian; [70] and a lively writer, observing the resemblance of climate, and, in his apprehension, of trade, has not hesitated to pronounce Colchos the Holland of antiquity. [71]

[Footnote 65: The Periplus, or circumnavigation of the Euxine Sea, was described in Latin by Sallust, and in Greek by Arrian: l. The former work, which no longer exists, has been restored by the singular diligence of M. de Brosses, first president of the parliament of Dijon, (Hist. de la Republique Romaine, tom. ii. l. iii. p. 199—298,) who ventures to assume the character of the Roman historian. His description of the Euxine is ingeniously formed of all the fragments of the original, and of all the Greeks and Latins whom Sallust might copy, or by whom he might be copied; and the merit of the execution atones for the whimsical design. 2. The Periplus of Arrian is addressed to the emperor Hadrian, (in Geograph. Minor. Hudson, tom. i.,) and contains whatever the governor of Pontus had seen from Trebizond to Dioscurias; whatever he had heard from Dioscurias to the Danube; and whatever he knew from the Danube to Trebizond.]

[Footnote 66: Besides the many occasional hints from the poets, historians &c., of antiquity, we may consult the geographical descriptions of Colchos, by Strabo (l. xi. p. 760—765) and Pliny, (Hist. Natur. vi. 5, 19, &c.)]

[Footnote 67: I shall quote, and have used, three modern descriptions of Mingrelia and the adjacent countries. 1. Of the Pere Archangeli Lamberti, (Relations de Thevenot, part i. p. 31-52, with a map,) who has all the knowledge and prejudices of a missionary. 2. Of Chardia, (Voyages en Perse, tom. i. p. 54, 68-168.) His observations are judicious and his own adventures in the country are still more instructive than his observations. 3. Of Peyssonel, (Observations sur les Peuples Barbares, p. 49, 50, 51, 58 62, 64, 65, 71, &c., and a more recent treatise, Sur le Commerce de la Mer Noire, tom. ii. p. 1—53.) He had long resided at Caffa, as consul of France; and his erudition is less valuable than his experience.]

[Footnote 68: Pliny, Hist. Natur. l. xxxiii. 15. The gold and silver mines of Colchos attracted the Argonauts, (Strab. l. i. p. 77.) The sagacious Chardin could find no gold in mines, rivers, or elsewhere. Yet a Mingrelian lost his hand and foot for showing some specimens at Constantinople of native gold]

[Footnote 69: Herodot. l. ii. c. 104, 105, p. 150, 151. Diodor. Sicul. l. i. p. 33, edit. Wesseling. Dionys. Perieget. 689, and Eustath. ad loc. Schohast ad Apollonium Argonaut. l. iv. 282-291.]

[Footnote 70: Montesquieu, Esprit des Loix, l. xxi. c. 6. L'Isthme... couvero de villes et nations qui ne sont plus.]

[Footnote 71: Bougainville, Memoires de l'Academie des Inscriptions, tom. xxvi. p. 33, on the African voyage of Hanno and the commerce of antiquity.]

But the riches of Colchos shine only through the darkness of conjecture or tradition; and its genuine history presents a uniform scene of rudeness and poverty. If one hundred and thirty languages were spoken in the market of Dioscurias, [72] they were the imperfect idioms of so many savage tribes or families, sequestered from each other in the valleys of Mount Caucasus; and their separation, which diminished the importance, must have multiplied the number, of their rustic capitals. In the present state of Mingrelia, a village is an assemblage of huts within a wooden fence; the fortresses are seated in the depths of forests; the princely town of Cyta, or Cotatis, consists of two hundred houses, and a stone edifice appertains only to the magnificence of kings. Twelve ships from Constantinople, and about sixty barks, laden with the fruits of industry, annually cast anchor on the coast; and the list of Colchian exports is much increased, since the natives had only slaves and hides to offer in exchange for the corn and salt which they purchased from the subjects of Justinian. Not a vestige can be found of the art, the knowledge, or the navigation, of the ancient Colchians: few Greeks desired or dared to pursue the footsteps of the Argonauts; and even the marks of an Egyptian colony are lost on a nearer approach. The rite of circumcision is practised only by the Mahometans of the Euxine; and the curled hair and swarthy complexion of Africa no longer disfigure the most perfect of the human race. It is in the adjacent climates of Georgia, Mingrelia, and Circassia, that nature has placed, at least to our eyes, the model of beauty in the shape of the limbs, the color of the skin, the symmetry of the features, and the expression of the countenance. [73] According to the destination of the two sexes, the men seemed formed for action, the women for love; and the perpetual supply of females from Mount Caucasus has purified the blood, and improved the breed, of the southern nations of Asia. The proper district of Mingrelia, a portion only of the ancient Colchos, has long sustained an exportation of twelve thousand slaves. The number of prisoners or criminals would be inadequate to the annual demand; but the common people are in a state of servitude to their lords; the exercise of fraud or rapine is unpunished in a lawless community; and the market is continually replenished by the abuse of civil and paternal authority. Such a trade, [74] which reduces the human species to the level of cattle, may tend to encourage marriage and population, since the multitude of children enriches their sordid and inhuman parent. But this source of impure wealth must inevitably poison the national manners, obliterate the sense of honor and virtue, and almost extinguish the instincts of nature: the Christians of Georgia and Mingrelia are the most dissolute of mankind; and their children, who, in a tender age, are sold into foreign slavery, have already learned to imitate the rapine of the father and the prostitution of the mother. Yet, amidst the rudest ignorance, the untaught natives discover a singular dexterity both of mind and hand; and although the want of union and discipline exposes them to their more powerful neighbors, a bold and intrepid spirit has animated the Colchians of every age. In the host of Xerxes, they served on foot; and their arms were a dagger or a javelin, a wooden casque, and a buckler of raw hides. But in their own country the use of cavalry has more generally prevailed: the meanest of the peasants disdained to walk; the martial nobles are possessed, perhaps, of two hundred horses; and above five thousand are numbered in the train of the prince of Mingrelia. The Colchian government has been always a pure and hereditary kingdom; and the authority of the sovereign is only restrained by the turbulence of his subjects. Whenever they were obedient, he could lead a numerous army into the field; but some faith is requisite to believe, that the single tribe of the Suanians as composed of two hundred thousand soldiers, or that the population of Mingrelia now amounts to four millions of inhabitants. [75]

[Footnote 72: A Greek historian, Timosthenes, had affirmed, in eam ccc. nationes dissimilibus linguis descendere; and the modest Pliny is content to add, et postea a nostris cxxx. interpretibus negotia ibi gesta, (vi. 5) But the words nunc deserta cover a multitude of past fictions.]

[Footnote 73: Buffon (Hist. Nat. tom. iii. p. 433—437) collects the unanimous suffrage of naturalists and travellers. If, in the time of Herodotus, they were, (and he had observed them with care,) this precious fact is an example of the influence of climate on a foreign colony.]

[Footnote 74: The Mingrelian ambassador arrived at Constantinople with two hundred persons; but he ate (sold) them day by day, till his retinue was diminished to a secretary and two valets, (Tavernier, tom. i. p. 365.) To purchase his mistress, a Mingrelian gentleman sold twelve priests and his wife to the Turks, (Chardin, tom. i. p. 66.)]

[Footnote 75: Strabo, l. xi. p. 765. Lamberti, Relation de la Mingrelie. Yet we must avoid the contrary extreme of Chardin, who allows no more than 20,000 inhabitants to supply an annual exportation of 12,000 slaves; an absurdity unworthy of that judicious traveller.]

PART IV

It was the boast of the Colchians, that their ancestors had checked the victories of Sesostris; and the defeat of the Egyptian is less incredible than his successful progress as far as the foot of Mount Caucasus. They sunk without any memorable effort, under the arms of Cyrus; followed in distant wars the standard of the great king, and presented him every fifth year with one hundred boys, and as many virgins, the fairest produce of the land. [76] Yet he accepted this gift like the gold and ebony of India, the frankincense of the Arabs, or the negroes and ivory of Aethiopia: the Colchians were not subject to the dominion of a satrap, and they continued to enjoy the name as well as substance of national independence. [77] After the fall of the Persian empire, Mithridates, king of Pontus, added Colchos to the wide circle of his dominions on the Euxine; and when the natives presumed to request that his son might reign over them, he bound the ambitious youth in chains of gold, and delegated a servant in his place. In pursuit of Mithridates, the Romans advanced to the banks of the Phasis, and their galleys ascended the river till they reached the camp of Pompey and his legions. [78] But the senate, and afterwards the emperors, disdained to reduce that distant and useless conquest into the form of a province. The family of a Greek rhetorician was permitted to reign in Colchos and the adjacent kingdoms from the time of Mark Antony to that of Nero; and after the race of Polemo [79] was extinct, the eastern Pontus, which preserved his name, extended no farther than the neighborhood of Trebizond. Beyond these limits the fortifications of Hyssus, of Apsarus, of the Phasis, of Dioscurias or Sebastopolis, and of Pityus, were guarded by sufficient detachments of horse and foot; and six princes of Colchos received their diadems from the lieutenants of Caesar. One of these lieutenants, the eloquent and philosophic Arrian, surveyed, and has described, the Euxine coast, under the reign of Hadrian. The garrison which he reviewed at the mouth of the Phasis consisted of four hundred chosen legionaries; the brick walls and towers, the double ditch, and the military engines on the rampart, rendered this place inaccessible to the Barbarians: but the new suburbs which had been built by the merchants and veterans, required, in the opinion of Arrian, some external defence. [80] As the strength of the empire was gradually impaired, the Romans stationed on the Phasis were neither withdrawn nor expelled; and the tribe of the Lazi, [81] whose posterity speak a foreign dialect, and inhabit the sea coast of Trebizond, imposed their name and dominion on the ancient kingdom of Colchos. Their independence was soon invaded by a formidable neighbor, who had acquired, by arms and treaties, the sovereignty of Iberia. The dependent king of Lazica received his sceptre at the hands of the Persian monarch, and the successors of Constantine acquiesced in this injurious claim, which was proudly urged as a right of immemorial prescription. In the beginning of the sixth century, their influence was restored by the introduction of Christianity, which the Mingrelians still profess with becoming zeal, without understanding the doctrines, or observing the precepts, of their religion. After the decease of his father, Zathus was exalted to the regal dignity by the favor of the great king; but the pious youth abhorred the ceremonies of the Magi, and sought, in the palace of Constantinople, an orthodox baptism, a noble wife, and the alliance of the emperor Justin. The king of Lazica was solemnly invested with the diadem, and his cloak and tunic of white silk, with a gold border, displayed, in rich embroidery, the figure of his new patron; who soothed the jealousy of the Persian court, and excused the revolt of Colchos, by the venerable names of hospitality and religion. The common interest of both empires imposed on the Colchians the duty of guarding the passes of Mount Caucasus, where a wall of sixty miles is now defended by the monthly service of the musketeers of Mingrelia. [82]

[Footnote 76: Herodot. l. iii. c. 97. See, in l. vii. c. 79, their arms and service in the expedition of Xerxes against Greece.]

[Footnote 77: Xenophon, who had encountered the Colchians in his retreat, (Anabasis, l. iv. p. 320, 343, 348, edit. Hutchinson; and Foster's Dissertation, p. liii—lviii., in Spelman's English version, vol. ii.,) styled them. Before the conquest of Mithridates, they are named by Appian, (de Bell. Mithridatico, c. 15, tom. i. p. 661, of the last and best edition, by John Schweighaeuser. Lipsae, 1785 8 vols. largo octavo.)]

[Footnote 78: The conquest of Colchos by Mithridates and Pompey is marked by Appian (de Bell. Mithridat.) and Plutarch, (in Vit. Pomp.)]

[Footnote 79: We may trace the rise and fall of the family of Polemo, in Strabo, (l. xi. p. 755, l. xii. p. 867,) Dion Cassius, or Xiphilin, (p. 588, 593, 601, 719, 754, 915, 946, edit. Reimar,) Suetonius, (in Neron. c. 18, in Vespasian, c. 8,) Eutropius, (vii. 14,) Josephus, (Antiq. Judaic. l. xx. c. 7, p. 970, edit. Havercamp,) and Eusebius, (Chron. with Scaliger, Animadvers. p. 196.)]

[Footnote 80: In the time of Procopius, there were no Roman forts on the Phasis. Pityus and Sebastopolis were evacuated on the rumor of the Persians, (Goth. l. iv. c. 4;) but the latter was afterwards restored by Justinian, (de Edif. l. iv. c. 7.)]

[Footnote 81: In the time of Pliny, Arrian, and Ptolemy, the Lazi were a particular tribe on the northern skirts of Colchos, (Cellarius, Geograph. Antiq. tom. ii. p. 222.) In the age of Justinian, they spread, or at least reigned, over the whole country. At present, they have migrated along the coast towards Trebizond, and compose a rude sea-faring people, with a peculiar language, (Chardin, p. 149. Peyssonel p. 64.)]

[Footnote 82: John Malala, Chron. tom. ii. p. 134—137 Theophanes, p. 144. Hist. Miscell. l. xv. p. 103. The fact is authentic, but the date seems too recent. In speaking of their Persian alliance, the Lazi contemporaries of Justinian employ the most obsolete words, &c. Could they belong to a connection which had not been dissolved above twenty years?]

But this honorable connection was soon corrupted by the avarice and ambition of the Romans. Degraded from the rank of allies, the Lazi were incessantly reminded, by words and actions, of their dependent state. At the distance of a day's journey beyond the Apsarus, they beheld the rising fortress of Petra, [83] which commanded the maritime country to the south of the Phasis. Instead of being protected by the valor, Colchos was insulted by the licentiousness, of foreign mercenaries; the benefits of commerce were converted into base and vexatious monopoly; and Gubazes, the native prince, was reduced to a pageant of royalty, by the superior influence of the officers of Justinian. Disappointed in their expectations of Christian virtue, the indignant Lazi reposed some confidence in the justice of an unbeliever. After a private assurance that their ambassadors should not be delivered to the Romans, they publicly solicited the friendship and aid of Chosroes. The sagacious monarch instantly discerned the use and importance of Colchos; and meditated a plan of conquest, which was renewed at the end of a thousand years by Shah Abbas, the wisest and most powerful of his successors. [84] His ambition was fired by the hope of launching a Persian navy from the Phasis, of commanding the trade and navigation of the Euxine Sea, of desolating the coast of Pontus and Bithynia, of distressing, perhaps of attacking, Constantinople, and of persuading the Barbarians of Europe to second his arms and counsels against the common enemy of mankind.

Under the pretence of a Scythian war, he silently led his troops to the frontiers of Iberia; the Colchian guides were prepared to conduct them through the woods and along the precipices of Mount Caucasus; and a narrow path was laboriously formed into a safe and spacious highway, for the march of cavalry, and even of elephants. Gubazes laid his person and diadem at the feet of the king of Persia; his Colchians imitated the submission of their prince; and after the walls of Petra had been shaken, the Roman garrison prevented, by a capitulation, the impending fury of the last assault. But the Lazi soon discovered, that their impatience had urged them to choose an evil more intolerable than the calamities which they strove to escape. The monopoly of salt and corn was effectually removed by the loss of those valuable commodities. The authority of a Roman legislator, was succeeded by the pride of an Oriental despot, who beheld, with equal disdain, the slaves whom he had exalted, and the kings whom he had humbled before the footstool of his throne. The adoration of fire was introduced into Colchos by the zeal of the Magi: their intolerant spirit provoked the fervor of a Christian people; and the prejudice of nature or education was wounded by the impious practice of exposing the dead bodies of their parents, on the summit of a lofty tower, to the crows and vultures of the air. [85] Conscious of the increasing hatred, which retarded the execution of his great designs, the just Nashirvan had secretly given orders to assassinate the king of the Lazi, to transplant the people into some distant land, and to fix a faithful and warlike colony on the banks of the Phasis. The watchful jealousy of the Colchians foresaw and averted the approaching ruin. Their repentance was accepted at Constantinople by the prudence, rather than clemency, of Justinian; and he commanded Dagisteus, with seven thousand Romans, and one thousand of the Zani, [85/1] to expel the Persians from the coast of the Euxine.

[Footnote 83: The sole vestige of Petra subsists in the writings of Procopius and Agathias. Most of the towns and castles of Lazica may be found by comparing their names and position with the map of Mingrelia, in Lamberti.]

[Footnote 84: See the amusing letters of Pietro della Valle, the Roman traveler, (Viaggi, tom. ii. 207, 209, 213, 215, 266, 286, 300, tom. iii. p. 54, 127.) In the years 1618, 1619, and 1620, he conversed with Shah Abbas, and strongly encouraged a design which might have united Persia and Europe against their common enemy the Turk.]

[Footnote 85: See Herodotus, (l. i. c. 140, p. 69,) who speaks with diffidence, Larcher, (tom. i. p. 399—401, Notes sur Herodote,) Procopius, (Persic. l. i. c. 11,) and Agathias, (l. ii. p. 61, 62.) This practice, agreeable to the Zendavesta, (Hyde, de Relig. Pers. c. 34, p. 414—421,) demonstrates that the burial of the Persian kings, (Xenophon, Cyropaed. l. viii. p. 658,) is a Greek fiction, and that their tombs could be no more than cenotaphs.]

[Footnote 85/1: These seem the same people called Suanians, p. 328—M.]

The siege of Petra, which the Roman general, with the aid of the Lazi, immediately undertook, is one of the most remarkable actions of the age. The city was seated on a craggy rock, which hung over the sea, and communicated by a steep and narrow path with the land. Since the approach was difficult, the attack might be deemed impossible: the Persian conqueror had strengthened the fortifications of Justinian; and the places least inaccessible were covered by additional bulwarks. In this important fortress, the vigilance of Chosroes had deposited a magazine of offensive and defensive arms, sufficient for five times the number, not only of the garrison, but of the besiegers themselves. The stock of flour and salt provisions was adequate to the consumption of five years; the want of wine was supplied by vinegar; and of grain from whence a strong liquor was extracted, and a triple aqueduct eluded the diligence, and even the suspicions, of the enemy. But the firmest defence of Petra was placed in the valor of fifteen hundred Persians, who resisted the assaults of the Romans, whilst, in a softer vein of earth, a mine was secretly perforated. The wall, supported by slender and temporary props, hung tottering in the air; but Dagisteus delayed the attack till he had secured a specific recompense; and the town was relieved before the return of his messenger from Constantinople. The Persian garrison was reduced to four hundred men, of whom no more than fifty were exempt from sickness or wounds; yet such had been their inflexible perseverance, that they concealed their losses from the enemy, by enduring, without a murmur, the sight and putrefying stench of the dead bodies of their eleven hundred companions. After their deliverance, the breaches were hastily stopped with sand-bags; the mine was replenished with earth; a new wall was erected on a frame of substantial timber; and a fresh garrison of three thousand men was stationed at Petra to sustain the labors of a second siege. The operations, both of the attack and defence, were conducted with skilful obstinacy; and each party derived useful lessons from the experience of their past faults. A battering-ram was invented, of light construction and powerful effect: it was transported and worked by the hands of forty soldiers; and as the stones were loosened by its repeated strokes, they were torn with long iron hooks from the wall. From those walls, a shower of darts was incessantly poured on the heads of the assailants; but they were most dangerously annoyed by a fiery composition of sulphur and bitumen, which in Colchos might with some propriety be named the oil of Medea. Of six thousand Romans who mounted the scaling-ladders, their general Bessas was the first, a gallant veteran of seventy years of age: the courage of their leader, his fall, and extreme danger, animated the irresistible effort of his troops; and their prevailing numbers oppressed the strength, without subduing the spirit, of the Persian garrison. The fate of these valiant men deserves to be more distinctly noticed. Seven hundred had perished in the siege, two thousand three hundred survived to defend the breach. One thousand and seventy were destroyed with fire and sword in the last assault; and if seven hundred and thirty were made prisoners, only eighteen among them were found without the marks of honorable wounds. The remaining five hundred escaped into the citadel, which they maintained without any hopes of relief, rejecting the fairest terms of capitulation and service, till they were lost in the flames. They died in obedience to the commands of their prince; and such examples of loyalty and valor might excite their countrymen to deeds of equal despair and more prosperous event. The instant demolition of the works of Petra confessed the astonishment and apprehension of the conqueror. A Spartan would have praised and pitied the virtue of these heroic slaves; but the tedious warfare and alternate success of the Roman and Persian arms cannot detain the attention of posterity at the foot of Mount Caucasus. The advantages obtained by the troops of Justinian were more frequent and splendid; but the forces of the great king were continually supplied, till they amounted to eight elephants and seventy thousand men, including twelve thousand Scythian allies, and above three thousand Dilemites, who descended by their free choice from the hills of Hyrcania, and were equally formidable in close or in distant combat. The siege of Archaeopolis, a name imposed or corrupted by the Greeks, was raised with some loss and precipitation; but the Persians occupied the passes of Iberia: Colchos was enslaved by their forts and garrisons; they devoured the scanty sustenance of the people; and the prince of the Lazi fled into the mountains. In the Roman camp, faith and discipline were unknown; and the independent leaders, who were invested with equal power, disputed with each other the preeminence of vice and corruption. The Persians followed, without a murmur, the commands of a single chief, who implicitly obeyed the instructions of their supreme lord. Their general was distinguished among the heroes of the East by his wisdom in council, and his valor in the field. The advanced age of Mermeroes, and the lameness of both his feet, could not diminish the activity of his mind, or even of his body; and, whilst he was carried in a litter in the front of battle, he inspired terror to the enemy, and a just confidence to the troops, who, under his banners, were always successful. After his death, the command devolved to Nacoragan, a proud satrap, who, in a conference with the Imperial chiefs, had presumed to declare that he disposed of victory as absolutely as of the ring on his finger. Such presumption was the natural cause and forerunner of a shameful defeat. The Romans had been gradually repulsed to the edge of the sea-shore; and their last camp, on the ruins of the Grecian colony of Phasis, was defended on all sides by strong intrenchments, the river, the Euxine, and a fleet of galleys. Despair united their counsels and invigorated their arms: they withstood the assault of the Persians and the flight of Nacoragan preceded or followed the slaughter of ten thousand of his bravest soldiers. He escaped from the Romans to fall into the hands of an unforgiving master who severely chastised the error of his own choice: the unfortunate general was flayed alive, and his skin, stuffed into the human form, was exposed on a mountain; a dreadful warning to those who might hereafter be intrusted with the fame and fortune of Persia. [86] Yet the prudence of Chosroes insensibly relinquished the prosecution of the Colchian war, in the just persuasion, that it is impossible to reduce, or, at least, to hold a distant country against the wishes and efforts of its inhabitants. The fidelity of Gubazes sustained the most rigorous trials. He patiently endured the hardships of a savage life, and rejected with disdain, the specious temptations of the Persian court. [86/1] The king of the Lazi had been educated in the Christian religion; his mother was the daughter of a senator; during his youth he had served ten years a silentiary of the Byzantine palace, [87] and the arrears of an unpaid salary were a motive of attachment as well as of complaint. But the long continuance of his sufferings extorted from him a naked representation of the truth; and truth was an unpardonable libel on the lieutenants of Justinian, who, amidst the delays of a ruinous war, had spared his enemies and trampled on his allies. Their malicious information persuaded the emperor that his faithless vassal already meditated a second defection: an order was surprised to send him prisoner to Constantinople; a treacherous clause was inserted, that he might be lawfully killed in case of resistance; and Gubazes, without arms, or suspicion of danger, was stabbed in the security of a friendly interview. In the first moments of rage and despair, the Colchians would have sacrificed their country and religion to the gratification of revenge. But the authority and eloquence of the wiser few obtained a salutary pause: the victory of the Phasis restored the terror of the Roman arms, and the emperor was solicitous to absolve his own name from the imputation of so foul a murder. A judge of senatorial rank was commissioned to inquire into the conduct and death of the king of the Lazi. He ascended a stately tribunal, encompassed by the ministers of justice and punishment: in the presence of both nations, this extraordinary cause was pleaded, according to the forms of civil jurisprudence, and some satisfaction was granted to an injured people, by the sentence and execution of the meaner criminals. [88]

[Footnote 86: The punishment of flaying alive could not be introduced into Persia by Sapor, (Brisson, de Regn. Pers. l. ii. p. 578,) nor could it be copied from the foolish tale of Marsyas, the Phrygian piper, most foolishly quoted as a precedent by Agathias, (l. iv. p. 132, 133.)]

[Footnote 86/1: According to Agathias, the death of Gubazos preceded the defeat of Nacoragan. The trial took place after the battle—M.]

[Footnote 87: In the palace of Constantinople there were thirty silentiaries, who were styled hastati, ante fores cubiculi, an honorable title which conferred the rank, without imposing the duties, of a senator, (Cod. Theodos. l. vi. tit. 23. Gothofred. Comment. tom. ii. p. 129.)]

[Footnote 88: On these judicial orations, Agathias (l. iii. p. 81-89, l. iv. p. 108—119) lavishes eighteen or twenty pages of false and florid rhetoric. His ignorance or carelessness overlooks the strongest argument against the king of Lazica—his former revolt. Note: The Orations in the third book of Agathias are not judicial, nor delivered before the Roman tribunal: it is a deliberative debate among the Colchians on the expediency of adhering to the Roman, or embracing the Persian alliance—M.]

In peace, the king of Persia continually sought the pretences of a rupture: but no sooner had he taken up arms, than he expressed his desire of a safe and honorable treaty. During the fiercest hostilities, the two monarchs entertained a deceitful negotiation; and such was the superiority of Chosroes, that whilst he treated the Roman ministers with insolence and contempt, he obtained the most unprecedented honors for his own ambassadors at the Imperial court. The successor of Cyrus assumed the majesty of the Eastern sun, and graciously permitted his younger brother Justinian to reign over the West, with the pale and reflected splendor of the moon. This gigantic style was supported by the pomp and eloquence of Isdigune, one of the royal chamberlains. His wife and daughters, with a train of eunuchs and camels, attended the march of the ambassador: two satraps with golden diadems were numbered among his followers: he was guarded by five hundred horse, the most valiant of the Persians; and the Roman governor of Dara wisely refused to admit more than twenty of this martial and hostile caravan. When Isdigune had saluted the emperor, and delivered his presents, he passed ten months at Constantinople without discussing any serious affairs. Instead of being confined to his palace, and receiving food and water from the hands of his keepers, the Persian ambassador, without spies or guards, was allowed to visit the capital; and the freedom of conversation and trade enjoyed by his domestics, offended the prejudices of an age which rigorously practised the law of nations, without confidence or courtesy. [89] By an unexampled indulgence, his interpreter, a servant below the notice of a Roman magistrate, was seated, at the table of Justinian, by the side of his master: and one thousand pounds of gold might be assigned for the expense of his journey and entertainment. Yet the repeated labors of Isdigune could procure only a partial and imperfect truce, which was always purchased with the treasures, and renewed at the solicitation, of the Byzantine court Many years of fruitless desolation elapsed before Justinian and Chosroes were compelled, by mutual lassitude, to consult the repose of their declining age. At a conference held on the frontier, each party, without expecting to gain credit, displayed the power, the justice, and the pacific intentions, of their respective sovereigns; but necessity and interest dictated the treaty of peace, which was concluded for a term of fifty years, diligently composed in the Greek and Persian languages, and attested by the seals of twelve interpreters. The liberty of commerce and religion was fixed and defined; the allies of the emperor and the great king were included in the same benefits and obligations; and the most scrupulous precautions were provided to prevent or determine the accidental disputes that might arise on the confines of two hostile nations. After twenty years of destructive though feeble war, the limits still remained without alteration; and Chosroes was persuaded to renounce his dangerous claim to the possession or sovereignty of Colchos and its dependent states. Rich in the accumulated treasures of the East, he extorted from the Romans an annual payment of thirty thousand pieces of gold; and the smallness of the sum revealed the disgrace of a tribute in its naked deformity. In a previous debate, the chariot of Sesostris, and the wheel of fortune, were applied by one of the ministers of Justinian, who observed that the reduction of Antioch, and some Syrian cities, had elevated beyond measure the vain and ambitious spirit of the Barbarian. "You are mistaken," replied the modest Persian: "the king of kings, the lord of mankind, looks down with contempt on such petty acquisitions; and of the ten nations, vanquished by his invincible arms, he esteems the Romans as the least formidable." [90] According to the Orientals, the empire of Nushirvan extended from Ferganah, in Transoxiana, to Yemen or Arabia Faelix. He subdued the rebels of Hyrcania, reduced the provinces of Cabul and Zablestan on the banks of the Indus, broke the power of the Euthalites, terminated by an honorable treaty the Turkish war, and admitted the daughter of the great khan into the number of his lawful wives. Victorious and respected among the princes of Asia, he gave audience, in his palace of Madain, or Ctesiphon, to the ambassadors of the world. Their gifts or tributes, arms, rich garments, gems, slaves or aromatics, were humbly presented at the foot of his throne; and he condescended to accept from the king of India ten quintals of the wood of aloes, a maid seven cubits in height, and a carpet softer than silk, the skin, as it was reported, of an extraordinary serpent. [91]

[Footnote 89: Procopius represents the practice of the Gothic court of Ravenna (Goth. l. i. c. 7;) and foreign ambassadors have been treated with the same jealousy and rigor in Turkey, (Busbequius, epist. iii. p. 149, 242, &c.,) Russia, (Voyage D'Olearius,) and China, (Narrative of A. de Lange, in Bell's Travels, vol. ii. p. 189—311.)]

[Footnote 90: The negotiations and treaties between Justinian and Chosroes are copiously explained by Procopius, (Persie, l. ii. c. 10, 13, 26, 27, 28. Gothic. l. ii. c. 11, 15,) Agathias, (l. iv. p. 141, 142,) and Menander, (in Excerpt. Legat. p. 132—147.) Consult Barbeyrac, Hist. des Anciens Traites, tom. ii. p. 154, 181—184, 193—200.]

[Footnote 91: D'Herbelot, Bibliot. Orient. p. 680, 681, 294, 295.]

Justinian had been reproached for his alliance with the Aethiopians, as if he attempted to introduce a people of savage negroes into the system of civilized society. But the friends of the Roman empire, the Axumites, or Abyssinians, may be always distinguished from the original natives of Africa. [92] The hand of nature has flattened the noses of the negroes, covered their heads with shaggy wool, and tinged their skin with inherent and indelible blackness. But the olive complexion of the Abyssinians, their hair, shape, and features, distinctly mark them as a colony of Arabs; and this descent is confirmed by the resemblance of language and manners the report of an ancient emigration, and the narrow interval between the shores of the Red Sea. Christianity had raised that nation above the level of African barbarism: [93] their intercourse with Egypt, and the successors of Constantine, [94] had communicated the rudiments of the arts and sciences; their vessels traded to the Isle of Ceylon, [95] and seven kingdoms obeyed the Negus or supreme prince of Abyssinia. The independence of the Homerites, [95/1] who reigned in the rich and happy Arabia, was first violated by an Aethiopian conqueror: he drew his hereditary claim from the queen of Sheba, [96] and his ambition was sanctified by religious zeal. The Jews, powerful and active in exile, had seduced the mind of Dunaan, prince of the Homerites. They urged him to retaliate the persecution inflicted by the Imperial laws on their unfortunate brethren: some Roman merchants were injuriously treated; and several Christians of Negra [97] were honored with the crown of martyrdom. [98] The churches of Arabia implored the protection of the Abyssinian monarch. The Negus passed the Red Sea with a fleet and army, deprived the Jewish proselyte of his kingdom and life, and extinguished a race of princes, who had ruled above two thousand years the sequestered region of myrrh and frankincense. The conqueror immediately announced the victory of the gospel, requested an orthodox patriarch, and so warmly professed his friendship to the Roman empire, that Justinian was flattered by the hope of diverting the silk trade through the channel of

Abyssinia, and of exciting the forces of Arabia against the Persian king. Nonnosus, descended from a family of ambassadors, was named by the emperor to execute this important commission. He wisely declined the shorter, but more dangerous, road, through the sandy deserts of Nubia; ascended the Nile, embarked on the Red Sea, and safely landed at the African port of Adulis. From Adulis to the royal city of Axume is no more than fifty leagues, in a direct line; but the winding passes of the mountains detained the ambassador fifteen days; and as he traversed the forests, he saw, and vaguely computed, about five thousand wild elephants. The capital, according to his report, was large and populous; and the village of Axume is still conspicuous by the regal coronations, by the ruins of a Christian temple, and by sixteen or seventeen obelisks inscribed with Grecian characters. [99] But the Negus [99/1] gave audience in the open field, seated on a lofty chariot, which was drawn by four elephants, superbly caparisoned, and surrounded by his nobles and musicians. He was clad in a linen garment and cap, holding in his hand two javelins and a light shield; and, although his nakedness was imperfectly covered, he displayed the Barbaric pomp of gold chains, collars, and bracelets, richly adorned with pearls and precious stones. The ambassador of Justinian knelt; the Negus raised him from the ground, embraced Nonnosus, kissed the seal, perused the letter, accepted the Roman alliance, and, brandishing his weapons, denounced implacable war against the worshipers of fire. But the proposal of the silk trade was eluded; and notwithstanding the assurances, and perhaps the wishes, of the Abyssinians, these hostile menaces evaporated without effect. The Homerites were unwilling to abandon their aromatic groves, to explore a sandy desert, and to encounter, after all their fatigues, a formidable nation from whom they had never received any personal injuries. Instead of enlarging his conquests, the king of Aethiopia was incapable of defending his possessions. Abrahah, [99/2] the slave of a Roman merchant of Adulis, assumed the sceptre of the Homerites,; the troops of Africa were seduced by the luxury of the climate; and Justinian solicited the friendship of the usurper, who honored with a slight tribute the supremacy of his prince. After a long series of prosperity, the power of Abrahah was overthrown before the gates of Mecca; and his children were despoiled by the Persian conqueror; and the Aethiopians were finally expelled from the continent of Asia. This narrative of obscure and remote events is not foreign to the decline and fall of the Roman empire. If a Christian power had been maintained in Arabia, Mahomet must have been crushed in his cradle, and Abyssinia would have prevented a revolution which has changed the civil and religious state of the world. [100] [100/1]

[Footnote 92: See Buffon, Hist. Naturelle, tom. iii. p. 449. This Arab cast of features and complexion, which has continued 3400 years (Ludolph. Hist. et Comment. Aethiopic. l. i. c. 4) in the colony of Abyssinia, will justify the suspicion, that race, as well as climate, must have contributed to form the negroes of the adjacent and similar regions. Note: Mr. Salt (Travels, vol. ii. p. 458) considers them to be distinct from the Arabs—"in feature, color, habit, and manners."—M.]

[Footnote 93: The Portuguese missionaries, Alvarez, (Ramusio, tom. i. fol. 204, rect. 274, vers.) Bermudez, (Purchas's Pilgrims, vol. ii. l. v. c. 7, p. 1149—1188,) Lobo, (Relation, &c., par M. le Grand, with xv. Dissertations, Paris, 1728,) and Tellez (Relations de Thevenot, part iv.) could only relate of modern Abyssinia what they had seen or invented. The erudition of Ludolphus, (Hist. Aethiopica, Francofurt, 1681. Commentarius, 1691. Appendix, 1694,) in twenty-five languages, could add little concerning its ancient history. Yet the fame of Caled, or Ellisthaeus, the conqueror of Yemen, is celebrated in national songs and legends.]

[Footnote 94: The negotiations of Justinian with the Axumites, or Aethiopians, are recorded by Procopius (Persic. l. i. c. 19, 20) and John Malala, (tom. ii. p. 163—165, 193—196.) The historian of Antioch quotes the original narrative of the ambassador Nonnosus, of which Photius (Bibliot. Cod. iii.) has preserved a curious extract.]

[Footnote 95: The trade of the Axumites to the coast of India and Africa, and the Isle of Ceylon, is curiously represented by Cosmas Indicopleustes, (Topograph. Christian. l. ii. p. 132, 138, 139, 140, l. xi. p. 338, 339.)]

[Footnote 95/1: It appears by the important inscription discovered by Mr. Salt at Axoum, and from a law of Constantius, (16th Jan. 356, inserted in the Theodosian Code, l. 12, c. 12,) that in the middle of the fourth century of our era the princes of the Axumites joined to their titles that of king of the Homerites. The conquests which they made over the Arabs in the sixth century were only a restoration of the ancient order of things. St. Martin vol. viii. p. 46—M.]

[Footnote 96: Ludolph. Hist. et Comment. Aethiop. l. ii. c. 3.]

[Footnote 97: The city of Negra, or Nag'ran, in Yemen, is surrounded with palm-trees, and stands in the high road between Saana, the capital, and Mecca; from the former ten, from the latter twenty days' journey of a caravan of camels, (Abulfeda, Descript. Arabiae, p. 52.)]

[Footnote 98: The martyrdom of St. Arethas, prince of Negra, and his three hundred and forty companions, is embellished in the legends of Metaphrastes and Nicephorus Callistus, copied by Baronius, (A. D 522, No. 22—66, A.D. 523, No. 16—29,) and refuted with obscure diligence, by Basnage, (Hist. des Juifs, tom. viii. l. xii. c. ii. p. 333—348,) who investigates the state of the Jews in Arabia and Aethiopia. Note: According to Johannsen, (Hist. Yemanae, Praef. p. 89,) Dunaan (Ds Nowas) massacred 20,000 Christians, and threw them into a pit, where they were burned. They are called in the Koran the companions of the pit (socii foveae.)—M.]

[Footnote 99: Alvarez (in Ramusio, tom. i. fol. 219, vers. 221, vers.) saw the flourishing state of Axume in the year 1520—luogomolto buono e grande. It was ruined in the same century by the Turkish invasion. No more than 100 houses remain; but the memory of its past greatness is preserved by the regal coronation, (Ludolph. Hist. et Comment. l. ii. c. 11.) Note: Lord Valentia's and Mr. Salt's Travels give a high notion of the ruins of Axum—M.]

[Footnote 99/1: The Negus is differently called Elesbaan, Elesboas, Elisthaeus, probably the same name, or rather appellation. See St. Martin, vol. viii. p. 49—M.]

[Footnote 99/2: According to the Arabian authorities, (Johannsen, Hist. Yemanae, p. 94, Bonn, 1828,) Abrahah was an Abyssinian, the rival of Ariathus, the brother of the Abyssinian king: he surprised and slew Ariathus, and by his craft appeased the resentment of Nadjash, the Abyssinian king. Abrahah was a Christian; he built a magnificent church at Sana, and dissuaded his subjects from their accustomed pilgrimages to Mecca. The church was defiled, it was supposed, by the Koreishites, and Abrahah took up arms to revenge himself on the temple at Mecca. He was repelled by miracle: his elephant would not advance, but knelt down before the sacred place; Abrahah fled, discomfited and mortally wounded, to Sana—M.]

[Footnote 100: The revolutions of Yemen in the sixth century must be collected from Procopius, (Persic. l. i. c. 19, 20,) Theophanes Byzant., (apud Phot. cod. lxiii. p. 80,) St. Theophanes, (in Chronograph. p. 144, 145, 188, 189, 206, 207, who is full of strange blunders,) Pocock, (Specimen Hist. Arab. p. 62, 65,) D'Herbelot, (Bibliot. Orientale, p. 12, 477,) and Sale's Preliminary Discourse and Koran, (c. 105.) The revolt of Abrahah is mentioned by Procopius; and his fall, though clouded with miracles, is an historical fact. Note: To the authors who have illustrated the obscure history of the Jewish and Abyssinian kingdoms in Homeritis may be added Schultens, Hist. Joctanidarum; Walch, Historia rerum in Homerite gestarum, in the 4th vol. of the Gottingen Transactions; Salt's Travels, vol. ii. p. 446, &c.: Sylvestre de Sacy, vol. i. Acad. des Inscrip. Jost, Geschichte der Israeliter; Johannsen, Hist. Yemanae; St. Martin's notes to Le Beau, t. vii p. 42—M.]

[Footnote 100/1: A period of sixty-seven years is assigned by most of the Arabian authorities to the Abyssinian kingdoms in Homeritis—M.]

CHAPTER XLIII

LAST VICTORY AND DEATH OF BELISARIUS, DEATH OF JUSTINIAN

PART I

REBELLIONS OF AFRICA—RESTORATION OF THE GOTHIC KINGDOM BY TOTILA—LOSS AND RECOVERY OF ROME—FINAL CONQUEST OF ITALY BY NARSES—EXTINCTION OF THE OSTROGOTHS—DEFEAT OF THE FRANKS AND ALEMANNI—LAST VICTORY, DISGRACE, AND DEATH OF BELISARIUS—DEATH AND CHARACTER OF JUSTINIAN—COMET, EARTHQUAKES, AND PLAGUE

The review of the nations from the Danube to the Nile has exposed, on every side, the weakness of the Romans; and our wonder is reasonably excited that they should presume to enlarge an empire whose ancient limits they were incapable of defending. But the wars, the conquests, and the triumphs of Justinian, are the feeble and pernicious efforts of old age, which exhaust the remains of strength, and accelerate the decay of the powers of life. He exulted in the glorious act of restoring Africa and Italy to the republic; but the calamities which followed the departure of Belisarius betrayed the impotence of the conqueror, and accomplished the ruin of those unfortunate countries.

From his new acquisitions, Justinian expected that his avarice, as well as pride, should be richly gratified. A rapacious minister of the finances closely pursued the footsteps of Belisarius; and as the old registers of tribute had been burnt by the Vandals, he indulged his fancy in a liberal calculation and arbitrary assessment of the wealth of Africa. [1] The increase of taxes, which were drawn away by a distant sovereign, and a general resumption of the patrimony or crown lands, soon dispelled the intoxication of the public joy: but the emperor was insensible to the modest complaints of the people, till he was awakened and alarmed by the clamors of military discontent. Many of the Roman soldiers had married the widows and daughters of the Vandals. As their own, by the double right of conquest and inheritance, they claimed the estates which Genseric had assigned to his victorious troops. They heard with disdain the cold and selfish representations of their officers, that the liberality of Justinian had raised them from a savage or servile condition; that they were already enriched by the spoils of Africa, the treasure, the slaves, and the movables of the vanquished Barbarians; and that the ancient and lawful patrimony of the emperors would be applied only to the support of that government on which their own safety and reward must ultimately depend. The mutiny was secretly inflamed by a thousand soldiers, for the most part Heruli, who had imbibed the doctrines, and were instigated by the clergy, of the Arian sect; and the cause of perjury and rebellion was sanctified by the dispensing powers of fanaticism. The Arians deplored the ruin of their church, triumphant above a century in Africa; and they were justly provoked by the laws of the conqueror, which interdicted the baptism of their children, and the exercise of all religious worship. Of the Vandals chosen by Belisarius, the far greater part, in the honors of the Eastern service, forgot their country and religion. But a generous band of four hundred obliged the mariners, when they were in sight of the Isle of Lesbos, to alter their course: they touched on Peloponnesus, ran ashore on a desert coast of Africa, and boldly erected, on Mount Aurasius, the standard of independence and revolt. While the troops of the provinces disclaimed the commands of their superiors, a conspiracy was formed at Carthage against the life of Solomon, who filled with honor the place of Belisarius; and the Arians had piously resolved to sacrifice the tyrant at the foot of the altar, during the awful mysteries of the festival of Easter. Fear or remorse restrained the daggers of the assassins, but the patience of Solomon emboldened their discontent; and, at the end of ten days, a furious sedition was kindled in the Circus, which desolated Africa above ten years. The pillage of the city, and the indiscriminate slaughter of its inhabitants, were suspended only by darkness, sleep, and intoxication: the governor, with seven companions, among whom was the historian Procopius, escaped to Sicily: two thirds of the army were involved in the guilt of treason; and eight thousand insurgents, assembling in the field of Bulla, elected Stoza for their chief, a private soldier, who possessed in a superior degree the virtues of a rebel. Under the mask of freedom, his eloquence could lead, or at least impel, the passions of his equals. He raised himself to a level with Belisarius, and the nephew of the emperor, by daring to encounter them in the field; and the victorious generals were compelled to acknowledge that Stoza deserved a purer cause, and a more legitimate command. Vanquished in battle, he dexterously employed the arts of negotiation; a Roman army was seduced from their allegiance, and the chiefs who had trusted to his faithless promise were murdered by his order in a church of Numidia. When every resource, either of force or perfidy, was exhausted, Stoza, with some desperate Vandals, retired to the wilds of Mauritania, obtained the daughter of a Barbarian prince, and eluded the pursuit of his enemies, by the report of his death. The personal weight of Belisarius, the rank, the spirit, and the temper, of Germanus, the emperor's nephew, and the vigor and success of the second administration of the eunuch Solomon, restored the modesty of the camp, and maintained for a while the tranquillity of Africa. But the vices of the Byzantine court were felt in that distant province; the troops complained that they were neither paid nor relieved, and as soon as the public disorders were sufficiently mature, Stoza was again alive, in arms, and at the gates of Carthage. He fell in a single combat, but he smiled in the agonies of death, when he was informed that his own javelin had reached the heart of his antagonist. [100/1] The example of Stoza, and the assurance that a fortunate soldier had been the first king, encouraged the ambition of Gontharis, and he promised, by a private treaty, to divide Africa with the Moors, if, with their dangerous aid, he should ascend the throne of Carthage. The feeble Areobindus, unskilled in the affairs of peace and war, was raised, by his marriage with the niece of Justinian, to the office of exarch. He was suddenly oppressed by a sedition of the guards, and his abject supplications, which provoked the contempt, could not move the pity, of the inexorable tyrant. After a reign of thirty days, Gontharis himself was stabbed at a banquet by the hand of Artaban; [100/2] and it is singular enough, that an Armenian prince, of the royal family of Arsaces, should reestablish at Carthage the authority of the Roman empire. In the conspiracy which unsheathed the dagger of Brutus against the life of Caesar, every circumstance is curious and important to the eyes of posterity; but the guilt or merit of these loyal or rebellious assassins could interest only the contemporaries of Procopius, who, by their hopes and fears, their friendship or resentment, were personally engaged in the revolutions of Africa. [2]

[Footnote 1: For the troubles of Africa, I neither have nor desire another guide than Procopius, whose eye contemplated the image, and whose ear collected the reports, of the memorable events of his own times. In the second book of the Vandalic war he relates the revolt of Stoza, (c. 14—24,) the return of Belisarius,

(c. 15,) the victory of Germanus, (c. 16, 17, 18,) the second administration of Solomon, (c. 19, 20, 21,) the government of Sergius, (c. 22, 23,) of Areobindus, (c. 24,) the tyranny and death of Gontharis, (c. 25, 26, 27, 28;) nor can I discern any symptoms of flattery or malevolence in his various portraits.]

[Footnote 100/1: Corippus gives a different account of the death of Stoza; he was transfixed by an arrow from the hand of John, (not the hero of his poem) who broke desperately through the victorious troops of the enemy. Stoza repented, says the poet, of his treasonous rebellion, and anticipated—another Cataline—eternal torments as his punishment.

Reddam, improba, poenas Quas merui. Furiis socius Catilina cruentis Exagitatus adest. Video jam Tartara, fundo Flammarumque globos, et clara incendia volvi. —Johannidos, book iv. line 211.

All the other authorities confirm Gibbon's account of the death of John by the hand of Stoza. This poem of Corippus, unknown to Gibbon, was first published by Mazzuchelli during the present century, and is reprinted in the new edition of the Byzantine writers—M]

[Footnote 100/2: This murder was prompted to the Armenian (according to Corippus) by Athanasius, (then praefect of Africa.)

Hunc placidus cana gravitate coegit
Inumitera mactare virum.
—Corripus, vol. iv. p. 237—M.]

[Footnote 2: Yet I must not refuse him the merit of painting, in lively colors, the murder of Gontharis. One of the assassins uttered a sentiment not unworthy of a Roman patriot: "If I fail," said Artasires, "in the first stroke, kill me on the spot, lest the rack should extort a discovery of my accomplices."]

That country was rapidly sinking into the state of barbarism from whence it had been raised by the Phoenician colonies and Roman laws; and every step of intestine discord was marked by some deplorable victory of savage man over civilized society. The Moors, [3] though ignorant of justice, were impatient of oppression: their vagrant life and boundless wilderness disappointed the arms, and eluded the chains, of a conqueror; and experience had shown, that neither oaths nor obligations could secure the fidelity of their attachment. The victory of Mount Auras had awed them into momentary submission; but if they respected the character of Solomon, they hated and despised the pride and luxury of his two nephews, Cyrus and Sergius, on whom their uncle had imprudently bestowed the provincial governments of Tripoli and Pentapolis. A Moorish tribe encamped under the walls of Leptis, to renew their alliance, and receive from the governor the customary gifts. Fourscore of their deputies were introduced as friends into the city; but on the dark suspicion of a conspiracy, they were massacred at the table of Sergius, and the clamor of arms and revenge was reechoed through the valleys of Mount Atlas from both the Syrtes to the Atlantic Ocean. A personal injury, the unjust execution or murder of his brother, rendered Antalas the enemy of the Romans. The defeat of the Vandals had formerly signalized his valor; the rudiments of justice and prudence were still more conspicuous in a Moor; and while he laid Adrumetum in ashes, he calmly admonished the emperor that the peace of Africa might be secured by the recall of Solomon and his unworthy nephews. The exarch led forth his troops from Carthage: but, at the distance of six days' journey, in the neighborhood of Tebeste, [4] he was astonished by the superior numbers and fierce aspect of the Barbarians. He proposed a treaty; solicited a reconciliation; and offered to bind himself by the most solemn oaths. "By what oaths can he bind himself?" interrupted the indignant Moors. "Will he swear by the Gospels, the divine books of the Christians? It was on those books that the faith of his nephew Sergius was pledged to eighty of our innocent and unfortunate brethren. Before we trust them a second time, let us try their efficacy in the chastisement of perjury and the vindication of their own honor." Their honor was vindicated in the field of Tebeste, by the death of Solomon, and the total loss of his army. [4/1] The arrival of fresh troops and more skilful commanders soon checked the insolence of the Moors: seventeen of their princes were slain in the same battle; and the doubtful and transient submission of their tribes was celebrated with lavish applause by the people of Constantinople. Successive inroads had reduced the province of Africa to one third of the measure of Italy; yet the Roman emperors continued to reign above a century over Carthage and the fruitful coast of the Mediterranean. But the victories and the losses of Justinian were alike pernicious to mankind; and such was the desolation of Africa, that in many parts a stranger might wander whole days without meeting the face either of a friend or an enemy. The nation of the Vandals had disappeared: they once amounted to a hundred and sixty thousand warriors, without including the children, the women, or the slaves. Their numbers were infinitely surpassed by the number of the Moorish families extirpated in a relentless war; and the same destruction was retaliated on the Romans and their allies, who perished by the climate, their mutual quarrels, and the rage of the Barbarians. When Procopius first landed, he admired the populousness of the cities and country, strenuously exercised in the labors of commerce and agriculture. In less than twenty years, that busy scene was converted into a silent solitude; the wealthy citizens escaped to Sicily and Constantinople; and the secret historian has confidently affirmed, that five millions of Africans were consumed by the wars and government of the emperor Justinian. [5]

[Footnote 3: The Moorish wars are occasionally introduced into the narrative of Procopius, (Vandal. l. ii. c. 19—23, 25, 27, 28. Gothic. l. iv. c. 17;) and Theophanes adds some prosperous and adverse events in the last years of Justinian.]

[Footnote 4: Now Tibesh, in the kingdom of Algiers. It is watered by a river, the Sujerass, which falls into the Mejerda, (Bagradas.) Tibesh is still remarkable for its walls of large stones, (like the Coliseum of Rome,) a fountain, and a grove of walnut-trees: the country is fruitful, and the neighboring Bereberes are warlike. It appears from an inscription, that, under the reign of Adrian, the road from Carthage to Tebeste was constructed by the third legion, (Marmol, Description de l'Afrique, tom. ii. p. 442, 443. Shaw's Travels, p. 64, 65, 66.)]

[Footnote 4/1: Corripus (Johannidos lib. iii. 417—441) describes the defeat and death of Solomon—M.]

[Footnote 5: Procopius, Anecdot. c. 18. The series of the African history at tests this melancholy truth.]

The jealousy of the Byzantine court had not permitted Belisarius to achieve the conquest of Italy; and his abrupt departure revived the courage of the Goths, [6] who respected his genius, his virtue, and even the laudable motive which had urged the servant of Justinian to deceive and reject them. They had lost their king, (an inconsiderable loss,) their capital, their treasures, the provinces from Sicily to the Alps, and the military force of two hundred thousand Barbarians, magnificently equipped with horses and arms. Yet all was not lost, as long as Pavia was defended by one thousand Goths, inspired by a sense of honor, the love of freedom, and the memory of their past greatness. The supreme command was unanimously offered to the brave Uraias; and it was in his eyes alone that the disgrace of his uncle Vitiges could appear as a reason of exclusion. His voice inclined the election in favor of Hildibald, whose personal merit was recommended by the vain hope that his kinsman Theudes, the Spanish monarch, would support the common interest of the Gothic nation. The success of his arms in Liguria and Venetia seemed to justify their choice; but he soon declared to the world that he was incapable of forgiving or commanding his benefactor. The consort of Hildibald was deeply wounded by the beauty, the riches, and the pride, of the wife of Uraias; and the death of that virtuous patriot excited the indignation of a free people. A bold assassin executed their sentence by striking off the head of Hildibald in the midst of a banquet; the Rugians, a foreign tribe, assumed the privilege of election: and Totila, [6/1] the nephew of the late king, was tempted, by revenge, to deliver himself and the garrison of Trevigo into the hands of the Romans.

But the gallant and accomplished youth was easily persuaded to prefer the Gothic throne before the service of Justinian; and as soon as the palace of Pavia had been purified from the Rugian usurper, he reviewed the national force of five thousand soldiers, and generously undertook the restoration of the kingdom of Italy.

[Footnote 6: In the second (c. 30) and third books, (c. 1—40,) Procopius continues the history of the Gothic war from the fifth to the fifteenth year of Justinian. As the events are less interesting than in the former period, he allots only half the space to double the time. Jornandes, and the Chronicle of Marcellinus, afford some collateral hints Sigonius, Pagi, Muratori, Mascou, and De Buat, are useful, and have been used.]

[Footnote 6/1: His real name, as appears by medals, was Baduilla, or Badiula. Totila signifies immortal: tod (in German) is death. Todilas, deathless. Compare St Martin, vol. ix. p. 37—M.]

The successors of Belisarius, eleven generals of equal rank, neglected to crush the feeble and disunited Goths, till they were roused to action by the progress of Totila and the reproaches of Justinian. The gates of Verona were secretly opened to Artabazus, at the head of one hundred Persians in the service of the empire. The Goths fled from the city. At the distance of sixty furlongs the Roman generals halted to regulate the division of the spoil. While they disputed, the enemy discovered the real number of the victors: the Persians were instantly overpowered, and it was by leaping from the wall that Artabazus preserved a life which he lost in a few days by the lance of a Barbarian, who had defied him to single combat. Twenty thousand Romans encountered the forces of Totila, near Faenza, and on the hills of Mugello, of the Florentine territory. The ardor of freedmen, who fought to regain their country, was opposed to the languid temper of mercenary troops, who were even destitute of the merits of strong and well-disciplined servitude. On the first attack, they abandoned their ensigns, threw down their arms, and dispersed on all sides with an active speed, which abated the loss, whilst it aggravated the shame, of their defeat. The king of the Goths, who blushed for the baseness of his enemies, pursued with rapid steps the path of honor and victory. Totila passed the Po, [6/2] traversed the Apennine, suspended the important conquest of Ravenna, Florence, and Rome, and marched through the heart of Italy, to form the siege or rather the blockade, of Naples. The Roman chiefs, imprisoned in their respective cities, and accusing each other of the common disgrace, did not presume to disturb his enterprise. But the emperor, alarmed by the distress and danger of his Italian conquests, despatched to the relief of Naples a fleet of galleys and a body of Thracian and Armenian soldiers. They landed in Sicily, which yielded its copious stores of provisions; but the delays of the new commander, an unwarlike magistrate, protracted the sufferings of the besieged; and the succors, which he dropped with a timid and tardy hand, were successively intercepted by the armed vessels stationed by Totila in the Bay of Naples. The principal officer of the Romans was dragged, with a rope round his neck, to the foot of the wall, from whence, with a trembling voice, he exhorted the citizens to implore, like himself, the mercy of the conqueror. They requested a truce, with a promise of surrendering the city, if no effectual relief should appear at the end of thirty days. Instead of one month, the audacious Barbarian granted them three, in the just confidence that famine would anticipate the term of their capitulation. After the reduction of Naples and Cumae, the provinces of Lucania, Apulia, and Calabria, submitted to the king of the Goths. Totila led his army to the gates of Rome, pitched his camp at Tibur, or Tivoli, within twenty miles of the capital, and calmly exhorted the senate and people to compare the tyranny of the Greeks with the blessings of the Gothic reign.

[Footnote 6/2: This is not quite correct: he had crossed the Po before the battle of Faenza—M.]

The rapid success of Totila may be partly ascribed to the revolution which three years' experience had produced in the sentiments of the Italians. At the command, or at least in the name, of a Catholic emperor, the pope, [7] their spiritual father, had been torn from the Roman church, and either starved or murdered on a desolate island. [8] The virtues of Belisarius were replaced by the various or uniform vices of eleven chiefs, at Rome, Ravenna, Florence, Perugia, Spoleto, &c., who abused their authority for the indulgence of lust or avarice. The improvement of the revenue was committed to Alexander, a subtle scribe, long practised in the fraud and oppression of the Byzantine schools, and whose name of Psalliction, the scissors, [9] was drawn from the dexterous artifice with which he reduced the size without defacing the figure, of the gold coin. Instead of expecting the restoration of peace and industry, he imposed a heavy assessment on the fortunes of the Italians. Yet his present or future demands were less odious than a prosecution of arbitrary rigor against the persons and property of all those who, under the Gothic kings, had been concerned in the receipt and expenditure of the public money. The subjects of Justinian, who escaped these partial vexations, were oppressed by the irregular maintenance of the soldiers, whom Alexander defrauded and despised; and their hasty sallies in quest of wealth, or subsistence, provoked the inhabitants of the country to await or implore their deliverance from the virtues of a Barbarian. Totila [10] was chaste and temperate; and none were deceived, either friends or enemies, who depended on his faith or his clemency. To the husbandmen of Italy the Gothic king issued a welcome proclamation, enjoining them to pursue their important labors, and to rest assured, that, on the payment of the ordinary taxes, they should be defended by his valor and discipline from the injuries of war. The strong towns he successively attacked; and as soon as they had yielded to his arms, he demolished the fortifications, to save the people from the calamities of a future siege, to deprive the Romans of the arts of defence, and to decide the tedious quarrel of the two nations, by an equal and honorable conflict in the field of battle. The Roman captives and deserters were tempted to enlist in the service of a liberal and courteous adversary; the slaves were attracted by the firm and faithful promise, that they should never be delivered to their masters; and from the thousand warriors of Pavia, a new people, under the same appellation of Goths, was insensibly formed in the camp of Totila. He sincerely accomplished the articles of capitulation, without seeking or accepting any sinister advantage from ambiguous expressions or unforeseen events: the garrison of Naples had stipulated that they should be transported by sea; the obstinacy of the winds prevented their voyage, but they were generously supplied with horses, provisions, and a safe-conduct to the gates of Rome. The wives of the senators, who had been surprised in the villas of Campania, were restored, without a ransom, to their husbands; the violation of female chastity was inexorably chastised with death; and in the salutary regulation of the edict of the famished Neapolitans, the conqueror assumed the office of a humane and attentive physician. The virtues of Totila are equally laudable, whether they proceeded from true policy, religious principle, or the instinct of humanity: he often harangued his troops; and it was his constant theme, that national vice and ruin are inseparably connected; that victory is the fruit of moral as well as military virtue; and that the prince, and even the people, are responsible for the crimes which they neglect to punish.

[Footnote 7: Sylverius, bishop of Rome, was first transported to Patara, in Lycia, and at length starved (sub eorum custodia inedia confectus) in the Isle of Palmaria, A.D. 538, June 20, (Liberat. in Breviar. c. 22.

Anastasius, in Sylverio. Baronius, A.D. 540, No. 2, 3. Pagi, in Vit. Pont. tom. i. p. 285, 286.) Procopius (Anecdot. c. 1) accuses only the empress and Antonina.]

[Footnote 8: Palmaria, a small island, opposite to Terracina and the coast of the Volsci, (Cluver. Ital. Antiq. l. iii. c. 7, p. 1014.)]

[Footnote 9: As the Logothete Alexander, and most of his civil and military colleagues, were either disgraced or despised, the ink of the Anecdotes (c. 4, 5, 18) is scarcely blacker than that of the Gothic History (l. iii. c. 1, 3, 4, 9, 20, 21, &c.)]

[Footnote 10: Procopius (l. iii. c. 2, 8, &c.,) does ample and willing justice to the merit of Totila. The Roman historians, from Sallust and Tacitus were happy to forget the vices of their countrymen in the contemplation of Barbaric virtue.]

The return of Belisarius to save the country which he had subdued, was pressed with equal vehemence by his friends and enemies; and the Gothic war was imposed as a trust or an exile on the veteran commander. A hero on the banks of the Euphrates, a slave in the palace of Constantinople, he accepted with reluctance the painful task of supporting his own reputation, and retrieving the faults of his successors. The sea was open to the Romans: the ships and soldiers were assembled at Salona, near the palace of Diocletian: he refreshed and reviewed his troops at Pola in Istria, coasted round the head of the Adriatic, entered the port of Ravenna, and despatched orders rather than supplies to the subordinate cities. His first public oration was addressed to the Goths and Romans, in the name of the emperor, who had suspended for a while the conquest of Persia, and listened to the prayers of his Italian subjects. He gently touched on the causes and the authors of the recent disasters; striving to remove the fear of punishment for the past, and the hope of impunity for the future, and laboring, with more zeal than success, to unite all the members of his government in a firm league of affection and obedience. Justinian, his gracious master, was inclined to pardon and reward; and it was their interest, as well as duty, to reclaim their deluded brethren, who had been seduced by the arts of the usurper. Not a man was tempted to desert the standard of the Gothic king. Belisarius soon discovered, that he was sent to remain the idle and impotent spectator of the glory of a young Barbarian; and his own epistle exhibits a genuine and lively picture of the distress of a noble mind. "Most excellent prince, we are arrived in Italy, destitute of all the necessary implements of war, men, horses, arms, and money. In our late circuit through the villages of Thrace and Illyricum, we have collected, with extreme difficulty, about four thousand recruits, naked, and unskilled in the use of weapons and the exercises of the camp. The soldiers already stationed in the province are discontented, fearful, and dismayed; at the sound of an enemy, they dismiss their horses, and cast their arms on the ground. No taxes can be raised, since Italy is in the hands of the Barbarians; the failure of payment has deprived us of the right of command, or even of admonition. Be assured, dread Sir, that the greater part of your troops have already deserted to the Goths. If the war could be achieved by the presence of Belisarius alone, your wishes are satisfied; Belisarius is in the midst of Italy. But if you desire to conquer, far other preparations are requisite: without a military force, the title of general is an empty name. It would be expedient to restore to my service my own veteran and domestic guards. Before I can take the field, I must receive an adequate supply of light and heavy armed troops; and it is only with ready money that you can procure the indispensable aid of a powerful body of the cavalry of the Huns." [11] An officer in whom Belisarius confided was sent from Ravenna to hasten and conduct the succors; but the message was neglected, and the messenger was detained at Constantinople by an advantageous marriage. After his patience had been exhausted by delay and disappointment, the Roman general repassed the Adriatic, and expected at Dyrrachium the arrival of the troops, which were slowly assembled among the subjects and allies of the empire. His powers were still inadequate to the deliverance of Rome, which was closely besieged by the Gothic king. The Appian way, a march of forty days, was covered by the Barbarians; and as the prudence of Belisarius declined a battle, he preferred the safe and speedy navigation of five days from the coast of Epirus to the mouth of the Tyber.

[Footnote 11: Procopius, l. iii. c. 12. The soul of a hero is deeply impressed on the letter; nor can we confound such genuine and original acts with the elaborate and often empty speeches of the Byzantine historians]

After reducing, by force, or treaty, the towns of inferior note in the midland provinces of Italy, Totila proceeded, not to assault, but to encompass and starve, the ancient capital. Rome was afflicted by the avarice, and guarded by the valor, of Bessas, a veteran chief of Gothic extraction, who filled, with a garrison of three thousand soldiers, the spacious circle of her venerable walls. From the distress of the people he extracted a profitable trade, and secretly rejoiced in the continuance of the siege. It was for his use that the granaries had been replenished: the charity of Pope Vigilius had purchased and embarked an ample supply of Sicilian corn; but the vessels which escaped the Barbarians were seized by a rapacious governor, who imparted a scanty sustenance to the soldiers, and sold the remainder to the wealthy Romans. The medimnus, or fifth part of the quarter of wheat, was exchanged for seven pieces of gold; fifty pieces were given for an ox, a rare and accidental prize; the progress of famine enhanced this exorbitant value, and the mercenaries were tempted to deprive themselves of the allowance which was scarcely sufficient for the support of life. A tasteless and unwholesome mixture, in which the bran thrice exceeded the quantity of flour, appeased the hunger of the poor; they were gradually reduced to feed on dead horses, dogs, cats, and mice, and eagerly to snatch the grass, and even the nettles, which grew among the ruins of the city. A crowd of spectres, pale and emaciated, their bodies oppressed with disease, and their minds with despair, surrounded the palace of the governor, urged, with unavailing truth, that it was the duty of a master to maintain his slaves, and humbly requested that he would provide for their subsistence, to permit their flight, or command their immediate execution. Bessas replied, with unfeeling tranquillity, that it was impossible to feed, unsafe to dismiss, and unlawful to kill, the subjects of the emperor. Yet the example of a private citizen might have shown his countrymen that a tyrant cannot withhold the privilege of death. Pierced by the cries of five children, who vainly called on their father for bread, he ordered them to follow his steps, advanced with calm and silent despair to one of the bridges of the Tyber, and, covering his face, threw himself headlong into the stream, in the presence of his family and the Roman people. To the rich and pusillammous, Bessas [12] sold the permission of departure; but the greatest part of the fugitives expired on the public highways, or were intercepted by the flying parties of Barbarians. In the mean while, the artful governor soothed the discontent, and revived the hopes of the Romans, by the vague reports of the fleets and armies which were hastening to their relief from the extremities of the East. They derived more rational comfort from the assurance that Belisarius had landed at the port; and, without numbering his forces, they firmly relied on the humanity, the courage, and the skill of their great deliverer.

[Footnote 12: The avarice of Bessas is not dissembled by Procopius, (l. iii. c. 17, 20.) He expiated the loss of Rome by the glorious conquest of Petraea, (Goth. l. iv. c. 12;) but the same vices followed him from the Tyber to the Phasis, (c. 13;) and the historian is equally true to the merits and defects of his character. The chastisement which the author of the romance of Belisaire has inflicted on the oppressor of Rome is more agreeable to justice than to history.]

PART II

The foresight of Totila had raised obstacles worthy of such an antagonist. Ninety furlongs below the city, in the narrowest part of the river, he joined the two banks by strong and solid timbers in the form of a bridge, on which he erected two lofty towers, manned by the bravest of his Goths, and profusely stored with missile weapons and engines of offence. The approach of the bridge and towers was covered by a strong and massy chain of iron; and the chain, at either end, on the opposite sides of the Tyber, was defended by a numerous and chosen detachment of archers. But the enterprise of forcing these barriers, and relieving the capital, displays a shining example of the boldness and conduct of Belisarius. His cavalry advanced from the port along the public road, to awe the motions, and distract the attention of the enemy. His infantry and provisions were distributed in two hundred large boats; and each boat was shielded by a high rampart of thick planks, pierced with many small holes for the discharge of missile weapons. In the front, two large vessels were linked together to sustain a floating castle, which commanded the towers of the bridge, and contained a magazine of fire, sulphur, and bitumen. The whole fleet, which the general led in person, was laboriously moved against the current of the river. The chain yielded to their weight, and the enemies who guarded the banks were either slain or scattered. As soon as they touched the principal barrier, the fire-ship was instantly grappled to the bridge; one of the towers, with two hundred Goths, was consumed by the flames; the assailants shouted victory; and Rome was saved, if the wisdom of Belisarius had not been defeated by the misconduct of his officers. He had previously sent orders to Bessas to second his operations by a timely sally from the town; and he had fixed his lieutenant, Isaac, by a peremptory command, to the station of the port. But avarice rendered Bessas immovable; while the youthful ardor of Isaac delivered him into the hands of a superior enemy. The exaggerated rumor of his defeat was hastily carried to the ears of Belisarius: he paused; betrayed in that single moment of his life some emotions of surprise and perplexity; and reluctantly sounded a retreat to save his wife Antonina, his treasures, and the only harbor which he possessed on the Tuscan coast. The vexation of his mind produced an ardent and almost mortal fever; and Rome was left without protection to the mercy or indignation of Totila. The continuance of hostilities had imbittered the national hatred: the Arian clergy was ignominiously driven from Rome; Pelagius, the archdeacon, returned without success from an embassy to the Gothic camp; and a Sicilian bishop, the envoy or nuncio of the pope, was deprived of both his hands, for daring to utter falsehoods in the service of the church and state.

Famine had relaxed the strength and discipline of the garrison of Rome. They could derive no effectual service from a dying people; and the inhuman avarice of the merchant at length absorbed the vigilance of the governor. Four Isaurian sentinels, while their companions slept, and their officers were absent, descended by a rope from the wall, and secretly proposed to the Gothic king to introduce his troops into the city. The offer was entertained with coldness and suspicion; they returned in safety; they twice repeated their visit; the place was twice examined; the conspiracy was known and disregarded; and no sooner had Totila consented to the attempt, than they unbarred the Asinarian gate, and gave admittance to the Goths. Till the dawn of day, they halted in order of battle, apprehensive of treachery or ambush; but the troops of Bessas, with their leader, had already escaped; and when the king was pressed to disturb their retreat, he prudently replied, that no sight could be more grateful than that of a flying enemy. The patricians, who were still possessed of horses, Decius, Basilius, &c. accompanied the governor; their brethren, among whom Olybrius, Orestes, and Maximus, are named by the historian, took refuge in the church of St. Peter: but the assertion, that only five hundred persons remained in the capital, inspires some doubt of the fidelity either of his narrative or of his text. As soon as daylight had displayed the entire victory of the Goths, their monarch devoutly visited the tomb of the prince of the apostles; but while he prayed at the altar, twenty-five soldiers, and sixty citizens, were put to the sword in the vestibule of the temple. The archdeacon Pelagius [13] stood before him, with the Gospels in his hand. "O Lord, be merciful to your servant." "Pelagius," said Totila, with an insulting smile, "your pride now condescends to become a suppliant." "I am a suppliant," replied the prudent archdeacon; "God has now made us your subjects, and as your subjects, we are entitled to your clemency." At his humble prayer, the lives of the Romans were spared; and the chastity of the maids and matrons was preserved inviolate from the passions of the hungry soldiers.

But they were rewarded by the freedom of pillage, after the most precious spoils had been reserved for the royal treasury. The houses of the senators were plentifully stored with gold and silver; and the avarice of Bessas had labored with so much guilt and shame for the benefit of the conqueror. In this revolution, the sons and daughters of Roman consuls lasted the misery which they had spurned or relieved, wandered in tattered garments through the streets of the city and begged their bread, perhaps without success, before the gates of their hereditary mansions. The riches of Rusticiana, the daughter of Symmachus and widow of Boethius, had been generously devoted to alleviate the calamities of famine. But the Barbarians were exasperated by the report, that she had prompted the people to overthrow the statues of the great Theodoric; and the life of that venerable matron would have been sacrificed to his memory, if Totila had not respected her birth, her virtues, and even the pious motive of her revenge. The next day he pronounced two orations, to congratulate and admonish his victorious Goths, and to reproach the senate, as the vilest of slaves, with their perjury, folly, and ingratitude; sternly declaring, that their estates and honors were justly forfeited to the companions of his arms. Yet he consented to forgive their revolt; and the senators repaid his clemency by despatching circular letters to their tenants and vassals in the provinces of Italy, strictly to enjoin them to desert the standard of the Greeks, to cultivate their lands in peace, and to learn from their masters the duty of obedience to a Gothic sovereign. Against the city which had so long delayed the course of his victories, he appeared inexorable: one third of the walls, in different parts, were demolished by his command; fire and engines prepared to consume or subvert the most stately works of antiquity; and the world was astonished by the fatal decree, that Rome should be changed into a pasture for cattle. The firm and temperate remonstrance of Belisarius suspended the execution; he warned the Barbarian not to sully his fame by the destruction of those monuments which were the glory of the dead, and the delight of the living; and Totila was persuaded, by the advice of an enemy, to preserve Rome as the ornament of his kingdom, or the fairest pledge of peace and reconciliation. When he had signified to the ambassadors of Belisarius his intention of sparing the city, he stationed an army at the distance of one hundred and twenty furlongs, to observe the motions of the Roman general. With the remainder of his forces he marched into Lucania and Apulia, and occupied on the summit of Mount Garganus [14] one of the camps of Hannibal. [15] The senators were dragged in his train, and afterwards confined in the fortresses of Campania: the citizens, with their wives and children, were dispersed in exile; and during forty days Rome was abandoned to desolate and dreary solitude. [16]

[Footnote 13: During the long exile, and after the death of Vigilius, the Roman church was governed, at first by the archdeacon, and at length (A. D 655) by the pope Pelagius, who was not thought guiltless of the sufferings of his predecessor. See the original lives of the popes under the name of Anastasius, (Muratori, Script. Rer. Italicarum, tom. iii. P. i. p. 130, 131,) who relates several curious incidents of the sieges of Rome and the wars of Italy.]

[Footnote 14: Mount Garganus, now Monte St. Angelo, in the kingdom of Naples, runs three hundred stadia into the Adriatic Sea, (Strab—vi. p. 436,) and in the darker ages was illustrated by the apparition, miracles, and church, of St. Michael the archangel. Horace, a native of Apulia or Lucania, had seen the *elms and oaks of Garganus laboring and bellowing with the north wind that blew on that lofty coast, (Carm. ii. 9, Epist. ii. i. 201.)]*

[Footnote 15: I cannot ascertain this particular camp of Hannibal; but the Punic quarters were long and often in the neighborhood of Arpi, (T. Liv. xxii. 9, 12, xxiv. 3, &c.)]

[Footnote 16: Totila.... Romam ingreditur.... ac evertit muros, domos aliquantas igni comburens, ac omnes Romanorum res in praedam ac cepit, hos ipsos Romanos in Campaniam captivos abduxit. Post quam devastationem, xl. autamp lius dies, Roma fuit ita desolata, ut nemo ibi hominum, nisi (nulloe?) bestiae morarentur, (Marcellin. in Chron. p. 54.)]

The loss of Rome was speedily retrieved by an action, to which, according to the event, the public opinion would apply the names of rashness or heroism. After the departure of Totila, the Roman general sallied from the port at the head of a thousand horse, cut in pieces the enemy who opposed his progress, and visited with pity and reverence the vacant space of the eternal city. Resolved to maintain a station so conspicuous in the eyes of mankind, he summoned the greatest part of his troops to the standard which he erected on the Capitol: the old inhabitants were recalled by the love of their country and the hopes of food; and the keys of Rome were sent a second time to the emperor Justinian. The walls, as far as they had been demolished by the Goths, were repaired with rude and dissimilar materials; the ditch was restored; iron spikes [17] were profusely scattered in the highways to annoy the feet of the horses; and as new gates could not suddenly be procured, the entrance was guarded by a Spartan rampart of his bravest soldiers. At the expiration of twenty-five days, Totila returned by hasty marches from Apulia to avenge the injury and disgrace. Belisarius expected his approach. The Goths were thrice repulsed in three general assaults; they lost the flower of their troops; the royal standard had almost fallen into the hands of the enemy, and the fame of Totila sunk, as it had risen, with the fortune of his arms. Whatever skill and courage could achieve, had been performed by the Roman general: it remained only that Justinian should terminate, by a strong and seasonable effort, the war which he had ambitiously undertaken. The indolence, perhaps the impotence, of a prince who despised his enemies, and envied his servants, protracted the calamities of Italy. After a long silence, Belisarius was commanded to leave a sufficient garrison at Rome, and to transport himself into the province of Lucania, whose inhabitants, inflamed by Catholic zeal, had cast away the yoke of their Arian conquerors. In this ignoble warfare, the hero, invincible against the power of the Barbarians, was basely vanquished by the delay, the disobedience, and the cowardice of his own officers. He reposed in his winter quarters of Crotona, in the full assurance, that the two passes of the Lucanian hills were guarded by his cavalry. They were betrayed by treachery or weakness; and the rapid march of the Goths scarcely allowed time for the escape of Belisarius to the coast of Sicily. At length a fleet and army were assembled for the relief of Ruscianum, or Rossano, [18] a fortress sixty furlongs from the ruins of Sybaris, where the nobles of Lucania had taken refuge. In the first attempt, the Roman forces were dissipated by a storm. In the second, they approached the shore; but they saw the hills covered with archers, the landing-place defended by a line of spears, and the king of the Goths impatient for battle. The conqueror of Italy retired with a sigh, and continued to languish, inglorious and inactive, till Antonina, who had been sent to Constantinople to solicit succors, obtained, after the death of the empress, the permission of his return.

[Footnote 17: The tribuli are small engines with four spikes, one fixed in the ground, the three others erect or adverse, (Procopius, Gothic. l. iii. c. 24. Just. Lipsius, Poliorcetwv, l. v. c. 3.) The metaphor was borrowed from the tribuli, (land-caltrops,) an herb with a prickly fruit, commex in Italy. (Martin, ad Virgil. Georgic. i. 153 vol. ii. p. 33.)]

[Footnote 18: Ruscia, the navale Thuriorum, was transferred to the distance of sixty stadia to Ruscianum, Rossano, an archbishopric without suffragans. The republic of Sybaris is now the estate of the duke of Corigliano. (Riedesel, Travels into Magna Graecia and Sicily, p. 166—171.)]

The five last campaigns of Belisarius might abate the envy of his competitors, whose eyes had been dazzled and wounded by the blaze of his former glory. Instead of delivering Italy from the Goths, he had wandered like a fugitive along the coast, without daring to march into the country, or to accept the bold and repeated challenge of Totila. Yet, in the judgment of the few who could discriminate counsels from events, and compare the instruments with the execution, he appeared a more consummate master of the art of war, than in the season of his prosperity, when he presented two captive kings before the throne of Justinian. The valor of Belisarius was not chilled by age: his prudence was matured by experience; but the moral virtues of humanity and justice seem to have yielded to the hard necessity of the times. The parsimony or poverty of the emperor compelled him to deviate from the rule of conduct which had deserved the love and confidence of the Italians. The war was maintained by the oppression of Ravenna, Sicily, and all the faithful subjects of the empire; and the rigorous prosecution of Herodian provoked that injured or guilty officer to deliver Spoleto into the hands of the enemy. The avarice of Antonina, which had been some times diverted by love, now reigned without a rival in her breast. Belisarius himself had always understood, that riches, in a corrupt age, are the support and ornament of personal merit. And it cannot be presumed that he should stain his honor for the public service, without applying a part of the spoil to his private emolument. The hero had escaped the sword of the Barbarians. But the dagger of conspiracy [19] awaited his return. In the midst of wealth and honors, Artaban, who had chastised the African tyrant, complained of the ingratitude of courts. He aspired to Praejecta, the emperor's niece, who wished to reward her deliverer; but the impediment of his previous marriage was asserted by the piety of Theodora. The pride of royal descent was irritated by flattery; and the service in which he gloried had proved him capable of bold and sanguinary deeds. The death of Justinian was resolved, but the conspirators delayed the execution till they could surprise Belisarius disarmed, and naked, in the palace of Constantinople. Not a hope could be entertained of shaking his long-tried fidelity; and they justly dreaded the revenge, or rather the justice, of the veteran general, who might speedily assemble an army in Thrace to punish the assassins, and perhaps to enjoy the fruits of their crime. Delay afforded time for rash communications and honest confessions: Artaban and his accomplices were condemned by the senate, but the extreme clemency of Justinian detained them in the gentle confinement of the palace, till he pardoned their flagitious attempt against his throne and life. If the emperor forgave his enemies, he must cordially embrace a friend whose victories were alone remembered, and who was endeared to his prince by the recent circumstances of their common danger. Belisarius reposed from his toils, in the high station of general of the East and count of the domestics; and the older consuls and patricians respectfully yielded the precedency of rank to the peerless merit of the first of the Romans. [20] The first of the Romans still submitted to be the slave of his wife; but the servitude of habit and affection became less disgraceful when the death of Theodora had removed the baser influence of fear. Joannina, their daughter, and the sole heiress of their fortunes, was betrothed to Anastasius, the grandson, or rather the nephew, of the empress, [21] whose kind interposition forwarded the consummation of their youthful loves. But the power of Theodora expired, the parents of Joannina returned, and her honor, perhaps her happiness, were sacrificed to the revenge of an unfeeling mother, who dissolved the imperfect nuptials before they had been ratified by the ceremonies of the church. [22]

[Footnote 19: This conspiracy is related by Procopius (Gothic. l. iii. c. 31, 32) with such freedom and candor, that the liberty of the Anecdotes gives him nothing to add.]

[Footnote 20: The honors of Belisarius are gladly commemorated by his secretary, (Procop. Goth. l. iii. c. 35, l. iv. c. 21.) This title is ill translated, at least in this instance, by praefectus praetorio; and to a military character, magister militum is more proper and applicable, (Ducange, Gloss. Graec. p. 1458, 1459.)]

[Footnote 21: Alemannus, (ad Hist. Arcanum, p. 68,) Ducange, (Familiae Byzant. p. 98,) and Heineccius, (Hist. Juris Civilis, p. 434,) all three represent Anastasius as the son of the daughter of Theodora; and their opinion firmly reposes on the unambiguous testimony of Procopius, (Anecdot. c. 4, 5,—twice repeated.) And yet I will remark, 1. That in the year 547, Theodora could sarcely have a grandson of the age of puberty; 2. That we are totally ignorant of this daughter and her husband; and, 3. That Theodora concealed her bastards, and that her grandson by Justinian would have been heir apparent of the empire.]

[Footnote 22: The sins of the hero in Italy and after his return, are manifested, and most probably swelled, by the author of the Anecdotes, (c. 4, 5.) The designs of Antonina were favored by the fluctuating jurisprudence of Justinian. On the law of marriage and divorce, that emperor was trocho versatilior, (Heineccius, Element Juris Civil. ad Ordinem Pandect. P. iv. No. 233.)]

Before the departure of Belisarius, Perusia was besieged, and few cities were impregnable to the Gothic arms. Ravenna, Ancona, and Crotona, still resisted the Barbarians; and when Totila asked in marriage one of the daughters of France, he was stung by the just reproach that the king of Italy was unworthy of his title till it was acknowledged by the Roman people. Three thousand of the bravest soldiers had been left to defend the capital. On the suspicion of a monopoly, they massacred the governor, and announced to Justinian, by a deputation of the clergy, that unless their offence was pardoned, and their arrears were satisfied, they should instantly accept the tempting offers of Totila. But the officer who succeeded to the command (his name was Diogenes) deserved their esteem and confidence; and the Goths, instead of finding an easy conquest, encountered a vigorous resistance from the soldiers and people, who patiently endured the loss of the port and of all maritime supplies. The siege of Rome would perhaps have been raised, if the liberality of Totila to the Isaurians had not encouraged some of their venal countrymen to copy the example of treason. In a dark night, while the Gothic trumpets sounded on another side, they silently opened the gate of St. Paul: the Barbarians rushed into the city; and the flying garrison was intercepted before they could reach the harbor of Centumcellae. A soldier trained in the school of Belisarius, Paul of Cilicia, retired with four hundred men to the mole of Hadrian. They repelled the Goths; but they felt the approach of famine; and their aversion to the taste of horse-flesh confirmed their resolution to risk the event of a desperate and decisive sally. But their spirit insensibly stooped to the offers of capitulation; they retrieved their arrears of pay, and preserved their arms and horses, by enlisting in the service of Totila; their chiefs, who pleaded a laudable attachment to their wives and children in the East, were dismissed with honor; and above four hundred enemies, who had taken refuge in the sanctuaries, were saved by the clemency of the victor. He no longer entertained a wish of destroying the edifices of Rome, [23] which he now respected as the seat of the Gothic kingdom: the senate and people were restored to their country; the means of subsistence were liberally provided; and Totila, in the robe of peace, exhibited the equestrian games of the circus. Whilst he amused the eyes of the multitude, four hundred vessels were prepared for the embarkation of his troops. The cities of Rhegium and Tarentum were reduced: he passed into Sicily, the object of his implacable resentment; and the island was stripped of its gold and silver, of the fruits of the earth, and of an infinite number of horses, sheep, and oxen. Sardinia and Corsica obeyed the fortune of Italy; and the sea-coast of Greece was visited by a fleet of three hundred galleys. [24] The Goths were landed in

Corcyra and the ancient continent of Epirus; they advanced as far as Nicopolis, the trophy of Augustus, and Dodona, [25] once famous by the oracle of Jove. In every step of his victories, the wise Barbarian repeated to Justinian the desire of peace, applauded the concord of their predecessors, and offered to employ the Gothic arms in the service of the empire.

[Footnote 23: The Romans were still attached to the monuments of their ancestors; and according to Procopius, (Goth. l. iv. c. 22,) the gallery of Aeneas, of a single rank of oars, 25 feet in breadth, 120 in length, was preserved entire in the navalia, near Monte Testaceo, at the foot of the Aventine, (Nardini, Roma Antica, l. vii. c. 9, p. 466. Donatus, Rom Antiqua, l. iv. c. 13, p. 334) But all antiquity is ignorant of relic.]

[Footnote 24: In these seas Procopius searched without success for the Isle of Calypso. He was shown, at Phaeacia, or Cocyra, the petrified ship of Ulysses, (Odyss. xiii. 163;) but he found it a recent fabric of many stones, dedicated by a merchant to Jupiter Cassius, (l. iv. c. 22.) Eustathius had supposed it to be the fanciful likeness of a rock.]

[Footnote 25: M. D'Anville (Memoires de l'Acad. tom. xxxii. p. 513—528) illustrates the Gulf of Ambracia; but he cannot ascertain the situation of Dodona. A country in sight of Italy is less known than the wilds of America. Note: On the site of Dodona compare Walpole's Travels in the East, vol. ii. p. 473; Col. Leake's Northern Greece, vol. iv. p. 163; and a dissertation by the present bishop of Lichfield (Dr. Butler) in the appendix to Hughes's Travels, vol. i. p. 511—M.]

Justinian was deaf to the voice of peace: but he neglected the prosecution of war; and the indolence of his temper disappointed, in some degree, the obstinacy of his passions. From this salutary slumber the emperor was awakened by the pope Vigilius and the patrician Cethegus, who appeared before his throne, and adjured him, in the name of God and the people, to resume the conquest and deliverance of Italy. In the choice of the generals, caprice, as well as judgment, was shown. A fleet and army sailed for the relief of Sicily, under the conduct of Liberius; but his youth [2511] and want of experience were afterwards discovered, and before he touched the shores of the island he was overtaken by his successor. In the place of Liberius, the conspirator Artaban was raised from a prison to military honors; in the pious presumption, that gratitude would animate his valor and fortify his allegiance. Belisarius reposed in the shade of his laurels, but the command of the principal army was reserved for Germanus, [26] the emperor's nephew, whose rank and merit had been long depressed by the jealousy of the court. Theodora had injured him in the rights of a private citizen, the marriage of his children, and the testament of his brother; and although his conduct was pure and blameless, Justinian was displeased that he should be thought worthy of the confidence of the malecontents. The life of Germanus was a lesson of implicit obedience: he nobly refused to prostitute his name and character in the factions of the circus: the gravity of his manners was tempered by innocent cheerfulness; and his riches were lent without interest to indigent or deserving friends. His valor had formerly triumphed over the Sclavonians of the Danube and the rebels of Africa: the first report of his promotion revived the hopes of the Italians; and he was privately assured, that a crowd of Roman deserters would abandon, on his approach, the standard of Totila. His second marriage with Malasontha, the granddaughter of Theodoric endeared Germanus to the Goths themselves; and they marched with reluctance against the father of a royal infant the last offspring of the line of Amali. [27] A splendid allowance was assigned by the emperor: the general contribute his private fortune: his two sons were popular and active and he surpassed, in the promptitude and success of his levies the expectation of mankind. He was permitted to select some squadrons of Thracian cavalry: the veterans, as well as the youth of Constantinople and Europe, engaged their voluntary service; and as far as the heart of Germany, his fame and liberality attracted the aid of the Barbarians. [2711] The Romans advanced to Sardica; an army of Sclavonians fled before their march; but within two days of their final departure, the designs of Germanus were terminated by his malady and death. Yet the impulse which he had given to the Italian war still continued to act with energy and effect. The maritime towns Ancona, Crotona, Centumcellae, resisted the assaults of Totila Sicily was reduced by the zeal of Artaban, and the Gothic navy was defeated near the coast of the Adriatic. The two fleets were almost equal, forty-seven to fifty galleys: the victory was decided by the knowledge and dexterity of the Greeks; but the ships were so closely grappled, that only twelve of the Goths escaped from this unfortunate conflict. They affected to depreciate an element in which they were unskilled; but their own experience confirmed the truth of a maxim, that the master of the sea will always acquire the dominion of the land. [28]

[Footnote 25/1: This is a singular mistake. Gibbon must have hastily caught at his inexperience, and concluded that it must have been from youth. Lord Mahon has pointed out this error, p. 401. I should add that in the last 4to. edition, corrected by Gibbon, it stands "want of youth and experience;"—but Gibbon can scarcely have intended such a phrase—M.]

[Footnote 26: See the acts of Germanus in the public (Vandal. l. ii, c. 16, 17, 18 Goth. l. iii. c. 31, 32) and private history, (Anecdot. c. 5,) and those of his son Justin, in Agathias, (l. iv. p. 130, 131.) Notwithstanding an ambiguous expression of Jornandes, fratri suo, Alemannus has proved that he was the son of the emperor's brother.]

[Footnote 27: Conjuncta Aniciorum gens cum Amala stirpe spem adhuc utii usque generis promittit, (Jornandes, c. 60, p. 703.) He wrote at Ravenna before the death of Totila]

[Footnote 2711: See note 31, p. 268—M.]

[Footnote 28: The third book of Procopius is terminated by the death of Germanus, (Add. l. iv. c. 23, 24, 25, 26.)]

After the loss of Germanus, the nations were provoked to smile, by the strange intelligence, that the command of the Roman armies was given to a eunuch. But the eunuch Narses [29] is ranked among the few who have rescued that unhappy name from the contempt and hatred of mankind. A feeble, diminutive body concealed the soul of a statesman and a warrior. His youth had been employed in the management of the loom and distaff, in the cares of the household, and the service of female luxury; but while his hands were busy, he secretly exercised the faculties of a vigorous and discerning mind. A stranger to the schools and the camp, he studied in the palace to dissemble, to flatter, and to persuade; and as soon as he approached the person of the emperor, Justinian listened with surprise and pleasure to the manly counsels of his chamberlain and private treasurer. [30] The talents of Narses were tried and improved in frequent embassies: he led an army into Italy acquired a practical knowledge of the war and the country, and presumed to strive with the genius of Belisarius. Twelve years after his return, the eunuch was chosen to achieve the conquest which had been left imperfect by the first of the Roman generals. Instead of being dazzled by vanity or emulation, he seriously declared that, unless he were armed with an adequate force, he would never consent to risk his own glory and that of his sovereign. Justinian granted to the favorite what he might have denied to the hero: the Gothic war was rekindled from its ashes, and the preparations were not unworthy of the ancient majesty of the empire. The key of the public treasure was put into his hand, to collect magazines, to levy soldiers, to purchase arms and horses, to discharge the arrears of pay, and to tempt the fidelity of the fugitives and deserters. The troops of Germanus were still in arms; they halted at Salona in the expectation of a new leader; and legions of subjects and allies were created by the well-known liberality of the eunuch Narses. The king of the Lombards [31] satisfied or surpassed the obligations of a treaty, by lending two thousand two hundred of his bravest warriors, [31/1] who were followed by three thousand of their martial attendants. Three thousand Heruli fought on horseback under Philemuth, their native chief; and the noble Aratus, who adopted the manners and discipline of Rome, conducted a band of veterans of the same nation. Dagistheus was released from prison to command the Huns; and Kobad, the grandson and nephew of the great king, was conspicuous by the regal tiara at the head of his faithful Persians, who had devoted themselves to the fortunes of their prince. [32] Absolute in the exercise of his authority, more absolute in the affection of his troops, Narses led a numerous and gallant army from Philippopolis to Salona, from whence he coasted the eastern side of the Adriatic as far as the confines of Italy. His progress was checked. The East could not supply vessels capable of transporting such multitudes of men and horses. The Franks, who, in the general confusion, had usurped the greater part of the Venetian province, refused a free passage to the friends of the Lombards. The station of Verona was occupied by Teias, with the flower of the Gothic forces; and that skilful commander had overspread the adjacent country with the fall of woods and the inundation of waters. [33] In this perplexity, an officer of experience proposed a measure, secure by the appearance of rashness; that the Roman army should cautiously advance along the seashore, while the fleet preceded their march, and successively cast a bridge of boats over the mouths of the rivers, the Timavus, the Brenta, the Adige, and the Po, that fall into the Adriatic to the north of Ravenna. Nine days he reposed in the city, collected the fragments of the Italian army, and marching towards Rimini to meet the defiance of an insulting enemy.

[Footnote 29: Procopius relates the whole series of this second Gothic war and the victory of Narses, (l. iv. c. 21, 26—35.) A splendid scene. Among the six subjects of epic poetry which Tasso revolved in his mind, he hesitated between the conquests of Italy by Belisarius and by Narses, (Hayley's Works, vol. iv. p. 70.)]

[Footnote 30: The country of Narses is unknown, since he must not be confounded with the Persarmenian. Procopius styles him (see Goth. l. ii. c. 13); Paul Warnefrid, (l. ii. c. 3, p. 776,) Chartularius: Marcellinus adds the name of Cubicularius. In an inscription on the Salarian bridge he is entitled Ex-consul, Ex-praepositus, Cubiculi Patricius, (Mascou, Hist. of the Germans, (l. xiii. c. 25.) The law of Theodosius against eunuchs was obsolete or abolished, Annotation xx.,) but the foolish prophecy of the Romans subsisted in full vigor, (Procop. l. iv. c. 21.) Note: Lord Mahon supposes them both to have been Persarmenians. Note, p. 256—M.]

[Footnote 31: Paul Warnefrid, the Lombard, records with complacency the succor, service, and honorable dismission of his countrymen—reipublicae Romanae adversus aemulos adjutores fuerant, (l. ii. c. i. p. 774, edit. Grot.) I am surprised that Alboin, their martial king, did not lead his subjects in person. Note: The Lombards were still at war with the Gepidae. See Procop. Goth. lib. iv. p. 25—M.]

[Footnote 31/1: Gibbon has blindly followed the translation of Maltretus: Bis mille ducentos—while the original Greek says expressly something else, (Goth. lib. iv. c. 26.) In like manner, (p. 266,) he draws volunteers from Germany, on the authority of Cousin, who, in one place, has mistaken Germanus for Germania. Yet only a few pages further we find Gibbon loudly condemning the French and Latin readers of Procopius. Lord Mahon, p. 403. The first of these errors remains uncorrected in the new edition of the Byzantines—M.]

[Footnote 32: He was, if not an impostor, the son of the blind Zames, saved by compassion, and educated in the Byzantine court by the various motives of policy, pride, and generosity, (Procop. Persic. l. i. c. 23.)]

[Footnote 33: In the time of Augustus, and in the middle ages, the whole waste from Aquileia to Ravenna was covered with woods, lakes, and morasses. Man has subdued nature, and the land has been cultivated since the waters are confined and embanked. See the learned researches of Muratori, (Antiquitat. Italiae Medii Aevi. tom. i. dissert xxi. p. 253, 254,) from Vitruvius, Strabo, Herodian, old charters, and local knowledge.]

PART III

The prudence of Narses impelled him to speedy and decisive action. His powers were the last effort of the state; the cost of each day accumulated the enormous account; and the nations, untrained to discipline or fatigue, might be rashly provoked to turn their arms against each other, or against their benefactor. The same considerations might have tempered the ardor of Totila. But he was conscious that the clergy and people of Italy aspired to a second revolution: he felt or suspected the rapid progress of treason; and he resolved to risk the Gothic kingdom on the chance of a day, in which the valiant would be animated by instant danger and the disaffected might be awed by mutual ignorance. In his march from Ravenna, the Roman general chastised the garrison of Rimini, traversed in a direct line the hills of Urbino, and reentered the Flaminian way, nine miles beyond the perforated rock, an obstacle of art and nature which might have stopped or retarded his progress. [34] The Goths were assembled in the neighborhood of Rome, they advanced without delay to seek a superior enemy, and the two armies approached each other at the distance of one hundred furlongs, between Tagina [35] and the sepulchres of the Gauls. [36] The haughty message of Narses was an offer, not of peace, but of pardon. The answer of the Gothic king declared his resolution to die or conquer. "What day," said the messenger, "will you fix for the combat?" "The eighth day," replied Totila; but early the next morning he attempted to surprise a foe, suspicious of deceit, and prepared for battle. Ten thousand Heruli and Lombards, of approved valor and doubtful faith, were placed in the centre. Each of the wings was composed of eight thousand Romans; the right was guarded by the cavalry of the Huns, the left was covered by fifteen hundred chosen horse, destined, according to the emergencies of action, to sustain the retreat of their friends, or to encompass the flank of the enemy. From his proper station at the head of the right wing, the eunuch rode along the line, expressing by his voice and countenance the assurance of victory; exciting the soldiers of the emperor to punish the guilt and madness of a band of robbers; and exposing to their view gold chains, collars, and bracelets, the rewards of military virtue. From the event of a single combat they drew an omen of success; and they beheld with pleasure the courage of fifty archers, who maintained a small eminence against three successive attacks of the Gothic cavalry. At the distance only of two bow-shots, the armies spent the morning in dreadful suspense, and the Romans tasted some necessary food, without unloosing the cuirass from their breast, or the bridle from their horses. Narses awaited the charge; and it was delayed by Totila till he had received his last succors of two thousand Goths. While he consumed the hours in fruitless treaty, the king exhibited in a narrow space the strength and agility of a warrior. His armor was enchased with gold; his purple banner floated with the wind: he cast his lance into the air; caught it with the right hand; shifted it to the left; threw himself backwards; recovered his seat; and managed a fiery steed in all the paces and evolutions of the equestrian school. As soon as the succors had arrived, he retired to his tent, assumed the dress and arms of a private soldier, and gave the signal of a battle. The first line of cavalry advanced with more courage than discretion, and left behind them the infantry of the second line. They were soon engaged between the horns of a crescent, into which the adverse wings had been insensibly curved, and were saluted from either side by the volleys of four thousand archers. Their ardor, and even their distress, drove them forwards to a close and unequal conflict, in which they could only use their lances against an enemy equally skilled in all the instruments of war. A generous emulation inspired the Romans and their Barbarian allies; and Narses, who calmly viewed and directed their efforts, doubted to whom he should adjudge the prize of superior bravery. The Gothic cavalry was astonished and disordered, pressed and broken; and the line of infantry, instead of presenting their spears, or opening their intervals, were trampled under the feet of the flying horse. Six thousand of the Goths were slaughtered without mercy in the field of Tagina. Their prince, with five attendants, was overtaken by Asbad, of the race of the Gepidae. "Spare the king of Italy," [36/1] cried a loyal voice, and Asbad struck his lance through the body of Totila. The blow was instantly revenged by the faithful Goths: they transported their dying monarch seven miles beyond the scene of his disgrace; and his last moments were not imbittered by the presence of an enemy. Compassion afforded him the shelter of an obscure tomb; but the Romans were not satisfied of their victory, till they beheld the corpse of the Gothic king. His hat, enriched with gems, and his bloody robe, were presented to Justinian by the messengers of triumph. [37]

[Footnote 34: The Flaminian way, as it is corrected from the Itineraries, and the best modern maps, by D'Anville, (Analyse de l'Italie, p. 147—162,) may be thus stated: Rome to Narni, 51 Roman miles; Terni, 57; Spoleto, 75; Foligno, 88; Nocera, 103; Cagli, 142; Intercisa, 157; Fossombrone, 160; Fano, 176; Pesaro, 184; Rimini, 208—about 189 English miles. He takes no notice of the death of Totila; but West selling (Itinerar. p. 614) exchanges, for the field of Taginas, the unknown appellation of Ptanias, eight miles from Nocera.]

[Footnote 35: Taginae, or rather Tadinae, is mentioned by Pliny; but the bishopric of that obscure town, a mile from Gualdo, in the plain, was united, in the year 1007, with that of Nocera. The signs of antiquity are preserved in the local appellations, Fossato, the camp; Capraia, Caprea; Bastia, Busta Gallorum. See Cluverius, (Italia Antiqua, l. ii. c. 6, p. 615, 616, 617,) Lucas Holstenius, (Annotat. ad Cluver. p. 85, 86,) Guazzesi, (Dissertat. p. 177—217, a professed inquiry,) and the maps of the ecclesiastical state and the march of Ancona, by Le Maire and Magini.]

[Footnote 36: The battle was fought in the year of Rome 458; and the consul Decius, by devoting his own life, assured the triumph of his country and his colleague Fabius, (T. Liv. x. 28, 29.) Procopius ascribes to Camillus the victory of the Busta Gallorum; and his error is branded by Cluverius with the national reproach of Graecorum nugamenta.]

[Footnote 36/1: "Dog, wilt thou strike thy Lord?" was the more characteristic exclamation of the Gothic youth. Procop. lib. iv. p. 32—M.]

[Footnote 37: Theophanes, Chron. p. 193. Hist. Miscell. l. xvi. p. 108.]

As soon as Narses had paid his devotions to the Author of victory, and the blessed Virgin, his peculiar patroness, [38] he praised, rewarded, and dismissed the Lombards. The villages had been reduced to ashes by these valiant savages; they ravished matrons and virgins on the altar; their retreat was diligently watched by a strong detachment of regular forces, who prevented a repetition of the like disorders. The victorious eunuch pursued his march through Tuscany, accepted the submission of the Goths, heard the acclamations, and often the complaints, of the Italians, and encompassed the walls of Rome with the remainder of his formidable host. Round the wide circumference, Narses assigned to himself, and to each of his lieutenants, a real or a feigned attack, while he silently marked the place of easy and unguarded entrance. Neither the fortifications of Hadrian's mole, nor of the port, could long delay the progress of the conqueror; and Justinian once more received the keys of Rome, which, under his reign, had been five times taken and recovered. [39] But the deliverance of Rome was the last calamity of the Roman people. The Barbarian allies of Narses too frequently confounded the privileges of peace and war. The despair of the flying Goths found some consolation in sanguinary revenge; and three hundred youths of the noblest families, who had been sent as hostages beyond the Po, were inhumanly slain by the successor of Totila. The fate of the senate suggests an awful lesson of the vicissitude of human affairs. Of the senators whom Totila had banished from their country, some were rescued by an officer of Belisarius, and transported from Campania to Sicily; while others were too guilty to confide in the clemency of Justinian, or too poor to provide horses for their escape to the sea-shore. Their brethren languished five years in a state of indigence and exile: the victory of Narses revived their hopes; but their premature return to the metropolis was prevented by the furious Goths; and all the fortresses of Campania were stained with patrician [40] blood. After a period of thirteen centuries, the institution of Romulus expired; and if the nobles of Rome still assumed the title of senators, few subsequent traces can be discovered of a public council, or constitutional order. Ascend six hundred years, and contemplate the kings of the earth soliciting an audience, as the slaves or freedmen of the Roman senate! [41]

[Footnote 38: Evagrius, l. iv. c. 24. The inspiration of the Virgin revealed to Narses the day, and the word, of battle, (Paul Diacon. l. ii. c. 3, p. 776)]

[Footnote 39: (Procop. Goth. lib. iv. p. 33.) In the year 536 by Belisarius, in 546 by Totila, in 547 by Belisarius, in 549 by Totila, and in 552 by Narses. Maltretus had inadvertently translated sextum; a mistake which he afterwards retracts; out the mischief was done; and Cousin, with a train of French and Latin readers, have fallen into the snare.]

[Footnote 40: Compare two passages of Procopius, (l. iii. c. 26, l. iv. c. 24,) which, with some collateral hints from Marcellinus and Jornandes, illustrate the state of the expiring senate.]

[Footnote 41: See, in the example of Prusias, as it is delivered in the fragments of Polybius, (Excerpt. Legat. xcvii. p. 927, 928,) a curious picture of a royal slave.]

The Gothic war was yet alive. The bravest of the nation retired beyond the Po; and Teias was unanimously chosen to succeed and revenge their departed hero. The new king immediately sent ambassadors to implore, or rather to purchase, the aid of the Franks, and nobly lavished, for the public safety, the riches which had been deposited in the palace of Pavia. The residue of the royal treasure was guarded by his brother Aligern, at Cumaea, in Campania; but the strong castle which Totila had fortified was closely besieged by the arms of Narses. From the Alps to the foot of Mount Vesuvius, the Gothic king, by rapid and secret marches, advanced to the relief of his brother, eluded the vigilance of the Roman chiefs, and pitched his camp on the banks of the Sarnus or Draco, [42] which flows from Nuceria into the Bay of Naples. The river separated the two armies: sixty days were consumed in distant and fruitless combats, and Teias maintained this important post till he was deserted by his fleet and the hope of subsistence. With reluctant steps he ascended the Lactarian mount, where the physicians of Rome, since the time of Galen, had sent their patients for the benefit of the air and the milk. [43] But the Goths soon embraced a more generous resolution: to descend the hill, to dismiss their horses, and to die in arms, and in the possession of freedom. The king marched at their head, bearing in his right hand a lance, and an ample buckler in his left: with the one he struck dead the foremost of the assailants; with the other he received the weapons which every hand was ambitious to aim against his life. After a combat of many hours, his left arm was fatigued by the weight of twelve javelins which hung from his shield. Without moving from his ground, or suspending his blows, the hero called aloud on his attendants for a fresh buckler; but in the moment while his side was uncovered, it was pierced by a mortal dart. He fell; and his head, exalted on a spear, proclaimed to the nations that the Gothic kingdom was no more. But the example of his death served only to animate the companions who had sworn to perish with their leader. They fought till darkness descended on the earth. They reposed on their arms. The combat was renewed with the return of light, and maintained with unabated vigor till the evening of the second day. The repose of a second night, the want of water, and the loss of their bravest champions, determined the surviving Goths to accept the fair capitulation which the prudence of Narses was inclined to propose. They embraced the alternative of residing in Italy, as the subjects and soldiers of Justinian, or departing with a portion of their private wealth, in search of some independent country. [44] Yet the oath of fidelity or exile was alike rejected by one thousand Goths, who broke away before the treaty was signed, and boldly effected their retreat to the walls of Pavia. The spirit, as well as the situation, of Aligern prompted him to imitate rather than to bewail his brother: a strong and dexterous archer, he transpierced with a single arrow the armor and breast of his antagonist; and his military conduct defended Cumae [45] above a year against the forces of the Romans.

Their industry had scooped the Sibyl's cave [46] into a prodigious mine; combustible materials were introduced to consume the temporary props: the wall and the gate of Cumae sunk into the cavern, but the ruins formed a deep and inaccessible precipice. On the fragment of a rock Aligern stood alone and unshaken, till he calmly surveyed the hopeless condition of his country, and judged it more honorable to be the friend of Narses, than the slave of the Franks. After the death of Teias, the Roman general separated his troops to reduce the cities of Italy; Lucca sustained a long and vigorous siege: and such was the humanity or the prudence of Narses, that the repeated perfidy of the inhabitants could not provoke him to exact the forfeit lives of their hostages. These hostages were dismissed in safety; and their grateful zeal at length subdued the obstinacy of their countrymen. [47]

[Footnote 42: The item of Procopius (Goth. l. iv. c. 35) is evidently the Sarnus. The text is accused or altered by the rash violence of Cluverius (l. iv. c. 3. p. 1156:) but Camillo Pellegrini of Naples (Discorsi sopra la Campania Felice, p. 330, 331) has proved from old records, that as early as the year 822 that river was called the Dracontio, or Draconcello.]

[Footnote 43: Galen (de Method. Medendi, l. v. apud Cluver. l. iv. c. 3, p. 1159, 1160) describes the lofty site, pure air, and rich milk, of Mount Lactarius, whose medicinal benefits were equally known and sought in the time of Symmachus (l. vi. epist. 18) and Cassiodorus, (Var. xi. 10.) Nothing is now left except the name of the town of Lettere.]

[Footnote 44: Buat (tom. xi. p. 2, &c.) conveys to his favorite Bavaria this remnant of Goths, who by others are buried in the mountains of Uri, or restored to their native isle of Gothland, (Mascou, Annot. xxi.)]

[Footnote 45: I leave Scaliger (Animadvers. in Euseb. p. 59) and Salmasius (Exercitat. Plinian. p. 51, 52) to quarrel about the origin of Cumae, the oldest of the Greek colonies in Italy, (Strab. l. v. p. 372, Velleius Paterculus, l. i. c. 4,) already vacant in Juvenal's time, (Satir. iii.,) and now in ruins.]

[Footnote 46: Agathias (l. i. c. 21) settles the Sibyl's cave under the wall of Cumae: he agrees with Servius, (ad. l. vi. Aeneid.;) nor can I perceive why their opinion should be rejected by Heyne, the excellent editor of Virgil, (tom. ii. p. 650, 651.) In urbe media secreta religio! But Cumae was not yet built; and the lines (l. vi. 96, 97) would become ridiculous, if Aeneas were actually in a Greek city.]

[Footnote 47: There is some difficulty in connecting the 35th chapter of the fourth book of the Gothic war of Procopius with the first book of the history of Agathias. We must now relinquish the statesman and soldier, to attend the footsteps of a poet and rhetorician, (l. i. p. 11, l. ii. p. 51, edit. Lonvre.)]

Before Lucca had surrendered, Italy was overwhelmed by a new deluge of Barbarians. A feeble youth, the grandson of Clovis, reigned over the Austrasians or oriental Franks. The guardians of Theodebald entertained with coldness and reluctance the magnificent promises of the Gothic ambassadors. But the spirit of a martial people outstripped the timid counsels of the court: two brothers, Lothaire and Buccelin, [48] the dukes of the Alemanni, stood forth as the leaders of the Italian war; and seventy-five thousand Germans descended in the autumn from the Rhaetian Alps into the plain of Milan. The vanguard of the Roman army was stationed near the Po, under the conduct of Fulcaris, a bold Herulian, who rashly conceived that personal bravery was the sole duty and merit of a commander. As he marched without order or precaution along the Aemilian way, an ambuscade of Franks suddenly rose from the amphitheatre of Parma; his troops were surprised and routed; but their leader refused to fly; declaring to the last moment, that death was less terrible than the angry countenance of Narses. [48/1] The death of Fulcaris, and the retreat of the surviving chiefs, decided the fluctuating and rebellious temper of the Goths; they flew to the standard of their deliverers, and admitted them into the cities which still resisted the arms of the Roman general. The conqueror of Italy opened a free passage to the irresistible torrent of Barbarians. They passed under the walls of Cesena, and answered by threats and reproaches the advice of Aligern, [48/2] that the Gothic treasures could no longer repay the labor of an invasion. Two thousand Franks were destroyed by the skill and valor of Narses himself, who sailed from Rimini at the head of three hundred horse, to chastise the licentious rapine of their march. On the confines of Samnium the two brothers divided their forces. With the right wing, Buccelin assumed the spoil of Campania, Lucania, and Bruttium; with the left, Lothaire accepted the plunder of Apulia and Calabria. They followed the coast of the Mediterranean and the Adriatic, as far as Rhegium and Otranto, and the extreme lands of Italy were the term of their destructive progress. The Franks, who were Christians and Catholics, contented themselves with simple pillage and occasional murder. But the churches which their piety had spared, were stripped by the sacrilegious hands of the Alamanni, who sacrificed horses' heads to their native deities of the woods and rivers; [49] they melted or profaned the consecrated vessels, and the ruins of shrines and altars were stained with the blood of the faithful. Buccelin was actuated by ambition, and Lothaire by avarice. The former aspired to restore the Gothic kingdom; the latter, after a promise to his brother of speedy succors, returned by the same road to deposit his treasure beyond the Alps. The strength of their armies was already wasted by the change of climate and contagion of disease: the Germans revelled in the vintage of Italy; and their own intemperance avenged, in some degree, the miseries of a defenceless people. [49/1]

[Footnote 48: Among the fabulous exploits of Buccelin, he discomfited and slew Belisarius, subdued Italy and Sicily, &c. See in the Historians of France, Gregory of Tours, (tom. ii. l. iii. c. 32, p. 203,) and Aimoin, (tom. iii. l. ii. de Gestis Francorum, c. 23, p. 59.)]

[Footnote 48/1:.... Agathius.]

[Footnote 48/2: Aligern, after the surrender of Cumae, had been sent to Cesent by Narses. Agathias—M.]

[Footnote 49: Agathias notices their superstition in a philosophic tone, (l. i. p. 18.) At Zug, in Switzerland, idolatry still prevailed in the year 613: St. Columban and St. Gaul were the apostles of that rude country; and the latter founded a hermitage, which has swelled into an ecclesiastical principality and a populous city, the seat of freedom and commerce.]

[Footnote 49/1: A body of Lothaire's troops was defeated near Fano, some were driven down precipices into the sea, others fled to the camp; many prisoners seized the opportunity of making their escape; and the Barbarians lost most of their booty in their precipitate retreat. Agathias—M.]

At the entrance of the spring, the Imperial troops, who had guarded the cities, assembled, to the number of eighteen thousand men, in the neighborhood of Rome. Their winter hours had not been consumed in idleness. By the command, and after the example, of Narses, they repeated each day their military exercise on foot and on horseback, accustomed their ear to obey the sound of the trumpet, and practised the steps and evolutions of the Pyrrhic dance. From the Straits of Sicily, Buccelin, with thirty thousand Franks and Alamanni, slowly moved towards Capua, occupied with a wooden tower the bridge of Casilinum, covered his right by the stream of the Vulturnus, and secured the rest of his encampment by a rampart of sharp stakes, and a circle of wagons, whose wheels were buried in the earth. He impatiently expected the return of Lothaire; ignorant, alas! that his brother could never return, and that the chief and his army had been swept away by a strange disease [50] on the banks of the Lake Benacus, between Trent and Verona. The banners of Narses soon approached the Vulturnus, and the eyes of Italy were anxiously fixed on the event of this final contest. Perhaps the talents of the Roman general were most conspicuous in the calm operations which precede the tumult of a battle. His skilful movements intercepted the subsistence of the Barbarian deprived him of the advantage of the bridge and river, and in the choice of the ground and moment of action reduced him to comply with the inclination of his enemy. On the morning of the important day, when the ranks were already formed, a servant, for some trivial fault, was killed by his master, one of the leaders of the Heruli. The justice or passion of Narses was awakened: he summoned the offender to his presence, and without listening to his excuses, gave the signal to the minister of death. If the cruel master had not infringed the laws of his nation, this arbitrary execution was not less unjust than it appears to have been imprudent. The Heruli felt the indignity; they halted: but the Roman general, without soothing their rage, or expecting their resolution, called aloud, as the trumpets sounded, that unless they hastened to occupy their place, they would lose the honor of the victory. His troops were disposed [51] in a long front, the cavalry on the wings; in the centre, the heavy-armed foot; the archers and slingers in the rear. The Germans advanced in a sharp-pointed column, of the form of a triangle or solid wedge. They pierced the feeble centre of Narses, who received them with a smile into the fatal snare, and directed his wings of cavalry insensibly to wheel on their flanks and encompass their rear. The host of the Franks and Alamanni consisted of infantry: a sword and buckler hung by their side; and they used, as their weapons of offence, a weighty hatchet and a hooked javelin, which were only formidable in close combat, or at a short distance. The flower of the Roman archers, on horseback, and in complete armor, skirmished without peril round this immovable phalanx; supplied by active speed the deficiency of number; and aimed their arrows against a crowd of Barbarians, who, instead of a cuirass and helmet, were covered by a loose garment of fur or linen. They paused, they trembled, their ranks were confounded, and in the decisive moment the Heruli, preferring glory to revenge, charged with rapid violence the head of the column. Their leader, Sinbal, and Aligern, the Gothic prince, deserved the prize of superior valor; and their example excited the victorious troops to achieve with swords and spears the destruction of the enemy. Buccelin, and the greatest part of his army, perished on the field of battle, in the waters of the Vulturnus, or by the hands of the enraged peasants: but it may seem incredible, that a victory, [52] which no more than five of the Alamanni survived, could be purchased with the loss of fourscore Romans. Seven thousand Goths, the relics of the war, defended the fortress of Campsa till the ensuing spring; and every messenger of Narses announced the reduction of the Italian cities, whose names were corrupted by the ignorance or vanity of the Greeks. [53] After the battle of Casilinum, Narses entered the capital; the arms and treasures of the

Goths, the Franks, and the Alamanni, were displayed; his soldiers, with garlands in their hands, chanted the praises of the conqueror; and Rome, for the last time, beheld the semblance of a triumph.

[Footnote 50: See the death of Lothaire in Agathias (l. ii. p. 38) and Paul Warnefrid, surnamed Diaconus, (l. ii. c. 3, 775.) The Greek makes him rave and tear his flesh. He had plundered churches.]

[Footnote 51: Pere Daniel (Hist. de la Milice Francoise, tom. i. p. 17—21) has exhibited a fanciful representation of this battle, somewhat in the manner of the Chevalier Folard, the once famous editor of Polybius, who fashioned to his own habits and opinions all the military operations of antiquity.]

[Footnote 52: Agathias (l. ii. p. 47) has produced a Greek epigram of six lines on this victory of Narses, which a favorably compared to the battles of Marathon and Plataea. The chief difference is indeed in their consequences—so trivial in the former instance—so permanent and glorious in the latter. Note: Not in the epigram, but in the previous observations—M.]

[Footnote 53: The Beroia and Brincas of Theophanes or his transcriber (p. 201) must be read or understood Verona and Brixia.]

After a reign of sixty years, the throne of the Gothic kings was filled by the exarchs of Ravenna, the representatives in peace and war of the emperor of the Romans. Their jurisdiction was soon reduced to the limits of a narrow province: but Narses himself, the first and most powerful of the exarchs, administered above fifteen years the entire kingdom of Italy. Like Belisarius, he had deserved the honors of envy, calumny, and disgrace: but the favorite eunuch still enjoyed the confidence of Justinian; or the leader of a victorious army awed and repressed the ingratitude of a timid court. Yet it was not by weak and mischievous indulgence that Narses secured the attachment of his troops. Forgetful of the past, and regardless of the future, they abused the present hour of prosperity and peace. The cities of Italy resounded with the noise of drinking and dancing; the spoils of victory were wasted in sensual pleasures; and nothing (says Agathias) remained unless to exchange their shields and helmets for the soft lute and the capacious hogshead. [54] In a manly oration, not unworthy of a Roman censor, the eunuch reproved these disorderly vices, which sullied their fame, and endangered their safety. The soldiers blushed and obeyed; discipline was confirmed; the fortifications were restored; a duke was stationed for the defence and military command of each of the principal cities; [55] and the eye of Narses pervaded the ample prospect from Calabria to the Alps. The remains of the Gothic nation evacuated the country, or mingled with the people; the Franks, instead of revenging the death of Buccelin, abandoned, without a struggle, their Italian conquests; and the rebellious Sinbal, chief of the Heruli, was subdued, taken and hung on a lofty gallows by the inflexible justice of the exarch. [56] The civil state of Italy, after the agitation of a long tempest, was fixed by a pragmatic sanction, which the emperor promulgated at the request of the pope. Justinian introduced his own jurisprudence into the schools and tribunals of the West; he ratified the acts of Theodoric and his immediate successors, but every deed was rescinded and abolished which force had extorted, or fear had subscribed, under the usurpation of Totila. A moderate theory was framed to reconcile the rights of property with the safety of prescription, the claims of the state with the poverty of the people, and the pardon of offences with the interest of virtue and order of society. Under the exarchs of Ravenna, Rome was degraded to the second rank. Yet the senators were gratified by the permission of visiting their estates in Italy, and of approaching, without obstacle, the throne of Constantinople: the regulation of weights and measures was delegated to the pope and senate; and the salaries of lawyers and physicians, of orators and grammarians, were destined to preserve, or rekindle, the light of science in the ancient capital. Justinian might dictate benevolent edicts, [57] and Narses might second his wishes by the restoration of cities, and more especially of churches. But the power of kings is most effectual to destroy; and the twenty years of the Gothic war had consummated the distress and depopulation of Italy. As early as the fourth campaign, under the discipline of Belisarius himself, fifty thousand laborers died of hunger [58] in the narrow region of Picenum; [59] and a strict interpretation of the evidence of Procopius would swell the loss of Italy above the total sum of her present inhabitants. [60]

[Footnote 54: (Agathias, l. ii. p. 48.) In the first scene of Richard III. our English poet has beautifully enlarged on this idea, for which, however, he was not indebted to the Byzantine historian.]

[Footnote 55: Maffei has proved, (Verona Illustrata. P. i. l. x. p. 257, 289,) against the common opinion, that the dukes of Italy were instituted before the conquest of the Lombards, by Narses himself. In the Pragmatic Sanction, (No. 23,) Justinian restrains the judices militares.]

[Footnote 56: See Paulus Diaconus, liii. c. 2, p. 776. Menander in (Excerp Legat. p. 133) mentions some risings in Italy by the Franks, and Theophanes (p. 201) hints at some Gothic rebellions.]

[Footnote 57: The Pragmatic Sanction of Justinian, which restores and regulates the civil state of Italy, consists of xxvii. articles: it is dated August 15, A.D. 554; is addressed to Narses, V. J. Praepositus Sacri Cubiculi, and to Antiochus, Praefectus Praetorio Italiae; and has been preserved by Julian Antecessor, and in the Corpus Juris Civilis, after the novels and edicts of Justinian, Justin, and Tiberius.]

[Footnote 58: A still greater number was consumed by famine in the southern provinces, without the Ionian Gulf. Acorns were used in the place of bread. Procopius had seen a deserted orphan suckled by a she-goat. Seventeen passengers were lodged, murdered, and eaten, by two women, who were detected and slain by the eighteenth, &c. Note: Denina considers that greater evil was inflicted upon Italy by the Urocian conquest than by any other invasion. Reveluz. d' Italia, t. i. l. v. p. 247—M.]

[Footnote 59: Quinta regio Piceni est; quondam uberrimae multitudinis, ccclx. millia Picentium in fidem P. R. venere, (Plin. Hist. Natur. iii. 18.) In the time of Vespasian, this ancient population was already diminished.]

[Footnote 60: Perhaps fifteen or sixteen millions. Procopius (Anecdot. c. 18) computes that Africa lost five millions, that Italy was thrice as extensive, and that the depopulation was in a larger proportion. But his reckoning is inflamed by passion, and clouded with uncertainty.]

I desire to believe, but I dare not affirm, that Belisarius sincerely rejoiced in the triumph of Narses. Yet the consciousness of his own exploits might teach him to esteem without jealousy the merit of a rival; and the repose of the aged warrior was crowned by a last victory, which saved the emperor and the capital. The Barbarians, who annually visited the provinces of Europe, were less discouraged by some accidental defeats, than they were excited by the double hope of spoil and of subsidy. In the thirty-second winter of Justinian's reign, the Danube was deeply frozen: Zabergan led the cavalry of the Bulgarians, and his standard was followed by a promiscuous multitude of Sclavonians. [60/1] The savage chief passed, without opposition, the river and the mountains, spread his troops over Macedonia and Thrace, and advanced with no more than seven thousand horse to the long wall, which should have defended the territory of Constantinople. But the works of man are impotent against the assaults of nature: a recent earthquake had shaken the foundations of the wall; and the forces of the empire were employed on the distant frontiers of Italy, Africa, and Persia. The seven schools, [61] or companies of the guards or domestic troops, had been augmented to the number of five thousand five hundred men, whose ordinary station was in the peaceful cities of Asia. But the places of the brave Armenians were insensibly supplied by lazy citizens, who purchased an exemption from the duties of civil life, without being exposed to the dangers of military service. Of such soldiers, few could be tempted to sally from the gates; and none could be persuaded to remain in the field, unless they wanted strength and speed to escape from the Bulgarians. The report of the fugitives exaggerated the numbers and fierceness of an enemy, who had polluted holy virgins, and abandoned new-born infants to the dogs and vultures; a crowd of rustics, imploring food and protection, increased the consternation of the city, and the tents of Zabergan were pitched at the distance of twenty miles, [62] on the banks of a small river, which encircles Melanthias, and afterwards falls into the Propontis. [63] Justinian trembled: and those who had only seen the emperor in his old age, were pleased to suppose, that he had lost the alacrity and vigor of his youth. By his command the vessels of gold and silver were removed from the churches in the neighborhood, and even the suburbs, of Constantinople; the ramparts were lined with trembling spectators; the golden gate was crowded with useless generals and tribunes, and the senate shared the fatigues and the apprehensions of the populace.

[Footnote 60/1: Zabergan was king of the Cutrigours, a tribe of Huns, who were neither Bulgarians nor Sclavonians. St. Martin, vol. ix. p. 408—420—M]

[Footnote 61: In the decay of these military schools, the satire of Procopius (Anecdot. c. 24, Aleman. p. 102, 103) is confirmed and illustrated by Agathias, (l. v. p. 159,) who cannot be rejected as a hostile witness.]

[Footnote 62: The distance from Constantinople to Melanthias, Villa Caesariana, (Ammian. Marcellin. xxx. 11,) is variously fixed at 102 or 140 stadia, (Suidas, tom. ii. p. 522, 523. Agathias, l. v. p. 158,) or xviii. or xix. miles, (Itineraria, p. 138, 230, 323, 332, and Wesseling's Observations.) The first xii. miles, as far as Rhegium, were paved by Justinian, who built a bridge over a morass or gullet between a lake and the sea, (Procop. de Edif. l. iv. c. 8.)]

[Footnote 63: The Atyras, (Pompon. Mela, l. ii. c. 2, p. 169, edit. Voss.) At the river's mouth, a town or castle of the same name was fortified by Justinian, (Procop. de Edif. l. iv. c. 2. Itinerar. p. 570, and Wesseling.)]

But the eyes of the prince and people were directed to a feeble veteran, who was compelled by the public danger to resume the armor in which he had entered Carthage and defended Rome. The horses of the royal stables, of private citizens, and even of the circus, were hastily collected; the emulation of the old and young was roused by the name of Belisarius, and his first encampment was in the presence of a victorious enemy. His prudence, and the labor of the friendly peasants, secured, with a ditch and rampart, the repose of the night; innumerable fires, and clouds of dust, were artfully contrived to magnify the opinion of his strength; his soldiers suddenly passed from despondency to presumption; and, while ten thousand voices demanded the battle, Belisarius dissembled his knowledge, that in the hour of trial he must depend on the firmness of three hundred veterans. The next morning the Bulgarian cavalry advanced to the charge. But they heard the shouts of multitudes, they beheld the arms and discipline of the front; they were assaulted on the flanks by two ambuscades which rose from the woods; their foremost warriors fell by the hand of the aged hero and his guards; and the swiftness of their evolutions was rendered useless by the close attack and rapid pursuit of the Romans. In this action (so speedy was their flight) the Bulgarians lost only four hundred horse; but Constantinople was saved; and Zabergan, who felt the hand of a master, withdrew to a respectful distance. But his friends were numerous in the councils of the emperor, and Belisarius obeyed with reluctance the commands of envy and Justinian, which forbade him to achieve the deliverance of his country. On his return to the city, the people, still conscious of their danger, accompanied his triumph with acclamations of joy and gratitude, which were imputed as a crime to the victorious general. But when he entered the palace, the courtiers were silent, and the emperor, after a cold and thankless embrace, dismissed him to mingle with the train of slaves. Yet so deep was the impression of his glory on the minds of men, that Justinian, in the seventy-seventh year of his age, was encouraged to advance near forty miles from the capital, and to inspect in person the restoration of the long wall. The Bulgarians wasted the summer in the plains of Thrace; but they were inclined to peace by the failure of their rash attempts on Greece and the Chersonesus. A menace of killing their prisoners quickened the payment of heavy ransoms; and the departure of Zabergan was hastened by the report, that double-prowed vessels were built on the Danube to intercept his passage. The danger was soon forgotten; and a vain question, whether their sovereign had shown more wisdom or weakness, amused the idleness of the city. [64]

[Footnote 64: The Bulgarian war, and the last victory of Belisarius, are imperfectly represented in the prolix declamation of Agathias. (l. 5, p. 154-174,) and the dry Chronicle of Theophanes, (p. 197 198.)]

PART IV

About two years after the last victory of Belisarius, the emperor returned from a Thracian journey of health, or business, or devotion. Justinian was afflicted by a pain in his head; and his private entry countenanced the rumor of his death. Before the third hour of the day, the bakers' shops were plundered of their bread, the houses were shut, and every citizen, with hope or terror, prepared for the impending tumult. The senators themselves, fearful and suspicious, were convened at the ninth hour; and the praefect received their commands to visit every quarter of the city, and proclaim a general illumination for the recovery of the emperor's health. The ferment subsided; but every accident betrayed the impotence of the government, and the factious temper of the people: the guards were disposed to mutiny as often as their quarters were changed, or their pay was withheld: the frequent calamities of fires and earthquakes afforded the opportunities of disorder; the disputes of the blues and greens, of the orthodox and heretics, degenerated into bloody battles; and, in the presence of the Persian ambassador, Justinian blushed for himself and for his subjects. Capricious pardon and arbitrary punishment imbittered the irksomeness and discontent of a long reign: a conspiracy was formed in the palace; and, unless we are deceived by the names of Marcellus and Sergius, the most virtuous and the most profligate of the courtiers were associated in the same designs. They had fixed the time of the execution; their rank gave them access to the royal banquet; and their black slaves [65] were stationed in the vestibule and porticos, to announce the death of the tyrant, and to excite a sedition in the capital. But the indiscretion of an accomplice saved the poor remnant of the days of Justinian. The conspirators were detected and seized, with daggers hidden under their garments: Marcellus died by his own hand, and Sergius was dragged from the sanctuary. [66] Pressed by remorse, or tempted by the hopes of safety, he accused two officers of the household of Belisarius; and torture forced them to declare that they had acted according to the secret instructions of their patron. [67] Posterity will not hastily believe that a hero who, in the vigor of life, had disdained the fairest offers of ambition and revenge, should stoop to the murder of his prince, whom he could not long expect to survive. His followers were impatient to fly; but flight must have been supported by rebellion, and he had lived enough for nature and for glory. Belisarius appeared before the council with less fear than indignation: after forty years' service, the emperor had prejudged his guilt; and injustice was sanctified by the presence and authority of the patriarch. The life of Belisarius was graciously spared; but his fortunes were sequestered, and, from December to July, he was guarded as a prisoner in his own palace. At length his innocence was acknowledged; his freedom and honor were restored; and death, which might be hastened by resentment and grief, removed him from the world in about eight months after his deliverance. The name of Belisarius can never die but instead of the funeral, the monuments, the statues, so justly due to his memory, I only read, that his treasures, the spoil of the Goths and Vandals, were immediately confiscated by the emperor. Some decent portion was reserved, however for the use of his widow: and as Antonina had much to repent, she devoted the last remains of her life and fortune to the foundation of a convent. Such is the simple and genuine narrative of the fall of Belisarius and the ingratitude of Justinian. [68] That he was deprived of his eyes, and reduced by envy to beg his bread, [68/1] "Give a penny to Belisarius the general!" is a fiction of later times, [69] which has obtained credit, or rather favor, as a strange example of the vicissitudes of fortune. [70]

[Footnote 65: They could scarcely be real Indians; and the Aethiopians, sometimes known by that name, were never used by the ancients as guards or followers: they were the trifling, though costly objects of female and royal luxury, (Terent. Eunuch. act. i. scene ii Sueton. in August. c. 83, with a good note of Casaubon, in Caligula, c. 57.)]

[Footnote 66: The Sergius (Vandal. l. ii. c. 21, 22, Anecdot. c. 5) and Marcellus (Goth. l. iii. c. 32) are mentioned by Procopius. See Theophanes, p. 197, 201. Note: Some words, "the acts of," or "the crimes cf," appear to have false from the text. The omission is in all the editions I have consulted—M.]

[Footnote 67: Alemannus, (p. quotes an old Byzantian Ms., which has been printed in the Imperium Orientale of Banduri.)]

[Footnote 68: Of the disgrace and restoration of Belisarius, the genuine original record is preserved in the Fragment of John Malala (tom. ii. p. 234—243) and the exact Chronicle of Theophanes, (p. 194—204.) Cedrenus (Compend. p. 387, 388) and Zonaras (tom. ii. l. xiv. p. 69) seem to hesitate between the obsolete truth and the growing falsehood.]

[Footnote 68/1: Le Beau, following Allemannus, conceives that Belisarius was confounded with John of Cappadocia, who was thus reduced to beggary, (vol. ix. p. 58, 449.) Lord Mahon has, with considerable learning, and on the authority of a yet unquoted writer of the eleventh century, endeavored to reestablish the old tradition. I cannot acknowledge that I have been convinced, and am inclined to subscribe to the theory of Le Beau—M.]

[Footnote 69: The source of this idle fable may be derived from a miscellaneous work of the xiith century, the Chiliads of John Tzetzes, a monk, (Basil. 1546, ad calcem Lycophront. Colon. Allobrog. 1614, in Corp. Poet. Graec.) He relates the blindness and beggary of Belisarius in ten vulgar or political verses, (Chiliad iii. No. 88, 339—348, in Corp. Poet. Graec. tom. ii. p. 311.) This moral or romantic tale was imported into Italy with the language and manuscripts of Greece; repeated before the end of the xvth century by Crinitus, Pontanus, and Volaterranus, attacked by Alciat, for the honor of the law; and defended by Baronius, (A.D. 561, No. 2, &c.,) for the honor of the church. Yet Tzetzes himself had read in other chronicles, that Belisarius did not lose his sight, and that he recovered his fame and fortunes. Note: I know not where Gibbon found Tzetzes to be a monk; I suppose he considered his bad verses a proof of his monachism. Compare to Gerbelius in Kiesling's edition of Tzetzes—M.]

[Footnote 70: The statue in the villa Borghese at Rome, in a sitting posture, with an open hand, which is vulgarly given to Belisarius, may be ascribed with more dignity to Augustus in the act of propitiating

Nemesis, (Winckelman, Hist. de l'Art, tom. iii. p. 266.) Ex nocturno visu etiam stipem, quotannis, die certo, emendicabat a populo, cavana manum asses porrigentibus praebens, (Sueton. in August. c. 91, with an excellent note of Casaubon.) Note: Lord Mahon abandons the statue, as altogether irreconcilable with the state of the arts at this period, (p. 472.)—M.]

If the emperor could rejoice in the death of Belisarius, he enjoyed the base satisfaction only eight months, the last period of a reign of thirty-eight years, and a life of eighty-three years. It would be difficult to trace the character of a prince who is not the most conspicuous object of his own times: but the confessions of an enemy may be received as the safest evidence of his virtues. The resemblance of Justinian to the bust of Domitian, is maliciously urged; [71] with the acknowledgment, however, of a well-proportioned figure, a ruddy complexion, and a pleasing countenance. The emperor was easy of access, patient of hearing, courteous and affable in discourse, and a master of the angry passions which rage with such destructive violence in the breast of a despot. Procopius praises his temper, to reproach him with calm and deliberate cruelty: but in the conspiracies which attacked his authority and person, a more candid judge will approve the justice, or admire the clemency, of Justinian. He excelled in the private virtues of chastity and temperance: but the impartial love of beauty would have been less mischievous than his conjugal tenderness for Theodora; and his abstemious diet was regulated, not by the prudence of a philosopher, but the superstition of a monk. His repasts were short and frugal: on solemn fasts, he contented himself with water and vegetables; and such was his strength, as well as fervor, that he frequently passed two days, and as many nights, without tasting any food. The measure of his sleep was not less rigorous: after the repose of a single hour, the body was awakened by the soul, and, to the astonishment of his chamberlain, Justinian walked or studied till the morning light. Such restless application prolonged his time for the acquisition of knowledge [72] and the despatch of business; and he might seriously deserve the reproach of confounding, by minute and preposterous diligence, the general order of his administration. The emperor professed himself a musician and architect, a poet and philosopher, a lawyer and theologian; and if he failed in the enterprise of reconciling the Christian sects, the review of the Roman jurisprudence is a noble monument of his spirit and industry. In the government of the empire, he was less wise, or less successful: the age was unfortunate; the people was oppressed and discontented; Theodora abused her power; a succession of bad ministers disgraced his judgment; and Justinian was neither beloved in his life, nor regretted at his death. The love of fame was deeply implanted in his breast, but he condescended to the poor ambition of titles, honors, and contemporary praise; and while he labored to fix the admiration, he forfeited the esteem and affection, of the Romans.

The design of the African and Italian wars was boldly conceived and executed; and his penetration discovered the talents of Belisarius in the camp, of Narses in the palace. But the name of the emperor is eclipsed by the names of his victorious generals; and Belisarius still lives, to upbraid the envy and ingratitude of his sovereign. The partial favor of mankind applauds the genius of a conqueror, who leads and directs his subjects in the exercise of arms. The characters of Philip the Second and of Justinian are distinguished by the cold ambition which delights in war, and declines the dangers of the field. Yet a colossal statue of bronze represented the emperor on horseback, preparing to march against the Persians in the habit and armor of Achilles. In the great square before the church of St. Sophia, this monument was raised on a brass column and a stone pedestal of seven steps; and the pillar of Theodosius, which weighed seven thousand four hundred pounds of silver, was removed from the same place by the avarice and vanity of Justinian. Future princes were more just or indulgent to his memory; the elder Andronicus, in the beginning of the fourteenth century, repaired and beautified his equestrian statue: since the fall of the empire it has been melted into cannon by the victorious Turks. [73]

[Footnote 71: The rubor of Domitian is stigmatized, quaintly enough, by the pen of Tacitus, (in Vit. Agricol. c. 45;) and has been likewise noticed by the younger Pliny, (Panegyr. c. 48,) and Suetonius, (in Domitian, c. 18, and Casaubon ad locum.) Procopius (Anecdot. c. 8) foolishly believes that only one bust of Domitian had reached the vith century.]

[Footnote 72: The studies and science of Justinian are attested by the confession (Anecdot. c. 8, 13) still more than by the praises (Gothic. l. iii. c. 31, de Edific. l. i. Proem. c. 7) of Procopius. Consult the copious index of Alemannus, and read the life of Justinian by Ludewig, (p. 135—142.)]

[Footnote 73: See in the C. P. Christiana of Ducange (l. i. c. 24, No. 1) a chain of original testimonies, from Procopius in the vith, to Gyllius in the xvith century.]

I shall conclude this chapter with the comets, the earthquakes, and the plague, which astonished or afflicted the age of Justinian. I. In the fifth year of his reign, and in the month of September, a comet [74] was seen during twenty days in the western quarter of the heavens, and which shot its rays into the north. Eight years afterwards, while the sun was in Capricorn, another comet appeared to follow in the Sagittary; the size was gradually increasing; the head was in the east, the tail in the west, and it remained visible above forty days. The nations, who gazed with astonishment, expected wars and calamities from their baleful influence; and these expectations were abundantly fulfilled. The astronomers dissembled their ignorance of the nature of these blazing stars, which they affected to represent as the floating meteors of the air; and few among them embraced the simple notion of Seneca and the Chaldeans, that they are only planets of a longer period and more eccentric motion. [75] Time and science have justified the conjectures and predictions of the Roman sage: the telescope has opened new worlds to the eyes of astronomers; [76] and, in the narrow space of history and fable, one and the same comet is already found to have revisited the earth in seven equal revolutions of five hundred and seventy-five years. The first, [77] which ascends beyond the Christian aera one thousand seven hundred and sixty-seven years, is coeval with Ogyges, the father of Grecian antiquity. And this appearance explains the tradition which Varro has preserved, that under his reign the planet Venus changed her color, size, figure, and course; a prodigy without example either in past or succeeding ages. [78] The second visit, in the year eleven hundred and ninety-three, is darkly implied in the fable of Electra, the seventh of the Pleiads, who have been reduced to six since the time of the Trojan war. That nymph, the wife of Dardanus, was unable to support the ruin of her country: she abandoned the dances of her sister orbs, fled from the zodiac to the north pole, and obtained, from her dishevelled locks, the name of the comet. The third period expires in the year six hundred and eighteen, a date that exactly agrees with the tremendous comet of the Sibyl, and perhaps of Pliny, which arose in the West two generations before the reign of Cyrus. The fourth apparition, forty-four years before the birth of Christ, is of all others the most splendid and important. After the death of Caesar, a long-haired star was conspicuous to Rome and to the nations, during the games which were exhibited by young Octavian in honor of Venus and his uncle. The vulgar opinion, that it conveyed to heaven the divine soul of the dictator, was cherished and consecrated by the piety of a statesman; while his secret superstition referred the comet to the glory of his own times. [79] The fifth visit has been already ascribed to the fifth year of Justinian, which coincides with the five hundred and thirty-first of the Christian aera. And it may deserve notice, that in this, as in the preceding instance, the comet was followed, though at a longer interval, by a remarkable paleness of the sun. The sixth return, in the year eleven hundred and six, is recorded by the chronicles of Europe and China: and in the first fervor of the crusades, the Christians and the Mahometans might surmise, with equal reason, that it portended the destruction of the Infidels. The seventh phenomenon, of one thousand six hundred and eighty, was presented to the eyes of an enlightened age. [80] The philosophy of Bayle dispelled a prejudice which Milton's muse had so recently adorned, that the comet, "from its horrid hair shakes pestilence and war." [81] Its road in the heavens was observed with exquisite skill by Flamstead and Cassini: and the mathematical science of Bernoulli, Newton [8111], and Halley, investigated the laws of its revolutions. At the eighth period, in the year two thousand three hundred and fifty-five, their calculations may perhaps be verified by the astronomers of some future capital in the Siberian or American wilderness.

[Footnote 74: The first comet is mentioned by John Malala (tom. ii. p. 190, 219) and Theophanes, (p. 154;) the second by Procopius, (Persic. l. ii. 4.) Yet I strongly suspect their identity. The paleness of the sun sum Vandal. (l. ii. c. 14) is applied by Theophanes (p. 158) to a different year. Note: See Lydus de Ostentis, particularly c 15, in which the author begins to show the signification of comets according to the part of the heavens in which they appear, and what fortunes they prognosticate to the Roman empire and their Persian enemies. The chapter, however, is imperfect. (Edit. Neibuhr, p. 290.)—M.]

[Footnote 75: Seneca's viith book of Natural Questions displays, in the theory of comets, a philosophic mind. Yet should we not too candidly confound a vague prediction, a venient tempus, &c., with the merit of real discoveries.]

[Footnote 76: Astronomers may study Newton and Halley. I draw my humble science from the article Comete, in the French Encyclopedie, by M. d'Alembert.]

[Footnote 77: Whiston, the honest, pious, visionary Whiston, had fancied for the aera of Noah's flood (2242 years before Christ) a prior apparition of the same comet which drowned the earth with its tail.]

[Footnote 78: A Dissertation of Freret (Memoires de l'Academie des Inscriptions, tom. x. p. 357-377) affords a happy union of philosophy and erudition. The phenomenon in the time of Ogyges was preserved by Varro, (Apud Augustin. de Civitate Dei, xxi. 8,) who quotes Castor, Dion of Naples, and Adastrus of Cyzicus—nobiles mathematici. The two subsequent periods are preserved by the Greek mythologists and the spurious books of Sibylline verses.]

[Footnote 79: Pliny (Hist. Nat. ii. 23) has transcribed the original memorial of Augustus. Mairan, in his most ingenious letters to the P. Parennin, missionary in China, removes the games and the comet of September, from the year 44 to the year 43, before the Christian aera; but I am not totally subdued by the criticism of the astronomer, (Opuscules, p. 275)]

[Footnote 80: This last comet was visible in the month of December, 1680. Bayle, who began his Pensees sur la Comete in January, 1681, (Oeuvres, tom. iii.,) was forced to argue that a supernatural comet would have confirmed the ancients in their idolatry. Bernoulli (see his Eloge, in Fontenelle, tom. v. p. 99) was forced to allow that the tail though not the head, was a sign of the wrath of God.]

[Footnote 81: Paradise Lost was published in the year 1667; and the famous lines (l. ii. 708, &c.) which startled the licenser, may allude to the recent comet of 1664, observed by Cassini at Rome in the presence of Queen Christina, (Fontenelle, in his Eloge, tom. v. p. 338.) Had Charles II. betrayed any symptoms of curiosity or fear?]

[Footnote 81/1: Compare Pingre, Histoire des Cometes—M.]

II. The near approach of a comet may injure or destroy the globe which we inhabit; but the changes on its surface have been hitherto produced by the action of volcanoes and earthquakes. [82] The nature of the soil may indicate the countries most exposed to these formidable concussions, since they are caused by subterraneous fires, and such fires are kindled by the union and fermentation of iron and sulphur. But their times and effects appear to lie beyond the reach of human curiosity; and the philosopher will discreetly abstain from the prediction of earthquakes, till he has counted the drops of water that silently filtrate on the inflammable mineral, and measured the caverns which increase by resistance the explosion of the imprisoned air. Without assigning the cause, history will distinguish the periods in which these calamitous events have been rare or frequent, and will observe, that this fever of the earth raged with uncommon violence during the reign of Justinian. [83] Each year is marked by the repetition of earthquakes, of such duration, that Constantinople has been shaken above forty days; of such extent, that the shock has been communicated to the whole surface of the globe, or at least of the Roman empire. An impulsive or vibratory motion was felt: enormous chasms were opened, huge and heavy bodies were discharged into the air, the sea alternately advanced and retreated beyond its ordinary bounds, and a mountain was torn from Libanus, [84] and cast into the waves, where it protected, as a mole, the new harbor of Botrys [85] in Phoenicia. The stroke that agitates an ant-hill may crush the insect-myriads in the dust; yet truth must extort confession that man has industriously labored for his own destruction. The institution of great cities, which include a nation within the limits of a wall, almost realizes the wish of Caligula, that the Roman people had but one neck. Two hundred and fifty thousand persons are said to have perished in the earthquake of Antioch, whose domestic multitudes were swelled by the conflux of strangers to the festival of the Ascension. The loss of Berytus [86] was of smaller account, but of much greater value. That city, on the coast of Phoenicia, was illustrated by the study of the civil law, which opened the surest road to wealth and dignity: the schools of Berytus were filled with the rising spirits of the age, and many a youth was lost in the earthquake, who might have lived to be the scourge or the guardian of his country. In these disasters, the architect becomes the enemy of mankind. The hut of a savage, or the tent of an Arab, may be thrown down without injury to the inhabitant; and the Peruvians had reason to deride the folly of their Spanish conquerors, who with so much cost and labor erected their own sepulchres. The rich marbles of a patrician are dashed on his own head: a whole people is buried under the ruins of public and private edifices, and the conflagration is kindled and propagated by the innumerable fires which are necessary for the subsistence and manufactures of a great city. Instead of the mutual sympathy which might comfort and assist the distressed, they dreadfully experience the vices and passions which are released from the fear of punishment: the tottering houses are pillaged by intrepid avarice; revenge embraces the moment, and selects the victim; and the earth often swallows the assassin, or the ravisher, in the consummation of their crimes. Superstition involves the present danger with invisible terrors; and if the image of death may sometimes be subservient to the virtue or repentance of individuals, an affrighted people is more forcibly moved to expect the end of the world, or to deprecate with servile homage the wrath of an avenging Deity.

[Footnote 82: For the cause of earthquakes, see Buffon, (tom. i. p. 502—536 Supplement a l'Hist. Naturelle, tom. v. p. 382-390, edition in 4to., Valmont de Bomare, Dictionnaire d'Histoire Naturelle, Tremblemen de Terre, Pyrites,) Watson, (Chemical Essays, tom. i. p. 181—209.)]

[Footnote 83: The earthquakes that shook the Roman world in the reign of Justinian are described or mentioned by Procopius, (Goth. l. iv. c. 25 Anecdot. c. 18,) Agathias, (l. ii. p. 52, 53, 54, l. v. p. 145-152,) John Malala, (Chron. tom. ii. p. 140-146, 176, 177, 183, 193, 220, 229, 231, 233, 234,) and Theophanes, (p. 151, 183, 189, 191-196.) Note: Compare Daubeny on Earthquakes, and Lyell's Geology, vol. ii. p. 161 et seq—M]

[Footnote 84: An abrupt height, a perpendicular cape, between Aradus and Botrys (Polyb. l. v. p. 411. Pompon. Mela, l. i. c. 12, p. 87, cum Isaac. Voss. Observat. Maundrell, Journey, p. 32, 33. Pocock's Description, vol. ii. p. 99.)]

[Footnote 85: Botrys was founded (ann. ante Christ. 935—903) by Ithobal, king of Tyre, (Marsham, Canon. Chron. p. 387, 388.) Its poor representative, the village of Patrone, is now destitute of a harbor.]

[Footnote 86: The university, splendor, and ruin of Berytus are celebrated by Heineccius (p. 351—356) as an essential part of the history of the Roman law. It was overthrown in the xxvth year of Justinian, A. D 551, July 9, (Theophanes, p. 192;) but Agathias (l. ii. p. 51, 52) suspends the earthquake till he has achieved the Italian war.]

III. Aethiopia and Egypt have been stigmatized, in every age, as the original source and seminary of the plague. [87] In a damp, hot, stagnating air, this African fever is generated from the putrefaction of animal substances, and especially from the swarms of locusts, not less destructive to mankind in their death than in their lives. The fatal disease which depopulated the earth in the time of Justinian and his successors, [88] first appeared in the neighborhood of Pelusium, between the Serbonian bog and the eastern channel of the Nile. From thence, tracing as it were a double path, it spread to the East, over Syria, Persia, and the Indies, and penetrated to the West, along the coast of Africa, and over the continent of Europe. In the spring of the second year, Constantinople, during three or four months, was visited by the pestilence; and Procopius, who observed its progress and symptoms with the eyes of a physician, [89] has emulated the skill and diligence of Thucydides in the description of the plague of Athens. [90] The infection was sometimes announced by the visions of a distempered fancy, and the victim despaired as soon as he had heard the menace and felt the stroke of an invisible spectre. But the greater number, in their beds, in the streets, in their usual occupation, were surprised by a slight fever; so slight, indeed, that neither the pulse nor the color of the patient gave any signs of the approaching danger. The same, the next, or the succeeding day, it was declared by the swelling of the glands, particularly those of the groin, of the armpits, and under the ear; and when these buboes or tumors were opened, they were found to contain a coal, or black substance, of the size of a lentil. If they came to a just swelling and suppuration, the patient was saved by this kind and natural discharge of the morbid humor. But if they continued hard and dry, a mortification quickly ensued, and the fifth day was commonly the term of his life. The fever was often accompanied with lethargy or delirium; the bodies of the sick were covered with black pustules or carbuncles, the symptoms of immediate death; and in the constitutions too feeble to produce an irruption, the vomiting of blood was followed by a mortification of the bowels. To pregnant women the plague was generally mortal: yet one infant was drawn alive from his dead mother, and three mothers survived the loss of their infected foetus. Youth was the most perilous season; and the female sex was less susceptible than the male: but every rank and profession was attacked with indiscriminate rage, and many of those who escaped were deprived of the use of their speech, without being secure from a return of the disorder. [91] The physicians of Constantinople were zealous and skilful; but their art was baffled by the various symptoms and pertinacious vehemence of the disease: the same remedies were productive of contrary effects, and the event capriciously disappointed their prognostics of death or recovery. The order of funerals, and the right of sepulchres, were confounded: those who were left without friends or servants, lay unburied in the streets, or in their desolate houses; and a magistrate was authorized to collect the promiscuous heaps of dead bodies, to transport them by land or water, and to inter them in deep pits beyond the precincts of the city. Their own danger, and the prospect of public distress, awakened some remorse in the minds of the most vicious of mankind: the confidence of health again revived their passions and habits; but philosophy must disdain the observation of Procopius, that the lives of such men were guarded by the peculiar favor of fortune or Providence. He forgot, or perhaps he secretly recollected, that the plague had touched the person of Justinian himself; but the abstemious diet of the emperor may suggest, as in the case of Socrates, a more rational and honorable cause for his recovery. [92] During his sickness, the public consternation was expressed in the habits of the citizens; and their idleness and despondence occasioned a general scarcity in the capital of the East. [Footnote 87: I have read with pleasure Mead's short, but elegant, treatise concerning Pestilential Disorders, the viiith edition, London, 1722.]

[Footnote 88: The great plague which raged in 542 and the following years (Pagi, Critica, tom. ii. p. 518) must be traced in Procopius, (Persic. l. ii. c. 22, 23,) Agathias, (l. v. p. 153, 154,) Evagrius, (l. iv. c. 29,) Paul Diaconus, (l. ii. c. iv. p. 776, 777,) Gregory of Tours, (tom. ii. l. iv. c. 5, p 205,) who styles it Lues Inguinaria, and the Chronicles of Victor Tunnunensis, (p. 9, in Thesaur. Temporum,) of Marcellinus, (p. 54,) and of Theophanes, (p. 153.)]

[Footnote 89: Dr. Friend (Hist. Medicin. in Opp. p. 416—420, Lond. 1733) is satisfied that Procopius must have studied physic, from his knowledge and use of the technical words. Yet many words that are now scientific were common and popular in the Greek idiom.]

[Footnote 90: See Thucydides, l. ii. c. 47—54, p. 127—133, edit. Duker, and the poetical description of the same plague by Lucretius. (l. vi. 1136—1284.) I was indebted to Dr. Hunter for an elaborate commentary on this part of Thucydides, a quarto of 600 pages, (Venet. 1603, apud Juntas,) which was pronounced in St. Mark's Library by Fabius Paullinus Utinensis, a physician and philosopher.]

[Footnote 91: Thucydides (c. 51) affirms, that the infection could only be once taken; but Evagrius, who had family experience of the plague, observes, that some persons, who had escaped the first, sunk under the second attack; and this repetition is confirmed by Fabius Paullinus, (p. 588.) I observe, that on this head physicians are divided; and the nature and operation of the disease may not always be similar.]

[Footnote 92: It was thus that Socrates had been saved by his temperance, in the plague of Athens, (Aul. Gellius, Noct. Attic. ii. l.) Dr. Mead accounts for the peculiar salubrity of religious houses, by the two advantages of seclusion and abstinence, (p. 18, 19.)]

Contagion is the inseparable symptom of the plague; which, by mutual respiration, is transfused from the infected persons to the lungs and stomach of those who approach them. While philosophers believe and tremble, it is singular, that the existence of a real danger should have been denied by a people most prone to vain and imaginary terrors. [93] Yet the fellow-citizens of Procopius were satisfied, by some short and partial experience, that the infection could not be gained by the closest conversation: [94] and this persuasion might support the assiduity of friends or physicians in the care of the sick, whom inhuman prudence would have condemned to solitude and despair. But the fatal security, like the predestination of the Turks, must have aided the progress of the contagion; and those salutary precautions to which Europe is indebted for her safety, were unknown to the government of Justinian. No restraints were imposed on the free and frequent intercourse of the Roman provinces: from Persia to France, the nations were mingled and infected by wars and emigrations; and the pestilential odor which lurks for years in a bale of cotton was imported, by the abuse of trade, into the most distant regions. The mode of its propagation is explained by the remark of Procopius himself, that it always spread from the sea-coast to the inland country: the most sequestered islands and mountains were successively visited; the places which had escaped the fury of its first passage were alone exposed to the contagion of the ensuing year. The winds might diffuse that subtile venom; but unless the atmosphere be previously disposed for its reception, the plague would soon expire in the cold or temperate climates of the earth. Such was the universal corruption of the air, that the pestilence which burst forth in the fifteenth year of Justinian was not checked or alleviated by any difference of the seasons. In time, its first malignity was abated and dispersed; the disease alternately languished and revived; but it was not till the end of a calamitous period of fifty-two years, that mankind recovered their health, or the air resumed its pure and salubrious quality.

No facts have been preserved to sustain an account, or even a conjecture, of the numbers that perished in this extraordinary mortality. I only find, that during three months, five, and at length ten, thousand persons died each day at Constantinople; that many cities of the East were left vacant, and that in several districts of Italy the harvest and the vintage withered on the ground. The triple scourge of war, pestilence, and famine, afflicted the subjects of Justinian; and his reign is disgraced by the visible decrease of the human species, which has never been repaired in some of the fairest countries of the globe. [95]

[Footnote 93: Mead proves that the plague is contagious from Thucydides, Lacretius, Aristotle, Galen, and common experience, (p. 10—20;) and he refutes (Preface, p. 2—13) the contrary opinion of the French physicians who visited Marseilles in the year 1720. Yet these were the recent and enlightened spectators of a plague which, in a few months, swept away 50,000 inhabitants (sur le Peste de Marseille, Paris, 1786) of a city that, in the present hour of prosperity and trade contains no more then 90,000 souls, (Necker, sur les Finances, tom. i. p. 231.)]

[Footnote 94: The strong assertions of Procopius are overthrown by the subsequent experience of Evagrius.]

[Footnote 95: After some figures of rhetoric, the sands of the sea, &c., Procopius (Anecdot. c. 18) attempts a more definite account; that it had been exterminated under the reign of the Imperial demon. The expression is obscure in grammar and arithmetic and a literal interpretation would produce several millions of millions Alemannus (p. 80) and Cousin (tom. iii. p. 178) translate this passage, "two hundred millions:" but I am ignorant of their motives. The remaining myriad of myriads, would furnish one hundred millions, a number not wholly inadmissible.]

CHAPTER XLIV

IDEA OF THE ROMAN JURISPRUDENCE

PART I

Idea Of The Roman Jurisprudence—The Laws Of The Kings—The Twelve Of The Decemvirs—The Laws Of The People—The Decrees Of The Senate—The Edicts Of The Magistrates And Emperors—Authority Of The Civilians—Code, Pandects, Novels, And Institutes Of Justinian:—I. Rights Of Persons—II. Rights Of Things—III. Private Injuries And Actions—IV. Crimes And Punishments.

Note: In the notes to this important chapter, which is received as the text-book on Civil Law in some of the foreign universities, I have consulted,

I. the newly-discovered Institutes of Gaius, (Gaii Institutiones, ed. Goeschen, Berlin, 1824,) with some other fragments of the Roman law, (Codicis Theodosiani Fragmenta inedita, ab Amadeo Peyron. Turin, 1824.)

II. The History of the Roman Law, by Professor Hugo, in the French translation of M. Jourdan. Paris, 1825.

III. Savigny, Geschichte des Romischen Rechts im Mittelalter, 6 bande, Heidelberg, 1815.

IV. Walther, Romische Rechts-Geschichte, Bonn. 1834. But I am particularly indebted to an edition of the French translation of this chapter, with additional notes, by one of the most learned civilians of Europe, Professor Warnkonig, published at Liege, 1821. I have inserted almost the whole of these notes, which are distinguished by the letter W—M. The vain titles of the victories of Justinian are crumbled into dust; but the name of the legislator is inscribed on a fair and everlasting monument. Under his reign, and by his care, the civil jurisprudence was digested in the immortal works of the Code, the Pandects, and the Institutes: [1] the public reason of the Romans has been silently or studiously transfused into the domestic institutions of Europe, [2], and the laws of Justinian still command the respect or obedience of independent nations. Wise or fortunate is the prince who connects his own reputation with the honor or interest of a perpetual order of men. The defence of their founder is the first cause, which in every age has exercised the zeal and industry of the civilians. They piously commemorate his virtues; dissemble or deny his failings; and fiercely chastise the guilt or folly of the rebels, who presume to sully the majesty of the purple. The idolatry of love has provoked, as it usually happens, the rancor of opposition; the character of Justinian has been exposed to the blind vehemence of flattery and invective; and the injustice of a sect (the Anti-Tribonians,) has refused all praise and merit to the prince, his ministers, and his laws. [3] Attached to no party, interested only for the truth and candor of history, and directed by the most temperate and skilful guides, [4] I enter with just diffidence on the subject of civil law, which has exhausted so many learned lives, and clothed the walls of such spacious libraries. In a single, if possible in a short, chapter, I shall trace the Roman jurisprudence from Romulus to Justinian, [5] appreciate the labors of that emperor, and pause to contemplate the principles of a science so important to the peace and happiness of society. The laws of a nation form the most instructive portion of its history; and although I have devoted myself to write the annals of a declining monarchy, I shall embrace the occasion to breathe the pure and invigorating air of the republic.

[Footnote 1: The civilians of the darker ages have established an absurd and incomprehensible mode of quotation, which is supported by authority and custom. In their references to the Code, the Pandects, and the Institutes, they mention the number, not of the book, but only of the law; and content themselves with reciting the first words of the title to which it belongs; and of these titles there are more than a thousand. Ludewig (Vit. Justiniani, p. 268) wishes to shake off this pedantic yoke; and I have dared to adopt the simple and rational method of numbering the book, the title, and the law. Note: The example of Gibbon has been followed by M Hugo and other civilians—M]

[Footnote 2: Germany, Bohemia, Hungary, Poland, and Scotland, have received them as common law or reason; in France, Italy, &c., they possess a direct or indirect influence; and they were respected in England, from Stephen to Edward I. our national Justinian, (Duck. de Usu et Auctoritate Juris Civilis, l. ii. c. 1, 8—15. Heineccius, Hist. Juris Germanici, c. 3, 4, No. 55-124, and the legal historians of each country.) Note: Although the restoration of the Roman law, introduced by the revival of this study in Italy, is one of the most important branches of history, it had been treated but imperfectly when Gibbon wrote his work. That of Arthur Duck is but an insignificant performance. But the researches of the learned have thrown much light upon the matter. The Sarti, the Tiraboschi, the Fantuzzi, the Savioli, had made some very interesting inquiries; but it was reserved for M. de Savigny, in a work entitled "The History of the Roman Law during the Middle Ages," to cast the strongest right on this part of history. He demonstrates incontestably the preservation of the Roman law from Justinian to the time of the Glossators, who by their indefatigable zeal, propagated the study of the Roman jurisprudence in all the countries of Europe. It is much to be desired that the author should continue this interesting work, and that the learned should engage in the inquiry in what manner the Roman law introduced itself into their respective countries, and the authority which it progressively acquired. For Belgium, there exists, on this subject, (proposed by the Academy of Brussels in 1781,) a Collection of Memoirs, printed at Brussels in 4to., 1783, among which should be distinguished those of M. de Berg. M. Berriat Saint Prix has given us hopes of the speedy appearance of a work in which he will discuss this question, especially in relation to France. M. Spangenberg, in his Introduction to the Study of the Corpus Juris Civilis Hanover, 1817, 1 vol. 8vo. p. 86, 116, gives us a general sketch of the history of the Roman law in different parts of Europe. We cannot avoid mentioning an elementary work by M. Hugo, in which he treats of the History of the Roman Law from Justinian to the present Time, 2d edit. Berlin 1818 W.]

[Footnote 3: Francis Hottoman, a learned and acute lawyer of the xvith century, wished to mortify Cujacius, and to please the Chancellor de l'Hopital. His Anti-Tribonianus (which I have never been able to procure) was published in French in 1609; and his sect was propagated in Germany, (Heineccius, Op. tom. iii. sylloge iii. p. 171—183.) Note: Though there have always been many detractors of the Roman law, no sect of Anti-Tribonians has ever existed under that name, as Gibbon seems to suppose—W.]

[Footnote 4: At the head of these guides I shall respectfully place the learned and perspicuous Heineccius, a German professor, who died at Halle in the year 1741, (see his Eloge in the Nouvelle Bibliotheque Germanique, tom. ii. p. 51—64.) His ample works have been collected in eight volumes in 4to. Geneva, 1743-1748. The treatises which I have separately used are, 1. Historia Juris Romani et Germanici, Lugd. Batav. 1740, in 8 vo. 2. Syntagma Antiquitatum Romanam Jurisprudentiam illustrantium, 2 vols. in 8 vo. Traject. ad Rhenum. 3. Elementa Juris Civilis secundum Ordinem Institutionum, Lugd. Bat. 1751, in 8 vo. 4. Elementa J. C. secundum Ordinem Pandectarum Traject. 1772, in 8vo. 2 vols. Note: Our author, who was not a lawyer, was necessarily obliged to content himself with following the opinions of those writers who were then of the greatest authority; but as Heineccius, notwithstanding his high reputation for the study of the Roman law, knew nothing of the subject on which he treated, but what he had learned from the compilations of various authors, it happened that, in following the sometimes rash opinions of these guides, Gibbon has fallen into many errors, which we shall endeavor in succession to correct. The work of Bach on the History of the Roman Jurisprudence, with which Gibbon was not acquainted, is far superior to that of Heineccius and since that time we have new obligations to the modern historic civilians, whose indefatigable researches have greatly enlarged the sphere of our knowledge in this important branch of history. We want a pen like that of Gibbon to give to the more accurate notions which we have acquired since his time, the brilliancy, the vigor, and the animation which Gibbon has bestowed on the opinions of Heineccius and his contemporaries—W]

[Footnote 5: Our original text is a fragment de Origine Juris (Pandect. l. i. tit. ii.) of Pomponius, a Roman lawyer, who lived under the Antonines, (Heinecc. tom. iii. syl. iii. p. 66—126.) It has been abridged, and probably corrupted, by Tribonian, and since restored by Bynkershoek (Opp. tom. i. p. 279—304.)]

The primitive government of Rome [6] was composed, with some political skill, of an elective king, a council of nobles, and a general assembly of the people. War and religion were administered by the supreme magistrate; and he alone proposed the laws, which were debated in the senate, and finally ratified or rejected by a majority of votes in the thirty curiae or parishes of the city. Romulus, Numa, and Servius Tullius, are celebrated as the most ancient legislators; and each of them claims his peculiar part in the threefold division of jurisprudence. [7] The laws of marriage, the education of children, and the authority of parents, which may seem to draw their origin from nature itself, are ascribed to the untutored wisdom of Romulus. The law of nations and of religious worship, which Numa introduced, was derived from his nocturnal converse with the nymph Egeria. The civil law is attributed to the experience of Servius: he balanced the rights and fortunes of the seven classes of citizens; and guarded, by fifty new regulations, the observance of contracts and the punishment of crimes. The state, which he had inclined towards a democracy, was changed by the last Tarquin into a lawless despotism; and when the kingly office was abolished, the patricians engrossed the benefits of freedom. The royal laws became odious or obsolete; the mysterious deposit was silently preserved by the priests and nobles; and at the end of sixty years, the citizens of Rome still complained that they were ruled by the arbitrary sentence of the magistrates. Yet the positive institutions of the kings had blended themselves with the public and private manners of the city, some fragments of that venerable jurisprudence [8] were compiled by the diligence of antiquarians, [9] and above twenty texts still speak the rudeness of the Pelasgic idiom of the Latins. [10]

[Footnote 6: The constitutional history of the kings of Rome may be studied in the first book of Livy, and more copiously in Dionysius Halicarnassensis, (l. li. p. 80—96, 119—130, l. iv. p. 198—220,) who sometimes betrays the character of a rhetorician and a Greek. Note: M. Warnkonig refers to the work of Beaufort, on the Uncertainty of the Five First Ages of the Roman History, with which Gibbon was probably acquainted, to Niebuhr, and to the less known volume of Wachsmuth, "Aeltere Geschichte des Rom. Staats." To these I would add A. W. Schlegel's Review of Niebuhr, and my friend Dr. Arnold's recently published volume, of which the chapter on the Law of the XII. Tables appears to me one of the most valuable, if not the most valuable, chapter—M.]

[Footnote 7: This threefold division of the law was applied to the three Roman kings by Justus Lipsius, (Opp. tom. iv. p. 279;) is adopted by Gravina, (Origines Juris Civilis, p. 28, edit. Lips. 1737:) and is reluctantly admitted by Mascou, his German editor. Note: Whoever is acquainted with the real notions of the Romans on the jus naturale, gentium et civile, cannot but disapprove of this explanation which has no relation to them, and might be taken for a pleasantry. It is certainly unnecessary to increase the confusion which already prevails among modern writers on the true sense of these ideas. Hugo—W]

[Footnote 8: The most ancient Code or Digest was styled Jus Papirianum, from the first compiler, Papirius, who flourished somewhat before or after the Regifugium, (Pandect. l. i. tit. ii.) The best judicial critics, even Bynkershoek (tom. i. p. 284, 285) and Heineccius, (Hist. J. C. R. l. i. c. 16, 17, and Opp. tom. iii. sylloge iv. p. 1—8,) give credit to this tale of Pomponius, without sufficiently adverting to the value and rarity of such a monument of the third century, of the illiterate city. I much suspect that the Caius Papirius, the Pontifex Maximus, who revived the laws of Numa (Dionys. Hal. l. iii. p. 171) left only an oral tradition; and that the Jus Papirianum of Granius Flaccus (Pandect. l. L. tit. xvi. leg. 144) was not a commentary, but an original work, compiled in the time of Caesar, (Censorin. de Die Natali, l. iii. p. 13, Duker de Latinitate J. C. p. 154.) Note: Niebuhr considers the Jus Papirianum, adduced by Verrius Flaccus, to be of undoubted authenticity. Rom. Geschichte, I. 257—M. Compare this with the work of M. Hugo—W.]

[Footnote 9: A pompous, though feeble attempt to restore the original, is made in the Histoire de la Jurisprudence Romaine of Terasson, p. 22—72, Paris, 1750, in folio; a work of more promise than performance.]

[Footnote 10: In the year 1444, seven or eight tables of brass were dug up between Cortona and Gubio. A part of these (for the rest is Etruscan) represents the primitive state of the Pelasgic letters and language, which are ascribed by Herodotus to that district of Italy, (l. i. c. 56, 57, 58;) though this difficult passage may be explained of a Crestona in Thrace, (Notes de Larcher, tom. i. p. 256—261.) The savage dialect of the Eugubine tables has exercised, and may still elude, the divination of criticism; but the root is undoubtedly Latin, of the same age and character as the Saliare Carmen, which, in the time of Horace, none could understand. The Roman idiom, by an infusion of Doric and Aeolic Greek, was gradually ripened into the style of the xii. tables, of the Duillian column, of Ennius, of Terence, and of Cicero, (Gruter. Inscript. tom. i. p. cxlii. Scipion Maffei, Istoria Diplomatica, p. 241—258. Bibliotheque Italique, tom. iii. p. 30—41, 174—205. tom. xiv. p. 1—52.) Note: The Eugubine Tables have exercised the ingenuity of the Italian and German critics; it seems admitted (O. Muller, die Etrusker, ii. 313) that they are Tuscan. See the works of Lanzi, Passeri, Dempster, and O. Muller—M]

I shall not repeat the well-known story of the Decemvirs, [11] who sullied by their actions the honor of inscribing on brass, or wood, or ivory, the Twelve Tables of the Roman laws. [12] They were dictated by the rigid and jealous spirit of an aristocracy, which had yielded with reluctance to the just demands of the people. But the substance of the Twelve Tables was adapted to the state of the city; and the Romans had emerged from Barbarism, since they were capable of studying and embracing the institutions of their more enlightened neighbors. [12/1] A wise Ephesian was driven by envy from his native country: before he could reach the shores of Latium, he had observed the various forms of human nature and civil society: he imparted his knowledge to the legislators of Rome, and a statue was erected in the forum to the perpetual memory of Hermodorus. [13] The names and divisions of the copper money, the sole coin of the infant state, were of Dorian origin: [14] the harvests of Campania and Sicily relieved the wants of a people whose agriculture was often interrupted by war and faction; and since the trade was established, [15] the deputies who sailed from the Tyber might return from the same harbors with a more precious cargo of political wisdom. The colonies of Great Greece had transported and improved the arts of their mother country. Cumae and Rhegium, Crotona and Tarentum, Agrigentum and Syracuse, were in the rank of the most flourishing cities. The disciples of Pythagoras applied philosophy to the use of government; the unwritten laws of Charondas accepted the aid of poetry and music, [16] and Zaleucus framed the republic of the Locrians, which stood without alteration above two hundred years. [17] From a similar motive of national pride, both Livy and Dionysius are willing to believe, that the deputies of Rome visited Athens under the wise and splendid administration of Pericles; and the laws of Solon were transfused into the twelve tables. If such an embassy had indeed been received from the Barbarians of Hesperia, the Roman name would have been familiar to the Greeks before the reign of Alexander; [18] and the faintest evidence would have been explored and celebrated by the curiosity of succeeding times. But the Athenian monuments are silent; nor will it seem credible that the patricians should undertake a long and perilous navigation to copy the purest model of democracy. In the comparison of the tables of Solon with those of the Decemvirs, some casual resemblance may be found; some rules which nature and reason have revealed to every society; some proofs of a common descent from Egypt or Phoenicia. [19] But in all the great lines of public and private jurisprudence, the legislators of Rome and Athens appear to be strangers or adverse at each other.

[Footnote 11: Compare Livy (l. iii. c. 31—59) with Dionysius Halicarnassensis, (l. x. p. 644—xi. p. 691.) How concise and animated is the Roman—how prolix and lifeless the Greek! Yet he has admirably judged the masters, and defined the rules, of historical composition.]

[Footnote 12: From the historians, Heineccius (Hist. J. R. l. i. No. 26) maintains that the twelve tables were of brass—aereas; in the text of Pomponius we read eboreas; for which Scaliger has substituted roboreas, (Bynkershoek, p. 286.) Wood, brass, and ivory, might be successively employed. Note: Compare Niebuhr, vol. ii. p. 349, &c—M.]

[Footnote 12/1: Compare Niebuhr, 355, note 720—M. It is a most important question whether the twelve tables in fact include laws imported from Greece. The negative opinion maintained by our author, is now almost universally adopted, particularly by Mm. Niebuhr, Hugo, and others. See my Institutiones Juris Romani privati Leodii, 1819, p. 311, 312—W. Dr. Arnold, p. 255, seems to incline to the opposite opinion. Compare some just and sensible observations in the Appendix to Mr. Travers Twiss's Epitome of Niebuhr, p. 347, Oxford, 1836—M.]

[Footnote 13: His exile is mentioned by Cicero, (Tusculan. Quaestion. v. 36; his statue by Pliny, (Hist. Nat. xxxiv. 11.) The letter, dream, and prophecy of Heraclitus, are alike spurious, (Epistolae Graec. Divers. p. 337.) Note: Compare Niebuhr, ii. 209—M. See the Mem de l'Academ. des Inscript. xxii. p. 48. It would be difficult to disprove, that a certain Hermodorus had some share in framing the Laws of the Twelve Tables. Pomponius even says that this Hermodorus was the author of the last two tables. Pliny calls him the Interpreter of the Decemvirs, which may lead us to suppose that he labored with them in drawing up that law. But it is astonishing that in his Dissertation, (De Hermodoro vero XII. Tabularum Auctore, Annales Academiae Groninganae anni 1817, 1818,) M. Gratama has ventured to advance two propositions entirely devoid of proof: "Decem priores tabulas ab ipsis Romanis non esse profectas, tota confirma Decemviratus Historia," et "Hermodorum legum decemviralium ceri nominis auctorem esse, qui eas composuerit suis ordinibus, disposuerit, suaque fecerit auctoritate, ut a decemviris reciperentur." This truly was an age in which the Roman Patricians would allow their laws to be dictated by a foreign Exile! Mr. Gratama does not attempt to prove the authenticity of the supposititious letter of Heraclitus. He contents himself with expressing his astonishment that M. Bonamy (as well as Gibbon) will be receive it as genuine—W.]

[Footnote 14: This intricate subject of the Sicilian and Roman money, is ably discussed by Dr. Bentley, (Dissertation on the Epistles of Phalaris, p. 427—479,) whose powers in this controversy were called forth by honor and resentment.]

[Footnote 15: The Romans, or their allies, sailed as far as the fair promontory of Africa, (Polyb. l. iii. p. 177, edit. Casaubon, in folio.) Their voyages to Cumae, &c., are noticed by Livy and Dionysius.]

[Footnote 16: This circumstance would alone prove the antiquity of Charondas, the legislator of Rhegium and Catana, who, by a strange error of Diodorus Siculus (tom. i. l. xii. p. 485—492) is celebrated long afterwards as the author of the policy of Thurium.]

[Footnote 17: Zaleucus, whose existence has been rashly attacked, had the merit and glory of converting a band of outlaws (the Locrians) into the most virtuous and orderly of the Greek republics. (See two Memoirs of the Baron de St. Croix, sur la Legislation de la Grande Grece Mem. de l'Academie, tom. xlii. p. 276—333.) But the laws of Zaleucus and Charondas, which imposed on Diodorus and Stobaeus, are the spurious composition of a Pythagorean sophist, whose fraud has been detected by the critical sagacity of Bentley, p. 335—377.]

[Footnote 18: I seize the opportunity of tracing the progress of this national intercourse 1. Herodotus and Thucydides (A. U. C. 300—350) appear ignorant of the name and existence of Rome, (Joseph. contra

Appion tom. ii. l. i. c. 12, p. 444, edit. Havercamp.) 2. Theopompus (A. U. C. 400, Plin. iii. 9) mentions the invasion of the Gauls, which is noticed in looser terms by Heraclides Ponticus, (Plutarch in Camillo, p. 292, edit. H. Stephan.) 3. The real or fabulous embassy of the Romans to Alexander (A. U. C. 430) is attested by Clitarchus, (Plin. iii. 9,) by Aristus and Asclepiades, (Arrian. l. vii. p. 294, 295,) and by Memnon of Heraclea, (apud Photium, cod. ccxxiv. p. 725,) though tacitly denied by Livy. 4. Theophrastus (A. U. C. 440) primus externorum aliqua de Romanis diligentius scripsit, (Plin. iii. 9.) 5. Lycophron (A. U. C. 480—500) scattered the first seed of a Trojan colony and the fable of the Aeneid, (Cassandra, 1226—1280.) A bold prediction before the end of the first Punic war! Note: Compare Niebuhr throughout. Niebuhr has written a dissertation (Kleine Schriften, i. p. 438,) arguing from this prediction, and on the other conclusive grounds, that the Lycophron, the author of the Cassandra, is not the Alexandrian poet. He had been anticipated in this sagacious criticism, as he afterwards discovered, by a writer of no less distinction than Charles James Fox—Letters to Wakefield. And likewise by the author of the extraordinary translation of this poem, that most promising scholar, Lord Royston. See the Remains of Lord Royston, by the Rev. Henry Pepys, London, 1838.]

[Footnote 19: The tenth table, de modo sepulturae, was borrowed from Solon, (Cicero de Legibus, ii. 23—26:) the furtem per lancem et licium conceptum, is derived by Heineccius from the manners of Athens, (Antiquitat. Rom. tom. ii. p. 167—175.) The right of killing a nocturnal thief was declared by Moses, Solon, and the Decemvirs, (Exodus xxii. 3. Demosthenes contra Timocratem, tom. i. p. 736, edit. Reiske. Macrob. Saturnalia, l. i. c. 4. Collatio Legum Mosaicarum et Romanatum, tit, vii. No. i. p. 218, edit. Cannegieter.) Note: Are not the same points of similarity discovered in the legislation of all actions in the infancy of their civilization?—W.]

PART II

Whatever might be the origin or the merit of the twelve tables, [20] they obtained among the Romans that blind and partial reverence which the lawyers of every country delight to bestow on their municipal institutions. The study is recommended by Cicero [21] as equally pleasant and instructive. "They amuse the mind by the remembrance of old words and the portrait of ancient manners; they inculcate the soundest principles of government and morals; and I am not afraid to affirm, that the brief composition of the Decemvirs surpasses in genuine value the libraries of Grecian philosophy. How admirable," says Tully, with honest or affected prejudice, "is the wisdom of our ancestors! We alone are the masters of civil prudence, and our superiority is the more conspicuous, if we deign to cast our eyes on the rude and almost ridiculous jurisprudence of Draco, of Solon, and of Lycurgus." The twelve tables were committed to the memory of the young and the meditation of the old; they were transcribed and illustrated with learned diligence; they had escaped the flames of the Gauls, they subsisted in the age of Justinian, and their subsequent loss has been imperfectly restored by the labors of modern critics. [22] But although these venerable monuments were considered as the rule of right and the fountain of justice, [23] they were overwhelmed by the weight and variety of new laws, which, at the end of five centuries, became a grievance more intolerable than the vices of the city. [24] Three thousand brass plates, the acts of the senate of the people, were deposited in the Capitol: [25] and some of the acts, as the Julian law against extortion, surpassed the number of a hundred chapters. [26] The Decemvirs had neglected to import the sanction of Zaleucus, which so long maintained the integrity of his republic. A Locrian, who proposed any new law, stood forth in the assembly of the people with a cord round his neck, and if the law was rejected, the innovator was instantly strangled.

[Footnote 20: It is the praise of Diodorus, (tom. i. l. xii. p. 494,) which may be fairly translated by the eleganti atque absoluta brevitate verborum of Aulus Gellius, (Noct. Attic. xxi. 1.)]

[Footnote 21: Listen to Cicero (de Legibus, ii. 23) and his representative Crassus, (de Oratore, i. 43, 44.)]

[Footnote 22: See Heineccius, (Hist. J. R. No. 29—33.) I have followed the restoration of the xii. tables by Gravina (Origines J. C. p. 280—307) and Terrasson, (Hist. de la Jurisprudence Romaine, p. 94—205.) Note: The wish expressed by Warnkonig, that the text and the conjectural emendations on the fragments of the xii. tables should be submitted to rigid criticism, has been fulfilled by Dirksen, Uebersicht der bisherigen Versuche Leipzig Kritik und Herstellung des Textes der Zwolf-Tafel-Fragmente, Leipzug, 1824—M.]

[Footnote 23: Finis aequi juris, (Tacit. Annal. iii. 27.) Fons omnis publici et privati juris, (T. Liv. iii. 34.) Note: From the context of the phrase in Tacitus, "Nam secutae leges etsi alquando in maleficos ex delicto; saepius tamen dissensione ordinum latae sunt," it is clear that Gibbon has rendered this sentence incorrectly. Hugo, Hist. p. 62—M.]

[Footnote 24: De principiis juris, et quibus modis ad hanc multitudinem infinitam ac varietatem legum perventum sit altius disseram, (Tacit. Annal. iii. 25.) This deep disquisition fills only two pages, but they are the pages of Tacitus. With equal sense, but with less energy, Livy (iii. 34) had complained, in hoc immenso aliarum super alias acervatarum legum cumulo, &c.]

[Footnote 25: Suetonius in Vespasiano, c. 8.]

[Footnote 26: Cicero ad Familiares, viii. 8.]

The Decemvirs had been named, and their tables were approved, by an assembly of the centuries, in which riches preponderated against numbers. To the first class of Romans, the proprietors of one hundred thousand pounds of copper, [27] ninety-eight votes were assigned, and only ninety-five were left for the six inferior classes, distributed according to their substance by the artful policy of Servius. But the tribunes soon established a more specious and popular maxim, that every citizen has an equal right to enact the laws which he is bound to obey. Instead of the centuries, they convened the tribes; and the patricians, after an impotent struggle, submitted to the decrees of an assembly, in which their votes were confounded with those of the meanest plebeians. Yet as long as the tribes successively passed over narrow bridges [28] and gave their voices aloud, the conduct of each citizen was exposed to the eyes and ears of his friends and countrymen. The insolvent debtor consulted the wishes of his creditor; the client would have blushed to oppose the views of his patron; the general was followed by his veterans, and the aspect of a grave magistrate was a living lesson to the multitude. A new method of secret ballot abolished the influence of fear and shame, of honor and interest, and the abuse of freedom accelerated the progress of anarchy and despotism. [29] The Romans had aspired to be equal; they were levelled by the equality of servitude; and the dictates of Augustus were patiently ratified by the formal consent of the tribes or centuries. Once, and once only, he experienced a sincere and strenuous opposition. His subjects had resigned all political liberty; they defended the freedom of domestic life. A law which enforced the obligation, and strengthened the bonds of marriage, was clamorously rejected; Propertius, in the arms of Delia, applauded the victory of licentious love; and the project of reform was suspended till a new and more tractable generation had arisen in the world. [30] Such an example was not necessary to instruct a prudent usurper of the mischief of popular assemblies; and their abolition, which Augustus had silently prepared, was accomplished without resistance, and almost without notice, on the accession of his successor. [31] Sixty thousand plebeian legislators, whom numbers made formidable, and poverty secure, were supplanted by six hundred senators, who held their honors, their fortunes, and their lives, by the clemency of the emperor. The loss of executive power was alleviated by the gift of legislative authority; and Ulpian might assert, after the practice of two hundred years, that the decrees of the senate obtained the force and validity of laws. In the times of freedom, the resolves of the people had often been dictated by the passion or error of the moment: the Cornelian, Pompeian, and Julian laws were adapted by a single hand to the prevailing disorders; but the senate, under the reign of the Caesars, was composed of magistrates and lawyers, and in questions of private jurisprudence, the integrity of their judgment was seldom perverted by fear or interest. [32]

[Footnote 27: Dionysius, with Arbuthnot, and most of the moderns, (except Eisenschmidt de Ponderibus, &c., p. 137—140,) represent the 100,000 asses by 10,000 Attic drachmae, or somewhat more than 300 pounds sterling. But their calculation can apply only to the latter times, when the as was diminished to 1-24th of its ancient weight: nor can I believe that in the first ages, however destitute of the precious metals, a single ounce of silver could have been exchanged for seventy pounds of copper or brass. A more simple and rational method is to value the copper itself according to the present rate, and, after comparing the mint and the market price, the Roman and avoirdupois weight, the primitive as or Roman pound of copper may be appreciated at one English shilling, and the 100,000 asses of the first class amounted to 5000 pounds sterling. It will appear from the same reckoning, that an ox was sold at Rome for five pounds, a sheep for ten shillings, and a quarter of wheat for one pound ten shillings, (Festus, p. 330, edit. Dacier. Plin. Hist. Natur. xviii. 4:) nor do I see any reason to reject these consequences, which moderate our ideas of the poverty of the first Romans. Note: Compare Niebuhr, English translation, vol. i. p. 448, &c—M.]

[Footnote 28: Consult the common writers on the Roman Comitia, especially Sigonius and Beaufort. Spanheim (de Praestantia et Usu Numismatum, tom. ii. dissert. x. p. 192, 193) shows, on a curious medal, the Cista, Pontes, Septa, Diribitor, &c.]

[Footnote 29: Cicero (de Legibus, iii. 16, 17, 18) debates this constitutional question, and assigns to his brother Quintus the most unpopular side.]

[Footnote 30: Prae tumultu recusantium perferre non potuit, (Sueton. in August. c. 34.) See Propertius, l. ii. eleg. 6. Heineccius, in a separate history, has exhausted the whole subject of the Julian and Papian Poppaean laws, (Opp. tom. vii. P. i. p. 1—479.)]

[Footnote 31: Tacit. Annal. i. 15. Lipsius, Excursus E. in Tacitum. Note: This error of Gibbon has been long detected. The senate, under Tiberius did indeed elect the magistrates, who before that emperor were elected in the comitia. But we find laws enacted by the people during his reign, and that of Claudius. For example; the Julia-Norbana, Vellea, and Claudia de tutela foeminarum. Compare the Hist. du Droit Romain, by M. Hugo, vol. ii. p. 55, 57. The comitia ceased imperceptibly as the republic gradually expired—W.]

[Footnote 32: Non ambigitur senatum jus facere posse, is the decision of Ulpian, (l. xvi. ad Edict. in Pandect. l. i. tit. iii. leg. 9.) Pomponius taxes the comitia of the people as a turba hominum, (Pandect. l. i. tit. ii. leg 9.) Note: The author adopts the opinion, that under the emperors alone the senate had a share in the legislative power. They had nevertheless participated in it under the Republic, since senatus-consulta relating to civil rights have been preserved, which are much earlier than the reigns of Augustus or Tiberius. It is true that, under the emperors, the senate exercised this right more frequently, and that *the assemblies of the people had become much more rare, though in law they were still permitted, in the time of Ulpian. (See the fragments of Ulpian.) Bach has clearly demonstrated that the senate had the same power in the time of the Republic. It is natural that the senatus-consulta should have been more frequent under the emperors, because they employed those means of flattering the pride of the senators, by granting them the right of deliberating on all affairs which did not intrench on the Imperial power. Compare the discussions of M. Hugo, vol. i. p. 284, et seq—W.]*

The silence or ambiguity of the laws was supplied by the occasional edicts [32/1] of those magistrates who were invested with the honors of the state. [33] This ancient prerogative of the Roman kings was transferred, in their respective offices, to the consuls and dictators, the censors and praetors; and a similar right was assumed by the tribunes of the people, the ediles, and the proconsuls. At Rome, and in the provinces, the duties of the subject, and the intentions of the governor, were proclaimed; and the civil jurisprudence was reformed by the annual edicts of the supreme judge, the praetor of the city. [33/1] As soon as he ascended his tribunal, he announced by the voice of the crier, and afterwards inscribed on a white wall, the rules which he proposed to follow in the decision of doubtful cases, and the relief which his equity would afford from the precise rigor of ancient statutes. A principle of discretion more congenial to monarchy was introduced into the republic: the art of respecting the name, and eluding the efficacy, of the laws, was improved by successive praetors; subtleties and fictions were invented to defeat the plainest meaning of the Decemvirs, and where the end was salutary, the means were frequently absurd. The secret or probable wish of the dead was suffered to prevail over the order of succession and the forms of testaments; and the claimant, who was excluded from the character of heir, accepted with equal pleasure from an indulgent praetor the possession of the goods of his late kinsman or benefactor. In the redress of private wrongs, compensations and fines were substituted to the obsolete rigor of the Twelve Tables; time and space were annihilated by fanciful suppositions; and the plea of youth, or fraud, or violence, annulled the obligation, or excused the performance, of an inconvenient contract. A jurisdiction thus vague and arbitrary was exposed to the most dangerous abuse: the substance, as well as the form, of justice were often sacrificed to the prejudices of virtue, the bias of laudable affection, and the grosser seductions of interest or resentment. But the errors or vices of each praetor expired with his annual office; such maxims alone as had been approved by reason and practice were copied by succeeding judges; the rule of proceeding was defined by the solution of new cases; and the temptations of injustice were removed by the Cornelian law, which compelled the praetor of the year to adhere to the spirit and letter of his first proclamation. [34] It was reserved for the curiosity and learning of Adrian, to accomplish the design which had been conceived by the genius of Caesar; and the praetorship of Salvius Julian, an eminent lawyer, was immortalized by the composition of the Perpetual Edict. This well-digested code was ratified by the emperor and the senate; the long divorce of law and equity was at length reconciled; and, instead of the Twelve Tables, the perpetual edict was fixed as the invariable standard of civil jurisprudence. [35]

[Footnote 32/1: There is a curious passage from Aurelius, a writer on Law, on the Praetorian Praefect, quoted in Lydus de Magistratibus, p. 32, edit. Hase. The Praetorian praefect was to the emperor what the master of the horse was to the dictator under the Republic. He was the delegate, therefore, of the full Imperial authority; and no appeal could be made or exception taken against his edicts. I had not observed this passage, when the third volume, where it would have been more appropriately placed, passed through the press—M]

[Footnote 33: The jus honorarium of the praetors and other magistrates is strictly defined in the Latin text to the Institutes, (l. i. tit. ii. No. 7,) and more loosely explained in the Greek paraphrase of Theophilus, (p. 33—38, edit. Reitz,) who drops the important word honorarium. Note: The author here

follows the opinion of Heineccius, who, according to the idea of his master Thomasius, was unwilling to suppose that magistrates exercising a judicial could share in the legislative power. For this reason he represents the edicts of the praetors as absurd. (See his work, Historia Juris Romani, 69, 74.) But Heineccius had altogether a false notion of this important institution of the Romans, to which we owe in a great degree the perfection of their jurisprudence. Heineccius, therefore, in his own days had many opponents of his system, among others the celebrated Ritter, professor at Wittemberg, who contested it in notes appended to the work of Heineccius, and retained in all subsequent editions of that book. After Ritter, the learned Bach undertook to vindicate the edicts of the praetors in his Historia Jurisprud. Rom. edit. 6, p. 218, 224. But it remained for a civilian of our own days to throw light on the spirit and true character of this institution. M. Hugo has completely demonstrated that the praetorian edicts furnished the salutary means of perpetually harmonizing the legislation with the spirit of the times. The praetors were the true organs of public opinion. It was not according to their caprice that they framed their regulations, but according to the manners and to the opinions of the great civil lawyers of their day. We know from Cicero himself, that it was esteemed a great honor among the Romans to publish an edict, well conceived and well drawn. The most distinguished lawyers of Rome were invited by the praetor to assist in framing this annual law, which, according to its principle, was only a declaration which the praetor made to the public, to announce the manner in which he would judge, and to guard against every charge of partiality. Those who had reason to fear his opinions might delay their cause till the following year. The praetor was responsible for all the faults which he committed. The tribunes could lodge an accusation against the praetor who issued a partial edict. He was bound strictly to follow and to observe the regulations published by him at the commencement of his year of office, according to the Cornelian law, by which these edicts were called perpetual, and he could make no change in a regulation once published. The praetor was obliged to submit to his own edict, and to judge his own affairs according to its provisions. These magistrates had no power of departing from the fundamental laws, or the laws of the Twelve Tables. The people held them in such consideration, that they rarely enacted laws contrary to their provisions; but as some provisions were found inefficient, others opposed to the manners of the people, and to the spirit of subsequent ages, the praetors, still maintaining respect for the laws, endeavored to bring them into accordance with the necessities of the existing time, by such fictions as best suited the nature of the case. In what legislation do we not find these fictions, which even yet exist, absurd and ridiculous as they are, among the ancient laws of modern nations? These always variable edicts at length comprehended the whole of the Roman legislature, and became the subject of the commentaries of the most celebrated lawyers. They must therefore be considered as the basis of all the Roman jurisprudence comprehended in the Digest of Justinian. —It is in this sense that M. Schrader has written on this important institution, proposing it for imitation as far as may be consistent with our manners, and agreeable to our political institutions, in order to avoid immature legislation becoming a permanent evil. See the History of the Roman Law by M. Hugo, vol. i. p. 296, &c., vol. ii. p. 30, et seq., 78. et seq., and the note in my elementary book on the Industries, p. 313. With regard to the works best suited to give information on the framing and the form of these edicts, see Haubold, Institutiones Literariae, tom. i. p. 321, 368. All that Heineccius says about the usurpation of the right of making these edicts by the praetors is false, and contrary to all historical testimony. A multitude of authorities proves that the magistrates were under an obligation to publish these edicts—W. —With the utmost deference for these excellent civilians, I cannot but consider this confusion of the judicial and legislative authority as a very perilous constitutional precedent. It might answer among a people so singularly trained as the Romans were by habit and national character in reverence for legal institutions, so as to be an aristocracy, if not a people, of legislators; but in most nations the investiture of a magistrate in such authority, leaving to his sole judgment the lawyers he might consult, and the view of public opinion which he might take, would be a very insufficient guaranty for right legislation—M.]

[Footnote 33/1: Compare throughout the brief but admirable sketch of the progress and growth of the Roman jurisprudence, the necessary operation of the jusgentium, when Rome became the sovereign of nations, upon the jus civile of the citizens of Rome, in the first chapter of Savigny. Geschichte des Romischen Rechts im Mittelalter—M.]

[Footnote 34: Dion Cassius (tom. i. l. xxxvi. p. 100) fixes the perpetual edicts in the year of Rome, 686. Their institution, however, is ascribed to the year 585 in the Acta Diurna, which have been published from the papers of Ludovicus Vives. Their authenticity is supported or allowed by Pighius, (Annal. Rom. tom. ii. p. 377, 378,) Graevius, (ad Sueton. p. 778,) Dodwell, (Praelection. Cambden, p. 665,) and Heineccius: but a single word, Scutum Cimbricum, detects the forgery, (Moyle's Works, vol. i. p. 303.)]

[Footnote 35: The history of edicts is composed, and the text of the perpetual edict is restored, by the master-hand of Heineccius, (Opp. tom. vii. P. ii. p. 1—564;) in whose researches I might safely acquiesce. In the Academy of Inscriptions, M. Bouchaud has given a series of memoirs to this interesting subject of law and literature. Note: This restoration was only the commencement of a work found among the papers of Heineccius, and published after his death—G. —Note: Gibbon has here fallen into an error, with Heineccius, and almost the whole literary world, concerning the real meaning of what is called the perpetual edict of Hadrian. Since the Cornelian law, the edicts were perpetual, but only in this sense, that the praetor could not change them during the year of his magistracy. And although it appears that under Hadrian, the civilian Julianus made, or assisted in making, a complete collection of the edicts, (which certainly had been done likewise before Hadrian, for example, by Ofilius, qui diligenter edictum composuit,) we have no sufficient proof to admit the common opinion, that the Praetorian edict was declared perpetually unalterable by Hadrian. The writers on law subsequent to Hadrian (and among the rest Pomponius, in his Summary of the Roman Jurisprudence) speak of the edict as it existed in the time of Cicero. They would not certainly have passed over in silence so remarkable a change in the most important source of the civil law. M. Hugo has conclusively shown that the various passages in authors, like Eutropius, are not sufficient to establish the opinion introduced by Heineccius. Compare Hugo, vol. ii. p. 78. A new proof of this is found in the Institutes of Gaius, who, in the first books of his work, expresses himself in the same manner, without mentioning any change made by Hadrian. Nevertheless, if it had taken place, he must have noticed it, as he does l. i. 8, the responsa prudentum, on the occasion of a rescript of Hadrian. There is no lacuna in the text. Why then should Gaius maintain silence concerning an innovation so much more important than that of which he speaks? After all, this question becomes of slight interest, since, in fact, we find no change in the perpetual edict inserted in the Digest, from the time of Hadrian to the end of that epoch, except that made by Julian, (compare Hugo, l. c.) The latter lawyers appear to follow, in their commentaries, the same texts as their predecessors. It is natural to suppose, that, after the labors of so many men distinguished in jurisprudence, the framing of the edict must have attained such perfection that it would have been difficult to have made any innovation. We nowhere find that the jurists of the Pandects disputed concerning the words, or the drawing up of the edict. What difference would, in fact, result from this with regard to our codes, and our modern legislation? Compare the learned Dissertation of M. Biener, De Salvii Juliani meritis in Edictum Praetorium recte aestimandis. Lipsae, 1809, 4to—W.]

From Augustus to Trajan, the modest Caesars were content to promulgate their edicts in the various characters of a Roman magistrate; [3511] and, in the decrees of the senate, the epistles and orations of the prince were respectfully inserted. Adrian [36] appears to have been the first who assumed, without disguise, the plenitude of legislative power. And this innovation, so agreeable to his active mind, was countenanced by the patience of the times, and his long absence from the seat of government. The same policy was embraced by succeeding monarchs, and, according to the harsh metaphor of Tertullian, "the gloomy and intricate forest of ancient laws was cleared away by the axe of royal mandates and constitutions." [37] During four centuries, from Adrian to Justinian the public and private jurisprudence was moulded by the will of the sovereign; and few institutions, either human or divine, were permitted to stand on their former basis. The origin of Imperial legislation was concealed by the darkness of ages and the terrors of armed despotism; and a double tiction was propagated by the servility, or perhaps the ignorance, of the civilians, who basked in the sunshine of the Roman and Byzantine courts. 1. To the prayer of the ancient Caesars, the people or the senate had sometimes granted a personal exemption from the obligation and penalty of particular statutes; and each indulgence was an act of jurisdiction exercised by the republic over the first of her citizens. His humble privilege was at length transformed into the prerogative of a tyrant; and the Latin expression of "released from the laws" [38] was supposed to exalt the emperor above all human restraints, and to leave his conscience and reason as the sacred measure of his conduct. 2. A similar dependence was implied in the decrees of the senate, which, in every reign, defined the titles and powers of an elective magistrate. But it was not before the ideas, and even the language, of the Romans had been corrupted, that a royal law, [39] and an irrevocable gift of the people, were created by the fancy of Ulpian, or more probably of Tribonian himself; [40] and the origin of Imperial power, though false in fact, and slavish in its consequence, was supported on a principle of freedom and justice. "The pleasure of the emperor has the vigor and effect of law, since the Roman people, by the royal law, have transferred to their prince the full extent of their own power and sovereignty." [41] The will of a single man, of a child perhaps, was allowed to prevail over the wisdom of ages and the inclinations of millions; and the degenerate Greeks were proud to declare, that in his hands alone the arbitrary exercise of legislation could be safely deposited. "What interest or passion," exclaims Theophilus in the court of Justinian, "can reach the calm and sublime elevation of the monarch? He is already master of the lives and fortunes of his subjects; and those who have incurred his displeasure are already numbered with the dead." [42] Disdaining the language of flattery, the historian may confess, that in questions of private jurisprudence, the absolute sovereign of a great empire can seldom be influenced by any personal considerations. Virtue, or even reason, will suggest to his impartial mind, that he is the guardian of peace and equity, and that the interest of society is inseparably connected with his own. Under the weakest and most vicious reign, the seat of justice was filled by the wisdom and integrity of Papinian and Ulpian; [43] and the purest materials of the Code and Pandects are inscribed with the names of Caracalla and his ministers. [44] The tyrant of Rome was sometimes the benefactor of the provinces. A dagger terminated the crimes of Domitian; but the prudence of Nerva confirmed his acts, which, in the joy of their deliverance, had been rescinded by an indignant senate. [45] Yet in the rescripts, [46] replies to the consultations of the magistrates, the wisest of princes might be deceived by a partial exposition of the case. And this abuse, which placed their hasty decisions on the same level with mature and deliberate acts of legislation, was ineffectually condemned by the sense and example of Trajan. The rescripts of the emperor, his grants and decrees, his edicts and pragmatic sanctions, were subscribed in purple ink, [47] and transmitted to the provinces as general or special laws, which the magistrates were bound to execute, and the people to obey. But as their number continually multiplied, the rule of obedience became each day more doubtful and obscure, till the will of the sovereign was fixed and ascertained in the Gregorian, the Hermogenian, and the Theodosian codes. [47/1] The two first, of which some fragments have escaped, were framed by two private lawyers, to preserve the constitutions of the Pagan emperors from Adrian to Constantine. The third, which is still extant, was digested in sixteen books by the order of the younger Theodosius to consecrate the laws of the Christian princes from Constantine to his own reign. But the three codes obtained an equal authority in the tribunals; and any act which was not included in the sacred deposit might be disregarded by the judge as epurious or obsolete. [48]

[Footnote 35/1: It is an important question in what manner the emperors were invested with this legislative power. The newly discovered Gaius distinctly states that it was in virtue of a law—Nec unquam dubitatum est, quin id legis vicem obtineat, cum ipse imperator per legem imperium accipiat. But it is still uncertain whether this was a general law, passed on the transition of the government from a republican to a monarchical form, or a law passed on the accession of each emperor. Compare Hugo, Hist. du Droit Romain, (French translation,) vol. ii. p. 8—M.]

[Footnote 36: His laws are the first in the code. See Dodwell, (Praelect. Cambden, p. 319—340,) who wanders from the subject in confused reading and feeble paradox. Note: This is again an error which Gibbon shares with Heineccius, and the generality of authors. It arises from having mistaken the insignificant edict of Hadrian, inserted in the Code of Justinian, (lib. vi, tit. xxiii. c. 11,) for the first constitutio principis, without attending to the fact, that the Pandects contain so many constitutions of the emperors, from Julius Caesar, (see l. i. Digest 29, l) M. Hugo justly observes, that the acta of Sylla, approved by the senate, were the same thing with the constitutions of those who after him usurped the sovereign power. Moreover, we find that Pliny, and other ancient authors, report a multitude of rescripts of the emperors from the time of Augustus. See Hugo, Hist. du Droit Romain, vol. ii. p. 24-27—W.]

[Footnote 37: Totam illam veterem et squalentem sylvam legum novis principalium rescriptorum et edictorum securibus truncatis et caeditis; (Apologet. c. 4, p. 50, edit. Havercamp.) He proceeds to praise the recent firmness of Severus, who repealed the useless or pernicious laws, without any regard to their age or authority.]

[Footnote 38: The constitutional style of Legibus Solutus is misinterpreted by the art or ignorance of Dion Cassius, (tom. i. l. liii. p. 713.) On this occasion, his editor, Reimer, joins the universal censure which freedom and criticism have pronounced against that slavish historian.]

[Footnote 39: The word (Lex Regia) was still more recent than the thing. The slaves of Commodus or Caracalla would have started at the name of royalty. Note: Yet a century before, Domitian was called not only by Martial but even in public documents, Dominus et Deus Noster. Sueton. Domit. cap. 13. Hugo—W.]

[Footnote 40: See Gravina (Opp. p. 501—512) and Beaufort, (Republique Romaine, tom. i. p. 255—274.) He has made a proper use of two dissertations by John Frederic Gronovius and Noodt, both translated, with valuable notes, by Barbeyrac, 2 vols. in 12mo. 1731.]

[Footnote 41: Institut. l. i. tit. ii. No. 6. Pandect. l. i. tit. iv. leg. 1. Cod. Justinian, l. i. tit. xvii. leg. 1, No. 7. In his Antiquities and Elements, Heineccius has amply treated de constitutionibus principum, which are illustrated by Godefroy (Comment. ad Cod. Theodos. l. i. tit. i. ii. iii.) and Gravina, (p. 87—90.) —Note: Gaius asserts that the Imperial edict or rescript has and always had, the force of law, because the Imperial authority rests upon law. Constitutio principis est, quod imperator decreto vel edicto, vel epistola constituit, nec unquam dubitatum, quin id legis, vicem obtineat, cum ipse imperator per legem imperium accipiat. Gaius, 6 Instit. i. 2—M.]

[Footnote 42: Theophilus, in Paraphras. Graec. Institut. p. 33, 34, edit. Reitz For his person, time, writings, see the Theophilus of J. H. Mylius, Excurs. iii. p. 1034—1073.]

[Footnote 43: There is more envy than reason in the complaint of Macrinus (Jul. Capitolin. c. 13:) Nefas esse leges videri Commodi et Caracalla at hominum imperitorum voluntates. Commodus was made a Divus by Severus, (Dodwell, Praelect. viii. p. 324, 325.) Yet he occurs only twice in the Pandects.]

[Footnote 44: Of Antoninus Caracalla alone 200 constitutions are extant in the Code, and with his father 160. These two princes are quoted fifty times in the Pandects, and eight in the Institutes, (Terasson, p. 265.)]

[Footnote 45: Plin. Secund. Epistol. x. 66. Sueton. in Domitian. c. 23.]

[Footnote 46: It was a maxim of Constantine, contra jus rescripta non valeant, (Cod. Theodos. l. i. tit. ii. leg. 1.) The emperors reluctantly allow some scrutiny into the law and the fact, some delay, petition, &c.; but these insufficient remedies are too much in the discretion and at the peril of the judge.]

[Footnote 47: A compound of vermilion and cinnabar, which marks the Imperial diplomas from Leo I. (A.D. 470) to the fall of the Greek empire, (Bibliotheque Raisonnee de la Diplomatique, tom. i. p. 504—515 Lami, de Eruditione Apostolorum, tom. ii. p. 720-726.)]

[Footnote 47/1: Savigny states the following as the authorities for the Roman law at the commencement of the fifth century:— 1. The writings of the jurists, according to the regulations of the Constitution of Valentinian III., first promulgated in the West, but by its admission into the Theodosian Code established likewise in the East. (This Constitution established the authority of the five great jurists, Papinian, Paulus, Caius, Ulpian, and Modestinus as interpreters of the ancient law. In case of difference of opinion among these five, a majority decided the case; where they were equal, the opinion of Papinian, where he was silent, the judge; but see p. 40, and Hugo, vol. ii. p. 89.) 2. The Gregorian and Hermogenian Collection of the Imperial Rescripts. 3. The Code of Theodosius II. 4. The particular Novellae, as additions and Supplements to this Code Savigny. vol. i. p 10—M.]

[Footnote 48: Schulting, Jurisprudentia Ante-Justinianea, p. 681-718. Cujacius assigned to Gregory the reigns from Hadrian to Gallienus. and the continuation to his fellow-laborer Hermogenes. This general division may be just, but they often trespassed on each other's ground]

PART III

Among savage nations, the want of letters is imperfectly supplied by the use of visible signs, which awaken attention, and perpetuate the remembrance of any public or private transaction. The jurisprudence of the first Romans exhibited the scenes of a pantomime; the words were adapted to the gestures, and the slightest error or neglect in the forms of proceeding was sufficient to annul the substance of the fairest claim. The communion of the marriage-life was denoted by the necessary elements of fire and water; [49] and the divorced wife resigned the bunch of keys, by the delivery of which she had been invested with the government of the family. The manumission of a son, or a slave, was performed by turning him round with a gentle blow on the cheek; a work was prohibited by the casting of a stone; prescription was interrupted by the breaking of a branch; the clinched fist was the symbol of a pledge or deposit; the right hand was the gift of faith and confidence. The indenture of covenants was a broken straw; weights and scales were introduced into every payment, and the heir who accepted a testament was sometimes obliged to snap his fingers, to cast away his garments, and to leap or dance with real or affected transport. [50] If a citizen pursued any stolen goods into a neighbor's house, he concealed his nakedness with a linen towel, and hid his face with a mask or basin, lest he should encounter the eyes of a virgin or a matron. [51] In a civil action the plaintiff touched the ear of his witness, seized his reluctant adversary by the neck, and implored, in solemn lamentation, the aid of his fellow-citizens. The two competitors grasped each other's hand as if they stood prepared for combat before the tribunal of the praetor; he commanded them to produce the object of the dispute; they went, they returned with measured steps, and a clod of earth was cast at his feet to represent the field for which they contended. This occult science of the words and actions of law was the inheritance of the pontiffs and patricians. Like the Chaldean astrologers, they announced to their clients the days of business and repose; these important trifles were interwoven with the religion of Numa; and after the publication of the Twelve Tables, the Roman people was still enslaved by the ignorance of judicial proceedings. The treachery of some plebeian officers at length revealed the profitable mystery: in a more enlightened age, the legal actions were derided and observed; and the same antiquity which sanctified the practice, obliterated the use and meaning of this primitive language. [52]

[Footnote 49: Scaevola, most probably Q. Cervidius Scaevola; the master of Papinian considers this acceptance of fire and water as the essence of marriage, (Pandect. l. xxiv. tit. 1, leg. 66. See Heineccius, Hist. J. R. No. 317.)]

[Footnote 50: Cicero (de Officiis, iii. 19) may state an ideal case, but St. Am brose (de Officiis, iii. 2,) appeals to the practice of his own times, which he understood as a lawyer and a magistrate, (Schulting ad Ulpian, Fragment. tit. xxii. No. 28, p. 643, 644.) Note: In this passage the author has endeavored to collect all the examples of judicial formularies which he could find. That which he adduces as the form of cretio haereditatis is absolutely false. It is sufficient to glance at the passage in Cicero which he cites, to see that it has no relation to it. The author appeals to the opinion of Schulting, who, in the passage quoted, himself protests against the ridiculous and absurd interpretation of the passage in Cicero, and observes that Graevius had already well explained the real sense. See in Gaius the form of cretio haereditatis Inst. l. ii. p. 166—W.]

[Footnote 51: The furtum lance licioque conceptum was no longer understood in the time of the Antonines, (Aulus Gellius, xvi. 10.) The Attic derivation of Heineccius, (Antiquitat. Rom. l. iv. tit. i. No. 13—21) is supported by the evidence of Aristophanes, his scholiast, and Pollux. Note: Nothing more is known of this ceremony; nevertheless we find that already in his own days Gaius turned it into ridicule. He says, (lib. iii. et p. 192, Sections 293,) prohibiti actio quadrupli ex edicto praetoris introducta est; lex autem eo nomine nullam poenam constituit. Hoc solum praecepit, ut qui quaerere velit, nudus quaerat, linteo cinctus, lancem habens; qui si quid invenerit. jubet id lex furtum manifestum esse. Quid sit autem linteum? quaesitum est. Sed verius est consuti genus esse, quo necessariae partes tegerentur. Quare lex tota ridicula est. Nam qui vestitum quaerere prohibet, is et nudum quaerere prohibiturus est; eo magis, quod invenerit ibi imponat, neutrum eorum procedit, si id quod quaeratur, ejus magnitudinis aut naturae sit ut neque subjici, neque ibi imponi possit. Certe non dubitatur, cujuscunque materiae sit ea lanx, satis legi fieri. We see moreover, from this passage, that the basin, as most authors, resting on the authority of Festus, have supposed, was not used to cover the figure—W. Gibbon says the face, though equally inaccurately. This passage of Gaius, I must observe, as well as others in M. Warnkonig's work, is very inaccurately printed—M.]

[Footnote 52: In his Oration for Murena, (c. 9—13,) Cicero turns into ridicule the forms and mysteries of the civilians, which are represented with more candor by Aulus Gellius, (Noct. Attic. xx. 10,) Gravina, (Opp p. 265, 266, 267,) and Heineccius, (Antiquitat. l. iv. tit. vi.) Note: Gibbon had conceived opinions too decided against the forms of procedure in use among the Romans. Yet it is on these solemn forms that the certainty of laws has been founded among all nations. Those of the Romans were very intimately allied with the ancient religion, and must of necessity have disappeared as Rome attained a higher degree of civilization. Have not modern nations, even the most civilized, overloaded their laws with a thousand forms, often absurd, almost always trivial? How many examples are afforded by the English law! See, on the nature of these forms, the work of M. de Savigny on the Vocation of our Age for Legislation and Jurisprudence, Heidelberg, 1814, p. 9, 10—W. This work of M. Savigny has been translated into English by Mr. Hayward—M.]

A more liberal art was cultivated, however, by the sage of Rome, who, in a stricter sense, may be considered as the authors of the civil law. The alteration of the idiom and manners of the Romans rendered the style of the Twelve Tables less familiar to each rising generation, and the doubtful passages were imperfectly explained by the study of legal antiquarians. To define the ambiguities, to circumscribe the latitude, to apply the principles, to extend the consequences, to reconcile the real or apparent contradictions, was a much nobler and more important task; and the province of legislation was silently invaded by the expounders of ancient statutes. Their subtle interpretations concurred with the equity of the praetor, to reform the tyranny of the darker ages: however strange or intricate the means, it was the aim of artificial jurisprudence to restore the simple dictates of nature and reason, and the skill of private citizens was usefully employed to undermine the public institutions of their country. [52/1] The revolution of almost one thousand years, from the Twelve Tables to the reign of Justinian, may be divided into three periods, almost equal in duration, and distinguished from each other by the mode of instruction and the character of the civilians. [53] Pride and ignorance contributed, during the first period, to confine within narrow limits the science of the Roman law. On the public days of market or assembly, the masters of the art were seen walking in the forum ready to impart the needful advice to the meanest of their fellow-citizens, from whose votes, on a future occasion, they might solicit a grateful return. As their years and honors increased, they seated themselves at home on a chair or throne, to expect with patient gravity the visits of their clients, who at the dawn of day, from the town and country, began to thunder at their door. The duties of social life, and the incidents of judicial proceeding, were the ordinary subject of these consultations, and the verbal or written opinion of the juris-consults was framed according to the rules of prudence and law. The youths of their own order and family were permitted to listen; their children enjoyed the benefit of more private lessons, and the Mucian race was long renowned for the hereditary knowledge of the civil law. The second period, the learned and splendid age of jurisprudence, may be extended from the birth of Cicero to the reign of Severus Alexander. A system was formed, schools were instituted, books were composed, and both the living and the dead became subservient to the instruction of the student. The tripartite of Aelius Paetus, surnamed Catus, or the Cunning, was preserved as the oldest work of Jurisprudence. Cato the censor derived some additional fame from his legal studies, and those of his son: the kindred appellation of Mucius Scaevola was illustrated by three sages of the law; but the perfection of the science was ascribed to Servius Sulpicius, their disciple, and the friend of Tully; and the long succession, which shone with equal lustre under the republic and under the Caesars, is finally closed by the respectable characters of Papinian, of Paul, and of Ulpian. Their names, and the various titles of their productions, have been minutely preserved, and the example of Labeo may suggest some idea of their diligence and fecundity. That eminent lawyer of the Augustan age divided the year between the city and country, between business and composition; and four hundred books are enumerated as the fruit of his retirement. Of the collection of his rival Capito, the two hundred and fifty-ninth book is expressly quoted; and few teachers could deliver their opinions in less than a century of volumes. In the third period, between the reigns of Alexander and Justinian, the oracles of jurisprudence were almost mute. The measure of curiosity had been filled: the throne was occupied by tyrants and Barbarians, the active spirits were diverted by religious disputes, and the professors of Rome, Constantinople, and Berytus, were humbly content to repeat the lessons of their more enlightened predecessors. From the slow advances and rapid decay of these legal studies, it may be inferred, that they require a state of peace and refinement. From the multitude of voluminous civilians who fill the intermediate space, it is evident that such studies may be pursued, and such works may be performed, with a common share of judgment, experience, and industry. The genius of Cicero and Virgil was more sensibly felt, as each revolving age had been found incapable of producing a similar or a second: but the most eminent teachers of the law were assured of leaving disciples equal or superior to themselves in merit and reputation.

[Footnote 52/1: Compare, on the Responsa Prudentum, Warnkonig, Histoire Externe du Droit Romain Bruxelles, 1836, p. 122—M.]

[Footnote 53: The series of the civil lawyers is deduced by Pomponius, (de Origine Juris Pandect. l. i. tit. ii.) The moderns have discussed, with learning and criticism, this branch of literary history; and among these I have chiefly been guided by Gravina (p. 41—79) and Hei neccius, (Hist. J. R. No. 113-351.) Cicero, more especially in his books de Oratore, de Claris Oratoribus, de Legibus, and the Clavie Ciceroniana of Ernesti (under the names of Mucius, &c.) afford much genuine and pleasing information. Horace often alludes to the morning labors of the civilians, (Serm. I. i. 10, Epist. II. i. 103, &c)

Agricolam laudat juris legumque peritus Sub galli cantum,
consultor ubi ostia pulsat.
Romae dulce diu fuit et solemne, reclusa Mane domo vigilare,
clienti promere jura.

Note: It is particularly in this division of the history of the Roman jurisprudence into epochs, that Gibbon displays his profound knowledge of the laws of this people. M. Hugo, adopting this division, prefaced these three periods with the history of the times anterior to the Law of the Twelve Tables, which are, as it were, the infancy of the Roman law—W]

The jurisprudence which had been grossly adapted to the wants of the first Romans, was polished and improved in the seventh century of the city, by the alliance of Grecian philosophy. The Scaevolas had been taught by use and experience; but Servius Sulpicius [5311] was the first civilian who established his art on a certain and general theory. [54] For the discernment of truth and falsehood he applied, as an infallible rule, the logic of Aristotle and the stoics, reduced particular cases to general principles, and diffused over the shapeless mass the light of order and eloquence. Cicero, his contemporary and friend, declined the reputation of a professed lawyer; but the jurisprudence of his country was adorned by his incomparable genius, which converts into gold every object that it touches. After the example of Plato, he composed a republic; and, for the use of his republic, a treatise of laws; in which he labors to deduce from a celestial origin the wisdom and justice of the Roman constitution. The whole universe, according to his sublime hypothesis, forms one immense commonwealth: gods and men, who participate of the same essence, are members of the same community; reason prescribes the law of nature and nations; and all positive institutions, however modified by accident or custom, are drawn from the rule of right, which the Deity has inscribed on every virtuous mind. From these philosophical mysteries, he mildly excludes the sceptics who refuse to believe, and the epicureans who are unwilling to act. The latter disdain the care of the republic: he advises them to slumber in their shady gardens. But he humbly entreats that the new academy would be silent, since her bold objections would too soon destroy the fair and well ordered structure of his lofty system. [55] Plato, Aristotle, and Zeno, he represents as the only teachers who arm and instruct a citizen for the duties of social life. Of these, the armor of the stoics

[56] was found to be of the firmest temper; and it was chiefly worn, both for use and ornament, in the schools of jurisprudence. From the portico, the Roman civilians learned to live, to reason, and to die: but they imbibed in some degree the prejudices of the sect; the love of paradox, the pertinacious habits of dispute, and a minute attachment to words and verbal distinctions. The superiority of form to matter was introduced to ascertain the right of property: and the equality of crimes is countenanced by an opinion of Trebatius, [57] that he who touches the ear, touches the whole body; and that he who steals from a heap of corn, or a hogshead of wine, is guilty of the entire theft. [58]

[Footnote 53/1: M. Hugo thinks that the ingenious system of the Institutes adopted by a great number of the ancient lawyers, and by Justinian himself, dates from Severus Sulpicius. Hist du Droit Romain, vol.iii.p. 119—W.]

[Footnote 54: Crassus, or rather Cicero himself, proposes (de Oratore, i. 41, 42) an idea of the art or science of jurisprudence, which the eloquent, but illiterate, Antonius (i. 58) affects to deride. It was partly executed by Servius Sulpicius, (in Bruto, c. 41,) whose praises are elegantly varied in the classic Latinity of the Roman Gravina, (p. 60.)]

[Footnote 55: Perturbatricem autem omnium harum rerum academiam, hanc ab Arcesila et Carneade recentem, exoremus ut sileat, nam si invaserit in haec, quae satis scite instructa et composita videantur, nimis edet ruinas, quam quidem ego placare cupio, submovere non audeo. (de Legibus, i. 13.) From this passage alone, Bentley (Remarks on Free-thinking, p. 250) might have learned how firmly Cicero believed in the specious doctrines which he has adorned.]

[Footnote 56: The stoic philosophy was first taught at Rome by Panaetius, the friend of the younger Scipio, (see his life in the Mem. de l'Academis des Inscriptions, tom. x. p. 75—89.)]

[Footnote 57: As he is quoted by Ulpian, (leg.40, 40, ad Sabinum in Pandect. l. xlvii. tit. ii. leg. 21.) Yet Trebatius, after he was a leading civilian, que qui familiam duxit, became an epicurean, (Cicero ad Fam. vii. 5.) Perhaps he was not constant or sincere in his new sect. Note: Gibbon had entirely misunderstood this phrase of Cicero. It was only since his time that the real meaning of the author was apprehended. Cicero, in enumerating the qualifications of Trebatius, says, Accedit etiam, quod familiam ducit in jure civili, singularis memoria, summa scientia, which means that Trebatius possessed a still further most important qualification for a student of civil law, a remarkable memory, &c. This explanation, already conjectured by G. Menage, Amaenit. Juris Civilis, c. 14, is found in the dictionary of Scheller, v. Familia, and in the History of the Roman Law by M. Hugo. Many authors have asserted, without any proof sufficient to warrant the conjecture, that Trebatius was of the school of Epicurus—W.]

[Footnote 58: See Gravina (p. 45—51) and the ineffectual cavils of Mascou. Heineccius (Hist. J. R. No. 125) quotes and approves a dissertation of Everard Otto, de Stoica Jurisconsultorum Philosophia.]

Arms, eloquence, and the study of the civil law, promoted a citizen to the honors of the Roman state; and the three professions were sometimes more conspicuous by their union in the same character. In the composition of the edict, a learned praetor gave a sanction and preference to his private sentiments; the opinion of a censor, or a counsel, was entertained with respect; and a doubtful interpretation of the laws might be supported by the virtues or triumphs of the civilian. The patrician arts were long protected by the veil of mystery; and in more enlightened times, the freedom of inquiry established the general principles of jurisprudence. Subtile and intricate cases were elucidated by the disputes of the forum: rules, axioms, and definitions, [59] were admitted as the genuine dictates of reason; and the consent of the legal professors was interwoven into the practice of the tribunals. But these interpreters could neither enact nor execute the laws of the republic; and the judges might disregard the authority of the Scaevolas themselves, which was often overthrown by the eloquence or sophistry of an ingenious pleader. [60] Augustus and Tiberius were the first to adopt, as a useful engine, the science of the civilians; and their servile labors accommodated the old system to the spirit and views of despotism. Under the fair pretence of securing the dignity of the art, the privilege of subscribing legal and valid opinions was confined to the sages of senatorian or equestrian rank, who had been previously approved by the judgment of the prince; and this monopoly prevailed, till Adrian restored the freedom of the profession to every citizen conscious of his abilities and knowledge. The discretion of the praetor was now governed by the lessons of his teachers; the judges were enjoined to obey the comment as well as the text of the law; and the use of codicils was a memorable innovation, which Augustus ratified by the advice of the civilians. [61] [61/1]

[Footnote 59: We have heard of the Catonian rule, the Aquilian stipulation, and the Manilian forms, of 211 maxims, and of 247 definitions, (Pandect. l. i. tit. xvi. xvii.)]

[Footnote 60: Read Cicero, l. i. de Oratore, Topica, pro Murena.]

[Footnote 61: See Pomponius, (de Origine Juris Pandect. l. i. tit. ii. leg. 2, No 47,) Heineccius, (ad Institut. l. i. tit. ii. No. 8, l. ii. tit. xxv. in Element et Antiquitat.,) and Gravina, (p. 41—45.) Yet the monopoly of Augustus, a harsh measure, would appear with some softening in contemporary evidence; and it was probably veiled by a decree of the senate]

[Footnote 61/1: The author here follows the then generally received opinion of Heineccius. The proofs which appear to confirm it are l. 2 47, D. l. 2, and 8. Instit. l. 2. The first of these passages speaks expressly of a privilege granted to certain lawyers, until the time of Adrian, publice respondendi jus ante Augusti tempora non dabatur. Primus Divus ut major juris auctoritas haberetur, constituit, ut ex auctoritate ejus responderent. The passage of the Institutes speaks of the different opinions of those, quibus est permissum jura condere. It is true that the first of these passages does not say that the opinion of these privileged lawyers had the force of a law for the judges. For this reason M. Hugo altogether rejects the opinion adopted by Heineccius, by Bach, and in general by all the writers who preceded him. He conceives that the 8 of the Institutes referred to the constitution of Valentinian III., which regulated the respective authority to be ascribed to the different writings of the great civilians. But we have now the following passage in the Institutes of Gaius: Responsa prudentum sunt sententiae et opiniones eorum, quibus permissum est jura condere; quorum omnium si in unum sententiae concorrupt, id quod ita sentiunt, legis vicem obtinet, si vero dissentiunt, judici licet, quam velit sententiam sequi, idque rescripto Divi Hadrian signiticatur. I do not know, how in opposition to this passage, the opinion of M. Hugo can be maintained. We must add to this the passage quoted from Pomponius and from such strong proofs, it seems incontestable that the emperors had granted some kind of privilege to certain civilians, quibus permissum erat jura condere. Their opinion had sometimes the force of law, legis vicem. M. Hugo, endeavoring to reconcile this phrase with his system, gives it a forced interpretation, which quite alters the sense; he supposes that the passage contains no more than what is evident of itself, that the authority of the civilians was to be respected, thus making a privilege of that which was free to all the world. It appears to me almost indisputable, that the emperors had sanctioned certain provisions relative to the authority of these civilians, consulted by the judges. But how far was their advice to be respected? This is a question which it is impossible to answer precisely, from the want of historic evidence. Is it not possible that the emperors established an authority to be consulted by the judges? and in this case this authority must have emanated from certain civilians named for this purpose by the emperors. See Hugo, l. c. Moreover, may not the passage of Suetonius, in the Life of Caligula, where he says that the emperor would no longer permit the civilians to give their advice, mean that Caligula entertained the design of suppressing this institution? See on this passage the Themis, vol. xi. p. 17, 36. Our author not being acquainted with the opinions opposed to Heineccius has not gone to the bottom of the subject—W.]

The most absolute mandate could only require that the judges should agree with the civilians, if the civilians agreed among themselves. But positive institutions are often the result of custom and prejudice; laws and language are ambiguous and arbitrary; where reason is incapable of pronouncing, the love of argument is inflamed by the envy of rivals, the vanity of masters, the blind attachment of their disciples; and the Roman jurisprudence was divided by the once famous sects of the Proculians and Sabinians. [62] Two sages of the law, Ateius Capito and Antistius Labeo, [63] adorned the peace of the Augustan age; the former distinguished by the favor of his sovereign; the latter more illustrious by his contempt of that favor, and his stern though harmless opposition to the tyrant of Rome. Their legal studies were influenced by the various colors of their temper and principles. Labeo was attached to the form of the old republic; his rival embraced the more profitable substance of the rising monarchy. But the disposition of a courtier is tame and submissive; and Capito seldom presumed to deviate from the sentiments, or at least from the words, of his predecessors; while the bold republican pursued his independent ideas without fear of paradox or innovations. The freedom of Labeo was enslaved, however, by the rigor of his own conclusions, and he decided, according to the letter of the law, the same questions which his indulgent competitor resolved with a latitude of equity more suitable to the common sense and feelings of mankind. If a fair exchange had been substituted to the payment of money, Capito still considered the transaction as a legal sale; [64] and he consulted nature for the age of puberty, without confining his definition to the precise period of twelve or fourteen years. [65] This opposition of sentiments was propagated in the writings and lessons of the two founders; the schools of Capito and Labeo maintained their inveterate conflict from the age of Augustus to that of Adrian; [66] and the two sects derived their appellations from Sabinus and Proculus, their most celebrated teachers. The names of Cassians and Pegasians were likewise applied to the same parties; but, by a strange reverse, the popular cause was in the hands of Pegasus, [67] a timid slave of Domitian, while the favorite of the Caesars was represented by Cassius, [68] who gloried in his descent from the patriot assassin. By the perpetual edict, the controversies of the sects were in a great measure determined. For that important work, the emperor Adrian preferred the chief of the Sabinians: the friends of monarchy prevailed; but the moderation of Salvius Julian insensibly reconciled the victors and the vanquished. Like the contemporary philosophers, the lawyers of the age of the Antonines disclaimed the authority of a master, and adopted from every system the most probable doctrines. [69] But their writings would have been less voluminous, had their choice been more unanimous. The conscience of the judge was perplexed by the number and weight of discordant testimonies, and every sentence that his passion or interest might pronounce was justified by the sanction of some venerable name. An indulgent edict of the younger Theodosius excused him from the labor of comparing and weighing their arguments. Five civilians, Caius, Papinian, Paul, Ulpian, and Modestinus, were established as the oracles of jurisprudence: a majority was decisive: but if their opinions were equally divided, a casting vote was ascribed to the superior wisdom of Papinian. [70]

[Footnote 62: I have perused the Diatribe of Gotfridus Mascovius, the learned Mascou, de Sectis Jurisconsultorum, (Lipsiae, 1728, in 12mo., p. 276,) a learned treatise on a narrow and barren ground.]

[Footnote 63: See the character of Antistius Labeo in Tacitus, (Annal. iii. 75,) and in an epistle of Ateius Capito, (Aul. Gellius, xiii. 12,) who accuses his rival of libertas nimia et vecors. Yet Horace would not have lashed a virtuous and respectable senator; and I must adopt the emendation of Bentley, who reads Labieno insanior, (Serm. l. iii. 82.) See Mascou, de Sectis, (c. i. p. 1—24.)]

[Footnote 64: Justinian (Institut. l. iii. tit. 23, and Theophil. Vers. Graec. p. 677, 680) has commemorated this weighty dispute, and the verses of Homer that were alleged on either side as legal authorities. It was decided by Paul, (leg. 33, ad Edict. in Pandect. l. xviii. tit. i. leg. 1,) since, in a simple exchange, the buyer could not be discriminated from the seller.]

[Footnote 65: This controversy was likewise given for the Proculians, to supersede the indecency of a search, and to comply with the aphorism of Hippocrates, who was attached to the septenary number of two weeks of years, or 700 of days, (Institut. l. i. tit. xxii.) Plutarch and the Stoics (de Placit. Philosoph. l. v. c. 24) assign a more natural reason. Fourteen years is the age. See the vestigia of the sects in Mascou, c. ix. p. 145—276.]

[Footnote 66: The series and conclusion of the sects are described by Mascou, (c. ii—vii. p. 24—120;) and it would be almost ridiculous to praise his equal justice to these obsolete sects. Note: The work of Gaius, subsequent to the time of Adrian, furnishes us with some information on this subject. The disputes which rose between these two sects appear to have been very numerous. Gaius avows himself a disciple of Sabinus and of Caius. Compare Hugo, vol. ii. p. 106—W.]

[Footnote 67: At the first summons he flies to the turbot-council; yet Juvenal (Satir. iv. 75—81) styles the praefect or bailiff of Rome sanctissimus legum interpres. From his science, says the old scholiast, he was called, not a man, but a book. He derived the singular name of Pegasus from the galley which his father commanded.]

[Footnote 68: Tacit. Annal. xvii. 7. Sueton. in Nerone, c. xxxvii.]

[Footnote 69: Mascou, de Sectis, c. viii. p. 120—144 de Herciscundis, a legal term which was applied to these eclectic lawyers: herciscere is synonymous to dividere. Note: This word has never existed. Cujacius is the author of it, who read me words terris condi in Servius ad Virg. herciscundi, to which he gave an erroneous interpretation—W.]

[Footnote 70: See the Theodosian Code, l. i. tit. iv. with Godefroy's Commentary, tom. i. p. 30—35. [! This decree might give occasion to Jesuitical disputes like those in the Lettres Provinciales, whether a Judge was obliged to follow the opinion of Papinian, or of a majority, against his judgment, against his conscience, &c. Yet a legislator might give that opinion, however false, the validity, not of truth, but of law. Note: We possess (since 1824) some interesting information as to the framing of the Theodosian Code, and its ratification at Rome, in the year 438. M. Closius, now professor at Dorpat in Russia, and M. Peyron, member of the Academy of Turin, have discovered, the one at Milan, the other at Turin, a great part of the five first books of the Code which were wanting, and besides this, the reports (gesta) of the sitting of the senate at Rome, in which the Code was published, in the year after the marriage of Valentinian III. Among these pieces are the constitutions which nominate commissioners for the formation of the Code; and though there are many points of considerable obscurity in these documents, they communicate many facts relative to this legislation. 1. That Theodosius designed a great reform in the legislation; to add to the Gregorian and Hermogenian codes all the new constitutions from Constantine to his own day; and to frame a second code for common use with extracts from the three codes, and from the works of the civil lawyers. All laws either abrogated or fallen into disuse were to be noted under their proper heads. 2. An Ordinance was issued in 429 to form a commission for this purpose *of nine persons, of which Antiochus, as quaestor and praefectus, was president. A second commission of sixteen members was issued in 435 under the same president. 3. A code, which we possess under the name of Codex Theodosianus, was finished in 438, published in the East, in an ordinance addressed to the Praetorian praefect, Florentinus, and intended to be published in the West. 4. Before it was published in the West, Valentinian submitted it to the senate. There is a report of the proceedings of the senate, which closed with loud acclamations and gratulations—From Warnkonig, Histoire du Droit Romain, p. 169-Wenck has published this work, Codicis Theodosiani libri priores. Leipzig, 1825—M.] Note: Closius of Tubingen communicated to M.Warnkonig the two following constitutions of the emperor Constantine, which he discovered in the Ambrosian library at Milan:— 1. Imper. Constantinus Aug. ad Maximum Praef. Praetorio. Perpetuas prudentum contentiones eruere cupientes, Ulpiani ac Pauli, in Papinianum notas, qui dum ingenii laudem sectantur, non tam corrigere eum quam depravere maluerunt, aboleri praecepimus. Dat. III. Kalend. Octob. Const. Cons. et Crispi, (321.) Idem. Aug. ad Maximium Praef Praet. Universa, quae scriptura Pauli continentur, recepta auctoritate firmanda runt, et omni veneratione celebranda. Ideoque sententiarum libros plepissima luce et perfectissima elocutione et justissima juris ratione succinctos in judiciis prolatos valere minimie dubitatur. Dat. V. Kalend. Oct. Trovia Coust. et Max. Coss. (327.)—W]*

PART IV

When Justinian ascended the throne, the reformation of the Roman jurisprudence was an arduous but indispensable task. In the space of ten centuries, the infinite variety of laws and legal opinions had filled many thousand volumes, which no fortune could purchase and no capacity could digest. Books could not easily be found; and the judges, poor in the midst of riches, were reduced to the exercise of their illiterate discretion. The subjects of the Greek provinces were ignorant of the language that disposed of their lives and properties; and the barbarous dialect of the Latins was imperfectly studied in the academies of Berytus and Constantinople. As an Illyrian soldier, that idiom was familiar to the infancy of Justinian; his youth had been instructed by the lessons of jurisprudence, and his Imperial choice selected the most learned civilians of the East, to labor with their sovereign in the work of reformation. [71] The theory of professors was assisted by the practice of advocates, and the experience of magistrates; and the whole undertaking was animated by the spirit of Tribonian. [72] This extraordinary man, the object of so much praise and censure, was a native of Side in Pamphylia; and his genius, like that of Bacon, embraced, as his own, all the business and knowledge of the age. Tribonian composed, both in prose and verse, on a strange diversity of curious and abstruse subjects: [73] a double panegyric of Justinian and the life of the philosopher Theodotus; the nature of happiness and the duties of government; Homer's catalogue and the four-and-twenty sorts of metre; the astronomical canon of Ptolemy; the changes of the months; the houses of the planets; and the harmonic system of the world. To the literature of Greece he added the use of the Latin tonque; the Roman civilians were deposited in his library and in his mind; and he most assiduously cultivated those arts which opened the road of wealth and preferment. From the bar of the Praetorian praefects, he raised himself to the honors of quaestor, of consul, and of master of the offices: the council of Justinian listened to his eloquence and wisdom; and envy was mitigated by the gentleness and affability of his manners. The reproaches of impiety and avarice have stained the virtue or the reputation of Tribonian. In a bigoted and persecuting court, the principal minister was accused of a secret aversion to the Christian faith, and was supposed to entertain the sentiments of an Atheist and a Pagan, which have been imputed, inconsistently enough, to the last philosophers of Greece. His avarice was more clearly proved and more sensibly felt. If he were swayed by gifts in the administration of justice, the example of Bacon will again occur; nor can the merit of

Tribonian atone for his baseness, if he degraded the sanctity of his profession; and if laws were every day enacted, modified, or repealed, for the base consideration of his private emolument. In the sedition of Constantinople, his removal was granted to the clamors, perhaps to the just indignation, of the people: but the quaestor was speedily restored, and, till the hour of his death, he possessed, above twenty years, the favor and confidence of the emperor. His passive and dutiful submission had been honored with the praise of Justinian himself, whose vanity was incapable of discerning how often that submission degenerated into the grossest adulation. Tribonian adored the virtues of his gracious of his gracious master; the earth was unworthy of such a prince; and he affected a pious fear, that Justinian, like Elijah or Romulus, would be snatched into the air, and translated alive to the mansions of celestial glory. [74]

[Footnote 71: For the legal labors of Justinian, I have studied the Preface to the Institutes; the 1st, 2d, and 3d Prefaces to the Pandects; the 1st and 2d Preface to the Code; and the Code itself, (l. i. tit. xvii. de Veteri Jure enucleando.) After these original testimonies, I have consulted, among the moderns, Heineccius, (Hist. J. R. No. 383—404,) Terasson. (Hist. de la Jurisprudence Romaine, p. 295—356,) Gravina, (Opp. p. 93-100,) and Ludewig, in his Life of Justinian, (p.19—123, 318-321; for the Code and Novels, p. 209—261; for the Digest or Pandects, p. 262—317.)]

[Footnote 72: For the character of Tribonian, see the testimonies of Procopius, (Persic. l. i. c. 23, 24. Anecdot. c. 13, 20,) and Suidas, (tom. iii. p. 501, edit. Kuster.) Ludewig (in Vit. Justinian, p. 175—209) works hard, very hard, to whitewash—the blackamoor.]

[Footnote 73: I apply the two passages of Suidas to the same man; every circumstance so exactly tallies. Yet the lawyers appear ignorant; and Fabricius is inclined to separate the two characters, (Bibliot. Grae. tom. i. p. 341, ii. p. 518, iii. p. 418, xii. p. 346, 353, 474.)]

[Footnote 74: This story is related by Hesychius, (de Viris Illustribus,) Procopius, (Anecdot. c. 13,) and Suidas, (tom. iii. p. 501.) Such flattery is incredible! —Nihil est quod credere de se Non possit, cum laudatur Diis aequa potestas. Fontenelle (tom. i. p. 32—39) has ridiculed the impudence of the modest Virgil. But the same Fontenelle places his king above the divine Augustus; and the sage Boileau has not blushed to say, "Le destin a ses yeux n'oseroit balancer" Yet neither Augustus nor Louis XIV. were fools.]

If Caesar had achieved the reformation of the Roman law, his creative genius, enlightened by reflection and study, would have given to the world a pure and original system of jurisprudence. Whatever flattery might suggest, the emperor of the East was afraid to establish his private judgment as the standard of equity: in the possession of legislative power, he borrowed the aid of time and opinion; and his laborious compilations are guarded by the sages and legislature of past times. Instead of a statue cast in a simple mould by the hand of an artist, the works of Justinian represent a tessellated pavement of antique and costly, but too often of incoherent, fragments. In the first year of his reign, he directed the faithful Tribonian, and nine learned associates, to revise the ordinances of his predecessors, as they were contained, since the time of Adrian, in the Gregorian Hermogenian, and Theodosian codes; to purge the errors and contradictions, to retrench whatever was obsolete or superfluous, and to select the wise and salutary laws best adapted to the practice of the tribunals and the use of his subjects. The work was accomplished in fourteen months; and the twelve books or tables, which the new decemvirs produced, might be designed to imitate the labors of their Roman predecessors. The new Code of Justinian was honored with his name, and confirmed by his royal signature: authentic transcripts were multiplied by the pens of notaries and scribes; they were transmitted to the magistrates of the European, the Asiatic, and afterwards the African provinces; and the law of the empire was proclaimed on solemn festivals at the doors of churches. A more arduous operation was still behind—to extract the spirit of jurisprudence from the decisions and conjectures, the questions and disputes, of the Roman civilians. Seventeen lawyers, with Tribonian at their head, were appointed by the emperor to exercise an absolute jurisdiction over the works of their predecessors. If they had obeyed his commands in ten years, Justinian would have been satisfied with their diligence; and the rapid composition of the Digest of Pandects, [75] in three years, will deserve praise or censure, according to the merit of the execution. From the library of Tribonian, they chose forty, the most eminent civilians of former times: [76] two thousand treatises were comprised in an abridgment of fifty books; and it has been carefully recorded, that three millions of lines or sentences, [77] were reduced, in this abstract, to the moderate number of one hundred and fifty thousand. The edition of this great work was delayed a month after that of the Institutes; and it seemed reasonable that the elements should precede the digest of the Roman law. As soon as the emperor had approved their labors, he ratified, by his legislative power, the speculations of these private citizens: their commentaries, on the twelve tables, the perpetual edict, the laws of the people, and the decrees of the senate, succeeded to the authority of the text; and the text was abandoned, as a useless, though venerable, relic of antiquity. The Code, the Pandects, and the Institutes, were declared to be the legitimate system of civil jurisprudence; they alone were admitted into the tribunals, and they alone were taught in the academies of Rome, Constantinople, and Berytus. Justinian addressed to the senate and provinces his eternal oracles; and his pride, under the mask of piety, ascribed the consummation of this great design to the support and inspiration of the Deity.

[Footnote 75: *General receivers* was a common title of the Greek miscellanies, (Plin. Praefat. ad Hist. Natur.) The Digesta of Scaevola, Marcellinus, Celsus, were already familiar to the civilians: but Justinian was in the wrong when he used the two appellations as synonymous. Is the word Pandects Greek or Latin—masculine or feminine? The diligent Brenckman will not presume to decide these momentous controversies, (Hist. Pandect. Florentine. p. 200—304.) Note: The word was formerly in common use. See the preface is Aulus Gellius—W]

[Footnote 76: Angelus Politianus (l. v. Epist. ult.) reckons thirty-seven (p. 192—200) civilians quoted in the Pandects—a learned, and for his times, an extraordinary list. The Greek index to the Pandects enumerates thirty-nine, and forty are produced by the indefatigable Fabricius, (Bibliot. Graec. tom. iii. p. 488—502.) Antoninus Augustus (de Nominibus Propriis Pandect. apud Ludewig, p. 283) is said to have added fifty-four names; but they must be vague or second-hand references.]

[Footnote 77: The item of the ancient Mss. may be strictly defined as sentences or periods of a complete sense, which, on the breadth of the parchment rolls or volumes, composed as many lines of unequal length. The number in each book served as a check on the errors of the scribes, (Ludewig, p. 211—215; and his original author Suicer. Thesaur. Ecclesiast. tom. i. p 1021-1036).]

Since the emperor declined the fame and envy of original composition, we can only require, at his hands, method choice, and fidelity, the humble, though indispensable, virtues of a compiler. Among the various combinations of ideas, it is difficult to assign any reasonable preference; but as the order of Justinian is different in his three works, it is possible that all may be wrong; and it is certain that two cannot be right. In the selection of ancient laws, he seems to have viewed his predecessors without jealousy, and with equal regard: the series could not ascend above the reign of Adrian, and the narrow distinction of Paganism and Christianity, introduced by the superstition of Theodosius, had been abolished by the consent of mankind. But the jurisprudence of the Pandects is circumscribed within a period of a hundred years, from the perpetual edict to the death of Severus Alexander: the civilians who lived under the first Caesars are seldom permitted to speak, and only three names can be attributed to the age of the republic. The favorite of Justinian (it has been fiercely urged) was fearful of encountering the light of freedom and the gravity of Roman sages.

Tribonian condemned to oblivion the genuine and native wisdom of Cato, the Scaevolas, and Sulpicius; while he invoked spirits more congenial to his own, the Syrians, Greeks, and Africans, who flocked to the Imperial court to study Latin as a foreign tongue, and jurisprudence as a lucrative profession. But the ministers of Justinian, [78] were instructed to labor, not for the curiosity of antiquarians, but for the immediate benefit of his subjects. It was their duty to select the useful and practical parts of the Roman law; and the writings of the old republicans, however curious on excellent, were no longer suited to the new system of manners, religion, and government. Perhaps, if the preceptors and friends of Cicero were still alive, our candor would acknowledge, that, except in purity of language, [79] their intrinsic merit was excelled by the school of Papinian and Ulpian. The science of the laws is the slow growth of time and experience, and the advantage both of method and materials, is naturally assumed by the most recent authors. The civilians of the reign of the Antonines had studied the works of their predecessors: their philosophic spirit had mitigated the rigor of antiquity, simplified the forms of proceeding, and emerged from the jealousy and prejudice of the rival sects. The choice of the authorities that compose the Pandects depended on the judgment of Tribonian: but the power of his sovereign could not absolve him from the sacred obligations of truth and fidelity. As the legislator of the empire, Justinian might repeal the acts of the Antonines, or condemn, as seditious, the free principles, which were maintained by the last of the Roman lawyers. [80] But the existence of past facts is placed beyond the reach of despotism; and the emperor was guilty of fraud and forgery, when he corrupted the integrity of their text, inscribed with their venerable names the words and ideas of his servile reign, [81] and suppressed, by the hand of power, the pure and authentic copies of their sentiments. The changes and interpolations of Tribonian and his colleagues are excused by the pretence of uniformity: but their cares have been insufficient, and the antinomies, or contradictions of the Code and Pandects, still exercise the patience and subtilty of modern civilians. [82]

[Footnote 78: An ingenious and learned oration of Schultingius (Jurisprudentia Ante-Justinianea, p. 883—907) justifies the choice of Tribonian, against the passionate charges of Francis Hottoman and his sectaries.]

[Footnote 79: Strip away the crust of Tribonian, and allow for the use of technical words, and the Latin of the Pandects will be found not unworthy of the silver age. It has been vehemently attacked by Laurentius Valla, a fastidious grammarian of the xvth century, and by his apologist Floridus Sabinus. It has been defended by Alciat, and a name less advocate, (most probably James Capellus.) Their various treatises are collected by Duker, (Opuscula de Latinitate veterum Jurisconsultorum, Lugd. Bat. 1721, in 12mo.) Note: Gibbon is mistaken with regard to Valla, who, though he inveighs against the barbarous style of the civilians of his own day, lavishes the highest praise on the admirable purity of the language of the ancient writers on civil law. (M. Warnkonig quotes a long passage of Valla in justification of this observation.) Since his time, this truth has been recognized by men of the highest eminence, such as Erasmus, David Hume and Runkhenius—W.]

[Footnote 80: Nomina quidem veteribus servavimus, legum autem veritatem nostram fecimus. Itaque siquid erat in illis seditiosum, multa autem talia erant ibi reposita, hoc decisum est et definitum, et in perspicuum finem deducta est quaeque lex, (Cod. Justinian. l. i. tit. xvii. leg. 3, No 10.) A frank confession! Note: Seditiosum, in the language of Justinian, means not seditious, but discounted—W.]

[Footnote 81: The number of these emblemata (a polite name for forgeries) is much reduced by Bynkershoek, (in the four last books of his Observations,) who poorly maintains the right of Justinian and the duty of Tribonian.]

[Footnote 82: The antinomies, or opposite laws of the Code and Pandects, are sometimes the cause, and often the excuse, of the glorious uncertainty of the civil law, which so often affords what Montaigne calls "Questions pour l'Ami." See a fine passage of Franciscus Balduinus in Justinian, (l. ii. p. 259, &c., apud Ludewig, p. 305, 306.)]

A rumor devoid of evidence has been propagated by the enemies of Justinian; that the jurisprudence of ancient Rome was reduced to ashes by the author of the Pandects, from the vain persuasion, that it was now either false or superfluous. Without usurping an office so invidious, the emperor might safely commit to ignorance and time the accomplishments of this destructive wish. Before the invention of printing and paper, the labor and the materials of writing could be purchased only by the rich; and it may reasonably be computed, that the price of books was a hundred fold their present value. [83] Copies were slowly multiplied and cautiously renewed: the hopes of profit tempted the sacrilegious scribes to erase the characters of antiquity, [83/1] and Sophocles or Tacitus were obliged to resign the parchment to missals, homilies, and the golden legend. [84] If such was the fate of the most beautiful compositions of genius, what stability could be expected for the dull and barren works of an obsolete science? The books of jurisprudence were interesting to few, and entertaining to none: their value was connected with present use, and they sunk forever as soon as that use was superseded by the innovations of fashion, superior merit, or public authority. In the age of peace and learning, between Cicero and the last of the Antonines, many losses had been already sustained, and some luminaries of the school, or forum, were known only to the curious by tradition and report. Three hundred and sixty years of disorder and decay accelerated the progress of oblivion; and it may fairly be presumed, that of the writings, which Justinian is accused of neglecting, many were no longer to be found in the libraries of the East. [85] The copies of Papinian, or Ulpian, which the reformer had proscribed, were deemed unworthy of future notice: the Twelve Tables and praetorian edicts insensibly vanished, and the monuments of ancient Rome were neglected or destroyed by the envy and ignorance of the Greeks. Even the Pandects themselves have escaped with difficulty and danger from the common shipwreck, and criticism has pronounced that all the editions and manuscripts of the West are derived from one original. [86] It was transcribed at Constantinople in the beginning of the seventh century, [87] was successively transported by the accidents of war and commerce to Amalphi, [88] Pisa, [89] and Florence, [90] and is now deposited as a sacred relic [91] in the ancient palace of the republic. [92]

[Footnote 83: When Faust, or Faustus, sold at Paris his first printed Bibles as manuscripts, the price of a parchment copy was reduced from four or five hundred to sixty, fifty, and forty crowns. The public was at first pleased with the cheapness, and at length provoked by the discovery of the fraud, (Mattaire, Annal. Typograph. tom. i. p. 12; first edit.)]

[Footnote 83/1: Among the works which have been recovered, by the persevering and successful endeavors of M. Mai and his followers to trace the imperfectly erased characters of the ancient writers on these Palimpsests, Gibbon at this period of his labors would have hailed with delight the recovery of the Institutes of Gaius, and the fragments of the Theodosian Code, published by M Keyron of Turin—M.]

[Footnote 84: This execrable practice prevailed from the viiith, and more especially from the xiith, century, when it became almost universal (Montfaucon, in the Memoires de l'Academie, tom. vi. p. 606, &c. Bibliotheque Raisonnee de la Diplomatique, tom. i. p. 176.)]

[Footnote 85: Pomponius (Pandect. l. i. tit. ii. leg. 2) observes, that of the three founders of the civil law, Mucius, Brutus, and Manilius, extant volumina, scripta Manilii monumenta; that of some old republican lawyers, haec versantur eorum scripta inter manus hominum. Eight of the Augustan sages were reduced to a compendium: of Cascellius, scripta non extant sed unus liber, &c.; of Trebatius, minus frequentatur; of Tubero, libri parum grati sunt. Many quotations in the Pandects are derived from books which Tribonian never saw; and in the long period from the viith to the xiiith century of Rome, the apparent reading of the moderns successively depends on the knowledge and veracity of their predecessors.]

[Footnote 86: All, in several instances, repeat the errors of the scribe and the transpositions of some leaves in the Florentine Pandects. This fact, if it be true, is decisive. Yet the Pandects are quoted by Ivo of Chartres, (who died in 1117,) by Theobald, archbishop of Canterbury, and by Vacarius, our first professor, in the year 1140, (Selden ad Fletam, c. 7, tom. ii. p. 1080—1085.) Have our British Mss. of the Pandects been collated?]

[Footnote 87: See the description of this original in Brenckman, (Hist. Pandect. Florent. l. i. c. 2, 3, p. 4—17, and l. ii.) Politian, an enthusiast, revered it as the authentic standard of Justinian himself, (p. 407, 408;) but this paradox is refuted by the abbreviations of the Florentine Ms. (l. ii. c. 3, p. 117-130.) It is composed of two quarto volumes, with large margins, on a thin parchment, and the Latin characters betray the hand of a Greek scribe.]

[Footnote 88: Brenckman, at the end of his history, has inserted two dissertations on the republic of Amalphi, and the Pisan war in the year 1135, &c.]

[Footnote 89: The discovery of the Pandects at Amalphi (A. D 1137) is first noticed (in 1501) by Ludovicus Bologninus, (Brenckman, l. i. c. 11, p. 73, 74, l. iv. c. 2, p. 417—425,) on the faith of a Pisan chronicle, (p. 409, 410,) without a name or a date. The whole story, though unknown to the xiith century, embellished by ignorant ages, and suspected by rigid criticism, is not, however, destitute of much internal probability, (l. i. c. 4—8, p. 17—50.) The Liber Pandectarum of Pisa was undoubtedly consulted in the xivth century by the great Bartolus, (p. 406, 407. See l. i. c. 9, p. 50—62.) Note: Savigny (vol. iii. p. 83, 89) examines and rejects the whole story. See likewise Hallam vol. iii. p. 514—M.]

[Footnote 90: Pisa was taken by the Florentines in the year 1406; and in 1411 the Pandects were transported to the capital. These events are authentic and famous.]

[Footnote 91: They were new bound in purple, deposited in a rich casket, and shown to curious travellers by the monks and magistrates bareheaded, and with lighted tapers, (Brenckman, l. i. c. 10, 11, 12, p. 62—93.)]

[Footnote 92: After the collations of Politian, Bologninus, and Antoninus Augustinus, and the splendid edition of the Pandects by Taurellus, (in 1551,) Henry Brenckman, a Dutchman, undertook a pilgrimage to Florence, where he employed several years in the study of a single manuscript. His Historia Pandectarum Florentinorum, (Utrecht, 1722, in 4to.,) though a monument of industry, is a small portion of his original design.]

It is the first care of a reformer to prevent any future reformation. To maintain the text of the Pandects, the Institutes, and the Code, the use of ciphers and abbreviations was rigorously proscribed; and as Justinian recollected, that the perpetual edict had been buried under the weight of commentators, he denounced the punishment of forgery against the rash civilians who should presume to interpret or pervert the will of their sovereign. The scholars of Accursius, of Bartolus, of Cujacius, should blush for their accumulated guilt, unless they dare to dispute his right of binding the authority of his successors, and the native freedom of the mind. But the emperor was unable to fix his own inconstancy; and, while he boasted of renewing the exchange of Diomede, of transmuting brass into gold, [93] discovered the necessity of purifying his gold from the mixture of baser alloy. Six years had not elapsed from the publication of the Code, before he condemned the imperfect attempt, by a new and more accurate edition of the same work; which he enriched with two hundred of his own laws, and fifty decisions of the darkest and most intricate points of jurisprudence. Every year, or, according to Procopius, each day, of his long reign, was marked by some legal innovation. Many of his acts were rescinded by himself; many were rejected by his successors; many have been obliterated by time; but the number of sixteen Edicts, and one hundred and sixty-eight Novels, [94] has been admitted into the authentic body of the civil jurisprudence. In the opinion of a philosopher superior to the prejudices of his profession, these incessant, and, for the most part, trifling alterations, can be only explained by the venal spirit of a prince, who sold without shame his judgments and his laws. [95] The charge of the secret historian is indeed explicit and vehement; but the sole instance, which he produces, may be ascribed to the devotion as well as to the avarice of Justinian. A wealthy bigot had bequeathed his inheritance to the church of Emesa; and its value was enhanced by the dexterity of an artist, who subscribed confessions of debt and promises of payment with the names of the richest Syrians. They pleaded the established prescription of thirty or forty years; but their defence was overruled by a retrospective edict, which extended the claims of the church to the term of a century; an edict so pregnant with injustice and disorder, that, after serving this occasional purpose, it was prudently abolished in the same reign. [96] If candor will acquit the emperor himself, and transfer the corruption to his wife and favorites, the suspicion of so foul a vice must still degrade the majesty of his laws; and the advocates of Justinian may acknowledge, that such levity, whatsoever be the motive, is unworthy of a legislator and a man.

[Footnote 93: Apud Homerum patrem omnis virtutis, (1st Praefat. ad Pandect.) A line of Milton or Tasso would surprise us in an act of parliament. Quae omnia obtinere sancimus in omne aevum. Of the first Code, he says, (2d Praefat.,) in aeternum valiturum. Man and forever!]

[Footnote 94: Novellae is a classic adjective, but a barbarous substantive, (Ludewig, p. 245.) Justinian never collected them himself; the nine collations, the legal standard of modern tribunals, consist of ninety-eight Novels; but the number was increased by the diligence of Julian, Haloander, and Contius, (Ludewig, p. 249, 258 Aleman. Not in Anecdot. p. 98.)]

[Footnote 95: Montesquieu, Considerations sur la Grandeur et la Decadence des Romains, c. 20, tom. iii. p. 501, in 4to. On this occasion he throws aside the gown and cap of a President a Mortier.]

[Footnote 96: Procopius, Anecdot. c. 28. A similar privilege was granted to the church of Rome, (Novel. ix.) For the general repeal of these mischievous indulgences, see Novel. cxi. and Edict. v.]

Monarchs seldom condescend to become the preceptors of their subjects; and some praise is due to Justinian, by whose command an ample system was reduced to a short and elementary treatise. Among the various institutes of the Roman law, [97] those of Caius [98] were the most popular in the East and West; and their use may be considered as an evidence of their merit. They were selected by the Imperial delegates, Tribonian, Theophilus, and Dorotheus; and the freedom and purity of the Antonines was incrusted with the coarser materials of a degenerate age. The same volume which introduced the youth of Rome, Constantinople, and Berytus, to the gradual study of the Code and Pandects, is still precious to the historian, the philosopher, and the magistrate. The Institutes of Justinian are divided into four books: they proceed, with no contemptible method, from, I. Persons, to, II. Things, and from things, to, III. Actions; and the article IV., of Private Wrongs, is terminated by the principles of Criminal Law. [98/1]

[Footnote 97: Lactantius, in his Institutes of Christianity, an elegant and specious work, proposes to imitate the title and method of the civilians. Quidam prudentes et arbitri aequitatis Institutiones Civilis Juris compositas ediderunt, (Institut. Divin. l. i. c. 1.) Such as Ulpian, Paul, Florentinus, Marcian.]

[Footnote 98: The emperor Justinian calls him suum, though he died before the end of the second century. His Institutes are quoted by Servius, Boethius, Priscian, &c.; and the Epitome by Arrian is still extant. (See the Prolegomena and notes to the edition of Schulting, in the Jurisprudentia Ante-Justinianea, Lugd. Bat. 1717. Heineccius, Hist. J R No. 313. Ludewig, in Vit. Just. p. 199.)]

[Footnote 98/1: Gibbon, dividing the Institutes into four parts, considers the appendix of the criminal law in the last title as a fourth part—W.]

PART V

The distinction of ranks and persons is the firmest basis of a mixed and limited government. In France, the remains of liberty are kept alive by the spirit, the honors, and even the prejudices, of fifty thousand nobles. [99] Two hundred families [99/1] supply, in lineal descent, the second branch of English legislature, which maintains, between the king and commons, the balance of the constitution. A gradation of patricians and plebeians, of strangers and subjects, has supported the aristocracy of Genoa, Venice, and ancient Rome. The perfect equality of men is the point in which the extremes of democracy and despotism are confounded; since the majesty of the prince or people would be offended, if any heads were exalted above the level of their fellow-slaves or fellow-citizens. In the decline of the Roman empire, the proud distinctions of the republic were gradually abolished, and the reason or instinct of Justinian completed the simple form of an absolute monarchy. The emperor could not eradicate the popular reverence which always waits on the possession of hereditary wealth, or the memory of famous ancestors. He delighted to honor, with titles and emoluments, his generals, magistrates, and senators; and his precarious indulgence communicated some rays of their glory to the persons of their wives and children. But in the eye of the law, all Roman citizens were equal, and all subjects of the empire were citizens of Rome. That inestimable character was degraded to an obsolete and empty name. The voice of a Roman could no longer enact his laws, or create the annual ministers of his power: his constitutional rights might have checked the arbitrary will of a master: and the bold adventurer from Germany or Arabia was admitted, with equal favor, to the civil and military command, which the citizen alone had been once entitled to assume over the conquests of his fathers. The first Caesars had scrupulously guarded the distinction of ingenuous and servile birth, which was decided by the condition of the mother; and the candor of the laws was satisfied, if her freedom could be ascertained, during a single moment, between the conception and the delivery. The slaves, who were liberated by a generous master, immediately entered into the middle class of libertines or freedmen; but they could never be enfranchised from the duties of obedience and gratitude; whatever were the fruits of their industry, their patron and his family inherited the third part; or even the whole of their fortune, if they died without children and without a testament. Justinian respected the rights of patrons; but his indulgence removed the badge of disgrace from the two inferior orders of freedmen; whoever ceased to be a slave, obtained, without reserve or delay, the station of a citizen; and at length the dignity of an ingenuous birth, which nature had refused, was created, or supposed, by the omnipotence of the emperor. Whatever restraints of age, or forms, or numbers, had been formerly introduced to check the abuse of manumissions, and the too rapid increase of vile and indigent Romans, he finally abolished; and the spirit of his laws promoted the extinction of domestic servitude. Yet the eastern provinces were filled, in the time of Justinian, with multitudes of slaves, either born or purchased for the use of their masters; and the price, from ten to seventy pieces of gold, was determined by their age, their strength, and their education. [100] But the hardships of this dependent state were continually diminished by the influence of government and religion: and the pride of a subject was no longer elated by his absolute dominion over the life and happiness of his bondsman. [101]

[Footnote 99: See the Annales Politiques de l'Abbe de St. Pierre, tom. i. p. 25 who dates in the year 1735. The most ancient families claim the immemorial possession of arms and fiefs. Since the Crusades, some, the most truly respectable, have been created by the king, for merit and services. The recent and vulgar crowd is derived from the multitude of venal offices without trust or dignity, which continually ennoble the wealthy plebeians.]

[Footnote 99/1: Since the time of Gibbon, the House of Peers has been more than doubled: it is above 400, exclusive of the spiritual peers—a wise policy to increase the patrician order in proportion to the general increase of the nation—M.]

[Footnote 100: If the option of a slave was bequeathed to several legatees, they drew lots, and the losers were entitled to their share of his value; ten pieces of gold for a common servant or maid under ten years: if above that age, twenty; if they knew a trade, thirty; notaries or writers, fifty; midwives or physicians, sixty; eunuchs under ten years, thirty pieces; above, fifty; if tradesmen, seventy, (Cod. l. vi. tit. xliii. leg. 3.) These legal prices are generally below those of the market.]

[Footnote 101: For the state of slaves and freedmen, see Institutes, l. i. tit. iii—viii. l. ii. tit. ix. l. iii. tit. viii. ix. Pandects or Digest, l. i. tit. v. vi. l. xxxviii. tit. i—iv., and the whole of the xlth book. Code, l. vi. tit. iv. v. l. vii. tit. i—xxiii. Be it henceforward understood that, with the original text of the Institutes and Pandects, the correspondent articles in the Antiquities and Elements of Heineccius are implicitly quoted; and with the xxvii. first books of the Pandects, the learned and rational Commentaries of Gerard Noodt, (Opera, tom. ii. p. 1—590, the end. Lugd. Bat. 1724.)]

The law of nature instructs most animals to cherish and educate their infant progeny. The law of reason inculcates to the human species the returns of filial piety. But the exclusive, absolute, and perpetual dominion of the father over his children, is peculiar to the Roman jurisprudence, [102] and seems to be coeval with the foundation of the city. [103] The paternal power was instituted or confirmed by Romulus himself; and, after the practice of three centuries, it was inscribed on the fourth table of the Decemvirs. In the forum, the senate, or the camp, the adult son of a Roman citizen enjoyed the public and private rights of a person: in his father's house he was a mere thing; [103/1] confounded by the laws with the movables, the cattle, and the slaves, whom the capricious master might alienate or destroy, without being responsible to any earthly tribunal. The hand which bestowed the daily sustenance might resume the voluntary gift, and whatever was acquired by the labor or fortune of the son was immediately lost in the property of the father. His stolen goods (his oxen or his children) might be recovered by the same action of theft; [104] and if either had been guilty of a trespass, it was in his own option to compensate the damage, or resign to the injured party the obnoxious animal. At the call of indigence or avarice, the master of a family could dispose of his children or his slaves. But the condition of the slave was far more advantageous, since he regained, by the first manumission, his alienated freedom: the son was again restored to his unnatural father; he might be condemned to servitude a second and a third time, and it was not till after the third sale and deliverance, [105] that he was enfranchised from the domestic power which had been so repeatedly abused. According to his discretion, a father might chastise the real or imaginary faults of his children, by stripes, by imprisonment, by exile, by sending them to the country to work in chains among the meanest of his servants. The majesty of a parent was armed with the power of life and death; [106] and the examples of such bloody executions, which were sometimes praised and never punished, may be traced in the annals of Rome beyond the times of Pompey and Augustus. Neither age, nor rank, nor the consular office, nor the honors of a triumph, could exempt the most illustrious citizen from the bonds of filial subjection: [107] his own descendants were included in the family of their common ancestor; and the claims of adoption were not less sacred or less rigorous than those of nature. Without fear, though not without danger of abuse, the Roman legislators had reposed an unbounded confidence in the sentiments of paternal love; and the oppression was tempered by the assurance that each generation must succeed in its turn to the awful dignity of parent and master.

[Footnote 102: See the patria potestas in the Institutes, (l. i. tit. ix.,) the Pandects, (l. i. tit. vi. vii.,) and the Code, (l. viii. tit. xlvii. xlviii. xlix.) Jus potestatis quod in liberos habemus proprium est civium Romanorum. Nulli enim alii sunt homines, qui talem in liberos habeant potestatem qualem nos habemus. Note: The newly-discovered Institutes of Gaius name one nation in which the same power was vested in the parent. Nec me praeterit Galatarum gentem credere, in potestate parentum liberos esse. Gaii Instit. edit. 1824, p. 257—M.]

[Footnote 103: Dionysius Hal. l. ii. p. 94, 95. Gravina (Opp. p. 286) produces the words of the xii. tables. Papinian (in Collatione Legum Roman et Mosaicarum, tit. iv. p. 204) styles this patria potestas, lex regia: Ulpian (ad Sabin. l. xxvi. in Pandect. l. i. tit. vi. leg. 8) says, jus potestatis moribus receptum; and furiosus filium in potestate habebit How sacred—or rather, how absurd! Note: All this is in strict accordance with the Roman character—W.]

[Footnote 103/1: This parental power was strictly confined to the Roman citizen. The foreigner, or he who had only jus Latii, did not possess it. If a Roman citizen unknowingly married a Latin or a foreign wife, he did not possess this power over his son, because the son, following the legal condition of the mother, was not a Roman citizen. A man, however, alleging sufficient cause for his ignorance, might raise both mother and child to the rights of citizenship. Gaius. p. 30—M.]

[Footnote 104: Pandect. l. xlvii. tit. ii. leg. 14, No. 13, leg. 38, No. 1. Such was the decision of Ulpian and Paul.]

[Footnote 105: The trina mancipatio is most clearly defined by Ulpian, (Fragment. x. p. 591, 592, edit. Schulting;) and best illustrated in the Antiquities of Heineccius. Note: The son of a family sold by his father did not become in every respect a slave, he was statu liber; that is to say, on paying the price for which he was sold, he became entirely free. See Hugo, Hist. Section 61—W.]

[Footnote 106: By Justinian, the old law, the jus necis of the Roman father (Institut. l. iv. tit. ix. No. 7) is reported and reprobated. Some legal vestiges are left in the Pandects (l. xliii. tit. xxix. leg. 3, No. 4) and the Collatio Legum Romanarum et Mosaicarum, (tit. ii. No. 3, p. 189.)]

[Footnote 107: Except on public occasions, and in the actual exercise of his office. In publicis locis atque muneribus, atque actionibus patrum, jura cum filiorum qui in magistratu sunt potestatibus collata *interquiescere paullulum et connivere, &c., (Aul. Gellius, Noctes Atticae, ii. 2.) The Lessons of the philosopher Taurus were justified by the old and memorable example of Fabius; and we may contemplate the same story in the style of Livy (xxiv. 44) and the homely idiom of Claudius Quadri garius the annalist.]*

The first limitation of paternal power is ascribed to the justice and humanity of Numa; and the maid who, with his father's consent, had espoused a freeman, was protected from the disgrace of becoming the wife of a slave. In the first ages, when the city was pressed, and often famished, by her Latin and Tuscan neighbors, the sale of children might be a frequent practice; but as a Roman could not legally purchase the liberty of his fellow-citizen, the market must gradually fail, and the trade would be destroyed by the conquests of the republic. An imperfect right of property was at length communicated to sons; and the threefold distinction of profectitious, adventitious, and professional was ascertained by the jurisprudence of the Code and Pandects. [108] Of all that proceeded from the father, he imparted only the use, and reserved the absolute dominion; yet if his goods were sold, the filial portion was excepted, by a favorable interpretation, from the demands of the creditors. In whatever accrued by marriage, gift, or collateral succession, the property was secured to the son; but the father, unless he had been specially excluded, enjoyed the usufruct during his life. As a just and prudent reward of military virtue, the spoils of the enemy were acquired, possessed, and bequeathed by the soldier alone; and the fair analogy was extended to the emoluments of any liberal profession, the salary of public service, and the sacred liberality of the emperor or empress. The life of a citizen was less exposed than his fortune to the abuse of paternal power. Yet his life might be adverse to the interest or passions of an unworthy father: the same crimes that flowed from the corruption, were more sensibly felt by the humanity, of the Augustan age; and the cruel Erixo, who whipped his son till he expired, was saved by the emperor from the just fury of the multitude. [109] The Roman father, from the license of servile dominion, was reduced to the gravity and moderation of a judge. The presence and opinion of Augustus confirmed the sentence of exile pronounced against an intentional parricide by the domestic tribunal of Arius. Adrian transported to an island the jealous parent, who, like a robber, had seized the opportunity of hunting, to assassinate a youth, the incestuous lover of his step-mother. [110] A private jurisdiction is repugnant to the spirit of monarchy; the parent was again reduced from a judge to an accuser; and the magistrates were enjoined by Severus Alexander to hear his complaints and execute his sentence. He could no longer take the life of a son without incurring the guilt and punishment of murder; and the pains of parricide, from which he had been excepted by the Pompeian law, were finally inflicted by the justice of Constantine. [111] The same protection was due to every period of existence; and reason must applaud the humanity of Paulus, for imputing the crime of murder to the father who strangles, or starves, or abandons his new-born infant; or exposes him in a public place to find the mercy which he himself had denied. But the exposition of children was the prevailing and stubborn vice of antiquity: it was sometimes prescribed, often permitted, almost always practised with impunity, by the nations who never entertained the Roman ideas of paternal power; and the dramatic poets, who appeal to the human heart, represent with indifference a popular custom which was palliated by the motives of economy and compassion. [112] If the father could subdue his own feelings, he might escape, though not the censure, at least the chastisement, of the laws; and the Roman empire was stained with the blood of infants, till such murders were included, by Valentinian and his colleagues, in the letter and spirit of the Cornelian law. The lessons of jurisprudence [113] and Christianity had been insufficient to eradicate this inhuman practice, till their gentle influence was fortified by the terrors of capital punishment. [114]

[Footnote 108: See the gradual enlargement and security of the filial peculium in the Institutes, (l. ii. tit. ix.,) the Pandects, (l. xv. tit. i. l. xli. tit. i.,) and the Code, (l. iv. tit. xxvi. xxvii.)]

[Footnote 109: The examples of Erixo and Arius are related by Seneca, (de Clementia, i. 14, 15,) the former with horror, the latter with applause.]

[Footnote 110: Quod latronis magis quam patris jure eum interfecit, nam patria potestas in pietate debet non in atrocitate consistere, (Marcian. Institut. l. xix. in Pandect. l. xlviii. tit. ix. leg.5.)]

[Footnote 111: The Pompeian and Cornelian laws de sicariis and parricidis are repeated, or rather abridged, with the last supplements of Alexander Severus, Constantine, and Valentinian, in the Pandects (l. xlviii. tit. viii ix,) and Code, (l. ix. tit. xvi. xvii.) See likewise the Theodosian Code, (l. ix. tit. xiv. xv.,) with Godefroy's Commentary, (tom. iii. p. 84—113) who pours a flood of ancient and modern learning over these penal laws.]

[Footnote 112: When the Chremes of Terence reproaches his wife for not obeying his orders and exposing their infant, he speaks like a father and a master, and silences the scruples of a foolish woman. See Apuleius, (Metamorph. l. x. p. 337, edit. Delphin.)]

[Footnote 113: The opinion of the lawyers, and the discretion of the magistrates, had introduced, in the time of Tacitus, some legal restraints, which might support his contrast of the boni mores of the Germans to the bonae leges alibi—that is to say, at Rome, (de Moribus Germanorum, c. 19.) Tertullian (ad Nationes, l. i. c. 15) refutes his own charges, and those of his brethren, against the heathen jurisprudence.]

[Footnote 114: The wise and humane sentence of the civilian Paul (l. ii. Sententiarum in Pandect, 1. xxv. tit. iii. leg. 4) is represented as a mere moral precept by Gerard Noodt, (Opp. tom. i. in Julius Paulus, p. 567—558, and Amica Responsio, p. 591-606,) who maintains the opinion of Justus Lipsius, (Opp. tom. ii. p. 409, ad Belgas. cent. i. epist. 85,) and as a positive binding law by Bynkershoek, (de Jure occidendi Liberos, Opp. tom. i. p. 318—340. Curae Secundae, p. 391—427.) In a learned out angry controversy, the two friends deviated into the opposite extremes.]

Experience has proved, that savages are the tyrants of the female sex, and that the condition of women is usually softened by the refinements of social life. In the hope of a robust progeny, Lycurgus had delayed the season of marriage: it was fixed by Numa at the tender age of twelve years, that the Roman husband might educate to his will a pure and obedient virgin. [115] According to the custom of antiquity, he bought his bride of her parents, and she fulfilled the coemption by purchasing, with three pieces of copper, a just introduction to his house and household deities. A sacrifice of fruits was offered by the pontiffs in the presence of ten witnesses; the contracting parties were seated on the same sheep-skin; they tasted a salt cake of far or rice; and this confarreation, [116] which denoted the ancient food of Italy, served as an emblem of their mystic union of mind and body. But this union on the side of the woman was rigorous and unequal; and she renounced the name and worship of her father's house, to embrace a new servitude, decorated only by the title of adoption, a fiction of the law, neither rational nor elegant, bestowed on the mother of a family [117] (her proper appellation) the strange characters of sister to her own children, and of daughter to her husband or master, who was invested with the plenitude of paternal power. By his judgment or caprice her behavior was approved, or censured, or chastised; he exercised the jurisdiction of life and death; and it was allowed, that in the cases of adultery or drunkenness, [118] the sentence might be properly inflicted. She acquired and inherited for the sole profit of her lord; and so clearly was woman defined, not as a person, but as a thing, that, if the original title were deficient, she might be claimed, like other movables, by the use and possession of an entire year. The inclination of the Roman husband discharged or withheld the conjugal debt, so scrupulously exacted by the Athenian and Jewish laws: [119] but as polygamy was unknown, he could never admit to his bed a fairer or a more favored partner.

[Footnote 115: Dionys. Hal. l. ii. p. 92, 93. Plutarch, in Numa, p. 140-141.]

[Footnote 116: Among the winter frunenta, the triticum, or bearded wheat; the siligo, or the unbearded; the far, adorea, oryza, whose description perfectly tallies with the rice of Spain and Italy. I adopt this identity on the credit of M. Paucton in his useful and laborious Metrologie, (p. 517—529.)]

[Footnote 117: Aulus Gellius (Noctes Atticae, xviii. 6) gives a ridiculous definition of Aelius Melissus, Matrona, quae semel materfamilias quae saepius peperit, as porcetra and scropha in the sow kind. He then adds the genuine meaning, quae in matrimonium vel in manum convenerat.]

[Footnote 118: It was enough to have tasted wine, or to have stolen the key of the cellar, (Plin. Hist. Nat. xiv. 14.)]

[Footnote 119: Solon requires three payments per month. By the Misna, a daily debt was imposed on an idle, vigorous, young husband; twice a week on a citizen; once on a peasant; once in thirty days on a camel-driver; once in six months on a seaman. But the student or doctor was free from tribute; and no wife, if she received a weekly sustenance, could sue for a divorce; for one week a vow of abstinence was allowed. Polygamy divided, without multiplying, the duties of the husband, (Selden, Uxor Ebraica, l. iii. c 6, in his works, vol ii. p. 717—720.)]

After the Punic triumphs, the matrons of Rome aspired to the common benefits of a free and opulent republic: their wishes were gratified by the indulgence of fathers and lovers, and their ambition was unsuccessfully resisted by the gravity of Cato the Censor. [120] They declined the solemnities of the old nuptiais; defeated the annual prescription by an absence of three days; and, without losing their name or independence, subscribed the liberal and definite terms of a marriage contract. Of their private fortunes, they communicated the use, and secured the property: the estates of a wife could neither be alienated nor mortgaged by a prodigal husband; their mutual gifts were prohibited by the jealousy of the laws; and the misconduct of either party might afford, under another name, a future subject for an action of theft. To this loose and voluntary compact, religious and civil rights were no longer essential; and, between persons of a similar rank, the apparent community of life was allowed as sufficient evidence of their nuptials. The dignity of marriage was restored by the Christians, who derived all spiritual grace from the prayers of the faithful and the benediction of the priest or bishop. The origin, validity, and duties of the holy institution were regulated by the tradition of the synagogue, the precepts of the gospel, and the canons of general or provincial synods; [121] and the conscience of the Christians was awed by the decrees and censures of their ecclesiastical rulers. Yet the magistrates of Justinian were not subject to the authority of the church: the emperor consulted the unbelieving civilians of antiquity, and the choice of matrimonial laws in the Code and Pandects, is directed by the earthly motives of justice, policy, and the natural freedom of both sexes. [122]

[Footnote 120: On the Oppian law we may hear the mitigating speech of Vaerius Flaccus, and the severe censorial oration of the elder Cato, (Liv. xxxiv. l—8.) But we shall rather hear the polished historian of the eighth, than the rough orators of the sixth, century of Rome. The principles, and even the style, of Cato are more accurately preserved by Aulus Gellius, (x. 23.)]

[Footnote 121: For the system of Jewish and Catholic matrimony, see Selden, (Uxor Ebraica, Opp. vol. ii. p. 529—860,) Bingham, (Christian Antiquities, l. xxii.,) and Chardon, (Hist. des Sacremens, tom. vi.)]

[Footnote 122: The civil laws of marriage are exposed in the Institutes, (l. i. tit. x.,) the Pandects, (l. xxiii. xxiv. xxv.,) and the Code, (l. v.;) but as the title de ritu nuptiarum is yet imperfect, we are obliged to explore the fragments of Ulpian (tit. ix. p. 590, 591,) and the Collatio Legum Mosaicarum, (tit. xvi. p. 790, 791,) with the notes of Pithaeus and Schulting. They find in the Commentary of Servius (on the 1st Georgia and the 4th Aeneid) two curious passages.]

Besides the agreement of the parties, the essence of every rational contract, the Roman marriage required the previous approbation of the parents. A father might be forced by some recent laws to supply the wants of a mature daughter; but even his insanity was not gradually allowed to supersede the necessity of his consent. The causes of the dissolution of matrimony have varied among the Romans; [123] but the most solemn sacrament, the confarreation itself, might always be done away by rites of a contrary tendency. In the first ages, the father of a family might sell his children, and his wife was reckoned in the number of his children: the domestic judge might pronounce the death of the offender, or his mercy might expel her from his bed and house; but the slavery of the wretched female was hopeless and perpetual, unless he asserted for his own convenience the manly prerogative of divorce. [123/1] The warmest applause has been lavished on the virtue of the Romans, who abstained from the exercise of this tempting privilege above five hundred years: [124] but the same fact evinces the unequal terms of a connection in which the slave was unable to renounce her tyrant, and the tyrant was unwilling to relinquish his slave. When the Roman matrons became the equal and voluntary companions of their lords, a new jurisprudence was introduced, that marriage, like other partnerships, might be dissolved by the abdication of one of the associates. In three centuries of prosperity and corruption, this principle was enlarged to frequent practice and pernicious abuse.

Passion, interest, or caprice, suggested daily motives for the dissolution of marriage; a word, a sign, a message, a letter, the mandate of a freedman, declared the separation; the most tender of human connections was degraded to a transient society of profit or pleasure. According to the various conditions of life, both sexes alternately felt the disgrace and injury: an inconstant spouse transferred her wealth to a new family, abandoning a numerous, perhaps a spurious, progeny to the paternal authority and care of her late husband; a beautiful virgin might be dismissed to the world, old, indigent, and friendless; but the reluctance of the Romans, when they were pressed to marriage by Augustus, sufficiently marks, that the prevailing institutions were least favorable to the males. A specious theory is confuted by this free and perfect experiment, which demonstrates, that the liberty of divorce does not contribute to happiness and virtue. The facility of separation would destroy all mutual confidence, and inflame every trifling dispute: the minute difference between a husband and a stranger, which might so easily be removed, might still more easily be forgotten; and the matron, who in five years can submit to the embraces of eight husbands, must cease to reverence the chastity of her own person. [125]

[Footnote 123: According to Plutarch, (p. 57,) Romulus allowed only three grounds of a divorce—drunkenness, adultery, and false keys. Otherwise, the husband who abused his supremacy forfeited half his goods to the wife, and half to the goddess Ceres, and offered a sacrifice (with the remainder?) to the terrestrial deities. This strange law was either imaginary or transient.]

[Footnote 123/1: Montesquieu relates and explains this fact in a different marnes Esprit des Loix, l. xvi. c. 16—G.]

[Footnote 124: In the year of Rome 523, Spurius Carvilius Ruga repudiated a fair, a good, but a barren, wife, (Dionysius Hal. l. ii. p. 93. Plutarch, in Numa, p. 141; Valerius Maximus, l. ii. c. 1; Aulus Gellius, iv. 3.) He was questioned by the censors, and hated by the people; but his divorce stood unimpeached in law.]

[Footnote 125:—Sic fiunt octo mariti Quinque per autumnos. Juvenal, Satir. vi. 20—A rapid succession, which may yet be credible, as well as the non consulum numero, sed maritorum annos suos computant, of Seneca, (de Beneficiis, iii. 16.) Jerom saw at Rome a triumphant husband bury his twenty-first wife, who had interred twenty-two of his less sturdy predecessors, (Opp. tom. i. p. 90, ad Gerontiam.) But the ten husbands in a month of the poet Martial, is an extravagant hyperbole, (l. 71. epigram 7.)]

Insufficient remedies followed with distant and tardy steps the rapid progress of the evil. The ancient worship of the Romans afforded a peculiar goddess to hear and reconcile the complaints of a married life; but her epithet of Viriplaca, [126] the appeaser of husbands, too clearly indicates on which side submission and repentance were always expected. Every act of a citizen was subject to the judgment of the censors; the first who used the privilege of divorce assigned, at their command, the motives of his conduct; [127] and a senator was expelled for dismissing his virgin spouse without the knowledge or advice of his friends. Whenever an action was instituted for the recovery of a marriage portion, the proetor, as the guardian of equity, examined the cause and the characters, and gently inclined the scale in favor of the guiltless and injured party. Augustus, who united the powers of both magistrates, adopted their different modes of repressing or chastising the license of divorce. [128] The presence of seven Roman witnesses was required for the validity of this solemn and deliberate act: if any adequate provocation had been given by the husband, instead of the delay of two years, he was compelled to refund immediately, or in the space of six months; but if he could arraign the manners of his wife, her guilt or levity was expiated by the loss of the sixth or eighth part of her marriage portion. The Christian princes were the first who specified the just causes of a private divorce; their institutions, from Constantine to Justinian, appear to fluctuate between the custom of the empire and the wishes of the church, [129] and the author of the Novels too frequently reforms the jurisprudence of the Code and Pandects. In the most rigorous laws, a wife was condemned to support a gamester, a drunkard, or a libertine, unless he were guilty of homicide, poison, or sacrilege, in which cases the marriage, as it should seem, might have been dissolved by the hand of the executioner. But the sacred right of the husband was invariably maintained, to deliver his name and family from the disgrace of adultery: the list of mortal sins, either male or female, was curtailed and enlarged by successive regulations, and the obstacles of incurable impotence, long absence, and monastic profession, were allowed to rescind the matrimonial obligation. Whoever transgressed the permission of the law, was subject to various and heavy penalties. The woman was stripped of her wealth and ornaments, without excepting the bodkin of her hair: if the man introduced a new bride into his bed, her fortune might be lawfully seized by the vengeance of his exiled wife. Forfeiture was sometimes commuted to a fine; the fine was sometimes aggravated by transportation to an island, or imprisonment in a monastery; the injured party was released from the bonds of marriage; but the offender, during life, or a term of years, was disabled from the repetition of nuptials. The successor of Justinian yielded to the prayers of his unhappy subjects, and restored the liberty of divorce by mutual consent: the civilians were unanimous, [130] the theologians were divided, [131] and the ambiguous word, which contains the precept of Christ, is flexible to any interpretation that the wisdom of a legislator can demand.

[Footnote 126: Sacellum Viriplacae, (Valerius Maximus, l. ii. c. 1,) in the Palatine region, appears in the time of Theodosius, in the description of Rome by Publius Victor.]

[Footnote 127: Valerius Maximus, l. ii. c. 9. With some propriety he judges divorce more criminal than celibacy: illo namque conjugalia sacre spreta tantum, hoc etiam injuriose tractata.]

[Footnote 128: See the laws of Augustus and his successors, in Heineccius, ad Legem Papiam-Poppaeam, c. 19, in Opp. tom. vi. P. i. p. 323—333.]

[Footnote 129: Aliae sunt leges Caesarum, aliae Christi; aliud Papinianus, aliud Paulus nocter praecipit, (Jerom. tom. i. p. 198. Selden, Uxor Ebraica l. iii. c. 31 p. 847—853.)]

[Footnote 130: The Institutes are silent; but we may consult the Codes of Theodosius (l. iii. tit. xvi., with Godefroy's Commentary, tom. i. p. 310—315) and Justinian, (l. v. tit. xvii.,) the Pandects (l. xxiv. tit. ii.) and the Novels, (xxii. cxvii. cxxvii. cxxxiv. cxl.) Justinian fluctuated to the last between civil and ecclesiastical law.]

[Footnote 131: In pure Greek, it is not a common word; nor can the proper meaning, fornication, be strictly applied to matrimonial sin. In a figurative sense, how far, and to what offences, may it be extended? Did Christ speak the Rabbinical or Syriac tongue? Of what original word is the translation? How variously is that Greek word translated in the versions ancient and modern! There are two (Mark, x. 11, Luke, xvi. 18) to one (Matthew, xix. 9) that such ground of divorce was not excepted by Jesus. Some critics have presumed to think, by an evasive answer, he avoided the giving offence either to the school of Sammai or to that of Hillel, (Selden, Uxor Ebraica, l. iii. c. 18—22, 28, 31.) Note: But these had nothing to do with the question of a divorce made by judicial authority—Hugo.]

The freedom of love and marriage was restrained among the Romans by natural and civil impediments. An instinct, almost innate and universal, appears to prohibit the incestuous commerce [132] of parents and children in the infinite series of ascending and descending generations. Concerning the oblique and collateral branches, nature is indifferent, reason mute, and custom various and arbitrary. In Egypt, the marriage of brothers and sisters was admitted without scruple or exception: a Spartan might espouse the daughter of his father, an Athenian, that of his mother; and the nuptials of an uncle with his niece were applauded at Athens as a happy union of the dearest relations. The profane lawgivers of Rome were never tempted by interest or superstition to multiply the forbidden degrees: but they inflexibly condemned the marriage of sisters and brothers, hesitated whether first cousins should be touched by the same interdict; revered the parental character of aunts and uncles, [132/1] and treated affinity and adoption as a just imitation of the ties of blood. According to the proud maxims of the republic, a legal marriage could only be contracted by free citizens; an honorable, at least an ingenuous birth, was required for the spouse of a senator: but the blood of kings could never mingle in legitimate nuptials with the blood of a Roman; and the name of Stranger degraded Cleopatra and Berenice, [133] to live the concubines of Mark Antony and Titus. [134] This appellation, indeed, so injurious to the majesty, cannot without indulgence be applied to the manners, of these Oriental queens. A concubine, in the strict sense of the civilians, was a woman of servile or plebeian extraction, the sole and faithful companion of a Roman citizen, who continued in a state of celibacy. Her modest station, below the honors of a wife, above the infamy of a prostitute, was acknowledged and approved by the laws: from the age of Augustus to the tenth century, the use of this secondary marriage prevailed both in the West and East; and the humble virtues of a concubine were often preferred to the pomp and insolence of a noble matron. In this connection, the two Antonines, the best of princes and of men, enjoyed the comforts of domestic love: the example was imitated by many citizens impatient of celibacy, but regardful of their families. If at any time they desired to legitimate their natural children, the conversion was instantly performed by the celebration of their nuptials with a partner whose faithfulness and fidelity they had already tried. [134/1] By this epithet of natural, the offspring of the concubine were distinguished from the spurious brood of adultery, prostitution, and incest, to whom Justinian reluctantly grants the necessary aliments of life; and these natural children alone were capable of succeeding to a sixth part of the inheritance of their reputed father. According to the rigor of law, bastards were entitled only to the name and condition of their mother, from whom they might derive the character of a slave, a stranger, or a citizen. The outcasts of every family were adopted without reproach as the children of the state. [135] [135/1]

[Footnote 132: The principles of the Roman jurisprudence are exposed by Justinian, (Institut. t. i. tit. x.;) and the laws and manners of the different nations of antiquity concerning forbidden degrees, &c., are copiously explained by Dr. Taylor in his Elements of Civil Law, (p. 108, 314—339,) a work of amusing, though various reading; but which cannot be praised for philosophical precision.]

[Footnote 132/1: According to the earlier law, (Gaii Instit. p. 27,) a man might marry his niece on the brother's, not on the sister's, side. The emperor Claudius set the example of the former. In the Institutes, this distinction was abolished and both declared illegal—M.]

[Footnote 133: When her father Agrippa died, (A.D. 44,) Berenice was sixteen years of age, (Joseph. tom. i. Antiquit. Judaic. l. xix. c. 9, p. 952, edit. Havercamp.) She was therefore above fifty years old when Titus (A.D. 79) invitus invitam invisit. This date would not have adorned the tragedy or pastoral of the tender Racine.]

[Footnote 134: The Aegyptia conjux of Virgil (Aeneid, viii. 688) seems to be numbered among the monsters who warred with Mark Antony against Augustus, the senate, and the gods of Italy.]

[Footnote 134/1: The Edict of Constantine first conferred this right; for Augustus had prohibited the taking as a concubine a woman who might be taken as a wife; and if marriage took place afterwards, this marriage made no change in the rights of the children born before it; recourse was then had to adoption, properly called arrogation—G.]

[Footnote 135: The humble but legal rights of concubines and natural children are stated in the Institutes, (l. i. tit. x.,) the Pandects, (l. i. tit. vii.,) the Code, (l. v. tit. xxv.,) and the Novels, (lxxiv. lxxxix.) The researches of Heineccius and Giannone, (ad Legem Juliam et Papiam-Poppaeam, c. iv. p. 164-175. Opere Posthume, p. 108—158) illustrate this interesting and domestic subject.]

[Footnote 135/1: See, however, the two fragments of laws in the newly discovered extracts from the Theodosian Code, published by M. A. Peyron, at Turin. By the first law of Constantine, the legitimate offspring could alone inherit; where there were no near legitimate relatives, the inheritance went to the fiscus. The son of a certain Licinianus, who had inherited his father's property under the supposition that he was legitimate, and had been promoted to a place of dignity, was to be degraded, his property confiscated, himself punished with stripes and imprisonment. By the second, all persons, even of the highest rank, senators, perfectissimi, decemvirs, were to be declared infamous, and out of the protection of the Roman law, if born ex ancilla, vel ancillae filia, vel liberta, vel libertae filia, sive Romana facta, seu Latina, vel scaenicae filia, vel ex tabernaria, vel ex tabernariae filia, vel humili vel abjecta, vel lenonis, aut arenarii filia, vel quae mercimoniis publicis praefuit. Whatever a fond father had conferred on such children was revoked, and either restored to the legitimate children, or confiscated to the state; the mothers, who were guilty of thus poisoning the minds of the fathers, were to be put to the torture (tormentis subici jubemus.) The unfortunate son of Licinianus, it appears from this second law, having fled, had been taken, and was ordered to be kept in chains to work in the Gynaeceum at Carthage. Cod. Theodor ab. A. Person, 87—90—M.]

PART VI

The relation of guardian and ward, or in Roman words of tutor and pupil, which covers so many titles of the Institutes and Pandects, [136] is of a very simple and uniform nature. The person and property of an orphan must always be trusted to the custody of some discreet friend. If the deceased father had not signified his choice, the agnats, or paternal kindred of the nearest degree, were compelled to act as the natural guardians: the Athenians were apprehensive of exposing the infant to the power of those most interested in his death; but an axiom of Roman jurisprudence has pronounced, that the charge of tutelage should constantly attend the emolument of succession. If the choice of the father, and the line of consanguinity, afforded no efficient guardian, the failure was supplied by the nomination of the praetor of the city, or the president of the province. But the person whom they named to this public office might be legally excused by insanity or blindness, by ignorance or inability, by previous enmity or adverse interest, by the number of children or guardianships with which he was already burdened, and by the immunities which were granted to the useful labors of magistrates, lawyers, physicians, and professors. Till the infant could speak, and think, he was represented by the tutor, whose authority was finally determined by the age of puberty. Without his consent, no act of the pupil could bind himself to his own prejudice, though it might oblige others for his personal benefit. It is needless to observe, that the tutor often gave security, and always rendered an account, and that the want of diligence or integrity exposed him to a civil and almost criminal action for the violation of his sacred trust. The age of puberty had been rashly fixed by the civilians at fourteen; [136/1] but as the faculties of the mind ripen more slowly than those of the body, a curator was interposed to guard the fortunes of a Roman youth from his own inexperience and headstrong passions. Such a trustee had been first instituted by the praetor, to save a family from the blind havoc of a prodigal or madman; and the minor was compelled, by the laws, to solicit the same protection, to give validity to his acts till he accomplished the full period of twenty-five years. Women were condemned to the perpetual tutelage of parents, husbands, or guardians; a sex created to please and obey was never supposed to have attained the age of reason and experience. Such, at least, was the stern and haughty spirit of the ancient law, which had been insensibly mollified before the time of Justinian.

[Footnote 136: See the article of guardians and wards in the Institutes, (l. i. tit. xiii—xxvi.,) the Pandects, (l. xxvi. xxvii.,) and the Code, (l. v. tit. xxviii—lxx.)]

[Footnote 136/1: Gibbon accuses the civilians of having "rashly fixed the age of puberty at twelve or fourteen years." It was not so; before Justinian, no law existed on this subject. Ulpian relates the discussions which took place on this point among the different sects of civilians. See the Institutes, l. i. tit. 22, and the fragments of Ulpian. Nor was the curatorship obligatory for all minors—W.]

II. The original right of property can only be justified by the accident or merit of prior occupancy; and on this foundation it is wisely established by the philosophy of the civilians. [137] The savage who hollows a tree, inserts a sharp stone into a wooden handle, or applies a string to an elastic branch, becomes in a state of nature the just proprietor of the canoe, the bow, or the hatchet. The materials were common to all, the new form, the produce of his time and simple industry, belongs solely to himself. His hungry brethren cannot, without a sense of their own injustice, extort from the hunter the game of the forest overtaken or slain by his personal strength and dexterity. If his provident care preserves and multiplies the tame animals, whose nature is tractable to the arts of education, he acquires a perpetual title to the use and service of their numerous progeny, which derives its existence from him alone. If he encloses and cultivates a field for their sustenance and his own, a barren waste is converted into a fertile soil; the seed, the manure, the labor, create a new value, and the rewards of harvest are painfully earned by the fatigues of the revolving year. In the successive states of society, the hunter, the shepherd, the husbandman, may defend their possessions by two reasons which forcibly appeal to the feelings of the human mind: that whatever they enjoy is the fruit of their own industry; and that every man who envies their felicity, may purchase similar acquisitions by the exercise of similar diligence. Such, in truth, may be the freedom and plenty of a small colony cast on a fruitful island. But the colony multiplies, while the space still continues the same; the common rights, the equal inheritance of mankind. are engrossed by the bold and crafty; each field and forest is circumscribed by the landmarks of a jealous master; and it is the peculiar praise of the Roman jurisprudence, that i asserts the claim of the first occupant to the wild animals of the earth, the air, and the waters. In the progress from primitive equity to final injustice, the steps are silent, the shades are almost imperceptible, and the absolute monopoly is guarded by positive laws and artificial reason. The active, insatiate principle of self-love can alone supply the arts of life and the wages of industry; and as soon as civil government and exclusive property have been introduced, they become necessary to the existence of the human race. Except in the singular institutions of Sparta, the wisest legislators have disapproved an agrarian law as a false and dangerous innovation. Among the Romans, the enormous disproportion of wealth surmounted the ideal restraints of a doubtful tradition, and an obsolete statute; a tradition that the poorest follower of Romulus had been endowed with the perpetual inheritance of two jugera; [138] a statute which confined the richest citizen to the measure of five hundred jugera, or three hundred and twelve acres of land. The original territory of Rome consisted only of some miles of wood and meadow along the banks of the Tyber; and domestic exchange could add nothing to the national stock. But the goods of an alien or enemy were lawfully exposed to the first hostile occupier; the city was enriched by the profitable trade of war; and the blood of her sons was the only price that was paid for the Volscian sheep, the slaves of Briton, or the gems and gold of Asiatic kingdoms. In the language of ancient jurisprudence, which was corrupted and forgotten before the age of Justinian, these spoils were distinguished by the name of manceps or manicipium, taken with the hand; and whenever they were sold or emancipated, the purchaser required some assurance that they had been the property of an enemy, and not of a fellow-citizen. [139] A citizen could only forfeit his rights by apparent dereliction, and such dereliction of a valuable interest could not easily be presumed. Yet, according to the Twelve Tables, a prescription of one year for movables, and of two years for immovables, abolished the claim of the ancient master, if the actual possessor had acquired them by a fair transaction from the person whom he believed to be the lawful proprietor. [140] Such conscientious injustice, without any mixture of fraud or force could seldom injure the members of a small republic; but the various periods of three, of ten, or of twenty years, determined by Justinian, are more suitable to the latitude of a great empire. It is only in the term of prescription that the distinction of real and personal fortune has been remarked by the civilians; and their general idea of property is that of simple, uniform, and absolute dominion. The subordinate exceptions of use, of usufruct, [141] of servitude, [142] imposed for the benefit of a neighbor on lands and houses, are abundantly explained by the professors of jurisprudence. The claims of property, as far as they are altered by the mixture, the division, or the transformation of substances, are investigated with metaphysical subtilty by the same civilians.

[Footnote 137: *Institut. l. ii. tit i. ii. Compare the pure and precise reasoning of Caius and Heineccius (l. ii. tit. i. p. 69-91) with the loose prolixity of Theophilus, (p. 207—265.) The opinions of Ulpian are preserved in the Pandects, (l. i. tit. viii. leg. 41, No. 1.)]*

[Footnote 138: The heredium of the first Romans is defined by Varro, (de Re Rustica, l. i. c. ii. p. 141, c. x. p. 160, 161, edit. Gesner,) and clouded by Pliny's declamation, (Hist. Natur. xviii. 2.) A just and learned comment is given in the Administration des Terres chez les Romains, (p. 12—66.) Note: On the duo jugera, compare Niebuhr, vol. i. p. 337—M.]

[Footnote 139: The res mancipi is explained from faint and remote lights by Ulpian (Fragment. tit. xviii. p. 618, 619) and Bynkershoek, (Opp tom. i. p. 306—315.) The definition is somewhat arbitrary; and as none except myself have assigned a reason, I am diffident of my own.]

[Footnote 140: From this short prescription, Hume (Essays, vol. i. p. 423) infers that there could not then be more order and settlement in Italy than now amongst the Tartars. By the civilian of his adversary Wallace, he is reproached, and not without reason, for overlooking the conditions, (Institut. l. ii. tit. vi.) Note: Gibbon acknowledges, in the former note, the obscurity of his views with regard to the res mancipi. The interpreters, who preceded him, are not agreed on this point, one of the most difficult in the ancient Roman law. The conclusions of Hume, of which the author here speaks, are grounded on false assumptions. Gibbon had conceived very inaccurate notions of Property among the Romans, and those of many authors in the present day are not less erroneous. We think it right, in this place, to develop the system of property among the Romans, as the result of the study of the extant original authorities on the ancient law, and as it has been demonstrated, recognized, and adopted by the most learned expositors of the Roman law. Besides the authorities formerly known, such as the Fragments of Ulpian, t. xix. and t. i. 16. Theoph. Paraph. i. 5, 4, may be consulted the Institutes of Gaius, i. 54, and ii. 40, et seq. The Roman laws protected all property acquired in a lawful manner. They imposed on those who had invaded it, the obligation of making restitution and reparation of all damage caused by that invasion; they punished it moreover, in many cases, by a pecuniary fine. But they did not always grant a recovery against the third person, who had become bona fide possessed of the property. He who had obtained possession of a thing belonging to another, knowing nothing of the prior rights of that person, maintained the possession. The law had expressly determined those cases, in which it permitted property to be reclaimed from an innocent possessor. In these cases possession had the characters of absolute proprietorship, called mancipium, jus Quiritium. To possess this right, it was not sufficient to have entered into possession of the thing in any manner; the acquisition was bound to have that character of publicity, which was given by the observation of solemn forms, prescribed by the laws, or the uninterrupted exercise of proprietorship during a certain time: the Roman citizen alone could acquire this proprietorship. Every other kind of possession, which might be named imperfect proprietorship, was called "in bonis habere." It was not till after the time of Cicero that the general name of Dominium was given to all proprietorship. It was then the publicity which constituted the distinctive character of absolute dominion. This publicity was grounded on the mode of acquisition, which the moderns have called Civil, (Modi adquirendi Civiles.) These modes of acquisition were, 1. Mancipium or mancipatio, which was nothing but the solemn delivering over of the thing in the presence of a determinate number of witnesses and a public officer; it was from this probably that proprietorship was named, 2. In jure cessio, which was a solemn delivering over before the praetor. 3. Adjudicatio, made by a judge, in a case of partition. 4. Lex, which comprehended modes of acquiring in particular cases determined by law; probably the law of the xii. tables; for instance, the sub corona emptio and the legatum. 5. Usna, called afterwards usacapio, and by the moderns prescription. This was only a year for movables; two years for things not movable. Its primary object was altogether different from that of prescription in the present day. It was originally introduced in order to transform the simple possession of a thing (in bonis habere) into Roman proprietorship. The public and uninterrupted possession of a thing, enjoyed for the space of one or two years, was sufficient to make known to the inhabitants of the city of Rome to whom the thing belonged. This last mode of acquisition completed the system of civil acquisitions. by legalizing. as it were, every other kind of acquisition which was not conferred, from the commencement, by the Jus Quiritium. V. Ulpian. Fragm. i. 16. Gaius, ii. 14. We believe, according to Gaius, 43, that this usucaption was extended to the case where a thing had been acquired from a person not the real proprietor; and that according to the time prescribed, it gave to the possessor the Roman proprietorship. But this does not appear to have been the original design of this Institution. Caeterum etiam earum rerum usucapio nobis competit, quae non a domino nobis tradita fuerint, si modo eas bona fide acceperimus Gaius, l ii. 43. As to things of smaller value, or those which it was difficult to distinguish from each other, the solemnities of which we speak were not requisite to obtain legal proprietorship. In this case simple delivery was sufficient. In proportion to the aggrandizement of the Republic, this latter principle became more important from the increase of the commerce and wealth of the state. It was necessary to know what were those things of which absolute property might be acquired by simple delivery, and what, on the contrary, those, the acquisition of which must be sanctioned by these solemnities. This question was necessarily to be decided by a general rule; and it is this rule which establishes the distinction between res mancipi and nec mancipi, a distinction about which the opinions of modern civilians differ so much that there are above ten conflicting systems on the subject. The system which accords best with a sound interpretation of the Roman laws, is that proposed by M. Trekel of Hamburg, and still further developed by M. Hugo, who has extracted it in the Magazine of Civil Law, vol. ii. p. 7. This is the system now almost universally adopted. Res mancipi (by contraction for mancipii) were things of which the absolute property (Jus Quiritium) might be acquired only by the solemnities mentioned above, at least by that of mancipation, which was, without doubt, the most easy and the most usual. Gaius, ii. 25. As for other things, the acquisition of which was not subject to these forms, in order to confer absolute right, they were called res nec mancipi. See Ulpian, Fragm. xix. 1. 3, 7. Ulpian and Varro enumerate the different kinds of res mancipi. Their enumerations do not quite agree; and various methods of reconciling them have been attempted. The authority of Ulpian, however, who wrote as a civilian, ought to have the greater weight on this subject. But why are these things alone res mancipi? This is one of the questions which have been most frequently agitated, and on which the opinions of civilians are most divided. M. Hugo has resolved it in the most natural and satisfactory manner. "All things which were easily known individually, which were of great value, with which the Romans were acquainted, and which they highly appreciated, were res mancipi. Of old mancipation or some other solemn form was required for the acquisition of these things, an account of their importance. Mancipation served to prove their acquisition, because they were easily distinguished one from the other." On this great historical discussion consult the Magazine of Civil Law by M. Hugo, vol. ii. p. 37, 38; the dissertation of M. J. M. Zachariae, de Rebus Mancipi et nec Mancipi Conjecturae, p. 11. Lipsiae, 1807; the History of Civil Law by M. Hugo; and my Institutiones Juris Romani Privati p. 108, 110. As a general rule, it may be said that all things are res nec mancipi; the res mancipi are the exception to this principle. The praetors changed the system of property by allowing a person, who had a thing in bonis, the right to recover before the prescribed term of usucaption had conferred absolute proprietorship. (Pauliana in rem actio.) Justinian went still further, in times when there was no longer any distinction between a Roman citizen and a stranger. He granted the right of recovering all things which had been acquired, whether by what were called civil or natural modes of acquisition, Cod. l. vii. t. 25, 31. And he so altered the theory of Gaius in his Institutes, ii. 1, that no trace remains of the doctrine taught by that civilian—W.]

[Footnote 141: See the Institutes (l. i. tit. iv. v.) and the Pandects, (l. vii.) Noodt has composed a learned and distinct treatise de Usufructu, (Opp. tom. i. p. 387—478.)]

[Footnote 142: The questions de Servitutibus are discussed in the Institutes (l. ii. tit. iii.) and Pandects, (l. viii.) Cicero (pro Murena, c. 9) and Lactantius (Institut. Divin. l. i. c. i.) affect to laugh at the insignificant doctrine, *de aqua de pluvia arcenda*, &c. Yet it might be of frequent use among litigious neighbors, both in town and country.]

The personal title of the first proprietor must be determined by his death: but the possession, without any appearance of change, is peaceably continued in his children, the associates of his toil, and the partners of his wealth. This natural inheritance has been protected by the legislators of every climate and age, and the father is encouraged to persevere in slow and distant improvements, by the tender hope, that a long posterity will enjoy the fruits of his labor. The principle of hereditary succession is universal; but the order has been variously established by convenience or caprice, by the spirit of national institutions, or by some partial example which was originally decided by fraud or violence. The jurisprudence of the Romans appear to have deviated from the inequality of nature much less than the Jewish, [143] the Athenian, [144] or the English institutions. [145] On the death of a citizen, all his descendants, unless they were already freed from his paternal power, were called to the inheritance of his possessions. The insolent prerogative of primogeniture was unknown; the two sexes were placed on a just level; all the sons and daughters were entitled to an equal portion of the patrimonial estate; and if any of the sons had been intercepted by a premature death, his person was represented, and his share was divided, by his surviving children. On the failure of the direct line, the right of succession must diverge to the collateral branches. The degrees of kindred [146] are numbered by the civilians, ascending from the last possessor to a common parent, and descending from the common parent to the next heir: my father stands in the first degree, my brother in the second, his children in the third, and the remainder of the series may be conceived by a fancy, or pictured in a genealogical table. In this computation, a distinction was made, essential to the laws and even the constitution of Rome; the agnats, or persons connected by a line of males, were called, as they stood in the nearest degree, to an equal partition; but a female was incapable of transmitting any legal claims; and the cognats of every rank, without excepting the dear relation of a mother and a son, were disinherited by the Twelve Tables, as strangers and aliens. Among the Romans agens or lineage was united by a common name and domestic rites; the various cognomens or surnames of Scipio, or Marcellus, distinguished from each other the subordinate branches or families of the Cornelian or Claudian race: the default of the agnats, of the same surname, was supplied by the larger denomination of gentiles; and the vigilance of the laws maintained, in the same name, the perpetual descent of religion and property. A similar principle dictated the Voconian law, [147] which abolished the right of female inheritance. As long as virgins were given or sold in marriage, the adoption of the wife extinguished the hopes of the daughter. But the equal succession of independent matrons supported their pride and luxury, and might transport into a foreign house the riches of their fathers.

While the maxims of Cato [148] were revered, they tended to perpetuate in each family a just and virtuous mediocrity: till female blandishments insensibly triumphed; and every salutary restraint was lost in the dissolute greatness of the republic. The rigor of the decemvirs was tempered by the equity of the praetors. Their edicts restored and emancipated posthumous children to the rights of nature; and upon the failure of the agnats, they preferred the blood of the cognats to the name of the gentiles whose title and character were insensibly covered with oblivion. The reciprocal inheritance of mothers and sons was established in the Tertullian and Orphitian decrees by the humanity of the senate. A new and more impartial order was introduced by the Novels of Justinian, who affected to revive the jurisprudence of the Twelve Tables. The lines of masculine and female kindred were confounded: the descending, ascending, and collateral series was accurately defined; and each degree, according tot he proximity of blood and affection, succeeded to the vacant possessions of a Roman citizen. [149]

[Footnote 143: Among the patriarchs, the first-born enjoyed a mystic and spiritual primogeniture, (Genesis, xxv. 31.) In the land of Canaan, he was entitled to a double portion of inheritance, (Deuteronomy, xxi. 17, with Le Clerc's judicious Commentary.)]

[Footnote 144: At Athens, the sons were equal; but the poor daughters were endowed at the discretion of their brothers. See the pleadings of Isaeus, (in the viith volume of the Greek Orators,) illustrated by the version and comment of Sir William Jones, a scholar, a lawyer, and a man of genius.]

[Footnote 145: In England, the eldest son also inherits all the land; a law, says the orthodox Judge Blackstone, (Commentaries on the Laws of England, vol. ii. p. 215,) unjust only in the opinion of younger brothers. It may be of some political use in sharpening their industry.]

[Footnote 146: Blackstone's Tables (vol. ii. p. 202) represent and compare the decrees of the civil with those of the canon and common law. A separate tract of Julius Paulus, de gradibus et affinibus, is inserted or abridged in the Pandects, (l. xxxviii. tit. x.) In the viith degrees he computes (No. 18) 1024 persons.]

[Footnote 147: The Voconian law was enacted in the year of Rome 584. The younger Scipio, who was then 17 years of age, (Frenshemius, Supplement. Livian. xlvi. 40,) found an occasion of exercising his generosity to his mother, sisters, &c. (Polybius, tom. ii. l. xxxi. p. 1453—1464, edit Gronov., a domestic witness.)]

[Footnote 148: Legem Voconiam (Ernesti, Clavis Ciceroniana) magna voce bonis lateribus (at lxv. years of age) suasissem, says old Cato, (de Senectute, c. 5,) Aulus Gellius (vii. 13, xvii. 6) has saved some passages.]

[Footnote 149: See the law of succession in the Institutes of Caius, (l. ii. tit. viii. p. 130—144,) and Justinian, (l. iii. tit. i—vi., with the Greek version of Theophilus, p. 515-575, 588—600,) the Pandects, (l. xxxviii. tit. vi—xvii.,) the Code, (l. vi. tit. lv—lx.,) and the Novels, (cxviii.)]

The order of succession is regulated by nature, or at least by the general and permanent reason of the lawgiver: but this order is frequently violated by the arbitrary and partial wills, which prolong the dominion of the testator beyond the grave. [150] In the simple state of society, this last use or abuse of the right of property is seldom indulged: it was introduced at Athens by the laws of Solon; and the private testaments of the father of a family are authorized by the Twelve Tables. Before the time of the decemvirs, [151] a Roman citizen exposed his wishes and motives to the assembly of the thirty curiae or parishes, and the general law of inheritance was suspended by an occasional act of the legislature. After the permission of the decemvirs, each private lawgiver promulgated his verbal or written testament in the presence of five citizens, who represented the five classes of the Roman people; a sixth witness attested their concurrence; a seventh weighed the copper money, which was paid by an imaginary purchaser; and the estate was emancipated by a fictitious sale and immediate release. This singular ceremony, [152] which excited the wonder of the Greeks, was still practised in the age of Severus; but the praetors had already approved a more simple testament, for which they required the seals and signatures of seven witnesses, free from all legal exception, and purposely summoned for the execution of that important act. A domestic monarch, who reigned over the lives and fortunes of his children, might distribute their respective shares according to the degrees of their merit or his affection; his arbitrary displeasure chastised an unworthy son by the loss of his inheritance, and the mortifying preference of a stranger. But the experience of unnatural parents recommended some limitations of their testamentary powers. A son, or, by the laws of Justinian, even a daughter, could no longer be disinherited by their silence: they were compelled to name the criminal, and to specify the offence; and the justice of the emperor enumerated the sole causes that could justify such a violation of the first principles of nature and society. [153] Unless a legitimate portion, a fourth part, had been reserved for the children, they were entitled to institute an action or complaint of inofficious testament; to suppose that their father's understanding was impaired by sickness or age; and respectfully to appeal from his rigorous sentence to the deliberate wisdom of the magistrate. In the Roman jurisprudence, an essential distinction was admitted between the inheritance and the legacies. The heirs who succeeded to the entire unity, or to any of the twelve fractions of the substance of the testator, represented his civil and religious character, asserted his rights, fulfilled his obligations, and discharged the gifts of friendship or liberality, which his last will had bequeathed under the name of legacies. But as the imprudence or prodigality of a dying man might exhaust the inheritance, and leave only risk and labor to his successor, he was empowered to retain the Falcidian portion; to deduct, before the payment of the legacies, a clear fourth for his own emolument. A reasonable time was allowed to examine the proportion between the debts and the estate, to decide whether he should accept or refuse the testament; and if he used the benefit of an inventory, the demands of the creditors could not exceed the valuation of the effects. The last will of a citizen might be altered during his life, or rescinded after his death: the persons whom he named might die before him, or reject the inheritance, or be exposed to some legal disqualification. In the contemplation of these events, he was permitted to substitute second and third heirs, to replace each other according to the order of the testament; and the incapacity of a madman or an infant to bequeath his property might be supplied by a similar substitution. [154] But the power of the testator expired with the acceptance of the testament: each Roman of mature age and discretion acquired the absolute dominion of his inheritance, and the simplicity of the civil law was never clouded by the long and intricate entails which confine the happiness and freedom of unborn generations.

[Footnote 150: That succession was the rule, testament the exception, is proved by Taylor, (Elements of Civil Law, p. 519-527,) a learned, rambling, spirited writer. In the iid and iiid books, the method of the Institutes is doubtless preposterous; and the Chancellor Daguesseau (Oeuvres, tom. i. p. 275) wishes his countryman Domat in the place of Tribonian. Yet covenants before successions is not surely the natural order of civil laws.]

[Footnote 151: Prior examples of testaments are perhaps fabulous. At Athens a childless father only could make a will, (Plutarch, in Solone, tom. i. p. 164. See Isaeus and Jones.)]

[Footnote 152: The testament of Augustus is specified by Suetonius, (in August, c. 101, in Neron. c. 4,) who may be studied as a code of Roman antiquities. Plutarch (Opuscul. tom. ii. p. 976) is surprised. The language of Ulpian (Fragment. tit. xx. p. 627, edit. Schulting) is almost too exclusive—solum in usu est.]

[Footnote 153: Justinian (Novell. cxv. No. 3, 4) enumerates only the public and private crimes, for which a son might likewise disinherit his father. Note: Gibbon has singular notions on the provisions of Novell. cxv. 3, 4, which probably he did not clearly understand—W]

[Footnote 154: The substitutions of fidei-commissaires of the modern civil law is a feudal idea grafted on the Roman jurisprudence, and bears scarcely any resemblance to the ancient fidei-commissa, (Institutions du Droit Francois, tom. i. p. 347-383. Denissart, Decisions de Jurisprudence, tom. iv. p. 577-604.) They were stretched to the fourth degree by an abuse of the clixth Novel; a partial, perplexed, declamatory law.]

Conquest and the formalities of law established the use of codicils. If a Roman was surprised by death in a remote province of the empire, he addressed a short epistle to his legitimate or testamentary heir; who fulfilled with honor, or neglected with impunity, this last request, which the judges before the age of Augustus were not authorized to enforce. A codicil might be expressed in any mode, or in any language; but the subscription of five witnesses must declare that it was the genuine composition of the author. His intention, however laudable, was sometimes illegal; and the invention of fidei-commissa, or trusts, arose form the struggle between natural justice and positive jurisprudence. A stranger of Greece or Africa might be the friend or benefactor of a childless Roman, but none, except a fellow-citizen, could act as his heir. The Voconian law, which abolished female succession, restrained the legacy or inheritance of a woman to the sum of one hundred thousand sesterces; [155] and an only daughter was condemned almost as an alien in her father's house. The zeal of friendship, and parental affection, suggested a liberal artifice: a qualified citizen was named in the testament, with a prayer or injunction that he would restore the inheritance to the person for whom it was truly intended. Various was the conduct of the trustees in this painful situation: they had sworn to observe the laws of their country, but honor prompted them to violate their oath; and if they preferred their interest under the mask of patriotism, they forfeited the esteem of every virtuous mind. The declaration of Augustus relieved their doubts, gave a legal sanction to confidential testaments and codicils, and gently unravelled the forms and restraints of the republican jurisprudence. [156] But as the new practice of trusts degenerated into some abuse, the trustee was enabled, by the Trebellian and Pegasian decrees, to reserve one fourth of the estate, or to transfer on the head of the real heir all the debts and actions of the succession. The interpretation of testaments was strict and literal; but the language of trusts and codicils was delivered from the minute and technical accuracy of the civilians. [157]

[Footnote 155: Dion Cassius (tom. ii. l. lvi. p. 814, with Reimar's Notes) specifies in Greek money the sum of 25,000 drachms.]

[Footnote 156: The revolutions of the Roman laws of inheritance are finely, though sometimes fancifully, deduced by Montesquieu, (Esprit des Loix, l. xxvii.)]

[Footnote 157: Of the civil jurisprudence of successions, testaments, codicils, legacies, and trusts, the principles are ascertained in the Institutes of Caius, (l. ii. tit. ii—ix. p. 91—144,) Justinian, (l. ii. tit. x—xxv.,) and Theophilus, (p. 328—514;) and the immense detail occupies twelve books (xxviii—xxxix.) of the Pandects.] III. The general duties of mankind are imposed by their public and private relations: but their specific obligations to each other can only be the effect of, 1. a promise, 2. a benefit, or 3. an injury: and when these obligations are ratified by law, the interested party may compel the performance by a judicial action. On this principle, the civilians of every country have erected a similar jurisprudence, the fair conclusion of universal reason and justice. [158]

[Footnote 158: The Institutes of Caius, (l. ii. tit. ix. x. p. 144—214,) of Justinian, (l. iii. tit. xiv—xxx. l. iv. tit. i—vi.,) and of Theophilus, (p. 616—837,) distinguish four sorts of obligations—aut re, aut verbis, aut literis aut consensu: but I confess myself partial to my own division. Note: It is not at all applicable to the Roman system of contracts, even if I were allowed to be good—M.]

PART VII

1. The goddess of faith (of human and social faith) was worshipped, not only in her temples, but in the lives of the Romans; and if that nation was deficient in the more amiable qualities of benevolence and generosity, they astonished the Greeks by their sincere and simple performance of the most burdensome engagements. [159] Yet among the same people, according to the rigid maxims of the patricians and decemvirs, a naked pact, a promise, or even an oath, did not create any civil obligation, unless it was confirmed by the legal form of a stipulation. Whatever might be the etymology of the Latin word, it conveyed the idea of a firm and irrevocable contract, which was always expressed in the mode of a question and answer. Do you promise to pay me one hundred pieces of gold? was the solemn interrogation of Seius. I do promise, was the reply of Sempronius. The friends of Sempronius, who answered for his ability and inclination, might be separately sued at the option of Seius; and the benefit of partition, or order of reciprocal actions, insensibly deviated from the strict theory of stipulation. The most cautious and deliberate consent was justly required to sustain the validity of a gratuitous promise; and the citizen who might have obtained a legal security, incurred the suspicion of fraud, and paid the forfeit of his neglect. But the ingenuity of the civilians successfully labored to convert simple engagements into the form of solemn stipulations. The praetors, as the guardians of social faith, admitted every rational evidence of a voluntary and deliberate act, which in their tribunal produced an equitable obligation, and for which they gave an action and a remedy. [160]

[Footnote 159: How much is the cool, rational evidence of Polybius (l. vi. p. 693, l. xxxi. p. 1459, 1460) superior to vague, indiscriminate applause—omnium maxime et praecipue fidem coluit, (A. Gellius, xx. l.)]

[Footnote 160: The Jus Praetorium de Pactis et Transactionibus is a separate and satisfactory treatise of Gerard Noodt, (Opp. tom. i. p. 483—564.) And I will here observe, that the universities of Holland and Brandenburg, in the beginning of the present century, appear to have studied the civil law on the most just and liberal principles. Note: Simple agreements (pacta) formed as valid an obligation as a solemn contract. Only an action, or the right to a direct judicial prosecution, was not permitted in every case of compact. In all other respects, the judge was bound to maintain an agreement made by pactum. The stipulation was a form common to every kind of agreement, by which the right of action was given to this—W.]

2. The obligations of the second class, as they were contracted by the delivery of a thing, are marked by the civilians with the epithet of real. [161] A grateful return is due to the author of a benefit; and whoever is intrusted with the property of another, has bound himself to the sacred duty of restitution. In the case of a friendly loan, the merit of generosity is on the side of the lender only; in a deposit, on the side of the receiver; but in a pledge, and the rest of the selfish commerce of ordinary life, the benefit is compensated by an equivalent, and the obligation to restore is variously modified by the nature of the transaction. The Latin language very happily expresses the fundamental difference between the commodatum and the mutuum, which our poverty is reduced to confound under the vague and common appellation of a loan. In the former, the borrower was obliged to restore the same individual thing with which he had been accommodated for the temporary supply of his wants; in the latter, it was destined for his use and consumption, and he discharged this mutual engagement, by substituting the same specific value according to a just estimation of number, of weight, and of measure. In the contract of sale, the absolute dominion is transferred to the purchaser, and he repays the benefit with an adequate sum of gold or silver, the price and universal standard of all earthly possessions. The obligation of another contract, that of location, is of a more complicated kind. Lands or houses, labor or talents, may be hired for a definite term; at the expiration of the time, the thing itself must be restored to the owner, with an additional reward for the beneficial occupation and employment. In these lucrative

contracts, to which may be added those of partnership and commissions, the civilians sometimes imagine the delivery of the object, and sometimes presume the consent of the parties. The substantial pledge has been refined into the invisible rights of a mortgage or hypotheca; and the agreement of sale, for a certain price, imputes, from that moment, the chances of gain or loss to the account of the purchaser. It may be fairly supposed, that every man will obey the dictates of his interest; and if he accepts the benefit, he is obliged to sustain the expense, of the transaction. In this boundless subject, the historian will observe the location of land and money, the rent of the one and the interest of the other, as they materially affect the prosperity of agriculture and commerce. The landlord was often obliged to advance the stock and instruments of husbandry, and to content himself with a partition of the fruits. If the feeble tenant was oppressed by accident, contagion, or hostile violence, he claimed a proportionate relief from the equity of the laws: five years were the customary term, and no solid or costly improvements could be expected from a farmer, who, at each moment might be ejected by the sale of the estate. [162] Usury, [163] the inveterate grievance of the city, had been discouraged by the Twelve Tables, [164] and abolished by the clamors of the people. It was revived by their wants and idleness, tolerated by the discretion of the praetors, and finally determined by the Code of Justinian. Persons of illustrious rank were confined to the moderate profit of four per cent.; six was pronounced to be the ordinary and legal standard of interest; eight was allowed for the convenience of manufactures and merchants; twelve was granted to nautical insurance, which the wiser ancients had not attempted to define; but, except in this perilous adventure, the practice of exorbitant usury was severely restrained. [165] The most simple interest was condemned by the clergy of the East and West; [166] but the sense of mutual benefit, which had triumphed over the law of the republic, has resisted with equal firmness the decrees of the church, and even the prejudices of mankind. [167]

[Footnote 161: The nice and various subject of contracts by consent is spread over four books (xvii—xx.) of the Pandects, and is one of the parts best deserving of the attention of an English student. Note: This is erroneously called "benefits." Gibbon enumerates various kinds of contracts, of which some alone are properly called benefits—W.]

[Footnote 162: The covenants of rent are defined in the Pandects (l. xix.) and the Code, (l. iv. tit. lxv.) The quinquennium, or term of five years, appears to have been a custom rather than a law; but in France all leases of land were determined in nine years. This limitation was removed only in the year 1775, (Encyclopedie Methodique, tom. i. de la Jurisprudence, p. 668, 669;) and I am sorry to observe that it yet prevails in the beauteous and happy country where I am permitted to reside.]

[Footnote 163: I might implicitly acquiesce in the sense and learning of the three books of G. Noodt, de foenore et usuris. (Opp. tom. i. p. 175—268.) The interpretation of the asses or centesimoe usuroe at twelve, the unciarioe at one per cent., is maintained by the best critics and civilians: Noodt, (l. ii. c. 2, p. 207,) Gravina, (Opp. p. 205, &c., 210,) Heineccius, (Antiquitat. ad Institut. l. iii. tit. xv.,) Montesquieu, (Esprit des Loix, l. xxii. c. 22, tom. ii. p. 36). Defense de l'Esprit des Loix, (tom. iii. p. 478, &c.,) and above all, John Frederic Gronovius (de Pecunia Veteri, l. iii. c. 13, p. 213—227,) and his three Antexegeses, (p. 455—655), the founder, or at least the champion, of this probable opinion; which is, however, perplexed with some difficulties.]

[Footnote 164: Primo xii. Tabulis sancitum est ne quis unciario foenore amplius exerceret, (Tacit. Annal. vi. 16.) Pour peu (says Montesquieu, Esprit des Loix, l. xxii. 22) qu'on soit verse dans l'histoire de Rome, on verra qu'une pareille loi ne devoit pas etre l'ouvrage des decemvirs. Was Tacitus ignorant—or stupid? But the wiser and more virtuous patricians might sacrifice their avarice to their ambition, and might attempt to check the odious practice by such interest as no lender would accept, and such penalties as no

debtor would incur. Note: The real nature of the foenus unciarium has been proved; it amounted in a year of twelve months to ten per cent. See, in the Magazine for Civil Law, by M. Hugo, vol. v. p. 180, 184, an article of M. Schrader, following up the conjectures of Niebuhr, Hist. Rom. tom. ii. p. 431—W. Compare a very clear account of this question in the appendix to Mr. Travers Twiss's Epitome of Niebuhr, vol. ii. p. 257—M.]

[Footnote 165: Justinian has not condescended to give usury a place in his Institutes; but the necessary rules and restrictions are inserted in the Pandects (l. xxii. tit. i. ii.) and the Code, (l. iv. tit. xxxii. xxxiii.)]

[Footnote 166: The Fathers are unanimous, (Barbeyrac, Morale des Peres, p. 144. &c.:) Cyprian, Lactantius, Basil, Chrysostom, (see his frivolous arguments in Noodt, l. i. c. 7, p. 188,) Gregory of Nyssa, Ambrose, Jerom, Augustin, and a host of councils and casuists.]

[Footnote 167: Cato, Seneca, Plutarch, have loudly condemned the practice or abuse of usury. According to the etymology of foenus, the principal is supposed to generate the interest: a breed of barren metal, exclaims Shakespeare—and the stage is the echo of the public voice.]

3. Nature and society impose the strict obligation of repairing an injury; and the sufferer by private injustice acquires a personal right and a legitimate action. If the property of another be intrusted to our care, the requisite degree of care may rise and fall according to the benefit which we derive from such temporary possession; we are seldom made responsible for inevitable accident, but the consequences of a voluntary fault must always be imputed to the author. [168] A Roman pursued and recovered his stolen goods by a civil action of theft; they might pass through a succession of pure and innocent hands, but nothing less than a prescription of thirty years could extinguish his original claim. They were restored by the sentence of the praetor, and the injury was compensated by double, or threefold, or even quadruple damages, as the deed had been perpetrated by secret fraud or open rapine, as the robber had been surprised in the fact, or detected by a subsequent research. The Aquilian law [169] defended the living property of a citizen, his slaves and cattle, from the stroke of malice or negligence: the highest price was allowed that could be ascribed to the domestic animal at any moment of the year preceding his death; a similar latitude of thirty days was granted on the destruction of any other valuable effects. A personal injury is blunted or sharpened by the manners of the times and the sensibility of the individual: the pain or the disgrace of a word or blow cannot easily be appreciated by a pecuniary equivalent. The rude jurisprudence of the decemvirs had confounded all hasty insults, which did not amount to the fracture of a limb, by condemning the aggressor to the common penalty of twenty-five asses. But the same denomination of money was reduced, in three centuries, from a pound to the weight of half an ounce: and the insolence of a wealthy Roman indulged himself in the cheap amusement of breaking and satisfying the law of the twelve tables. Veratius ran through the streets striking on the face the inoffensive passengers, and his attendant purse-bearer immediately silenced their clamors by the legal tender of twenty-five pieces of copper, about the value of one shilling. [170] The equity of the praetors examined and estimated the distinct merits of each particular complaint. In the adjudication of civil damages, the magistrate assumed a right to consider the various circumstances of time and place, of age and dignity, which may aggravate the shame and sufferings of the injured person; but if he admitted the idea of a fine, a punishment, an example, he invaded the province, though, perhaps, he supplied the defects, of the criminal law. [Footnote 168: Sir William Jones has given an ingenious and rational Essay on the law of Bailment, (London, 1781, p. 127, in 8vo.) He is perhaps the only lawyer equally conversant with the year-books of Westminster, the Commentaries of Ulpian, the Attic pleadings of Isaeus, and the sentences of Arabian and Persian cadhis.]

[Footnote 169: Noodt (Opp. tom. i. p. 137—172) has composed a separate treatise, ad Legem Aquilian, (Pandect. l. ix. tit. ii.)]

[Footnote 170: Aulus Gellius (Noct. Attic. xx. i.) borrowed this story from the Commentaries of Q. Labeo on the xii. tables.]

The execution of the Alban dictator, who was dismembered by eight horses, is represented by Livy as the first and the fast instance of Roman cruelty in the punishment of the most atrocious crimes. [171] But this act of justice, or revenge, was inflicted on a foreign enemy in the heat of victory, and at the command of a single man. The twelve tables afford a more decisive proof of the national spirit, since they were framed by the wisest of the senate, and accepted by the free voices of the people; yet these laws, like the statutes of Draco, [172] are written in characters of blood. [173] They approve the inhuman and unequal principle of retaliation; and the forfeit of an eye for an eye, a tooth for a tooth, a limb for a limb, is rigorously exacted, unless the offender can redeem his pardon by a fine of three hundred pounds of copper. The decemvirs distributed with much liberality the slighter chastisements of flagellation and servitude; and nine crimes of a very different complexion are adjudged worthy of death.

1. Any act of treason against the state, or of correspondence with the public enemy. The mode of execution was painful and ignominious: the head of the degenerate Roman was shrouded in a veil, his hands were tied behind his back, and after he had been scourged by the lictor, he was suspended in the midst of the forum on a cross, or inauspicious tree.

2. Nocturnal meetings in the city; whatever might be the pretence, of pleasure, or religion, or the public good.

3. The murder of a citizen; for which the common feelings of mankind demand the blood of the murderer. Poison is still more odious than the sword or dagger; and we are surprised to discover, in two flagitious events, how early such subtle wickedness had infected the simplicity of the republic, and the chaste virtues of the Roman matrons. [174] The parricide, who violated the duties of nature and gratitude, was cast into the river or the sea, enclosed in a sack; and a cock, a viper, a dog, and a monkey, were successively added, as the most suitable companions. [175] Italy produces no monkeys; but the want could never be felt, till the middle of the sixth century first revealed the guilt of a parricide. [176]

4. The malice of an incendiary. After the previous ceremony of whipping, he himself was delivered to the flames; and in this example alone our reason is tempted to applaud the justice of retaliation.

5. Judicial perjury. The corrupt or malicious witness was thrown headlong from the Tarpeian rock, to expiate his falsehood, which was rendered still more fatal by the severity of the penal laws, and the deficiency of written evidence.

6. The corruption of a judge, who accepted bribes to pronounce an iniquitous sentence.

7. Libels and satires, whose rude strains sometimes disturbed the peace of an illiterate city. The author was beaten with clubs, a worthy chastisement, but it is not certain that he was left to expire under the blows of the executioner. [177]

8. The nocturnal mischief of damaging or destroying a neighbor's corn. The criminal was suspended as a grateful victim to Ceres. But the sylvan deities were less implacable, and the extirpation of a more valuable tree was compensated by the moderate fine of twenty-five pounds of copper.

9. Magical incantations; which had power, in the opinion of the Latin shepherds, to exhaust the strength of an enemy, to extinguish his life, and to remove from their seats his deep-rooted plantations.

The cruelty of the twelve tables against insolvent debtors still remains to be told; and I shall dare to prefer the literal sense of antiquity to the specious refinements of modern criticism. [178] [178/1] After the judicial proof or confession of the debt, thirty days of grace were allowed before a Roman was delivered into the power of his fellow-citizen. In this private prison, twelve ounces of rice were his daily food; he might be bound with a chain of fifteen pounds weight; and his misery was thrice exposed in the market place, to solicit the compassion of his friends and countrymen. At the expiration of sixty days, the debt was discharged by the loss of liberty or life; the insolvent debtor was either put to death, or sold in foreign slavery beyond the Tyber: but, if several creditors were alike obstinate and unrelenting, they might legally dismember his body, and satiate their revenge by this horrid partition. The advocates for this savage law have insisted, that it must strongly operate in deterring idleness and fraud from contracting debts which they were unable to discharge; but experience would dissipate this salutary terror, by proving that no creditor could be found to exact this unprofitable penalty of life or limb. As the manners of Rome were insensibly polished, the criminal code of the decemvirs was abolished by the humanity of accusers, witnesses, and judges; and impunity became the consequence of immoderate rigor. The Porcian and Valerian laws prohibited the magistrates from inflicting on a free citizen any capital, or even corporal, punishment; and the obsolete statutes of blood were artfully, and perhaps truly, ascribed to the spirit, not of patrician, but of regal, tyranny.

[Footnote 171: The narrative of Livy (i. 28) is weighty and solemn. At tu, Albane, maneres, is a harsh reflection, unworthy of Virgil's humanity, (Aeneid, viii. 643.) Heyne, with his usual good taste, observes that the subject was too horrid for the shield of Aencas, (tom. iii. p. 229.)]

[Footnote 172: The age of Draco (Olympiad xxxix. I) is fixed by Sir John Marsham (Canon Chronicus, p. 593—596) and Corsini, (Fasti Attici, tom. iii. p. 62.) For his laws, see the writers on the government of Athens, Sigonius, Meursius, Potter, &c.]

[Footnote 173: The viith, de delictis, of the xii. tables is delineated by Gravina, (Opp. p. 292, 293, with a commentary, p. 214—230.) Aulus Gellius (xx. 1) and the Collatio Legum Mosaicarum et Romanarum afford much original information.]

[Footnote 174: Livy mentions two remarkable and flagitious aeras, of 3000 persons accused, and of 190 noble matrons convicted, of the crime of poisoning, (xl. 43, viii. 18.) Mr. Hume discriminates the ages of private and public virtue, (Essays, vol. i. p. 22, 23.) I would rather say that such ebullitions of mischief (as in France in the year 1680) are accidents and prodigies which leave no marks on the manners of a nation.]

[Footnote 175: The xii. tables and Cicero (pro Roscio Amerino, c. 25, 26) are content with the sack; Seneca (Excerpt. Controvers. v 4) adorns it with serpents; Juvenal pities the guiltless monkey (innoxia simia—156.) Adrian (apud Dositheum Magistrum, l. iii. c. p. 874—876, with Schulting's Note,) Modestinus, (Pandect. xlviii. tit. ix. leg. 9,) Constantine, (Cod. l. ix. tit. xvii.,) and Justinian, (Institut. l. iv. tit. xviii.,) enumerate all the companions of the parricide. But this fanciful execution was simplified in *practice. Hodie tamen viv exuruntur vel ad bestias dantur, (Paul. Sentent. Recept. l. v. tit. xxiv p. 512, edit. Schulting.)]*

[Footnote 176: The first parricide at Rome was L. Ostius, after the second Punic war, (Plutarch, in Romulo, tom. i. p. 54.) During the Cimbric, P. Malleolus was guilty of the first matricide, (Liv. Epitom. l. lxviii.)]

[Footnote 177: Horace talks of the formidine fustis, (l. ii. epist. ii. 154,) but Cicero (de Republica, l. iv. apud Augustin. de Civitat. Dei, ix. 6, in Fragment. Philosoph. tom. iii. p. 393, edit. Olivet) affirms that the decemvirs made libels a capital offence: cum perpaucas res capite sanxisent—perpaucus!]

[Footnote 178: Bynkershoek (Observat. Juris Rom. l. i. c. 1, in Opp. tom. i. p. 9, 10, 11) labors to prove that the creditors divided not the body, but the price, of the insolvent debtor. Yet his interpretation is one perpetual harsh metaphor; nor can he surmount the Roman authorities of Quintilian, Caecilius, Favonius, and Tertullian. See Aulus Gellius, Noct. Attic. xxi.]

[Footnote 178/1: Hugo (Histoire du Droit Romain, tom. i. p. 234) concurs with Gibbon See Niebuhr, vol. ii. p. 313—M.]

In the absence of penal laws, and the insufficiency of civil actions, the peace and justice of the city were imperfectly maintained by the private jurisdiction of the citizens. The malefactors who replenish our jails are the outcasts of society, and the crimes for which they suffer may be commonly ascribed to ignorance, poverty, and brutal appetite. For the perpetration of similar enormities, a vile plebeian might claim and abuse the sacred character of a member of the republic: but, on the proof or suspicion of guilt, the slave, or the stranger, was nailed to a cross; and this strict and summary justice might be exercised without restraint over the greatest part of the populace of Rome.

Each family contained a domestic tribunal, which was not confined, like that of the praetor, to the cognizance of external actions: virtuous principles and habits were inculcated by the discipline of education; and the Roman father was accountable to the state for the manners of his children, since he disposed, without appeal, of their life, their liberty, and their inheritance. In some pressing emergencies, the citizen was authorized to avenge his private or public wrongs. The consent of the Jewish, the Athenian, and the Roman laws approved the slaughter of the nocturnal thief; though in open daylight a robber could not be slain without some previous evidence of danger and complaint. Whoever surprised an adulterer in his nuptial bed might freely exercise his revenge; [179] the most bloody and wanton outrage was excused by the provocation; [180] nor was it before the reign of Augustus that the husband was reduced to weigh the rank of the offender, or that the parent was condemned to sacrifice his daughter with her guilty seducer. After the expulsion of the kings, the ambitious Roman, who should dare to assume their title or imitate their tyranny, was devoted to the infernal gods: each of his fellow-citizens was armed with the sword of justice; and the act of Brutus, however repugnant to gratitude or prudence, had been already sanctified by the judgment of his country. [181] The barbarous practice of wearing arms in the midst of peace, [182] and the bloody maxims of honor, were unknown to the Romans; and, during the two purest ages, from the establishment of equal freedom to the end of the Punic wars, the city was never disturbed by sedition, and rarely polluted with atrocious crimes. The failure of penal laws was more sensibly felt, when every vice was inflamed by faction at home and dominion abroad. In the time of Cicero, each private citizen enjoyed the privilege of anarchy; each minister of the republic was exalted to the temptations of regal power, and their virtues are entitled to the warmest praise, as the spontaneous fruits of nature or philosophy. After a triennial indulgence of lust, rapine, and cruelty, Verres, the tyrant of Sicily, could only be sued for the pecuniary restitution of three hundred thousand pounds sterling; and such was the temper of the laws, the judges, and perhaps the accuser himself, [183] that, on refunding a thirteenth part of his plunder, Verres could retire to an easy and luxurious exile. [184]

[Footnote 179: The first speech of Lysias (Reiske, Orator. Graec. tom. v. p. 2—48) is in defence of a husband who had killed the adulterer. The rights of husbands and fathers at Rome and Athens are discussed with much learning by Dr. Taylor, (Lectiones Lysiacae, c. xi. in Reiske, tom. vi. p. 301—308.)]

[Footnote 180: See Casaubon ad Athenaeum, l. i. c. 5, p. 19. Percurrent raphanique mugilesque, (Catull. p. 41, 42, edit. Vossian.) Hunc mugilis intrat, (Juvenal. Satir. x. 317.) Hunc perminxere calones, (Horat l. i. Satir. ii. 44.) Familiae stuprandum dedit.. fraudi non fuit, (Val. Maxim. l. vi. c. l, No. 13.)]

[Footnote 181: This law is noticed by Livy (ii. 8) and Plutarch, (in Publiccla, tom. i. p. 187,) and it fully justifies the public opinion on the death of Caesar which Suetonius could publish under the Imperial government. Jure caesus existimatur, (in Julio, c. 76.) Read the letters that passed between Cicero and Matius a few months after the ides of March (ad Fam. xi. 27, 28.)]

[Footnote 182: Thucydid. l. i. c. 6 The historian who considers this circumstance as the test of civilization, would disdain the barbarism of a European court]

[Footnote 183: He first rated at millies (800,000 L.) the damages of Sicily, (Divinatio in Caecilium, c. 5,) which he afterwards reduced to quadringenties, (320,000 L—1 Actio in Verrem, c. 18,) and was finally content with tricies, (24,000l L.) Plutarch (in Ciceron. tom. iii. p. 1584) has not dissembled the popular suspicion and report.]

[Footnote 184: Verres lived near thirty years after his trial, till the second triumvirate, when he was proscribed by the taste of Mark Antony for the sake of his Corinthian plate, (Plin. Hist. Natur. xxxiv. 3.)]

The first imperfect attempt to restore the proportion of crimes and punishments was made by the dictator Sylla, who, in the midst of his sanguinary triumph, aspired to restrain the license, rather than to oppress the liberty, of the Romans. He gloried in the arbitrary proscription of four thousand seven hundred citizens. [185] But, in the character of a legislator, he respected the prejudices of the times; and, instead of pronouncing a sentence of death against the robber or assassin, the general who betrayed an army, or the magistrate who ruined a province, Sylla was content to aggravate the pecuniary damages by the penalty of exile, or, in more constitutional language, by the interdiction of fire and water. The Cornelian, and afterwards the Pompeian and Julian, laws introduced a new system of criminal jurisprudence; [186] and the emperors, from Augustus to Justinian, disguised their increasing rigor under the names of the original authors. But the invention and frequent use of extraordinary pains proceeded from the desire to extend and conceal the progress of despotism. In the condemnation of illustrious Romans, the senate was always prepared to confound, at the will of their masters, the judicial and legislative powers. It was the duty of the governors to maintain the peace of their province, by the arbitrary and rigid administration of justice; the freedom of the city evaporated in the extent of empire, and the Spanish malefactor, who claimed the privilege of a Roman, was elevated by the command of Galba on a fairer and more lofty cross. [187] Occasional rescripts issued from the throne to decide the questions which, by their novelty or importance, appeared to surpass the authority and discernment of a proconsul. Transportation and beheading were reserved for honorable persons; meaner criminals were either hanged, or burnt, or buried in the mines, or exposed to the wild beasts of the amphitheatre.

Armed robbers were pursued and extirpated as the enemies of society; the driving away horses or cattle was made a capital offence; [188] but simple theft was uniformly considered as a mere civil and private injury. The degrees of guilt, and the modes of punishment, were too often determined by the discretion of the rulers, and the subject was left in ignorance of the legal danger which he might incur by every action of his life.

[Footnote 185: Such is the number assigned by Valer'us Maximus, (l. ix. c. 2, No. 1,) Florus (iv. 21) distinguishes 2000 senators and knights. Appian (de Bell. Civil. l. i. c. 95, tom. ii. p. 133, edit. Schweighauser) more accurately computes forty victims of the senatorian rank, and 1600 of the equestrian census or order.]

[Footnote 186: For the penal laws (Leges Corneliae, Pompeiae, Julae, of Sylla, Pompey, and the Caesars) see the sentences of Paulus, (l. iv. tit. xviii—xxx. p. 497—528, edit. Schulting,) the Gregorian Code, (Fragment. l. xix. p. 705, 706, in Schulting,) the Collatio Legum Mosaicarum et Romanarum, (tit. i—xv.,) the Theodosian Code, (l. ix.,) the Code of Justinian, (l. ix.,) the Pandects, (xlviii.,) the Institutes, (l. iv. tit. xviii.,) and the Greek version of Theophilus, (p. 917—926.)]

[Footnote 187: It was a guardian who had poisoned his ward. The crime was atrocious: yet the punishment is reckoned by Suetonius (c. 9) among the acts in which Galba showed himself acer, vehemens, et in delictis coercendis immodicus.]

[Footnote 188: The abactores or abigeatores, who drove one horse, or two mares or oxen, or five hogs, or ten goats, were subject to capital punishment, (Paul, Sentent. Recept. l. iv. tit. xviii. p. 497, 498.) Hadrian, (ad Concil. Baeticae,) most severe where the offence was most frequent, condemns the criminals, ad gladium, ludi damnationem, (Ulpian, de Officio Proconsulis, l. viii. in Collatione Legum Mosaic. et Rom. tit. xi p. 235.)]

A sin, a vice, a crime, are the objects of theology, ethics, and jurisprudence. Whenever their judgments agree, they corroborate each other; but, as often as they differ, a prudent legislator appreciates the guilt and punishment according to the measure of social injury. On this principle, the most daring attack on the life and property of a private citizen is judged less atrocious than the crime of treason or rebellion, which invades the majesty of the republic: the obsequious civilians unanimously pronounced, that the republic is contained in the person of its chief; and the edge of the Julian law was sharpened by the incessant diligence of the emperors. The licentious commerce of the sexes may be tolerated as an impulse of nature, or forbidden as a source of disorder and corruption; but the fame, the fortunes, the family of the husband, are seriously injured by the adultery of the wife. The wisdom of Augustus, after curbing the freedom of revenge, applied to this domestic offence the animadversion of the laws: and the guilty parties, after the payment of heavy forfeitures and fines, were condemned to long or perpetual exile in two separate islands. [189] Religion pronounces an equal censure against the infidelity of the husband; but, as it is not accompanied by the same civil effects, the wife was never permitted to vindicate her wrongs; [190] and the distinction of simple or double adultery, so familiar and so important in the canon law, is unknown to the jurisprudence of the Code and the Pandects. I touch with reluctance, and despatch with impatience, a more odious vice, of which modesty rejects the name, and nature abominates the idea. The primitive Romans were infected by the example of the Etruscans [191] and Greeks: [192] and in the mad abuse of prosperity and power, every pleasure that is innocent was deemed insipid; and the Scatinian law, [193] which had been extorted by an act of violence, was insensibly abolished by the lapse of time and the multitude of criminals. By this law, the rape, perhaps the seduction, of an ingenuous youth, was compensated, as a personal injury, by the poor damages of ten thousand sesterces, or fourscore pounds; the ravisher might be slain by the resistance or revenge of chastity; and I wish to believe, that at Rome, as in Athens, the voluntary and effeminate deserter of his sex was degraded from the honors and the rights of a citizen. [194] But the practice of vice was not discouraged by the severity of opinion: the indelible stain of manhood was confounded with the more venial transgressions of fornication and adultery, nor was the licentious lover exposed to the same dishonor which he impressed on the male or female partner of his guilt. From Catullus to Juvenal, [195] the poets accuse and celebrate the degeneracy of the times; and the reformation of manners was feebly attempted by the reason and authority of the civilians till the most virtuous of the Caesars proscribed the sin against nature as a crime against society. [196]

[Footnote 189: Till the publication of the Julius Paulus of Schulting, (l. ii. tit. xxvi. p. 317—323,) it was affirmed and believed that the Julian laws punished adultery with death; and the mistake arose from the fraud or error of Tribonian. Yet Lipsius had suspected the truth from the narratives of Tacitus, (Annal. ii. 50, iii. 24, iv. 42,) and even from the practice of Augustus, who distinguished the treasonable frailties of his female kindred.]

[Footnote 190: In cases of adultery, Severus confined to the husband the right of public accusation, (Cod. Justinian, l. ix. tit. ix. leg. 1.) Nor is this privilege unjust—so different are the effects of male or female infidelity.]

[Footnote 191: Timon (l. i.) and Theopompus (l. xliii. apud Athenaeum, l. xii. p. 517) describe the luxury and lust of the Etruscans. About the same period (A. U. C. 445) the Roman youth studied in Etruria, (liv. ix. 36.)]

[Footnote 192: The Persians had been corrupted in the same school, (Herodot. l. i. c. 135.) A curious dissertation might be formed on the introduction of paederasty after the time of Homer, its progress among the Greeks of Asia and Europe, the vehemence of their passions, and the thin device of virtue and friendship which amused the philosophers of Athens. But scelera ostendi oportet dum puniuntur, abscondi flagitia.]

[Footnote 193: The name, the date, and the provisions of this law are equally doubtful, (Gravina, Opp. p. 432, 433. Heineccius, Hist. Jur. Rom. No. 108. Ernesti, Clav. Ciceron. in Indice Legum.) But I will observe that the nefanda Venus of the honest German is styled aversa by the more polite Italian.]

[Footnote 194: See the oration of Aeschines against the catamite Timarchus, (in Reiske, Orator. Graec. tom. iii. p. 21—184.)]

[Footnote 195: A crowd of disgraceful passages will force themselves on the memory of the classic reader: I will only remind him of the cool declaration of Ovid:— Odi concubitus qui non utrumque resolvant. Hoc est quod puerum tangar amore minus.]

[Footnote 196: Aelius Lampridius, in Vit. Heliogabal. in Hist. August p. 112 Aurelius Victor, in Philippo, Codex Theodos. l. ix. tit. vii. leg. 7, and Godefroy's Commentary, tom. iii. p. 63. Theodosius abolished the subterraneous brothels of Rome, in which the prostitution of both sexes was acted with impunity.]

A new spirit of legislation, respectable even in its error, arose in the empire with the religion of Constantine. [197] The laws of Moses were received as the divine original of justice, and the Christian princes adapted their penal statutes to the degrees of moral and religious turpitude. Adultery was first declared to be a capital offence: the frailty of the sexes was assimilated to poison or assassination, to sorcery or parricide; the same penalties were inflicted on the passive and active guilt of paederasty; and all criminals of free or servile condition were either drowned or beheaded, or cast alive into the avenging flames. The adulterers were spared by the common sympathy of mankind; but the lovers of their own sex were pursued by general and pious indignation: the impure manners of Greece still prevailed in the cities of Asia, and every vice was fomented by the celibacy of the monks and clergy. Justinian relaxed the punishment at least of female infidelity: the guilty spouse was only condemned to solitude and penance, and at the end of two years she might be recalled to the arms of a forgiving husband. But the same emperor declared himself the implacable enemy of unmanly lust, and the cruelty of his persecution can scarcely be excused by the purity of his motives. [198] In defiance of every principle of justice, he stretched to past as well as future offences the operations of his edicts, with the previous allowance of a short respite for confession and pardon. A painful death was inflicted by the amputation of the sinful instrument, or the insertion of sharp reeds into the pores and tubes of most exquisite sensibility; and Justinian defended the propriety of the execution, since the criminals would have lost their hands, had they been convicted of sacrilege. In this state of disgrace and agony, two bishops, Isaiah of Rhodes and Alexander of Diospolis, were dragged through the streets of Constantinople, while their brethren were admonished, by the voice of a crier, to observe this awful lesson, and not to pollute the sanctity of their character. Perhaps these prelates were innocent. A sentence of death and infamy was often founded on the slight and suspicious evidence of a child or a servant: the guilt of the green faction, of the rich, and of the enemies of Theodora, was presumed by the judges, and paederasty became the crime of those to whom no crime could be imputed. A French philosopher [199] has dared to remark that whatever is secret must be doubtful, and that our natural horror of vice may be abused as an engine of tyranny. But the favorable persuasion of the same writer, that a legislator may confide in the taste and reason of mankind, is impeached by the unwelcome discovery of the antiquity and extent of the disease. [200]

[Footnote 197: See the laws of Constantine and his successors against adultery, sodomy &c., in the Theodosian, (l. ix. tit. vii. leg. 7, l. xi. tit. xxxvi leg. 1, 4) and Justinian Codes, (l. ix. tit. ix. leg. 30, 31.) These princes speak the language of passion as well as of justice, and fraudulently ascribe their own severity to the first Caesars.]

[Footnote 198: Justinian, Novel. lxxvii. cxxxiv. cxli. Procopius in Anecdot. c. 11, 16, with the notes of Alemannus. Theophanes, p. 151. Cedrenus. p. 688. Zonaras, l. xiv. p. 64.]

[Footnote 199: Montesquieu, Esprit des Loix, l. xii. c. 6. That eloquent philosopher conciliates the rights of liberty and of nature, which should never be placed in opposition to each other.]

[Footnote 200: For the corruption of Palestine, 2000 years before the Christian aera, see the history and laws of Moses. Ancient Gaul is stigmatized by Diodorus Siculus, (tom. i. l. v. p. 356,) China by the Mahometar and Christian travellers, (Ancient Relations of India and China, p. 34 translated by Renaudot, and his bitter critic the Pere Premare, Lettres Edifiantes, tom. xix. p. 435,) and native America by the Spanish historians, (Garcilasso de la Vega, l. iii. c. 13, Rycaut's translation; and Dictionnaire de Bayle, tom. iii. p. 88.) I believe, and hope, that the negroes, in their own country, were exempt from this moral pestilence.]

The free citizens of Athens and Rome enjoyed, in all criminal cases, the invaluable privilege of being tried by their country. [201] 1. The administration of justice is the most ancient office of a prince: it was exercised by the Roman kings, and abused by Tarquin; who alone, without law or council, pronounced his arbitrary judgments. The first consuls succeeded to this regal prerogative; but the sacred right of appeal soon abolished the jurisdiction of the magistrates, and all public causes were decided by the supreme tribunal of the people. But a wild democracy, superior to the forms, too often disdains the essential principles, of justice: the pride of despotism was envenomed by plebeian envy, and the heroes of Athens might sometimes applaud the happiness of the Persian, whose fate depended on the caprice of a single tyrant. Some salutary restraints, imposed by the people or their own passions, were at once the cause and effect of the gravity and temperance of the Romans. The right of accusation was confined to the magistrates.

A vote of the thirty five tribes could inflict a fine; but the cognizance of all capital crimes was reserved by a fundamental law to the assembly of the centuries, in which the weight of influence and property was sure to preponderate. Repeated proclamations and adjournments were interposed, to allow time for prejudice and resentment to subside: the whole proceeding might be annulled by a seasonable omen, or the opposition of a tribune; and such popular trials were commonly less formidable to innocence than they were favorable to guilt. But this union of the judicial and legislative powers left it doubtful whether the accused party was pardoned or acquitted; and, in the defence of an illustrious client, the orators of Rome and Athens address their arguments to the policy and benevolence, as well as to the justice, of their sovereign. 2. The task of convening the citizens for the trial of each offender became more difficult, as the citizens and the offenders continually multiplied; and the ready expedient was adopted of delegating the jurisdiction of the people to the ordinary magistrates, or to extraordinary inquisitors. In the first ages these questions were rare and occasional. In the beginning of the seventh century of Rome they were made perpetual: four praetors were annually empowered to sit in judgment on the state offences of treason, extortion, peculation, and bribery; and Sylla added new praetors and new questions for those crimes which more directly injure the safety of individuals. By these inquisitors the trial was prepared and directed; but they could only pronounce the sentence of the majority of judges, who with some truth, and more prejudice, have been compared to the English juries. [202] To discharge this important, though burdensome office, an annual list of ancient and respectable citizens was formed by the praetor. After many constitutional struggles, they were chosen in equal numbers from the senate, the equestrian order, and the people; four hundred and fifty were appointed for single questions; and the various rolls or decuries of judges must have contained the names of some thousand Romans, who represented the judicial authority of the state. In each particular cause, a sufficient number was drawn from the urn; their integrity was guarded by an oath; the mode of ballot secured their independence; the suspicion of partiality was removed by the mutual challenges of the accuser and defendant; and the judges of Milo, by the retrenchment of fifteen on each side, were reduced to fifty-one voices or tablets, of acquittal, of condemnation, or of favorable doubt. [203] 3. In his civil jurisdiction, the praetor of the city was truly a judge, and almost a legislator; but, as soon as he had prescribed the action of law, he often referred to a delegate the determination of the fact. With the increase of legal proceedings, the tribunal of the centumvirs, in which he presided, acquired more weight and reputation. But whether he acted alone, or with the advice of his council, the most absolute powers might be trusted to a magistrate who was annually chosen by the votes of the people. The rules and precautions of freedom have required some explanation; the order of despotism is simple and inanimate. Before the age of Justinian, or perhaps of Diocletian, the decuries of Roman judges had sunk to an empty title: the humble advice of the assessors might be accepted or despised; and in each tribunal the civil and criminal jurisdiction was administered by a single magistrate, who was raised and disgraced by the will of the emperor.

[Footnote 201: The important subject of the public questions and judgments at Rome, is explained with much learning, and in a classic style, by Charles Sigonius, (l. iii. de Judiciis, in Opp. tom. iii. p. 679—864;) and a good abridgment may be found in the Republique Romaine of Beaufort, (tom. ii. l. v. p. 1—121.) Those who wish for more abstruse law may study Noodt, (de Jurisdictione et Imperio Libri duo, tom. i. p. 93—134,) Heineccius, (ad Pandect. l. i. et ii. ad Institut. l. iv. tit. xvii Element. ad Antiquitat.) and Gravina (Opp. 230—251.)]

[Footnote 202: The office, both at Rome and in England, must be considered as an occasional duty, and not a magistracy, or profession. But the obligation of a unanimous verdict is peculiar to our laws, which condemn the jurymen to undergo the torture from whence they have exempted the criminal.]

[Footnote 203: We are indebted for this interesting fact to a fragment of Asconius Pedianus, who flourished under the reign of Tiberius. The loss of his Commentaries on the Orations of Cicero has deprived us of a valuable fund of historical and legal knowledge.]

A Roman accused of any capital crime might prevent the sentence of the law by voluntary exile, or death. Till his guilt had been legally proved, his innocence was presumed, and his person was free: till the votes of the last century had been counted and declared, he might peaceably secede to any of the allied cities of Italy, or Greece, or Asia. [204] His fame and fortunes were preserved, at least to his children, by this civil death; and he might still be happy in every rational and sensual enjoyment, if a mind accustomed to the ambitious tumult of Rome could support the uniformity and silence of Rhodes or Athens. A bolder effort was required to escape from the tyranny of the Caesars; but this effort was rendered familiar by the maxims of the stoics, the example of the bravest Romans, and the legal encouragements of suicide. The bodies of condemned criminals were exposed to public ignominy, and their children, a more serious evil, were reduced to poverty by the confiscation of their fortunes. But, if the victims of Tiberius and Nero anticipated the decree of the prince or senate, their courage and despatch were recompensed by the applause of the public, the decent honors of burial, and the validity of their testaments. [205] The exquisite avarice and cruelty of Domitian appear to have deprived the unfortunate of this last consolation, and it was still denied even by the clemency of the Antonines. A voluntary death, which, in the case of a capital offence, intervened between the accusation and the sentence, was admitted as a confession of guilt, and the spoils of the deceased were seized by the inhuman claims of the treasury. [206] Yet the civilians have always respected the natural right of a citizen to dispose of his life; and the posthumous disgrace invented by Tarquin, [207] to check the despair of his subjects, was never revived or imitated by succeeding tyrants. The powers of this world have indeed lost their dominion over him who is resolved on death; and his arm can only be restrained by the religious apprehension of a future state. Suicides are enumerated by Virgil among the unfortunate, rather than the guilty; [208] and the poetical fables of the infernal shades could not seriously influence the faith or practice of mankind. But the precepts of the gospel, or the church, have at length imposed a pious servitude on the minds of Christians, and condemn them to expect, without a murmur, the last stroke of disease or the executioner.

[Footnote 204: Polyb. l. vi. p. 643. The extension of the empire and city of Rome obliged the exile to seek a more distant place of retirement.]

[Footnote 205: Qui de se statuebant, humabanta corpora, manebant testamenta; pretium festinandi. Tacit. Annal. vi. 25, with the Notes of Lipsius.]

[Footnote 206: Julius Paulus, (Sentent. Recept. l. v. tit. xii. p. 476,) the Pandects, (xlviii. tit. xxi.,) the Code, (l. ix. tit. l.,) Bynkershoek, (tom. i. p. 59, Observat. J. C. R. iv. 4,) and Montesquieu, (Esprit des Loix, l. xxix. c. ix.,) define the civil limitations of the liberty and privileges of suicide. The criminal penalties are the production of a later and darker age.]

[Footnote 207: Plin. Hist. Natur. xxxvi. 24. When he fatigued his subjects in building the Capitol, many of the laborers were provoked to despatch themselves: he nailed their dead bodies to crosses.]

[Footnote 208: The sole resemblance of a violent and premature death has engaged Virgil (Aeneid, vi. 434—439) to confound suicides with infants, lovers, and persons unjustly condemned. Heyne, the best of his editors, is at a loss to deduce the idea, or ascertain the jurisprudence, of the Roman poet.]

The penal statutes form a very small proportion of the sixty-two books of the Code and Pandects; and in all judicial proceedings, the life or death of a citizen is determined with less caution or delay than the most ordinary question of covenant or inheritance. This singular distinction, though something may be allowed for the urgent necessity of defending the peace of society, is derived from the nature of criminal and civil jurisprudence. Our duties to the state are simple and uniform: the law by which he is condemned is inscribed not only on brass or marble, but on the conscience of the offender, and his guilt is commonly proved by the testimony of a single fact. But our relations to each other are various and infinite; our obligations are created, annulled, and modified, by injuries, benefits, and promises; and the interpretation of voluntary contracts and testaments, which are often dictated by fraud or ignorance, affords a long and laborious exercise to the sagacity of the judge. The business of life is multiplied by the extent of commerce and dominion, and the residence of the parties in the distant provinces of an empire is productive of doubt, delay, and inevitable appeals from the local to the supreme magistrate. Justinian, the Greek emperor of Constantinople and the East, was the legal successor of the Latin shepherd who had planted a colony on the banks of the Tyber. In a period of thirteen hundred years, the laws had reluctantly followed the changes of government and manners; and the laudable desire of conciliating ancient names with recent institutions destroyed the harmony, and swelled the magnitude, of the obscure and irregular system. The laws which excuse, on any occasions, the ignorance of their subjects, confess their own imperfections: the civil jurisprudence, as it was abridged by Justinian, still continued a mysterious science, and a profitable trade, and the innate perplexity of the study was involved in tenfold darkness by the private industry of the practitioners. The expense of the pursuit sometimes exceeded the value of the prize, and the fairest rights were abandoned by the poverty or prudence of the claimants. Such costly justice might tend to abate the spirit of litigation, but the unequal pressure serves only to increase the influence of the rich, and to aggravate the misery of the poor. By these dilatory and expensive proceedings, the wealthy pleader obtains a more certain advantage than he could hope from the accidental corruption of his judge. The experience of an abuse, from which our own age and country are not perfectly exempt, may sometimes provoke a generous indignation, and extort the hasty wish of exchanging our elaborate jurisprudence for the simple and summary decrees of a Turkish cadhi. Our calmer reflection will suggest, that such forms and delays are necessary to guard the person and property of the citizen; that the discretion of the judge is the first engine of tyranny; and that the laws of a free people should foresee and determine every question that may probably arise in the exercise of power and the transactions of industry. But the government of Justinian united the evils of liberty and servitude; and the Romans were oppressed at the same time by the multiplicity of their laws and the arbitrary will of their master.

CHAPTER XLV

STATE OF ITALY UNDER THE LOMBARDS

PART I

REIGN OF THE YOUNGER JUSTIN—EMBASSY OF THE AVARS—THEIR SETTLEMENT ON THE DANUBE—CONQUEST OF ITALY BY THE LOMBARDS—ADOPTION AND REIGN OF TIBERIUS—OF MAURICE—STATE OF ITALY UNDER THE LOMBARDS AND THE EXARCHS—OF RAVENNA—DISTRESS OF ROME—CHARACTER AND PONTIFICATE OF GREGORY THE FIRST

During the last years of Justinian, his infirm mind was devoted to heavenly contemplation, and he neglected the business of the lower world. His subjects were impatient of the long continuance of his life and reign: yet all who were capable of reflection apprehended the moment of his death, which might involve the capital in tumult, and the empire in civil war. Seven nephews [1] of the childless monarch, the sons or grandsons of his brother and sister, had been educated in the splendor of a princely fortune; they had been shown in high commands to the provinces and armies; their characters were known, their followers were zealous, and, as the jealousy of age postponed the declaration of a successor, they might expect with equal hopes the inheritance of their uncle. He expired in his palace, after a reign of thirty-eight years; and the decisive opportunity was embraced by the friends of Justin, the son of Vigilantia. [2] At the hour of midnight, his domestics were awakened by an importunate crowd, who thundered at his door, and obtained admittance by revealing themselves to be the principal members of the senate. These welcome deputies announced the recent and momentous secret of the emperor's decease; reported, or perhaps invented, his dying choice of the best beloved and most deserving of his nephews, and conjured Justin to prevent the disorders of the multitude, if they should perceive, with the return of light, that they were left without a master. After composing his countenance to surprise, sorrow, and decent modesty, Justin, by the advice of his wife Sophia, submitted to the authority of the senate. He was conducted with speed and silence to the palace; the guards saluted their new sovereign; and the martial and religious rites of his coronation were diligently accomplished. By the hands of the proper officers he was invested with the Imperial garments, the red buskins, white tunic, and purple robe.

A fortunate soldier, whom he instantly promoted to the rank of tribune, encircled his neck with a military collar; four robust youths exalted him on a shield; he stood firm and erect to receive the adoration of his subjects; and their choice was sanctified by the benediction of the patriarch, who imposed the diadem on the head of an orthodox prince. The hippodrome was already filled with innumerable multitudes; and no sooner did the emperor appear on his throne, than the voices of the blue and the green factions were confounded in the same loyal acclamations. In the speeches which Justin addressed to the senate and people, he promised to correct the abuses which had disgraced the age of his predecessor, displayed the maxims of a just and beneficent government, and declared that, on the approaching calends of January, [3] he would revive in his own person the name and liberty of a Roman consul. The immediate discharge of his uncle's debts exhibited a solid pledge of his faith and generosity: a train of porters, laden with bags of gold, advanced into the midst of the hippodrome, and the hopeless creditors of Justinian accepted this equitable payment as a voluntary gift. Before the end of three years, his example was imitated and surpassed by the empress Sophia, who delivered many indigent citizens from the weight of debt and usury: an act of benevolence the best entitled to gratitude, since it relieves the most intolerable distress; but in which the bounty of a prince is the most liable to be abused by the claims of prodigality and fraud. [4]

[Footnote 1: See the family of Justin and Justinian in the Familiae Byzantine of Ducange, p. 89—101. The devout civilians, Ludewig (in Vit. Justinian. p. 131) and Heineccius (Hist. Juris. Roman. p. 374) have since illustrated the genealogy of their favorite prince.]

[Footnote 2: In the story of Justin's elevation I have translated into simple and concise prose the eight hundred verses of the two first books of Corippus, de Laudibus Justini Appendix Hist. Byzant. p. 401—416 Rome 1777.]

[Footnote 3: It is surprising how Pagi (Critica. in Annal. Baron. tom. ii. p 639) could be tempted by any chronicles to contradict the plain and decisive text of Corippus, (vicina dona, l. ii. 354, vicina dies, l. iv. 1,) and to postpone, till A.D. 567, the consulship of Justin.]

[Footnote 4: Theophan. Chronograph. p. 205. Whenever Cedrenus or Zonaras are mere transcribers, it is superfluous to allege their testimony.]

On the seventh day of his reign, Justin gave audience to the ambassadors of the Avars, and the scene was decorated to impress the Barbarians with astonishment, veneration, and terror. From the palace gate, the spacious courts and long porticos were lined with the lofty crests and gilt bucklers of the guards, who presented their spears and axes with more confidence than they would have shown in a field of battle. The officers who exercised the power, or attended the person, of the prince, were attired in their richest habits, and arranged according to the military and civil order of the hierarchy. When the veil of the sanctuary was withdrawn, the ambassadors beheld the emperor of the East on his throne, beneath a canopy, or dome, which was supported by four columns, and crowned with a winged figure of Victory. In the first emotions of surprise, they submitted to the servile adoration of the Byzantine court; but as soon as they rose from the ground, Targetius, the chief of the embassy, expressed the freedom and pride of a Barbarian. He extolled, by the tongue of his interpreter, the greatness of the chagan, by whose clemency the kingdoms of the South were permitted to exist, whose victorious subjects had traversed the frozen rivers of Scythia, and who now covered the banks of the Danube with innumerable tents. The late emperor had cultivated, with annual and costly gifts, the friendship of a grateful monarch, and the enemies of Rome had respected the allies of the Avars. The same prudence would instruct the nephew of Justinian to imitate the liberality of his uncle, and to purchase the blessings of peace from an invincible people, who delighted and excelled in the exercise of war. The reply of the emperor was delivered in the same strain of haughty defiance, and he derived his confidence from the God of the Christians, the ancient glory of Rome, and the recent triumphs of Justinian. "The empire," said he, "abounds with men and horses, and arms sufficient to defend our frontiers, and to chastise the Barbarians. You offer aid, you threaten hostilities: we despise your enmity and your aid. The conquerors of the Avars solicit our alliance; shall we dread their fugitives and exiles? [5] The bounty of our uncle was granted to your misery, to your humble prayers. From us you shall receive a more important obligation, the knowledge of your own weakness. Retire from our presence; the lives of ambassadors are safe; and, if you return to implore our pardon, perhaps you will taste of our benevolence." [6] On the report of his ambassadors, the chagan was awed by the apparent firmness of a Roman emperor of whose character and resources he was ignorant. Instead of executing his threats against the Eastern empire, he marched into the poor and savage countries of Germany, which were subject to the dominion of the Franks. After two doubtful battles, he consented to retire, and the Austrasian king relieve the distress of his camp with an immediate supply of corn and cattle. [7] Such repeated disappointments had chilled the spirit of the Avars, and their power would have dissolved away in the Sarmatian desert, if the alliance of Alboin, king of the Lombards, had not given a new object to their arms, and a lasting settlement to their wearied fortunes.

[Footnote 5: Corippus, l. iii. 390. The unquestionable sense relates to the Turks, the conquerors of the Avars; but the word scultor has no apparent meaning, and the sole Ms. of Corippus, from whence the first edition (1581, apud Plantin) was printed, is no longer visible. The last editor, Foggini of Rome, has inserted the conjectural emendation of soldan: but the proofs of Ducange, (Joinville, Dissert. xvi. p. 238—240,) for the early use of this title among the Turks and Persians, are weak or ambiguous. And I must incline to the authority of D'Herbelot, (Bibliotheque Orient. p. 825,) who ascribes the word to the Arabic and Chaldaean tongues, and the date to the beginning of the xith century, when it was bestowed by the khalif of Bagdad on Mahmud, prince of Gazna, and conqueror of India.]

[Footnote 6: For these characteristic speeches, compare the verse of Corippus (l. iii. 251—401) with the prose of Menander, (Excerpt. Legation. p 102, 103.) Their diversity proves that they did not copy each other their resemblance, that they drew from a common original.]

[Footnote 7: For the Austrasian war, see Menander (Excerpt. Legat. p. 110,) Gregory of Tours, (Hist. Franc. l. iv. c 29,) and Paul the deacon, (de Gest. Langobard. l. ii. c. 10.)]

While Alboin served under his father's standard, he encountered in battle, and transpierced with his lance, the rival prince of the Gepidae. The Lombards, who applauded such early prowess, requested his father, with unanimous acclamations, that the heroic youth, who had shared the dangers of the field, might be admitted to the feast of victory. "You are not unmindful," replied the inflexible Audoin, "of the wise customs of our ancestors. Whatever may be his merit, a prince is incapable of sitting at table with his father till he has received his arms from a foreign and royal hand." Alboin bowed with reverence to the institutions of his country, selected forty companions, and boldly visited the court of Turisund, king of the Gepidae, who embraced and entertained, according to the laws of hospitality, the murderer of his son. At the banquet, whilst Alboin occupied the seat of the youth whom he had slain, a tender remembrance arose in the mind of Turisund. "How dear is that place! how hateful is that person!" were the words that escaped, with a sigh, from the indignant father. His grief exasperated the national resentment of the Gepidae; and Cunimund, his surviving son, was provoked by wine, or fraternal affection, to the desire of vengeance. "The Lombards," said the rude Barbarian, "resemble, in figure and in smell, the mares of our Sarmatian plains." And this insult was a coarse allusion to the white bands which enveloped their legs. "Add another resemblance," replied an audacious Lombard; "you have felt how strongly they kick. Visit the plain of Asfield, and seek for the bones of thy brother: they are mingled with those of the vilest animals." The Gepidae, a nation of warriors, started from their seats, and the fearless Alboin, with his forty companions, laid their hands on their swords. The tumult was appeased by the venerable interposition of Turisund. He saved his own honor, and the life of his guest; and, after the solemn rites of investiture, dismissed the stranger in the bloody arms of his son; the gift of a weeping parent. Alboin returned in triumph; and the Lombards, who celebrated his matchless intrepidity, were compelled to praise the virtues of an enemy. [8] In this extraordinary visit he had probably seen the daughter of Cunimund, who soon after ascended the throne of the Gepidae. Her name was Rosamond, an appellation expressive of female beauty, and which our own history or romance has consecrated to amorous tales. The king of the Lombards (the father of Alboin no longer lived) was contracted to the granddaughter of Clovis; but the restraints of faith and policy soon yielded to the hope of possessing the fair Rosamond, and of insulting her family and nation. The arts of persuasion were tried without success;

and the impatient lover, by force and stratagem, obtained the object of his desires. War was the consequence which he foresaw and solicited; but the Lombards could not long withstand the furious assault of the Gepidae, who were sustained by a Roman army. And, as the offer of marriage was rejected with contempt, Alboin was compelled to relinquish his prey, and to partake of the disgrace which he had inflicted on the house of Cunimund. [9]

[Footnote 8: Paul Warnefrid, the deacon of Friuli, de Gest. Langobard. l. i. c. 23, 24. His pictures of national manners, though rudely sketched are more lively and faithful than those of Bede, or Gregory of Tours]

[Footnote 9: The story is told by an impostor, (Theophylact. Simocat. l. vi. c. 10;) but he had art enough to build his fictions on public and notorious facts.]

When a public quarrel is envenomed by private injuries, a blow that is not mortal or decisive can be productive only of a short truce, which allows the unsuccessful combatant to sharpen his arms for a new encounter. The strength of Alboin had been found unequal to the gratification of his love, ambition, and revenge: he condescended to implore the formidable aid of the chagan; and the arguments that he employed are expressive of the art and policy of the Barbarians. In the attack of the Gepidae, he had been prompted by the just desire of extirpating a people whom their alliance with the Roman empire had rendered the common enemies of the nations, and the personal adversaries of the chagan. If the forces of the Avars and the Lombards should unite in this glorious quarrel, the victory was secure, and the reward inestimable: the Danube, the Hebrus, Italy, and Constantinople, would be exposed, without a barrier, to their invincible arms. But, if they hesitated or delayed to prevent the malice of the Romans, the same spirit which had insulted would pursue the Avars to the extremity of the earth. These specious reasons were heard by the chagan with coldness and disdain: he detained the Lombard ambassadors in his camp, protracted the negotiation, and by turns alleged his want of inclination, or his want of ability, to undertake this important enterprise. At length he signified the ultimate price of his alliance, that the Lombards should immediately present him with a tithe of their cattle; that the spoils and captives should be equally divided; but that the lands of the Gepidae should become the sole patrimony of the Avars. Such hard conditions were eagerly accepted by the passions of Alboin; and, as the Romans were dissatisfied with the ingratitude and perfidy of the Gepidae, Justin abandoned that incorrigible people to their fate, and remained the tranquil spectator of this unequal conflict. The despair of Cunimund was active and dangerous. He was informed that the Avars had entered his confines; but, on the strong assurance that, after the defeat of the Lombards, these foreign invaders would easily be repelled, he rushed forwards to encounter the implacable enemy of his name and family. But the courage of the Gepidae could secure them no more than an honorable death. The bravest of the nation fell in the field of battle; the king of the Lombards contemplated with delight the head of Cunimund; and his skull was fashioned into a cup to satiate the hatred of the conqueror, or, perhaps, to comply with the savage custom of his country. [10] After this victory, no further obstacle could impede the progress of the confederates, and they faithfully executed the terms of their agreement. [11] The fair countries of Walachia, Moldavia, Transylvania, and the other parts of Hungary beyond the Danube, were occupied, without resistance, by a new colony of Scythians; and the Dacian empire of the chagans subsisted with splendor above two hundred and thirty years. The nation of the Gepidae was dissolved; but, in the distribution of the captives, the slaves of the Avars were less fortunate than the companions of the Lombards, whose generosity adopted a valiant foe, and whose freedom was incompatible with cool and deliberate tyranny. One moiety of the spoil introduced into the camp of Alboin more wealth than a Barbarian could readily compute. The fair Rosamond was persuaded, or compelled, to acknowledge the rights of her victorious lover; and the daughter of Cunimund appeared to forgive those crimes which might be imputed to her own irresistible charms.

[Footnote 10: It appears from Strabo, Pliny, and Ammianus Marcellinus, that the same practice was common among the Scythian tribes, (Muratori, Scriptores Rer. Italic. tom. i. p. 424.) The scalps of North America are likewise trophies of valor. The skull of Cunimund was preserved above two hundred years among the Lombards; and Paul himself was one of the guests to whom Duke Ratchis exhibited this cup on a high festival, (l. ii. c. 28.)]

[Footnote 11: Paul, l. i. c. 27. Menander, in Excerpt Legat. p. 110, 111.]

The destruction of a mighty kingdom established the fame of Alboin. In the days of Charlemagne, the Bavarians, the Saxons, and the other tribes of the Teutonic language, still repeated the songs which described the heroic virtues, the valor, liberality, and fortune of the king of the Lombards. [12] But his ambition was yet unsatisfied; and the conqueror of the Gepidae turned his eyes from the Danube to the richer banks of the Po, and the Tyber. Fifteen years had not elapsed, since his subjects, the confederates of Narses, had visited the pleasant climate of Italy: the mountains, the rivers, the highways, were familiar to their memory: the report of their success, perhaps the view of their spoils, had kindled in the rising generation the flame of emulation and enterprise. Their hopes were encouraged by the spirit and eloquence of Alboin: and it is affirmed, that he spoke to their senses, by producing at the royal feast, the fairest and most exquisite fruits that grew spontaneously in the garden of the world. No sooner had he erected his standard, than the native strength of the Lombard was multiplied by the adventurous youth of Germany and Scythia. The robust peasantry of Noricum and Pannonia had resumed the manners of Barbarians; and the names of the Gepidae, Bulgarians, Sarmatians, and Bavarians, may be distinctly traced in the provinces of Italy. [13] Of the Saxons, the old allies of the Lombards, twenty thousand warriors, with their wives and children, accepted the invitation of Alboin. Their bravery contributed to his success; but the accession or the absence of their numbers was not sensibly felt in the magnitude of his host. Every mode of religion was freely practised by its respective votaries. The king of the Lombards had been educated in the Arian heresy; but the Catholics, in their public worship, were allowed to pray for his conversion; while the more stubborn Barbarians sacrificed a she-goat, or perhaps a captive, to the gods of their fathers. [14] The Lombards, and their confederates, were united by their common attachment to a chief, who excelled in all the virtues and vices of a savage hero; and the vigilance of Alboin provided an ample magazine of offensive and defensive arms for the use of the expedition. The portable wealth of the Lombards attended the march: their lands they cheerfully relinquished to the Avars, on the solemn promise, which was made and accepted without a smile, that if they failed in the conquest of Italy, these voluntary exiles should be reinstated in their former possessions.

[Footnote 12: Ut hactenus etiam tam apud Bajoarior um gentem, quam et Saxmum, sed et alios ejusdem linguae homines..... in eorum carmini bus celebretur. Paul, l. i. c. 27. He died A.D. 799, (Muratori, in Praefat. tom. i. p. 397.) These German songs, some of which might be as old as Tacitus, (de Moribus Germ. c. 2,) were compiled and transcribed by Charlemagne. Barbara et antiquissima carmina, quibus veterum regum actus et bella canebantur scripsit memoriaeque mandavit, (Eginard, in Vit. Carol. Magn. c. 29, p. 130, 131.) The poems, which Goldast commends, (Animadvers. ad Eginard. p. 207,) appear to be recent and contemptible romances.]

[Footnote 13: The other nations are rehearsed by Paul, (l. ii. c. 6, 26,) Muratori (Antichita Italiane, tom. i. dissert. i. p. 4) has discovered the village of the Bavarians, three miles from Modena.]

[Footnote 14: Gregory the Roman (Dialog. l. i. iii. c. 27, 28, apud Baron. Annal Eccles. A.D. 579, No. 10) supposes that they likewise adored this she-goat. I know but of one religion in which the god and the victim are the same.]

They might have failed, if Narses had been the antagonist of the Lombards; and the veteran warriors, the associates of his Gothic victory, would have encountered with reluctance an enemy whom they dreaded and esteemed. But the weakness of the Byzantine court was subservient to the Barbarian cause; and it was for the ruin of Italy, that the emperor once listened to the complaints of his subjects. The virtues of Narses were stained with avarice; and, in his provincial reign of fifteen years, he accumulated a treasure of gold and silver which surpassed the modesty of a private fortune. His government was oppressive or unpopular, and the general discontent was expressed with freedom by the deputies of Rome. Before the throne of Justinian they boldly declared, that their Gothic servitude had been more tolerable than the despotism of a Greek eunuch; and that, unless their tyrant were instantly removed, they would consult their own happiness in the choice of a master. The apprehension of a revolt was urged by the voice of envy and detraction, which had so recently triumphed over the merit of Belisarius. A new exarch, Longinus, was appointed to supersede the conqueror of Italy, and the base motives of his recall were revealed in the insulting mandate of the empress Sophia, "that he should leave to men the exercise of arms, and return to his proper station among the maidens of the palace, where a distaff should be again placed in the hand of the eunuch." "I will spin her such a thread as she shall not easily unravel!" is said to have been the reply which indignation and conscious virtue extorted from the hero. Instead of attending, a slave and a victim, at the gate of the Byzantine palace, he retired to Naples, from whence (if any credit is due to the belief of the times) Narses invited the Lombards to chastise the ingratitude of the prince and people. [15] But the passions of the people are furious and changeable, and the Romans soon recollected the merits, or dreaded the resentment, of their victorious general. By the mediation of the pope, who undertook a special pilgrimage to Naples, their repentance was accepted; and Narses, assuming a milder aspect and a more dutiful language, consented to fix his residence in the Capitol. His death, [16] though in the extreme period of old age, was unseasonable and premature, since his genius alone could have repaired the last and fatal error of his life. The reality, or the suspicion, of a conspiracy disarmed and disunited the Italians. The soldiers resented the disgrace, and bewailed the loss, of their general. They were ignorant of their new exarch; and Longinus was himself ignorant of the state of the army and the province. In the preceding years Italy had been desolated by pestilence and famine, and a disaffected people ascribed the calamities of nature to the guilt or folly of their rulers. [17]

[Footnote 15: The charge of the deacon against Narses (l. ii. c. 5) may be groundless; but the weak apology of the Cardinal (Baron. Annal Eccles. A.D. 567, No. 8—12) is rejected by the best critics—Pagi (tom. ii. p. 639, 640,) Muratori, (Annali d' Italia, tom. v. p. 160—163,) and the last editors, Horatius Blancus, (Script. Rerum Italic. tom. i. p. 427, 428,) and Philip Argelatus, (Sigon. Opera, tom. ii. p. 11, 12.) The Narses who assisted at the coronation of Justin (Corippus, l. iii. 221) is clearly understood to be a different person.]

[Footnote 16: The death of Narses is mentioned by Paul, l. ii. c. 11. Anastas. in Vit. Johan. iii. p. 43. Agnellus, Liber Pontifical. Raven. in Script. Rer. Italicarum, tom. ii. part i. p. 114, 124. Yet I cannot believe with Agnellus that Narses was ninety-five years of age. Is it probable that all his exploits were performed at fourscore?]

[Footnote 17: The designs of Narses and of the Lombards for the invasion of Italy are exposed in the last chapter of the first book, and the seven last chapters of the second book, of Paul the deacon.]

Whatever might be the grounds of his security, Alboin neither expected nor encountered a Roman army in the field. He ascended the Julian Alps, and looked down with contempt and desire on the fruitful plains to which his victory communicated the perpetual appellation of Lombardy. A faithful chieftain, and a select band, were stationed at Forum Julii, the modern Friuli, to guard the passes of the mountains. The Lombards respected the strength of Pavia, and listened to the prayers of the Trevisans: their slow and heavy multitudes proceeded to occupy the palace and city of Verona; and Milan, now rising from her ashes, was invested by the powers of Alboin five months after his departure from Pannonia. Terror preceded his march: he found every where, or he left, a dreary solitude; and the pusillanimous Italians presumed, without a trial, that the stranger was invincible. Escaping to lakes, or rocks, or morasses, the affrighted crowds concealed some fragments of their wealth, and delayed the moment of their servitude. Paulinus, the patriarch of Aquileia, removed his treasures, sacred and profane, to the Isle of Grado, [18] and his successors were adopted by the infant republic of Venice, which was continually enriched by the public calamities. Honoratus, who filled the chair of St. Ambrose, had credulously accepted the faithless offers of a capitulation; and the archbishop, with the clergy and nobles of Milan, were driven by the perfidy of Alboin to seek a refuge in the less accessible ramparts of Genoa. Along the maritime coast, the courage of the inhabitants was supported by the facility of supply, the hopes of relief, and the power of escape; but from the Trentine hills to the gates of Ravenna and Rome the inland regions of Italy became, without a battle or a siege, the lasting patrimony of the Lombards. The submission of the people invited the Barbarian to assume the character of a lawful sovereign, and the helpless exarch was confined to the office of announcing to the emperor Justin the rapid and irretrievable loss of his provinces and cities. [19] One city, which had been diligently fortified by the Goths, resisted the arms of a new invader; and while Italy was subdued by the flying detachments of the Lombards, the royal camp was fixed above three years before the western gate of Ticinum, or Pavia. The same courage which obtains the esteem of a civilized enemy provokes the fury of a savage, and the impatient besieger had bound himself by a tremendous oath, that age, and sex, and dignity, should be confounded in a general massacre. The aid of famine at length enabled him to execute his bloody vow; but, as Alboin entered the gate, his horse stumbled, fell, and could not be raised from the ground. One of his attendants was prompted by compassion, or piety, to interpret this miraculous sign of the wrath of Heaven: the conqueror paused and relented; he sheathed his sword, and peacefully reposing himself in the palace of Theodoric, proclaimed to the trembling multitude that they should live and obey. Delighted with the situation of a city which was endeared to his pride by the difficulty of the purchase, the prince of the Lombards disdained the ancient glories of Milan; and Pavia, during some ages, was respected as the capital of the kingdom of Italy. [20]

[Footnote 18: Which from this translation was called New Aquileia, (Chron. Venet. p. 3.) The patriarch of Grado soon became the first citizen of the republic, (p. 9, &c.,) but his seat was not removed to Venice till the year 1450. He is now decorated with titles and honors; but the genius of the church has bowed to that of the state, and the government of a Catholic city is strictly Presbyterian. Thomassin, Discipline de l'Eglise, tom. i. p. 156, 157, 161—165. Amelot de la Houssaye, Gouvernement de Venise, tom. i. p. 256—261.]

[Footnote 19: Paul has given a description of Italy, as it was then divided into eighteen regions, (l. ii. c. 14—24.) The Dissertatio Chorographica de Italia Medii Aevi, by Father Beretti, a Benedictine monk, and regius professor at Pavia, has been usefully consulted.]

[Footnote 20: For the conquest of Italy, see the original materials of Paul, (l. p. 7—10, 12, 14, 25, 26, 27,) the eloquent narrative of Sigonius, (tom. il. de Regno Italiae, l. i. p. 13—19,) and the correct and critical review el Muratori, (Annali d' Italia, tom. v. p. 164—180.)]

The reign of the founder was splendid and transient; and, before he could regulate his new conquests, Alboin fell a sacrifice to domestic treason and female revenge. In a palace near Verona, which had not been erected for the Barbarians, he feasted the companions of his arms; intoxication was the reward of valor, and the king himself was tempted by appetite, or vanity, to exceed the ordinary measure of his intemperance. After draining many capacious bowls of Rhaetian or Falernian wine, he called for the skull of Cunimund, the noblest and most precious ornament of his sideboard. The cup of victory was accepted with horrid applause by the circle of the Lombard chiefs. "Fill it again with wine," exclaimed the inhuman conqueror, "fill it to the brim: carry this goblet to the queen, and request in my name that she would rejoice with her father." In an agony of grief and rage, Rosamond had strength to utter, "Let the will of my lord be obeyed!" and, touching it with her lips, pronounced a silent imprecation, that the insult should be washed away in the blood of Alboin. Some indulgence might be due to the resentment of a daughter, if she had not already violated the duties of a wife. Implacable in her enmity, or inconstant in her love, the queen of Italy had stooped from the throne to the arms of a subject, and Helmichis, the king's armor-bearer, was the secret minister of her pleasure and revenge. Against the proposal of the murder, he could no longer urge the scruples of fidelity or gratitude; but Helmichis trembled when he revolved the danger as well as the guilt, when he recollected the matchless strength and intrepidity of a warrior whom he had so often attended in the field of battle. He pressed and obtained, that one of the bravest champions of the Lombards should be associated to the enterprise; but no more than a promise of secrecy could be drawn from the gallant Peredeus, and the mode of seduction employed by Rosamond betrays her shameless insensibility both to honor and love. She supplied the place of one of her female attendants who was beloved by Peredeus, and contrived some excuse for darkness and silence, till she could inform her companion that he had enjoyed the queen of the Lombards, and that his own death, or the death of Alboin, must be the consequence of such treasonable adultery. In this alternative he chose rather to be the accomplice than the victim of Rosamond, [21] whose undaunted spirit was incapable of fear or remorse. She expected and soon found a favorable moment, when the king, oppressed with wine, had retired from the table to his afternoon slumbers. His faithless spouse was anxious for his health and repose: the gates of the palace were shut, the arms removed, the attendants dismissed, and Rosamond, after lulling him to rest by her tender caresses, unbolted the chamber door, and urged the reluctant conspirators to the instant execution of the deed. On the first alarm, the warrior started from his couch: his sword, which he attempted to draw, had been fastened to the scabbard by the hand of Rosamond; and a small stool, his only weapon, could not long protect him from the spears of the assassins. The daughter of Cunimund smiled in his fall: his body was buried under the staircase of the palace; and the grateful posterity of the Lombards revered the tomb and the memory of their victorious leader.

[Footnote 21: The classical reader will recollect the wife and murder of Candaules, so agreeably told in the first book of Herodotus. The choice of Gyges, may serve as the excuse of Peredeus; and this soft insinuation of an odious idea has been imitated by the best writers of antiquity, (Graevius, ad Ciceron. Orat. pro Miloue c. 10)]

PART II

The ambitious Rosamond aspired to reign in the name of her lover; the city and palace of Verona were awed by her power; and a faithful band of her native Gepidae was prepared to applaud the revenge, and to second the wishes, of their sovereign. But the Lombard chiefs, who fled in the first moments of consternation and disorder, had resumed their courage and collected their powers; and the nation, instead of submitting to her reign, demanded, with unanimous cries, that justice should be executed on the guilty spouse and the murderers of their king. She sought a refuge among the enemies of her country; and a criminal who deserved the abhorrence of mankind was protected by the selfish policy of the exarch. With her daughter, the heiress of the Lombard throne, her two lovers, her trusty Gepidae, and the spoils of the palace of Verona, Rosamond descended the Adige and the Po, and was transported by a Greek vessel to the safe harbor of Ravenna. Longinus beheld with delight the charms and the treasures of the widow of Alboin: her situation and her past conduct might justify the most licentious proposals; and she readily listened to the passion of a minister, who, even in the decline of the empire, was respected as the equal of kings. The death of a jealous lover was an easy and grateful sacrifice; and, as Helmichis issued from the bath, he received the deadly potion from the hand of his mistress. The taste of the liquor, its speedy operation, and his experience of the character of Rosamond, convinced him that he was poisoned: he pointed his dagger to her breast, compelled her to drain the remainder of the cup, and expired in a few minutes, with the consolation that she could not survive to enjoy the fruits of her wickedness. The daughter of Alboin and Rosamond, with the richest spoils of the Lombards, was embarked for Constantinople: the surprising strength of Peredeus amused and terrified the Imperial court: [21/1] his blindness and revenge exhibited an imperfect copy of the adventures of Samson. By the free suffrage of the nation, in the assembly of Pavia, Clepho, one of their noblest chiefs, was elected as the successor of Alboin. Before the end of eighteen months, the throne was polluted by a second murder: Clepho was stabbed by the hand of a domestic; the regal office was suspended above ten years during the minority of his son Autharis; and Italy was divided and oppressed by a ducal aristocracy of thirty tyrants. [22]

[Footnote 21/1: He killed a lion. His eyes were put out by the timid Justin. Peredeus requesting an interview, Justin substituted two patricians, whom the blinded Barbarian stabbed to the heart with two concealed daggers. See Le Beau, vol. x. p. 99—M.]

[Footnote 22: See the history of Paul, l. ii. c. 28—32. I have borrowed some interesting circumstances from the Liber Pontificalis of Agnellus, in Script. Rer. Ital. tom. ii. p. 124. Of all chronological guides, Muratori is the safest.]

When the nephew of Justinian ascended the throne, he proclaimed a new aera of happiness and glory. The annals of the second Justin [23] are marked with disgrace abroad and misery at home. In the West, the Roman empire was afflicted by the loss of Italy, the desolation of Africa, and the conquests of the Persians. Injustice prevailed both in the capital and the provinces: the rich trembled for their property, the poor for their safety, the ordinary magistrates were ignorant or venal, the occasional remedies appear to have been arbitrary and violent, and the complaints of the people could no longer be silenced by the splendid names of a legislator and a conqueror. The opinion which imputes to the prince all the calamities of his times may be countenanced by the historian as a serious truth or a salutary prejudice. Yet a candid suspicion will arise, that the sentiments of Justin were pure and benevolent, and that he might have filled his station without reproach, if the faculties of his mind had not been impaired by disease, which deprived the emperor of the use of his feet, and confined him to the palace, a stranger to the complaints of the people and the vices of the government. The tardy knowledge of his own impotence determined him to lay down the weight of the diadem; and, in the choice of a worthy substitute, he showed some symptoms of a discerning and even magnanimous spirit. The only son of

Justin and Sophia died in his infancy; their daughter Arabia was the wife of Baduarius, [24] superintendent of the palace, and afterwards commander of the Italian armies, who vainly aspired to confirm the rights of marriage by those of adoption. While the empire appeared an object of desire, Justin was accustomed to behold with jealousy and hatred his brothers and cousins, the rivals of his hopes; nor could he depend on the gratitude of those who would accept the purple as a restitution, rather than a gift. Of these competitors, one had been removed by exile, and afterwards by death; and the emperor himself had inflicted such cruel insults on another, that he must either dread his resentment or despise his patience. This domestic animosity was refined into a generous resolution of seeking a successor, not in his family, but in the republic; and the artful Sophia recommended Tiberius, [25] his faithful captain of the guards, whose virtues and fortune the emperor might cherish as the fruit of his judicious choice. The ceremony of his elevation to the rank of Caesar, or Augustus, was performed in the portico of the palace, in the presence of the patriarch and the senate. Justin collected the remaining strength of his mind and body; but the popular belief that his speech was inspired by the Deity betrays a very humble opinion both of the man and of the times. [26] "You behold," said the emperor, "the ensigns of supreme power. You are about to receive them, not from my hand, but from the hand of God. Honor them, and from them you will derive honor. Respect the empress your mother: you are now her son; before, you were her servant. Delight not in blood; abstain from revenge; avoid those actions by which I have incurred the public hatred; and consult the experience, rather than the example, of your predecessor. As a man, I have sinned; as a sinner, even in this life, I have been severely punished: but these servants, (and we pointed to his ministers,) who have abused my confidence, and inflamed my passions, will appear with me before the tribunal of Christ. I have been dazzled by the splendor of the diadem: be thou wise and modest; remember what you have been, remember what you are. You see around us your slaves, and your children: with the authority, assume the tenderness, of a parent. Love your people like yourself; cultivate the affections, maintain the discipline, of the army; protect the fortunes of the rich, relieve the necessities of the poor." [27] The assembly, in silence and in tears, applauded the counsels, and sympathized with the repentance, of their prince the patriarch rehearsed the prayers of the church; Tiberius received the diadem on his knees; and Justin, who in his abdication appeared most worthy to reign, addressed the new monarch in the following words: "If you consent, I live; if you command, I die: may the God of heaven and earth infuse into your heart whatever I have neglected or forgotten." The four last years of the emperor Justin were passed in tranquil obscurity: his conscience was no longer tormented by the remembrance of those duties which he was incapable of discharging; and his choice was justified by the filial reverence and gratitude of Tiberius.

[Footnote 23: The original authors for the reign of Justin the younger are Evagrius, Hist. Eccles. l. v. c. 1—12; Theophanes, in Chonograph. p. 204—210; Zonaras, tom. ii. l. xiv. p. 70-72; Cedrenus, in Compend. p. 388—392.]

[Footnote 24: Dispositorque novus sacrae Baduarius aulae. Successor soceri mox factus Cura-palati—Cerippus. Baduarius is enumerated among the descendants and allies of the house of Justinian. A family of noble Venetians (Casa Badoero) built churches and gave dukes to the republic as early as the ninth century; and, if their descent be admitted, no kings in Europe can produce a pedigree so ancient and illustrious. Ducange, Fam. Byzantin, p. 99 Amelot de la Houssaye, Gouvernement de Venise, tom. ii. p. 555.]

[Footnote 25: The praise bestowed on princes before their elevation is the purest and most weighty. Corippus has celebrated Tiberius at the time of the accession of Justin, (l. i. 212—222.) Yet even a captain of the guards might attract the flattery of an African exile.]

[Footnote 26: Evagrius (l. v. c. 13) has added the reproach to his ministers He applies this speech to the ceremony when Tiberius was invested with the rank of Caesar. The loose expression, rather than the positive error, of Theophanes, &c., has delayed it to his Augustan investitura immediately before the death of Justin.]

[Footnote 27: Theophylact Simocatta (l. iii. c. 11) declares that he shall give to posterity the speech of Justin as it was pronounced, without attempting to correct the imperfections of language or rhetoric. Perhaps the vain sophist would have been incapable of producing such sentiments.]

Among the virtues of Tiberius, [28] his beauty (he was one of the tallest and most comely of the Romans) might introduce him to the favor of Sophia; and the widow of Justin was persuaded, that she should preserve her station and influence under the reign of a second and more youthful husband. But, if the ambitious candidate had been tempted to flatter and dissemble, it was no longer in his power to fulfil her expectations, or his own promise. The factions of the hippodrome demanded, with some impatience, the name of their new empress: both the people and Sophia were astonished by the proclamation of Anastasia, the secret, though lawful, wife of the emperor Tiberius. Whatever could alleviate the disappointment of Sophia, Imperial honors, a stately palace, a numerous household, was liberally bestowed by the piety of her adopted son; on solemn occasions he attended and consulted the widow of his benefactor; but her ambition disdained the vain semblance of royalty, and the respectful appellation of mother served to exasperate, rather than appease, the rage of an injured woman. While she accepted, and repaid with a courtly smile, the fair expressions of regard and confidence, a secret alliance was concluded between the dowager empress and her ancient enemies; and Justinian, the son of Germanus, was employed as the instrument of her revenge. The pride of the reigning house supported, with reluctance, the dominion of a stranger: the youth was deservedly popular; his name, after the death of Justin, had been mentioned by a tumultuous faction; and his own submissive offer of his head with a treasure of sixty thousand pounds, might be interpreted as an evidence of guilt, or at least of fear. Justinian received a free pardon, and the command of the eastern army. The Persian monarch fled before his arms; and the acclamations which accompanied his triumph declared him worthy of the purple. His artful patroness had chosen the month of the vintage, while the emperor, in a rural solitude, was permitted to enjoy the pleasures of a subject. On the first intelligence of her designs, he returned to Constantinople, and the conspiracy was suppressed by his presence and firmness. From the pomp and honors which she had abused, Sophia was reduced to a modest allowance: Tiberius dismissed her train, intercepted her correspondence, and committed to a faithful guard the custody of her person. But the services of Justinian were not considered by that excellent prince as an aggravation of his offences: after a mild reproof, his treason and ingratitude were forgiven; and it was commonly believed, that the emperor entertained some thoughts of contracting a double alliance with the rival of his throne. The voice of an angel (such a fable was propagated) might reveal to the emperor, that he should always triumph over his domestic foes; but Tiberius derived a firmer assurance from the innocence and generosity of his own mind.

[Footnote 28: For the character and reign of Tiberius, see Evagrius, l v. c. 13. Theophylact, l. iii. c. 12, &c. Theophanes, in Chron. p. 2 0—213. Zonaras, tom. ii. l. xiv. p. 72. Cedrenus, p. 392. Paul Warnefrid, de Gestis Langobard. l. iii. c. 11, 12. The deacon of Forum Juli appears to have possessed some curious and authentic facts.]

With the odious name of Tiberius, he assumed the more popular appellation of Constantine, and imitated the purer virtues of the Antonines. After recording the vice or folly of so many Roman princes, it is pleasing to repose, for a moment, on a character conspicuous by the qualities of humanity, justice, temperance, and fortitude; to contemplate a sovereign affable in his palace, pious in the church, impartial on the seat of judgment, and victorious, at least by his generals, in the Persian war. The most glorious trophy of his victory consisted in a multitude of captives, whom Tiberius entertained, redeemed, and dismissed to their native homes with the charitable spirit of a Christian hero. The merit or misfortunes of his own subjects had a dearer claim to his beneficence, and he measured his bounty not so much by their expectations as by his own dignity. This maxim, however dangerous in a trustee of the public wealth, was balanced by a principle of humanity and justice, which taught him to abhor, as of the basest alloy, the gold that was extracted from the tears of the people. For their relief, as often as they had suffered by natural or hostile calamities, he was impatient to remit the arrears of the past, or the demands of future taxes: he sternly rejected the servile offerings of his ministers, which were compensated by tenfold oppression; and the wise and equitable laws of Tiberius excited the praise and regret of succeeding times. Constantinople believed that the emperor had discovered a treasure: but his genuine treasure consisted in the practice of liberal economy, and the contempt of all vain and superfluous expense. The Romans of the East would have been happy, if the best gift of Heaven, a patriot king, had been confirmed as a proper and permanent blessing. But in less than four years after the death of Justin, his worthy successor sunk into a mortal disease, which left him only sufficient time to restore the diadem, according to the tenure by which he held it, to the most deserving of his fellow-citizens. He selected Maurice from the crowd, a judgment more precious than the purple itself: the patriarch and senate were summoned to the bed of the dying prince: he bestowed his daughter and the empire; and his last advice was solemnly delivered by the voice of the quaestor. Tiberius expressed his hope that the virtues of his son and successor would erect the noblest mausoleum to his memory. His memory was embalmed by the public affliction; but the most sincere grief evaporates in the tumult of a new reign, and the eyes and acclamations of mankind were speedily directed to the rising sun. The emperor Maurice derived his origin from ancient Rome; [29] but his immediate parents were settled at Arabissus in Cappadocia, and their singular felicity preserved them alive to behold and partake the fortune of their august son. The youth of Maurice was spent in the profession of arms: Tiberius promoted him to the command of a new and favorite legion of twelve thousand confederates; his valor and conduct were signalized in the Persian war; and he returned to Constantinople to accept, as his just reward, the inheritance of the empire. Maurice ascended the throne at the mature age of forty-three years; and he reigned above twenty years over the East and over himself; [30] expelling from his mind the wild democracy of passions, and establishing (according to the quaint expression of Evagrius) a perfect aristocracy of reason and virtue. Some suspicion will degrade the testimony of a subject, though he protests that his secret praise should never reach the ear of his sovereign, [31] and some failings seem to place the character of Maurice below the purer merit of his predecessor. His cold and reserved demeanor might be imputed to arrogance; his justice was not always exempt from cruelty, nor his clemency from weakness; and his rigid economy too often exposed him to the reproach of avarice. But the rational wishes of an absolute monarch must tend to the happiness of his people. Maurice was endowed with sense and courage to promote that happiness, and his administration was directed by the principles and example of Tiberius. The pusillanimity of the Greeks had introduced so complete a separation between the offices of king and of general, that a private soldier, who had deserved and obtained the purple, seldom or never appeared at the head of his armies. Yet the emperor Maurice enjoyed the glory of restoring the Persian monarch to his throne; his lieutenants waged a doubtful war against the Avars of the Danube; and he cast an eye of pity, of ineffectual pity, on the abject and distressful state of his Italian provinces.

[Footnote 29: It is therefore singular enough that Paul (l. iii. c. 15) should distinguish him as the first Greek emperor—primus ex Graecorum genere in Imperio constitutus. His immediate predecessors had in

deed been born in the Latin provinces of Europe: and a various reading, in Graecorum Imperio, would apply the expression to the empire rather than the prince.]

[Footnote 30: Consult, for the character and reign of Maurice, the fifth and sixth books of Evagrius, particularly l. vi. c. l; the eight books of his prolix and florid history by Theophylact Simocatta; Theophanes, p. 213, &c.; Zonaras, tom. ii. l. xiv. p. 73; Cedrenus, p. 394.]

[Footnote 31: Evagrius composed his history in the twelfth year of Maurice; and he had been so wisely indiscreet that the emperor know and rewarded his favorable opinion, (l. vi. c. 24.)]

From Italy the emperors were incessantly tormented by tales of misery and demands of succor, which extorted the humiliating confession of their own weakness. The expiring dignity of Rome was only marked by the freedom and energy of her complaints: "If you are incapable," she said, "of delivering us from the sword of the Lombards, save us at least from the calamity of famine." Tiberius forgave the reproach, and relieved the distress: a supply of corn was transported from Egypt to the Tyber; and the Roman people, invoking the name, not of Camillus, but of St. Peter repulsed the Barbarians from their walls. But the relief was accidental, the danger was perpetual and pressing; and the clergy and senate, collecting the remains of their ancient opulence, a sum of three thousand pounds of gold, despatched the patrician Pamphronius to lay their gifts and their complaints at the foot of the Byzantine throne. The attention of the court, and the forces of the East, were diverted by the Persian war: but the justice of Tiberius applied the subsidy to the defence of the city; and he dismissed the patrician with his best advice, either to bribe the Lombard chiefs, or to purchase the aid of the kings of France. Notwithstanding this weak invention, Italy was still afflicted, Rome was again besieged, and the suburb of Classe, only three miles from Ravenna, was pillaged and occupied by the troops of a simple duke of Spoleto. Maurice gave audience to a second deputation of priests and senators: the duties and the menaces of religion were forcibly urged in the letters of the Roman pontiff; and his nuncio, the deacon Gregory, was alike qualified to solicit the powers either of heaven or of the earth.

The emperor adopted, with stronger effect, the measures of his predecessor: some formidable chiefs were persuaded to embrace the friendship of the Romans; and one of them, a mild and faithful Barbarian, lived and died in the service of the exarchs: the passes of the Alps were delivered to the Franks; and the pope encouraged them to violate, without scruple, their oaths and engagements to the misbelievers. Childebert, the great-grandson of Clovis, was persuaded to invade Italy by the payment of fifty thousand pieces; but, as he had viewed with delight some Byzantine coin of the weight of one pound of gold, the king of Austrasia might stipulate, that the gift should be rendered more worthy of his acceptance, by a proper mixture of these respectable medals. The dukes of the Lombards had provoked by frequent inroads their powerful neighbors of Gaul. As soon as they were apprehensive of a just retaliation, they renounced their feeble and disorderly independence: the advantages of real government, union, secrecy, and vigor, were unanimously confessed; and Autharis, the son of Clepho, had already attained the strength and reputation of a warrior. Under the standard of their new king, the conquerors of Italy withstood three successive invasions, one of which was led by Childebert himself, the last of the Merovingian race who descended from the Alps. The first expedition was defeated by the jealous animosity of the Franks and Alemanni. In the second they were vanquished in a bloody battle, with more loss and dishonor than they had sustained since the foundation of their monarchy. Impatient for revenge, they returned a third time with accumulated force, and Autharis yielded to the fury of the torrent. The troops and treasures of the Lombards were distributed in the walled towns between the Alps and the Apennine. A nation, less sensible of danger than of fatigue and delay, soon murmured against the folly of their twenty commanders; and the hot vapors of an Italian sun infected with disease those tramontane bodies which had already suffered the vicissitudes of intemperance and famine. The powers that were inadequate to the conquest, were more than sufficient for the desolation, of the country; nor could the trembling natives distinguish between their enemies and their deliverers. If the junction of the Merovingian and Imperial forces had been effected in the neighborhood of Milan, perhaps they might have subverted the throne of the Lombards; but the Franks expected six days the signal of a flaming village, and the arms of the Greeks were idly employed in the reduction of Modena and Parma, which were torn from them after the retreat of their transalpine allies. The victorious Autharis asserted his claim to the dominion of Italy. At the foot of the Rhaetian Alps, he subdued the resistance, and rifled the hidden treasures, of a sequestered island in the Lake of Comum. At the extreme point of the Calabria, he touched with his spear a column on the sea-shore of Rhegium, [32] proclaiming that ancient landmark to stand the immovable boundary of his kingdom. [33]

[Footnote 32: *The Columna Rhegina, in the narrowest part of the Faro of Messina, one hundred stadia from Rhegium itself, is frequently mentioned in ancient geography. Cluver. Ital. Antiq. tom. ii. p. 1295. Lucas Holsten. Annotat. ad Cluver. p. 301. Wesseling, Itinerar. p. 106.*]

[Footnote 33: *The Greek historians afford some faint hints of the wars of Italy (Menander, in Excerpt. Legat. p. 124, 126. Theophylact, l. iii. c. 4.) The Latins are more satisfactory; and especially Paul Warnefrid, (l iii. c. 13—34,) who had read the more ancient histories of Secundus and Gregory of Tours. Baronius produces some letters of the popes, &c.; and the times are measured by the accurate scale of Pagi and Muratori.*]

During a period of two hundred years, Italy was unequally divided between the kingdom of the Lombards and the exarchate of Ravenna. The offices and professions, which the jealousy of Constantine had separated, were united by the indulgence of Justinian; and eighteen successive exarchs were invested, in the decline of the empire, with the full remains of civil, of military, and even of ecclesiastical, power. Their immediate jurisdiction, which was afterwards consecrated as the patrimony of St. Peter, extended over the modern Romagna, the marshes or valleys of Ferrara and Commachio, [34] five maritime cities from Rimini to Ancona, and a second inland Pentapolis, between the Adriatic coast and the hills of the Apennine. Three subordinate provinces, of Rome, of Venice, and of Naples, which were divided by hostile lands from the palace of Ravenna, acknowledged, both in peace and war, the supremacy of the exarch. The duchy of Rome appears to have included the Tuscan, Sabine, and Latin conquests, of the first four hundred years of the city, and the limits may be distinctly traced along the coast, from Civita Vecchia to Terracina, and with the course of the Tyber from Ameria and Narni to the port of Ostia. The numerous islands from Grado to Chiozza composed the infant dominion of Venice: but the more accessible towns on the Continent were overthrown by the Lombards, who beheld with impotent fury a new capital rising from the waves. The power of the dukes of Naples was circumscribed by the bay and the adjacent isles, by the hostile territory of Capua, and by the Roman colony of Amalphi, [35] whose industrious citizens, by the invention of the mariner's compass, have unveiled the face of the globe. The three islands of Sardinia, Corsica, and Sicily, still adhered to the empire; and the acquisition of the farther Calabria removed the landmark of Autharis from the shore of Rhegium to the Isthmus of Consentia. In Sardinia, the savage mountaineers preserved the liberty and religion of their ancestors; and the husbandmen of Sicily were chained to their rich and cultivated soil. Rome was oppressed by the iron sceptre of the exarchs, and a Greek, perhaps a eunuch, insulted with impunity the ruins of the Capitol. But Naples soon acquired the privilege of electing her own dukes: [36] the independence of Amalphi was the fruit of commerce; and the voluntary attachment of Venice was finally ennobled by an equal alliance with the Eastern empire. On the map of Italy, the measure of the exarchate occupies a very inadequate space, but it included an ample proportion of wealth, industry, and population. The most faithful and valuable subjects escaped from the Barbarian yoke; and the banners of Pavia and Verona, of Milan and Padua, were displayed in their respective quarters by the new inhabitants of Ravenna. The remainder of Italy was possessed by the Lombards; and from Pavia, the royal seat, their kingdom was extended to the east, the north, and the west, as far as the confines of the Avars, the Bavarians, and the Franks of Austrasia and Burgundy. In the language of modern geography, it is now represented by the Terra Firma of the Venetian republic, Tyrol, the Milanese, Piedmont, the coast of Genoa, Mantua, Parma, and Modena, the grand duchy of Tuscany, and a large portion of the ecclesiastical state from Perugia to the Adriatic. The dukes, and at length the princes, of Beneventum, survived the monarchy, and propagated the name of the Lombards. From Capua to Tarentum, they reigned near five hundred years over the greatest part of the present kingdom of Naples. [37]

[Footnote 34: The papal advocates, Zacagni and Fontanini, might justly claim the valley or morass of Commachio as a part of the exarchate. But the ambition of including Modena, Reggio, Parma, and Placentia, has darkened a geographical question somewhat doubtful and obscure Even Muratori, as the servant of the house of Este, is not free from partiality and prejudice.]

[Footnote 35: See Brenckman, Dissert. Ima de Republica Amalphitana, p. 1—42, ad calcem Hist. Pandect. Florent.]

[Footnote 36: Gregor. Magn. l. iii. epist. 23, 25.]

[Footnote 37: I have described the state of Italy from the excellent Dissertation of Beretti. Giannone (Istoria Civile, tom. i. p. 374—387) has followed the learned Camillo Pellegrini in the geography of the kingdom of Naples. After the loss of the true Calabria, the vanity of the Greeks substituted that name instead of the more ignoble appellation of Bruttium; and the change appears to have taken place before the time of Charlemagne, (Eginard, p. 75.)]

In comparing the proportion of the victorious and the vanquished people, the change of language will afford the most probably inference. According to this standard, it will appear, that the Lombards of Italy, and the Visigoths of Spain, were less numerous than the Franks or Burgundians; and the conquerors of Gaul must yield, in their turn, to the multitude of Saxons and Angles who almost eradicated the idioms of Britain. The modern Italian has been insensibly formed by the mixture of nations: the awkwardness of the Barbarians in the nice management of declensions and conjugations reduced them to the use of articles and auxiliary verbs; and many new ideas have been expressed by Teutonic appellations. Yet the principal stock of technical and familiar words is found to be of Latin derivation; [38] and, if we were sufficiently conversant with the obsolete, the rustic, and the municipal dialects of ancient Italy, we should trace the origin of many terms which might, perhaps, be rejected by the classic purity of Rome. A numerous army constitutes but a small nation, and the powers of the Lombards were soon diminished by the retreat of twenty thousand Saxons, who scorned a dependent situation, and returned, after many bold and perilous adventures, to their native country. [39] The camp of Alboin was of formidable extent, but the extent of a camp would be easily circumscribed within the limits of a city; and its martial in habitants must be thinly scattered over the face of a large country. When Alboin descended from the Alps, he invested his nephew, the first duke of Friuli, with the command of the province and the people: but the prudent Gisulf would have declined the dangerous office, unless he had been permitted to choose, among the nobles of the Lombards, a sufficient number of families [40] to form a perpetual colony of soldiers and subjects. In the progress of conquest, the same option could not be granted to the dukes of Brescia or Bergamo, or Pavia or Turin, of Spoleto or Beneventum; but each of these, and each of their colleagues, settled in his appointed district with a band of followers who resorted to his standard in war and his tribunal in peace. Their attachment was free and honorable: resigning the gifts and benefits which they had accepted, they might emigrate with their families into the jurisdiction of another duke; but their absence from the kingdom was punished with death, as a crime of military desertion. [41] The posterity of the first conquerors struck a deeper root into the soil, which, by every motive of interest and honor, they were bound to defend. A Lombard was born the soldier of his king and his duke; and the civil assemblies of the nation displayed the banners, and assumed the appellation, of a regular army. Of this army, the pay and the rewards were drawn from the conquered provinces; and the distribution, which was not effected till after the death of Alboin, is disgraced by the foul marks of injustice and rapine. Many of the most wealthy Italians were slain or banished; the remainder were divided among the strangers, and a tributary obligation was imposed (under the name of hospitality) of paying to the Lombards a third part of the fruits of the earth. Within less than seventy years, this artificial system was abolished by a more simple and solid tenure. [42] Either the Roman landlord was expelled by his strong and insolent guest, or the annual payment, a third of the produce, was exchanged by a more equitable transaction for an adequate proportion of landed property. Under these foreign masters, the business of agriculture, in the cultivation of corn, wines, and olives, was exercised with degenerate skill and industry by the labor of the slaves and natives. But the occupations of a pastoral life were more pleasing to the idleness of the Barbarian. In the rich meadows of Venetia, they restored and improved the breed of horses, for which that province had once been illustrious; [43] and the Italians beheld with astonishment a foreign race of oxen or buffaloes. [44] The depopulation of Lombardy, and the increase of forests, afforded an ample range for the pleasures of the chase. [45] That marvellous art which teaches the birds of the air to acknowledge the voice, and execute the commands, of their master, had been unknown to the ingenuity of the Greeks and Romans. [46] Scandinavia and Scythia produce the boldest and most tractable falcons: [47] they were tamed and educated by the roving inhabitants, always on horseback and in the field. This favorite amusement of our ancestors was introduced by the Barbarians into the Roman provinces; and the laws of Italy esteemed the sword and the hawk as of equal dignity and importance in the hands of a noble Lombard. [48]

[Footnote 38: Maffei (Verona Illustrata, part i. p. 310—321) and Muratori (Antichita Italiane, tom. ii. Dissertazione xxxii. xxxiii. p. 71—365) have asserted the native claims of the Italian idiom; the former with enthusiasm, the latter with discretion; both with learning, ingenuity, and truth. Note: Compare the admirable sketch of the degeneracy of the Latin language and the formation of the Italian in Hallam, Middle Ages, vol. iii. p. 317 329—M.]

[Footnote 39: Paul, de Gest. Langobard. l. iii. c. 5, 6, 7.]

[Footnote 40: Paul, l. ii. c. 9. He calls these families or generations by the Teutonic name of Faras, which is likewise used in the Lombard laws. The humble deacon was not insensible of the nobility of his own race. See l. iv. c. 39.]

[Footnote 41: Compare No. 3 and 177 of the Laws of Rotharis.]

[Footnote 42: Paul, l. ii. c. 31, 32, l. iii. c. 16. The Laws of Rotharis, promulgated A.D. 643, do not contain the smallest vestige of this payment of thirds; but they preserve many curious circumstances of the state of Italy and the manners of the Lombards.]

[Footnote 43: The studs of Dionysius of Syracuse, and his frequent victories in the Olympic games, had diffused among the Greeks the fame of the Venetian horses; but the breed was extinct in the time of

Strabo, (l. v. p. 325.) Gisulf obtained from his uncle generosarum equarum greges. Paul, l. ii. c. 9. The Lombards afterwards introduced caballi sylvatici—wild horses. Paul, l. iv. c. 11.]

[Footnote 44: Tunc (A.D. 596) primum, bubali in Italiam delati Italiae populis miracula fuere, (Paul Warnefrid, l. iv. c. 11.) The buffaloes, whose native climate appears to be Africa and India, are unknown to Europe, except in Italy, where they are numerous and useful. The ancients were ignorant of these animals, unless Aristotle (Hist. Anim. l. ii. c. 1, p. 58, Paris, 1783) has described them as the wild oxen of Arachosia. See Buffon, Hist. Naturelle, tom. xi. and Supplement, tom. vi. Hist. Generale des Voyages, tom. i. p. 7, 481, ii. 105, iii. 291, iv. 234, 461, v. 193, vi. 491, viii. 400, x. 666. Pennant's Quadrupedes, p. 24. Dictionnaire d'Hist. Naturelle, par Valmont de Bomare, tom. ii. p. 74. Yet I must not conceal the suspicion that Paul, by a vulgar error, may have applied the name of bubalus to the aurochs, or wild bull, of ancient Germany.]

[Footnote 45: Consult the xxist Dissertation of Muratori.]

[Footnote 46: Their ignorance is proved by the silence even of those who professedly treat of the arts of hunting and the history of animals. Aristotle, (Hist. Animal. l. ix. c. 36, tom. i. p. 586, and the Notes of his last editor, M. Camus, tom. ii. p. 314,) Pliny, (Hist. Natur. l. x. c. 10,) Aelian (de Natur. Animal. l. ii. c. 42,) and perhaps Homer, (Odyss. xxii. 302-306,) describe with astonishment a tacit league and common chase between the hawks and the Thracian fowlers.]

[Footnote 47: Particularly the gerfaut, or gyrfalcon, of the size of a small eagle. See the animated description of M. de Buffon, Hist. Naturelle, tom. xvi. p. 239, &c.]

[Footnote 48: Script. Rerum Italicarum, tom. i. part ii. p. 129. This is the xvith law of the emperor Lewis the Pious. His father Charlemagne had falconers in his household as well as huntsmen, (Memoires sur l'ancienne Chevalerie, par M. de St. Palaye, tom. iii. p. 175.) I observe in the laws of Rotharis a more early mention of the art of hawking, (No. 322;) and in Gaul, in the fifth century, it is celebrated by Sidonius Apollinaris among the talents of Avitus, (202—207.) Note: See Beckman, Hist. of Inventions, vol. i. p. 319—M.]

PART III

So rapid was the influence of climate and example, that the Lombards of the fourth generation surveyed with curiosity and affright the portraits of their savage forefathers. [49] Their heads were shaven behind, but the shaggy locks hung over their eyes and mouth, and a long beard represented the name and character of the nation. Their dress consisted of loose linen garments, after the fashion of the Anglo-Saxons, which were decorated, in their opinion, with broad stripes or variegated colors. The legs and feet were clothed in long hose, and open sandals; and even in the security of peace a trusty sword was constantly girt to their side. Yet this strange apparel, and horrid aspect, often concealed a gentle and generous disposition; and as soon as the rage of battle had subsided, the captives and subjects were sometimes surprised by the humanity of the victor. The vices of the Lombards were the effect of passion, of ignorance, of intoxication; their virtues are the more laudable, as they were not affected by the hypocrisy of social manners, nor imposed by the rigid constraint of laws and education. I should not be apprehensive of deviating from my subject, if it were in my power to delineate the private life of the conquerors of Italy; and I shall relate with pleasure the adventurous gallantry of Autharis, which breathes the true spirit of chivalry and romance. [50] After the loss of his promised bride, a Merovingian princess, he sought in marriage the daughter of the king of Bavaria; and Garribald accepted the alliance of the Italian monarch. Impatient of the slow progress of negotiation, the ardent lover escaped from his palace, and visited the court of Bavaria in the train of his own embassy. At the public audience, the unknown stranger advanced to the throne, and informed Garribald that the ambassador was indeed the minister of state, but that he alone was the friend of Autharis, who had trusted him with the delicate commission of making a faithful report of the charms of his spouse. Theudelinda was summoned to undergo this important examination; and, after a pause of silent rapture, he hailed her as the queen of Italy, and humbly requested that, according to the custom of the nation, she would present a cup of wine to the first of her new subjects. By the command of her father she obeyed: Autharis received the cup in his turn, and, in restoring it to the princess, he secretly touched her hand, and drew his own finger over his face and lips. In the evening, Theudelinda imparted to her nurse the indiscreet familiarity of the stranger, and was comforted by the assurance, that such boldness could proceed only from the king her husband, who, by his beauty and courage, appeared worthy of her love. The ambassadors were dismissed: no sooner did they reach the confines of Italy than Autharis, raising himself on his horse, darted his battle-axe against a tree with incomparable strength and dexterity. "Such," said he to the astonished Bavarians, "such are the strokes of the king of the Lombards." On the approach of a French army, Garribald and his daughter took refuge in the dominions of their ally; and the marriage was consummated in the palace of Verona. At the end of one year, it was dissolved by the death of Autharis: but the virtues of Theudelinda [51] had endeared her to the nation, and she was permitted to bestow, with her hand, the sceptre of the Italian kingdom.

[Footnote 49: The epitaph of Droctulf (Paul, l. iii. c. 19) may be applied to many of his countrymen:— Terribilis visu facies, sed corda benignus Longaque robusto pectore barba fuit. The portraits of the old Lombards might still be seen in the palace of Monza, twelve miles from Milan, which had been founded or restored by Queen Theudelinda, (l. iv. 22, 23.) See Muratori, tom. i. disserta, xxiii. p. 300.]

[Footnote 50: The story of Autharis and Theudelinda is related by Paul, l. iii. 29, 34; and any fragment of Bavarian antiquity excites the indefatigable diligence of the count de Buat, Hist. des Peuples de l'Europe, ton. xi. p. 595—635, tom. xii. p. 1-53.]

[Footnote 51: Giannone (Istoria Civile de Napoli, tom. i. p. 263) has justly censured the impertinence of Boccaccio, (Gio. iii. Novel. 2,) who, without right, or truth, or pretence, has given the pious queen Theudelinda to the arms of a muleteer.]

From this fact, as well as from similar events, [52] it is certain that the Lombards possessed freedom to elect their sovereign, and sense to decline the frequent use of that dangerous privilege. The public revenue arose from the produce of land and the profits of justice. When the independent dukes agreed that Autharis should ascend the throne of his father, they endowed the regal office with a fair moiety of their respective domains. The proudest nobles aspired to the honors of servitude near the person of their prince: he rewarded the fidelity of his vassals by the precarious gift of pensions and benefices; and atoned for the injuries of war by the rich foundation of monasteries and churches. In peace a judge, a leader in war, he never usurped the powers of a sole and absolute legislator. The king of Italy convened the national assemblies in the palace, or more probably in the fields, of Pavia: his great council was composed of the persons most eminent by their birth and dignities; but the validity, as well as the execution, of their decrees depended on the approbation of the faithful people, the fortunate army of the Lombards. About fourscore years after the conquest of Italy, their traditional customs were transcribed in Teutonic Latin, [53] and ratified by the consent of the prince and people: some new regulations were introduced, more suitable to their present condition; the example of Rotharis was imitated by the wisest of his successors; and the laws of the Lombards have been esteemed the least imperfect of the Barbaric codes. [54] Secure by their courage in the possession of liberty, these rude and hasty legislators were incapable of balancing the powers of the constitution, or of discussing the nice theory of political government. Such crimes as threatened the life of the sovereign, or the safety of the state, were adjudged worthy of death; but their attention was principally confined to the defence of the person and property of the subject. According to the strange jurisprudence of the times, the guilt of blood might be redeemed by a fine; yet the high price of nine hundred pieces of gold declares a just sense of the value of a simple citizen. Less atrocious injuries, a wound, a fracture, a blow, an opprobrious word, were measured with scrupulous and almost ridiculous diligence; and the prudence of the legislator encouraged the ignoble practice of bartering honor and revenge for a pecuniary compensation. The ignorance of the Lombards in the state of Paganism or Christianity gave implicit credit to the malice and mischief of witchcraft, but the judges of the seventeenth century might have been instructed and confounded by the wisdom of Rotharis, who derides the absurd superstition, and protects the wretched victims of popular or judicial cruelty. [55] The same spirit of a legislator, superior to his age and country, may be ascribed to Luitprand, who condemns, while he tolerates, the impious and inveterate abuse of duels, [56] observing, from his own experience, that the juster cause had often been oppressed by successful violence. Whatever merit may be discovered in the laws of the Lombards, they are the genuine fruit of the reason of the Barbarians, who never admitted the bishops of Italy to a seat in their legislative councils. But the succession of their kings is marked with virtue and ability; the troubled series of their annals is adorned with fair intervals of peace, order, and domestic happiness; and the Italians enjoyed a milder and more equitable government, than any of the other kingdoms which had been founded on the ruins of the Western empire. [57]

[Footnote 52: Paul, l. iii. c. 16. The first dissertations of Muratori, and the first volume of Giannone's history, may be consulted for the state of the kingdom of Italy.]

[Footnote 53: The most accurate edition of the Laws of the Lombards is to be found in the Scriptores Rerum Italicarum, tom. i. part ii. p. 1—181, collated from the most ancient Mss. and illustrated by the critical notes of Muratori.]

[Footnote 54: Montesquieu, Esprit des Loix, l. xxviii. c. 1. Les loix des Bourguignons sont assez judicieuses; celles de Rotharis et des autres princes Lombards le sont encore plus.]

[Footnote 55: See Leges Rotharis, No. 379, p. 47. Striga is used as the name of a witch. It is of the purest classic origin, (Horat. epod. v. 20. Petron. c. 134;) and from the words of Petronius, (quae striges comederunt nervos tuos?) it may be inferred that the prejudice was of Italian rather than Barbaric extraction.]

[Footnote 56: Quia incerti sumus de judicio Dei, et multos audivimus per pugnam sine justa causa suam causam perdere. Sed propter consuetudinom gentem nostram Langobardorum legem impiam vetare non possumus. See p. 74, No. 65, of the Laws of Luitprand, promulgated A.D. 724.]

[Footnote 57: Read the history of Paul Warnefrid; particularly l. iii. c. 16. Baronius rejects the praise, which appears to contradict the invectives of Pope Gregory the Great; but Muratori (Annali d' Italia, tom. v. p. 217) presumes to insinuate that the saint may have magnified the faults of Arians and enemies.]

Amidst the arms of the Lombards, and under the despotism of the Greeks, we again inquire into the fate of Rome, [58] which had reached, about the close of the sixth century, the lowest period of her depression. By the removal of the seat of empire, and the successive loss of the provinces, the sources of public and private opulence were exhausted: the lofty tree, under whose shade the nations of the earth had reposed, was deprived of its leaves and branches, and the sapless trunk was left to wither on the ground. The ministers of command, and the messengers of victory, no longer met on the Appian or Flaminian way; and the hostile approach of the Lombards was often felt, and continually feared. The inhabitants of a potent and peaceful capital, who visit without an anxious thought the garden of the adjacent country, will faintly picture in their fancy the distress of the Romans: they shut or opened their gates with a trembling hand, beheld from the walls the flames of their houses, and heard the lamentations of their brethren, who were coupled together like dogs, and dragged away into distant slavery beyond the sea and the mountains. Such incessant alarms must annihilate the pleasures and interrupt the labors of a rural life; and the Campagna of Rome was speedily reduced to the state of a dreary wilderness, in which the land is barren, the waters are impure, and the air is infectious. Curiosity and ambition no longer attracted the nations to the capital of the world: but, if chance or necessity directed the steps of a wandering stranger, he contemplated with horror the vacancy and solitude of the city, and might be tempted to ask, Where is the senate, and where are the people? In a season of excessive rains, the Tyber swelled above its banks, and rushed with irresistible violence into the valleys of the seven hills. A pestilential disease arose from the stagnation of the deluge, and so rapid was the contagion, that fourscore persons expired in an hour in the midst of a solemn procession, which implored the mercy of Heaven. [59] A society in which marriage is encouraged and industry prevails soon repairs the accidental losses of pestilence and war: but, as the far greater part of the Romans was condemned to hopeless indigence and celibacy, the depopulation was constant and visible, and the gloomy enthusiasts might expect the approaching failure of the human race. [60] Yet the number of citizens still exceeded the measure of subsistence: their precarious food was supplied from the harvests of Sicily or Egypt; and the frequent repetition of famine betrays the inattention of the emperor to a distant province. The edifices of Rome were exposed to the same ruin and decay: the mouldering fabrics were easily overthrown by inundations, tempests, and earthquakes: and the monks, who had occupied the most advantageous stations, exulted in their base triumph over the ruins of antiquity. [61] It is commonly believed, that Pope Gregory the First attacked the temples and mutilated the statues of the city; that, by the command of the Barbarian, the Palatine library was reduced to ashes, and that the history of Livy was the peculiar mark of his absurd and mischievous fanaticism. The writings of Gregory himself reveal his implacable aversion to the monuments of classic genius; and he points his severest censure against the profane learning of a bishop, who taught the art of grammar, studied the Latin poets, and pronounced with the same voice the praises of Jupiter and those of Christ. But the evidence of his destructive rage is doubtful and recent: the Temple of Peace, or the theatre of Marcellus, have been demolished by the slow operation of ages, and a formal proscription would have multiplied the copies of Virgil and Livy in the countries which were not subject to the ecclesiastical dictator. [62]

[Footnote 58: *The passages of the homilies of Gregory, which represent the miserable state of the city and country, are transcribed in the Annals of Baronius, A.D. 590, No. 16, A.D. 595, No. 2, &c., &c.*]

[Footnote 59: *The inundation and plague were reported by a deacon, whom his bishop, Gregory of Tours, had despatched to Rome for some relics The ingenious messenger embellished his tale and the river with a great dragon and a train of little serpents, (Greg. Turon. l. x. c. 1.)*]

[Footnote 60: *Gregory of Rome (Dialog. l. ii. c. 15) relates a memorable prediction of St. Benedict. Roma a Gentilibus non exterminabitur sed tempestatibus, coruscis turbinibus ac terrae motu in semetipsa* marces cet. Such a prophecy melts into true history, and becomes the evidence of the fact after which it was invented.]

[Footnote 61: Quia in uno se ore cum Jovis laudibus, Christi laudes non capiunt, et quam grave nefandumque sit episcopis canere quod nec laico religioso conveniat, ipse considera, (l. ix. ep. 4.) The writings of Gregory himself attest his innocence of any classic taste or literature]

[Footnote 62: Bayle, (Dictionnaire Critique, tom. ii. 598, 569,) in a very good article of Gregoire I., has quoted, for the buildings and statues, Platina in Gregorio I.; for the Palatine library, John of Salisbury, (de Nugis Curialium, l. ii. c. 26;) and for Livy, Antoninus of Florence: the oldest of the three lived in the xiith century.]

Like Thebes, or Babylon, or Carthage, the names of Rome might have been erased from the earth, if the city had not been animated by a vital principle, which again restored her to honor and dominion. A vague tradition was embraced, that two Jewish teachers, a tent-maker and a fisherman, had formerly been executed in the circus of Nero, and at the end of five hundred years, their genuine or fictitious relics were adored as the Palladium of Christian Rome. The pilgrims of the East and West resorted to the holy threshold; but the shrines of the apostles were guarded by miracles and invisible terrors; and it was not without fear that the pious Catholic approached the object of his worship. It was fatal to touch, it was dangerous to behold, the bodies of the saints; and those who, from the purest motives, presumed to disturb the repose of the sanctuary, were affrighted by visions, or punished with sudden death. The unreasonable request of an empress, who wished to deprive the Romans of their sacred treasure, the head of St. Paul, was rejected with the deepest abhorrence; and the pope asserted, most probably with truth, that a linen which had been sanctified in the neighborhood of his body, or the filings of his chain, which it was sometimes easy and sometimes impossible to obtain, possessed an equal degree of miraculous virtue. [63] But the power as well as virtue of the apostles resided with living energy in the breast of their successors; and the chair of St. Peter was filled under the reign of Maurice by the first and greatest of the name of Gregory. [64] His grandfather Felix had himself been pope, and as the bishops were already bound by the laws of celibacy, his consecration must have been preceded by the death of his wife. The parents of Gregory, Sylvia, and Gordian, were the noblest of the senate, and the most pious of the church of Rome; his female relations were numbered among the saints and virgins; and his own figure, with those of his father and mother, were represented near three hundred years in a family portrait, [65] which he offered to the monastery of St. Andrew. The design and coloring of this picture afford an honorable testimony that the art of painting was cultivated by the Italians of the sixth century; but the most abject ideas must be entertained of their taste and learning, since the epistles of Gregory, his sermons, and his dialogues, are the work of a man who was second in erudition to none of his contemporaries: [66] his birth and abilities had raised him to the office of praefect of the city, and he enjoyed the merit of renouncing the pomps and vanities of this world. His ample patrimony was dedicated to the foundation of seven monasteries, [67] one in Rome, [68] and six in Sicily; and it was the wish of Gregory that he might be unknown in this life, and glorious only in the next. Yet his devotion (and it might be sincere) pursued the path which would have been chosen by a crafty and ambitious statesman. The talents of Gregory, and the splendor which accompanied his retreat, rendered him dear and useful to the church; and implicit obedience has always been inculcated as the first duty of a monk. As soon as he had received the character of deacon, Gregory was sent to reside at the Byzantine court, the nuncio or minister of the apostolic see; and he boldly assumed, in the name of St. Peter, a tone of independent dignity, which would have been criminal and dangerous in the most illustrious layman of the empire. He returned to Rome with a just increase of reputation, and, after a short exercise of the monastic virtues, he was dragged from the cloister to the papal throne, by the unanimous voice of the clergy, the senate, and the people. He alone resisted, or seemed to resist, his own elevation; and his humble petition, that Maurice would be pleased to reject the choice of the Romans, could only serve to exalt his character in the eyes of the emperor and the public. When the fatal mandate was proclaimed, Gregory solicited the aid of some friendly merchants to convey him in a basket beyond the gates of Rome, and modestly concealed himself some days among the woods and mountains, till his retreat was discovered, as it is said, by a celestial light. [Footnote 63: Gregor. l. iii. epist. 24, edict. 12, &c. From the epistles of Gregory, and the viiith volume of the Annals of Baronius, the pious reader may collect the particles of holy iron which were inserted in keys or crosses of gold, and distributed in Britain, Gaul, Spain, Africa, Constantinople, and Egypt. The pontifical smith who handled the file must have understood the miracles which it was in his own power to operate or withhold; a circumstance which abates the superstition of Gregory at the expense of his veracity.]

[Footnote 64: Besides the epistles of Gregory himself, which are methodized by Dupin, (Bibliotheque Eccles. tom. v. p. 103—126,) we have three lives of the pope; the two first written in the viiith and ixth centuries, (de Triplici Vita St. Greg. Preface to the ivth volume of the Benedictine edition,) by the deacons Paul (p. 1—18) and John, (p. 19—188,) and containing much original, though doubtful, evidence; the third, a long and labored compilation by the Benedictine editors, (p. 199—305.) The annals of Baronius are a copious but partial history. His papal prejudices are tempered by the good sense of Fleury, (Hist. Eccles. tom. viii.,) and his chronology has been rectified by the criticism of Pagi and Muratori.]

[Footnote 65: John the deacon has described them like an eye-witness, (l. iv. c. 83, 84;) and his description is illustrated by Angelo Rocca, a Roman antiquary, (St. Greg. Opera, tom. iv. p. 312—326;) who observes that some mosaics of the popes of the viith century are still preserved in the old churches of Rome, (p. 321—323) The same walls which represented Gregory's family are now decorated with the martyrdom of St. Andrew, the noble contest of Dominichino and Guido.]

[Footnote 66: Disciplinis vero liberalibus, hoc est grammatica, rhetorica, dialectica ita apuero est institutus, ut quamvis eo tempore florerent adhuc Romae studia literarum, tamen nulli in urbe ipsa secundus putaretur. Paul. Diacon. in Vit. St. Gregor. c. 2.]

[Footnote 67: The Benedictines (Vit. Greg. l. i. p. 205—208) labor to reduce the monasteries of Gregory within the rule of their own order; but, as the question is confessed to be doubtful, it is clear that these powerful monks are in the wrong. See Butler's Lives of the Saints, vol. iii. p. 145; a work of merit: the sense and learning belong to the author—his prejudices are those of his profession.]

[Footnote 68: Monasterium Gregorianum in ejusdem Beati Gregorii aedibus ad clivum Scauri prope ecclesiam SS. Johannis et Pauli in honorem St. Andreae, (John, in Vit. Greg. l. i. c. 6. Greg. l. vii. epist. 13.) This house and monastery were situate on the side of the Caelian hill which fronts the Palatine; they are now occupied by the Camaldoli: San Gregorio triumphs, and St. Andrew has retired to a small chapel Nardini, Roma Antica, l. iii. c. 6, p. 100. Descrizzione di Roma, tom. i. p. 442—446.]

The pontificate of Gregory the Great, which lasted thirteen years, six months, and ten days, is one of the most edifying periods of the history of the church. His virtues, and even his faults, a singular mixture of simplicity and cunning, of pride and humility, of sense and superstition, were happily suited to his station and to the temper of the times. In his rival, the patriarch of Constantinople, he condemned the anti-Christian title of universal bishop, which the successor of St. Peter was too haughty to concede, and too feeble to assume; and the ecclesiastical jurisdiction of Gregory was confined to the triple character of Bishop of Rome, Primate of Italy, and Apostle of the West. He frequently ascended the pulpit, and kindled, by his rude, though pathetic, eloquence, the congenial passions of his audience: the language of the Jewish prophets was interpreted and applied; and the minds of a people, depressed by their present calamities, were directed to the hopes and fears of the invisible world. His precepts and example defined the model of the Roman liturgy; [69] the distribution of the parishes, the calendar of the festivals, the order of processions, the service of the priests and deacons, the variety and change of sacerdotal garments. Till the last days of his life, he officiated in the canon of the mass, which continued above three hours: the Gregorian chant [70] has preserved the vocal and instrumental music of the theatre, and the rough voices of the Barbarians attempted to imitate the melody of the Roman school. [71] Experience had shown him the efficacy of these solemn and pompous rites, to soothe the distress, to confirm the faith, to mitigate the fierceness, and to dispel the dark enthusiasm of the vulgar, and he readily forgave their tendency to promote the reign of priesthood and superstition. The bishops of Italy and the adjacent islands acknowledged the Roman pontiff as their special metropolitan. Even the existence, the union, or the translation of episcopal seats was decided by his absolute discretion: and his successful inroads into the provinces of Greece, of Spain, and of Gaul, might countenance the more lofty pretensions of succeeding popes. He interposed to prevent the abuses of popular elections; his jealous care maintained the purity of faith and discipline; and the apostolic shepherd assiduously watched over the faith and discipline of the subordinate pastors. Under his reign, the Arians of Italy and Spain were reconciled to the Catholic church, and the conquest of Britain reflects less glory on the name of Caesar, than on that of Gregory the First. Instead of six legions, forty monks were embarked for that distant island, and the pontiff lamented the austere duties which forbade him to partake the perils of their spiritual warfare. In less than two years, he could announce to the archbishop of Alexandria, that they had baptized the king of Kent with ten thousand of his Anglo-Saxons, and that the Roman missionaries, like those of the primitive church, were armed only with spiritual and supernatural powers. The credulity or the prudence of Gregory was always disposed to confirm the truths of religion by the evidence of ghosts, miracles, and resurrections; [72] and posterity has paid to his memory the same tribute which he freely granted to the virtue of his own or the preceding generation. The celestial honors have been liberally bestowed by the authority of the popes, but Gregory is the last of their own order whom they have presumed to inscribe in the calendar of saints.

[Footnote 69: *The Lord's Prayer consists of half a dozen lines; the Sacramentarius and Antiphonarius of Gregory fill 880 folio pages, (tom. iii. p. i. p. 1—880;) yet these only constitute a part of the Ordo Romanus, which Mabillon has illustrated and Fleury has abridged, (Hist. Eccles. tom. viii. p. 139—152.)*]

[Footnote 70: *I learn from the Abbe Dobos, (Reflexions sur la Poesie et la Peinture, tom. iii. p. 174, 175,) that the simplicity of the Ambrosian chant was confined to four modes, while the more perfect harmony of the Gregorian comprised the eight modes or fifteen chords of the ancient music. He observes (p. 332) that the connoisseurs admire the preface and many passages of the Gregorian office.*]

[Footnote 71: *John the deacon (in Vit. Greg. l. ii. c. 7) expresses the early contempt of the Italians for tramontane singing. Alpina scilicet corpora vocum suarum tonitruis altisone perstrepentia, susceptae modulationis dulcedinem proprie non resultant: quia bibuli gutturis barbara feritas dum inflexionibus et repercussionibus mitem nititur edere cantilenam, naturali quodam fragore, quasi plaustra per gradus confuse sonantia, rigidas voces jactat, &c. In the time of Charlemagne, the Franks, though with some reluctance, admitted the justice of the reproach. Muratori, Dissert. xxv.*]

[Footnote 72: *A French critic (Petrus Gussanvillus, Opera, tom. ii. p. 105—112) has vindicated the right of Gregory to the entire nonsense of the Dialogues. Dupin (tom. v. p. 138) does not think that any one will vouch for the truth of all these miracles: I should like to know how many of them he believed himself.*]

Their temporal power insensibly arose from the calamities of the times: and the Roman bishops, who have deluged Europe and Asia with blood, were compelled to reign as the ministers of charity and peace. I. The church of Rome, as it has been formerly observed, was endowed with ample possessions in Italy, Sicily, and the more distant provinces; and her agents, who were commonly sub-deacons, had acquired a civil, and even criminal, jurisdiction over their tenants and husbandmen. The successor of St. Peter administered his patrimony with the temper of a vigilant and moderate landlord; [73] and the epistles of Gregory are filled with salutary instructions to abstain from doubtful or vexatious lawsuits; to preserve the integrity of weights and measures; to grant every reasonable delay; and to reduce the capitation of the slaves of the glebe, who purchased the right of marriage by the payment of an arbitrary fine. [74] The rent or the produce of these estates was transported to the mouth of the Tyber, at the risk and expense of the pope: in the use of wealth he acted like a faithful steward of the church and the poor, and liberally applied to their wants the inexhaustible resources of abstinence and order. The voluminous account of his receipts and disbursements was kept above three hundred years in the Lateran, as the model of Christian economy. On the four great festivals, he divided their quarterly allowance to the clergy, to his domestics, to the monasteries, the churches, the places of burial, the almshouses, and the hospitals of Rome, and the rest of the diocese. On the first day of every month, he distributed to the poor, according to the season, their stated portion of corn, wine, cheese, vegetables, oil, fish, fresh provisions, clothes, and money; and his treasurers were continually summoned to satisfy, in his name, the extraordinary demands of indigence and merit. The instant distress of the sick and helpless, of strangers and pilgrims, was relieved by the bounty of each day, and of every hour; nor would the pontiff indulge himself in a frugal repast, till he had sent the dishes from his own table to some objects deserving of his compassion. The misery of the times had reduced the nobles and matrons of Rome to accept, without a blush, the benevolence of the church: three thousand virgins received their food and raiment from the hand of their benefactor; and many bishops of Italy escaped from the Barbarians to the hospitable threshold of the Vatican. Gregory might justly be styled the Father of his Country; and such was the extreme sensibility of his conscience, that, for the death of a beggar who had perished in the streets, he interdicted himself during several days from the exercise of sacerdotal functions. II. The misfortunes of Rome involved the apostolical pastor in the business of peace and war; and it might be doubtful to himself, whether piety or ambition prompted him to supply the place of his absent sovereign. Gregory awakened the emperor from a long slumber; exposed the guilt or incapacity of the exarch and his inferior ministers; complained that the veterans were withdrawn from Rome for the defence of Spoleto; encouraged the Italians to guard their cities and altars; and condescended, in the crisis of danger, to name the tribunes, and to direct the operations, of the provincial troops. But the martial spirit of the pope was checked by the scruples of humanity and religion: the imposition of tribute, though it was employed in the Italian war, he freely condemned as odious and oppressive; whilst he protected, against the Imperial edicts, the pious cowardice of the soldiers who deserted a military for a monastic life If we may credit his own declarations, it would have been easy for Gregory to exterminate the Lombards by their domestic factions, without leaving a king, a duke, or a count, to save that unfortunate nation from the vengeance of their foes As a Christian bishop, he preferred the salutary offices of peace; his mediation appeased the tumult of arms: but he was too conscious of the arts of the Greeks, and the passions of the Lombards, to engage his sacred promise for the observance of the truce. Disappointed in the hope of a general and lasting treaty, he presumed to save his country without the consent of the emperor or the exarch. The sword of the enemy was suspended over Rome; it was averted by the mild eloquence and seasonable gifts of the pontiff, who commanded the respect of heretics and Barbarians. The merits of Gregory were treated by the Byzantine court with reproach and insult; but in the attachment of a grateful people, he found the purest reward of a citizen, and the best right of a sovereign. [75]

[Footnote 73: Baronius is unwilling to expatiate on the care of the patrimonies, lest he should betray that they consisted not of kingdoms, but farms. The French writers, the Benedictine editors, (tom. iv. l. iii. p. 272, &c.,) and Fleury, (tom. viii. p. 29, &c.,) are not afraid of entering into these humble, though useful, details; and the humanity of Fleury dwells on the social virtues of Gregory.]

[Footnote 74: I much suspect that this pecuniary fine on the marriages of villains produced the famous, and often fabulous right, de cuissage, de marquette, &c. With the consent of her husband, a handsome bride might commute the payment in the arms of a young landlord, and the mutual favor might afford a precedent of local rather than legal tyranny]

[Footnote 75: The temporal reign of Gregory I. is ably exposed by Sigonius in the first book, de Regno Italiae. See his works, tom. ii. p. 44—75]

CHAPTER XLVI

TROUBLES IN PERSIA

PART I

REVOLUTIONS ON PERSIA AFTER THE DEATH OF CHOSROES ON NUSHIRVAN—HISSON HORMOUZ, A TYRANT IS DEPOSED—USURPATION OF BAHARAM—FLIGHT AND RESTORATION OF CHOSROES II—HIS GRATITIUDE TO THE ROMANS—THE CHAGAN OF THE AVARS—REVOLT OF THE ARMY AGAINST MAURICE—HIS DEATH—TYRANNY OF PHOCAS—ELEVATION OF HERACLIUS—THE PERSIAN WAR—CHOSROES SUBDUES SYRIA, EGYPT, AND ASIA MINOR—SIEGE OF CONSTANTINOPLE BY THE PERSIANS AND AVARS—PERSIAN EXPEDITIONS—VICTORIES AND TRIUMPH OF HERACLIUS

The conflict of Rome and Persia was prolonged from the death of Craesus to the reign of Heraclius. An experience of seven hundred years might convince the rival nations of the impossibility of maintaining their conquests beyond the fatal limits of the Tigris and Euphrates. Yet the emulation of Trajan and Julian was awakened by the trophies of Alexander, and the sovereigns of Persia indulged the ambitious hope of restoring the empire of Cyrus. [1] Such extraordinary efforts of power and courage will always command the attention of posterity; but the events by which the fate of nations is not materially changed, leave a faint impression on the page of history, and the patience of the reader would be exhausted by the repetition of the same hostilities, undertaken without cause, prosecuted without glory, and terminated without effect. The arts of negotiation, unknown to the simple greatness of the senate and the Caesars, were assiduously cultivated by the Byzantine princes; and the memorials of their perpetual embassies [2] repeat, with the same uniform prolixity, the language of falsehood and declamation, the insolence of the Barbarians, and the servile temper of the tributary Greeks. Lamenting the barren superfluity of materials, I have studied to compress the narrative of these uninteresting transactions: but the just Nushirvan is still applauded as the model of Oriental kings, and the ambition of his grandson Chosroes prepared the revolution of the East, which was speedily accomplished by the arms and the religion of the successors of Mahomet.

[Footnote 1: Missis qui... reposcerent... veteres Persarum ac Macedonum terminos, seque invasurum possessa Cyro et post Alexandro, per vaniloquentiam ac minas jaciebat. Tacit. Annal. vi. 31. Such was the language of the Arsacides. I have repeatedly marked the lofty claims of the Sassanians.]

[Footnote 2: See the embassies of Menander, extracted and preserved in the tenth century by the order of Constantine Porphyrogenitus.]

In the useless altercations, that precede and justify the quarrels of princes, the Greeks and the Barbarians accused each other of violating the peace which had been concluded between the two empires about four years before the death of Justinian. The sovereign of Persia and India aspired to reduce under his obedience the province of Yemen or Arabia [3] Felix; the distant land of myrrh and frankincense, which had escaped, rather than opposed, the conquerors of the East. After the defeat of Abrahah under the walls of Mecca, the discord of his sons and brothers gave an easy entrance to the Persians: they chased the strangers of Abyssinia beyond the Red Sea; and a native prince of the ancient Homerites was restored to the throne as the vassal or viceroy of the great Nushirvan. [4] But the nephew of Justinian declared his resolution to avenge the injuries of his Christian ally the prince of Abyssinia, as they suggested a decent pretence to discontinue the annual tribute, which was poorly disguised by the name of pension. The churches of Persarmenia were oppressed by the intolerant spirit of the Magi; [4/1] they secretly invoked the protector of the Christians, and, after the pious murder of their satraps, the rebels were avowed and supported as the brethren and subjects of the Roman emperor. The complaints of Nushirvan were disregarded by the Byzantine court; Justin yielded to the importunities of the Turks, who offered an alliance against the common enemy; and the Persian monarchy was threatened at the same instant by the united forces of Europe, of Aethiopia, and of Scythia. At the age of fourscore the sovereign of the East would perhaps have chosen the peaceful enjoyment of his glory and greatness; but as soon as war became inevitable, he took the field with the alacrity of youth, whilst the aggressor trembled in the palace of Constantinople. Nushirvan, or Chosroes, conducted in person the siege of Dara; and although that important fortress had been left destitute of troops and magazines, the valor of the inhabitants resisted above five months the archers, the elephants, and the military engines of the Great King. In the mean while his general Adarman advanced from Babylon, traversed the desert, passed the Euphrates, insulted the suburbs of Antioch, reduced to ashes the city of Apamea, and laid the spoils of Syria at the feet of his master, whose perseverance in the midst of winter at length subverted the bulwark of the East. But these losses, which astonished the provinces and the court, produced a salutary effect in the repentance and abdication of the emperor Justin: a new spirit arose in the Byzantine councils; and a truce of three years was obtained by the prudence of Tiberius. That seasonable interval was employed in the preparations of war; and the voice of rumor proclaimed to the world, that from the distant countries of the Alps and the Rhine, from Scythia, Maesia, Pannonia, Illyricum, and Isauria, the strength of the Imperial cavalry was reenforced with one hundred and fifty thousand soldiers. Yet the king of Persia, without fear, or without faith, resolved to prevent the attack of the enemy; again passed the Euphrates, and dismissing the ambassadors of Tiberius, arrogantly commanded them to await his arrival at Caesarea, the metropolis of the Cappadocian provinces. The two armies encountered each other in the battle of Melitene: [4/2] the Barbarians, who darkened the air with a cloud of arrows, prolonged their line, and extended their wings across the plain; while the Romans, in deep and solid bodies, expected to prevail in closer action, by the weight of their swords and lances. A Scythian chief, who commanded their right wing, suddenly turned the flank of the enemy, attacked their rear-guard in the presence of Chosroes, penetrated to the midst of the camp, pillaged the royal tent, profaned the eternal fire, loaded a train of camels with the spoils of Asia, cut his way through the Persian host, and returned with songs of victory to his friends, who had consumed the day in single combats, or ineffectual skirmishes. The darkness of the night, and the separation of the Romans, afforded the Persian monarch an opportunity of revenge; and one of their camps was swept away by a rapid and impetuous assault. But the review of his loss, and the consciousness of his danger, determined Chosroes to a speedy retreat: he burnt, in his passage, the vacant town of Melitene; and, without consulting the safety of his troops, boldly swam the Euphrates on the back of an elephant. After this unsuccessful campaign, the want of magazines, and perhaps some inroad of the Turks, obliged him to disband or divide his forces; the Romans were left masters of the field, and their general Justinian, advancing to the relief of the Persarmenian rebels, erected his standard on the banks of the Araxes. The great Pompey had formerly halted within three days' march of the Caspian: [5] that inland sea was explored, for the first time, by a hostile fleet, [6] and seventy thousand captives were transplanted from Hyrcania to the Isle of Cyprus. On the return of spring, Justinian descended into the fertile plains of Assyria; the flames of war approached the residence of Nushirvan; the indignant monarch sunk into the grave; and his last edict restrained his successors from exposing their person in battle against the Romans. [6/1] Yet the memory of this transient affront was lost in the glories of a long reign; and his formidable enemies, after indulging their dream of conquest, again solicited a short respite from the calamities of war. [7]

[Footnote 3: The general independence of the Arabs, which cannot be admitted without many limitations, is blindly asserted in a separate dissertation of the authors of the Universal History, vol. xx. p. 196—250. A perpetual miracle is supposed to have guarded the prophecy in favor of the posterity of Ishmael; and these learned bigots are not afraid to risk the truth of Christianity on this frail and slippery foundation. Note: It certainly appears difficult to extract a prediction of the perpetual independence of the Arabs from the text in Genesis, which would have received an ample fulfilment during centuries of uninvaded freedom. But the disputants appear to forget the inseparable connection in the prediction between the wild, the Bedoween habits of the Ismaelites, with their national independence. The stationary and civilized descendant of Ismael forfeited, as it were, his birthright, and ceased to be a genuine son of the "wild man" The phrase, "dwelling in the presence of his brethren," is interpreted by Rosenmuller (in loc.) and others, according to the Hebrew geography, "to the East" of his brethren, the legitimate race of Abraham—M.]

[Footnote 4: D'Herbelot, Biblioth. Orient. p. 477. Pocock, Specimen Hist. Arabum, p. 64, 65. Father Pagi (Critica, tom. ii. p. 646) has proved that, after ten years' peace, the Persian war, which continued twenty years, was renewed A.D. 571. Mahomet was born A.D. 569, in the year of the elephant, or the defeat of Abrahah, (Gagnier, Vie de Mahomet, tom. i. p. 89, 90, 98;) and this account allows two years for the conquest of Yemen. Note: Abrahah, according to some accounts, was succeeded by his son Taksoum, who reigned seventeen years; his brother Mascouh, who was slain in battle against the Persians, twelve. But this chronology is irreconcilable with the Arabian conquests of Nushirvan the Great. Either Seif, or his son Maadi Karb, was the native prince placed on the throne by the Persians. St. Martin, vol. x. p. 78. See likewise Johannsen, Hist. Yemanae—M.]

[Footnote 4/1: Persarmenia was long maintained in peace by the tolerant administration of Mejej, prince of the Gnounians. On his death he was succeeded by a persecutor, a Persian, named Ten-Schahpour, who attempted to propagate Zoroastrianism by violence. Nushirvan, on an appeal to the throne by the Armenian clergy, replaced Ten-Schahpour, in 552, by Veschnas-Vahram. The new marzban, or governor, was instructed to repress the bigoted Magi in their persecutions of the Armenians, but the Persian converts to Christianity were still exposed to cruel sufferings. The most distinguished of them, Izdbouzid, was crucified at Dovin in the presence of a vast multitude. The fame of this martyr spread to the West. Menander, the historian, not only, as appears by a fragment published by Mai, related this event in his history, but, according to M. St. Martin, wrote a tragedy on the subject. This, however, is an unwarrantable inference from the phrase which merely means that he related the tragic event in his history. An epigram on the same subject, preserved in the Anthology, Jacob's Anth. Palat. i. 27, belongs to the historian. Yet Armenia remained in peace under the government of Veschnas-Vahram and his successor Varazdat. The tyranny of his successor Surena led to the insurrection under Vartan, the Mamigonian, who revenged the death of his brother on the marzban Surena, surprised Dovin, and put to the sword the governor, the soldiers, and the Magians. From St. Martin, vol x. p. 79—89—M.]

[Footnote 4/2: Malathiah. It was in the lesser Armenia—M.]

[Footnote 5: He had vanquished the Albanians, who brought into the field 12,000 horse and 60,000 foot; but he dreaded the multitude of venomous reptiles, whose existence may admit of some doubt, as well as that of the neighboring Amazons. Plutarch, in Pompeio, tom. ii. p. 1165, 1166.]

[Footnote 6: In the history of the world I can only perceive two navies on the Caspian: 1. Of the Macedonians, when Patrocles, the admiral of the kings of Syria, Seleucus and Antiochus, descended most probably the River Oxus, from the confines of India, (Plin. Hist. Natur. vi. 21.) 2. Of the Russians, when Peter the First conducted a fleet and army from the neighborhood of Moscow to the coast of Persia, (Bell's Travels, vol. ii. p. 325—352.) He justly observes, that such martial pomp had never been displayed on the Volga.]

[Footnote 6/1: This circumstance rests on the statements of Evagrius and Theophylaci Simocatta. They are not of sufficient authority to establish a fact so improbable. St. Martin, vol. x. p. 140—M.]

[Footnote 7: For these Persian wars and treaties, see Menander, in Excerpt. Legat. p. 113—125. Theophanes Byzant. apud Photium, cod. lxiv p. 77, 80, 81. Evagrius, l. v. c. 7—15. Theophylact, l. iii. c. 9—16 Agathias, l. iv. p. 140.]

The throne of Chosroes Nushirvan was filled by Hormouz, or Hormisdas, the eldest or the most favored of his sons. With the kingdoms of Persia and India, he inherited the reputation and example of his father, the service, in every rank, of his wise and valiant officers, and a general system of administration, harmonized by time and political wisdom to promote the happiness of the prince and people. But the royal youth enjoyed a still more valuable blessing, the friendship of a sage who had presided over his education, and who always preferred the honor to the interest of his pupil, his interest to his inclination. In a dispute with the Greek and Indian philosophers, Buzurg [8] had once maintained, that the most grievous misfortune of life is old age without the remembrance of virtue; and our candor will presume that the same principle compelled him, during three years, to direct the councils of the Persian empire. His zeal was rewarded by the gratitude and docility of Hormouz, who acknowledged himself more indebted to his preceptor than to his parent: but when age and labor had impaired the strength, and perhaps the faculties, of this prudent counsellor, he retired from court, and abandoned the youthful monarch to his own passions and those of his favorites. By the fatal vicissitude of human affairs, the same scenes were renewed at Ctesiphon, which had been exhibited at Rome after the death of Marcus Antoninus. The ministers of flattery and corruption, who had been banished by his father, were recalled and cherished by the son; the disgrace and exile of the friends of Nushirvan established their tyranny; and virtue was driven by degrees from the mind of Hormouz, from his palace, and from the government of the state. The faithful agents, the eyes and ears of the king, informed him of the progress of disorder, that the provincial governors flew to their prey with the fierceness of lions and eagles, and that their rapine and injustice would teach the most loyal of his subjects to abhor the name and authority of their sovereign. The sincerity of this advice was punished with death; the murmurs of the cities were despised, their tumults were quelled by military execution: the intermediate powers between the throne and the people were abolished; and the childish vanity of Hormouz, who affected the daily use of the tiara, was fond of declaring, that he alone would be the judge as well as the master of his kingdom.

In every word, and in every action, the son of Nushirvan degenerated from the virtues of his father. His avarice defrauded the troops; his jealous caprice degraded the satraps; the palace, the tribunals, the waters of the Tigris, were stained with the blood of the innocent, and the tyrant exulted in the sufferings and execution of thirteen thousand victims. As the excuse of his cruelty, he sometimes condescended to observe, that the fears of the Persians would be productive of hatred, and that their hatred must terminate in rebellion but he forgot that his own guilt and folly had inspired the sentiments which he deplored, and prepared the event which he so justly apprehended. Exasperated by long and hopeless oppression, the provinces of Babylon, Susa, and Carmania, erected the standard of revolt; and the princes of Arabia, India, and Scythia, refused the customary tribute to the unworthy successor of Nushirvan. The arms of the Romans, in slow sieges and frequent inroads, afflicted the frontiers of Mesopotamia and Assyria: one of their generals professed himself the disciple of Scipio; and the soldiers were animated by a miraculous image of Christ, whose mild aspect should never have been displayed in the front of battle. [9] At the same time, the eastern provinces of Persia were invaded by the great khan, who passed the Oxus at the head of three or four hundred thousand Turks. The imprudent Hormouz accepted their perfidious and formidable aid; the cities of Khorassan or Bactriana were commanded to open their gates the march of the Barbarians towards the mountains of Hyrcania revealed the correspondence of the Turkish and Roman arms; and their union must have subverted the throne of the house of Sassan.

[Footnote 8: Buzurg Mihir may be considered, in his character and station, as the Seneca of the East; but his virtues, and perhaps his faults, are less known than those of the Roman, who appears to have been much more loquacious. The Persian sage was the person who imported from India the game of chess and the fables of Pilpay. Such has been the fame of his wisdom and virtues, that the Christians claim him as a believer in the gospel; and the Mahometans revere Buzurg as a premature Mussulman. D'Herbelot, Bibliotheque Orientale, p. 218.]

[Footnote 9: See the imitation of Scipio in Theophylact, l. i. c. 14; the image of Christ, l. ii. c. 3. Hereafter I shall speak more amply of the Christian images—I had almost said idols. This, if I am not mistaken, is the oldest of divine manufacture; but in the next thousand years, many others issued from the same workshop.]

Persia had been lost by a king; it was saved by a hero. After his revolt, Varanes or Bahram is stigmatized by the son of Hormouz as an ungrateful slave; the proud and ambiguous reproach of despotism, since he was truly descended from the ancient princes of Rei, [10] one of the seven families whose splendid, as well as substantial, prerogatives exalted them above the heads of the Persian nobility. [11] At the siege of Dara, the valor of Bahram was signalized under the eyes of Nushirvan, and both the father and son successively promoted him to the command of armies, the government of Media, and the superintendence of the palace. The popular prediction which marked him as the deliverer of Persia, might be inspired by his past victories and extraordinary figure: the epithet Giubin [11/1] is expressive of the quality of dry wood: he had the strength and stature of a giant; and his savage countenance was fancifully compared to that of a wild cat. While the nation trembled, while Hormouz disguised his terror by the name of suspicion, and his servants concealed their disloyalty under the mask of fear, Bahram alone displayed his undaunted courage and apparent fidelity: and as soon as he found that no more than twelve thousand soldiers would follow him against the enemy; he prudently declared, that to this fatal number Heaven had reserved the honors of the triumph. [11/2] The steep and narrow descent of the Pule Rudbar, [12] or Hyrcanian rock, is the only pass through which an army can penetrate into the territory of Rei and the plains of Media. From the commanding heights, a band of resolute men might overwhelm with stones and darts the myriads of the Turkish host: their emperor and his son were transpierced with arrows; and the fugitives were left, without counsel or provisions, to the revenge of an injured people. The patriotism of the Persian general was stimulated by his affection for the city of his forefathers: in the hour of victory, every peasant became a soldier, and every soldier a hero; and their ardor was kindled by the gorgeous spectacle of beds, and thrones, and tables of massy gold, the spoils of Asia, and the luxury of the hostile camp. A prince of a less malignant temper could not easily have forgiven his benefactor; and the secret hatred of Hormouz was envenomed by a malicious report, that Bahram had privately retained the most precious fruits of his Turkish victory. But the approach of a Roman army on the side of the Araxes compelled the implacable tyrant to smile and to applaud; and the toils of Bahram were rewarded with the permission of encountering a new enemy, by their skill and discipline more formidable than a Scythian multitude. Elated by his recent success, he despatched a herald with a bold defiance to the camp of the Romans, requesting them to fix a day of battle, and to choose whether they would pass the river themselves, or allow a free passage to the arms of the great king. The lieutenant of the emperor Maurice preferred the safer alternative; and this local circumstance, which would have enhanced the victory of the Persians, rendered their defeat more bloody and their escape more difficult. But the loss of his subjects, and the danger of his kingdom, were overbalanced in the mind of Hormouz by the disgrace of his personal enemy; and no sooner had Bahram collected and reviewed his forces, than he received from a royal messenger the insulting gift of a distaff, a spinning-wheel, and a complete suit of female apparel. Obedient to the will of his sovereign he showed himself to the soldiers in this unworthy disguise they resented his ignominy and their own; a shout of rebellion ran through the ranks; and the general accepted their oath of fidelity and vows of revenge. A second messenger, who had been commanded to bring the rebel in chains, was trampled under the feet of an elephant, and manifestos were diligently circulated, exhorting the Persians to assert their freedom against an odious and contemptible tyrant. The defection was rapid and universal; his loyal slaves were sacrificed to the public fury; the troops deserted to the standard of Bahram; and the provinces again saluted the deliverer of his country.

[Footnote 10: Ragae, or Rei, is mentioned in the Apocryphal book of Tobit as already flourishing, 700 years before Christ, under the Assyrian empire. Under the foreign names of Europus and Arsacia, this city, 500 stadia to the south of the Caspian gates, was successively embellished by the Macedonians and Parthians, (Strabo, l. xi. p. 796.) Its grandeur and populousness in the ixth century are exaggerated beyond the bounds of credibility; but Rei has been since ruined by wars and the unwholesomeness of the air. Chardin, Voyage en Perse, tom. i. p. 279, 280. D'Herbelot, Biblioth. Oriental. p. 714.]

[Footnote 11: Theophylact. l. iii. c. 18. The story of the seven Persians is told in the third book of Herodotus; and their noble descendants are often mentioned, especially in the fragments of Ctesias. Yet the independence of Otanes (Herodot. l. iii. c. 83, 84) is hostile to the spirit of despotism, and it may not seem probable that the seven families could survive the revolutions of eleven hundred years. They might, however, be represented by the seven ministers, (Brisson, de Regno Persico, l. i. p. 190;) and some Persian nobles, like the kings of Pontus (Polyb l. v. p. 540) and Cappadocia, (Diodor. Sicul. l. xxxi. tom. ii. p. 517,) might claim their descent from the bold companions of Darius.]

[Footnote 11/1: He is generally called Baharam Choubeen, Baharam, the stick-like, probably from his appearance. Malcolm, vol. i. p. 120—M.]

[Footnote 11/2: The Persian historians say, that Hormouz entreated his general to increase his numbers; but Baharam replied, that experience had taught him that it was the quality, not the number of soldiers, which gave success. No man in his army was under forty years, and none above fifty. Malcolm, vol. i. p. 121—M.]

[Footnote 12: See an accurate description of this mountain by Olearius, (Voyage en Perse, p. 997, 998,) who ascended it with much difficulty and danger in his return from Ispahan to the Caspian Sea.]

As the passes were faithfully guarded, Hormouz could only compute the number of his enemies by the testimony of a guilty conscience, and the daily defection of those who, in the hour of his distress, avenged their wrongs, or forgot their obligations. He proudly displayed the ensigns of royalty; but the city and palace of Modain had already escaped from the hand of the tyrant. Among the victims of his cruelty, Bindoes, a Sassanian prince, had been cast into a dungeon; his fetters were broken by the zeal and courage of a brother; and he stood before the king at the head of those trusty guards, who had been chosen as the ministers of his confinement, and perhaps of his death. Alarmed by the hasty intrusion and bold reproaches of the captive, Hormouz looked round, but in vain, for advice or assistance; discovered that his strength consisted in the obedience of others; and patiently yielded to the single arm of Bindoes, who dragged him from the throne to the same dungeon in which he himself had been so lately confined. At the first tumult, Chosroes, the eldest of the sons of Hormouz, escaped from the city; he was persuaded to return by the pressing and friendly invitation of Bindoes, who promised to seat him on his father's throne, and who expected to reign under the name of an inexperienced youth. In the just assurance, that his accomplices could neither forgive nor hope to be forgiven, and that every Persian might be trusted as the judge and enemy of the tyrant, he instituted a public trial without a precedent and without a copy in the annals of the East. The son of Nushirvan, who had requested to plead in his own defence, was introduced as a criminal into the full assembly of the nobles and satraps. [13] He was heard with decent attention as long as he expatiated on the advantages of order and obedience, the danger of innovation, and the inevitable discord of those who had encouraged each other to trample on their lawful and hereditary sovereign. By a pathetic appeal to their humanity, he extorted that pity which is seldom refused to the fallen fortunes of a king; and while they beheld the abject posture and squalid appearance of the prisoner, his tears, his chains, and the marks of ignominious stripes, it was impossible to forget how recently they had adored the divine splendor of his diadem and purple. But an angry murmur arose in the assembly as soon as he presumed to vindicate his conduct, and to applaud the victories of his reign. He defined the duties of a king, and the Persian nobles listened with a smile of contempt; they were fired with indignation when he dared to vilify the character of Chosroes; and by the indiscreet offer of resigning the sceptre to the second of his sons, he subscribed his own condemnation, and sacrificed the life of his own innocent favorite. The mangled bodies of the boy and his mother were exposed to the people; the eyes of Hormouz were pierced with a hot needle; and the punishment of the father was succeeded by the coronation of his eldest son. Chosroes had ascended the throne without guilt, and his piety strove to alleviate the misery of the abdicated monarch; from the dungeon he removed Hormouz to an apartment of the palace, supplied with liberality the consolations of sensual enjoyment, and patiently endured the furious sallies of his resentment and despair. He might despise the resentment of a blind and unpopular tyrant, but the tiara was trembling on his head, till he could subvert the power, or acquire the friendship, of the great Bahram, who sternly denied the justice of a revolution, in which himself and his soldiers, the true representatives of Persia, had never been consulted. The offer of a general amnesty, and of the second rank in his kingdom, was answered by an epistle from Bahram, friend of the gods, conqueror of men, and enemy of tyrants, the satrap of satraps, general of the Persian armies, and a prince adorned with the title of eleven virtues. [14] He commands Chosroes, the son of Hormouz, to shun the example and fate of his father, to confine the traitors who had been released from their chains, to deposit in some holy place the diadem which he had usurped, and to accept from his gracious benefactor the pardon of his faults and the government of a province. The rebel might not be proud, and the king most assuredly was not humble; but the one was conscious of his strength, the other was sensible of his weakness; and even the modest language of his reply still left room for treaty and reconciliation. Chosroes led into the field the slaves of the palace and the populace of the capital: they beheld with terror the banners of a veteran army; they were encompassed and surprised by the evolutions of the general; and the satraps who had deposed Hormouz, received the punishment of their revolt, or expiated their first treason by a second and more criminal act of disloyalty. The life and liberty of Chosroes were saved, but he was reduced to the necessity of imploring aid or refuge in some foreign land; and the implacable Bindoes, anxious to secure an unquestionable title, hastily returned to the palace, and ended, with a bowstring, the wretched existence of the son of Nushirvan. [15]

[Footnote 13: The Orientals suppose that Bahram convened this assembly and proclaimed Chosroes; but Theophylact is, in this instance, more distinct and credible. Note: Yet Theophylact seems to have seized the opportunity to indulge his propensity for writing orations; and the orations read rather like those of a Grecian sophist than of an Eastern assembly—M.]

[Footnote 14: See the words of Theophylact, l. iv. c. 7., &c. In answer, Chosroes styles himself in genuine Oriental bombast.]

[Footnote 15: Theophylact (l. iv. c. 7) imputes the death of Hormouz to his son, by whose command he was beaten to death with clubs. I have followed the milder account of Khondemir and Eutychius, and shall always be content with the slightest evidence to extenuate the crime of parricide. Note: Malcolm concurs in ascribing his death to Bundawee, (Bindoes,) vol. i. p. 123. The Eastern writers generally impute the crime to the uncle St. Martin, vol. x. p. 300—M.]

While Chosroes despatched the preparations of his retreat, he deliberated with his remaining friends, [16] whether he should lurk in the valleys of Mount Caucasus, or fly to the tents of the Turks, or solicit the protection of the emperor. The long emulation of the successors of Artaxerxes and Constantine increased his reluctance to appear as a suppliant in a rival court; but he weighed the forces of the Romans, and prudently considered that the neighborhood of Syria would render his escape more easy and their succors more effectual. Attended only by his concubines, and a troop of thirty guards, he secretly departed from the capital, followed the banks of the Euphrates, traversed the desert, and halted at the distance of ten miles from Circesium. About the third watch of the night, the Roman praefect was informed of his approach, and he introduced the royal stranger to the fortress at the dawn of day. From thence the king of Persia was conducted to the more honorable residence of Hierapolis; and Maurice dissembled his pride, and displayed his benevolence, at the reception of the letters and ambassadors of the grandson of Nushirvan. They humbly represented the vicissitudes of fortune and the common interest of princes, exaggerated the ingratitude of Bahram, the agent of the evil principle, and urged, with specious argument, that it was for the advantage of the Romans themselves to support the two monarchies which balance the world, the two great luminaries by whose salutary influence it is vivified and adorned. The anxiety of Chosroes was soon relieved by the assurance, that the emperor had espoused the cause of justice and royalty; but Maurice prudently declined the expense and delay of his useless visit to Constantinople. In the name of his generous benefactor, a rich diadem was presented to the fugitive prince, with an inestimable gift of jewels and gold; a powerful army was assembled on the frontiers of Syria and Armenia, under the command of the valiant and faithful Narses, [17] and this general, of his own nation, and his own choice, was directed to pass the Tigris, and never to sheathe his sword till he had restored Chosroes to the throne of his ancestors. [17/1] The enterprise, however splendid, was less arduous than it might appear. Persia had already repented of her fatal rashness, which betrayed the heir of the house of Sassan to the ambition of a rebellious subject: and the bold refusal of the Magi to consecrate his usurpation, compelled Bahram to assume the sceptre, regardless of the laws and prejudices of the nation. The palace was soon distracted with conspiracy, the city with tumult, the provinces with insurrection; and the cruel execution of the guilty and the suspected served to irritate rather than subdue the public discontent. No sooner did the grandson of Nushirvan display his own and the Roman banners beyond the Tigris, than he was joined, each day, by the increasing multitudes of the nobility and people; and as he advanced, he received from every side the grateful offerings of the keys of his cities and the heads of his enemies. As soon as Modain was freed from the presence of the usurper, the loyal inhabitants obeyed the first summons of Mebodes at the head of only two thousand horse, and Chosroes accepted the sacred and precious ornaments of the palace as the pledge of their truth and the presage of his approaching success. After the junction of the Imperial troops, which Bahram vainly struggled to prevent, the contest was decided by two battles on the banks of the Zab, and the confines of Media. The Romans, with the faithful subjects of Persia, amounted to sixty thousand, while the whole force of the usurper did not exceed forty thousand men: the two generals signalized their valor and ability; but the victory was finally determined by the prevalence of numbers and discipline. With the remnant of a broken army, Bahram fled towards the eastern provinces of the Oxus: the enmity of Persia reconciled him to the Turks; but his days were shortened by poison, perhaps the most incurable of poisons; the stings of remorse and despair, and the bitter remembrance of lost glory. Yet the modern Persians still commemorate the exploits of Bahram; and some excellent laws have prolonged the duration of his troubled and transitory reign. [17/1]

[Footnote 16: After the battle of Pharsalia, the Pompey of Lucan (l. viii. 256—455) holds a similar debate. He was himself desirous of seeking the Parthians: but his companions abhorred the unnatural alliance and the adverse prejudices might operate as forcibly on Chosroes and his companions, who could describe, with the same vehemence, the contrast of laws, religion, and manners, between the East and West.]

[Footnote 17: In this age there were three warriors of the name of Narses, who have been often confounded, (Pagi, Critica, tom. ii. p. 640:) 1. A Persarmenian, the brother of Isaac and Armatius, who, after a successful action against Belisarius, deserted from his Persian sovereign, and afterwards served in the Italian war—2. The eunuch who conquered Italy—3. The restorer of Chosroes, who is celebrated in the poem of Corippus (l. iii. 220—327) as excelsus super omnia vertico agmina.... habitu modestus.... morum probitate placens, virtute verendus; fulmineus, cautus, vigilans, &c.]

[Footnote 17/1: The Armenians adhered to Chosroes. St. Martin, vol. x. p. 312—M.]

[Footnote 17/2: According to Mivkhond and the Oriental writers, Bahram received the daughter of the Khakan in marriage, and commanded a body of Turks in an invasion of Persia. Some say that he was assassinated; Malcolm adopts the opinion that he was poisoned. His sister Gourdieh, the companion of his flight, is celebrated in the Shah Nameh. She was afterwards one of the wives of Chosroes. St. Martin. vol. x. p. 331—M.]

The restoration of Chosroes was celebrated with feasts and executions; and the music of the royal banquet was often disturbed by the groans of dying or mutilated criminals. A general pardon might have diffused comfort and tranquillity through a country which had been shaken by the late revolutions; yet, before the sanguinary temper of Chosroes is blamed, we should learn whether the Persians had not been accustomed either to dread the rigor, or to despise the weakness, of their sovereign. The revolt of Bahram, and the conspiracy of the satraps, were impartially punished by the revenge or justice of the conqueror; the merits of Bindoes himself could not purify his hand from the guilt of royal blood: and the son of Hormouz was desirous to assert his own innocence, and to vindicate the sanctity of kings. During the vigor of the Roman power, several princes were seated on the throne of Persia by the arms and the authority of the first Caesars. But their new subjects were soon disgusted with the vices or virtues which they had imbibed in a foreign land; the instability of their dominion gave birth to a vulgar observation, that the choice of Rome was solicited and rejected with equal ardor by the capricious levity of Oriental slaves. But the glory of Maurice was conspicuous in the long and fortunate reign of his son and his ally. A band of a thousand Romans, who continued to guard the person of Chosroes, proclaimed his confidence in the fidelity of the strangers; his growing strength enabled him to dismiss this unpopular aid, but he steadily professed the same gratitude and reverence to his adopted father; and till the death of Maurice, the peace and alliance of the two empires were faithfully maintained. [18] Yet the mercenary friendship of the Roman prince had been purchased with costly and important gifts; the strong cities of Martyropolis and Dara [18/1] were restored, and the Persarmenians became the willing subjects of an empire, whose eastern limit was extended, beyond the example of former times, as far as the banks of the Araxes, and the neighborhood of the Caspian. A pious hope was indulged, that the church as well as the state might triumph in this revolution: but if Chosroes had sincerely listened to the Christian bishops, the impression was erased by the zeal and eloquence of the Magi: if he was armed with philosophic indifference, he accommodated his belief, or rather his professions, to the various circumstances of an exile and a sovereign. The imaginary conversion of the king of Persia was reduced to a local and superstitious veneration for Sergius, [19] one of the saints of Antioch, who heard his prayers and appeared to him in dreams; he enriched the shrine with offerings of gold and silver, and ascribed to this invisible patron the success of his arms, and the pregnancy of Sira, a devout Christian and the best beloved of his wives. [20] The beauty of Sira, or Schirin, [21] her wit, her musical talents, are still famous in the history, or rather in the romances, of the East: her own name is expressive, in the Persian tongue, of sweetness and grace; and the epithet of Parviz alludes to the charms of her royal lover. Yet Sira never shared the passions which she inspired, and the bliss of Chosroes was tortured by a jealous doubt, that while he possessed her person, she had bestowed her affections on a meaner favorite. [22]

[Footnote 18: Experimentis cognitum est Barbaros malle Roma petere reges quam habere. These experiments are admirably represented in the invitation and expulsion of Vonones, (Annal. ii. 1—3,) Tiridates, (Annal. vi. 32-44,) and Meherdates, (Annal. xi. 10, xii. 10-14.) The eye of Tacitus seems to have transpierced the camp of the Parthians and the walls of the harem.]

[Footnote 18/1: Concerning Nisibis, see St. Martin and his Armenian authorities, vol. x p. 332, and Memoires sur l'Armenie, tom. i. p. 25—M.]

[Footnote 19: Sergius and his companion Bacchus, who are said to have suffered in the persecution of Maximian, obtained divine honor in France, Italy, Constantinople, and the East. Their tomb at Rasaphe was famous for miracles, and that Syrian town acquired the more honorable name of Sergiopolis. Tillemont, Mem. Eccles. tom. v. p. 481—496. Butler's Saints, vol. x. p. 155.]

[Footnote 20: Evagrius (l. vi. c. 21) and Theophylact (l. v. c. 13, 14) have preserved the original letters of Chosroes, written in Greek, signed with his own hand, and afterwards inscribed on crosses and tables of gold, which were deposited in the church of Sergiopolis. They had been sent to the bishop of Antioch, as primate of Syria. Note: St. Martin thinks that they were first written in Syriac, and then translated into the bad Greek in which they appear, vol. x. p. 334—M.]

[Footnote 21: The Greeks only describe her as a Roman by birth, a Christian by religion: but she is represented as the daughter of the emperor Maurice in the Persian and Turkish romances which celebrate the love of Khosrou for Schirin, of Schirin for Ferhad, the most beautiful youth of the East, D'Herbelot, Biblioth. Orient. p. 789, 997, 998. Note: Compare M. von Hammer's preface to, and poem of, Schirin in which he gives an account of the various Persian poems, of which he has endeavored to extract the essence in his own work—M.]

[Footnote 22: The whole series of the tyranny of Hormouz, the revolt of Bahram, and the flight and restoration of Chosroes, is related by two contemporary Greeks—more concisely by Evagrius, (l. vi. c. 16, 17, 18, 19,) and most diffusely by Theophylact Simocatta, (l. iii. c. 6—18, l. iv. c. 1—16, l. v. c. 1-15:) succeeding compilers, Zonaras and Cedrenus, can only transcribe and abridge. The Christian Arabs, Eutychius (Annal. tom. ii. p. 200—208) and Abulpharagius (Dynast. p. 96—98) appear to have consulted some particular memoirs. The great Persian historians of the xvth century, Mirkhond and Khondemir, are only known to me by the imperfect extracts of Schikard, (Tarikh, p. 150—155,) Texeira, or rather Stevens, (Hist. of Persia, p. 182—186,) a Turkish Ms. translated by the Abbe Fourmount, (Hist. de l'Academie des Inscriptions, tom. vii. p. 325—334,) and D'Herbelot, (aux mots Hormouz, p. 457—459. Bahram, p. 174. Khosrou Parviz, p. 996.) Were I perfectly satisfied of their authority, I could wish these Oriental materials had been more copious.]

PART II

While the majesty of the Roman name was revived in the East, the prospect of Europe is less pleasing and less glorious. By the departure of the Lombards, and the ruin of the Gepidae, the balance of power was destroyed on the Danube; and the Avars spread their permanent dominion from the foot of the Alps to the sea-coast of the Euxine. The reign of Baian is the brightest aera of their monarchy; their chagan, who occupied the rustic palace of Attila, appears to have imitated his character and policy; [23] but as the same scenes were repeated in a smaller circle, a minute representation of the copy would be devoid of the greatness and novelty of the original. The pride of the second Justin, of Tiberius, and Maurice, was humbled by a proud Barbarian, more prompt to inflict, than exposed to suffer, the injuries of war; and as often as Asia was threatened by the Persian arms, Europe was oppressed by the dangerous inroads, or costly friendship, of the Avars. When the Roman envoys approached the presence of the chagan, they were commanded to wait at the door of his tent, till, at the end perhaps of ten or twelve days, he condescended to admit them. If the substance or the style of their message was offensive to his ear, he insulted, with real or affected fury, their own dignity, and that of their prince; their baggage was plundered, and their lives were only saved by the promise of a richer present and a more respectful address. But his sacred ambassadors enjoyed and abused an unbounded license in the midst of Constantinople: they urged, with importunate clamors, the increase of tribute, or the restitution of captives and deserters: and the majesty of the empire was almost equally degraded by a base compliance, or by the false and fearful excuses with which they eluded such insolent demands. The chagan had never seen an elephant; and his curiosity was excited by the strange, and perhaps fabulous, portrait of that wonderful animal. At his command, one of the largest elephants of the Imperial stables was equipped with stately caparisons, and conducted by a numerous train to the royal village in the plains of Hungary. He surveyed the enormous beast with surprise, with disgust, and possibly with terror; and smiled at the vain industry of the Romans, who, in search of such useless rarities, could explore the limits of the land and sea. He wished, at the expense of the emperor, to repose in a golden bed. The wealth of Constantinople, and the skilful diligence of her artists, were instantly devoted to the gratification of his caprice; but when the work was finished, he rejected with scorn a present so unworthy the majesty of a great king. [24] These were the casual sallies of his pride; but the avarice of the chagan was a more steady and tractable passion: a rich and regular supply of silk apparel, furniture, and plate, introduced the rudiments of art and luxury among the tents of the Scythians; their appetite was stimulated by the pepper and cinnamon of India; [25] the annual subsidy or tribute was raised from fourscore to one hundred and twenty thousand pieces of gold; and after each hostile interruption, the payment of the arrears, with exorbitant interest, was always made the first condition of the new treaty. In the language of a Barbarian, without guile, the prince of the Avars affected to complain of the insincerity of the Greeks; [26] yet he was not inferior to the most civilized nations in the refinement of dissimulation and perfidy. As the successor of the Lombards, the chagan asserted his claim to the important city of Sirmium, the ancient bulwark of the Illyrian provinces. [27] The plains of the Lower Hungary were covered with the Avar horse and a fleet of large boats was built in the Hercynian wood, to descend the Danube, and to transport into the Save the materials of a bridge. But as the strong garrison of Singidunum, which commanded the conflux of the two rivers, might have stopped their passage and baffled his designs, he dispelled their apprehensions by a solemn oath that his views were not hostile to the empire. He swore by his sword, the symbol of the god of war, that he did not, as the enemy of Rome, construct a bridge upon the Save. "If I violate my oath," pursued the intrepid Baian, "may I myself, and the last of my nation, perish by the sword! May the heavens, and fire, the deity of the heavens, fall upon our heads! May the forests and mountains bury us in their ruins! and the Save returning, against the laws of nature, to his source, overwhelm us in his angry waters!" After this barbarous imprecation, he calmly inquired, what oath was most sacred and venerable among the Christians, what guilt or perjury it was most dangerous to incur. The bishop of Singidunum presented the gospel, which the chagan received with devout reverence. "I swear," said he, "by the God who has spoken in this holy book, that I have neither falsehood on my tongue, nor treachery in my heart." As soon as he rose from his knees, he accelerated the labor of the bridge, and despatched an envoy to proclaim what he no longer wished to conceal. "Inform the emperor," said the perfidious Baian, "that Sirmium is invested on every side. Advise his prudence to withdraw the citizens and their effects, and to resign a city which it is now impossible to relieve or defend." Without the hope of relief, the defence of Sirmium was prolonged above three years: the walls were still untouched; but famine was enclosed within the walls, till a merciful capitulation allowed the escape of the naked and hungry inhabitants. Singidunum, at the distance of fifty miles, experienced a more cruel fate: the buildings were razed, and the vanquished people was condemned to servitude and exile. Yet the ruins of Sirmium are no longer visible; the advantageous situation of Singidunum soon attracted a new colony of Sclavonians, and the conflux of the Save and Danube is still guarded by the fortifications of Belgrade, or the White City, so often and so obstinately disputed by the Christian and Turkish arms. [28] From Belgrade to the walls of Constantinople a line may be measured of six hundred miles: that line was marked with flames and with blood; the horses of the Avars were alternately bathed in the Euxine and the Adriatic; and the Roman pontiff, alarmed by the approach of a more savage enemy, [29] was reduced to cherish the Lombards, as the protectors of Italy. The despair of a captive, whom his country refused to ransom, disclosed to the Avars the invention and practice of military engines. [30] But in the first attempts they were rudely framed, and awkwardly managed; and the resistance of Diocletianopolis and Beraea, of Philippopolis and Adrianople, soon exhausted the skill and patience of the besiegers. The warfare of Baian was that of a Tartar; yet his mind was susceptible of a humane and generous sentiment: he spared Anchialus, whose salutary waters had restored the health of the best beloved of his wives; and the Romans confessed, that their starving army was fed and dismissed by the liberality of a foe. His empire extended over Hungary, Poland, and Prussia, from the mouth of the Danube to that of the Oder; [31] and his new subjects were divided and transplanted by the jealous policy of the conqueror. [32] The eastern regions of Germany, which had been left vacant by the emigration of the Vandals, were replenished with Sclavonian colonists; the same tribes are discovered in the neighborhood of the Adriatic and of the Baltic, and with the name of Baian himself, the Illyrian cities of Neyss and Lissa are again found in the heart of Silesia. In the disposition both of his troops and provinces the chagan exposed the vassals, whose lives he disregarded, [33] to the first assault; and the swords of the enemy were blunted before they encountered the native valor of the Avars.

[Footnote 23: A general idea of the pride and power of the chagan may be taken from Menander (Excerpt. Legat. p. 118, &c.) and Theophylact, (l. i. c. 3, l. vii. c. 15,) whose eight books are much more honorable to the Avar than to the Roman prince. The predecessors of Baian had tasted the liberality of Rome, and he survived the reign of Maurice, (Buat, Hist. des Peuples Barbares, tom. xi. p. 545.) The chagan who invaded Italy, A.D. 611, (Muratori, Annali, tom. v. p. 305,) was then invenili aetate florentem, (Paul Warnefrid, de Gest. Langobard. l v c 38,) the son, perhaps, or the grandson, of Baian.]

[Footnote 24: Theophylact, l. i. c. 5, 6.]

[Footnote 25: Even in the field, the chagan delighted in the use of these aromatics. He solicited, as a gift, and received. Theophylact, l. vii. c. 13. The Europeans of the ruder ages consumed more spices in their meat and drink than is compatible with the delicacy of a modern palate. Vie Privee des Francois, tom. ii. p. 162, 163.]

[Footnote 26: Theophylact, l. vi. c. 6, l. vii. c. 15. The Greek historian confesses the truth and justice of his reproach]

[Footnote 27: Menander (in Excerpt. Legat. p. 126—132, 174, 175) describes the perjury of Baian and the surrender of Sirmium. We have lost his account of the siege, which is commended by Theophylact, l. i. c. 3. Note: Compare throughout Schlozer Nordische Geschichte, p. 362—373—M.]

[Footnote 28: See D'Anville, in the Memoires de l'Acad. des Inscriptions, tom. xxviii. p. 412—443. The Sclavonic name of Belgrade is mentioned in the xth century by Constantine Porphyrogenitus: the Latin appellation of Alba Croeca is used by the Franks in the beginning of the ixth, (p. 414.)]

[Footnote 29: Baron. Annal. Eccles. A. B. 600, No. 1. Paul Warnefrid (l. iv. c. 38) relates their irruption into Friuli, and (c. 39) the captivity of his ancestors, about A.D. 632. The Sclavi traversed the Adriatic cum multitudine navium, and made a descent in the territory of Sipontum, (c. 47.)]

[Footnote 30: Even the helepolis, or movable turret. Theophylact, l. ii. 16, 17.]

[Footnote 31: The arms and alliances of the chagan reached to the neighborhood of a western sea, fifteen months' journey from Constantinople. The emperor Maurice conversed with some itinerant harpers from that remote country, and only seems to have mistaken a trade for a nation Theophylact, l. vi. c. 2.]

[Footnote 32: This is one of the most probable and luminous conjectures of the learned count de Buat, (Hist. des Peuples Barbares, tom. xi. p. 546—568.) The Tzechi and Serbi are found together near Mount Caucasus, in Illyricum, and on the lower Elbe. Even the wildest traditions of the Bohemians, &c., afford some color to his hypothesis.]

[Footnote 33: See Fredegarius, in the Historians of France, tom. ii. p. 432. Baian did not conceal his proud insensibility.]

The Persian alliance restored the troops of the East to the defence of Europe: and Maurice, who had supported ten years the insolence of the chagan, declared his resolution to march in person against the Barbarians. In the space of two centuries, none of the successors of Theodosius had appeared in the field: their lives were supinely spent in the palace of Constantinople; and the Greeks could no longer understand, that the name of emperor, in its primitive sense, denoted the chief of the armies of the republic. The martial ardor of Maurice was opposed by the grave flattery of the senate, the timid superstition of the patriarch, and the tears of the empress Constantina; and they all conjured him to devolve on some meaner general the fatigues and perils of a Scythian campaign. Deaf to their advice and entreaty, the emperor boldly advanced [34] seven miles from the capital; the sacred ensign of the cross was displayed in the front; and Maurice reviewed, with conscious pride, the arms and numbers of the veterans who had fought and conquered beyond the Tigris. Anchialus was the last term of his progress by sea and land; he solicited, without success, a miraculous answer to his nocturnal prayers; his mind was confounded by the death of a favorite horse, the encounter of a wild boar, a storm of wind and rain, and the birth of a monstrous child; and he forgot that the best of omens is to unsheathe our sword in the defence of our country. [35] Under the pretence of receiving the ambassadors of Persia, the emperor returned to Constantinople, exchanged the thoughts of war for those of devotion, and disappointed the public hope by his absence and the choice of his lieutenants. The blind partiality of fraternal love might excuse the promotion of his brother Peter, who fled with equal disgrace from the Barbarians, from his own soldiers and from the inhabitants of a Roman city. That city, if we may credit the resemblance of name and character, was the famous Azimuntium, [36] which had alone repelled the tempest of Attila. The example of her warlike youth was propagated to succeeding generations; and they obtained, from the first or the second Justin, an honorable privilege, that their valor should be always reserved for the defence of their native country. The brother of Maurice attempted to violate this privilege, and to mingle a patriot band with the mercenaries of his camp; they retired to the church, he was not awed by the sanctity of the place; the people rose in their cause, the gates were shut, the ramparts were manned; and the cowardice of Peter was found equal to his arrogance and injustice. The military fame of Commentiolus [37] is the object of satire or comedy rather than of serious history, since he was even deficient in the vile and vulgar qualification of personal courage. His solemn councils, strange evolutions, and secret orders, always supplied an apology for flight or delay. If he marched against the enemy, the pleasant valleys of Mount Haemus opposed an insuperable barrier; but in his retreat, he explored, with fearless curiosity, the most difficult and obsolete paths, which had almost escaped the memory of the oldest native. The only blood which he lost was drawn, in a real or affected malady, by the lancet of a surgeon; and his health, which felt with exquisite sensibility the approach of the Barbarians, was uniformly restored by the repose and safety of the winter season. A prince who could promote and support this unworthy favorite must derive no glory from the accidental merit of his colleague Priscus. [38] In five successive battles, which seem to have been conducted with skill and resolution, seventeen thousand two hundred Barbarians were made prisoners: near sixty thousand, with four sons of the chagan, were slain: the Roman general surprised a peaceful district of the Gepidae, who slept under the protection of the Avars; and his last trophies were erected on the banks of the Danube and the Teyss. Since the death of Trajan the arms of the empire had not penetrated so deeply into the old Dacia: yet the success of Priscus was transient and barren; and he was soon recalled by the apprehension that Baian, with dauntless spirit and recruited forces, was preparing to avenge his defeat under the walls of Constantinople. [39]

[Footnote 34: See the march and return of Maurice, in Theophylact, l. v. c. 16 l. vi. c. 1, 2, 3. If he were a writer of taste or genius, we might suspect him of an elegant irony: but Theophylact is surely harmless.]

[Footnote 35: Iliad, xii. 243. This noble verse, which unites the spirit of a hero with the reason of a sage, may prove that Homer was in every light superior to his age and country.]

[Footnote 36: Theophylact, l. vii. c. 3. On the evidence of this fact, which had not occurred to my memory, the candid reader will correct and excuse a note in Chapter XXXIV., note 86 of this History, which hastens the decay of Asimus, or Azimuntium; another century of patriotism and valor is cheaply purchased by such a confession.]

[Footnote 37: See the shameful conduct of Commentiolus, in Theophylact, l. ii. c. 10—15, l. vii. c. 13, 14, l. viii. c. 2, 4.]

[Footnote 38: See the exploits of Priscus, l. viii. c. 23.]

[Footnote 39: The general detail of the war against the Avars may be traced in the first, second, sixth, seventh, and eighth books of the history of the emperor Maurice, by Theophylact Simocatta. As he wrote in the reign of Heraclius, he had no temptation to flatter; but his want of judgment renders him diffuse in trifles, and concise in the most interesting facts.]

The theory of war was not more familiar to the camps of Caesar and Trajan, than to those of Justinian and Maurice. [40] The iron of Tuscany or Pontus still received the keenest temper from the skill of the Byzantine workmen. The magazines were plentifully stored with every species of offensive and defensive arms. In the construction and use of ships, engines, and fortifications, the Barbarians admired the superior ingenuity of a people whom they had so often vanquished in the field. The science of tactics, the order, evolutions, and stratagems of antiquity, was transcribed and studied in the books of the Greeks and Romans. But the solitude or degeneracy of the provinces could no longer supply a race of men to handle those weapons, to guard those walls, to navigate those ships, and to reduce the theory of war into bold and successful practice. The genius of Belisarius and Narses had been formed without a master, and expired without a disciple Neither honor, nor patriotism, nor generous superstition, could animate the lifeless bodies of slaves and strangers, who had succeeded to the honors of the legions: it was in the camp alone that the emperor should have exercised a despotic command; it was only in the camps that his authority was disobeyed and insulted: he appeased and inflamed with gold the licentiousness of the troops; but their vices were inherent, their victories were accidental, and their costly maintenance exhausted the substance of a state which they were unable to defend. After a long and pernicious indulgence, the cure of this inveterate evil was undertaken by Maurice; but the rash attempt, which drew destruction on his own head, tended only to aggravate the disease. A reformer should be exempt from the suspicion of interest, and he must possess the confidence and esteem of those whom he proposes to reclaim. The troops of Maurice might listen to the voice of a victorious leader; they disdained the admonitions of statesmen and sophists; and, when they received an edict which deducted from their pay the price of their arms and clothing, they execrated the avarice of a prince insensible of the dangers and fatigues from which he had escaped.

The camps both of Asia and Europe were agitated with frequent and furious seditions; [41] the enraged soldiers of Edessa pursued with reproaches, with threats, with wounds, their trembling generals; they overturned the statues of the emperor, cast stones against the miraculous image of Christ, and either rejected the yoke of all civil and military laws, or instituted a dangerous model of voluntary subordination. The monarch, always distant and often deceived, was incapable of yielding or persisting, according to the exigence of the moment. But the fear of a general revolt induced him too readily to accept any act of valor, or any expression of loyalty, as an atonement for the popular offence; the new reform was abolished as hastily as it had been announced, and the troops, instead of punishment and restraint, were agreeably surprised by a gracious proclamation of immunities and rewards. But the soldiers accepted without gratitude the tardy and reluctant gifts of the emperor: their insolence was elated by the discovery of his weakness and their own strength; and their mutual hatred was inflamed beyond the desire of forgiveness or the hope of reconciliation. The historians of the times adopt the vulgar suspicion, that Maurice conspired to destroy the troops whom he had labored to reform; the misconduct and favor of Commentiolus are imputed to this malevolent design; and every age must condemn the inhumanity of avarice [42] of a prince, who, by the trifling ransom of six thousand pieces of gold, might have prevented the massacre of twelve thousand prisoners in the hands of the chagan. In the just fervor of indignation, an order was signified to the army of the Danube, that they should spare the magazines of the province, and establish their winter quarters in the hostile country of the Avars. The measure of their grievances was full: they pronounced Maurice unworthy to reign, expelled or slaughtered his faithful adherents, and, under the command of Phocas, a simple centurion, returned by hasty marches to the neighborhood of Constantinople. After a long series of legal succession, the military disorders of the third century were again revived; yet such was the novelty of the enterprise, that the insurgents were awed by their own rashness. They hesitated to invest their favorite with the vacant purple; and, while they rejected all treaty with Maurice himself, they held a friendly correspondence with his son Theodosius, and with Germanus, the father-in-law of the royal youth. So obscure had been the former condition of Phocas, that the emperor was ignorant of the name and character of his rival; but as soon as he learned, that the centurion, though bold in sedition, was timid in the face of danger, "Alas!" cried the desponding prince, "if he is a coward, he will surely be a murderer."

[Footnote 40: Maurice himself composed xii books on the military art, which are still extant, and have been published (Upsal, 1664) by John Schaeffer, at the end of the Tactics of Arrian, (Fabricius, Bibliot Graeca, l. iv. c. 8, tom. iii. p. 278,) who promises to speak more fully of his work in its proper place.]

[Footnote 41: See the mutinies under the reign of Maurice, in Theophylact l iii c. 1—4,.vi. c. 7, 8, 10, l. vii. c. 1 l. viii. c. 6, &c.]

[Footnote 42: Theophylact and Theophanes seem ignorant of the conspiracy and avarice of Maurice. These charges, so unfavorable to the memory of that emperor, are first mentioned by the author of the Paschal Chronicle, (p. 379, 280;) from whence Zonaras (tom. ii. l. xiv. p. 77, 78) has transcribed them. Cedrenus (p. 399) has followed another computation of the ransom.]

Yet if Constantinople had been firm and faithful, the murderer might have spent his fury against the walls; and the rebel army would have been gradually consumed or reconciled by the prudence of the emperor. In the games of the Circus, which he repeated with unusual pomp, Maurice disguised, with smiles of confidence, the anxiety of his heart, condescended to solicit the applause of the factions, and flattered their pride by accepting from their respective tribunes a list of nine hundred blues and fifteen hundred greens, whom he affected to esteem as the solid pillars of his throne Their treacherous or languid support betrayed his weakness and hastened his fall: the green faction were the secret accomplices of the rebels, and the blues recommended lenity and moderation in a contest with their Roman brethren The rigid and parsimonious virtues of Maurice had long since alienated the hearts of his subjects: as he walked barefoot in a religious procession, he was rudely assaulted with stones, and his guards were compelled to present their iron maces in the defence of his person. A fanatic monk ran through the streets with a drawn sword, denouncing against him the wrath and the sentence of God; and a vile plebeian, who represented his countenance and apparel, was seated on an ass, and pursued by the imprecations of the multitude. [43] The emperor suspected the popularity of Germanus with the soldiers and citizens: he feared, he threatened, but he delayed to strike; the patrician fled to the sanctuary of the church; the people rose in his defence, the walls were deserted by the guards, and the lawless city was abandoned to the flames and rapine of a nocturnal tumult. In a small bark, the unfortunate Maurice, with his wife and nine children, escaped to the Asiatic shore; but the violence of the wind compelled him to land at the church of St. Autonomus, [44] near Chalcedon, from whence he despatched Theodosius, his eldest son, to implore the gratitude and friendship of the Persian monarch. For himself, he refused to fly: his body was tortured with sciatic pains, [45] his mind was enfeebled by superstition; he patiently awaited the event of the revolution, and addressed a fervent and public prayer to the Almighty, that the punishment of his sins might be inflicted in this world rather than in a future life. After the abdication of Maurice, the two factions disputed the choice of an emperor; but the favorite of the blues was rejected by the jealousy of their antagonists, and Germanus himself was hurried along by the crowds who rushed to the palace of Hebdomon, seven miles from the city, to adore the majesty of Phocas the centurion. A modest wish of resigning the purple to the rank and merit of Germanus was opposed by his resolution, more obstinate and equally sincere; the senate and clergy obeyed his summons; and, as soon as the patriarch was assured of his orthodox belief, he consecrated the successful usurper in the church of St. John the Baptist. On the third day, amidst the acclamations of a thoughtless people, Phocas made his public entry in a chariot drawn by four white horses: the revolt of the troops was rewarded by a lavish donative; and the new sovereign, after visiting the palace, beheld from his throne the games of the hippodrome. In a dispute of precedency between the two factions, his partial judgment inclined in favor of the greens. "Remember that Maurice is still alive," resounded from the opposite side; and the indiscreet clamor of the blues admonished and stimulated the cruelty of the tyrant. The ministers of death were despatched to Chalcedon: they dragged the emperor from his sanctuary; and the five sons of Maurice were successively murdered before the eyes of their agonizing parent. At each stroke, which he felt in his heart, he found strength to rehearse a pious ejaculation: "Thou art just, O Lord! and thy judgments are righteous." And such, in the last moments, was his rigid attachment to truth and justice, that he revealed to the soldiers the pious falsehood of a nurse who presented her own child in the place of a royal infant. [46] The tragic scene was finally closed by the execution of the emperor himself, in the twentieth year of his reign, and the sixty-third of his age. The bodies of the father and his five sons were cast into the sea; their heads were exposed at Constantinople to the insults or pity of the multitude; and it was not till some signs of putrefaction had appeared, that Phocas connived at the private burial of these venerable remains. In that grave, the faults and errors of Maurice were kindly interred. His fate alone was remembered; and at the end of twenty years, in the recital of the history of Theophylact, the mournful tale was interrupted by the tears of the audience. [47]

[Footnote 43: In their clamors against Maurice, the people of Constantinople branded him with the name of Marcionite or Marcionist; a heresy (says Theophylact, l. viii. c. 9). Did they only cast out a vague reproach—or had the emperor really listened to some obscure teacher of those ancient Gnostics?]

[Footnote 44: The church of St. Autonomous (whom I have not the honor to know) was 150 stadia from Constantinople, (Theophylact, l. viii. c. 9.) The port of Eutropius, where Maurice and his children were murdered, is described by Gyllius (de Bosphoro Thracio, l. iii. c. xi.) as one of the two harbors of Chalcedon.]

[Footnote 45: The inhabitants of Constantinople were generally subject; and Theophylact insinuates, (l. viii. c. 9,) that if it were consistent with the rules of history, he could assign the medical cause. Yet such a digression would not have been more impertinent than his inquiry (l. vii. c. 16, 17) into the annual inundations of the Nile, and all the opinions of the Greek philosophers on that subject.]

[Footnote 46: From this generous attempt, Corneille has deduced the intricate web of his tragedy of Heraclius, which requires more than one representation to be clearly understood, (Corneille de Voltaire, tom. v. p. 300;) and which, after an interval of some years, is said to have puzzled the author himself, (Anecdotes Dramatiques, tom. i. p. 422.)]

[Footnote 47: The revolt of Phocas and death of Maurice are told by Theophylact Simocatta, (l. viii. c. 7—12,) the Paschal Chronicle, (p. 379, 380,) Theophanes, (Chronograph. p. 238-244,) Zonaras, (tom. ii. l. xiv. p. 77—80,) and Cedrenus, (p. 399—404.)]

Such tears must have flowed in secret, and such compassion would have been criminal, under the reign of Phocas, who was peaceably acknowledged in the provinces of the East and West. The images of the emperor and his wife Leontia were exposed in the Lateran to the veneration of the clergy and senate of Rome, and afterwards deposited in the palace of the Caesars, between those of Constantine and Theodosius. As a subject and a Christian, it was the duty of Gregory to acquiesce in the established government; but the joyful applause with which he salutes the fortune of the assassin, has sullied, with indelible disgrace, the character of the saint. The successor of the apostles might have inculcated with decent firmness the guilt of blood, and the necessity of repentance; he is content to celebrate the deliverance of the people and the fall of the oppressor; to rejoice that the piety and benignity of Phocas have been raised by Providence to the Imperial throne; to pray that his hands may be strengthened against all his enemies; and to express a wish, perhaps a prophecy, that, after a long and triumphant reign, he may be transferred from a temporal to an everlasting kingdom. [48] I have already traced the steps of a revolution so pleasing, in Gregory's opinion, both to heaven and earth; and Phocas does not appear less hateful in the exercise than in the acquisition of power The pencil of an impartial historian has delineated the portrait of a monster: [49] his diminutive and deformed person, the closeness of his shaggy eyebrows, his red hair, his beardless chin, and his cheek disfigured and discolored by a formidable scar. Ignorant of letters, of laws, and even of arms, he indulged in the supreme rank a more ample privilege of lust and drunkenness; and his brutal pleasures were either injurious to his subjects or disgraceful to himself. Without assuming the office of a prince, he renounced the profession of a soldier; and the reign of Phocas afflicted Europe with ignominious peace, and Asia with desolating war. His savage temper was inflamed by passion, hardened by fear, and exasperated by resistance of reproach. The flight of Theodosius to the Persian court had been intercepted by a rapid pursuit, or a deceitful message: he was beheaded at Nice, and the last hours of the young prince were soothed by the comforts of religion and the consciousness of innocence. Yet his phantom disturbed the repose of the usurper: a whisper was circulated through the East, that the son of Maurice was still alive: the people expected their avenger, and the widow and daughters of the late emperor would have adopted as their son and brother the vilest of mankind. In the massacre of the Imperial family, [50] the mercy, or rather the discretion, of Phocas had spared these unhappy females, and they were decently confined to a private house. But the spirit of the empress Constantina, still mindful of her father, her husband, and her sons, aspired to freedom and revenge. At the dead of night, she escaped to the sanctuary of St. Sophia; but her tears, and the gold of her associate Germanus, were insufficient to provoke an insurrection. Her life was forfeited to revenge, and even to justice: but the patriarch obtained and pledged an oath for her safety: a monastery was allotted for her prison, and the widow of Maurice accepted and abused the lenity of his assassin. The discovery or the suspicion of a second conspiracy, dissolved the engagements, and rekindled the fury, of Phocas. A matron who commanded the respect and pity of mankind, the daughter, wife, and mother of emperors, was tortured like the vilest malefactor, to force a confession of her designs and associates; and the empress Constantina, with her three innocent daughters, was beheaded at Chalcedon, on the same ground which had been stained with the blood of her husband and five sons. After such an example, it would be superfluous to enumerate the names and sufferings of meaner victims. Their condemnation was seldom preceded by the forms of trial, and their punishment was embittered by the refinements of cruelty: their eyes were pierced, their tongues were torn from the root, the hands and feet were amputated; some expired under the lash, others in the flames; others again were transfixed with arrows; and a simple speedy death was mercy which they could rarely obtain. The hippodrome, the sacred asylum of the pleasures and the liberty of the Romans, was polluted with heads and limbs, and mangled bodies; and the companions of Phocas were the most sensible, that neither his favor, nor their services, could protect them from a tyrant, the worthy rival of the Caligulas and Domitians of the first age of the empire. [51]

[Footnote 48: Gregor. l. xi. epist. 38, indict. vi. Benignitatem vestrae pietatis ad Imperiale fastigium pervenisse gaudemus. Laetentur coeli et exultet terra, et de vestris benignis actibus universae republicae populus nunc usque vehementer afflictus hilarescat, &c. This base flattery, the topic of Protestant invective, is justly censured by the philosopher Bayle, (Dictionnaire Critique, Gregoire I. Not. H. tom. ii. p. 597 598.) Cardinal Baronius justifies the pope at the expense of the fallen emperor.]

[Footnote 49: The images of Phocas were destroyed; but even the malice of his enemies would suffer one copy of such a portrait or caricature (Cedrenus, p. 404) to escape the flames.]

[Footnote 50: The family of Maurice is represented by Ducange, (Familiae By zantinae, p. 106, 107, 108;) his eldest son Theodosius had been crowned emperor, when he was no more than four years and a half old, and he is always joined with his father in the salutations of Gregory. With the Christian daughters, Anastasia and Theocteste, I am surprised to find the Pagan name of Cleopatra.]

[Footnote 51: Some of the cruelties of Phocas are marked by Theophylact, l. viii. c. 13, 14, 15. George of Pisidia, the poet of Heraclius, styles him (Bell. Avaricum, p. 46, Rome, 1777). The latter epithet is just—but the corrupter of life was easily vanquished.]

PART III

A daughter of Phocas, his only child, was given in marriage to the patrician Crispus, [52] and the royal images of the bride and bridegroom were indiscreetly placed in the circus, by the side of the emperor. The father must desire that his posterity should inherit the fruit of his crimes, but the monarch was offended by this premature and popular association: the tribunes of the green faction, who accused the officious error of their sculptors, were condemned to instant death: their lives were granted to the prayers of the people; but Crispus might reasonably doubt, whether a jealous usurper could forget and pardon his involuntary competition. The green faction was alienated by the ingratitude of Phocas and the loss of their privileges; every province of the empire was ripe for rebellion; and Heraclius, exarch of Africa, persisted above two years in refusing all tribute and obedience to the centurion who disgraced the throne of Constantinople. By the secret emissaries of Crispus and the senate, the independent exarch was solicited to save and to govern his country; but his ambition was chilled by age, and he resigned the dangerous enterprise to his son Heraclius, and to Nicetas, the son of Gregory, his friend and lieutenant. The powers of Africa were armed by the two adventurous youths; they agreed that the one should navigate the fleet from Carthage to Constantinople, that the other should lead an army through Egypt and Asia, and that the Imperial purple should be the reward of diligence and success. A faint rumor of their undertaking was conveyed to the ears of Phocas, and the wife and mother of the younger Heraclius were secured as the hostages of his faith: but the treacherous heart of Crispus extenuated the distant peril, the means of defence were neglected or delayed, and the tyrant supinely slept till the African navy cast anchor in the Hellespont. Their standard was joined at Abidus by the fugitives and exiles who thirsted for revenge; the ships of Heraclius, whose lofty masts were adorned with the holy symbols of religion, [53] steered their triumphant course through the Propontis; and Phocas beheld from the windows of the palace his approaching and inevitable fate. The green faction was tempted, by gifts and promises, to oppose a feeble and fruitless resistance to the landing of the Africans: but the people, and even the guards, were determined by the well-timed defection of Crispus; and they tyrant was seized by a private enemy, who boldly invaded the solitude of the palace. Stripped of the diadem and purple, clothed in a vile habit, and loaded with chains, he was transported in a small boat to the Imperial galley of Heraclius, who reproached him with the crimes of his abominable reign. "Wilt thou govern better?" were the last words of the despair of Phocas. After suffering each variety of insult and torture, his head was severed from his body, the mangled trunk was cast into the flames, and the same treatment was inflicted on the statues of the vain usurper, and the seditious banner of the green faction. The voice of the clergy, the senate, and the people, invited Heraclius to ascend the throne which he had purified from guilt and ignominy; after some graceful hesitation, he yielded to their entreaties. His coronation was accompanied by that of his wife Eudoxia; and their posterity, till the fourth generation, continued to reign over the empire of the East. The voyage of Heraclius had been easy and prosperous; the tedious march of Nicetas was not accomplished before the decision of the contest: but he submitted without a murmur to the fortune of his friend, and his laudable intentions were rewarded with an equestrian statue, and a daughter of the emperor. It was more difficult to trust the fidelity of Crispus, whose recent services were recompensed by the command of the Cappadocian army. His arrogance soon provoked, and seemed to excuse, the ingratitude of his new sovereign. In the presence of the senate, the son-in-law of Phocas was condemned to embrace the monastic life; and the sentence was justified by the weighty observation of Heraclius, that the man who had betrayed his father could never be faithful to his friend. [54]

[Footnote 52: In the writers, and in the copies of those writers, there is such hesitation between the names of Priscus and Crispus, (Ducange, Fam Byzant. p. 111,) that I have been tempted to identify the son-in-law of Phocas with the hero five times victorious over the Avars.]

[Footnote 53: According to Theophanes. Cedrenus adds, which Heraclius bore as a banner in the first Persian expedition. See George Pisid. Acroas L 140. The manufacture seems to have flourished; but Foggini, the Roman editor, (p. 26,) is at a loss to determine whether this picture was an original or a copy.]

[Footnote 54: See the tyranny of Phocas and the elevation of Heraclius, in Chron. Paschal. p. 380—383. Theophanes, p. 242-250. Nicephorus, p. 3—7. Cedrenus, p. 404—407. Zonaras, tom. ii. l. xiv. p. 80—82.]

Even after his death the republic was afflicted by the crimes of Phocas, which armed with a pious cause the most formidable of her enemies. According to the friendly and equal forms of the Byzantine and Persian courts, he announced his exaltation to the throne; and his ambassador Lilius, who had presented him with the heads of Maurice and his sons, was the best qualified to describe the circumstances of the tragic scene. [55] However it might be varnished by fiction or sophistry, Chosroes turned with horror from the assassin, imprisoned the pretended envoy, disclaimed the usurper, and declared himself the avenger of his father and benefactor. The sentiments of grief and resentment, which humanity would feel, and honor would dictate, promoted on this occasion the interest of the Persian king; and his interest was powerfully magnified by the national and religious prejudices of the Magi and satraps. In a strain of artful adulation, which assumed the language of freedom, they presumed to censure the excess of his gratitude and friendship for the Greeks; a nation with whom it was dangerous to conclude either peace or alliance; whose superstition was devoid of truth and justice, and who must be incapable of any virtue, since they could perpetrate the most atrocious of crimes, the impious murder of their sovereign. [56] For the crime of an ambitious centurion, the nation which he oppressed was chastised with the calamities of war; and the same calamities, at the end of twenty years, were retaliated and redoubled on the heads of the Persians. [57] The general who had restored Chosroes to the throne still commanded in the East; and the name of Narses was the formidable sound with which the Assyrian mothers were accustomed to terrify their infants. It is not improbable, that a native subject of Persia should encourage his master and his friend to deliver and possess the provinces of Asia. It is still more probable, that Chosroes should animate his troops by the assurance that the sword which they dreaded the most would remain in its scabbard, or be drawn in their favor. The hero could not depend on the faith of a tyrant; and the tyrant was conscious how little he deserved the obedience of a hero. Narses was removed from his military command; he reared an independent standard at Hierapolis, in Syria: he was betrayed by fallacious promises, and burnt alive in the market-place of Constantinople. Deprived of the only chief whom they could fear or esteem, the bands which he had led to victory were twice broken by the cavalry, trampled by the elephants, and pierced by the arrows of the Barbarians; and a great number of the captives were beheaded on the field of battle by the sentence of the victor, who might justly condemn these seditious mercenaries as the authors or accomplices of the death of Maurice. Under the reign of Phocas, the fortifications of Merdin, Dara, Amida, and Edessa, were successively besieged, reduced, and destroyed, by the Persian monarch: he passed the Euphrates, occupied the Syrian cities, Hierapolis, Chalcis, and Berrhaea or Aleppo, and soon encompassed the walls of Antioch with his irresistible arms. The rapid tide of success discloses the decay of the empire, the incapacity of Phocas, and the disaffection of his subjects; and Chosroes provided a decent apology for their submission or revolt, by an impostor, who attended his camp as the son of Maurice [58] and the lawful heir of the monarchy.

[Footnote 55: Theophylact, l. viii. c. 15. The life of Maurice was composed about the year 628 (l. viii. c. 13) by Theophylact Simocatta, ex-praefect, a native of Egypt. Photius, who gives an ample extract of the work, (cod. lxv. p. 81—100,) gently reproves the affectation and allegory of the style. His preface is a dialogue between Philosophy and History; they seat themselves under a plane-tree, and the latter touches her lyre.]

[Footnote 56: Christianis nec pactum esse, nec fidem nec foedus ..... quod si ulla illis fides fuisset, regem suum non occidissent. Eutych. Annales tom. ii. p. 211, vers. Pocock.]

[Footnote 57: We must now, for some ages, take our leave of contemporary historians, and descend, if it be a descent, from the affectation of rhetoric to the rude simplicity of chronicles and abridgments. Those of Theophanes (Chronograph. p. 244—279) and Nicephorus (p. 3—16) supply a regular, but imperfect, series of the Persian war; and for any additional facts I quote my special authorities. Theophanes, a courtier who became a monk, was born A.D. 748; Nicephorus patriarch of Constantinople, who died A.D. 829, was somewhat younger: they both suffered in the cause of images Hankius, de Scriptoribus Byzantinis, p. 200-246.]

[Footnote 58: The Persian historians have been themselves deceived: but Theophanes (p. 244) accuses Chosroes of the fraud and falsehood; and Eutychius believes (Annal. tom. ii. p. 212) that the son of Maurice, who was saved from the assassins, lived and died a monk on Mount Sinai.]

The first intelligence from the East which Heraclius received, [59] was that of the loss of Antioch; but the aged metropolis, so often overturned by earthquakes, and pillaged by the enemy, could supply but a small and languid stream of treasure and blood. The Persians were equally successful, and more fortunate, in the sack of Caesarea, the capital of Cappadocia; and as they advanced beyond the ramparts of the frontier, the boundary of ancient war, they found a less obstinate resistance and a more plentiful harvest. The pleasant vale of Damascus has been adorned in every age with a royal city: her obscure felicity has hitherto escaped the historian of the Roman empire: but Chosroes reposed his troops in the paradise of Damascus before he ascended the hills of Libanus, or invaded the cities of the Phoenician coast. The conquest of Jerusalem, [60] which had been meditated by Nushirvan, was achieved by the zeal and avarice of his grandson; the ruin of the proudest monument of Christianity was vehemently urged by the intolerant spirit of the Magi; and he could enlist for this holy warfare with an army of six-and-twenty thousand Jews, whose furious bigotry might compensate, in some degree, for the want of valor and discipline. [60/1] After the reduction of Galilee, and the region beyond the Jordan, whose resistance appears to have delayed the fate of the capital, Jerusalem itself was taken by assault. The sepulchre of Christ, and the stately churches of Helena and Constantine, were consumed, or at least damaged, by the flames; the devout offerings of three hundred years were rifled in one sacrilegious day; the Patriarch Zachariah, and the true cross, were transported into Persia; and the massacre of ninety thousand Christians is imputed to the Jews and Arabs, who swelled the disorder of the Persian march. The fugitives of Palestine were entertained at Alexandria by the charity of John the Archbishop, who is distinguished among a crowd of saints by the epithet of almsgiver: [61] and the revenues of the church, with a treasure of three hundred thousand pounds, were restored to the true proprietors, the poor of every country and every denomination. But Egypt itself, the only province which had been exempt, since the time of Diocletian, from foreign and domestic war, was again subdued by the successors of Cyrus. Pelusium, the key of that impervious country, was surprised by the cavalry of the Persians: they passed, with impunity, the innumerable channels of the Delta, and explored the long valley of the Nile, from the pyramids of Memphis to the confines of Aethiopia. Alexandria might have been relieved by a naval force, but the archbishop and the praefect embarked for Cyprus; and Chosroes entered the second city of the empire, which still preserved a wealthy remnant of industry and commerce. His western trophy was erected, not on the walls of Carthage, [62] but in the neighborhood of Tripoli; the Greek colonies of Cyrene were finally extirpated; and the conqueror, treading in the footsteps of Alexander, returned in triumph through the sands of the Libyan desert. In the same campaign, another army advanced from the Euphrates to the Thracian Bosphorus; Chalcedon surrendered after a long siege, and a Persian camp was maintained above ten years in the presence of Constantinople. The sea-coast of Pontus, the city of Ancyra, and the Isle of Rhodes, are enumerated among the last conquests of the great king; and if Chosroes had possessed any maritime power, his boundless ambition would have spread slavery and desolation over the provinces of Europe.

[Footnote 59: Eutychius dates all the losses of the empire under the reign of Phocas; an error which saves the honor of Heraclius, whom he brings not from Carthage, but Salonica, with a fleet laden with vegetables for the relief of Constantinople, (Annal. tom. ii. p. 223, 224.) The other Christians of the East, Barhebraeus, (apud Asseman, Bibliothec. Oriental. tom. iii. p. 412, 413,) Elmacin, (Hist. Saracen. p. 13—16,) Abulpharagius, (Dynast. p. 98, 99,) are more sincere and accurate. The years of the Persian war are disposed in the chronology of Pagi.]

[Footnote 60: On the conquest of Jerusalem, an event so interesting to the church, see the Annals of Eutychius, (tom. ii. p. 212—223,) and the lamentations of the monk Antiochus, (apud Baronium, Annal. Eccles. A.D. 614, No. 16—26,) whose one hundred and twenty-nine homilies are still extant, if what no one reads may be said to be extant.]

[Footnote 60/1: See Hist. of Jews, vol. iii. p. 240—M.]

[Footnote 61: The life of this worthy saint is composed by Leontius, a contemporary bishop; and I find in Baronius (Annal. Eccles. A.D. 610, No. 10, &c.) and Fleury (tom. viii. p. 235-242) sufficient extracts of this edifying work.]

[Footnote 62: The error of Baronius, and many others who have carried the arms of Chosroes to Carthage instead of Chalcedon, is founded on the near resemblance of the Greek words, in the text of Theophanes, &c., which have been sometimes confounded by transcribers, and sometimes by critics.]

From the long-disputed banks of the Tigris and Euphrates, the reign of the grandson of Nushirvan was suddenly extended to the Hellespont and the Nile, the ancient limits of the Persian monarchy. But the provinces, which had been fashioned by the habits of six hundred years to the virtues and vices of the Roman government, supported with reluctance the yoke of the Barbarians. The idea of a republic was kept alive by the institutions, or at least by the writings, of the Greeks and Romans, and the subjects of Heraclius had been educated to pronounce the words of liberty and law. But it has always been the pride and policy of Oriental princes to display the titles and attributes of their omnipotence; to upbraid a nation of slaves with their true name and abject condition, and to enforce, by cruel and insolent threats, the rigor of their absolute commands. The Christians of the East were scandalized by the worship of fire, and the impious doctrine of the two principles: the Magi were not less intolerant than the bishops; and the martyrdom of some native Persians, who had deserted the religion of Zoroaster, [63] was conceived to be the prelude of a fierce and general persecution. By the oppressive laws of Justinian, the adversaries of the church were made the enemies of the state; the alliance of the Jews, Nestorians, and Jacobites, had contributed to the success of Chosroes, and his partial favor to the sectaries provoked the hatred and fears of the Catholic clergy. Conscious of their fear and hatred, the Persian conqueror governed his new subjects with an iron sceptre; and, as if he suspected the stability of his dominion, he exhausted their wealth by exorbitant tributes and licentious rapine despoiled or demolished the temples of the East; and transported to his hereditary realms the gold, the silver, the precious marbles, the arts, and the artists of the Asiatic cities. In the obscure picture of the calamities of the empire, [64] it is not easy to discern the figure of Chosroes himself, to separate his actions from those of his lieutenants, or to ascertain his personal merit in the general blaze of glory and magnificence. He enjoyed with ostentation the fruits of victory, and frequently retired from the hardships of war to the luxury of the palace. But in the space of twenty-four years, he was deterred by superstition or resentment from approaching the gates of Ctesiphon: and his favorite residence of Artemita, or Dastagerd, was situate beyond the Tigris, about sixty miles to the north of the capital. [65] The adjacent pastures were covered with flocks and herds: the paradise or park was replenished with pheasants, peacocks, ostriches, roebucks, and wild boars, and the noble game of lions and tigers was sometimes turned loose for the bolder pleasures of the chase. Nine hundred and sixty elephants were maintained for the use or splendor of the great king: his tents and baggage were carried into the field by twelve thousand great camels and eight thousand of a smaller size; [66] and the royal stables were filled with six thousand mules and horses, among whom the names of Shebdiz and Barid are renowned for their speed or beauty. [66/1] Six thousand guards successively mounted before the palace gate; the service of the interior apartments was performed by twelve thousand slaves, and in the number of three thousand virgins, the fairest of Asia, some happy concubine might console her master for the age or the indifference of Sira.

The various treasures of gold, silver, gems, silks, and aromatics, were deposited in a hundred subterraneous vaults and the chamber Badaverd denoted the accidental gift of the winds which had wafted the spoils of Heraclius into one of the Syrian harbors of his rival. The vice of flattery, and perhaps of fiction, is not ashamed to compute the thirty thousand rich hangings that adorned the walls; the forty thousand columns of silver, or more probably of marble, and plated wood, that supported the roof; and the thousand globes of gold suspended in the dome, to imitate the motions of the planets and the constellations of the zodiac. [67] While the Persian monarch contemplated the wonders of his art and power, he received an epistle from an obscure citizen of Mecca, inviting him to acknowledge Mahomet as the apostle of God. He rejected the invitation, and tore the epistle. "It is thus," exclaimed the Arabian prophet, "that God will tear the kingdom, and reject the supplications of Chosroes." [68] [68/1] Placed on the verge of the two great empires of the East, Mahomet observed with secret joy the progress of their mutual destruction; and in the midst of the Persian triumphs, he ventured to foretell, that before many years should elapse, victory should again return to the banners of the Romans. [69]

[Footnote 63: The genuine acts of St. Anastasius are published in those of the with general council, from whence Baronius (Annal. Eccles. A.D. 614, 626, 627) and Butler (Lives of the Saints, vol. i. p. 242—248) have taken their accounts. The holy martyr deserted from the Persian to the Roman army, became a monk at Jerusalem, and insulted the worship of the Magi, which was then established at Caesarea in Palestine.]

[Footnote 64: Abulpharagius, Dynast. p. 99. Elmacin, Hist. Saracen. p. 14.]

[Footnote 65: D'Anville, Mem. de l'Academie des Inscriptions, tom. xxxii. p. 568—571.]

[Footnote 66: The difference between the two races consists in one or two humps; the dromedary has only one; the size of the proper camel is larger; the country he comes from, Turkistan or Bactriana; the dromedary is confined to Arabia and Africa. Buffon, Hist. Naturelle, tom. xi. p. 211, &c. Aristot. Hist. Animal. tom. i. l. ii. c. 1, tom. ii. p. 185.]

[Footnote 66/1: The ruins of these scenes of Khoosroo's magnificence have been visited by Sir R. K. Porter. At the ruins of Tokht i Bostan, he saw a gorgeous picture of a hunt, singularly illustrative of this passage. Travels, vol. ii. p. 204. Kisra Shirene, which he afterwards examined, appears to have been the palace of Dastagerd. Vol. ii. p. 173—175—M.]

[Footnote 67: Theophanes, Chronograph. p. 268. D'Herbelot, Bibliotheque Orientale, p. 997. The Greeks describe the decay, the Persians the splendor, of Dastagerd; but the former speak from the modest witness of the eye, the latter from the vague report of the ear.]

[Footnote 68: The historians of Mahomet, Abulfeda (in Vit. Mohammed, p. 92, 93) and Gagnier, (Vie de Mahomet, tom. ii. p. 247,) date this embassy in the viith year of the Hegira, which commences A.D. 628, May 11. Their chronology is erroneous, since Chosroes died in the month of February of the same year, (Pagi, Critica, tom. ii. p. 779.) The count de Boulainvilliers (Vie de Mahomed, p. 327, 328) places this embassy about A.D. 615, soon after the conquest of Palestine. Yet Mahomet would scarcely have ventured so soon on so bold a step.]

[Footnote 68/1: Khoosroo Purveez was encamped on the banks of the Karasoo River when he received the letter of Mahomed. He tore the letter and threw it into the Karasoo. For this action, the moderate author of the Zeenut-ul-Tuarikh calls him a wretch, and rejoices in all his subsequent misfortunes. These impressions still exist. I remarked to a Persian, when encamped near the Karasoo, in 1800, that the banks were very high, which must make it difficult to apply its waters to irrigation. "It once fertilized the whole country," said the zealous Mahomedan, "but its channel sunk with honor from its banks, when that madman, Khoosroo, threw our holy Prophet's letter into its stream; which has ever since been accursed and useless." Malcolm's Persia, vol. i. p. 126—M.]

[Footnote 69: See the xxxth chapter of the Koran, entitled the Greeks. Our honest and learned translator, Sale, (p. 330, 331,) fairly states this conjecture, guess, wager, of Mahomet; but Boulainvilliers, (p. 329—344,) with wicked intentions, labors to establish this evident prophecy of a future event, which must, in his opinion, embarrass the Christian polemics.]

At the time when this prediction is said to have been delivered, no prophecy could be more distant from its accomplishment, since the first twelve years of Heraclius announced the approaching dissolution of the empire. If the motives of Chosroes had been pure and honorable, he must have ended the quarrel with the death of Phocas, and he would have embraced, as his best ally, the fortunate African who had so generously avenged the injuries of his benefactor Maurice. The prosecution of the war revealed the true character of the Barbarian; and the suppliant embassies of Heraclius to beseech his clemency, that he would spare the innocent, accept a tribute, and give peace to the world, were rejected with contemptuous silence or insolent menace. Syria, Egypt, and the provinces of Asia, were subdued by the Persian arms, while Europe, from the confines of Istria to the long wall of Thrace, was oppressed by the Avars, unsatiated with the blood and rapine of the Italian war. They had coolly massacred their male captives in the sacred field of Pannonia; the women and children were reduced to servitude, and the noblest virgins were abandoned to the promiscuous lust of the Barbarians. The amorous matron who opened the gates of Friuli passed a short night in the arms of her royal lover; the next evening, Romilda was condemned to the embraces of twelve Avars, and the third day the Lombard princess was impaled in the sight of the camp, while the chagan observed with a cruel smile, that such a husband was the fit recompense of her lewdness and perfidy. [70] By these implacable enemies, Heraclius, on either side, was insulted and besieged: and the Roman empire was reduced to the walls of Constantinople, with the remnant of Greece, Italy, and Africa, and some maritime cities, from Tyre to Trebizond, of the Asiatic coast. After the loss of Egypt, the capital was afflicted by famine and pestilence; and the emperor, incapable of resistance, and hopeless of relief, had resolved to transfer his person and government to the more secure residence of Carthage. His ships were already laden with the treasures of the palace; but his flight was arrested by the patriarch, who armed the powers of religion in the defence of his country; led Heraclius to the altar of St. Sophia, and extorted a solemn oath, that he would live and die with the people whom God had intrusted to his care. The chagan was encamped in the plains of Thrace; but he dissembled his perfidious designs, and solicited an interview with the emperor near the town of Heraclea. Their reconciliation was celebrated with equestrian games; the senate and people, in their gayest apparel, resorted to the festival of peace; and the Avars beheld, with envy and desire, the spectacle of Roman luxury. On a sudden the hippodrome was encompassed by the Scythian cavalry, who had pressed their secret and nocturnal march: the tremendous sound of the chagan's whip gave the signal of the assault, and Heraclius, wrapping his diadem round his arm, was saved with extreme hazard, by the fleetness of his horse. So rapid was the pursuit, that the Avars almost entered the golden gate of Constantinople with the flying crowds: [71] but the plunder of the suburbs rewarded their treason, and they transported beyond the Danube two hundred and seventy thousand captives. On the shore of Chalcedon, the emperor held a safer conference with a more honorable foe, who, before Heraclius descended from his galley, saluted with reverence and pity the majesty of the purple. The friendly offer of Sain, the Persian general, to conduct an embassy to the presence of the great king, was accepted with the warmest gratitude, and the prayer for pardon and peace was humbly presented by the Praetorian praefect, the praefect of the city, and one of the first ecclesiastics of the patriarchal church. [72] But the lieutenant of Chosroes had fatally mistaken the intentions of his master. "It was not an embassy," said the tyrant of Asia, "it was the person of Heraclius, bound in chains, that he should have brought to the foot of my throne. I will never give peace to the emperor of Rome, till he had abjured his crucified God, and embraced the worship of the sun." Sain was flayed alive, according to the inhuman practice of his country; and the separate and rigorous confinement of the ambassadors violated the law of nations, and the faith of an express stipulation. Yet the experience of six years at length persuaded the Persian monarch to renounce the conquest of Constantinople, and to specify the annual tribute or ransom of the Roman empire; a thousand talents of gold, a thousand talents of silver, a thousand silk robes, a thousand horses, and a thousand virgins. Heraclius subscribed these ignominious terms; but the time and space which he obtained to collect such treasures from the poverty of the East, was industriously employed in the preparations of a bold and desperate attack. [Footnote 70: Paul Warnefrid, de Gestis Langobardorum, l. iv. c. 38, 42. Muratori, Annali d'Italia, tom. v. p. 305, &c.]

[Footnote 71: The Paschal Chronicle, which sometimes introduces fragments of history into a barren list of names and dates, gives the best account of the treason of the Avars, p. 389, 390. The number of captives is added by Nicephorus.]

[Footnote 72: Some original pieces, such as the speech or letter of the Roman ambassadors, (p. 386—388,) likewise constitute the merit of the Paschal Chronicle, which was composed, perhaps at Alexandria, under the reign of Heraclius.]

Of the characters conspicuous in history, that of Heraclius is one of the most extraordinary and inconsistent. In the first and last years of a long reign, the emperor appears to be the slave of sloth, of pleasure, or of superstition, the careless and impotent spectator of the public calamities. But the languid mists of the morning and evening are separated by the brightness of the meridian sun; the Arcadius of the palace arose the Caesar of the camp; and the honor of Rome and Heraclius was gloriously retrieved by the exploits and trophies of six adventurous campaigns. It was the duty of the Byzantine historians to have revealed the causes of his slumber and vigilance. At this distance we can only conjecture, that he was endowed with more personal courage than political resolution; that he was detained by the charms, and perhaps the arts, of his niece Martina, with whom, after the death of Eudocia, he contracted an incestuous marriage; [73] and that he yielded to the base advice of the counsellors, who urged, as a fundamental law, that the life of the emperor should never be exposed in the field. [74] Perhaps he was awakened by the last insolent demand of the Persian conqueror; but at the moment when Heraclius assumed the spirit of a hero, the only hopes of the Romans were drawn from the vicissitudes of fortune, which might threaten the proud prosperity of Chosroes, and must be favorable to those who had attained the lowest period of depression. [75] To provide for the expenses of war, was the first care of the emperor; and for the purpose of collecting the tribute, he was allowed to solicit the benevolence of the eastern provinces. But the revenue no longer flowed in the usual channels; the credit of an arbitrary prince is annihilated by his power; and the courage of Heraclius was first displayed in daring to borrow the consecrated wealth of churches, under the solemn vow of restoring, with usury, whatever he had been compelled to employ in the service of religion and the empire. The clergy themselves appear to have sympathized with the public distress; and the discreet patriarch of Alexandria, without admitting the precedent of sacrilege, assisted his sovereign by the miraculous or seasonable revelation of a secret treasure. [76] Of the soldiers who had conspired with Phocas, only two were found to have survived the stroke of time and of the Barbarians; [77] the loss, even of these seditious veterans, was imperfectly supplied by the new levies of Heraclius, and the gold of the sanctuary united, in the same camp, the names, and arms, and languages of the East and West. He would have been content with the neutrality of the Avars; and his friendly entreaty, that the chagan would act, not as the enemy, but as the guardian, of the empire, was accompanied with a more persuasive donative of two hundred thousand pieces of gold. Two days after the festival of Easter, the emperor, exchanging his purple for the simple garb of a penitent and warrior, [78] gave the signal of his departure. To the faith of the people Heraclius recommended his children; the civil and military powers were vested in the most deserving hands, and the discretion of the patriarch and senate was authorized to save or surrender the city, if they should be oppressed in his absence by the superior forces of the enemy. [Footnote 73: Nicephorus, (p. 10, 11,) is happy to observe, that of two sons, its incestuous fruit, the elder was marked by Providence with a stiff neck, the younger with the loss of hearing.]

[Footnote 74: George of Pisidia, (Acroas. i. 112—125, p. 5,) who states the opinions, acquits the pusillanimous counsellors of any sinister views. Would he have excused the proud and contemptuous admonition of Crispus?]

[Footnote 75: George Pisid. Acroas. i. 51, &c. p: 4. The Orientals are not less fond of remarking this strange vicissitude; and I remember some story of Khosrou Parviz, not very unlike the ring of Polycrates of Samos.]

[Footnote 76: Baronius gravely relates this discovery, or rather transmutation, of barrels, not of honey, but of gold, (Annal. Eccles. A.D. 620, No. 3, &c.) Yet the loan was arbitrary, since it was collected by soldiers, who were ordered to leave the patriarch of Alexandria no more than one hundred pounds of gold. Nicephorus, (p. 11,) two hundred years afterwards, speaks with ill humor of this contribution, which the church of Constantinople might still feel.]

[Footnote 77: Theophylact Symocatta, l. viii. c. 12. This circumstance need not excite our surprise. The muster-roll of a regiment, even in time of peace, is renewed in less than twenty or twenty-five years.]

[Footnote 78: He changed his purple for black, buckskins, and dyed them red in the blood of the Persians, (Georg. Pisid. Acroas. iii. 118, 121, 122 See the notes of Foggini, p. 35.)]

The neighboring heights of Chalcedon were covered with tents and arms: but if the new levies of Heraclius had been rashly led to the attack, the victory of the Persians in the sight of Constantinople might have been the last day of the Roman empire. As imprudent would it have been to advance into the provinces of Asia, leaving their innumerable cavalry to intercept his convoys, and continually to hang on the lassitude and disorder of his rear. But the Greeks were still masters of the sea; a fleet of galleys, transports, and store-ships, was assembled in the harbor; the Barbarians consented to embark; a steady wind carried them through the Hellespont the western and southern coast of Asia Minor lay on their left hand; the spirit of their chief was first displayed in a storm, and even the eunuchs of his train were excited to suffer and to work by the example of their master. He landed his troops on the confines of Syria and Cilicia, in the Gulf of Scanderoon, where the coast suddenly turns to the south; [79] and his discernment was expressed in the choice of this important post. [80] From all sides, the scattered garrisons of the maritime cities and the mountains might repair with speed and safety to his Imperial standard. The natural fortifications of Cilicia protected, and even concealed, the camp of Heraclius, which was pitched near Issus, on the same ground where Alexander had vanquished the host of Darius. The angle which the emperor occupied was deeply indented into a vast semicircle of the Asiatic,

Armenian, and Syrian provinces; and to whatsoever point of the circumference he should direct his attack, it was easy for him to dissemble his own motions, and to prevent those of the enemy. In the camp of Issus, the Roman general reformed the sloth and disorder of the veterans, and educated the new recruits in the knowledge and practice of military virtue. Unfolding the miraculous image of Christ, he urged them to revenge the holy altars which had been profaned by the worshippers of fire; addressing them by the endearing appellations of sons and brethren, he deplored the public and private wrongs of the republic. The subjects of a monarch were persuaded that they fought in the cause of freedom; and a similar enthusiasm was communicated to the foreign mercenaries, who must have viewed with equal indifference the interest of Rome and of Persia. Heraclius himself, with the skill and patience of a centurion, inculcated the lessons of the school of tactics, and the soldiers were assiduously trained in the use of their weapons, and the exercises and evolutions of the field. The cavalry and infantry in light or heavy armor were divided into two parties; the trumpets were fixed in the centre, and their signals directed the march, the charge, the retreat or pursuit; the direct or oblique order, the deep or extended phalanx; to represent in fictitious combat the operations of genuine war. Whatever hardships the emperor imposed on the troops, he inflicted with equal severity on himself; their labor, their diet, their sleep, were measured by the inflexible rules of discipline; and, without despising the enemy, they were taught to repose an implicit confidence in their own valor and the wisdom of their leader. Cilicia was soon encompassed with the Persian arms; but their cavalry hesitated to enter the defiles of Mount Taurus, till they were circumvented by the evolutions of Heraclius, who insensibly gained their rear, whilst he appeared to present his front in order of battle. By a false motion, which seemed to threaten Armenia, he drew them, against their wishes, to a general action. They were tempted by the artful disorder of his camp; but when they advanced to combat, the ground, the sun, and the expectation of both armies, were unpropitious to the Barbarians; the Romans successfully repeated their tactics in a field of battle, [81] and the event of the day declared to the world, that the Persians were not invincible, and that a hero was invested with the purple. Strong in victory and fame, Heraclius boldly ascended the heights of Mount Taurus, directed his march through the plains of Cappadocia, and established his troops, for the winter season, in safe and plentiful quarters on the banks of the River Halys. [82] His soul was superior to the vanity of entertaining Constantinople with an imperfect triumph; but the presence of the emperor was indispensably required to soothe the restless and rapacious spirit of the Avars.

[Footnote 79: George of Pisidia, (Acroas. ii. 10, p. 8) has fixed this important point of the Syrian and Cilician gates. They are elegantly described by Xenophon, who marched through them a thousand years before. A narrow pass of three stadia between steep, high rocks, and the Mediterranean, was closed at each end by strong gates, impregnable to the land, accessible by sea, (Anabasis, l. i. p. 35, 36, with Hutchinson's Geographical Dissertation, p. vi.) The gates were thirty-five parasangs, or leagues, from Tarsus, (Anabasis, l. i. p. 33, 34,) and eight or ten from Antioch. Compare Itinerar. Wesseling, p. 580, 581. Schultens, Index Geograph. ad calcem Vit. Saladin. p. 9. Voyage en Turquie et en Perse, par M. Otter, tom. i. p. 78, 79.]

[Footnote 80: Heraclius might write to a friend in the modest words of Cicero: "Castra habuimus ea ipsa quae contra Darium habuerat apud Issum Alexander, imperator haud paulo melior quam aut tu aut ego." Ad Atticum, v. 20. Issus, a rich and flourishing city in the time of Xenophon, was ruined by the prosperity of Alexandria or Scanderoon, on the other side of the bay.]

[Footnote 81: Foggini (Annotat. p. 31) suspects that the Persians were deceived by the of Aelian, (Tactic. c. 48,) an intricate spiral motion of the army. He observes (p. 28) that the military descriptions of George of Pisidia are transcribed in the Tactics of the emperor Leo.]

[Footnote 82: George of Pisidia, an eye-witness, (Acroas. ii. 122, &c.,) described in three acroaseis, or cantos, the first expedition of Heraclius. The poem has been lately (1777) published at Rome; but such vague and declamatory praise is far from corresponding with the sanguine hopes of Pagi, D'Anville, &c.]

Since the days of Scipio and Hannibal, no bolder enterprise has been attempted than that which Heraclius achieved for the deliverance of the empire [83] He permitted the Persians to oppress for a while the provinces, and to insult with impunity the capital of the East; while the Roman emperor explored his perilous way through the Black Sea, [84] and the mountains of Armenia, penetrated into the heart of Persia, [85] and recalled the armies of the great king to the defence of their bleeding country. With a select band of five thousand soldiers, Heraclius sailed from Constantinople to Trebizond; assembled his forces which had wintered in the Pontic regions; and, from the mouth of the Phasis to the Caspian Sea, encouraged his subjects and allies to march with the successor of Constantine under the faithful and victorious banner of the cross. When the legions of Lucullus and Pompey first passed the Euphrates, they blushed at their easy victory over the natives of Armenia. But the long experience of war had hardened the minds and bodies of that effeminate peeple; their zeal and bravery were approved in the service of a declining empire; they abhorred and feared the usurpation of the house of Sassan, and the memory of persecution envenomed their pious hatred of the enemies of Christ. The limits of Armenia, as it had been ceded to the emperor Maurice, extended as far as the Araxes: the river submitted to the indignity of a bridge, [86] and Heraclius, in the footsteps of Mark Antony, advanced towards the city of Tauris or Gandzaca, [87] the ancient and modern capital of one of the provinces of Media. At the head of forty thousand men, Chosroes himself had returned from some distant expedition to oppose the progress of the Roman arms; but he retreated on the approach of Heraclius, declining the generous alternative of peace or of battle. Instead of half a million of inhabitants, which have been ascribed to Tauris under the reign of the Sophys, the city contained no more than three thousand houses; but the value of the royal treasures was enhanced by a tradition, that they were the spoils of Croesus, which had been transported by Cyrus from the citadel of Sardes. The rapid conquests of Heraclius were suspended only by the winter season; a motive of prudence, or superstition, [88] determined his retreat into the province of Albania, along the shores of the Caspian; and his tents were most probably pitched in the plains of Mogan, [89] the favorite encampment of Oriental princes. In the course of this successful inroad, he signalized the zeal and revenge of a Christian emperor: at his command, the soldiers extinguished the fire, and destroyed the temples, of the Magi; the statues of Chosroes, who aspired to divine honors, were abandoned to the flames; and the ruins of Thebarma or Ormia, [90] which had given birth to Zoroaster himself, made some atonement for the injuries of the holy sepulchre. A purer spirit of religion was shown in the relief and deliverance of fifty thousand captives. Heraclius was rewarded by their tears and grateful acclamations; but this wise measure, which spread the fame of his benevolence, diffused the murmurs of the Persians against the pride and obstinacy of their own sovereign. [Footnote 83: Theophanes (p. 256) carries Heraclius swiftly into Armenia. Nicephorus, (p. 11,) though he confounds the two expeditions, defines the province of Lazica. Eutychius (Annal. tom. ii. p. 231) has given the 5000 men, with the more probable station of Trebizond.]

[Footnote 84: From Constantinople to Trebizond, with a fair wind, four or five days; from thence to Erzerom, five; to Erivan, twelve; to Taurus, ten; in all, thirty-two. Such is the Itinerary of Tavernier, (Voyages, tom. i. p. 12—56,) who was perfectly conversant with the roads of Asia. Tournefort, who travelled with a pacha, spent ten or twelve days between Trebizond and Erzerom, (Voyage du Levant, tom. iii. lettre xviii.;) and Chardin (Voyages, tom. i. p. 249—254) gives the more correct distance of fifty-three parasangs, each of 5000 paces, (what paces?) between Erivan and Tauris.]

[Footnote 85: The expedition of Heraclius into Persia is finely illustrated by M. D'Anville, (Memoires de l'Academie des Inscriptions, tom. xxviii. p. 559—573.) He discovers the situation of Gandzaca, Thebarma, Dastagerd, &c., with admirable skill and learning; but the obscure campaign of 624 he passes over in silence.]

[Footnote 86: Et pontem indignatus Araxes—Virgil, Aeneid, viii. 728. The River Araxes is noisy, rapid, vehement, and, with the melting of the snows, irresistible: the strongest and most massy bridges are swept away by the current; and its indignation is attested by the ruins of many arches near the old town of Zulfa. Voyages de Chardin, tom. i. p. 252.]

[Footnote 87: Chardin, tom. i. p. 255—259. With the Orientals, (D'Herbelot, Biblioth. Orient. p. 834,) he ascribes the foundation of Tauris, or Tebris, to Zobeide, the wife of the famous Khalif Haroun Alrashid; but it appears to have been more ancient; and the names of Gandzaca, Gazaca, Gaza, are expressive of the royal treasure. The number of 550,000 inhabitants is reduced by Chardin from 1,100,000, the popular estimate.]

[Footnote 88: He opened the gospel, and applied or interpreted the first casual passage to the name and situation of Albania. Theophanes, p. 258.]

[Footnote 89: The heath of Mogan, between the Cyrus and the Araxes, is sixty parasangs in length and twenty in breadth, (Olearius, p. 1023, 1024,) abounding in waters and fruitful pastures, (Hist. de Nadir Shah, translated by Mr. Jones from a Persian Ms., part ii. p. 2, 3.) See the encampments of Timur, (Hist. par Sherefeddin Ali, l. v. c. 37, l. vi. c. 13,) and the coronation of Nadir Shah, (Hist. Persanne, p. 3—13 and the English Life by Mr. Jones, p. 64, 65.)]

[Footnote 90: Thebarma and Ormia, near the Lake Spauta, are proved to be the same city by D'Anville, (Memoires de l'Academie, tom. xxviii. p. 564, 565.) It is honored as the birthplace of Zoroaster, according to the Persians, (Schultens, Index Geograph. p. 48;) and their tradition is fortified by M. Perron d'Anquetil, (Mem. de l'Acad. des Inscript. tom. xxxi. p. 375,) with some texts from his, or their, Zendavesta. Note: D'Anville (Mem. de l'Acad. des Inscript. tom. xxxii. p. 560) labored to prove the identity of these two cities; but according to M. St. Martin, vol. xi. p. 97, not with perfect success. Ourmiah. called Ariema in the ancient Pehlvi books, is considered, both by the followers of Zoroaster and by the Mahometans, as his birthplace. It is situated in the southern part of Aderbidjan—M.]

PART IV

Amidst the glories of the succeeding campaign, Heraclius is almost lost to our eyes, and to those of the Byzantine historians. [91] From the spacious and fruitful plains of Albania, the emperor appears to follow the chain of Hyrcanian Mountains, to descend into the province of Media or Irak, and to carry his victorious arms as far as the royal cities of Casbin and Ispahan, which had never been approached by a Roman conqueror. Alarmed by the danger of his kingdom, the powers of Chosroes were already recalled from the Nile and the Bosphorus, and three formidable armies surrounded, in a distant and hostile land, the camp of the emperor. The Colchian allies prepared to desert his standard; and the fears of the bravest veterans were expressed, rather than concealed, by their desponding silence. "Be not terrified," said the intrepid Heraclius, "by the multitude of your foes. With the aid of Heaven, one Roman may triumph over a thousand Barbarians. But if we devote our lives for the salvation of our brethren, we shall obtain the crown of martyrdom, and our immortal reward will be liberally paid by God and posterity." These magnanimous sentiments were supported by the vigor of his actions. He repelled the threefold attack of the Persians, improved the divisions of their chiefs, and, by a well-concerted train of marches, retreats, and successful actions, finally chased them from the field into the fortified cities of Media and Assyria. In the severity of the winter season, Sarbaraza deemed himself secure in the walls of Salban: he was surprised by the activity of Heraclius, who divided his troops, and performed a laborious march in the silence of the night. The flat roofs of the houses were defended with useless valor against the darts and torches of the Romans: the satraps and nobles of Persia, with their wives and children, and the flower of their martial youth, were either slain or made prisoners. The general escaped by a precipitate flight, but his golden armor was the prize of the conqueror; and the soldiers of Heraclius enjoyed the wealth and repose which they had so nobly deserved. On the return of spring, the emperor traversed in seven days the mountains of Curdistan, and passed without resistance the rapid stream of the Tigris. Oppressed by the weight of their spoils and captives, the Roman army halted under the walls of Amida; and Heraclius informed the senate of Constantinople of his safety and success, which they had already felt by the retreat of the besiegers. The bridges of the Euphrates were destroyed by the Persians; but as soon as the emperor had discovered a ford, they hastily retired to defend the banks of the Sarus, [92] in Cilicia. That river, an impetuous torrent, was about three hundred feet broad; the bridge was fortified with strong turrets; and the banks were lined with Barbarian archers. After a bloody conflict, which continued till the evening, the Romans prevailed in the assault; and a Persian of gigantic size was slain and thrown into the Sarus by the hand of the emperor himself. The enemies were dispersed and dismayed; Heraclius pursued his march to Sebaste in Cappadocia; and at the expiration of three years, the same coast of the Euxine applauded his return from a long and victorious expedition. [93]

[Footnote 91: I cannot find, and (what is much more,) M. D'Anville does not attempt to seek, the Salban, Tarantum, territory of the Huns, &c., mentioned by Theophanes, (p. 260-262.) Eutychius, (Annal. tom. ii. p. 231, 232,) an insufficient author, names Asphahan; and Casbin is most probably the city of Sapor. Ispahan is twenty-four days' journey from Tauris, and Casbin half way between, them (Voyages de Tavernier, tom. i. p. 63—82.)]

[Footnote 92: At ten parasangs from Tarsus, the army of the younger Cyrus passed the Sarus, three plethra in breadth: the Pyramus, a stadium in breadth, ran five parasangs farther to the east, (Xenophon, Anabas. l. i. p 33, 34.) Note: Now the Sihan—M.]

[Footnote 93: George of Pisidia (Bell. Abaricum, 246—265, p. 49) celebrates with truth the persevering courage of the three campaigns against the Persians.]

Instead of skirmishing on the frontier, the two monarchs who disputed the empire of the East aimed their desperate strokes at the heart of their rival. The military force of Persia was wasted by the marches and combats of twenty years, and many of the veterans, who had survived the perils of the sword and the climate, were still detained in the fortresses of Egypt and Syria. But the revenge and ambition of Chosroes exhausted his kingdom; and the new levies of subjects, strangers, and slaves, were divided into three formidable bodies. [94] The first army of fifty thousand men, illustrious by the ornament and title of the golden spears, was destined to march against Heraclius; the second was stationed to prevent his junction with the troops of his brother Theodorus; and the third was commanded to besiege Constantinople, and to second the operations of the chagan, with whom the Persian king had ratified a treaty of alliance and partition. Sarbar, the general of the third army, penetrated through the provinces of Asia to the well-known camp of Chalcedon, and amused himself with the destruction of the sacred and profane buildings of the Asiatic suburbs, while he impatiently waited the arrival of his Scythian friends on the opposite side of the Bosphorus. On the twenty-ninth of June, thirty thousand Barbarians, the vanguard of the Avars, forced the long wall, and drove into the capital a promiscuous crowd of peasants, citizens, and soldiers. Fourscore thousand [95] of his native subjects, and of the vassal tribes of Gepidae, Russians, Bulgarians, and Sclavonians, advanced under the standard of the chagan; a month was spent in marches and negotiations, but the whole city was invested on the thirty-first of July, from the suburbs of Pera and Galata to the Blachernae and seven towers; and the inhabitants descried with terror the flaming signals of the European and Asiatic shores. In the mean while, the magistrates of Constantinople repeatedly strove to purchase the retreat of the chagan; but their deputies were rejected and insulted; and he suffered the patricians to stand before his throne, while the Persian envoys, in silk robes, were seated by his side. "You see," said the haughty Barbarian, "the proofs of my perfect union with the great king; and his lieutenant is ready to send into my camp a select band of three thousand warriors. Presume no longer to tempt your master with a partial and inadequate ransom your wealth and your city are the only presents worthy of my acceptance. For yourselves, I shall permit you to depart, each with an under-garment and a shirt; and, at my entreaty, my friend Sarbar will not refuse a passage through his lines. Your absent prince, even now a captive or a fugitive, has left Constantinople to its fate; nor can you escape the arms of the Avars and Persians, unless you could soar into the air like birds, unless like fishes you could dive into the waves." [96] During ten successive days, the capital was assaulted by the Avars, who had made some progress in the science of attack; they advanced to sap or batter the wall, under the cover of the impenetrable tortoise; their engines discharged a perpetual volley of stones and darts; and twelve lofty towers of wood exalted the combatants to the height of the neighboring ramparts.

But the senate and people were animated by the spirit of Heraclius, who had detached to their relief a body of twelve thousand cuirassiers; the powers of fire and mechanics were used with superior art and success in the defence of Constantinople; and the galleys, with two and three ranks of oars, commanded the Bosphorus, and rendered the Persians the idle spectators of the defeat of their allies. The Avars were repulsed; a fleet of Sclavonian canoes was destroyed in the harbor; the vassals of the chagan threatened to desert, his provisions were exhausted, and after burning his engines, he gave the signal of a slow and formidable retreat. The devotion of the Romans ascribed this signal deliverance to the Virgin Mary; but the mother of Christ would surely have condemned their inhuman murder of the Persian envoys, who were entitled to the rights of humanity, if they were not protected by the laws of nations. [97]

[Footnote 94: Petavius (Annotationes ad Nicephorum, p. 62, 63, 64) discriminates the names and actions of five Persian generals who were successively sent against Heraclius.]

[Footnote 95: This number of eight myriads is specified by George of Pisidia, (Bell. Abar. 219.) The poet (50—88) clearly indicates that the old chagan lived till the reign of Heraclius, and that his son and successor was born of a foreign mother. Yet Foggini (Annotat. p. 57) has given another interpretation to this passage.]

[Footnote 96: A bird, a frog, a mouse, and five arrows, had been the present of the Scythian king to Darius, (Herodot. l. iv. c. 131, 132.) Substituez une lettre a ces signes (says Rousseau, with much good taste) plus elle sera menacante moins elle effrayera; ce ne sera qu'une fanfarronade dont Darius n'eut fait que rire, (Emile, tom. iii. p. 146.) Yet I much question whether the senate and people of Constantinople laughed at this message of the chagan.]

[Footnote 97: The Paschal Chronicle (p. 392—397) gives a minute and authentic narrative of the siege and deliverance of Constantinople Theophanes (p. 264) adds some circumstances; and a faint light may be obtained from the smoke of George of Pisidia, who has composed a poem (de Bello Abarico, p. 45—54) to commemorate this auspicious event.]

After the division of his army, Heraclius prudently retired to the banks of the Phasis, from whence he maintained a defensive war against the fifty thousand gold spears of Persia. His anxiety was relieved by the deliverance of Constantinople; his hopes were confirmed by a victory of his brother Theodorus; and to the hostile league of Chosroes with the Avars, the Roman emperor opposed the useful and honorable alliance of the Turks. At his liberal invitation, the horde of Chozars [98] transported their tents from the plains of the Volga to the mountains of Georgia; Heraclius received them in the neighborhood of Teflis, and the khan with his nobles dismounted from their horses, if we may credit the Greeks, and fell prostrate on the ground, to adore the purple of the Caesars. Such voluntary homage and important aid were entitled to the warmest acknowledgments; and the emperor, taking off his own diadem, placed it on the head of the Turkish prince, whom he saluted with a tender embrace and the appellation of son. After a sumptuous banquet, he presented Ziebel with the plate and ornaments, the gold, the gems, and the silk, which had been used at the Imperial table, and, with his own hand, distributed rich jewels and ear-rings to his new allies. In a secret interview, he produced the portrait of his daughter Eudocia, [99] condescended to flatter the Barbarian with the promise of a fair and august bride; obtained an immediate succor of forty thousand horse, and negotiated a strong diversion of the Turkish arms on the side of the Oxus. [100] The Persians, in their turn, retreated with precipitation; in the camp of Edessa, Heraclius reviewed an army of seventy thousand Romans and strangers; and some months were successfully employed in the recovery of the cities of Syria, Mesopotamia and Armenia, whose fortifications had been imperfectly restored. Sarbar still maintained the important station of Chalcedon; but the jealousy of Chosroes, or the artifice of Heraclius, soon alienated the mind of that powerful satrap from the service of his king and country. A messenger was intercepted with a real or fictitious mandate to the cadarigan, or second in command, directing him to send, without delay, to the throne, the head of a guilty or unfortunate general. The despatches were transmitted to Sarbar himself; and as soon as he read the sentence of his own death, he dexterously inserted the names of four hundred officers, assembled a military council, and asked the cadarigan whether he was prepared to execute the commands of their tyrant. The Persians unanimously declared, that Chosroes had forfeited the sceptre; a separate treaty was concluded with the government of Constantinople; and if some considerations of honor or policy restrained Sarbar from joining the standard of Heraclius, the emperor was assured that he might prosecute, without interruption, his designs of victory and peace.

[Footnote 98: The power of the Chozars prevailed in the viith, viiith, and ixth centuries. They were known to the Greeks, the Arabs, and under the name of Kosa, to the Chinese themselves. De Guignes, Hist. des Huns, tom. ii. part ii. p. 507—509. Note: Moses of Chorene speaks of an invasion of Armenia by the Khazars in the second century, l. ii. c. 62. M. St. Martin suspects them to be the same with the Hunnish nation of the Acatires or Agazzires. They are called by the Greek historians Eastern Turks; like the Madjars and other Hunnish or Finnish tribes, they had probably received some admixture from the genuine Turkish races. Ibn. Hankal (Oriental Geography) says that their language was like the Bulgarian, and considers them a people of Finnish or Hunnish race. Klaproth, Tabl. Hist. p. 268-273. Abel Remusat, Rech. sur les Langues Tartares, tom. i. p. 315, 316. St. Martin, vol. xi. p. 115—M]

[Footnote 99: Epiphania, or Eudocia, the only daughter of Heraclius and his first wife Eudocia, was born at Constantinople on the 7th of July, A.D. 611, baptized the 15th of August, and crowned (in the oratory of St. Stephen in the palace) the 4th of October of the same year. At this time she was about fifteen.

Eudocia was afterwards sent to her Turkish husband, but the news of his death stopped her journey, and prevented the consummation, (Ducange, Familiae Byzantin. p. 118.)]

[Footnote 100: Elmcain (Hist. Saracen. p. 13—16) gives some curious and probable facts; but his numbers are rather too high—300,000 Romans assembled at Edessa—500,000 Persians killed at Nineveh. The abatement of a cipher is scarcely enough to restore his sanity]

Deprived of his firmest support, and doubtful of the fidelity of his subjects, the greatness of Chosroes was still conspicuous in its ruins. The number of five hundred thousand may be interpreted as an Oriental metaphor, to describe the men and arms, the horses and elephants, that covered Media and Assyria against the invasion of Heraclius. Yet the Romans boldly advanced from the Araxes to the Tigris, and the timid prudence of Rhazates was content to follow them by forced marches through a desolate country, till he received a peremptory mandate to risk the fate of Persia in a decisive battle. Eastward of the Tigris, at the end of the bridge of Mosul, the great Nineveh had formerly been erected: [101] the city, and even the ruins of the city, had long since disappeared; [102] the vacant space afforded a spacious field for the operations of the two armies. But these operations are neglected by the Byzantine historians, and, like the authors of epic poetry and romance, they ascribe the victory, not to the military conduct, but to the personal valor, of their favorite hero. On this memorable day, Heraclius, on his horse Phallas, surpassed the bravest of his warriors: his lip was pierced with a spear; the steed was wounded in the thigh; but he carried his master safe and victorious through the triple phalanx of the Barbarians. In the heat of the action, three valiant chiefs were successively slain by the sword and lance of the emperor: among these was Rhazates himself; he fell like a soldier, but the sight of his head scattered grief and despair through the fainting ranks of the Persians. His armor of pure and massy gold, the shield of one hundred and twenty plates, the sword and belt, the saddle and cuirass, adorned the triumph of Heraclius; and if he had not been faithful to Christ and his mother, the champion of Rome might have offered the fourth opime spoils to the Jupiter of the Capitol. [103] In the battle of Nineveh, which was fiercely fought from daybreak to the eleventh hour, twenty-eight standards, besides those which might be broken or torn, were taken from the Persians; the greatest part of their army was cut in pieces, and the victors, concealing their own loss, passed the night on the field. They acknowledged, that on this occasion it was less difficult to kill than to discomfit the soldiers of Chosroes; amidst the bodies of their friends, no more than two bow-shot from the enemy the remnant of the Persian cavalry stood firm till the seventh hour of the night; about the eighth hour they retired to their unrifled camp, collected their baggage, and dispersed on all sides, from the want of orders rather than of resolution. The diligence of Heraclius was not less admirable in the use of victory; by a march of forty-eight miles in four-and-twenty hours, his vanguard occupied the bridges of the great and the lesser Zab; and the cities and palaces of Assyria were open for the first time to the Romans. By a just gradation of magnificent scenes, they penetrated to the royal seat of Dastagerd, [103/1] and, though much of the treasure had been removed, and much had been expended, the remaining wealth appears to have exceeded their hopes, and even to have satiated their avarice. Whatever could not be easily transported, they consumed with fire, that Chosroes might feel the anguish of those wounds which he had so often inflicted on the provinces of the empire: and justice might allow the excuse, if the desolation had been confined to the works of regal luxury, if national hatred, military license, and religious zeal, had not wasted with equal rage the habitations and the temples of the guiltless subject. The recovery of three hundred Roman standards, and the deliverance of the numerous captives of Edessa and Alexandria, reflect a purer glory on the arms of Heraclius. From the palace of Dastagerd, he pursued his march within a few miles of Modain or Ctesiphon, till he was stopped, on the banks of the Arba, by the difficulty of the passage, the rigor of the season, and perhaps the fame of an impregnable capital. The return of the emperor is marked by the modern name of the city of Sherhzour: he fortunately passed Mount Zara, before the snow, which fell incessantly thirty-four days; and the citizens of Gandzca, or Tauris, were compelled to entertain the soldiers and their horses with a hospitable reception. [104]

[Footnote 101: Ctesias (apud Didor. Sicul. tom. i. l. ii. p. 115, edit. Wesseling) assigns 480 stadia (perhaps only 32 miles) for the circumference of Nineveh. Jonas talks of three days' journey: the 120,000 persons described by the prophet as incapable of discerning their right hand from their left, may afford about 700,000 persons of all ages for the inhabitants of that ancient capital, (Goguet, Origines des Loix, &c., tom. iii. part i. p. 92, 93,) which ceased to exist 600 years before Christ. The western suburb still subsisted, and is mentioned under the name of Mosul in the first age of the Arabian khalifs.]

[Footnote 102: Niebuhr (Voyage en Arabie, &c., tom. ii. p. 286) passed over Nineveh without perceiving it. He mistook for a ridge of hills the old rampart of brick or earth. It is said to have been 100 feet high, flanked with 1500 towers, each of the height of 200 feet.]

[Footnote 103: Rex regia arma fero (says Romulus, in the first consecration).... bina postea (continues Livy, i. 10) inter tot bella, opima parta sunt spolia, adeo rara ejus fortuna decoris. If Varro (apud Pomp Festum, p. 306, edit. Dacier) could justify his liberality in granting the opime spoils even to a common soldier who had slain the king or general of the enemy, the honor would have been much more cheap and common]

[Footnote 103/1: Macdonald Kinneir places Dastagerd at Kasr e Shirin, the palace of Sira on the banks of the Diala between Holwan and Kanabee. Kinnets Geograph. Mem. p. 306—M.]

[Footnote 104: In describing this last expedition of Heraclius, the facts, the places, and the dates of Theophanes (p. 265—271) are so accurate and authentic, that he must have followed the original letters of the emperor, of which the Paschal Chronicle has preserved (p. 398—402) a very curious specimen.]

When the ambition of Chosroes was reduced to the defence of his hereditary kingdom, the love of glory, or even the sense of shame, should have urged him to meet his rival in the field. In the battle of Nineveh, his courage might have taught the Persians to vanquish, or he might have fallen with honor by the lance of a Roman emperor. The successor of Cyrus chose rather, at a secure distance, to expect the event, to assemble the relics of the defeat, and to retire, by measured steps, before the march of Heraclius, till he beheld with a sigh the once loved mansions of Dastagerd. Both his friends and enemies were persuaded, that it was the intention of Chosroes to bury himself under the ruins of the city and palace: and as both might have been equally adverse to his flight, the monarch of Asia, with Sira, [104/1] and three concubines, escaped through a hole in the wall nine days before the arrival of the Romans. The slow and stately procession in which he showed himself to the prostrate crowd, was changed to a rapid and secret journey; and the first evening he lodged in the cottage of a peasant, whose humble door would scarcely give admittance to the great king. [105] His superstition was subdued by fear: on the third day, he entered with joy the fortifications of Ctesiphon; yet he still doubted of his safety till he had opposed the River Tigris to the pursuit of the Romans. The discovery of his flight agitated with terror and tumult the palace, the city, and the camp of Dastagerd: the satraps hesitated whether they had most to fear from their sovereign or the enemy; and the females of the harem were astonished and pleased by the sight of mankind, till the jealous husband of three thousand wives again confined them to a more distant castle. At his command, the army of Dastagerd retreated to a new camp: the front was covered by the Arba, and a line of two hundred elephants; the troops of the more distant provinces successively arrived, and the vilest domestics of the king and satraps were enrolled for the last defence of the throne. It was still in the power of Chosroes to obtain a reasonable peace; and he was repeatedly pressed by the messengers of Heraclius to spare the blood of his subjects, and to relieve a humane conqueror from the painful duty of carrying fire and sword through the fairest countries of Asia. But the pride of the Persian had not yet sunk to the level of his fortune; he derived a momentary confidence from the retreat of the emperor; he wept with impotent rage over the ruins of his Assyrian palaces, and disregarded too long the rising murmurs of the nation, who complained that their lives and fortunes were sacrificed to the obstinacy of an old man. That unhappy old man was himself tortured with the sharpest pains both of mind and body; and, in the consciousness of his approaching end, he resolved to fix the tiara on the head of Merdaza, the most favored of his sons. But the will of Chosroes was no longer revered, and Siroes, [105/1] who gloried in the rank and merit of his mother Sira, had conspired with the malecontents to assert and anticipate the rights of primogeniture. [106] Twenty-two satraps (they styled themselves patriots) were tempted by the wealth and honors of a new reign: to the soldiers, the heir of Chosroes promised an increase of pay; to the Christians, the free exercise of their religion; to the captives, liberty and rewards; and to the nation, instant peace and the reduction of taxes. It was determined by the conspirators, that Siroes, with the ensigns of royalty, should appear in the camp; and if the enterprise should fail, his escape was contrived to the Imperial court. But the new monarch was saluted with unanimous acclamations; the flight of Chosroes (yet where could he have fled?) was rudely arrested, eighteen sons were massacred [106/1] before his face, and he was thrown into a dungeon, where he expired on the fifth day. The Greeks and modern Persians minutely describe how Chosroes was insulted, and famished, and tortured, by the command of an inhuman son, who so far surpassed the example of his father: but at the time of his death, what tongue would relate the story of the parricide? what eye could penetrate into the tower of darkness? According to the faith and mercy of his Christian enemies, he sunk without hope into a still deeper abyss; [107] and it will not be denied, that tyrants of every age and sect are the best entitled to such infernal abodes. The glory of the house of Sassan ended with the life of Chosroes: his unnatural son enjoyed only eight months the fruit of his crimes: and in the space of four years, the regal title was assumed by nine candidates, who disputed, with the sword or dagger, the fragments of an exhausted monarchy. Every province, and each city of Persia, was the scene of independence, of discord, and of blood; and the state of anarchy prevailed about eight years longer, [107/1] till the factions were silenced and united under the common yoke of the Arabian caliphs. [108]

[Footnote 104/1: The Schirin of Persian poetry. The love of Chosru and Schirin rivals in Persian romance that of Joseph with Zuleika the wife of Potiphar, of Solomon with the queen of Sheba, and that of Mejnoun and Leila. The number of Persian poems on the subject may be seen in M. von Hammer's preface to his poem of Schirin—M]

[Footnote 105: The words of Theophanes are remarkable. Young princes who discover a propensity to war should repeatedly transcribe and translate such salutary texts.]

[Footnote 105/1: His name was Kabad (as appears from an official letter in the Paschal Chronicle, p. 402.) St. Martin considers the name Siroes, Schirquieh of Schirwey, derived from the word schir, royal. St. Martin, xi. 153—M.]

[Footnote 106: The authentic narrative of the fall of Chosroes is contained in the letter of Heraclius (Chron. Paschal. p. 398) and the history of Theophanes, (p. 271.)]

[Footnote 106/1: According to Le Beau, this massacre was perpetrated at Mahuza in Babylonia, not in the presence of Chosroes. The Syrian historian, Thomas of Maraga, gives Chosroes twenty-four sons; Mirkhond, (translated by De Sacy,) fifteen; the inedited Modjmel-alte-warikh, agreeing with Gibbon, eighteen, with their names. Le Beau and St. Martin, xi. 146—M.]

[Footnote 107: On the first rumor of the death of Chosroes, an Heracliad in two cantos was instantly published at Constantinople by George of Pisidia, (p. 97—105.) A priest and a poet might very properly exult in the damnation of the public enemy but such mean revenge is unworthy of a king and a conqueror; and I am sorry to find so much black superstition in the letter of Heraclius: he almost applauds the parricide of Siroes as an act of piety and justice. Note: The Mahometans show no more charity towards the memory of Chosroes or Khoosroo Purveez. All his reverses are ascribed to the just indignation of God, upon a monarch who had dared, with impious and accursed hands, to tear the letter of the Holy Prophet Mahomed. Compare note, p. 231—M.]

[Footnote 107/1: Yet Gibbon himself places the flight and death of Yesdegird III., the last king of Persia, in 651. The famous era of Yesdegird dates from his accession, June 16 632—M.]

[Footnote 108: The best Oriental accounts of this last period of the Sassanian kings are found in Eutychius, (Annal. tom. ii. p. 251—256,) who dissembles the parricide of Siroes, D'Herbelot (Bibliotheque Orientale, p. 789,) and Assemanni, (Bibliothec. Oriental. tom. iii. p. 415—420.)]

As soon as the mountains became passable, the emperor received the welcome news of the success of the conspiracy, the death of Chosroes, and the elevation of his eldest son to the throne of Persia. The authors of the revolution, eager to display their merits in the court or camp of Tauris, preceded the ambassadors of Siroes, who delivered the letters of their master to his brother the emperor of the Romans. [109] In the language of the usurpers of every age, he imputes his own crimes to the Deity, and, without degrading his equal majesty, he offers to reconcile the long discord of the two nations, by a treaty of peace and alliance more durable than brass or iron. The conditions of the treaty were easily defined and faithfully executed. In the recovery of the standards and prisoners which had fallen into the hands of the Persians, the emperor imitated the example of Augustus: their care of the national dignity was celebrated by the poets of the times, but the decay of genius may be measured by the distance between Horace and George of Pisidia: the subjects and brethren of Heraclius were redeemed from persecution, slavery, and exile; but, instead of the Roman eagles, the true wood of the holy cross was restored to the importunate demands of the successor of Constantine. The victor was not ambitious of enlarging the weakness of the empire; the son of Chosroes abandoned without regret the conquests of his father; the Persians who evacuated the cities of Syria and Egypt were honorably conducted to the frontier, and a war which had wounded the vitals of the two monarchies, produced no change in their external and relative situation. The return of Heraclius from Tauris to Constantinople was a perpetual triumph; and after the exploits of six glorious campaigns, he peaceably enjoyed the Sabbath of his toils. After a long impatience, the senate, the clergy, and the people, went forth to meet their hero, with tears and acclamations, with olive branches and innumerable lamps; he entered the capital in a chariot drawn by four elephants; and as soon as the emperor could disengage himself from the tumult of public joy, he tasted more genuine satisfaction in the embraces of his mother and his son. [110]

[Footnote 109: The letter of Siroes in the Paschal Chronicle (p. 402) unfortunately ends before he proceeds to business. The treaty appears in its execution in the histories of Theophanes and Nicephorus. Note: M. Mai. Script. Vet. Nova Collectio, vol. i. P. 2, p. 223, has added some lines, but no clear sense can be made out of the fragment—M.]

[Footnote 110: The burden of Corneille's song, "Montrez Heraclius au peuple qui l'attend," is much better suited to the present occasion. See his triumph in Theophanes (p. 272, 273) and Nicephorus, (p. 15, 16.)

The life of the mother and tenderness of the son are attested by George of Pisidia, (Bell. Abar. 255, &c., p. 49.) The metaphor of the Sabbath is used somewhat profanely by these Byzantine Christians.]

The succeeding year was illustrated by a triumph of a very different kind, the restitution of the true cross to the holy sepulchre. Heraclius performed in person the pilgrimage of Jerusalem, the identity of the relic was verified by the discreet patriarch, [111] and this august ceremony has been commemorated by the annual festival of the exaltation of the cross. Before the emperor presumed to tread the consecrated ground, he was instructed to strip himself of the diadem and purple, the pomp and vanity of the world: but in the judgment of his clergy, the persecution of the Jews was more easily reconciled with the precepts of the gospel. [111/1] He again ascended his throne to receive the congratulations of the ambassadors of France and India: and the fame of Moses, Alexander, and Hercules, [112] was eclipsed in the popular estimation, by the superior merit and glory of the great Heraclius. Yet the deliverer of the East was indigent and feeble. Of the Persian spoils, the most valuable portion had been expended in the war, distributed to the soldiers, or buried, by an unlucky tempest, in the waves of the Euxine. The conscience of the emperor was oppressed by the obligation of restoring the wealth of the clergy, which he had borrowed for their own defence: a perpetual fund was required to satisfy these inexorable creditors; the provinces, already wasted by the arms and avarice of the Persians, were compelled to a second payment of the same taxes; and the arrears of a simple citizen, the treasurer of Damascus, were commuted to a fine of one hundred thousand pieces of gold. The loss of two hundred thousand soldiers [113] who had fallen by the sword, was of less fatal importance than the decay of arts, agriculture, and population, in this long and destructive war: and although a victorious army had been formed under the standard of Heraclius, the unnatural effort appears to have exhausted rather than exercised their strength. While the emperor triumphed at Constantinople or Jerusalem, an obscure town on the confines of Syria was pillaged by the Saracens, and they cut in pieces some troops who advanced to its relief; an ordinary and trifling occurrence, had it not been the prelude of a mighty revolution. These robbers were the apostles of Mahomet; their fanatic valor had emerged from the desert; and in the last eight years of his reign, Heraclius lost to the Arabs the same provinces which he had rescued from the Persians.

[Footnote 111: See Baronius, (Annal. Eccles. A.D. 628, No. 1-4,) Eutychius, (Annal. tom. ii. p. 240—248,) Nicephorus, (Brev. p. 15.) The seals of the case had never been broken; and this preservation of the cross is ascribed (under God) to the devotion of Queen Sira.]

[Footnote 111/1: If the clergy imposed upon the kneeling and penitent emperor the persecution of the Jews, it must be acknowledge that provocation was not wanting; for how many of them had been eye-witnesses of, perhaps sufferers in, the horrible atrocities committed on the capture of the city! Yet we have no authentic account of great severities exercised by Heraclius. The law of Hadrian was reenacted, which prohibited the Jews from approaching within three miles of the city—a law, which, in the present exasperated state of the Christians, might be a measure of security of mercy, rather than of oppression. Milman, Hist. of the Jews, iii. 242—M.]

[Footnote 112: George of Pisidia, Acroas. iii. de Expedit. contra Persas, 415, &c., and Heracleid. Acroas. i. 65—138. I neglect the meaner parallels of Daniel, Timotheus, &c.; Chosroes and the chagan were of course compared to Belshazzar, Pharaoh, the old serpent, &c.]

[Footnote 13: Suidas (in Excerpt. Hist. Byzant. p. 46) gives this number; but either the Persian must be read for the Isaurian war, or this passage does not belong to the emperor Heraclius.]

CHAPTER XLVII

ECCLESIASTICAL DISCORD

PART I

THEOLOGICAL HISTORY OF THE DOCTRINE OF THE INCARNATION—The HUMAN AND DIVINE NATURE OF CHRIST—ENMITY OF THE PATRIARCHS OF ALEXANDRIA AND CONSTANTINOPLE—ST. CYRIL AND NESTORIUS. THIRD GENERAL COUNCIL OF EPHESUS—HERESY OF EUTYCHES—FOURTH GENERAL COUNCIL OF CHALCEDON—CIVIL AND ECCLESIASTICAL DISCORD—INTOLERANCE OF JUSTINIAN—THE THREE CHAPTERS—THE MONOTHELITE CONTROVERSY—STATE OF THE ORIGINAL SECTS:—I. THE NESTORIANS—II. THE JACOBITES—III. THE MARONITES—IV. THE ARMENIANS—V. THE COPTS AND ABYSSINIANS

After the extinction of paganism, the Christians in peace and piety might have enjoyed their solitary triumph. But the principle of discord was alive in their bosom, and they were more solicitous to explore the nature, than to practice the laws, of their founder. I have already observed, that the disputes of the Trinity were succeeded by those of the Incarnation; alike scandalous to the church, alike pernicious to the state, still more minute in their origin, still more durable in their effects.

It is my design to comprise in the present chapter a religious war of two hundred and fifty years, to represent the ecclesiastical and political schism of the Oriental sects, and to introduce their clamorous or sanguinary contests, by a modest inquiry into the doctrines of the primitive church. [1]

[Footnote 1: By what means shall I authenticate this previous inquiry, which I have studied to circumscribe and compress?—If I persist in supporting each fact or reflection by its proper and special evidence, every line would demand a string of testimonies, and every note would swell to a critical dissertation. But the numberless passages of antiquity which I have seen with my own eyes, are compiled, digested and illustrated by Petavius and Le Clerc, by Beausobre and Mosheim. I shall be content to fortify my narrative by the names and characters of these respectable guides; and in the contemplation of a minute or remote object, I am not ashamed to borrow the aid of the strongest glasses: 1. The Dogmata Theologica of Petavius are a work of incredible labor and compass; the volumes which relate solely to the Incarnation (two folios, vth and vith, of 837 pages) are divided into xvi. books—the first of history, the remainder of controversy and doctrine. The Jesuit's learning is copious and correct; his Latinity is pure, his method clear, his argument profound and well connected; but he is the slave of the fathers, the scourge of heretics, and the enemy of truth and candor, as often as they are inimical to the Catholic cause. 2. The Arminian Le Clerc, who has composed in a quarto volume (Amsterdam, 1716) the ecclesiastical history of the two first centuries, was free both in his temper and situation; his sense is clear, but his thoughts are narrow; he reduces the reason or folly of ages to the standard of his private judgment, and his impartiality is sometimes quickened, and sometimes tainted by his opposition to the fathers. See the heretics (Cerinthians, lxxx. Ebionites, ciii. Carpocratians, cxx. Valentinijns, cxxi. Basilidians, cxxiii. Marcionites, cxli., &c.) under their proper dates. 3. The Histoire Critique du Manicheisme (Amsterdam, 1734, 1739, in two vols. in 4to., with a posthumous dissertation sur les Nazarenes, Lausanne, 1745) of M. de Beausobre is a treasure of ancient philosophy and theology. The learned historian spins with incomparable art the systematic thread of opinion, and transforms himself by turns into the person of a saint, a sage, or a heretic. Yet his refinement is sometimes excessive;

he betrays an amiable partiality in favor of the weaker side, and, while he guards against calumny, he does not allow sufficient scope for superstition and fanaticism. A copious table of contents will direct the reader to any point that he wishes to examine. 4. Less profound than Petavius, less independent than Le Clerc, less ingenious than Beausobre, the historian Mosheim is full, rational, correct, and moderate. In his learned work, De Rebus Christianis ante Constantinum (Helmstadt 1753, in 4to.,) see the Nazarenes and Ebionites, p. 172—179, 328—332. The Gnostics in general, p. 179, &c. Cerinthus, p. 196—202. Basilides, p. 352—361. Carpocrates, p. 363—367. Valentinus, p. 371—389 Marcion, p. 404—410. The Manichaeans, p. 829-837, &c.]

I. A laudable regard for the honor of the first proselyte has countenanced the belief, the hope, the wish, that the Ebionites, or at least the Nazarenes, were distinguished only by their obstinate perseverance in the practice of the Mosaic rites.

Their churches have disappeared, their books are obliterated: their obscure freedom might allow a latitude of faith, and the softness of their infant creed would be variously moulded by the zeal or prudence of three hundred years. Yet the most charitable criticism must refuse these sectaries any knowledge of the pure and proper divinity of Christ. Educated in the school of Jewish prophecy and prejudice, they had never been taught to elevate their hopes above a human and temporal Messiah. [2] If they had courage to hail their king when he appeared in a plebeian garb, their grosser apprehensions were incapable of discerning their God, who had studiously disguised his celestial character under the name and person of a mortal. [3] The familiar companions of Jesus of Nazareth conversed with their friend and countryman, who, in all the actions of rational and animal life, appeared of the same species with themselves. His progress from infancy to youth and manhood was marked by a regular increase in stature and wisdom; and after a painful agony of mind and body, he expired on the cross. He lived and died for the service of mankind: but the life and death of Socrates had likewise been devoted to the cause of religion and justice; and although the stoic or the hero may disdain the humble virtues of Jesus, the tears which he shed over his friend and country may be esteemed the purest evidence of his humanity. The miracles of the gospel could not astonish a people who held with intrepid faith the more splendid prodigies of the Mosaic law. The prophets of ancient days had cured diseases, raised the dead, divided the sea, stopped the sun, and ascended to heaven in a fiery chariot. And the metaphorical style of the Hebrews might ascribe to a saint and martyr the adoptive title of Son of God.

[Footnote 2: Jew Tryphon, (Justin. Dialog. p. 207) in the name of his countrymen, and the modern Jews, the few who divert their thoughts from money to religion, still hold the same language, and allege the literal sense of the prophets. Note: See on this passage Bp. Kaye, Justin Martyr, p. 25—M. Note: Most of the modern writers, who have closely examined this subject, and who will not be suspected of any theological bias, Rosenmuller on Isaiah ix. 5, and on Psalm xlv. 7, and Bertholdt, Christologia Judaeorum, c. xx., rightly ascribe much higher notions of the Messiah to the Jews. In fact, the dispute seems to rest on the notion that there was a definite and authorized notion of the Messiah, among the Jews, whereas it was probably so vague, as to admit every shade of difference, from the vulgar expectation of a mere temporal king, to the philosophic notion of an emanation from the Deity—M.]

[Footnote 3: Chrysostom (Basnage, Hist. des Juifs, tom. v. c. 9, p. 183) and Athanasius (Petav. Dogmat. Theolog. tom. v. l. i. c. 2, p. 3) are obliged to confess that the Divinity of Christ is rarely mentioned by himself or his apostles.]

Yet in the insufficient creed of the Nazarenes and the Ebionites, a distinction is faintly noticed between the heretics, who confounded the generation of Christ in the common order of nature, and the less guilty schismatics, who revered the virginity of his mother, and excluded the aid of an earthly father. The incredulity of the former was countenanced by the visible circumstances of his birth, the legal marriage of the reputed parents, Joseph and Mary, and his lineal claim to the kingdom of David and the inheritance of Judah. But the secret and authentic history has been recorded in several copies of the Gospel according to St. Matthew, [4] which these sectaries long preserved in the original Hebrew, [5] as the sole evidence of their faith. The natural suspicions of the husband, conscious of his own chastity, were dispelled by the assurance (in a dream) that his wife was pregnant of the Holy Ghost: and as this distant and domestic prodigy could not fall under the personal observation of the historian, he must have listened to the same voice which dictated to Isaiah the future conception of a virgin. The son of a virgin, generated by the ineffable operation of the Holy Spirit, was a creature without example or resemblance, superior in every attribute of mind and body to the children of Adam. Since the introduction of the Greek or Chaldean philosophy, [6] the Jews [7] were persuaded of the preexistence, transmigration, and immortality of souls; and providence was justified by a supposition, that they were confined in their earthly prisons to expiate the stains which they had contracted in a former state. [8] But the degrees of purity and corruption are almost immeasurable. It might be fairly presumed, that the most sublime and virtuous of human spirits was infused into the offspring of Mary and the Holy Ghost; [9] that his abasement was the result of his voluntary choice; and that the object of his mission was, to purify, not his own, but the sins of the world. On his return to his native skies, he received the immense reward of his obedience; the everlasting kingdom of the Messiah, which had been darkly foretold by the prophets, under the carnal images of peace, of conquest, and of dominion. Omnipotence could enlarge the human faculties of Christ to the extend of is celestial office. In the language of antiquity, the title of God has not been severely confined to the first parent, and his incomparable minister, his only-begotten son, might claim, without presumption, the religious, though secondary, worship of a subject of a subject world.

[Footnote 4: The two first chapters of St. Matthew did not exist in the Ebionite copies, (Epiphan. Haeres. xxx. 13;) and the miraculous conception is one of the last articles which Dr. Priestley has curtailed from his scanty creed. Note: The distinct allusion to the facts related in the two first chapters of the Gospel, in a work evidently written about the end of the reign of Nero, the Ascensio Isaiae, edited by Archbishop Lawrence, seems convincing evidence that they are integral parts of the authentic Christian history—M.]

[Footnote 5: It is probable enough that the first of the Gospels for the use of the Jewish converts was composed in the Hebrew or Syriac idiom: the fact is attested by a chain of fathers—Papias, Irenaeus, Origen, Jerom, &c. It is devoutly believed by the Catholics, and admitted by Casaubon, Grotius, and Isaac Vossius, among the Protestant critics. But this Hebrew Gospel of St. Matthew is most unaccountably lost; and we may accuse the diligence or fidelity of the primitive churches, who have preferred the unauthorized version of some nameless Greek. Erasmus and his followers, who respect our Greek text as the original Gospel, deprive themselves of the evidence which declares it to be the work of an apostle. See Simon, Hist. Critique, &c., tom. iii. c. 5—9, p. 47—101, and the Prolegomena of Mill and Wetstein to the New Testament. Note: Surely the extinction of the Judaeo-Christian community related from Mosheim by Gibbon himself (c. xv.) accounts both simply and naturally for the loss of a composition, which had become of no use—nor does it follow that the Greek Gospel of St. Matthew is unauthorized—M.]

[Footnote 6: The metaphysics of the soul are disengaged by Cicero (Tusculan. l. i.) and Maximus of Tyre (Dissertat. xvi.) from the intricacies of dialogue, which sometimes amuse, and often perplex, the readers of the Phoedrus, the Phoedon, and the Laws of Plato.]

[Footnote 7: The disciples of Jesus were persuaded that a man might have sinned before he was born, (John, ix. 2,) and the Pharisees held the transmigration of virtuous souls, (Joseph. de Bell. Judaico, l. ii. c. 7;) and a modern Rabbi is modestly assured, that Hermes, Pythagoras, Plato, &c., derived their metaphysics from his illustrious countrymen.]

[Footnote 8: Four different opinions have been entertained concerning the origin of human souls: 1. That they are eternal and divine. 2. That they were created in a separate state of existence, before their union with the body. 3. That they have been propagated from the original stock of Adam, who contained in himself the mental as well as the corporeal seed of his posterity. 4. That each soul is occasionally created and embodied in the moment of conception—The last of these sentiments appears to have prevailed among the moderns; and our spiritual history is grown less sublime, without becoming more intelligible.]

[Footnote 9: It was one of the fifteen heresies imputed to Origen, and denied by his apologist, (Photius, Bibliothec. cod. cxvii. p. 296.) Some of the Rabbis attribute one and the same soul to the persons of Adam, David, and the Messiah.]

II. The seeds of the faith, which had slowly arisen in the rocky and ungrateful soil of Judea, were transplanted, in full maturity, to the happier climes of the Gentiles; and the strangers of Rome or Asia, who never beheld the manhood, were the more readily disposed to embrace the divinity, of Christ. The polytheist and the philosopher, the Greek and the Barbarian, were alike accustomed to conceive a long succession, an infinite chain of angels or daemons, or deities, or aeons, or emanations, issuing from the throne of light. Nor could it seem strange or incredible, that the first of these aeons, the Logos, or Word of God, of the same substance with the Father, should descend upon earth, to deliver the human race from vice and error, and to conduct them in the paths of life and immortality. But the prevailing doctrine of the eternity and inherent pravity of matter infected the primitive churches of the East. Many among the Gentile proselytes refused to believe that a celestial spirit, an undivided portion of the first essence, had been personally united with a mass of impure and contaminated flesh; and, in their zeal for the divinity, they piously abjured the humanity, of Christ. While his blood was still recent on Mount Calvary, [10] the Docetes, a numerous and learned sect of Asiatics, invented the phantastic system, which was afterwards propagated by the Marcionites, the Manichaeans, and the various names of the Gnostic heresy. [11] They denied the truth and authenticity of the Gospels, as far as they relate the conception of Mary, the birth of Christ, and the thirty years that preceded the exercise of his ministry. He first appeared on the banks of the Jordan in the form of perfect manhood; but it was a form only, and not a substance; a human figure created by the hand of Omnipotence to imitate the faculties and actions of a man, and to impose a perpetual illusion on the senses of his friends and enemies. Articulate sounds vibrated on the ears of the disciples; but the image which was impressed on their optic nerve eluded the more stubborn evidence of the touch; and they enjoyed the spiritual, not the corporeal, presence of the Son of God. The rage of the Jews was idly wasted against an impassive phantom; and the mystic scenes of the passion and death, the resurrection and ascension, of Christ were represented on the theatre of Jerusalem for the benefit of mankind. If it were urged, that such ideal mimicry, such incessant deception, was unworthy of the God of truth, the Docetes agreed with too many of their orthodox brethren in the justification of pious falsehood. In the system of the Gnostics, the Jehovah of Israel, the Creator of this lower world, was a rebellious, or at least an ignorant, spirit. The Son of God descended upon earth to abolish his temple and his law; and, for the accomplishment of this salutary end, he dexterously transferred to his own person the hope and prediction of a temporal Messiah.

[Footnote 10: Apostolis adhuc in seculo superstitibus, apud Judaeam Christi sanguine recente, Phantasma domini corpus asserebatur. Hieronym, advers. Lucifer. c. 8. The epistle of Ignatius to the

Smyrnaeans, and even the Gospel according to St. John, are levelled against the growing error of the Docetes, who had obtained too much credit in the world, (1 John, iv. 1—5.)]

[Footnote 11: About the year 200 of the Christian aera, Irenaeus and Hippolytus efuted the thirty-two sects, which had multiplied to fourscore in the time of Epiphanius, (Phot. Biblioth. cod. cxx. cxxi. cxxii.) The five books of Irenaeus exist only in barbarous Latin; but the original might perhaps be found in some monastery of Greece.]

One of the most subtile disputants of the Manichaean school has pressed the danger and indecency of supposing, that the God of the Christians, in the state of a human foetus, emerged at the end of nine months from a female womb. The pious horror of his antagonists provoked them to disclaim all sensual circumstances of conception and delivery; to maintain that the divinity passed through Mary like a sunbeam through a plate of glass; and to assert, that the seal of her virginity remained unbroken even at the moment when she became the mother of Christ. But the rashness of these concessions has encouraged a milder sentiment of those of the Docetes, who taught, not that Christ was a phantom, but that he was clothed with an impassible and incorruptible body. Such, indeed, in the more orthodox system, he has acquired since his resurrection, and such he must have always possessed, if it were capable of pervading, without resistance or injury, the density of intermediate matter. Devoid of its most essential properties, it might be exempt from the attributes and infirmities of the flesh. A foetus that could increase from an invisible point to its full maturity; a child that could attain the stature of perfect manhood without deriving any nourishment from the ordinary sources, might continue to exist without repairing a daily waste by a daily supply of external matter. Jesus might share the repasts of his disciples without being subject to the calls of thirst or hunger; and his virgin purity was never sullied by the involuntary stains of sensual concupiscence. Of a body thus singularly constituted, a question would arise, by what means, and of what materials, it was originally framed; and our sounder theology is startled by an answer which was not peculiar to the Gnostics, that both the form and the substance proceeded from the divine essence. The idea of pure and absolute spirit is a refinement of modern philosophy: the incorporeal essence, ascribed by the ancients to human souls, celestial beings, and even the Deity himself, does not exclude the notion of extended space; and their imagination was satisfied with a subtile nature of air, or fire, or aether, incomparably more perfect than the grossness of the material world. If we define the place, we must describe the figure, of the Deity. Our experience, perhaps our vanity, represents the powers of reason and virtue under a human form. The Anthropomorphites, who swarmed among the monks of Egypt and the Catholics of Africa, could produce the express declaration of Scripture, that man was made after the image of his Creator. [12] The venerable Serapion, one of the saints of the Nitrian deserts, relinquished, with many a tear, his darling prejudice; and bewailed, like an infant, his unlucky conversion, which had stolen away his God, and left his mind without any visible object of faith or devotion. [13]

[Footnote 12: The pilgrim Cassian, who visited Egypt in the beginning of the vth century, observes and laments the reign of anthropomorphism among the monks, who were not conscious that they embraced the system of Epicurus, (Cicero, de Nat. Deorum, i. 18, 34.) Ab universo propemodum genere monachorum, qui per totam provinciam Egyptum morabantur, pro simplicitatis errore susceptum est, ut e contraric memoratum pontificem (Theophilus) velut haeresi gravissima depravatum, pars maxima seniorum ab universo fraternitatis corpore decerneret detestandum, (Cassian, Collation. x. 2.) As long as St. Augustin remained a Manichaean, he was scandalized by the anthropomorphism of the vulgar Catholics.]

[Footnote 13: Ita est in oratione senex mente confusus, eo quod illam imaginem Deitatis, quam proponere sibi in oratione consueverat, aboleri de suo corde sentiret, ut in amarissimos fletus, crebrosque singultus repente prorumpens, in terram prostratus, cum ejulatu validissimo proclamaret; "Heu me miserum! tulerunt a me Deum meum, et quem nunc teneam non habeo, vel quem adorem, aut interpallam am nescio." Cassian, Collat. x. 2.]

III. Such were the fleeting shadows of the Docetes. A more substantial, though less simple, hypothesis, was contrived by Cerinthus of Asia, [14] who dared to oppose the last of the apostles. Placed on the confines of the Jewish and Gentile world, he labored to reconcile the Gnostic with the Ebionite, by confessing in the same Messiah the supernatural union of a man and a God; and this mystic doctrine was adopted with many fanciful improvements by Carpocrates, Basilides, and Valentine, [15] the heretics of the Egyptian school. In their eyes, Jesus of Nazareth was a mere mortal, the legitimate son of Joseph and Mary: but he was the best and wisest of the human race, selected as the worthy instrument to restore upon earth the worship of the true and supreme Deity. When he was baptized in the Jordan, the Christ, the first of the aeons, the Son of God himself, descended on Jesus in the form of a dove, to inhabit his mind, and direct his actions during the allotted period of his ministry. When the Messiah was delivered into the hands of the Jews, the Christ, an immortal and impassible being, forsook his earthly tabernacle, flew back to the pleroma or world of spirits, and left the solitary Jesus to suffer, to complain, and to expire. But the justice and generosity of such a desertion are strongly questionable; and the fate of an innocent martyr, at first impelled, and at length abandoned, by his divine companion, might provoke the pity and indignation of the profane. Their murmurs were variously silenced by the sectaries who espoused and modified the double system of Cerinthus. It was alleged, that when Jesus was nailed to the cross, he was endowed with a miraculous apathy of mind and body, which rendered him insensible of his apparent sufferings. It was affirmed, that these momentary, though real, pangs would be abundantly repaid by the temporal reign of a thousand years reserved for the Messiah in his kingdom of the new Jerusalem. It was insinuated, that if he suffered, he deserved to suffer; that human nature is never absolutely perfect; and that the cross and passion might serve to expiate the venial transgressions of the son of Joseph, before his mysterious union with the Son of God. [16]

[Footnote 14: St. John and Cerinthus (A.D. 80. Cleric. Hist. Eccles. p. 493) accidentally met in the public bath of Ephesus; but the apostle fled from the heretic, lest the building should tumble on their heads. This foolish story, reprobated by Dr. Middleton, (Miscellaneous Works, vol. ii.,) is related, however, by Irenaeus, (iii. 3,) on the evidence of Polycarp, and was probably suited to the time and residence of Cerinthus. The obsolete, yet probably the true, reading of 1 John, iv. 3 alludes to the double nature of that primitive heretic. Note: Griesbach asserts that all the Greek Mss., all the translators, and all the Greek fathers, support the common reading—Nov. Test. in loc—M]

[Footnote 15: The Valentinians embraced a complex, and almost incoherent, system. 1. Both Christ and Jesus were aeons, though of different degrees; the one acting as the rational soul, the other as the divine spirit of the Savior. 2. At the time of the passion, they both retired, and left only a sensitive soul and a human body. 3. Even that body was aethereal, and perhaps apparent—Such are the laborious conclusions of Mosheim. But I much doubt whether the Latin translator understood Irenaeus, and whether Irenaeus and the Valetinians understood themselves.]

[Footnote 16: The heretics abused the passionate exclamation of "My God, my God, why hast thou forsaken me?" Rousseau, who has drawn an eloquent, but indecent, parallel between Christ and Socrates, forgets that not a word of impatience or despair escaped from the mouth of the dying *philosopher. In the Messiah, such sentiments could be only apparent; and such ill-sounding words were properly explained as the application of a psalm and prophecy.]*

IV. All those who believe the immateriality of the soul, a specious and noble tenet, must confess, from their present experience, the incomprehensible union of mind and matter. A similar union is not inconsistent with a much higher, or even with the highest, degree of mental faculties; and the incarnation of an aeon or archangel, the most perfect of created spirits, does not involve any positive contradiction or absurdity. In the age of religious freedom, which was determined by the council of Nice, the dignity of Christ was measured by private judgment according to the indefinite rule of Scripture, or reason, or tradition. But when his pure and proper divinity had been established on the ruins of Arianism, the faith of the Catholics trembled on the edge of a precipice where it was impossible to recede, dangerous to stand, dreadful to fall and the manifold inconveniences of their creed were aggravated by the sublime character of their theology. They hesitated to pronounce; that God himself, the second person of an equal and consubstantial trinity, was manifested in the flesh; [17] that a being who pervades the universe, had been confined in the womb of Mary; that his eternal duration had been marked by the days, and months, and years of human existence; that the Almighty had been scourged and crucified; that his impassible essence had felt pain and anguish; that his omniscience was not exempt from ignorance; and that the source of life and immortality expired on Mount Calvary. These alarming consequences were affirmed with unblushing simplicity by Apollinaris, [18] bishop of Laodicea, and one of the luminaries of the church. The son of a learned grammarian, he was skilled in all the sciences of Greece; eloquence, erudition, and philosophy, conspicuous in the volumes of Apollinaris, were humbly devoted to the service of religion. The worthy friend of Athanasius, the worthy antagonist of Julian, he bravely wrestled with the Arians and Polytheists, and though he affected the rigor of geometrical demonstration, his commentaries revealed the literal and allegorical sense of the Scriptures. A mystery, which had long floated in the looseness of popular belief, was defined by his perverse diligence in a technical form; and he first proclaimed the memorable words, "One incarnate nature of Christ," which are still reechoed with hostile clamors in the churches of Asia, Egypt, and Aethiopia. He taught that the Godhead was united or mingled with the body of a man; and that the Logos, the eternal wisdom, supplied in the flesh the place and office of a human soul. Yet as the profound doctor had been terrified at his own rashness, Apollinaris was heard to mutter some faint accents of excuse and explanation. He acquiesced in the old distinction of the Greek philosophers between the rational and sensitive soul of man; that he might reserve the Logos for intellectual functions, and employ the subordinate human principle in the meaner actions of animal life.

With the moderate Docetes, he revered Mary as the spiritual, rather than as the carnal, mother of Christ, whose body either came from heaven, impassible and incorruptible, or was absorbed, and as it were transformed, into the essence of the Deity. The system of Apollinaris was strenuously encountered by the Asiatic and Syrian divines whose schools are honored by the names of Basil, Gregory and Chrysostom, and tainted by those of Diodorus, Theodore, and Nestorius. But the person of the aged bishop of Laedicea, his character and dignity, remained inviolate; and his rivals, since we may not suspect them of the weakness of toleration, were astonished, perhaps, by the novelty of the argument, and diffident of the final sentence of the Catholic church. Her judgment at length inclined in their favor; the heresy of Apollinaris was condemned, and the separate congregations of his disciples were proscribed by the Imperial laws. But his principles were secretly entertained in the monasteries of Egypt, and his enemies felt the hatred of Theophilus and Cyril, the successive patriarchs of Alexandria.

[Footnote 17: This strong expression might be justified by the language of St. Paul, (1 Tim. iii. 16;) but we are deceived by our modern Bibles. The word which was altered to God at Constantinople in the beginning of the vith century: the true reading, which is visible in the Latin and Syriac versions, still exists in the reasoning of the Greek, as well as of the Latin fathers; and this fraud, with that of the three witnesses of St. John, is admirably detected by Sir Isaac Newton. (See his two letters translated by M. de Missy, in the Journal Britannique, tom. xv. p. 148—190, 351—390.) I have weighed the arguments, and may yield to the authority of the first of philosophers, who was deeply skilled in critical and theological studies. Note: It should be Griesbach in loc. The weight of authority is so much against the common reading in both these points, that they are no longer urged by prudent controversialists. Would Gibbon's deference for the first of philosophers have extended to all his theological conclusions?—M.]

[Footnote 18: For Apollinaris and his sect, see Socrates, l. ii. c. 46, l. iii. c. 16 Sazomen, l. v. c. 18, 1. vi. c. 25, 27. Theodoret, l. v. 3, 10, 11. Tillemont, Memoires Ecclesiastiques, tom. vii. p. 602—638. Not. p. 789—794, in 4to. Venise, 1732. The contemporary saint always mentions the bishop of Laodicea as a friend and brother. The style of the more recent historians is harsh and hostile: yet Philostorgius compares him (l. viii. c. 11-15) to Basil and Gregory.]

V. The grovelling Ebionite, and the fantastic Docetes, were rejected and forgotten: the recent zeal against the errors of Apollinaris reduced the Catholics to a seeming agreement with the double nature of Cerinthus. But instead of a temporary and occasional alliance, they established, and we still embrace, the substantial, indissoluble, and everlasting union of a perfect God with a perfect man, of the second person of the trinity with a reasonable soul and human flesh. In the beginning of the fifth century, the unity of the two natures was the prevailing doctrine of the church. On all sides, it was confessed, that the mode of their coexistence could neither be represented by our ideas, nor expressed by our language. Yet a secret and incurable discord was cherished, between those who were most apprehensive of confounding, and those who were most fearful of separating, the divinity, and the humanity, of Christ. Impelled by religious frenzy, they fled with adverse haste from the error which they mutually deemed most destructive of truth and salvation. On either hand they were anxious to guard, they were jealous to defend, the union and the distinction of the two natures, and to invent such forms of speech, such symbols of doctrine, as were least susceptible of doubt or ambiguity. The poverty of ideas and language tempted them to ransack art and nature for every possible comparison, and each comparison mislead their fancy in the explanation of an incomparable mystery. In the polemic microscope, an atom is enlarged to a monster, and each party was skilful to exaggerate the absurd or impious conclusions that might be extorted from the principles of their adversaries. To escape from each other, they wandered through many a dark and devious thicket, till they were astonished by the horrid phantoms of Cerinthus and Apollinaris, who guarded the opposite issues of the theological labyrinth. As soon as they beheld the twilight of sense and heresy, they started, measured back their steps, and were again involved in the gloom of impenetrable orthodoxy. To purge themselves from the guilt or reproach of damnable error, they disavowed their consequences, explained their principles, excused their indiscretions, and unanimously pronounced the sounds of concord and faith. Yet a latent and almost invisible spark still lurked among the embers of controversy: by the breath of prejudice and passion, it was quickly kindled to a mighty flame, and the verbal disputes [19] of the Oriental sects have shaken the pillars of the church and state.

[Footnote 19: I appeal to the confession of two Oriental prelates, Gregory Abulpharagius the Jacobite primate of the East, and Elias the Nestorian metropolitan of Damascus, (see Asseman, Bibliothec. Oriental. tom. ii. p. 291, tom. iii. p. 514, &c.,) that the Melchites, Jacobites, Nestorians, &c., agree in the doctrine, and differ only in the expression. Our most learned and rational divines—Basnage, Le Clerc, Beausobre, La Croze, Mosheim, Jablonski—are inclined to favor this charitable judgment; but the zeal of Petavius is loud and angry, and the moderation of Dupin is conveyed in a whisper.]

The name of Cyril of Alexandria is famous in controversial story, and the title of saint is a mark that his opinions and his party have finally prevailed. In the house of his uncle, the archbishop Theophilus, he imbibed the orthodox lessons of zeal and dominion, and five years of his youth were profitably spent in the adjacent monasteries of Nitria. Under the tuition of the abbot Serapion, he applied himself to ecclesiastical studies, with such indefatigable ardor, that in the course of one sleepless night, he has perused the four Gospels, the Catholic Epistles, and the Epistle to the Romans. Origen he detested; but the writings of Clemens and Dionysius, of Athanasius and Basil, were continually in his hands: by the theory and practice of dispute, his faith was confirmed and his wit was sharpened; he extended round his cell the cobwebs of scholastic theology, and meditated the works of allegory and metaphysics, whose remains, in seven verbose folios, now peaceably slumber by the side of their rivals. [20] Cyril prayed and fasted in the desert, but his thoughts (it is the reproach of a friend) [21] were still fixed on the world; and the call of Theophilus, who summoned him to the tumult of cities and synods, was too readily obeyed by the aspiring hermit. With the approbation of his uncle, he assumed the office, and acquired the fame, of a popular preacher. His comely person adorned the pulpit; the harmony of his voice resounded in the cathedral; his friends were stationed to lead or second the applause of the congregation; [22] and the hasty notes of the scribes preserved his discourses, which in their effect, though not in their composition, might be compared with those of the Athenian orators. The death of Theophilus expanded and realized the hopes of his nephew. The clergy of Alexandria was divided; the soldiers and their general supported the claims of the archdeacon; but a resistless multitude, with voices and with hands, asserted the cause of their favorite; and after a period of thirty-nine years, Cyril was seated on the throne of Athanasius. [23]

[Footnote 20: La Croze (Hist. du Christianisme des Indes, tom. i. p. 24) avows his contempt for the genius and writings of Cyril. De tous les on vrages des anciens, il y en a peu qu'on lise avec moins d'utilite: and Dupin, (Bibliotheque Ecclesiastique, tom. iv. p. 42—52,) in words of respect, teaches us to despise them.]

[Footnote 21: Of Isidore of Pelusium, (l. i. epist. 25, p. 8.) As the letter is not of the most creditable sort, Tillemont, less sincere than the Bollandists, affects a doubt whether this Cyril is the nephew of Theophilus, (Mem. Eccles. tom. xiv. p. 268.)]

[Footnote 22: A grammarian is named by Socrates (l. vii. c. 13).]

[Footnote 23: See the youth and promotion of Cyril, in Socrates, (l. vii. c. 7) and Renaudot, (Hist. Patriarchs. Alexandrin. p. 106, 108.) The Abbe Renaudot drew his materials from the Arabic history of Severus, bishop of Hermopolis Magma, or Ashmunein, in the xth century, who can never be trusted, unless our assent is extorted by the internal evidence of facts.]

PART II

The prize was not unworthy of his ambition. At a distance from the court, and at the head of an immense capital, the patriarch, as he was now styled, of Alexandria had gradually usurped the state and authority of a civil magistrate. The public and private charities of the city were blindly obeyed by his numerous and fanatic parabolani, [24] familiarized in their daily office with scenes of death; and the praefects of Egypt were awed or provoked by the temporal power of these Christian pontiffs. Ardent in the prosecution of heresy, Cyril auspiciously opened his reign by oppressing the Novatians, the most innocent and harmless of the sectaries. The interdiction of their religious worship appeared in his eyes a just and meritorious act; and he confiscated their holy vessels, without apprehending the guilt of sacrilege. The toleration, and even the privileges of the Jews, who had multiplied to the number of forty thousand, were secured by the laws of the Caesars and Ptolemies, and a long prescription of seven hundred years since the foundation of Alexandria. Without any legal sentence, without any royal mandate, the patriarch, at the dawn of day, led a seditious multitude to the attack of the synagogues. Unarmed and unprepared, the Jews were incapable of resistance; their houses of prayer were levelled with the ground, and the episcopal warrior, after-rewarding his troops with the plunder of their goods, expelled from the city the remnant of the unbelieving nation. Perhaps he might plead the insolence of their prosperity, and their deadly hatred of the Christians, whose blood they had recently shed in a malicious or accidental tumult.

Such crimes would have deserved the animadversion of the magistrate; but in this promiscuous outrage, the innocent were confounded with the guilty, and Alexandria was impoverished by the loss of a wealthy and industrious colony. The zeal of Cyril exposed him to the penalties of the Julian law; but in a feeble government and a superstitious age, he was secure of impunity, and even of praise. Orestes complained; but his just complaints were too quickly forgotten by the ministers of Theodosius, and too deeply remembered by a priest who affected to pardon, and continued to hate, the praefect of Egypt. As he passed through the streets, his chariot was assaulted by a band of five hundred of the Nitrian monks his guards fled from the wild beasts of the desert; his protestations that he was a Christian and a Catholic were answered by a volley of stones, and the face of Orestes was covered with blood. The loyal citizens of Alexandria hastened to his rescue; he instantly satisfied his justice and revenge against the monk by whose hand he had been wounded, and Ammonius expired under the rod of the lictor. At the command of Cyril his body was raised from the ground, and transported, in solemn procession, to the cathedral; the name of Ammonius was changed to that of Thaumasius the wonderful; his tomb was decorated with the trophies of martyrdom, and the patriarch ascended the pulpit to celebrate the magnanimity of an assassin and a rebel. Such honors might incite the faithful to combat and die under the banners of the saint; and he soon prompted, or accepted, the sacrifice of a virgin, who professed the religion of the Greeks, and cultivated the friendship of Orestes. Hypatia, the daughter of Theon the mathematician, [25] was initiated in her father's studies; her learned comments have elucidated the geometry of Apollonius and Diophantus, and she publicly taught, both at Athens and Alexandria, the philosophy of Plato and Aristotle. In the bloom of beauty, and in the maturity of wisdom, the modest maid refused her lovers and instructed her disciples; the persons most illustrious for their rank or merit were impatient to visit the female philosopher; and Cyril beheld, with a jealous eye, the gorgeous train of horses and slaves who crowded the door of her academy. A rumor was spread among the Christians, that the daughter of Theon was the only obstacle to the reconciliation of the praefect and the archbishop; and that obstacle was speedily removed. On a fatal day, in the holy season of Lent, Hypatia was torn from her chariot, stripped naked, dragged to the church, and inhumanly butchered by the hands of Peter the reader, and a troop of savage and merciless fanatics: her flesh was scraped from her bones with sharp cyster shells, [26] and her quivering limbs were delivered to the flames. The just progress of inquiry and punishment was stopped by seasonable gifts; but the murder of Hypatia has imprinted an indelible stain on the character and religion of Cyril of Alexandria. [27]

[Footnote 24: The Parabolani of Alexandria were a charitable corporation, instituted during the plague of Gallienus, to visit the sick and to bury the dead. They gradually enlarged, abused, and sold the privileges of their order. Their outrageous conduct during the reign of Cyril provoked the emperor to deprive the patriarch of their nomination, and to restrain their number to five or six hundred. But these restraints were transient and ineffectual. See the Theodosian Code, l. xvi. tit. ii. and Tillemont, Mem. Eccles. tom. xiv. p. 276—278.]

[Footnote 25: For Theon and his daughter Hypatia. see Fabricius, Bibliothec. tom. viii. p. 210, 211. Her article in the Lexicon of Suidas is curious and original. Hesychius (Meursii Opera, tom. vii. p. 295, 296) observes, that he was persecuted; and an epigram in the Greek Anthology (l. i. c. 76, p. 159, edit. Brodaei) celebrates her knowledge and eloquence. She is honorably mentioned (Epist. 10, 15 16, 33—80, 124, 135, 153) by her friend and disciple the philosophic bishop Synesius.]

[Footnote 26: Oyster shells were plentifully strewed on the sea-beach before the Caesareum. I may therefore prefer the literal sense, without rejecting the metaphorical version of tegulae, tiles, which is used by M. de Valois ignorant, and the assassins were probably regardless, whether their victim was yet alive.]

[Footnote 27: These exploits of St. Cyril are recorded by Socrates, (l. vii. c. 13, 14, 15;) and the most reluctant bigotry is compelled to copy an historian who coolly styles the murderers of Hypatia. At the mention of that injured name, I am pleased to observe a blush even on the cheek of Baronius, (A.D. 415, No. 48.)]

Superstition, perhaps, would more gently expiate the blood of a virgin, than the banishment of a saint; and Cyril had accompanied his uncle to the iniquitous synod of the Oak. When the memory of Chrysostom was restored and consecrated, the nephew of Theophilus, at the head of a dying faction, still maintained the justice of his sentence; nor was it till after a tedious delay and an obstinate resistance, that he yielded to the consent of the Catholic world. [28] His enmity to the Byzantine pontiffs [29] was a sense of interest, not a sally of passion: he envied their fortunate station in the sunshine of the Imperial court; and he dreaded their upstart ambition. which oppressed the metropolitans of Europe and Asia, invaded the provinces of Antioch and Alexandria, and measured their diocese by the limits of the empire. The long moderation of Atticus, the mild usurper of the throne of Chrysostom, suspended the animosities of the Eastern patriarchs; but Cyril was at length awakened by the exaltation of a rival more worthy of his esteem and hatred. After the short and troubled reign of Sisinnius, bishop of Constantinople, the factions of the clergy and people were appeased by the choice of the emperor, who, on this occasion, consulted the voice of fame, and invited the merit of a stranger.

Nestorius, [30] native of Germanicia, and a monk of Antioch, was recommended by the austerity of his life, and the eloquence of his sermons; but the first homily which he preached before the devout Theodosius betrayed the acrimony and impatience of his zeal. "Give me, O Caesar!" he exclaimed, "give me the earth purged of heretics, and I will give you in exchange the kingdom of heaven. Exterminate with me the heretics; and with you I will exterminate the Persians." On the fifth day as if the treaty had been already signed, the patriarch of Constantinople discovered, surprised, and attacked a secret conventicle of the Arians: they preferred death to submission; the flames that were kindled by their despair, soon spread to the neighboring houses, and the triumph of Nestorius was clouded by the name of incendiary. On either side of the Hellespont his episcopal vigor imposed a rigid formulary of faith and discipline; a chronological error concerning the festival of Easter was punished as an offence against the church and state. Lydia and Caria, Sardes and Miletus, were purified with the blood of the obstinate Quartodecimans; and the edict of the emperor, or rather of the patriarch, enumerates three-and-twenty degrees and denominations in the guilt and punishment of heresy. [31] But the sword of persecution which Nestorius so furiously wielded was soon turned against his own breast. Religion was the pretence; but, in the judgment of a contemporary saint, ambition was the genuine motive of episcopal warfare. [32]

[Footnote 28: He was deaf to the entreaties of Atticus of Constantinople, and of Isidore of Pelusium, and yielded only (if we may believe Nicephorus, l. xiv. c. 18) to the personal intercession of the Virgin. Yet in his last years he still muttered that John Chrysostom had been justly condemned, (Tillemont, Mem. Eccles. tom. xiv. p. 278—282. Baronius Annal. Eccles. A.D. 412, No. 46—64.)]

[Footnote 29: See their characters in the history of Socrates, (l. vii. c. 25—28;) their power and pretensions, in the huge compilation of Thomassin, (Discipline de l'Eglise, tom. i. p. 80-91.)]

[Footnote 30: His elevation and conduct are described by Socrates, (l. vii. c. 29 31;) and Marcellinus seems to have applied the eloquentiae satis, sapi entiae parum, of Sallust.]

[Footnote 31: Cod. Theodos. l. xvi. tit. v. leg. 65, with the illustrations of Baronius, (A.D. 428, No. 25, &c.,) Godefroy, (ad locum,) and Pagi, Critica, (tom. ii. p. 208.)]

[Footnote 32: Isidore of Pelusium, (l. iv. Epist. 57.) His words are strong and scandalous. Isidore is a saint, but he never became a bishop; and I half suspect that the pride of Diogenes trampled on the pride of Plato.]

In the Syrian school, Nestorius had been taught to abhor the confusion of the two natures, and nicely to discriminate the humanity of his master Christ from the divinity of the Lord Jesus. [33] The Blessed Virgin he revered as the mother of Christ, but his ears were offended with the rash and recent title of mother of God, [34] which had been insensibly adopted since the origin of the Arian controversy. From the pulpit of Constantinople, a friend of the patriarch, and afterwards the patriarch himself, repeatedly preached against the use, or the abuse, of a word [35] unknown to the apostles, unauthorized by the church, and which could only tend to alarm the timorous, to mislead the simple, to amuse the profane, and to justify, by a seeming resemblance, the old genealogy of Olympus. [36] In his calmer moments Nestorius confessed, that it might be tolerated or excused by the union of the two natures, and the communication of their idioms: [37] but he was exasperated, by contradiction, to disclaim the worship of a new-born, an infant Deity, to draw his inadequate similes from the conjugal or civil partnerships of life, and to describe the manhood of Christ as the robe, the instrument, the tabernacle of his Godhead. At these blasphemous sounds, the pillars of the sanctuary were shaken. The unsuccessful competitors of Nestorius indulged their pious or personal resentment, the Byzantine clergy was secretly displeased with the intrusion of a stranger: whatever is superstitious or absurd, might claim the protection of the monks; and the people were interested in the glory of their virgin patroness. [38] The sermons of the archbishop, and the service of the altar, were disturbed by seditious clamor; his authority and doctrine were renounced by separate congregations; every wind scattered round the empire the leaves of controversy; and the voice of the combatants on a sonorous theatre reechoed in the cells of Palestine and Egypt. It was the duty of Cyril to enlighten the zeal and ignorance of his innumerable monks: in the school of Alexandria, he had imbibed and professed the incarnation of one nature; and the successor of Athanasius consulted his pride and ambition, when he rose in arms against another Arius, more formidable and more guilty, on the second throne of the hierarchy. After a short correspondence, in which the rival prelates disguised their hatred in the hollow language of respect and charity, the patriarch of Alexandria denounced to the prince and people, to the East and to the West, the damnable errors of the Byzantine pontiff. From the East, more especially from Antioch, he obtained the ambiguous counsels of toleration and silence, which were addressed to both parties while they favored the cause of Nestorius. But the Vatican received with open arms the messengers of Egypt. The vanity of Celestine was flattered by the appeal; and the partial version of a monk decided the faith of the pope, who with his Latin clergy was ignorant of the language, the arts, and the theology of the Greeks. At the head of an

Italian synod, Celestine weighed the merits of the cause, approved the creed of Cyril, condemned the sentiments and person of Nestorius, degraded the heretic from his episcopal dignity, allowed a respite of ten days for recantation and penance, and delegated to his enemy the execution of this rash and illegal sentence. But the patriarch of Alexandria, while he darted the thunders of a god, exposed the errors and passions of a mortal; and his twelve anathemas [39] still torture the orthodox slaves, who adore the memory of a saint, without forfeiting their allegiance to the synod of Chalcedon. These bold assertions are indelibly tinged with the colors of the Apollinarian heresy; but the serious, and perhaps the sincere professions of Nestorius have satisfied the wiser and less partial theologians of the present times. [40]

[Footnote 33: La Croze (Christianisme des Indes, tom. i. p. 44-53. Thesaurus Epistolicus, La Crozianus, tom. iii. p. 276—280) has detected the use, which, in the ivth, vth, and vith centuries, discriminates the school of Diodorus of Tarsus and his Nestorian disciples.]

[Footnote 34: Deipara; as in zoology we familiarly speak of oviparous and viviparous animals. It is not easy to fix the invention of this word, which La Croze (Christianisme des Indes, tom. i. p. 16) ascribes to Eusebius of Caesarea and the Arians. The orthodox testimonies are produced by Cyril and Petavius, (Dogmat. Theolog. tom. v. l. v. c. 15, p. 254, &c.;) but the veracity of the saint is questionable, and the epithet so easily slides from the margin to the text of a Catholic Ms]

[Footnote 35: Basnage, in his Histoire de l'Eglise, a work of controversy, (tom l. p. 505,) justifies the mother, by the blood, of God, (Acts, xx. 28, with Mill's various readings.) But the Greek Mss. are far from unanimous; and the primitive style of the blood of Christ is preserved in the Syriac version, even in those copies which were used by the Christians of St. Thomas on the coast of Malabar, (La Croze, Christianisme des Indes, tom. i. p. 347.) The jealousy of the Nestorians and Monophysites has guarded the purity of their text.]

[Footnote 36: The Pagans of Egypt already laughed at the new Cybele of the Christians, (Isidor. l. i. epist. 54;) a letter was forged in the name of Hypatia, to ridicule the theology of her assassin, (Synodicon, c. 216, in iv. tom. Concil. p. 484.) In the article of Nestorius, Bayle has scattered some loose philosophy on the worship of the Virgin Mary.]

[Footnote 37: The item of the Greeks, a mutual loan or transfer of the idioms or properties of each nature to the other—of infinity to man, possibility to God, &c. Twelve rules on this nicest of subjects compose the Theological Grammar of Petavius, (Dogmata Theolog. tom. v. l. iv. c. 14, 15, p 209, &c.)]

[Footnote 38: See Ducange, C. P. Christiana, l. i. p. 30, &c.]

[Footnote 39: Concil. tom. iii. p. 943. They have never been directly approved by the church, (Tillemont. Mem. Eccles. tom. xiv. p. 368—372.) I almost pity the agony of rage and sophistry with which Petavius seems to be agitated in the vith book of his Dogmata Theologica]

[Footnote 40: Such as the rational Basnage (ad tom. i. Variar. Lection. Canisine in Praefat. c. 2, p. 11—23) and La Croze, the universal scholar, (Christianisme des Indes, tom. i. p. 16—20. De l'Ethiopie, p. 26, 27. The saur. Epist. p. 176, &c., 283, 285.) His free sentence is confirmed by that of his friends Jablonski (Thesaur. Epist. tom. i. p. 193—201) and Mosheim, (idem. p. 304, Nestorium crimine caruisse est et mea sententia;) and three more respectable judges will not easily be found. Asseman, a learned and modest slave, can hardly discern (Bibliothec. Orient. tom. iv. p. 190—224) the guilt and error of the Nestorians.]

Yet neither the emperor nor the primate of the East were disposed to obey the mandate of an Italian priest; and a synod of the Catholic, or rather of the Greek church, was unanimously demanded as the sole remedy that could appease or decide this ecclesiastical quarrel. [41] Ephesus, on all sides accessible by sea and land, was chosen for the place, the festival of Pentecost for the day, of the meeting; a writ of summons was despatched to each metropolitan, and a guard was stationed to protect and confine the fathers till they should settle the mysteries of heaven, and the faith of the earth. Nestorius appeared not as a criminal, but as a judge; he depended on the weight rather than the number of his prelates, and his sturdy slaves from the baths of Zeuxippus were armed for every service of injury or defence. But his adversary Cyril was more powerful in the weapons both of the flesh and of the spirit. Disobedient to the letter, or at least to the meaning, of the royal summons, he was attended by fifty Egyptian bishops, who expected from their patriarch's nod the inspiration of the Holy Ghost. He had contracted an intimate alliance with Memnon, bishop of Ephesus. The despotic primate of Asia disposed of the ready succors of thirty or forty episcopal votes: a crowd of peasants, the slaves of the church, was poured into the city to support with blows and clamors a metaphysical argument; and the people zealously asserted the honor of the Virgin, whose body reposed within the walls of Ephesus. [42] The fleet which had transported Cyril from Alexandria was laden with the riches of Egypt; and he disembarked a numerous body of mariners, slaves, and fanatics, enlisted with blind obedience under the banner of St. Mark and the mother of God. The fathers, and even the guards, of the council were awed by this martial array; the adversaries of Cyril and Mary were insulted in the streets, or threatened in their houses; his eloquence and liberality made a daily increase in the number of his adherents; and the Egyptian soon computed that he might command the attendance and the voices of two hundred bishops. [43] But the author of the twelve anathemas foresaw and dreaded the opposition of John of Antioch, who, with a small, but respectable, train of metropolitans and divines, was advancing by slow journeys from the distant capital of the East. Impatient of a delay, which he stigmatized as voluntary and culpable, [44] Cyril announced the opening of the synod sixteen days after the festival of Pentecost. Nestorius, who depended on the near approach of his Eastern friends, persisted, like his predecessor Chrysostom, to disclaim the jurisdiction, and to disobey the summons, of his enemies: they hastened his trial, and his accuser presided in the seat of judgment. Sixty-eight bishops, twenty-two of metropolitan rank, defended his cause by a modest and temperate protest: they were excluded from the councils of their brethren. Candidian, in the emperor's name, requested a delay of four days; the profane magistrate was driven with outrage and insult from the assembly of the saints. The whole of this momentous transaction was crowded into the compass of a summer's day: the bishops delivered their separate opinions; but the uniformity of style reveals the influence or the hand of a master, who has been accused of corrupting the public evidence of their acts and subscriptions. [45] Without a dissenting voice, they recognized in the epistles of Cyril the Nicene creed and the doctrine of the fathers: but the partial extracts from the letters and homilies of Nestorius were interrupted by curses and anathemas: and the heretic was degraded from his episcopal and ecclesiastical dignity. The sentence, maliciously inscribed to the new Judas, was affixed and proclaimed in the streets of Ephesus: the weary prelates, as they issued from the church of the mother of God, were saluted as her champions; and her victory was celebrated by the illuminations, the songs, and the tumult of the night.

[Footnote 41: *The origin and progress of the Nestorian controversy, till the synod of Ephesus, may be found in Socrates, (l. vii. c. 32,) Evagrius, (l. i. c. 1, 2,) Liberatus, (Brev. c. 1—4,) the original Acts, (Concil. tom. iii. p. 551—991, edit. Venice, 1728,) the Annals of Baronius and Pagi, and the faithful collections of Tillemont, (Mem. Eccles. tom. xiv p. 283—377.)]*

[Footnote 42: The Christians of the four first centuries were ignorant of the death and burial of Mary. The tradition of Ephesus is affirmed by the synod, (Concil. tom. iii. p. 1102;) yet it has been superseded by the claim of Jerusalem; and her empty sepulchre, as it was shown to the pilgrims, produced the fable of her resurrection and assumption, in which the Greek and Latin churches have piously acquiesced. See Baronius (Annal. Eccles. A.D. 48, No. 6, &c.) and Tillemont, (Mem. Eccles. tom. i. p. 467—477.)]

[Footnote 43: The Acts of Chalcedon (Concil. tom. iv. p. 1405, 1408) exhibit a lively picture of the blind, obstinate servitude of the bishops of Egypt to their patriarch.]

[Footnote 44: Civil or ecclesiastical business detained the bishops at Antioch till the 18th of May. Ephesus was at the distance of thirty days' journey; and ten days more may be fairly allowed for accidents and repose. The march of Xenophon over the same ground enumerates above 260 parasangs or leagues; and this measure might be illustrated from ancient and modern itineraries, if I knew how to compare the speed of an army, a synod, and a caravan. John of Antioch is reluctantly acquitted by Tillemont himself, (Mem. Eccles. tom. xiv. p. 386—389.)]

[Footnote 45: Evagrius, l. i. c. 7. The same imputation was urged by Count Irenaeus, (tom. iii. p. 1249;) and the orthodox critics do not find it an easy task to defend the purity of the Greek or Latin copies of the Acts.]

On the fifth day, the triumph was clouded by the arrival and indignation of the Eastern bishops. In a chamber of the inn, before he had wiped the dust from his shoes, John of Antioch gave audience to Candidian, the Imperial minister; who related his ineffectual efforts to prevent or to annul the hasty violence of the Egyptian. With equal haste and violence, the Oriental synod of fifty bishops degraded Cyril and Memnon from their episcopal honors, condemned, in the twelve anathemas, the purest venom of the Apollinarian heresy, and described the Alexandrian primate as a monster, born and educated for the destruction of the church. [46] His throne was distant and inaccessible; but they instantly resolved to bestow on the flock of Ephesus the blessing of a faithful shepherd. By the vigilance of Memnon, the churches were shut against them, and a strong garrison was thrown into the cathedral. The troops, under the command of Candidian, advanced to the assault; the outguards were routed and put to the sword, but the place was impregnable: the besiegers retired; their retreat was pursued by a vigorous sally; they lost their horses, and many of their soldiers were dangerously wounded with clubs and stones. Ephesus, the city of the Virgin, was defiled with rage and clamor, with sedition and blood; the rival synods darted anathemas and excommunications from their spiritual engines; and the court of Theodosius was perplexed by the adverse and contradictory narratives of the Syrian and Egyptian factions. During a busy period of three months, the emperor tried every method, except the most effectual means of indifference and contempt, to reconcile this theological quarrel. He attempted to remove or intimidate the leaders by a common sentence, of acquittal or condemnation; he invested his representatives at Ephesus with ample power and military force; he summoned from either party eight chosen deputies to a free and candid conference in the neighborhood of the capital, far from the contagion of popular frenzy. But the Orientals refused to yield, and the Catholics, proud of their numbers and of their Latin allies, rejected all terms of union or toleration. The patience of the meek Theodosius was provoked; and he dissolved in anger this episcopal tumult, which at the distance of thirteen centuries assumes the venerable aspect of the third oecumenical council. [47] "God is my witness," said the pious prince, "that I am not the author of this confusion. His providence will discern and punish the guilty. Return to your provinces, and may your private virtues repair the mischief and scandal of your meeting." They returned to their provinces; but the same passions which had distracted the synod of Ephesus were diffused over the Eastern world. After three obstinate and equal campaigns,

John of Antioch and Cyril of Alexandria condescended to explain and embrace: but their seeming reunion must be imputed rather to prudence than to reason, to the mutual lassitude rather than to the Christian charity of the patriarchs.

[Footnote 46: After the coalition of John and Cyril these invectives were mutually forgotten. The style of declamation must never be confounded with the genuine sense which respectable enemies entertain of each other's merit, (Concil tom. iii. p. 1244.)]

[Footnote 47: See the acts of the synod of Ephesus in the original Greek, and a Latin version almost contemporary, (Concil. tom. iii. p. 991—1339, with the Synodicon adversus Tragoediam Irenaei, tom. iv. p. 235—497,) the Ecclesiastical Histories of Socrates (l. vii. c. 34) and Evagrius, (l i. c. 3, 4, 5,) and the Breviary of Liberatus, (in Concil. tom. vi. p. 419—459, c. 5, 6,) and the Memoires Eccles. of Tillemont, (tom. xiv p. 377-487.)]

The Byzantine pontiff had instilled into the royal ear a baleful prejudice against the character and conduct of his Egyptian rival. An epistle of menace and invective, [48] which accompanied the summons, accused him as a busy, insolent, and envious priest, who perplexed the simplicity of the faith, violated the peace of the church and state, and, by his artful and separate addresses to the wife and sister of Theodosius, presumed to suppose, or to scatter, the seeds of discord in the Imperial family. At the stern command of his sovereign. Cyril had repaired to Ephesus, where he was resisted, threatened, and confined, by the magistrates in the interest of Nestorius and the Orientals; who assembled the troops of Lydia and Ionia to suppress the fanatic and disorderly train of the patriarch. Without expecting the royal license, he escaped from his guards, precipitately embarked, deserted the imperfect synod, and retired to his episcopal fortress of safety and independence. But his artful emissaries, both in the court and city, successfully labored to appease the resentment, and to conciliate the favor, of the emperor. The feeble son of Arcadius was alternately swayed by his wife and sister, by the eunuchs and women of the palace: superstition and avarice were their ruling passions; and the orthodox chiefs were assiduous in their endeavors to alarm the former, and to gratify the latter. Constantinople and the suburbs were sanctified with frequent monasteries, and the holy abbots, Dalmatius and Eutyches, [49] had devoted their zeal and fidelity to the cause of Cyril, the worship of Mary, and the unity of Christ. From the first moment of their monastic life, they had never mingled with the world, or trod the profane ground of the city. But in this awful moment of the danger of the church, their vow was superseded by a more sublime and indispensable duty. At the head of a long order of monks and hermits, who carried burning tapers in their hands, and chanted litanies to the mother of God, they proceeded from their monasteries to the palace. The people was edified and inflamed by this extraordinary spectacle, and the trembling monarch listened to the prayers and adjurations of the saints, who boldly pronounced, that none could hope for salvation, unless they embraced the person and the creed of the orthodox successor of Athanasius. At the same time, every avenue of the throne was assaulted with gold. Under the decent names of eulogies and benedictions, the courtiers of both sexes were bribed according to the measure of their power and rapaciousness. But their incessant demands despoiled the sanctuaries of Constantinople and Alexandria; and the authority of the patriarch was unable to silence the just murmur of his clergy, that a debt of sixty thousand pounds had already been contracted to support the expense of this scandalous corruption. [50] Pulcheria, who relieved her brother from the weight of an empire, was the firmest pillar of orthodoxy; and so intimate was the alliance between the thunders of the synod and the whispers of the court, that Cyril was assured of success if he could displace one eunuch, and substitute another in the favor of Theodosius. Yet the Egyptian could not boast of a glorious or decisive victory. The emperor, with unaccustomed firmness, adhered to his promise of protecting the innocence of the Oriental bishops; and Cyril softened his anathemas, and confessed, with ambiguity and reluctance, a twofold nature of Christ, before he was permitted to satiate his revenge against the unfortunate Nestorius. [51]

[Footnote 48: I should be curious to know how much Nestorius paid for these expressions, so mortifying to his rival.]

[Footnote 49: Eutyches, the heresiarch Eutyches, is honorably named by Cyril as a friend, a saint, and the strenuous defender of the faith. His brother, the abbot Dalmatus, is likewise employed to bind the emperor and all his chamberlains terribili conjuratione. Synodicon. c. 203, in Concil. tom. iv p. 467.]

[Footnote 50: Clerici qui hic sunt contristantur, quod ecclesia Alexandrina nudata sit hujus causa turbelae: et debet praeter illa quae hinc transmissa sint auri libras mille quingentas. Et nunc ei scriptum est ut praestet; sed de tua ecclesia praesta avaritiae quorum nosti, &c. This curious and original letter, from Cyril's archdeacon to his creature the new bishop of Constantinople, has been unaccountably preserved in an old Latin version, (Synodicon, c. 203, Concil. tom. iv. p. 465—468.) The mask is almost dropped, and the saints speak the honest language of interest and confederacy.]

[Footnote 51: The tedious negotiations that succeeded the synod of Ephesus are diffusely related in the original acts, (Concil. tom. iii. p. 1339—1771, ad fin. vol. and the Synodicon, in tom. iv.,) Socrates, (l. vii. c. 28, 35, 40, 41,) Evagrius, (l. i. c. 6, 7, 8, 12,) Liberatus, (c. 7—10, 7-10,) Tillemont, (Mem. Eccles. tom. xiv. p. 487—676.) The most patient reader will thank me for compressing so much nonsense and falsehood in a few lines.]

The rash and obstinate Nestorius, before the end of the synod, was oppressed by Cyril, betrayed by the court, and faintly supported by his Eastern friends. A sentiment or fear or indignation prompted him, while it was yet time, to affect the glory of a voluntary abdication: [52] his wish, or at least his request, was readily granted; he was conducted with honor from Ephesus to his old monastery of Antioch; and, after a short pause, his successors, Maximian and Proclus, were acknowledged as the lawful bishops of Constantinople. But in the silence of his cell, the degraded patriarch could no longer resume the innocence and security of a private monk. The past he regretted, he was discontented with the present, and the future he had reason to dread: the Oriental bishops successively disengaged their cause from his unpopular name, and each day decreased the number of the schismatics who revered Nestorius as the confessor of the faith. After a residence at Antioch of four years, the hand of Theodosius subscribed an edict, [53] which ranked him with Simon the magician, proscribed his opinions and followers, condemned his writings to the flames, and banished his person first to Petra, in Arabia, and at length to Oasis, one of the islands of the Libyan desert. [54] Secluded from the church and from the world, the exile was still pursued by the rage of bigotry and war. A wandering tribe of the Blemmyes or Nubians invaded his solitary prison: in their retreat they dismissed a crowd of useless captives: but no sooner had Nestorius reached the banks of the Nile, than he would gladly have escaped from a Roman and orthodox city, to the milder servitude of the savages. His flight was punished as a new crime: the soul of the patriarch inspired the civil and ecclesiastical powers of Egypt; the magistrates, the soldiers, the monks, devoutly tortured the enemy of Christ and St. Cyril; and, as far as the confines of Aethiopia, the heretic was alternately dragged and recalled, till his aged body was broken by the hardships and accidents of these reiterated journeys. Yet his mind was still independent and erect; the president of Thebais was awed by his pastoral letters; he survived the Catholic tyrant of Alexandria, and, after sixteen years' banishment, the synod of Chalcedon would perhaps have restored him to the honors, or at least to the communion, of the church. The death of Nestorius prevented his obedience to their welcome summons; [55] and his disease might afford some color to the scandalous report, that his tongue, the organ of blasphemy, had been eaten by the worms. He was buried in a city of Upper Egypt, known by the names of Chemnis, or Panopolis, or Akmim; [56] but the immortal malice of the Jacobites has persevered for ages to cast stones against his sepulchre, and to propagate the foolish tradition, that it was never watered by the rain of heaven, which equally descends on the righteous and the ungodly. [57] Humanity may drop a tear on the fate of Nestorius; yet justice must observe, that he suffered the persecution which he had approved and inflicted. [58]

[Footnote 52: Evagrius, l. i. c. 7. The original letters in the Synodicon (c. 15, 24, 25, 26) justify the appearance of a voluntary resignation, which is asserted by Ebed-Jesu, a Nestorian writer, apud Asseman. Bibliot. Oriental. tom. iii. p. 299, 302.]

[Footnote 53: See the Imperial letters in the Acts of the Synod of Ephesus, (Concil. tom. iii. p. 1730—1735.) The odious name of Simonians, which was affixed to the disciples of this. Yet these were Christians! who differed only in names and in shadows.]

[Footnote 54: The metaphor of islands is applied by the grave civilians (Pandect. l. xlviii. tit. 22, leg. 7) to those happy spots which are discriminated by water and verdure from the Libyan sands. Three of these under the common name of Oasis, or Alvahat: 1. The temple of Jupiter Ammon. 2. The middle Oasis, three days' journey to the west of Lycopolis. 3. The southern, where Nestorius was banished in the first climate, and only three days' journey from the confines of Nubia. See a learned note of Michaelis, (ad Descript. Aegypt. Abulfedae, p. 21-34.) Note: 1. The Oasis of Sivah has been visited by Mons. Drovetti and Mr. Browne. 2. The little Oasis, that of El Kassar, was visited and described by Belzoni. 3. The great Oasis, and its splendid ruins, have been well described in the travels of Sir A. Edmonstone. To these must be added another Western Oasis also visited by Sir A. Edmonstone—M.]

[Footnote 55: The invitation of Nestorius to the synod of Chalcedon, is related by Zacharias, bishop of Melitene (Evagrius, l. ii. c. 2. Asseman. Biblioth. Orient. tom. ii. p. 55,) and the famous Xenaias or Philoxenus, bishop of Hierapolis, (Asseman. Bibliot. Orient. tom. ii. p. 40, &c.,) denied by Evagrius and Asseman, and stoutly maintained by La Croze, (Thesaur. Epistol. tom. iii. p. 181, &c.) The fact is not improbable; yet it was the interest of the Monophysites to spread the invidious report, and Eutychius (tom. ii. p. 12) affirms, that Nestorius died after an exile of seven years, and consequently ten years before the synod of Chalcedon.]

[Footnote 56: Consult D'Anville, (Memoire sur l'Egypte, p. 191,) Pocock. (Description of the East, vol. i. p. 76,) Abulfeda, (Descript. Aegypt, p. 14,) and his commentator Michaelis, (Not. p. 78—83,) and the Nubian Geographer, (p. 42,) who mentions, in the xiith century, the ruins and the sugar-canes of Akmim.]

[Footnote 57: Eutychius (Annal. tom. ii. p. 12) and Gregory Bar-Hebraeus, of Abulpharagius, (Asseman, tom. ii. p. 316,) represent the credulity of the xth and xiith centuries.]

[Footnote 58: We are obliged to Evagrius (l. i. c. 7) for some extracts from the letters of Nestorius; but the lively picture of his sufferings is treated with insult by the hard and stupid fanatic.]

PART III

The death of the Alexandrian primate, after a reign of thirty-two years, abandoned the Catholics to the intemperance of zeal and the abuse of victory. [59] The monophysite doctrine (one incarnate nature) was rigorously preached in the churches of Egypt and the monasteries of the East; the primitive creed of Apollinarius was protected by the sanctity of Cyril; and the name of Eutyches, his venerable friend, has been applied to the sect most adverse to the Syrian heresy of Nestorius. His rival Eutyches was the abbot, or archimandrite, or superior of three hundred monks, but the opinions of a simple and illiterate recluse might have expired in the cell, where he had slept above seventy years, if the resentment or indiscretion of Flavian, the Byzantine pontiff, had not exposed the scandal to the eyes of the Christian world. His domestic synod was instantly convened, their proceedings were sullied with clamor and artifice, and the aged heretic was surprised into a seeming confession, that Christ had not derived his body from the substance of the Virgin Mary. From their partial decree, Eutyches appealed to a general council; and his cause was vigorously asserted by his godson Chrysaphius, the reigning eunuch of the palace, and his accomplice Dioscorus, who had succeeded to the throne, the creed, the talents, and the vices, of the nephew of Theophilus. By the special summons of Theodosius, the second synod of Ephesus was judiciously composed of ten metropolitans and ten bishops from each of the six dioceses of the Eastern empire: some exceptions of favor or merit enlarged the number to one hundred and thirty-five; and the Syrian Barsumas, as the chief and representative of the monks, was invited to sit and vote with the successors of the apostles. But the despotism of the Alexandrian patriarch again oppressed the freedom of debate: the same spiritual and carnal weapons were again drawn from the arsenals of Egypt: the Asiatic veterans, a band of archers, served under the orders of Dioscorus; and the more formidable monks, whose minds were inaccessible to reason or mercy, besieged the doors of the cathedral. The general, and, as it should seem, the unconstrained voice of the fathers, accepted the faith and even the anathemas of Cyril; and the heresy of the two natures was formally condemned in the persons and writings of the most learned Orientals. "May those who divide Christ be divided with the sword, may they be hewn in pieces, may they be burned alive!" were the charitable wishes of a Christian synod. [60] The innocence and sanctity of Eutyches were acknowledged without hesitation; but the prelates, more especially those of Thrace and Asia, were unwilling to depose their patriarch for the use or even the abuse of his lawful jurisdiction. They embraced the knees of Dioscorus, as he stood with a threatening aspect on the footstool of his throne, and conjured him to forgive the offences, and to respect the dignity, of his brother. "Do you mean to raise a sedition?" exclaimed the relentless tyrant. "Where are the officers?" At these words a furious multitude of monks and soldiers, with staves, and swords, and chains, burst into the church; the trembling bishops hid themselves behind the altar, or under the benches, and as they were not inspired with the zeal of martyrdom, they successively subscribed a blank paper, which was afterwards filled with the condemnation of the Byzantine pontiff. Flavian was instantly delivered to the wild beasts of this spiritual amphitheatre: the monks were stimulated by the voice and example of Barsumas to avenge the injuries of Christ: it is said that the patriarch of Alexandria reviled, and buffeted, and kicked, and trampled his brother of Constantinople: [61] it is certain, that the victim, before he could reach the place of his exile, expired on the third day of the wounds and bruises which he had received at Ephesus. This second synod has been justly branded as a gang of robbers and assassins; yet the accusers of Dioscorus would magnify his violence, to alleviate the cowardice and inconstancy of their own behavior.

[Footnote 59: Dixi Cyrillum dum viveret, auctoritate sua effecisse, ne Eutychianismus et Monophysitarum error in nervum erumperet: idque verum puto...aliquo... honesto modo cecinerat. The learned but cautious Jablonski did not always speak the whole truth. Cum Cyrillo lenius omnino egi, quam si tecum aut cum aliis rei hujus probe gnaris et aequis rerum aestimatoribus sermones privatos conferrem, (Thesaur. Epistol. La Crozian. tom. i. p. 197, 198) an excellent key to his dissertations on the Nestorian controversy!]

[Footnote 60: At the request of Dioscorus, those who were not able to roar, stretched out their hands. At Chalcedon, the Orientals disclaimed these exclamations: but the Egyptians more consistently declared. (Concil. tom. iv. p. 1012.)]

[Footnote 61: (Eusebius, bishop of Dorylaeum): and this testimony of Evagrius (l. ii. c. 2) is amplified by the historian Zonaras, (tom. ii. l. xiii. p. 44,) who affirms that Dioscorus kicked like a wild ass. But the language of Liberatus (Brev. c. 12, in Concil. tom. vi. p. 438) is more cautious; and the Acts of Chalcedon, which lavish the names of homicide, Cain, &c., do not justify so pointed a charge. The monk Barsumas is more particularly accused, (Concil. tom. iv. p. 1418.)]

The faith of Egypt had prevailed: but the vanquished party was supported by the same pope who encountered without fear the hostile rage of Attila and Genseric. The theology of Leo, his famous tome or epistle on the mystery of the incarnation, had been disregarded by the synod of Ephesus: his authority, and that of the Latin church, was insulted in his legates, who escaped from slavery and death to relate the melancholy tale of the tyranny of Dioscorus and the martyrdom of Flavian. His provincial synod annulled the irregular proceedings of Ephesus; but as this step was itself irregular, he solicited the convocation of a general council in the free and orthodox provinces of Italy. From his independent throne, the Roman bishop spoke and acted without danger as the head of the Christians, and his dictates were obsequiously transcribed by Placidia and her son Valentinian; who addressed their Eastern colleague to restore the peace and unity of the church. But the pageant of Oriental royalty was moved with equal dexterity by the hand of the eunuch; and Theodosius could pronounce, without hesitation, that the church was already peaceful and triumphant, and that the recent flame had been extinguished by the just punishment of the Nestorians. Perhaps the Greeks would be still involved in the heresy of the Monophysites, if the emperor's horse had not fortunately stumbled; Theodosius expired; his orthodox sister Pulcheria, with a nominal husband, succeeded to the throne; Chrysaphius was burnt, Dioscorus was disgraced, the exiles were recalled, and the tome of Leo was subscribed by the Oriental bishops. Yet the pope was disappointed in his favorite project of a Latin council: he disdained to preside in the Greek synod, which was speedily assembled at Nice in Bithynia; his legates required in a peremptory tone the presence of the emperor; and the weary fathers were transported to Chalcedon under the immediate eye of Marcian and the senate of Constantinople. A quarter of a mile from the Thracian Bosphorus, the church of St. Euphemia was built on the summit of a gentle though lofty ascent: the triple structure was celebrated as a prodigy of art, and the boundless prospect of the land and sea might have raised the mind of a sectary to the contemplation of the God of the universe. Six hundred and thirty bishops were ranged in order in the nave of the church; but the patriarchs of the East were preceded by the legates, of whom the third was a simple priest; and the place of honor was reserved for twenty laymen of consular or senatorian rank. The gospel was ostentatiously displayed in the centre, but the rule of faith was defined by the Papal and Imperial ministers, who moderated the thirteen sessions of the council of Chalcedon. [62] Their partial interposition silenced the intemperate shouts and execrations, which degraded the episcopal gravity; but, on the formal accusation of the legates, Dioscorus was compelled to descend from his throne to the rank of a criminal, already condemned in the opinion of his judges. The Orientals, less adverse to Nestorius than to Cyril, accepted the Romans as their deliverers: Thrace, and Pontus, and Asia, were exasperated against the murderer of Flavian, and the new patriarchs of Constantinople and Antioch secured their places by the sacrifice of their benefactor. The bishops of Palestine, Macedonia, and Greece, were attached to the faith of Cyril; but in the face of the synod, in the heat of the battle, the leaders, with their obsequious train, passed from the right to the left wing, and decided the victory by this seasonable desertion. Of the seventeen suffragans who sailed from Alexandria, four were tempted from their allegiance, and the thirteen, falling prostrate on the ground, implored the mercy of the council, with sighs and tears, and a pathetic declaration, that, if they yielded, they should be massacred, on their return to Egypt, by the indignant people. A tardy repentance was allowed to expiate the guilt or error of the accomplices of Dioscorus: but their sins were accumulated on his head; he neither asked nor hoped for pardon, and the moderation of those who pleaded for a general amnesty was drowned in the prevailing cry of victory and revenge.

To save the reputation of his late adherents, some personal offences were skilfully detected; his rash and illegal excommunication of the pope, and his contumacious refusal (while he was detained a prisoner) to attend to the summons of the synod. Witnesses were introduced to prove the special facts of his pride, avarice, and cruelty; and the fathers heard with abhorrence, that the alms of the church were lavished on the female dancers, that his palace, and even his bath, was open to the prostitutes of Alexandria, and that the infamous Pansophia, or Irene, was publicly entertained as the concubine of the patriarch. [63]

[Footnote 62: The Acts of the Council of Chalcedon (Concil. tom. iv. p. 761—2071) comprehend those of Ephesus, (p. 890—1189,) which again comprise the synod of Constantinople under Flavian, (p. 930—1072;) and at requires some attention to disengage this double involution. The whole business of Eutyches, Flavian, and Dioscorus, is related by Evagrius (l. i. c. 9—12, and l. ii. c. 1, 2, 3, 4,) and Liberatus, (Brev. c. 11, 12, 13, 14.) Once more, and almost for the last time, I appeal to the diligence of Tillemont, (Mem. Eccles. tom. xv. p. 479-719.) The annals of Baronius and Pagi will accompany me much further on my long and laborious journey.]

[Footnote 63: (Concil. tom. iv. p. 1276.) A specimen of the wit and malice of the people is preserved in the Greek Anthology, (l. ii. c. 5, p. 188, edit. Wechel,) although the application was unknown to the editor Brodaeus. The nameless epigrammatist raises a tolerable pun, by confounding the episcopal salutation of "Peace be to all!" with the genuine or corrupted name of the bishop's concubine: I am ignorant whether the patriarch, who seems to have been a jealous lover, is the Cimon of a preceding epigram, was viewed with envy and wonder by Priapus himself.]

For these scandalous offences, Dioscorus was deposed by the synod, and banished by the emperor; but the purity of his faith was declared in the presence, and with the tacit approbation, of the fathers. Their prudence supposed rather than pronounced the heresy of Eutyches, who was never summoned before their tribunal; and they sat silent and abashed, when a bold Monophysite casting at their feet a volume of Cyril, challenged them to anathematize in his person the doctrine of the saint. If we fairly peruse the acts of Chalcedon as they are recorded by the orthodox party, [64] we shall find that a great majority of the bishops embraced the simple unity of Christ; and the ambiguous concession that he was formed Of or From two natures, might imply either their previous existence, or their subsequent confusion, or some dangerous interval between the conception of the man and the assumption of the God. The Roman theology, more positive and precise, adopted the term most offensive to the ears of the Egyptians, that Christ existed In two natures; and this momentous particle [65] (which the memory, rather than the understanding, must retain) had almost produced a schism among the Catholic bishops. The tome of Leo had been respectfully, perhaps sincerely, subscribed; but they protested, in two successive debates, that it was neither expedient nor lawful to transgress the sacred landmarks which had been fixed at Nice, Constantinople, and Ephesus, according to the rule of Scripture and tradition. At length they yielded to the importunities of their masters; but their infallible decree, after it had been ratified with deliberate votes and vehement acclamations, was overturned in the next session by the opposition of the legates and their Oriental friends. It was in vain that a multitude of episcopal voices repeated in chorus, "The definition of the fathers is orthodox and immutable! The heretics are now discovered! Anathema to the Nestorians! Let them depart from the synod! Let them repair to Rome." [66] The legates threatened, the emperor was absolute, and a committee of eighteen bishops prepared a new decree, which was imposed on the reluctant assembly. In the name of the fourth general council, the Christ in one person, but in two natures, was announced to the Catholic world: an invisible line was drawn between the heresy of Apollinaris and the faith of St. Cyril; and the road to paradise, a bridge as sharp as a razor, was suspended over the abyss by the master-hand of the theological artist. During ten centuries of blindness and servitude, Europe received her religious opinions from the oracle of the Vatican; and the same doctrine, already varnished with the rust of antiquity, was admitted without dispute into the creed of the reformers, who disclaimed the supremacy of the Roman pontiff. The synod of Chalcedon still triumphs in the Protestant churches; but the ferment of controversy has subsided, and the most pious Christians of the present day are ignorant, or careless, of their own belief concerning the mystery of the incarnation.

[Footnote 64: Those who reverence the infallibility of synods, may try to ascertain their sense. The leading bishops were attended by partial or careless scribes, who dispersed their copies round the world. Our Greek Mss. are sullied with the false and prescribed reading of (Concil. tom. iii. p. 1460:) the authentic translation of Pope Leo I. does not seem to have been executed, and the old Latin versions materially differ from the present Vulgate, which was revised (A.D. 550) by Rusticus, a Roman priest, from the best Mss. at Constantinople, (Ducange, C. P. Christiana, l. iv. p. 151,) a famous monastery of Latins, Greeks, and Syrians. See Concil. tom. iv. p. 1959—2049, and Pagi, Critica, tom. ii. p. 326, &c.]

[Footnote 65: It is darkly represented in the microscope of Petavius, (tom. v. l. iii. c. 5;) yet the subtle theologian is himself afraid—ne quis fortasse supervacaneam, et nimis anxiam putet hujusmodi vocularum inquisitionem, et ab instituti theologici gravitate alienam, (p. 124.)]

[Footnote 66: (Concil. tom. iv. p. 1449.) Evagrius and Liberatus present only the placid face of the synod, and discreetly slide over these embers, suppositos cineri doloso.]

Far different was the temper of the Greeks and Egyptians under the orthodox reigns of Leo and Marcian. Those pious emperors enforced with arms and edicts the symbol of their faith; [67] and it was declared by the conscience or honor of five hundred bishops, that the decrees of the synod of Chalcedon might be lawfully supported, even with blood. The Catholics observed with satisfaction, that the same synod was odious both to the Nestorians and the Monophysites; [68] but the Nestorians were less angry, or less powerful, and the East was distracted by the obstinate and sanguinary zeal of the Monophysites. Jerusalem was occupied by an army of monks; in the name of the one incarnate nature, they pillaged, they burnt, they murdered; the sepulchre of Christ was defiled with blood; and the gates of the city were guarded in tumultuous rebellion against the troops of the emperor. After the disgrace and exile of Dioscorus, the Egyptians still regretted their spiritual father; and detested the usurpation of his successor, who was introduced by the fathers of Chalcedon. The throne of Proterius was supported by a guard of two thousand soldiers: he waged a five years' war against the people of Alexandria; and on the first intelligence of the death of Marcian, he became the victim of their zeal. On the third day before the festival of Easter, the patriarch was besieged in the cathedral, and murdered in the baptistery. The remains of his mangled corpse were delivered to the flames, and his ashes to the wind; and the deed was inspired by the vision of a pretended angel: an ambitious monk, who, under the name of Timothy the Cat, [69] succeeded to the place and opinions of Dioscorus. This deadly superstition was inflamed, on either side, by the principle and the practice of retaliation: in the pursuit of a metaphysical quarrel, many thousands [70] were slain, and the Christians of every degree were deprived of the substantial enjoyments of social life, and of the invisible gifts of baptism and the holy communion. Perhaps an extravagant fable of the times may conceal an allegorical picture of these fanatics, who tortured each other and themselves. "Under the consulship of Venantius and Celer," says a grave bishop, "the people of Alexandria, and all Egypt, were seized with a strange and diabolical frenzy: great and small, slaves and freedmen, monks and clergy, the natives of the land, who opposed the synod of Chalcedon, lost their speech and reason, barked like dogs, and tore, with their own teeth the flesh from their hands and arms." [71]

[Footnote 67: See, in the Appendix to the Acts of Chalcedon, the confirmation of the Synod by Marcian, (Concil. tom. iv. p. 1781, 1783;) his letters to the monks of Alexandria, (p. 1791,) of Mount Sinai, (p. 1793,) of Jerusalem and Palestine, (p. 1798;) his laws against the Eutychians, (p. 1809, 1811, 1831;) the correspondence of Leo with the provincial synods on the revolution of Alexandria, (p. 1835—1930.)]

[Footnote 68: Photius (or rather Eulogius of Alexandria) confesses, in a fine passage, the specious color of this double charge against Pope Leo and his synod of Chalcedon, (Bibliot. cod. ccxxv. p. 768.) He waged a double war against the enemies of the church, and wounded either foe with the darts of his adversary. Against Nestorius he seemed to introduce Monophysites; against Eutyches he appeared to countenance the Nestorians. The apologist claims a charitable interpretation for the saints: if the same had been extended to the heretics, the sound of the controversy would have been lost in the air]

[Footnote 69: From his nocturnal expeditions. In darkness and disguise he crept round the cells of the monastery, and whispered the revelation to his slumbering brethren, (Theodor. Lector. l. i.)]

[Footnote 70: Such is the hyperbolic language of the Henoticon.]

[Footnote 71: See the Chronicle of Victor Tunnunensis, in the Lectiones Antiquae of Canisius, republished by Basnage, tom. 326.]

The disorders of thirty years at length produced the famous Henoticon [72] of the emperor Zeno, which in his reign, and in that of Anastasius, was signed by all the bishops of the East, under the penalty of degradation and exile, if they rejected or infringed this salutary and fundamental law. The clergy may smile or groan at the presumption of a layman who defines the articles of faith; yet if he stoops to the humiliating task, his mind is less infected by prejudice or interest, and the authority of the magistrate can only be maintained by the concord of the people. It is in ecclesiastical story, that Zeno appears least contemptible; and I am not able to discern any Manichaean or Eutychian guilt in the generous saying of Anastasius. That it was unworthy of an emperor to persecute the worshippers of Christ and the citizens of Rome. The Henoticon was most pleasing to the Egyptians; yet the smallest blemish has not been described by the jealous, and even jaundiced eyes of our orthodox schoolmen, and it accurately represents the Catholic faith of the incarnation, without adopting or disclaiming the peculiar terms of tenets of the hostile sects. A solemn anathema is pronounced against Nestorius and Eutyches; against all heretics by whom Christ is divided, or confounded, or reduced to a phantom. Without defining the number or the article of the word nature, the pure system of St. Cyril, the faith of Nice, Constantinople, and Ephesus, is respectfully confirmed; but, instead of bowing at the name of the fourth council, the subject is dismissed by the censure of all contrary doctrines, if any such have been taught either elsewhere or at Chalcedon. Under this ambiguous expression, the friends and the enemies of the last synod might unite in a silent embrace. The most reasonable Christians acquiesced in this mode of toleration; but their reason was feeble and inconstant, and their obedience was despised as timid and servile by the vehement spirit of their brethren. On a subject which engrossed the thoughts and discourses of men, it was difficult to preserve an exact neutrality; a book, a sermon, a prayer, rekindled the flame of controversy; and the bonds of communion were alternately broken and renewed by the private animosity of the bishops. The space between Nestorius and Eutyches was filled by a thousand shades of language and opinion; the acephali [73] of Egypt, and the Roman pontiffs, of equal valor, though of unequal strength, may be found at the two extremities of the theological scale. The acephali, without a king or a bishop, were separated above three hundred years from the patriarchs of Alexandria, who had accepted the communion of Constantinople, without exacting a formal condemnation of the synod of Chalcedon. For accepting the communion of Alexandria, without a formal approbation of the same synod, the patriarchs of Constantinople were anathematized by the popes. Their inflexible despotism involved the most orthodox of the Greek churches in this spiritual contagion, denied or doubted the validity of their sacraments, [74] and fomented, thirty-five years, the schism of the East and West, till they finally abolished the memory of four Byzantine pontiffs, who had dared to oppose the supremacy of St. Peter. [75] Before that period, the precarious truce of Constantinople and Egypt had been violated by the zeal of the rival prelates. Macedonius, who was suspected of the Nestorian heresy, asserted, in disgrace and exile, the synod of Chalcedon, while the successor of Cyril would have purchased its overthrow with a bribe of two thousand pounds of gold.

[Footnote 72: The Henoticon is transcribed by Evagrius, (l. iii. c. 13,) and translated by Liberatus, (Brev. c. 18.) Pagi (Critica, tom. ii. p. 411) and (Bibliot. Orient. tom. i. p. 343) are satisfied that it is free from heresy; but Petavius (Dogmat. Theolog. tom. v. l. i. c. 13, p. 40) most unaccountably affirms Chalcedonensem ascivit. An adversary would prove that he had never read the Henoticon.]

[Footnote 73: See Renaudot, (Hist. Patriarch. Alex. p. 123, 131, 145, 195, 247.) They were reconciled by the care of Mark I. (A.D. 799—819;) he promoted their chiefs to the bishoprics of Athribis and Talba, (perhaps Tava. See D'Anville, p. 82,) and supplied the sacraments, which had failed for want of an episcopal ordination.]

[Footnote 74: De his quos baptizavit, quos ordinavit Acacius, majorum traditione confectam et veram, praecipue religiosae solicitudini congruam praebemus sine difficultate medicinam, (Galacius, in epist. i. ad Euphemium, Concil. tom. v. 286.) The offer of a medicine proves the disease, and numbers must have perished before the arrival of the Roman physician. Tillemont himself (Mem. Eccles. tom. xvi. p. 372, 642, &c.) is shocked at the proud, uncharitable temper of the popes; they are now glad, says he, to invoke St. Flavian of Antioch, St. Elias of Jerusalem, &c., to whom they refused communion whilst upon earth. But Cardinal Baronius is firm and hard as the rock of St. Peter.]

[Footnote 75: Their names were erased from the diptych of the church: ex venerabili diptycho, in quo piae memoriae transitum ad coelum habentium episcoporum vocabula continentur, (Concil. tom. iv. p. 1846.) This ecclesiastical record was therefore equivalent to the book of life.]

In the fever of the times, the sense, or rather the sound of a syllable, was sufficient to disturb the peace of an empire. The Trisagion [76] (thrice holy,) "Holy, holy, holy, Lord God of Hosts!" is supposed, by the Greeks, to be the identical hymn which the angels and cherubim eternally repeat before the throne of God, and which, about the middle of the fifth century, was miraculously revealed to the church of Constantinople. The devotion of Antioch soon added, "who was crucified for us!" and this grateful address, either to Christ alone, or to the whole Trinity, may be justified by the rules of theology, and has been gradually adopted by the Catholics of the East and West. But it had been imagined by a Monophysite bishop; [77] the gift of an enemy was at first rejected as a dire and dangerous blasphemy, and the rash innovation had nearly cost the emperor Anastasius his throne and his life. [78] The people of Constantinople was devoid of any rational principles of freedom; but they held, as a lawful cause of rebellion, the color of a livery in the races, or the color of a mystery in the schools. The Trisagion, with and without this obnoxious addition, was chanted in the cathedral by two adverse choirs, and when their lungs were exhausted, they had recourse to the more solid arguments of sticks and stones; the aggressors were punished by the emperor, and defended by the patriarch; and the crown and mitre were staked on the event of this momentous quarrel. The streets were instantly crowded with innumerable swarms of men, women, and children; the legions of monks, in regular array, marched, and shouted, and fought at their head, "Christians! this is the day of martyrdom: let us not desert our spiritual father; anathema to the Manichaean tyrant! he is unworthy to reign." Such was the Catholic cry; and the galleys of Anastasius lay upon their oars before the palace, till the patriarch had pardoned his penitent, and hushed the waves of the troubled multitude. The triumph of Macedonius was checked by a speedy exile; but the zeal of his flock was again exasperated by the same question, "Whether one of the Trinity had been crucified?" On this momentous occasion, the blue and green factions of Constantinople suspended their discord, and the civil and military powers were annihilated in their presence. The keys of the city, and the standards of the guards, were deposited in the forum of Constantine, the principal station and camp of the faithful. Day and night they were incessantly busied either in singing hymns to the honor of their God, or in pillaging and murdering the servants of their prince. The head of his favorite monk, the friend, as they styled him, of the enemy of the Holy Trinity, was borne aloft on a spear; and the firebrands, which had been darted against heretical structures, diffused the undistinguishing flames over the most orthodox buildings. The statues of the emperor were broken, and his person was concealed in a suburb, till, at the end of three days, he dared to implore the mercy of his subjects. Without his diadem, and in the posture of a suppliant, Anastasius appeared on the throne of the circus. The Catholics, before his face, rehearsed their genuine Trisagion; they exulted in the offer, which he proclaimed by the voice of a herald, of abdicating the purple; they listened to the admonition, that, since all could not reign, they should previously agree in the choice of a sovereign; and they accepted the blood of two unpopular ministers, whom their master, without hesitation, condemned to the lions. These furious but transient seditions were encouraged by the success of Vitalian, who, with an army of Huns and Bulgarians, for the most part idolaters, declared himself the champion of the Catholic faith. In this pious rebellion he depopulated Thrace, besieged Constantinople, exterminated sixty-five thousand of his fellow-Christians, till he obtained the recall of the bishops, the satisfaction of the pope, and the establishment of the council of Chalcedon, an orthodox treaty, reluctantly signed by the dying Anastasius, and more faithfully performed by the uncle of Justinian. And such was the event of the first of the religious wars which have been waged in the name and by the disciples, of the God of peace. [79]

[Footnote 76: Petavius (Dogmat. Theolog. tom. v. l. v. c. 2, 3, 4, p. 217-225) and Tillemont (Mem. Eccles. tom. xiv. p. 713, &c., 799) represent the history and doctrine of the Trisagion. In the twelve centuries between Isaiah and St. Proculs's boy, who was taken up into heaven before the bishop and people of Constantinople, the song was considerably improved. The boy heard the angels sing, "Holy God! Holy strong! Holy immortal!"]

[Footnote 77: Peter Gnapheus, the fuller, (a trade which he had exercised in his monastery,) patriarch of Antioch. His tedious story is discussed in the Annals of Pagi (A.D. 477—490) and a dissertation of M. de Valois at the end of his Evagrius.]

[Footnote 78: The troubles under the reign of Anastasius must be gathered from the Chronicles of Victor, Marcellinus, and Theophanes. As the last was not published in the time of Baronius, his critic Pagi is more copious, as well as more correct.]

[Footnote 79: The general history, from the council of Chalcedon to the death of Anastasius, may be found in the Breviary of Liberatus, (c. 14—19,) the iid and iiid books of Evagrius, the abstract of the two books of Theodore the Reader, the Acts of the Synods, and the Epistles of the Pope, (Concil. tom. v.) The series is continued with some disorder in the xvth and xvith tomes of the Memoires Ecclesiastiques of Tillemont. And here I must take leave forever of that incomparable guide—whose bigotry is overbalanced by the merits of erudition, diligence, veracity, and scrupulous minuteness. He was prevented by death from completing, as he designed, the vith century of the church and empire.]

PART IV

Justinian has been already seen in the various lights of a prince, a conqueror, and a lawgiver: the theologian [80] still remains, and it affords an unfavorable prejudice, that his theology should form a very prominent feature of his portrait. The sovereign sympathized with his subjects in their superstitious reverence for living and departed saints: his Code, and more especially his Novels, confirm and enlarge the privileges of the clergy; and in every dispute between a monk and a layman, the partial judge was inclined to pronounce, that truth, and innocence, and justice, were always on the side of the church. In his public and private devotions, the emperor was assiduous and exemplary; his prayers, vigils, and fasts, displayed the austere penance of a monk; his fancy was amused by the hope, or belief, of personal inspiration; he had secured the patronage of the Virgin and St. Michael the archangel; and his recovery from a dangerous disease was ascribed to the miraculous succor of the holy martyrs Cosmas and Damian. The capital and the provinces of the East were decorated with the monuments of his religion; [81] and though the far greater part of these costly structures may be attributed to his taste or ostentation, the zeal of the royal architect was probably quickened by a genuine sense of love and gratitude towards his invisible benefactors. Among the titles of Imperial greatness, the name of Pious was most pleasing to his ear; to promote the temporal and spiritual interest of the church was the serious business of his life; and the duty of father of his country was often sacrificed to that of defender of the faith. The controversies of the times were congenial to his temper and understanding and the theological professors must inwardly deride the diligence of a stranger, who cultivated their art and neglected his own. "What can ye fear," said a bold conspirator to his associates, "from your bigoted tyrant? Sleepless and unarmed, he sits whole nights in his closet, debating with reverend graybeards, and turning over the pages of ecclesiastical volumes." [82] The fruits of these lucubrations were displayed in many a conference, where Justinian might shine as the loudest and most subtile of the disputants; in many a sermon, which, under the name of edicts and epistles, proclaimed to the empire the theology of their master. While the Barbarians invaded the provinces, while the victorious legion marched under the banners of Belisarius and Narses, the successor of Trajan, unknown to the camp, was content to vanquish at the head of a synod. Had he invited to these synods a disinterested and rational spectator, Justinian might have learned, "that religious controversy is the offspring of arrogance and folly; that true piety is most laudably expressed by silence and submission; that man, ignorant of his own nature, should not presume to scrutinize the nature of his God; and that it is sufficient for us to know, that power and benevolence are the perfect attributes of the Deity." [83]

[Footnote 80: The strain of the Anecdotes of Procopius, (c. 11, 13, 18, 27, 28,) with the learned remarks of Alemannus, is confirmed, rather than contradicted, by the Acts of the Councils, the fourth book of Evagrius, and the complaints of the African Facundus, in his xiith book—de tribus capitulis, "cum videri doctus appetit importune...spontaneis quaestionibus ecclesiam turbat." See Procop. de Bell. Goth. l. iii. c. 35.]

[Footnote 81: Procop. de Edificiis, l. i. c. 6, 7, &c., passim.]

[Footnote 82: Procop. de Bell. Goth. l. iii. c. 32. In the life of St. Eutychius (apud Aleman. ad Procop. Arcan. c. 18) the same character is given with a design to praise Justinian.]

[Footnote 83: For these wise and moderate sentiments, Procopius (de Bell. Goth. l. i. c. 3) is scourged in the preface of Alemannus, who ranks him among the political Christians—sed longe verius haeresium omnium sentinas, prorsusque Atheos—abominable Atheists, who preached the imitation of God's mercy to man, (ad Hist. Arcan. c. 13.)]

Toleration was not the virtue of the times, and indulgence to rebels has seldom been the virtue of princes. But when the prince descends to the narrow and peevish character of a disputant, he is easily provoked to supply the defect of argument by the plenitude of power, and to chastise without mercy the perverse blindness of those who wilfully shut their eyes against the light of demonstration. The reign of Justinian was a uniform yet various scene of persecution; and he appears to have surpassed his indolent predecessors, both in the contrivance of his laws and the rigor of their execution. The insufficient term of three months was assigned for the conversion or exile of all heretics; [84] and if he still connived at their precarious stay, they were deprived, under his iron yoke, not only of the benefits of society, but of the common birth-right of men and Christians. At the end of four hundred years, the Montanists of Phrygia [85] still breathed the wild enthusiasm of perfection and prophecy which they had imbibed from their male and female apostles, the special organs of the Paraclete. On the approach of the Catholic priests and soldiers, they grasped with alacrity the crown of martyrdom the conventicle and the congregation perished in the flames, but these primitive fanatics were not extinguished three hundred years after the death of their tyrant. Under the protection of their Gothic confederates, the church of the Arians at Constantinople had braved the severity of the laws: their clergy equalled the wealth and magnificence of the senate; and the gold and silver which were seized by the rapacious hand of Justinian might perhaps be claimed as the spoils of the provinces, and the trophies of the Barbarians. A secret remnant of Pagans, who still lurked in the most refined and most rustic conditions of mankind, excited the indignation of the Christians, who were perhaps unwilling that any strangers should be the witnesses of their intestine quarrels. A bishop was named as the inquisitor of the faith, and his diligence soon discovered, in the court and city, the magistrates, lawyers, physicians, and sophists, who still cherished the superstition of the Greeks. They were sternly informed that they must choose without delay between the displeasure of Jupiter or Justinian, and that their aversion to the gospel could no longer be distinguished under the scandalous mask of indifference or impiety. The patrician Photius, perhaps, alone was resolved to live and to die like his ancestors: he enfranchised himself with the stroke of a dagger, and left his tyrant the poor consolation of exposing with ignominy the lifeless corpse of the fugitive. His weaker brethren submitted to their earthly monarch, underwent the ceremony of baptism, and labored, by their extraordinary zeal, to erase the suspicion, or to expiate the guilt, of idolatry. The native country of Homer, and the theatre of the Trojan war, still retained the last sparks of his mythology: by the care of the same bishop, seventy thousand Pagans were detected and converted in Asia, Phrygia, Lydia, and Caria; ninety-six churches were built for the new proselytes; and linen vestments, Bibles, and liturgies, and vases of gold and silver, were supplied by the pious munificence of Justinian. [86] The Jews, who had been gradually stripped of their immunities, were oppressed by a vexatious law, which compelled them to observe the festival of Easter the same day on which it was celebrated by the Christians. [87] And they might complain with the more reason, since the Catholics themselves did not agree with the astronomical calculations of their sovereign: the people of Constantinople delayed the beginning of their Lent a whole week after it had been ordained by authority; and they had the pleasure of fasting seven days, while meat was exposed for sale by the command of the emperor. The Samaritans of Palestine [88] were a motley race, an ambiguous sect, rejected as Jews by the Pagans, by the Jews as schismatics, and by the Christians as idolaters. The abomination of the cross had already been planted on their holy mount of Garizim, [89] but the persecution of Justinian offered only the alternative of baptism or rebellion. They chose the latter: under the standard of a desperate leader, they rose in arms, and retaliated their wrongs on the lives, the property, and the temples, of a defenceless people. The Samaritans were finally subdued by the regular forces of the East: twenty thousand were slain, twenty thousand were sold by the Arabs to the infidels of Persia and India, and the remains of that unhappy nation atoned for the crime of treason by the sin of hypocrisy. It has been computed that one hundred thousand Roman subjects were extirpated in the Samaritan war, [90] which converted the once fruitful province into a desolate and smoking wilderness. But in the creed of Justinian, the guilt of murder could not be applied to the slaughter of unbelievers; and he piously labored to establish with fire and sword the unity of the Christian faith. [91]

[Footnote 84: This alternative, a precious circumstance, is preserved by John Malala, (tom. ii. p. 63, edit. Venet. 1733,) who deserves more credit as he draws towards his end. After numbering the heretics, Nestorians, Eutychians, &c., ne expectent, says Justinian, ut digni venia judicen tur: jubemus, enim ut...convicti et aperti haeretici justae et idoneae animadversioni subjiciantur. Baronius copies and applauds this edict of the Code, (A.D. 527, No. 39, 40.)]

[Footnote 85: See the character and principles of the Montanists, in Mosheim, Rebus Christ. ante Constantinum, p. 410—424.]

[Footnote 86: Theophan. Chron. p. 153. John, the Monophysite bishop of Asia, is a more authentic witness of this transaction, in which he was himself employed by the emperor, (Asseman. Bib. Orient. tom. ii. p. 85.)]

[Footnote 87: Compare Procopius (Hist. Arcan. c. 28, and Aleman's Notes) with Theophanes, (Chron. p. 190.) The council of Nice has intrusted the patriarch, or rather the astronomers, of Alexandria, with the annual proclamation of Easter; and we still read, or rather we do not read, many of the Paschal epistles of St. Cyril. Since the reign of Monophytism in Egypt, the Catholics were perplexed by such a foolish prejudice as that which so long opposed, among the Protestants, the reception of the Gregorian style.]

[Footnote 88: For the religion and history of the Samaritans, consult Basnage, Histoire des Juifs, a learned and impartial work.]

[Footnote 89: Sichem, Neapolis, Naplous, the ancient and modern seat of the Samaritans, is situate in a valley between the barren Ebal, the mountain of cursing to the north, and the fruitful Garizim, or mountain of cursing to the south, ten or eleven hours' travel from Jerusalem. See Maundrel, Journey from Aleppo &c.]

[Footnote 90: Procop. Anecdot. c. 11. Theophan. Chron. p. 122. John Malala Chron. tom. ii. p. 62. I remember an observation, half philosophical. half superstitious, that the province which had been ruined by the bigotry of Justinian, was the same through which the Mahometans penetrated into the empire.]

[Footnote 91: The expression of Procopius is remarkable. Anecdot. c. 13.]

With these sentiments, it was incumbent on him, at least, to be always in the right. In the first years of his administration, he signalized his zeal as the disciple and patron of orthodoxy: the reconciliation of the Greeks and Latins established the tome of St. Leo as the creed of the emperor and the empire; the Nestorians and Eutychians were exposed. on either side, to the double edge of persecution; and the four synods of Nice, Constantinople, Ephesus, and Chalcedon, were ratified by the code of a Catholic lawgiver. [92] But while Justinian strove to maintain the uniformity of faith and worship, his wife Theodora, whose vices were not incompatible with devotion, had listened to the Monophysite teachers; and the open or clandestine enemies of the church revived and multiplied at the smile of their gracious patroness. The capital, the palace, the nuptial bed, were torn by spiritual discord; yet so doubtful was the sincerity of the royal consorts, that their seeming disagreement was imputed by many to a secret and mischievous confederacy against the religion and happiness of their people. [93] The famous dispute of the Three Chapters, [94] which has filled more volumes than it deserves lines, is deeply marked with this subtile and disingenuous spirit. It was now three hundred years since the body of Origen [95] had been eaten by the worms: his soul, of which he held the preexistence, was in the hands of its Creator; but his writings were eagerly perused by the monks of Palestine. In these writings, the piercing eye of Justinian descried more than ten metaphysical errors; and the primitive doctor, in the company of Pythagoras and Plato, was devoted by the clergy to the eternity of hell-fire, which he had presumed to deny. Under the cover of this precedent, a treacherous blow was aimed at the council of Chalcedon. The fathers had listened without impatience to the praise of Theodore of Mopsuestia; [96] and their justice or indulgence had restored both Theodore of Cyrrhus, and Ibas of Edessa, to the communion of the church. But the characters of these Oriental bishops were tainted with the reproach of heresy; the first had been the master, the two others were the friends, of Nestorius; their most suspicious passages were accused under the title of the three chapters; and the condemnation of their memory must involve the honor of a synod, whose name was pronounced with sincere or affected reverence by the Catholic world. If these bishops, whether innocent or guilty, were annihilated in the sleep of death, they would not probably be awakened by the clamor which, after the a hundred years, was raised over their grave. If they were already in the fangs of the daemon, their torments could neither be aggravated nor assuaged by human industry. If in the company of saints and angels they enjoyed the rewards of piety, they must have smiled at the idle fury of the theological insects who still crawled on the surface of the earth. The foremost of these insects, the emperor of the Romans, darted his sting, and distilled his venom, perhaps without discerning the true motives of Theodora and her ecclesiastical faction. The victims were no longer subject to his power, and the vehement style of his edicts could only proclaim their damnation, and invite the clergy of the East to join in a full chorus of curses and anathemas. The East, with some hesitation, consented to the voice of her sovereign: the fifth general council, of three patriarchs and one hundred and sixty-five bishops, was held at Constantinople; and the authors, as well as the defenders, of the three chapters were separated from the communion of the saints, and solemnly delivered to the prince of darkness. But the Latin churches were more jealous of the honor of Leo and the synod of Chalcedon: and if they had fought as they usually did under the standard of Rome, they might have prevailed in the cause of reason and humanity. But their chief was a prisoner in the hands of the enemy; the throne of St. Peter, which had been disgraced by the simony, was betrayed by the cowardice, of Vigilius, who yielded, after a long and inconsistent struggle, to the despotism of Justinian and the sophistry of the Greeks. His apostasy provoked the indignation of the Latins, and no more than two bishops could be found who would impose their hands on his deacon and successor Pelagius. Yet the perseverance of the popes insensibly transferred to their adversaries the appellation of schismatics; the Illyrian, African, and Italian churches were oppressed by the civil and ecclesiastical powers, not without some effort of military force; [97] the distant Barbarians transcribed the creed of the Vatican, and, in the period of a century, the schism of the three chapters expired in an obscure angle of the Venetian province. [98] But the religious discontent of the Italians had already promoted the conquests of the Lombards, and the Romans themselves were accustomed to suspect the faith and to detest the government of their Byzantine tyrant.

[Footnote 92: See the Chronicle of Victor, p. 328, and the original evidence of the laws of Justinian. During the first years of his reign, Baronius himself is in extreme good humor with the emperor, who courted the popes, till he got them into his power.]

[Footnote 93: Procopius, Anecdot. c. 13. Evagrius, l. iv. c. 10. If the ecclesiastical never read the secret historian, their common suspicion proves at least the general hatred.]

[Footnote 94: On the subject of the three chapters, the original acts of the vth general council of Constantinople supply much useless, though authentic, knowledge, (Concil. tom. vi. p. 1-419.) The Greek Evagrius is less copious and correct (l. iv. c. 38) than the three zealous Africans, Facundus, (in his twelve books, de tribus capitulis, which are most correctly published by Sirmond,) Liberatus, (in his Breviarium, c. 22, 23, 24,) and Victor Tunnunensis in his Chronicle, (in tom. i. Antiq. Lect. Canisii, 330—334.) The Liber Pontificalis, or Anastasius, (in Vigilio, Pelagio, &c.,) is original Italian evidence. The modern reader will derive some information from Dupin (Bibliot. Eccles. tom. v. p. 189—207) and Basnage, (Hist. de l'Eglise, tom. i. p. 519—541;) yet the latter is too firmly resolved to depreciate the authority and character of the popes.]

[Footnote 95: Origen had indeed too great a propensity to imitate the old philosophers, (Justinian, ad Mennam, in Concil. tom. vi. p. 356.) His moderate opinions were too repugnant to the zeal of the church, and he was found guilty of the heresy of reason.]

[Footnote 96: Basnage (Praefat. p. 11—14, ad tom. i. Antiq. Lect. Canis.) has fairly weighed the guilt and innocence of Theodore of Mopsuestia. If he composed 10,000 volumes, as many errors would be a charitable allowance. In all the subsequent catalogues of heresiarchs, he alone, without his two brethren, is included; and it is the duty of Asseman (Bibliot. Orient. tom. iv. p. 203—207) to justify the sentence.]

[Footnote 97: See the complaints of Liberatus and Victor, and the exhortations of Pope Pelagius to the conqueror and exarch of Italy. Schisma.. per potestates publicas opprimatur, &c., (Concil. tom. vi. p. 467, &c.) An army was detained to suppress the sedition of an Illyrian city. See Procopius, (de Bell. Goth. l. iv. c. 25:). He seems to promise an ecclesiastical history. It would have been curious and impartial.]

[Footnote 98: The bishops of the patriarchate of Aquileia were reconciled by Pope Honorius, A.D. 638, (Muratori, Annali d' Italia, tom. v. p. 376;) but they again relapsed, and the schism was not finally extinguished till 698. Fourteen years before, the church of Spain had overlooked the vth general council with contemptuous silence, (xiii. Concil. Toretan. in Concil. tom. vii. p. 487—494.)]

Justinian was neither steady nor consistent in the nice process of fixing his volatile opinions and those of his subjects. In his youth he was, offended by the slightest deviation from the orthodox line; in his old age he transgressed the measure of temperate heresy, and the Jacobites, not less than the Catholics, were scandalized by his declaration, that the body of Christ was incorruptible, and that his manhood was never subject to any wants and infirmities, the inheritance of our mortal flesh. This fantastic opinion was announced in the last edicts of Justinian; and at the moment of his seasonable departure, the clergy had refused to subscribe, the prince was prepared to persecute, and the people were resolved to suffer or resist. A bishop of Treves, secure beyond the limits of his power, addressed the monarch of the East in the language of authority and affection. "Most gracious Justinian, remember your baptism and your creed. Let not your gray hairs be defiled with heresy. Recall your fathers from exile, and your followers from perdition. You cannot be ignorant, that Italy and Gaul, Spain and Africa, already deplore your fall, and anathematize your name. Unless, without delay, you destroy what you have taught; unless you exclaim with a loud voice, I have erred, I have sinned, anathema to Nestorius, anathema to Eutyches, you deliver your soul to the same flames in which they will eternally burn." He died and made no sign. [99] His death restored in some degree the peace of the church, and the reigns of his four successors, Justin Tiberius, Maurice, and Phocas, are distinguished by a rare, though fortunate, vacancy in the ecclesiastical history of the East. [100]

[Footnote 99: Nicetus, bishop of Treves, (Concil. tom. vi. p. 511-513:) he himself, like most of the Gallican prelates, (Gregor. Epist. l. vii. 5 in Concil. tom. vi. p. 1007,) was separated from the communion of the four patriarchs by his refusal to condemn the three chapters. Baronius almost pronounces the damnation of Justinian, (A.D. 565, No. 6.)]

[Footnote 100: After relating the last heresy of Justinian, (l. iv. c. 39, 40, 41,) and the edict of his successor, (l. v. c. 3,) the remainder of the history of Evagrius is filled with civil, instead of ecclesiastical events.]

The faculties of sense and reason are least capable of acting on themselves; the eye is most inaccessible to the sight, the soul to the thought; yet we think, and even feel, that one will, a sole principle of action, is essential to a rational and conscious being. When Heraclius returned from the Persian war, the orthodox hero consulted his bishops, whether the Christ whom he adored, of one person, but of two natures, was actuated by a single or a double will. They replied in the singular, and the emperor was encouraged to hope that the Jacobites of Egypt and Syria might be reconciled by the profession of a doctrine, most certainly harmless, and most probably true, since it was taught even by the Nestorians themselves. [101] The experiment was tried without effect, and the timid or vehement Catholics condemned even the semblance of a retreat in the presence of a subtle and audacious enemy. The orthodox (the prevailing) party devised new modes of speech, and argument, and interpretation: to either nature of Christ they speciously applied a proper and distinct energy; but the difference was no longer visible when they allowed that the human and the divine will were invariably the same. [102] The disease was attended with the customary symptoms: but the Greek clergy, as if satiated with the endless controversy of the incarnation, instilled a healing counsel into the ear of the prince and people. They declared themselves Monothelites, (asserters of the unity of will,) but they treated the words as new, the questions as superfluous; and recommended a religious silence as the most agreeable to the prudence and charity of the gospel. This law of silence was successively imposed by the ecthesis or exposition of Heraclius, the type or model of his grandson Constans; [103] and the Imperial edicts were subscribed with alacrity or reluctance by the four patriarchs of Rome, Constantinople, Alexandria, and Antioch. But the bishop and monks of Jerusalem sounded the alarm: in the language, or even in the silence, of the Greeks, the Latin churches detected a latent heresy: and the obedience of Pope Honorius to the commands of his sovereign was retracted and censured by the bolder ignorance of his successors. They condemned the execrable and abominable heresy of the Monothelites, who revived the errors of Manes, Apollinaris, Eutyches, &c.; they signed the sentence of excommunication on the tomb of St. Peter; the ink was mingled with the sacramental wine, the blood of Christ; and no ceremony was omitted that could fill the superstitious mind with horror and affright. As the representative of the Western church, Pope Martin and his Lateran synod anathematized the perfidious and guilty silence of the Greeks: one hundred and five bishops of Italy, for the most part the subjects of Constans, presumed to reprobate his wicked type, and the impious ecthesis of his grandfather; and to confound the authors and their adherents with the twenty-one notorious heretics, the apostates from the church, and the organs of the devil. Such an insult under the tamest reign could not pass with impunity. Pope Martin ended his days on the inhospitable shore of the Tauric Chersonesus, and his oracle, the abbot Maximus, was inhumanly chastised by the amputation of his tongue and his right hand. [104] But the same invincible spirit survived in their successors; and the triumph of the Latins avenged their recent defeat, and obliterated the disgrace of the three chapters. The synods of Rome were confirmed by the sixth general council of Constantinople, in the palace and the presence of a new Constantine, a descendant of Heraclius. The royal convert converted the Byzantine pontiff and a majority of the bishops; [105] the dissenters, with their chief, Macarius of Antioch, were condemned to the spiritual and temporal pains of heresy; the East condescended to accept the lessons of the West; and the creed was finally settled, which teaches the Catholics of every age, that two wills or energies are harmonized in the person of Christ. The majesty of the pope and the Roman synod was represented by two priests, one deacon, and three bishops; but these obscure Latins had neither arms to compel, nor treasures to bribe, nor language to persuade; and I am ignorant by what arts they could determine the lofty emperor of the Greeks to abjure the catechism of his infancy, and to persecute the religion of his fathers. Perhaps the monks and people of Constantinople [106] were favorable to the Lateran creed, which is indeed the least reasonable of the two: and the suspicion is countenanced by the unnatural moderation of the Greek clergy, who appear in this quarrel to be conscious of their weakness. While the synod debated, a fanatic proposed a more summary decision, by raising a dead man to life: the prelates assisted at the trial; but the acknowledged failure may serve to indicate, that the passions and prejudices of the multitude were not enlisted on the side of the Monothelites. In the next generation, when the son of Constantine was deposed and slain by the disciple of Macarius, they tasted the feast of revenge and dominion: the image or monument of the sixth council was defaced, and the original acts were committed to the flames. But in the second year, their patron was cast headlong from the throne, the bishops of the East were released from their occasional conformity, the Roman faith was more firmly replanted by the orthodox successors of Bardanes, and the fine problems of the incarnation were forgotten in the more popular and visible quarrel of the worship of images. [107]

[Footnote 101: This extraordinary, and perhaps inconsistent, doctrine of the Nestorians, had been observed by La Croze, (Christianisme des Indes, tom. i. p. 19, 20,) and is more fully exposed by Abulpharagius, (Bibliot. Orient. tom. ii. p. 292. Hist. Dynast. p. 91, vers. Latin. Pocock.) and Asseman himself, (tom. iv. p. 218.) They seem ignorant that they might allege the positive authority of the ecthesis. (the common reproach of the Monophysites) (Concil. tom. vii. p. 205.)]

[Footnote 102: See the Orthodox faith in Petavius, (Dogmata Theolog. tom. v. l. ix. c. 6—10, p. 433—447:) all the depths of this controversy in the Greek dialogue between Maximus and Pyrrhus, (acalcem tom. viii. Annal. Baron. p. 755—794,) which relates a real conference, and produced as short-lived a conversion.]

[Footnote 103: Impiissimam ecthesim.... scelerosum typum (Concil. tom. vii p. 366) diabolicae operationis genimina, (fors. germina, or else the Greek in the original. Concil. p. 363, 364,) are the expressions of the xviiith anathema. The epistle of Pope Martin to Amandus, Gallican bishop, stigmatizes the Monothelites and their heresy with equal virulence, (p. 392.)]

[Footnote 104: The sufferings of Martin and Maximus are described with simplicity in their original letters and acts, (Concil. tom. vii. p. 63—78. Baron. Annal. Eccles. A.D. 656, No. 2, et annos subsequent.) Yet the chastisement of their disobedience had been previously announced in the Type of Constans, (Concil. tom. vii. p. 240.)]

[Footnote 105: Eutychius (Annal. tom. ii. p. 368) most erroneously supposes that the 124 bishops of the Roman synod transported themselves to Constantinople; and by adding them to the 168 Greeks, thus composes the sixth council of 292 fathers.]

[Footnote 106: The Monothelite Constans was hated by all, (says Theophanes, Chron. p. 292). When the Monothelite monk failed in his miracle, the people shouted, (Concil. tom. vii. p. 1032.) But this was a natural and transient emotion; and I much fear that the latter is an anticipation of the good people of Constantinople.]

[Footnote 107: The history of Monothelitism may be found in the Acts of the Synods of Rome (tom. vii. p. 77—395, 601—608) and Constantinople, (p. 609—1429.) Baronius extracted some original documents from the Vatican library; and his chronology is rectified by the diligence of Pagi. Even Dupin (Bibliotheque Eccles. tom. vi. p. 57—71) and Basnage (Hist. de l'Eglise, tom. i. p. 451—555) afford a tolerable abridgment.]

Before the end of the seventh century, the creed of the incarnation, which had been defined at Rome and Constantinople, was uniformly preached in the remote islands of Britain and Ireland; [108] the same ideas were entertained, or rather the same words were repeated, by all the Christians whose liturgy was performed in the Greek or the Latin tongue. Their numbers, and visible splendor, bestowed an imperfect claim to the appellation of Catholics: but in the East, they were marked with the less honorable name of Melchites, or Royalists; [109] of men, whose faith, instead of resting on the basis of Scripture, reason, or tradition, had been established, and was still maintained, by the arbitrary power of a temporal monarch. Their adversaries might allege the words of the fathers of Constantinople, who profess themselves the slaves of the king; and they might relate, with malicious joy, how the decrees of Chalcedon had been inspired and reformed by the emperor Marcian and his virgin bride. The prevailing faction will naturally inculcate the duty of submission, nor is it less natural that dissenters should feel and assert the principles of freedom. Under the rod of persecution, the Nestorians and Monophysites degenerated into rebels and fugitives; and the most ancient and useful allies of Rome were taught to consider the emperor not as the chief, but as the enemy of the Christians. Language, the leading principle which unites or separates the tribes of mankind, soon discriminated the sectaries of the East, by a peculiar and perpetual badge, which abolished the means of intercourse and the hope of reconciliation. The long dominion of the Greeks, their colonies, and, above all, their eloquence, had propagated a language doubtless the most perfect that has been contrived by the art of man. Yet the body of the people, both in Syria and Egypt, still persevered in the use of their national idioms; with this difference, however, that the Coptic was confined to the rude and illiterate peasants of the Nile, while the Syriac, [110] from the mountains of Assyria to the Red Sea, was adapted to the higher topics of poetry and argument. Armenia and Abyssinia were infected by the speech or learning of the Greeks; and their Barbaric tongues, which have been revived in the studies of modern Europe, were unintelligible to the inhabitants of the Roman empire. The Syriac and the Coptic, the Armenian and the Aethiopic, are consecrated in the service of their respective churches: and their theology is enriched by domestic versions [111] both of the Scriptures and of the most popular fathers. After a period of thirteen hundred and sixty years, the spark of controversy, first kindled by a sermon of Nestorius, still burns in the bosom of the East, and the hostile communions still maintain the faith and discipline of their founders. In the most abject state of ignorance, poverty, and servitude, the Nestorians and Monophysites reject the spiritual supremacy of Rome, and cherish the toleration of their Turkish masters, which allows them to anathematize, on the one hand, St. Cyril and the synod of Ephesus: on the other, Pope Leo and the council of Chalcedon. The weight which they cast into the downfall of the Eastern empire demands our notice, and the reader may be amused with the various prospect of, I. The Nestorians; II. The Jacobites; [112] III. The Maronites; IV.

The Armenians; V. The Copts; and, VI. The Abyssinians. To the three former, the Syriac is common; but of the latter, each is discriminated by the use of a national idiom.

Yet the modern natives of Armenia and Abyssinia would be incapable of conversing with their ancestors; and the Christians of Egypt and Syria, who reject the religion, have adopted the language of the Arabians. The lapse of time has seconded the sacerdotal arts; and in the East, as well as in the West, the Deity is addressed in an obsolete tongue, unknown to the majority of the congregation.

[Footnote 108: In the Lateran synod of 679, Wilfred, an Anglo-Saxon bishop, subscribed pro omni Aquilonari parte Britanniae et Hiberniae, quae ab Anglorum et Britonum, necnon Scotorum et Pictorum gentibus colebantur, (Eddius, in Vit. St. Wilfrid. c. 31, apud Pagi, Critica, tom. iii. p. 88.) Theodore (magnae insulae Britanniae archiepiscopus et philosophus) was long expected at Rome, (Concil. tom. vii. p. 714,) but he contented himself with holding (A.D. 680) his provincial synod of Hatfield, in which he received the decrees of Pope Martin and the first Lateran council against the Monothelites, (Concil. tom. vii. p. 597, &c.) Theodore, a monk of Tarsus in Cilicia, had been named to the primacy of Britain by Pope Vitalian, (A.D. 688; see Baronius and Pagi,) whose esteem for his learning and piety was tainted by some distrust of his national character—ne quid contrarium veritati fidei, Graecorum more, in ecclesiam cui praeesset introduceret. The Cilician was sent from Rome to Canterbury under the tuition of an African guide, (Bedae Hist. Eccles. Anglorum. l. iv. c. 1.) He adhered to the Roman doctrine; and the same creed of the incarnation has been uniformly transmitted from Theodore to the modern primates, whose sound understanding is perhaps seldom engaged with that abstruse mystery.]

[Footnote 109: This name, unknown till the xth century, appears to be of Syriac origin. It was invented by the Jacobites, and eagerly adopted by the Nestorians and Mahometans; but it was accepted without shame by the Catholics, and is frequently used in the Annals of Eutychius, (Asseman. Bibliot. Orient. tom. ii. p. 507, &c., tom. iii. p. 355. Renaudot, Hist. Patriarch. Alexandrin. p. 119.), was the acclamation of the fathers of Constantinople, (Concil. tom. vii. p. 765.)]

[Footnote 110: The Syriac, which the natives revere as the primitive language, was divided into three dialects. 1. The Aramoean, as it was refined at Edessa and the cities of Mesopotamia. 2. The Palestine, which was used in Jerusalem, Damascus, and the rest of Syria. 3. The Nabathoean, the rustic idiom of the mountains of Assyria and the villages of Irak, (Gregor, Abulpharag. Hist. Dynast. p. 11.) On the Syriac, sea Ebed-Jesu, (Asseman. tom. iii. p. 326, &c.,) whose prejudice alone could prefer it to the Arabic.]

[Footnote 111: I shall not enrich my ignorance with the spoils of Simon, Walton, Mill, Wetstein, Assemannus, Ludolphus, La Croze, whom I have consulted with some care. It appears, 1. That, of all the versions which are celebrated by the fathers, it is doubtful whether any are now extant in their pristine integrity. 2. That the Syriac has the best claim, and that the consent of the Oriental sects is a proof that it is more ancient than their schism.]

[Footnote 112: In the account of the Monophysites and Nestorians, I am deeply indebted to the Bibliotheca Orientalis Clementino-Vaticana of Joseph Simon Assemannus. That learned Maronite was despatched, in the year 1715, by Pope Clement XI. to visit the monasteries of Egypt and Syria, in search of Mss. His four folio volumes, published at Rome 1719—1728, contain a part only, though perhaps the most valuable, of his extensive project. As a native and as a scholar, he possessed the Syriac literature; and though a dependent of Rome, he wishes to be moderate and candid.]

PART V

I - Both in his native and his episcopal province, the heresy of the unfortunate Nestorius was speedily obliterated. The Oriental bishops, who at Ephesus had resisted to his face the arrogance of Cyril, were mollified by his tardy concessions. The same prelates, or their successors, subscribed, not without a murmur, the decrees of Chalcedon; the power of the Monophysites reconciled them with the Catholics in the conformity of passion, of interest, and, insensibly, of belief; and their last reluctant sigh was breathed in the defence of the three chapters. Their dissenting brethren, less moderate, or more sincere, were crushed by the penal laws; and, as early as the reign of Justinian, it became difficult to find a church of Nestorians within the limits of the Roman empire. Beyond those limits they had discovered a new world, in which they might hope for liberty, and aspire to conquest. In Persia, notwithstanding the resistance of the Magi, Christianity had struck a deep root, and the nations of the East reposed under its salutary shade. The catholic, or primate, resided in the capital: in his synods, and in their dioceses, his metropolitans, bishops, and clergy, represented the pomp and order of a regular hierarchy: they rejoiced in the increase of proselytes, who were converted from the Zendavesta to the gospel, from the secular to the monastic life; and their zeal was stimulated by the presence of an artful and formidable enemy. The Persian church had been founded by the missionaries of Syria; and their language, discipline, and doctrine, were closely interwoven with its original frame. The catholics were elected and ordained by their own suffragans; but their filial dependence on the patriarchs of Antioch is attested by the canons of the Oriental church. [113] In the Persian school of Edessa, [114] the rising generations of the faithful imbibed their theological idiom: they studied in the Syriac version the ten thousand volumes of Theodore of Mopsuestia; and they revered the apostolic faith and holy martyrdom of his disciple Nestorius, whose person and language were equally unknown to the nations beyond the Tigris. The first indelible lesson of Ibas, bishop of Edessa, taught them to execrate the Egyptians, who, in the synod of Ephesus, had impiously confounded the two natures of Christ. The flight of the masters and scholars, who were twice expelled from the Athens of Syria, dispersed a crowd of missionaries inflamed by the double zeal of religion and revenge. And the rigid unity of the Monophysites, who, under the reigns of Zeno and Anastasius, had invaded the thrones of the East, provoked their antagonists, in a land of freedom, to avow a moral, rather than a physical, union of the two persons of Christ. Since the first preaching of the gospel, the Sassanian kings beheld with an eye of suspicion a race of aliens and apostates, who had embraced the religion, and who might favor the cause, of the hereditary foes of their country. The royal edicts had often prohibited their dangerous correspondence with the Syrian clergy: the progress of the schism was grateful to the jealous pride of Perozes, and he listened to the eloquence of an artful prelate, who painted Nestorius as the friend of Persia, and urged him to secure the fidelity of his Christian subjects, by granting a just preference to the victims and enemies of the Roman tyrant. The Nestorians composed a large majority of the clergy and people: they were encouraged by the smile, and armed with the sword, of despotism; yet many of their weaker brethren were startled at the thought of breaking loose from the communion of the Christian world, and the blood of seven thousand seven hundred Monophysites, or Catholics, confirmed the uniformity of faith and discipline in the churches of Persia. [115] Their ecclesiastical institutions are distinguished by a liberal principle of reason, or at least of policy: the austerity of the cloister was relaxed and gradually forgotten; houses of charity were endowed for the education of orphans and foundlings; the law of celibacy, so forcibly recommended to the Greeks and Latins, was disregarded by the Persian clergy; and the number of the elect was multiplied by the public and reiterated nuptials of the priests, the bishops, and even the patriarch himself. To this standard of natural and religious freedom, myriads of fugitives resorted from all the provinces of the Eastern empire; the narrow bigotry of Justinian was punished by the emigration of his most industrious subjects; they transported into Persia the arts both of peace and war: and those who deserved the favor, were promoted in the service, of a discerning monarch. The arms of Nushirvan, and his fiercer grandson, were assisted with advice, and money, and troops, by the desperate sectaries who still lurked in their native cities of the East: their zeal was rewarded with the gift of the Catholic churches; but when those cities and churches were recovered by Heraclius, their open profession of treason and heresy compelled them to seek a refuge in the realm of their foreign ally. But the seeming tranquillity of the Nestorians was often endangered, and sometimes overthrown. They were involved in the common evils of Oriental despotism: their enmity to Rome could not always atone for their attachment to the gospel: and a colony of three hundred thousand Jacobites, the captives of Apamea and Antioch, was permitted to erect a hostile altar in the face of the catholic, and in the sunshine of the court. In his last treaty, Justinian introduced some conditions which tended to enlarge and fortify the toleration of Christianity in Persia. The emperor, ignorant of the rights of conscience, was incapable of pity or esteem for the heretics who denied the authority of the holy synods: but he flattered himself that they would gradually perceive the temporal benefits of union with the empire and the church of Rome; and if he failed in exciting their gratitude, he might hope to provoke the jealousy of their sovereign. In a later age the Lutherans have been burnt at Paris, and protected in Germany, by the superstition and policy of the most Christian king.

[Footnote 113: See the Arabic canons of Nice in the translation of Abraham Ecchelensis, No. 37, 38, 39, 40. Concil. tom. ii. p. 335, 336, edit. Venet. These vulgar titles, Nicene and Arabic, are both apocryphal. The council of Nice enacted no more than twenty canons, (Theodoret. Hist. Eccles. l. i. c. 8;) and the remainder, seventy or eighty, were collected from the synods of the Greek church. The Syriac edition of Maruthas is no longer extant, (Asseman. Bibliot. Oriental. tom. i. p. 195, tom. iii. p. 74,) and the Arabic version is marked with many recent interpolations. Yet this Code contains many curious relics of ecclesiastical discipline; and since it is equally revered by all the Eastern communions, it was probably finished before the schism of the Nestorians and Jacobites, (Fabric. Bibliot. Graec. tom. xi. p. 363—367.)]

[Footnote 114: Theodore the Reader (l. ii. c. 5, 49, ad calcem Hist. Eccles.) has noticed this Persian school of Edessa. Its ancient splendor, and the two aeras of its downfall, (A.D. 431 and 489) are clearly discussed by Assemanni, (Biblioth. Orient. tom. ii. p. 402, iii. p. 376, 378, iv. p. 70, 924.)]

[Footnote 115: A dissertation on the state of the Nestorians has swelled in the bands of Assemanni to a folio volume of 950 pages, and his learned researches are digested in the most lucid order. Besides this ivth volume of the Bibliotheca Orientalis, the extracts in the three preceding tomes (tom. i. p. 203, ii. p. 321-463, iii. 64—70, 378—395, &c., 405—408, 580—589) may be usefully consulted.]

The desire of gaining souls for God and subjects for the church, has excited in every age the diligence of the Christian priests. From the conquest of Persia they carried their spiritual arms to the north, the east, and the south; and the simplicity of the gospel was fashioned and painted with the colors of the Syriac theology. In the sixth century, according to the report of a Nestorian traveller, [116] Christianity was successfully preached to the Bactrians, the Huns, the Persians, the Indians, the Persarmenians, the Medes, and the Elamites: the Barbaric churches, from the Gulf of Persia to the Caspian Sea, were almost infinite; and their recent faith was conspicuous in the number and sanctity of their monks and martyrs. The pepper coast of Malabar, and the isles of the ocean, Socotora and Ceylon, were peopled with an increasing multitude of Christians; and the bishops and clergy of those sequestered regions derived their ordination from the Catholic of Babylon. In a subsequent age the zeal of the Nestorians overleaped the limits which had confined the ambition and curiosity both of the Greeks and Persians. The missionaries of Balch and Samarcand pursued without fear the footsteps of the roving Tartar, and insinuated themselves into the camps of the valleys of Imaus and the banks of the Selinga. They exposed a metaphysical creed to those illiterate shepherds: to those sanguinary warriors, they recommended humanity and repose. Yet a khan, whose power they vainly magnified, is said to have received at their hands the rites of baptism, and even of ordination; and the fame of Prester or Presbyter John [117] has long amused the credulity of Europe. The royal convert was indulged in the use of a portable altar; but he despatched an embassy to the patriarch, to inquire how, in the season of Lent, he should abstain from animal food, and how he might celebrate the Eucharist in a desert that produced neither corn nor wine. In their progress by sea and land, the Nestorians entered China by the port of Canton and the northern residence of Sigan. Unlike the senators of Rome, who assumed with a smile the characters of priests and augurs, the mandarins, who affect in public the reason of philosophers, are devoted in private to every mode of popular superstition. They cherished and they confounded the gods of Palestine and of India; but the propagation of Christianity awakened the jealousy of the state, and, after a short vicissitude of favor and persecution, the foreign sect expired in ignorance and oblivion. [118] Under the reign of the caliphs, the Nestorian church was diffused from China to Jerusalem and Cyrus; and their numbers, with those of the Jacobites, were computed to surpass the Greek and Latin communions. [119] Twenty-five metropolitans or archbishops composed their hierarchy; but several of these were dispensed, by the distance and danger of the way, from the duty of personal attendance, on the easy condition that every six years they should testify their faith and obedience to the catholic or patriarch of Babylon, a vague appellation which has been successively applied to the royal seats of Seleucia, Ctesiphon, and Bagdad. These remote branches are long since withered; and the old patriarchal trunk [120] is now divided by the Elijahs of Mosul, the representatives almost on lineal descent of the genuine and primitive succession; the Josephs of Amida, who are reconciled to the church of Rome: [121] and the Simeons of Van or Ormia, whose revolt, at the head of forty thousand families, was promoted in the sixteenth century by the Sophis of Persia. The number of three hundred thousand is allowed for the whole body of the Nestorians, who, under the name of Chaldeans or Assyrians, are confounded with the most learned or the most powerful nation of Eastern antiquity.

[Footnote 116: See the Topographia Christiana of Cosmas, surnamed Indicopleustes, or the Indian navigator, l. iii. p. 178, 179, l. xi. p. 337. The entire work, of which some curious extracts may be found in Photius, (cod. xxxvi. p. 9, 10, edit. Hoeschel,) Thevenot, (in the 1st part of his Relation des Voyages, &c.,) and Fabricius, (Bibliot. Graec. l. iii. c. 25, tom. ii. p. 603-617,) has been published by Father Montfaucon at Paris, 1707, in the Nova Collectio Patrum, (tom. ii. p. 113—346.) It was the design of the author to confute the impious heresy of those who maintained that the earth is a globe, and not a flat, oblong table, as it is represented in the Scriptures, (l. ii. p. 138.) But the nonsense of the monk is mingled with the practical knowledge of the traveller, who performed his voyage A.D. 522, and published his book at Alexandria, A.D. 547, (l. ii. p. 140, 141. Montfaucon, Praefat. c. 2.) The Nestorianism of Cosmas, unknown to his learned editor, was detected by La Croze, (Christianisme des Indes, tom. i. p. 40—55,) and is confirmed by Assemanni, (Bibliot. Orient. tom. iv. p. 605, 606.)]

[Footnote 117: In its long progress to Mosul, Jerusalem, Rome, &c., the story of Prester John evaporated in a monstrous fable, of which some features have been borrowed from the Lama of Thibet, (Hist. Genealogique des Tartares, P. ii. p. 42. Hist. de Gengiscan, p. 31, &c.,) and were ignorantly transferred by the Portuguese to the emperor of Abyssinia, (Ludolph. Hist. Aethiop. Comment. l. ii. c. 1.) Yet it is probable that in the xith and xiith centuries, Nestorian Christianity was professed in the horde of the Keraites, (D'Herbelot, p. 256, 915, 959. Assemanni, tom. iv. p. 468—504.) Note: The extent to which Nestorian Christianity prevailed among the Tartar tribes is one of the most curious questions in Oriental history. M. Schmidt (Geschichte der Ost Mongolen, notes, p. 383) appears to question the Christianity of Ong Chaghan, and his Keraite subjects—M.]

[Footnote 118: The Christianity of China, between the seventh and the thirteenth century, is invincibly proved by the consent of Chinese, Arabian, Syriac, and Latin evidence, (Assemanni, Biblioth. Orient. tom. iv. p. 502—552. Mem. de l'Academie des Inscript. tom. xxx. p. 802—819.) The inscription of Siganfu which describes the fortunes of the Nestorian church, from the first mission, A.D. 636, to the current year 781, is accused of forgery by La Croze, Voltaire, &c., who become the dupes of their own cunning, while they are afraid of a Jesuitical fraud. Note: This famous monument, the authenticity of which many have attempted to impeach, rather from hatred to the Jesuits, by whom it was made known, than by a candid examination of its contents, is now generally considered above all suspicion. The Chinese text and the facts which it relates are equally strong proofs of its authenticity. This monument was raised as a memorial of the establishment of Christianity in China. It is dated the year 1092 of the era of the Greeks, or the Seleucidae, A.D. 781, in the time of the Nestorian patriarch Anan-jesu. It was raised by Iezdbouzid, priest and chorepiscopus of Chumdan, that is, of the capital of the Chinese empire, and the son of a priest who came from Balkh in Tokharistan. Among the various arguments which may be urged in favor of the authenticity of this monument, and which has not yet been advanced, may be reckoned the name of the priest by whom it was raised. The name is Persian, and at the time the monument was discovered, it would have been impossible to have imagined it; for there was no work extant from whence the knowledge of it could be derived. I do not believe that ever since this period, any book has been published in which it can be found a second time. It is very celebrated amongst the Armenians, and is derived from a martyr, a Persian by birth, of the royal race, who perished towards the middle of the seventh century, and rendered his name celebrated among the Christian nations of the East. St. Martin, vol. i. p. 69. M. Remusat has also strongly expressed his conviction of the authenticity of this monument. Melanges Asiatiques, P. i. p. 33. Yet M. Schmidt (Geschichte der Ost Mongolen, p. 384) denies that there is any satisfactory proof that much a monument was ever found in China, or that it was not manufactured in Europe. But if the Jesuits had attempted such a forgery, would it not have been more adapted to further their peculiar views?—M.]

[Footnote 119: Jacobitae et Nestorianae plures quam Graeci et Latini Jacob a Vitriaco, Hist. Hierosol. l. ii. c. 76, p. 1093, in the Gesta Dei per Francos. The numbers are given by Thomassin, Discipline de l'Eglise, tom. i. p. 172.]

[Footnote 120: The division of the patriarchate may be traced in the Bibliotheca Orient. of Assemanni, tom. i. p. 523—549, tom. ii. p. 457, &c., tom. iii. p. 603, p. 621—623, tom. iv. p. 164-169, p. 423, p. 622—629, &c.]

[Footnote 121: The pompous language of Rome on the submission of a Nestorian patriarch, is elegantly represented in the viith book of Fra Paola, Babylon, Nineveh, Arbela, and the trophies of Alexander, Tauris, and Ecbatana, the Tigris and Indus.]

According to the legend of antiquity, the gospel was preached in India by St. Thomas. [122] At the end of the ninth century, his shrine, perhaps in the neighborhood of Madras, was devoutly visited by the ambassadors of Alfred; and their return with a cargo of pearls and spices rewarded the zeal of the English monarch, who entertained the largest projects of trade and discovery. [123] When the Portuguese first opened the navigation of India, the Christians of St. Thomas had been seated for ages on the coast of Malabar, and the difference of their character and color attested the mixture of a foreign race. In arms, in arts, and possibly in virtue, they excelled the natives of Hindostan; the husbandmen cultivated the palm-tree, the merchants were enriched by the pepper trade, the soldiers preceded the nairs or nobles of Malabar, and their hereditary privileges were respected by the gratitude or the fear of the king of Cochin and the Zamorin himself. They acknowledged a Gentoo of sovereign, but they were governed, even in temporal concerns, by the bishop of Angamala. He still asserted his ancient title of metropolitan of India, but his real jurisdiction was exercised in fourteen hundred churches, and he was intrusted with the care of two hundred thousand souls. Their religion would have rendered them the firmest and most cordial allies of the Portuguese; but the inquisitors soon discerned in the Christians of St. Thomas the unpardonable guilt of heresy and schism. Instead of owning themselves the subjects of the Roman pontiff, the spiritual and temporal monarch of the globe, they adhered, like their ancestors, to the communion of the Nestorian patriarch; and the bishops whom he ordained at Mosul, traversed the dangers of the sea and land to reach their diocese on the coast of Malabar. In their Syriac liturgy the names of Theodore and Nestorius were piously commemorated: they united their adoration of the two persons of Christ; the title of Mother of God was offensive to their ear, and they measured with scrupulous avarice the honors of the Virgin Mary, whom the superstition of the Latins had almost exalted to the rank of a goddess. When her image was first presented to the disciples of St. Thomas, they indignantly exclaimed, "We are Christians, not idolaters!" and their simple devotion was content with the veneration of the cross. Their separation from the Western world had left them in ignorance of the improvements, or corruptions, of a thousand years; and their conformity with the faith and practice of the fifth century would equally disappoint the prejudices of a Papist or a Protestant. It was the first care of the ministers of Rome to intercept all correspondence with the Nestorian patriarch, and several of his bishops expired in the prisons of the holy office.

The flock, without a shepherd, was assaulted by the power of the Portuguese, the arts of the Jesuits, and the zeal of Alexis de Menezes, archbishop of Goa, in his personal visitation of the coast of Malabar. The synod of Diamper, at which he presided, consummated the pious work of the reunion; and rigorously imposed the doctrine and discipline of the Roman church, without forgetting auricular confession, the strongest engine of ecclesiastical torture. The memory of Theodore and Nestorius was condemned, and Malabar was reduced under the dominion of the pope, of the primate, and of the Jesuits who invaded the see of Angamala or Cranganor. Sixty years of servitude and hypocrisy were patiently endured; but as soon as the Portuguese empire was shaken by the courage and industry of the Dutch, the Nestorians asserted, with vigor and effect, the religion of their fathers. The Jesuits were incapable of defending the power which they had abused; the arms of forty thousand Christians were pointed against their falling tyrants; and the Indian archdeacon assumed the character of bishop till a fresh supply of episcopal gifts and Syriac missionaries could be obtained from the patriarch of Babylon. Since the expulsion of the Portuguese, the Nestorian creed is freely professed on the coast of Malabar. The trading companies of Holland and England are the friends of toleration; but if oppression be less mortifying than contempt, the Christians of St. Thomas have reason to complain of the cold and silent indifference of their brethren of Europe. [124]

[Footnote 122: The Indian missionary, St. Thomas, an apostle, a Manichaean, or an Armenian merchant, (La Croze, Christianisme des Indes, tom. i. p. 57—70,) was famous, however, as early as the time of Jerom, (ad Marcellam, epist. 148.) Marco-Polo was informed on the spot that he suffered martyrdom in the city of Malabar, or Meliapour, a league only from Madras, (D'Anville, Eclaircissemens sur l'Inde, p. 125,) where the Portuguese founded an episcopal church under the name of St. Thome, and where the saint performed an annual miracle, till he was silenced by the profane neighborhood of the English, (La Croze, tom. ii. p. 7-16.)]

[Footnote 123: Neither the author of the Saxon Chronicle (A.D. 833) not William of Malmesbury (de Gestis Regum Angliae, l. ii. c. 4, p. 44) were capable, in the twelfth century, of inventing this extraordinary fact; they are incapable of explaining the motives and measures of Alfred; and their hasty notice serves only to provoke our curiosity. William of Malmesbury feels the difficulty of the enterprise,

quod quivis in hoc saeculo miretur; and I almost suspect that the English ambassadors collected their cargo and legend in Egypt. The royal author has not enriched his Orosius (see Barrington's Miscellanies) with an Indian, as well as a Scandinavian, voyage.]

[Footnote 124: Concerning the Christians of St. Thomas, see Assemann. Bibliot Orient. tom. iv. p. 391—407, 435—451; Geddes's Church History of Malabar; and, above all, La Croze, Histoire du Christianisme des Indes, in 2 vols. 12mo., La Haye, 1758, a learned and agreeable work. They have drawn from the same source, the Portuguese and Italian narratives; and the prejudices of the Jesuits are sufficiently corrected by those of the Protestants. Note: The St. Thome Christians had excited great interest in the ancient mind of the admirable Bishop Heber. See his curious and, to his friends, highly characteristic letter to Mar Athanasius, Appendix to Journal. The arguments of his friend and coadjutor, Mr. Robinson, (Last Days of Bishop Heber,) have not convinced me that the Christianity of India is older than the Nestorian dispersion—M]

II. The history of the Monophysites is less copious and interesting than that of the Nestorians. Under the reigns of Zeno and Anastasius, their artful leaders surprised the ear of the prince, usurped the thrones of the East, and crushed on its native soil the school of the Syrians. The rule of the Monophysite faith was defined with exquisite discretion by Severus, patriarch of Antioch: he condemned, in the style of the Henoticon, the adverse heresies of Nestorius; and Eutyches maintained against the latter the reality of the body of Christ, and constrained the Greeks to allow that he was a liar who spoke truth. [125] But the approximation of ideas could not abate the vehemence of passion; each party was the more astonished that their blind antagonist could dispute on so trifling a difference; the tyrant of Syria enforced the belief of his creed, and his reign was polluted with the blood of three hundred and fifty monks, who were slain, not perhaps without provocation or resistance, under the walls of Apamea. [126] The successor of Anastasius replanted the orthodox standard in the East; Severus fled into Egypt; and his friend, the eloquent Xenaias, [127] who had escaped from the Nestorians of Persia, was suffocated in his exile by the Melchites of Paphlagonia. Fifty-four bishops were swept from their thrones, eight hundred ecclesiastics were cast into prison, [128] and notwithstanding the ambiguous favor of Theodora, the Oriental flocks, deprived of their shepherds, must insensibly have been either famished or poisoned. In this spiritual distress, the expiring faction was revived, and united, and perpetuated, by the labors of a monk; and the name of James Baradaeus [129] has been preserved in the appellation of Jacobites, a familiar sound, which may startle the ear of an English reader. From the holy confessors in their prison of Constantinople, he received the powers of bishop of Edessa and apostle of the East, and the ordination of fourscore thousand bishops, priests, and deacons, is derived from the same inexhaustible source. The speed of the zealous missionary was promoted by the fleetest dromedaries of a devout chief of the Arabs; the doctrine and discipline of the Jacobites were secretly established in the dominions of Justinian; and each Jacobite was compelled to violate the laws and to hate the Roman legislator. The successors of Severus, while they lurked in convents or villages, while they sheltered their proscribed heads in the caverns of hermits, or the tents of the Saracens, still asserted, as they now assert, their indefeasible right to the title, the rank, and the prerogatives of patriarch of Antioch: under the milder yoke of the infidels, they reside about a league from Merdin, in the pleasant monastery of Zapharan, which they have embellished with cells, aqueducts, and plantations. The secondary, though honorable, place is filled by the maphrian, who, in his station at Mosul itself, defies the Nestorian catholic with whom he contests the primacy of the East. Under the patriarch and the maphrian, one hundred and fifty archbishops and bishops have been counted in the different ages of the Jacobite church; but the order of the hierarchy is relaxed or dissolved, and the greater part of their dioceses is confined to the neighborhood of the Euphrates and the Tigris. The cities of Aleppo and Amida, which are often visited by the patriarch, contain some wealthy merchants and industrious mechanics, but the multitude derive their scanty sustenance from their daily labor: and poverty, as well as superstition, may impose their excessive fasts: five annual lents, during which both the clergy and laity abstain not only from flesh or eggs, but even from the taste of wine, of oil, and of fish. Their present numbers are esteemed from fifty to fourscore thousand souls, the remnant of a populous church, which was gradually decreased under the impression of twelve centuries. Yet in that long period, some strangers of merit have been converted to the Monophysite faith, and a Jew was the father of Abulpharagius, [130] primate of the East, so truly eminent both in his life and death. In his life he was an elegant writer of the Syriac and Arabic tongues, a poet, physician, and historian, a subtile philosopher, and a moderate divine. In his death, his funeral was attended by his rival the Nestorian patriarch, with a train of Greeks and Armenians, who forgot their disputes, and mingled their tears over the grave of an enemy. The sect which was honored by the virtues of Abulpharagius appears, however, to sink below the level of their Nestorian brethren. The superstition of the Jacobites is more abject, their fasts more rigid, [131] their intestine divisions are more numerous, and their doctors (as far as I can measure the degrees of nonsense) are more remote from the precincts of reason. Something may possibly be allowed for the rigor of the Monophysite theology; much more for the superior influence of the monastic order. In Syria, in Egypt, in Ethiopia, the Jacobite monks have ever been distinguished by the austerity of their penance and the absurdity of their legends. Alive or dead, they are worshipped as the favorites of the Deity; the crosier of bishop and patriarch is reserved for their venerable hands; and they assume the government of men, while they are yet reeking with the habits and prejudices of the cloister. [132]

[Footnote 125: Is the expression of Theodore, in his Treatise of the Incarnation, p. 245, 247, as he is quoted by La Croze, (Hist. du Christianisme d'Ethiopie et d'Armenie, p. 35,) who exclaims, perhaps too hastily, "Quel pitoyable raisonnement!" Renaudot has touched (Hist. Patriarch. Alex. p. 127—138) the Oriental accounts of Severus; and his authentic creed may be found in the epistle of John the Jacobite patriarch of Antioch, in the xth century, to his brother Mannas of Alexandria, (Asseman. Bibliot. Orient. tom. ii. p. 132—141.)]

[Footnote 126: Epist. Archimandritarum et Monachorum Syriae Secundae ad Papam Hormisdam, Concil. tom. v. p. 598—602. The courage of St. Sabas, ut leo animosus, will justify the suspicion that the arms of these monks were not always spiritual or defensive, (Baronius, A.D. 513, No. 7, &c.)]

[Footnote 127: Assemanni (Bibliot. Orient. tom. ii. p. 10—46) and La Croze (Christianisme d'Ethiopie, p. 36—40) will supply the history of Xenaias, or Philoxenus, bishop of Mabug, or Hierapolis, in Syria. He was a perfect master of the Syriac language, and the author or editor of a version of the New Testament.]

[Footnote 128: The names and titles of fifty-four bishops who were exiled by Justin, are preserved in the Chronicle of Dionysius, (apud Asseman. tom. ii. p. 54.) Severus was personally summoned to Constantinople—for his trial, says Liberatus (Brev. c. 19)—that his tongue might be cut out, says Evagrius, (l. iv. c. iv.) The prudent patriarch did not stay to examine the difference. This ecclesiastical revolution is fixed by Pagi to the month of September of the year 518, (Critica, tom. ii. p. 506.)]

[Footnote 129: The obscure history of James or Jacobus Baradaeus, or Zanzalust may be gathered from Eutychius, (Annal. tom. ii. p. 144, 147,) Renau dot, (Hist. Patriarch. Alex. p. 133,) and Assemannus, (Bibliot. Orient. tom. i. p. 424, tom. ii. p. 62-69, 324—332, 414, tom. iii. p. 385—388.) He seems to be unknown to the Greeks. The Jacobites themselves had rather deduce their name and pedigree from St. James the apostle.]

[Footnote 130: The account of his person and writings is perhaps the most curious article in the Bibliotheca of Assemannus, (tom. ii. p. 244—321, under the name of Gregorius Bar-Hebroeus.) La Croze (Christianisme d'Ethiopie, p. 53—63) ridicules the prejudice of the Spaniards against the Jewish blood which secretly defiles their church and state.]

[Footnote 131: This excessive abstinence is censured by La Croze, (p. 352,) and even by the Syrian Assemannus, (tom. i. p. 226, tom. ii. p. 304, 305.)]

[Footnote 132: The state of the Monophysites is excellently illustrated in a dissertation at the beginning of the iid volume of Assemannus, which contains 142 pages. The Syriac Chronicle of Gregory Bar-Hebraeus, or Abulpharagius, (Bibliot. Orient. tom. ii. p. 321—463,) pursues the double series of the Nestorian Catholics and the Maphrians of the Jacobites.]

III. In the style of the Oriental Christians, the Monothelites of every age are described under the appellation of Maronites, [133] a name which has been insensibly transferred from a hermit to a monastery, from a monastery to a nation. Maron, a saint or savage of the fifth century, displayed his religious madness in Syria; the rival cities of Apamea and Emesa disputed his relics, a stately church was erected on his tomb, and six hundred of his disciples united their solitary cells on the banks of the Orontes. In the controversies of the incarnation they nicely threaded the orthodox line between the sects of Nestorians and Eutyches; but the unfortunate question of one will or operation in the two natures of Christ, was generated by their curious leisure. Their proselyte, the emperor Heraclius, was rejected as a Maronite from the walls of Emesa, he found a refuge in the monastery of his brethren; and their theological lessons were repaid with the gift a spacious and wealthy domain. The name and doctrine of this venerable school were propagated among the Greeks and Syrians, and their zeal is expressed by Macarius, patriarch of Antioch, who declared before the synod of Constantinople, that sooner than subscribe the two wills of Christ, he would submit to be hewn piecemeal and cast into the sea. [134] A similar or a less cruel mode of persecution soon converted the unresisting subjects of the plain, while the glorious title of Mardaites, [135] or rebels, was bravely maintained by the hardy natives of Mount Libanus. John Maron, one of the most learned and popular of the monks, assumed the character of patriarch of Antioch; his nephew, Abraham, at the head of the Maronites, defended their civil and religious freedom against the tyrants of the East. The son of the orthodox Constantine pursued with pious hatred a people of soldiers, who might have stood the bulwark of his empire against the common foes of Christ and of Rome. An army of Greeks invaded Syria; the monastery of St. Maron was destroyed with fire; the bravest chieftains were betrayed and murdered, and twelve thousand of their followers were transplanted to the distant frontiers of Armenia and Thrace. Yet the humble nation of the Maronites had survived the empire of Constantinople, and they still enjoy, under their Turkish masters, a free religion and a mitigated servitude. Their domestic governors are chosen among the ancient nobility: the patriarch, in his monastery of Canobin, still fancies himself on the throne of Antioch: nine bishops compose his synod, and one hundred and fifty priests, who retain the liberty of marriage, are intrusted with the care of one hundred thousand souls. Their country extends from the ridge of Mount Libanus to the shores of Tripoli; and the gradual descent affords, in a narrow space, each variety of soil and climate, from the Holy Cedars, erect under the weight of snow, [136] to the vine, the mulberry, and the olive-trees of the fruitful valley. In the twelfth century, the Maronites, abjuring the Monothelite error were reconciled to the Latin churches of Antioch and Rome, [137] and the same alliance has been frequently renewed by the ambition of the popes and the distress of the Syrians. But it may reasonably be questioned, whether their union has ever been perfect or sincere; and the learned Maronites of the college of Rome have vainly labored to absolve their ancestors from the guilt of heresy and schism. [138]

[Footnote 133: The synonymous use of the two words may be proved from Eutychius, (Annal. tom. ii. p. 191, 267, 332,) and many similar passages which may be found in the methodical table of Pocock. He was not actuated by any prejudice against the Maronites of the xth century; and we may believe a Melchite, whose testimony is confirmed by the Jacobites and Latins.]

[Footnote 134: Concil. tom. vii. p. 780. The Monothelite cause was supported with firmness and subtilty by Constantine, a Syrian priest of Apamea, (p. 1040, &c.)]

[Footnote 135: Theophanes (Chron. p. 295, 296, 300, 302, 306) and Cedrenus (p. 437, 440) relates the exploits of the Mardaites: the name (Mard, in Syriac, rebellavit) is explained by La Roque, (Voyage de la Syrie, tom. ii. p. 53;) and dates are fixed by Pagi, (A.D. 676, No. 4—14, A.D. 685, No. 3, 4;) and even the obscure story of the patriarch John Maron (Asseman. Bibliot. Orient. tom. i. p. 496—520) illustrates from the year 686 to 707, the troubles of Mount Libanus. Note: Compare on the Mardaites Anquetil du Perron, in the fiftieth volume of the Mem. de l'Acad. des Inscriptions; and Schlosser, Bildersturmendes Kaiser, p. 100—M]

[Footnote 136: In the last century twenty large cedars still remained, (Voyage de la Roque, tom. i. p. 68—76;) at present they are reduced to four or five, (Volney, tom. i. p. 264.) These trees, so famous in Scripture, were guarded by excommunication: the wood was sparingly borrowed for small crosses, &c.; an annual mass was chanted under their shade; and they were endowed by the Syrians with a sensitive power of erecting their branches to repel the snow, to which Mount Libanus is less faithful than it is painted by Tacitus: inter ardores opacum fidumque nivibus—a daring metaphor, (Hist. v. 6.) Note: Of the oldest and best looking trees, I counted eleven or twelve twenty-five very large ones; and about fifty of middling size; and more than three hundred smaller and young ones. Burckhardt's Travels in Syria p. 19—M]

[Footnote 137: The evidence of William of Tyre (Hist. in Gestis Dei per Francos, l. xxii. c. 8, p. 1022) is copied or confirmed by Jacques de Vitra, (Hist. Hierosolym. l. ii. c. 77, p. 1093, 1094.) But this unnatural league expired with the power of the Franks; and Abulpharagius (who died in 1286) considers the Maronites as a sect of Monothelites, (Bibliot. Orient. tom. ii. p. 292.)]

[Footnote 138: I find a description and history of the Maronites in the Voyage de la Syrie et du Mont Liban par la Roque, (2 vols. in 12mo., Amsterdam, 1723; particularly tom. i. p. 42—47, p. 174—184, tom. ii. p. 10—120.) In the ancient part, he copies the prejudices of Nairon and the other Maronites of Rome, which Assemannus is afraid to renounce and ashamed to support. Jablonski, (Institut. Hist. Christ. tom. iii. p. 186.) Niebuhr, (Voyage de l'Arabie, &c., tom. ii. p. 346, 370—381,) and, above all, the judicious Volney, (Voyage en Egypte et en Syrie, tom. ii. p. 8—31, Paris, 1787,) may be consulted.]

IV. Since the age of Constantine, the Armenians [139] had signalized their attachment to the religion and empire of the Christians. [139/1] The disorders of their country, and their ignorance of the Greek tongue, prevented their clergy from assisting at the synod of Chalcedon, and they floated eighty-four years [140] in a state of indifference or suspense, till their vacant faith was finally occupied by the missionaries of Julian of Halicarnassus, [141] who in Egypt, their common exile, had been vanquished by the arguments or the influence of his rival Severus, the Monophysite patriarch of Antioch. The Armenians alone are the pure disciples of Eutyches, an unfortunate parent, who has been renounced by the greater part of his spiritual progeny. They alone persevere in the opinion, that the manhood of Christ was created, or existed without creation, of a divine and incorruptible substance. Their adversaries reproach them with the adoration of a phantom; and they retort the accusation, by deriding or execrating the blasphemy of the Jacobites, who impute to the Godhead the vile infirmities of the flesh, even the natural effects of nutrition and digestion. The religion of Armenia could not derive much glory from the learning or the power of its inhabitants. The royalty expired with the origin of their schism; and their Christian kings, who arose and fell in the thirteenth century on the confines of Cilicia, were the clients of the Latins and the vassals of the Turkish sultan of Iconium. The helpless nation has seldom been permitted to enjoy the tranquillity of servitude. From the earliest period to the present hour, Armenia has been the theatre of perpetual war: the lands between Tauris and Erivan were dispeopled by the cruel policy of the Sophis; and myriads of Christian families were transplanted, to perish or to propagate in the distant provinces of Persia. Under the rod of oppression, the zeal of the Armenians is fervent and intrepid; they have often preferred the crown of martyrdom to the white turban of Mahomet; they devoutly hate the error and idolatry of the Greeks; and their transient union with the Latins is not less devoid of truth, than the thousand bishops, whom their patriarch offered at the feet of the Roman pontiff. [142] The catholic, or patriarch, of the Armenians resides in the monastery of Ekmiasin, three leagues from Erivan. Forty-seven archbishops, each of whom may claim the obedience of four or five suffragans, are consecrated by his hand; but the far greater part are only titular prelates, who dignify with their presence and service the simplicity of his court. As soon as they have performed the liturgy, they cultivate the garden; and our bishops will hear with surprise, that the austerity of their life increases in just proportion to the elevation of their rank.

In the fourscore thousand towns or villages of his spiritual empire, the patriarch receives a small and voluntary tax from each person above the age of fifteen; but the annual amount of six hundred thousand crowns is insufficient to supply the incessant demands of charity and tribute. Since the beginning of the last century, the Armenians have obtained a large and lucrative share of the commerce of the East: in their return from Europe, the caravan usually halts in the neighborhood of Erivan, the altars are enriched with the fruits of their patient industry; and the faith of Eutyches is preached in their recent congregations of Barbary and Poland. [143]

[Footnote 139: The religion of the Armenians is briefly described by La Croze, (Hist. du Christ. de l'Ethiopie et de l'Armenie, p. 269—402.) He refers to the great Armenian History of Galanus, (3 vols. in fol. Rome, 1650—1661,) and commends the state of Armenia in the iiid volume of the Nouveaux Memoires des Missions du Levant. The work of a Jesuit must have sterling merit when it is praised by La Croze.]

[Footnote 139/1: See vol. iii. ch. xx. p. 271—M.]

[Footnote 140: The schism of the Armenians is placed 84 years after the council of Chalcedon, (Pagi, Critica, ad A.D. 535.) It was consummated at the end of seventeen years; and it is from the year of Christ 552 that we date the aera of the Armenians, (L'Art de verifier les Dates, p. xxxv.)]

[Footnote 141: The sentiments and success of Julian of Halicarnassus may be seen in Liberatus, (Brev. c. 19,) Renaudot, (Hist. Patriarch. Alex. p. 132, 303,) and Assemannus, (Bibliot. Orient. tom. ii. Dissertat. Monophysitis, l. viii. p. 286.)]

[Footnote 142: See a remarkable fact of the xiith century in the History of Nicetas Choniates, (p. 258.) Yet three hundred years before, Photius (Epistol. ii. p. 49, edit. Montacut.) had gloried in the conversion of the Armenians.]

[Footnote 143: The travelling Armenians are in the way of every traveller, and their mother church is on the high road between Constantinople and Ispahan; for their present state, see Fabricius, (Lux Evangelii, &c., c. xxxviii. p. 40—51,) Olearius, (l. iv. c. 40,) Chardin, (vol. ii. p. 232,) Teurnefort, (lettre xx.,) and, above all, Tavernier, (tom. i. p. 28—37, 510-518,) that rambling jeweller, who had read nothing, but had seen so much and so well]

V. In the rest of the Roman empire, the despotism of the prince might eradicate or silence the sectaries of an obnoxious creed. But the stubborn temper of the Egyptians maintained their opposition to the synod of Chalcedon, and the policy of Justinian condescended to expect and to seize the opportunity of discord. The Monophysite church of Alexandria [144] was torn by the disputes of the corruptibles and incorruptibles, and on the death of the patriarch, the two factions upheld their respective candidates. [145] Gaian was the disciple of Julian, Theodosius had been the pupil of Severus: the claims of the former were supported by the consent of the monks and senators, the city and the province; the latter depended on the priority of his ordination, the favor of the empress Theodora, and the arms of the eunuch Narses, which might have been used in more honorable warfare. The exile of the popular candidate to Carthage and Sardinia inflamed the ferment of Alexandria; and after a schism of one hundred and seventy years, the Gaianites still revered the memory and doctrine of their founder. The strength of numbers and of discipline was tried in a desperate and bloody conflict; the streets were filled with the dead bodies of citizens and soldiers; the pious women, ascending the roofs of their houses, showered down every sharp or ponderous utensil on the heads of the enemy; and the final victory of Narses was owing to the flames, with which he wasted the third capital of the Roman world. But the lieutenant of Justinian had not conquered in the cause of a heretic; Theodosius himself was speedily, though gently, removed; and Paul of Tanis, an orthodox monk, was raised to the throne of Athanasius. The powers of government were strained in his support; he might appoint or displace the dukes and tribunes of Egypt; the allowance of bread, which Diocletian had granted, was suppressed, the churches were shut, and a nation of schismatics was deprived at once of their spiritual and carnal food. In his turn, the tyrant was excommunicated by the zeal and revenge of the people: and none except his servile Melchites would salute him as a man, a Christian, or a bishop. Yet such is the blindness of ambition, that, when Paul was expelled on a charge of murder, he solicited, with a bribe of seven hundred pounds of gold, his restoration to the same station of hatred and ignominy. His successor Apollinaris entered the hostile city in military array, alike qualified for prayer or for battle. His troops, under arms, were distributed through the streets; the gates of the cathedral were guarded, and a chosen band was stationed in the choir, to defend the person of their chief. He stood erect on his throne, and, throwing aside the upper garment of a warrior, suddenly appeared before the eyes of the multitude in the robes of patriarch of Alexandria. Astonishment held them mute; but no sooner had Apollinaris begun to read the tome of St. Leo, than a volley of curses, and invectives, and stones, assaulted the odious minister of the emperor and the synod. A charge was instantly sounded by the successor of the apostles; the soldiers waded to their knees in blood; and two hundred thousand Christians are said to have fallen by the sword: an incredible account, even if it be extended from the slaughter of a day to the eighteen years of the reign of Apollinaris. Two succeeding patriarchs, Eulogius [146] and John, [147] labored in the conversion of heretics, with arms and arguments more worthy of their evangelical profession. The theological knowledge of Eulogius was displayed in many a volume, which magnified the errors of Eutyches and Severus, and attempted to reconcile the ambiguous language of St. Cyril with the orthodox creed of Pope Leo and the fathers of Chalcedon. The bounteous alms of John the eleemosynary were dictated by superstition, or benevolence, or policy. Seven thousand five hundred poor were maintained at his expense; on his accession he found eight thousand pounds of gold in the treasury of the church; he collected ten thousand from the liberality of the faithful; yet the primate could boast in his testament, that he left behind him no more than the third part of the smallest of the silver coins. The churches of Alexandria were delivered to the Catholics, the religion of the Monophysites was proscribed in Egypt, and a law was revived which excluded the natives from the honors and emoluments of the state.

[Footnote 144: The history of the Alexandrian patriarchs, from Dioscorus to Benjamin, is taken from Renaudot, (p. 114—164,) and the second tome of the Annals of Eutychius.]

[Footnote 145: Liberat. Brev. c. 20, 23. Victor. Chron. p. 329 330. Procop. Anecdot. c. 26, 27.]

[Footnote 146: Eulogius, who had been a monk of Antioch, was more conspicuous for subtilty than eloquence. He proves that the enemies of the faith, the Gaianites and Theodosians, ought not to be reconciled; that the same proposition may be orthodox in the mouth of St. Cyril, heretical in that of Severus; that the opposite assertions of St. Leo are equally true, &c. His writings are no longer extant except in the Extracts of Photius, who had perused them with care and satisfaction, ccviii. ccxxv. ccxxvi. ccxxvii. ccxxx. cclxxx.]

[Footnote 147: See the Life of John the eleemosynary by his contemporary Leontius, bishop of Neapolis in Cyrus, whose Greek text, either lost or hidden, is reflected in the Latin version of Baronius, (A.D. 610, No. 9, A.D. 620, No. 8.) Pagi (Critica, tom. ii. p. 763) and Fabricius (l. v c. 11, tom. vii. p. 454) have made some critical observations]

PART VI

A more important conquest still remained, of the patriarch, the oracle and leader of the Egyptian church. Theodosius had resisted the threats and promises of Justinian with the spirit of an apostle or an enthusiast. "Such," replied the patriarch, "were the offers of the tempter when he showed the kingdoms of the earth. But my soul is far dearer to me than life or dominion. The churches are in the hands of a prince who can kill the body; but my conscience is my own; and in exile, poverty, or chains, I will steadfastly adhere to the faith of my holy predecessors, Athanasius, Cyril, and Dioscorus. Anathema to the tome of Leo and the synod of Chalcedon! Anathema to all who embrace their creed! Anathema to them now and forevermore! Naked came I out of my mother's womb, naked shall I descend into the grave. Let those who love God follow me and seek their salvation." After comforting his brethren, he embarked for Constantinople, and sustained, in six successive interviews, the almost irresistible weight of the royal presence. His opinions were favorably entertained in the palace and the city; the influence of Theodora assured him a safe conduct and honorable dismission; and he ended his days, though not on the throne, yet in the bosom, of his native country. On the news of his death, Apollinaris indecently feasted the nobles and the clergy; but his joy was checked by the intelligence of a new election; and while he enjoyed the wealth of Alexandria, his rivals reigned in the monasteries of Thebais, and were maintained by the voluntary oblations of the people. A perpetual succession of patriarchs arose from the ashes of Theodosius; and the Monophysite churches of Syria and Egypt were united by the name of Jacobites and the communion of the faith. But the same faith, which has been confined to a narrow sect of the Syrians, was diffused over the mass of the Egyptian or Coptic nation; who, almost unanimously, rejected the decrees of the synod of Chalcedon. A thousand years were now elapsed since Egypt had ceased to be a kingdom, since the conquerors of Asia and Europe had trampled on the ready necks of a people, whose ancient wisdom and power ascend beyond the records of history. The conflict of zeal and persecution rekindled some sparks of their national spirit. They abjured, with a foreign heresy, the manners and language of the Greeks: every Melchite, in their eyes, was a stranger, every Jacobite a citizen; the alliance of marriage, the offices of humanity, were condemned as a deadly sin the natives renounced all allegiance to the emperor; and his orders, at a distance from Alexandria, were obeyed only under the pressure of military force. A generous effort might have edeemed the religion and liberty of Egypt, and her six hundred monasteries might have poured forth their myriads of holy warriors, for whom death should have no terrors, since life had no comfort or delight. But experience has proved the distinction of active and passive courage; the fanatic who endures without a groan the torture of the rack or the stake, would tremble and fly before the face of an armed enemy. The pusillanimous temper of the Egyptians could only hope for a change of masters; the arms of Chosroes depopulated the land, yet under his reign the Jacobites enjoyed a short and precarious respite. The victory of Heraclius renewed and aggravated the persecution, and the patriarch again escaped from Alexandria to the desert. In his flight, Benjamin was encouraged by a voice, which bade him expect, at the end of ten years, the aid of a foreign nation, marked, like the Egyptians themselves, with the ancient rite of circumcision. The character of these deliverers, and the nature of the deliverance, will be hereafter explained; and I shall step over the interval of eleven centuries to observe the present misery of the Jacobites of Egypt. The populous city of Cairo affords a residence, or rather a shelter, for their indigent patriarch, and a remnant of ten bishops; forty monasteries have survived the inroads of the Arabs; and the progress of servitude and apostasy has reduced the Coptic nation to the despicable number of twenty-five or thirty thousand families; [148] a race of illiterate beggars, whose only consolation is derived from the superior wretchedness of the Greek patriarch and his diminutive congregation. [149]

[Footnote 148: This number is taken from the curious Recherches sur les Egyptiens et les Chinois, (tom. ii. p. 192, 193,) and appears more probable than the 600,000 ancient, or 15,000 modern, Copts of Gemelli Carreri Cyril Lucar, the Protestant patriarch of Constantinople, laments that those heretics were ten times more numerous than his orthodox Greeks, ingeniously applying Homer, (Iliad, ii. 128,) the most perfect expression of contempt, (Fabric. Lux Evangelii, 740.)]

[Footnote 149: The history of the Copts, their religion, manners, &c., may be found in the Abbe Renaudot's motley work, neither a translation nor an original; the Chronicon Orientale of Peter, a Jacobite; in the two versions of Abraham Ecchellensis, Paris, 1651; and John Simon Asseman, Venet. 1729. These annals descend no lower than the xiiith century. The more recent accounts must be searched for in the travellers into Egypt and the Nouveaux Memoires des Missions du Levant. In the last century, Joseph Abudacnus, a native of Cairo, published at Oxford, in thirty pages, a slight Historia Jacobitarum, 147, post p.150]

VI. The Coptic patriarch, a rebel to the Caesars, or a slave to the khalifs, still gloried in the filial obedience of the kings of Nubia and Aethiopia. He repaid their homage by magnifying their greatness; and it was boldly asserted that they could bring into the field a hundred thousand horse, with an equal number of camels; [150] that their hand could pour out or restrain the waters of the Nile; [151] and the peace and plenty of Egypt was obtained, even in this world, by the intercession of the patriarch. In exile at Constantinople, Theodosius recommended to his patroness the conversion of the black nations of Nubia, from the tropic of Cancer to the confines of Abyssinia. [152] Her design was suspected and emulated by the more orthodox emperor. The rival missionaries, a Melchite and a Jacobite, embarked at the same time; but the empress, from a motive of love or fear, was more effectually obeyed; and the Catholic priest was detained by the president of Thebais, while the king of Nubia and his court were hastily baptized in the faith of Dioscorus. The tardy envoy of Justinian was received and dismissed with honor: but when he accused the heresy and treason of the Egyptians, the negro convert was instructed to reply that he would never abandon his brethren, the true believers, to the persecuting ministers of the synod of Chalcedon. [153] During several ages, the bishops of Nubia were named and consecrated by the Jacobite patriarch of Alexandria: as late as the twelfth century, Christianity prevailed; and some rites, some ruins, are still visible in the savage towns of Sennaar and Dongola. [154] But the Nubians at length executed their threats of returning to the worship of idols; the climate required the indulgence of polygamy, and they have finally preferred the triumph of the Koran to the abasement of the Cross. A metaphysical religion may appear too refined for the capacity of the negro race: yet a black or a parrot might be taught to repeat the words of the Chalcedonian or Monophysite creed.

[Footnote 150: About the year 737. See Renaudot, Hist. Patriarch. Alex p. 221, 222. Elmacin, Hist. Saracen. p. 99.]

[Footnote 151: Ludolph. Hist. Aethiopic. et Comment. l. i. c. 8. Renaudot Hist. Patriarch. Alex. p. 480, &c. This opinion, introduced into Egypt and Europe by the artifice of the Copts, the pride of the Abyssinians, the fear and ignorance of the Turks and Arabs, has not even the semblance of truth. The rains of Aethiopia do not, in the increase of the Nile, consult the will of the monarch. If the river approaches at Napata within three days' journey of the Red Sea (see D'Anville's Maps,) a canal that should divert its course would demand, and most probably surpass, the power of the Caesars.]

[Footnote 152: The Abyssinians, who still preserve the features and olive complexion of the Arabs, afford a proof that two thousand years are not sufficient to change the color of the human race. The Nubians, an African race, are pure negroes, as black as those of Senegal or Congo, with flat noses, thick lips, and woolly hair, (Buffon, Hist. Naturelle, tom. v. p. 117, 143, 144, 166, 219, edit. in 12mo., Paris, 1769.) The ancients beheld, without much attention, the extraordinary phenomenon which has exercised the philosophers and theologians of modern times]

[Footnote 153: Asseman. Bibliot. Orient. tom. i. p. 329.]

[Footnote 154: The Christianity of the Nubians (A.D. 1153) is attested by the sheriff al Edrisi, falsely described under the name of the Nubian geographer, (p. 18,) who represents them as a nation of Jacobites. The rays of historical light that twinkle in the history of Ranaudot (p. 178, 220—224, 281—286, 405, 434, 451, 464) are all previous to this aera. See the modern state in the Lettres Edifiantes (Recueil, iv.) and Busching, (tom. ix. p. 152—139, par Berenger.)]

Christianity was more deeply rooted in the Abyssinian empire; and, although the correspondence has been sometimes interrupted above seventy or a hundred years, the mother-church of Alexandria retains her colony in a state of perpetual pupilage. Seven bishops once composed the Aethiopic synod: had their number amounted to ten, they might have elected an independent primate; and one of their kings was ambitious of promoting his brother to the ecclesiastical throne. But the event was foreseen, the increase was denied: the episcopal office has been gradually confined to the abuna, [155] the head and author of the Abyssinian priesthood; the patriarch supplies each vacancy with an Egyptian monk; and the character of a stranger appears more venerable in the eyes of the people, less dangerous in those of the monarch. In the sixth century, when the schism of Egypt was confirmed, the rival chiefs, with their patrons, Justinian and Theodora, strove to outstrip each other in the conquest of a remote and independent province. The industry of the empress was again victorious, and the pious Theodora has established in that sequestered church the faith and discipline of the Jacobites. [156] Encompassed on all sides by the enemies of their religion, the Aethiopians slept near a thousand years, forgetful of the world, by whom they were forgotten. They were awakened by the Portuguese, who, turning the southern promontory of Africa, appeared in India and the Red Sea, as if they had descended through the air from a distant planet. In the first moments of their interview, the subjects of Rome and Alexandria observed the resemblance, rather than the difference, of their faith; and each nation expected the most important benefits from an alliance with their Christian brethren. In their lonely situation, the Aethiopians had almost relapsed into the savage life. Their vessels, which had traded to Ceylon, scarcely presumed to navigate the rivers of Africa; the ruins of Axume were deserted, the nation was scattered in villages, and the emperor, a pompous name, was content, both in peace and war, with the immovable residence of a camp. Conscious of their own indigence, the Abyssinians had formed the rational project of importing the arts and ingenuity of Europe; [157] and their ambassadors at Rome and Lisbon were instructed to solicit a colony of smiths, carpenters, tilers, masons, printers, surgeons, and physicians, for the use of their country. But the public danger soon called for the instant and effectual aid of arms and soldiers, to defend an unwarlike people from the Barbarians who ravaged the inland country and the Turks and Arabs who advanced from the sea-coast in more formidable array. Aethiopia was saved by four hundred and fifty Portuguese, who displayed in the field the native valor of Europeans, and the artificial power of the musket and cannon. In a moment of terror, the emperor had promised to reconcile himself and his subjects to the Catholic faith; a Latin patriarch represented the supremacy of the pope: [158] the empire, enlarged in a tenfold proportion, was supposed to contain more gold than the mines of America; and the wildest hopes of avarice and zeal were built on the willing submission of the Christians of Africa.

[Footnote 155: The abuna is improperly dignified by the Latins with the title of patriarch. The Abyssinians acknowledge only the four patriarchs, and their chief is no more than a metropolitan or national primate, (Ludolph. Hist. Aethiopic. et Comment. l. iii. c. 7.) The seven bishops of Renaudot, (p. 511,) who existed A.D. 1131, are unknown to the historian.]

[Footnote 156: I know not why Assemannus (Bibliot. Orient. tom. ii. p. 384) should call in question these probable missions of Theodora into Nubia and Aethiopia. The slight notices of Abyssinia till the year 1500 are supplied by Renaudot (p. 336-341, 381, 382, 405, 443, &c., 452, 456, 463, 475, 480, 511, 525, 559—564) from the Coptic writers. The mind of Ludolphus was a perfect blank.]

[Footnote 157: Ludolph. Hist. Aethiop. l. iv. c. 5. The most necessary arts are now exercised by the Jews, and the foreign trade is in the hands of the Armenians. What Gregory principally admired and envied was the industry of Europe—artes et opificia.]

[Footnote 158: John Bermudez, whose relation, printed at Lisbon, 1569, was translated into English by Purchas, (Pilgrims, l. vii. c. 7, p. 1149, &c.,) and from thence into French by La Croze, (Christianisme d'Ethiopie, p. 92—265.) The piece is curious; but the author may be suspected of deceiving Abyssinia, Rome, and Portugal. His title to the rank of patriarch is dark and doubtful, (Ludolph. Comment. No. 101, p. 473.)]

But the vows which pain had extorted were forsworn on the return of health. The Abyssinians still adhered with unshaken constancy to the Monophysite faith; their languid belief was inflamed by the exercise of dispute; they branded the Latins with the names of Arians and Nestorians, and imputed the adoration of four gods to those who separated the two natures of Christ. Fremona, a place of worship, or rather of exile, was assigned to the Jesuit missionaries. Their skill in the liberal and mechanic arts, their theological learning, and the decency of their manners, inspired a barren esteem; but they were not endowed with the gift of miracles, [159] and they vainly solicited a reenforcement of European troops. The patience and dexterity of forty years at length obtained a more favorable audience, and two emperors of Abyssinia were persuaded that Rome could insure the temporal and everlasting happiness of her votaries. The first of these royal converts lost his crown and his life; and the rebel army was sanctified by the abuna, who hurled an anathema at the apostate, and absolved his subjects from their oath of fidelity. The fate of Zadenghel was revenged by the courage and fortune of Susneus, who ascended the throne under the name of Segued, and more vigorously prosecuted the pious enterprise of his kinsman. After the amusement of some unequal combats between the Jesuits and his illiterate priests, the emperor declared himself a proselyte to the synod of Chalcedon, presuming that his clergy and people would embrace without delay the religion of their prince. The liberty of choice was succeeded by a law, which imposed, under pain of death, the belief of the two natures of Christ: the Abyssinians were enjoined to work and to play on the Sabbath; and Segued, in the face of Europe and Africa, renounced his connection with the Alexandrian church. A Jesuit, Alphonso Mendez, the Catholic patriarch of Aethiopia, accepted, in the name of Urban VIII., the homage and abjuration of the penitent. "I confess," said the emperor on his knees, "I confess that the pope is the vicar of Christ, the successor of St. Peter, and the sovereign of the world. To him I swear true obedience, and at his feet I offer my person and kingdom." A similar oath was repeated by his son, his brother, the clergy, the nobles, and even the ladies of the court: the Latin patriarch was invested with honors and wealth; and his missionaries erected their churches or citadels in the most convenient stations of the empire. The Jesuits themselves deplore the fatal indiscretion of their chief, who forgot the mildness of the gospel and the policy of his order, to introduce with hasty violence the liturgy of Rome and the inquisition of Portugal. He condemned the ancient practice of circumcision, which health, rather than superstition, had first invented in the climate of Aethiopia. [160] A new baptism, a new ordination, was inflicted on the natives; and they trembled with horror when the most holy of the dead were torn from their graves, when the most illustrious of the living were excommunicated by a foreign priest. In the defense of their religion and liberty, the Abyssinians rose in arms, with desperate but unsuccessful zeal. Five rebellions were extinguished in the blood of the insurgents: two abunas were slain in battle, whole legions were slaughtered in the field, or suffocated in their caverns; and neither merit, nor rank, nor sex, could save from an ignominious death the enemies of Rome. But the victorious monarch was finally subdued by the constancy of the nation, of his mother, of his son, and of his most faithful friends. Segued listened to the voice of pity, of reason, perhaps of fear: and his edict of liberty of conscience instantly revealed the tyranny and weakness of the Jesuits. On the death of his father, Basilides expelled the Latin patriarch, and restored to the wishes of the nation the faith and the discipline of Egypt. The Monophysite churches resounded with a song of triumph, "that the sheep of Aethiopia were now delivered from the hyaenas of the West;" and the gates of that solitary realm were forever shut against the arts, the science, and the fanaticism of Europe. [161]

[Footnote 159: *Religio Romana...nec precibus patrum nec miraculis ab ipsis editis suffulciebatur*, is the uncontradicted assurance of the devout emperor Susneus to his patriarch Mendez, (Ludolph. Comment. No. 126, p. 529;) and such assurances should be preciously kept, as an antidote against any marvellous legends.]

[Footnote 160: *I am aware how tender is the question of circumcision. Yet I will affirm, 1. That the Aethiopians have a physical reason for the circumcision of males, and even of females, (Recherches Philosophiques sur les Americains, tom. ii.) 2. That it was practised in Aethiopia long before the introduction of Judaism or Christianity, (Herodot. l. ii. c. 104. Marsham, Canon. Chron. p. 72, 73.) "Infantes circumcidunt ob consuetudinemn, non ob Judaismum," says Gregory the Abyssinian priest, (apud Fabric. Lux Christiana, p. 720.) Yet in the heat of dispute, the Portuguese were sometimes branded with the name of uncircumcised, (La Croze, p. 90. Ludolph. Hist. and Comment. l. iii. c. l.)]*

[Footnote 161: The three Protestant historians, Ludolphus, (Hist. Aethiopica, Francofurt. 1681; Commentarius, 1691; Relatio Nova, &c., 1693, in folio,) Geddes, (Church History of Aethiopia, London, 1696, in 8vo..) and La Croze, (Hist. du Christianisme d'Ethiopie et d'Armenie, La Haye, 1739, in 12mo.,) have drawn their principal materials from the Jesuits, especially from the General History of Tellez, published in Portuguese at Coimbra, 1660. We might be surprised at their frankness; but their most flagitious vice, the spirit of persecution, was in their eyes the most meritorious virtue. Ludolphus possessed some, though a slight, advantage from the Aethiopic language, and the personal conversation of Gregory, a free-spirited Abyssinian priest, whom he invited from Rome to the court of Saxe-Gotha. See the Theologia Aethiopica of Gregory, in (Fabric. Lux Evangelii, p. 716—734.) Note: The travels of Bruce, illustrated by those of Mr. Salt, and the narrative of Nathaniel Pearce, have brought us again acquainted with this remote region. Whatever may be their speculative opinions the barbarous manners of the Ethiopians seem to be gaining more and more the ascendency over the practice of Christianity—M.]

CHAPTER XLVIII

SUCCESSION AND CHARACTERS OF THE GREEK EMPERORS

PART I

PLAN OF THE LAST TWO VOLUMES—SUCCESSION AND CHARACTERS OF THE GREEK EMPERORS OF CONSTANTINOPLE, FROM THE TIME OF HERACLIUS TO THE LATIN CONQUEST

I have now deduced from Trajan to Constantine, from Constantine to Heraclius, the regular series of the Roman emperors; and faithfully exposed the prosperous and adverse fortunes of their reigns. Five centuries of the decline and fall of the empire have already elapsed; but a period of more than eight hundred years still separates me from the term of my labors, the taking of Constantinople by the Turks. Should I persevere in the same course, should I observe the same measure, a prolix and slender thread would be spun through many a volume, nor would the patient reader find an adequate reward of instruction or amusement. At every step, as we sink deeper in the decline and fall of the Eastern empire, the annals of each succeeding reign would impose a more ungrateful and melancholy task. These annals must continue to repeat a tedious and uniform tale of weakness and misery; the natural connection of causes and events would be broken by frequent and hasty transitions, and a minute accumulation of circumstances must destroy the light and effect of those general pictures which compose the use and ornament of a remote history. From the time of Heraclius, the Byzantine theatre is contracted and darkened: the line of empire, which had been defined by the laws of Justinian and the arms of Belisarius, recedes on all sides from our view; the Roman name, the proper subject of our inquiries, is reduced to a narrow corner of Europe, to the lonely suburbs of Constantinople; and the fate of the Greek empire has been compared to that of the Rhine, which loses itself in the sands, before its waters can mingle with the ocean. The scale of dominion is diminished to our view by the distance of time and place; nor is the loss of external splendor compensated by the nobler gifts of virtue and genius. In the last moments of her decay, Constantinople was doubtless more opulent and populous than Athens at her most flourishing aera, when a scanty sum of six thousand talents, or twelve hundred thousand pounds sterling was possessed by twenty-one thousand male citizens of an adult age. But each of these citizens was a freeman, who dared to assert the liberty of his thoughts, words, and actions, whose person and property were guarded by equal law; and who exercised his independent vote in the government of the republic. Their numbers seem to be multiplied by the strong and various discriminations of character;

under the shield of freedom, on the wings of emulation and vanity, each Athenian aspired to the level of the national dignity; from this commanding eminence, some chosen spirits soared beyond the reach of a vulgar eye; and the chances of superior merit in a great and populous kingdom, as they are proved by experience, would excuse the computation of imaginary millions. The territories of Athens, Sparta, and their allies, do not exceed a moderate province of France or England; but after the trophies of Salamis and Platea, they expand in our fancy to the gigantic size of Asia, which had been trampled under the feet of the victorious Greeks. But the subjects of the Byzantine empire, who assume and dishonor the names both of Greeks and Romans, present a dead uniformity of abject vices, which are neither softened by the weakness of humanity, nor animated by the vigor of memorable crimes. The freemen of antiquity might repeat with generous enthusiasm the sentence of Homer, "that on the first day of his servitude, the captive is deprived of one half of his manly virtue." But the poet had only seen the effects of civil or domestic slavery, nor could he foretell that the second moiety of manhood must be annihilated by the spiritual despotism which shackles not only the actions, but even the thoughts, of the prostrate votary. By this double yoke, the Greeks were oppressed under the successors of Heraclius; the tyrant, a law of eternal justice, was degraded by the vices of his subjects; and on the throne, in the camp, in the schools, we search, perhaps with fruitless diligence, the names and characters that may deserve to be rescued from oblivion. Nor are the defects of the subject compensated by the skill and variety of the painters. Of a space of eight hundred years, the four first centuries are overspread with a cloud interrupted by some faint and broken rays of historic light: in the lives of the emperors, from Maurice to Alexius, Basil the Macedonian has alone been the theme of a separate work; and the absence, or loss, or imperfection of contemporary evidence, must be poorly supplied by the doubtful authority of more recent compilers. The four last centuries are exempt from the reproach of penury; and with the Comnenian family, the historic muse of Constantinople again revives, but her apparel is gaudy, her motions are without elegance or grace. A succession of priests, or courtiers, treads in each other's footsteps in the same path of servitude and superstition: their views are narrow, their judgment is feeble or corrupt; and we close the volume of copious barrenness, still ignorant of the causes of events, the characters of the actors, and the manners of the times which they celebrate or deplore. The observation which has been applied to a man, may be extended to a whole people, that the energy of the sword is communicated to the pen; and it will be found by experience, that the tone of history will rise or fall with the spirit of the age.

From these considerations, I should have abandoned without regret the Greek slaves and their servile historians, had I not reflected that the fate of the Byzantine monarchy is passively connected with the most splendid and important revolutions which have changed the state of the world. The space of the lost provinces was immediately replenished with new colonies and rising kingdoms: the active virtues of peace and war deserted from the vanquished to the victorious nations; and it is in their origin and conquests, in their religion and government, that we must explore the causes and effects of the decline and fall of the Eastern empire. Nor will this scope of narrative, the riches and variety of these materials, be incompatible with the unity of design and composition. As, in his daily prayers, the Mussulman of Fez or Delhi still turns his face towards the temple of Mecca, the historian's eye shall be always fixed on the city of Constantinople. The excursive line may embrace the wilds of Arabia and Tartary, but the circle will be ultimately reduced to the decreasing limit of the Roman monarchy.

On this principle I shall now establish the plan of the last two volumes of the present work. The first chapter will contain, in a regular series, the emperors who reigned at Constantinople during a period of six hundred years, from the days of Heraclius to the Latin conquest; a rapid abstract, which may be supported by a general appeal to the order and text of the original historians. In this introduction, I shall confine myself to the revolutions of the throne, the succession of families, the personal characters of the Greek princes, the mode of their life and death, the maxims and influence of their domestic government, and the tendency of their reign to accelerate or suspend the downfall of the Eastern empire. Such a chronological review will serve to illustrate the various argument of the subsequent chapters; and each circumstance of the eventful story of the Barbarians will adapt itself in a proper place to the Byzantine annals. The internal state of the empire, and the dangerous heresy of the Paulicians, which shook the East and enlightened the West, will be the subject of two separate chapters; but these inquiries must be postponed till our further progress shall have opened the view of the world in the ninth and tenth centuries of the Christian area. After this foundation of Byzantine history, the following nations will pass before our eyes, and each will occupy the space to which it may be entitled by greatness or merit, or the degree of connection with the Roman world and the present age. I. The Franks; a general appellation which includes all the Barbarians of France, Italy, and Germany, who were united by the sword and sceptre of Charlemagne. The persecution of images and their votaries separated Rome and Italy from the Byzantine throne, and prepared the restoration of the Roman empire in the West. II. The Arabs or Saracens. Three ample chapters will be devoted to this curious and interesting object. In the first, after a picture of the country and its inhabitants, I shall investigate the character of Mahomet; the character, religion, and success of the prophet. In the second, I shall lead the Arabs to the conquest of Syria, Egypt, and Africa, the provinces of the Roman empire; nor can I check their victorious career till they have overthrown the monarchies of Persia and Spain. In the third, I shall inquire how Constantinople and Europe were saved by the luxury and arts, the division and decay, of the empire of the caliphs. A single chapter will include, III. The Bulgarians, IV. Hungarians, and, V. Russians, who assaulted by sea or by land the provinces and the capital; but the last of these, so important in their present greatness, will excite some curiosity in their origin and infancy. VI. The Normans; or rather the private adventurers of that warlike people, who founded a powerful kingdom in Apulia and Sicily, shook the throne of Constantinople, displayed the trophies of chivalry, and almost realized the wonders of romance.

VII. The Latins; the subjects of the pope, the nations of the West, who enlisted under the banner of the cross for the recovery or relief of the holy sepulchre. The Greek emperors were terrified and preserved by the myriads of pilgrims who marched to Jerusalem with Godfrey of Bouillon and the peers of Christendom. The second and third crusades trod in the footsteps of the first: Asia and Europe were mingled in a sacred war of two hundred years; and the Christian powers were bravely resisted, and finally expelled by Saladin and the Mamelukes of Egypt. In these memorable crusades, a fleet and army of French and Venetians were diverted from Syria to the Thracian Bosphorus: they assaulted the capital, they subverted the Greek monarchy: and a dynasty of Latin princes was seated near threescore years on the throne of Constantine. VII. The Greeks themselves, during this period of captivity and exile, must be considered as a foreign nation; the enemies, and again the sovereigns of Constantinople. Misfortune had rekindled a spark of national virtue; and the Imperial series may be continued with some dignity from their restoration to the Turkish conquest. IX. The Moguls and Tartars. By the arms of Zingis and his descendants, the globe was shaken from China to Poland and Greece: the sultans were overthrown: the caliphs fell, and the Caesars trembled on their throne. The victories of Timour suspended above fifty years the final ruin of the Byzantine empire. X. I have already noticed the first appearance of the Turks; and the names of the fathers, of Seljuk and Othman, discriminate the two successive dynasties of the nation, which emerged in the eleventh century from the Scythian wilderness. The former established a splendid and potent kingdom from the banks of the Oxus to Antioch and Nice; and the first crusade was provoked by the violation of Jerusalem and the danger of Constantinople. From an humble origin, the Ottomans arose, the scourge and terror of Christendom. Constantinople was besieged and taken by Mahomet II., and his triumph annihilates the remnant, the image, the title, of the Roman empire in the

East. The schism of the Greeks will be connected with their last calamities, and the restoration of learning in the Western world.

I shall return from the captivity of the new, to the ruins of ancient Rome; and the venerable name, the interesting theme, will shed a ray of glory on the conclusion of my labors.

The emperor Heraclius had punished a tyrant and ascended his throne; and the memory of his reign is perpetuated by the transient conquest, and irreparable loss, of the Eastern provinces. After the death of Eudocia, his first wife, he disobeyed the patriarch, and violated the laws, by his second marriage with his niece Martina; and the superstition of the Greeks beheld the judgment of Heaven in the diseases of the father and the deformity of his offspring. But the opinion of an illegitimate birth is sufficient to distract the choice, and loosen the obedience, of the people: the ambition of Martina was quickened by maternal love, and perhaps by the envy of a step-mother; and the aged husband was too feeble to withstand the arts of conjugal allurements. Constantine, his eldest son, enjoyed in a mature age the title of Augustus; but the weakness of his constitution required a colleague and a guardian, and he yielded with secret reluctance to the partition of the empire. The senate was summoned to the palace to ratify or attest the association of Heracleonas, the son of Martina: the imposition of the diadem was consecrated by the prayer and blessing of the patriarch; the senators and patricians adored the majesty of the great emperor and the partners of his reign; and as soon as the doors were thrown open, they were hailed by the tumultuary but important voice of the soldiers. After an interval of five months, the pompous ceremonies which formed the essence of the Byzantine state were celebrated in the cathedral and the hippodrome; the concord of the royal brothers was affectedly displayed by the younger leaning on the arm of the elder; and the name of Martina was mingled in the reluctant or venal acclamations of the people. Heraclius survived this association about two years: his last testimony declared his two sons the equal heirs of the Eastern empire, and commanded them to honor his widow Martina as their mother and their sovereign.

When Martina first appeared on the throne with the name and attributes of royalty, she was checked by a firm, though respectful, opposition; and the dying embers of freedom were kindled by the breath of superstitious prejudice. "We reverence," exclaimed the voice of a citizen, "we reverence the mother of our princes; but to those princes alone our obedience is due; and Constantine, the elder emperor, is of an age to sustain, in his own hands, the weight of the sceptre. Your sex is excluded by nature from the toils of government. How could you combat, how could you answer, the Barbarians, who, with hostile or friendly intentions, may approach the royal city? May Heaven avert from the Roman republic this national disgrace, which would provoke the patience of the slaves of Persia!" Martina descended from the throne with indignation, and sought a refuge in the female apartment of the palace. The reign of Constantine the Third lasted only one hundred and three days: he expired in the thirtieth year of his age, and, although his life had been a long malady, a belief was entertained that poison had been the means, and his cruel step-mother the author, of his untimely fate. Martina reaped indeed the harvest of his death, and assumed the government in the name of the surviving emperor; but the incestuous widow of Heraclius was universally abhorred; the jealousy of the people was awakened, and the two orphans whom Constantine had left became the objects of the public care. It was in vain that the son of Martina, who was no more than fifteen years of age, was taught to declare himself the guardian of his nephews, one of whom he had presented at the baptismal font: it was in vain that he swore on the wood of the true cross, to defend them against all their enemies. On his death-bed, the late emperor had despatched a trusty servant to arm the troops and provinces of the East in the defence of his helpless children: the eloquence and liberality of Valentin had been successful, and from his camp of Chalcedon, he boldly demanded the punishment of the assassins, and the restoration of the lawful heir. The license of the soldiers, who devoured the grapes and drank the wine of their Asiatic vineyards, provoked the citizens of Constantinople against the domestic authors of their calamities, and the dome of St. Sophia reechoed, not with prayers and hymns, but with the clamors and imprecations of an enraged multitude. At their imperious command, Heracleonas appeared in the pulpit with the eldest of the royal orphans; Constans alone was saluted as emperor of the Romans, and a crown of gold, which had been taken from the tomb of Heraclius, was placed on his head, with the solemn benediction of the patriarch.

But in the tumult of joy and indignation, the church was pillaged, the sanctuary was polluted by a promiscuous crowd of Jews and Barbarians; and the Monothelite Pyrrhus, a creature of the empress, after dropping a protestation on the altar, escaped by a prudent flight from the zeal of the Catholics. A more serious and bloody task was reserved for the senate, who derived a temporary strength from the consent of the soldiers and people.

The spirit of Roman freedom revived the ancient and awful examples of the judgment of tyrants, and the Imperial culprits were deposed and condemned as the authors of the death of Constantine. But the severity of the conscript fathers was stained by the indiscriminate punishment of the innocent and the guilty: Martina and Heracleonas were sentenced to the amputation, the former of her tongue, the latter of his nose; and after this cruel execution, they consumed the remainder of their days in exile and oblivion. The Greeks who were capable of reflection might find some consolation for their servitude, by observing the abuse of power when it was lodged for a moment in the hands of an aristocracy.

We shall imagine ourselves transported five hundred years backwards to the age of the Antonines, if we listen to the oration which Constans II. pronounced in the twelfth year of his age before the Byzantine senate. After returning his thanks for the just punishment of the assassins, who had intercepted the fairest hopes of his father's reign, "By the divine Providence," said the young emperor, "and by your righteous decree, Martina and her incestuous progeny have been cast headlong from the throne. Your majesty and wisdom have prevented the Roman state from degenerating into lawless tyranny. I therefore exhort and beseech you to stand forth as the counsellors and judges of the common safety." The senators were gratified by the respectful address and liberal donative of their sovereign; but these servile Greeks were unworthy and regardless of freedom; and in his mind, the lesson of an hour was quickly erased by the prejudices of the age and the habits of despotism. He retained only a jealous fear lest the senate or people should one day invade the right of primogeniture, and seat his brother Theodosius on an equal throne. By the imposition of holy orders, the grandson of Heraclius was disqualified for the purple; but this ceremony, which seemed to profane the sacraments of the church, was insufficient to appease the suspicions of the tyrant, and the death of the deacon Theodosius could alone expiate the crime of his royal birth. [1111] His murder was avenged by the imprecations of the people, and the assassin, in the fullness of power, was driven from his capital into voluntary and perpetual exile. Constans embarked for Greece and, as if he meant to retort the abhorrence which he deserved he is said, from the Imperial galley, to have spit against the walls of his native city. After passing the winter at Athens, he sailed to Tarentum in Italy, visited Rome, [1112] and concluded a long pilgrimage of disgrace and sacrilegious rapine, by fixing his residence at Syracuse. But if Constans could fly from his people, he could not fly from himself. The remorse of his conscience created a phantom who pursued him by land and sea, by day and by night; and the visionary Theodosius, presenting to his lips a cup of blood, said, or seemed to say, "Drink, brother, drink;" a sure emblem of the aggravation of his guilt, since he had received from the hands of the deacon the mystic cup of the blood of Christ. Odious to himself and to mankind, Constans perished by domestic, perhaps by episcopal, treason, in the capital of Sicily. A servant who waited in the bath, after pouring warm water on his head, struck him violently with the vase. He fell, stunned by the blow, and suffocated by the water; and his attendants, who wondered at the tedious delay, beheld with indifference the corpse of their lifeless emperor. The troops of Sicily invested with the purple an obscure youth, whose inimitable beauty eluded, and it might easily elude, the declining art of the painters and sculptors of the age.

[Footnote 1111: His soldiers (according to Abulfaradji. Chron. Syr. p. 112) called him another Cain. St. Martin, t. xi. p. 379—M.]

[Footnote 1112: He was received in Rome, and pillaged the churches. He carried off the brass roof of the Pantheon to Syracuse, or, as Schlosser conceives, to Constantinople Schlosser Geschichte der bilder-sturmenden Kaiser p. 80—M.]

Constans had left in the Byzantine palace three sons, the eldest of whom had been clothed in his infancy with the purple. When the father summoned them to attend his person in Sicily, these precious hostages were detained by the Greeks, and a firm refusal informed him that they were the children of the state. The news of his murder was conveyed with almost supernatural speed from Syracuse to Constantinople; and Constantine, the eldest of his sons, inherited his throne without being the heir of the public hatred. His subjects contributed, with zeal and alacrity, to chastise the guilt and presumption of a province which had usurped the rights of the senate and people; the young emperor sailed from the Hellespont with a powerful fleet; and the legions of Rome and Carthage were assembled under his standard in the harbor of Syracuse. The defeat of the Sicilian tyrant was easy, his punishment just, and his beauteous head was exposed in the hippodrome: but I cannot applaud the clemency of a prince, who, among a crowd of victims, condemned the son of a patrician, for deploring with some bitterness the execution of a virtuous father. The youth was castrated: he survived the operation, and the memory of this indecent cruelty is preserved by the elevation of Germanus to the rank of a patriarch and saint. After pouring this bloody libation on his father's tomb, Constantine returned to his capital; and the growth of his young beard during the Sicilian voyage was announced, by the familiar surname of Pogonatus, to the Grecian world. But his reign, like that of his predecessor, was stained with fraternal discord. On his two brothers, Heraclius and Tiberius, he had bestowed the title of Augustus; an empty title, for they continued to languish, without trust or power, in the solitude of the palace. At their secret instigation, the troops of the Anatolian theme or province approached the city on the Asiatic side, demanded for the royal brothers the partition or exercise of sovereignty, and supported their seditious claim by a theological argument. They were Christians, (they cried,) and orthodox Catholics; the sincere votaries of the holy and undivided Trinity. Since there are three equal persons in heaven, it is reasonable there should be three equal persons upon earth. The emperor invited these learned divines to a friendly conference, in which they might propose their arguments to the senate: they obeyed the summons, but the prospect of their bodies hanging on the gibbet in the suburb of Galata reconciled their companions to the unity of the reign of Constantine. He pardoned his brothers, and their names were still pronounced in the public acclamations: but on the repetition or suspicion of a similar offence, the obnoxious princes were deprived of their titles and noses, [1113] in the presence of the Catholic bishops who were assembled at Constantinople in the sixth general synod. In the close of his life, Pogonatus was anxious only to establish the right of primogeniture: the heir of his two sons, Justinian and Heraclius, was offered on the shrine of St. Peter, as a symbol of their spiritual adoption by the pope; but the elder was alone exalted to the rank of Augustus, and the assurance of the empire.

[Footnote 1113: Schlosser (Geschichte der bilder sturmenden Kaiser, p. 90) supposed that the young princes were mutilated after the first insurrection; that after this the acts were still inscribed with their names, the princes being closely secluded in the palace. The improbability of this circumstance may be weighed against Gibbon's want of authority for his statement—M.]

After the decease of his father, the inheritance of the Roman world devolved to Justinian II.; and the name of a triumphant lawgiver was dishonored by the vices of a boy, who imitated his namesake only in the expensive luxury of building. His passions were strong; his understanding was feeble; and he was intoxicated with a foolish pride, that his birth had given him the command of millions, of whom the smallest community would not have chosen him for their local magistrate. His favorite ministers were two beings the least susceptible of human sympathy, a eunuch and a monk: to the one he abandoned the palace, to the other the finances; the former corrected the emperor's mother with a scourge, the latter suspended the insolvent tributaries, with their heads downwards, over a slow and smoky fire. Since the days of Commodus and Caracalla, the cruelty of the Roman princes had most commonly been the effect of their fear; but Justinian, who possessed some vigor of character, enjoyed the sufferings, and braved the revenge, of his subjects, about ten years, till the measure was full, of his crimes and of their patience. In a dark dungeon, Leontius, a general of reputation, had groaned above three years, with some of the noblest and most deserving of the patricians: he was suddenly drawn forth to assume the government of Greece; and this promotion of an injured man was a mark of the contempt rather than of the confidence of his prince. As he was followed to the port by the kind offices of his friends, Leontius observed, with a sigh, that he was a victim adorned for sacrifice, and that inevitable death would pursue his footsteps. They ventured to reply, that glory and empire might be the recompense of a generous resolution; that every order of men abhorred the reign of a monster; and that the hands of two hundred thousand patriots expected only the voice of a leader. The night was chosen for their deliverance; and in the first effort of the conspirators, the praefect was slain, and the prisons were forced open: the emissaries of Leontius proclaimed in every street, "Christians, to St. Sophia!" and the seasonable text of the patriarch, "This is the day of the Lord!" was the prelude of an inflammatory sermon. From the church the people adjourned to the hippodrome: Justinian, in whose cause not a sword had been drawn, was dragged before these tumultuary judges, and their clamors demanded the instant death of the tyrant. But Leontius, who was already clothed with the purple, cast an eye of pity on the prostrate son of his own benefactor and of so many emperors. The life of Justinian was spared; the amputation of his nose, perhaps of his tongue, was imperfectly performed: the happy flexibility of the Greek language could impose the name of Rhinotmetus; and the mutilated tyrant was banished to Chersonae in Crim-Tartary, a lonely settlement, where corn, wine, and oil, were imported as foreign luxuries.

On the edge of the Scythian wilderness, Justinian still cherished the pride of his birth, and the hope of his restoration. After three years' exile, he received the pleasing intelligence that his injury was avenged by a second revolution, and that Leontius in his turn had been dethroned and mutilated by the rebel Apsimar, who assumed the more respectable name of Tiberius. But the claim of lineal succession was still formidable to a plebeian usurper; and his jealousy was stimulated by the complaints and charges of the Chersonites, who beheld the vices of the tyrant in the spirit of the exile. With a band of followers, attached to his person by common hope or common despair, Justinian fled from the inhospitable shore to the horde of the Chozars, who pitched their tents between the Tanais and Borysthenes. The khan entertained with pity and respect the royal suppliant: Phanagoria, once an opulent city, on the Asiatic side of the lake Moeotis, was assigned for his residence; and every Roman prejudice was stifled in his marriage with the sister of the Barbarian, who seems, however, from the name of Theodora, to have received the sacrament of baptism. But the faithless Chozar was soon tempted by the gold of Constantinople: and had not the design been revealed by the conjugal love of Theodora, her husband must have been assassinated or betrayed into the power of his enemies. After strangling, with his own hands, the two emissaries of the khan, Justinian sent back his wife to her brother, and embarked on the Euxine in search of new and more faithful allies. His vessel was assaulted by a violent tempest; and one of his pious companions advised him to deserve the mercy of God by a vow of general forgiveness, if he should be restored to the throne. "Of forgiveness?" replied the intrepid tyrant: "may I perish this instant—may the Almighty whelm me in the waves—if I consent to spare a single head of my enemies!" He survived this impious menace, sailed into the mouth of the Danube, trusted his person in the royal village of the Bulgarians, and purchased the aid of Terbelis, a pagan conqueror, by the promise of his daughter and a fair partition of the treasures of the empire. The Bulgarian kingdom extended to the confines of Thrace; and the two princes besieged Constantinople at the head of fifteen thousand horse. Apsimar was dismayed by the sudden and hostile apparition of his rival whose head had been promised by the Chozar, and of whose evasion he was yet ignorant. After an absence of ten years, the crimes of Justinian were faintly remembered, and the birth and misfortunes of their hereditary sovereign excited the pity of the multitude, ever discontented with the ruling powers; and by the active diligence of his adherents, he was introduced into the city and palace of Constantine.

PART II

In rewarding his allies, and recalling his wife, Justinian displayed some sense of honor and gratitude; [1114] and Terbelis retired, after sweeping away a heap of gold coin, which he measured with his Scythian whip. But never was vow more religiously performed than the sacred oath of revenge which he had sworn amidst the storms of the Euxine. The two usurpers (for I must reserve the name of tyrant for the conqueror) were dragged into the hippodrome, the one from his prison, the other from his palace. Before their execution, Leontius and Apsimar were cast prostrate in chains beneath the throne of the emperor; and Justinian, planting a foot on each of their necks, contemplated above an hour the chariot-race, while the inconstant people shouted, in the words of the Psalmist, "Thou shalt trample on the asp and basilisk, and on the lion and dragon shalt thou set thy foot!" The universal defection which he had once experienced might provoke him to repeat the wish of Caligula, that the Roman people had but one head. Yet I shall presume to observe, that such a wish is unworthy of an ingenious tyrant, since his revenge and cruelty would have been extinguished by a single blow, instead of the slow variety of tortures which Justinian inflicted on the victims of his anger. His pleasures were inexhaustible: neither private virtue nor public service could expiate the guilt of active, or even passive, obedience to an established government; and, during the six years of his new reign, he considered the axe, the cord, and the rack, as the only instruments of royalty. But his most implacable hatred was pointed against the Chersonites, who had insulted his exile and violated the laws of hospitality. Their remote situation afforded some means of defence, or at least of escape; and a grievous tax was imposed on Constantinople, to supply the preparations of a fleet and army. "All are guilty, and all must perish," was the mandate of Justinian; and the bloody execution was intrusted to his favorite Stephen, who was recommended by the epithet of the savage. Yet even the savage Stephen imperfectly accomplished the intentions of his sovereign. The slowness of his attack allowed the greater part of the inhabitants to withdraw into the country; and the minister of vengeance contented himself with reducing the youth of both sexes to a state of servitude, with roasting alive seven of the principal citizens, with drowning twenty in the sea, and with reserving forty-two in chains to receive their doom from the mouth of the emperor. In their return, the fleet was driven on the rocky shores of Anatolia; and Justinian applauded the obedience of the Euxine, which had involved so many thousands of his subjects and enemies in a common shipwreck: but the tyrant was still insatiate of blood; and a second expedition was commanded to extirpate the remains of the proscribed colony. In the short interval, the Chersonites had returned to their city, and were prepared to die in arms; the khan of the Chozars had renounced the cause of his odious brother; the exiles of every province were assembled in Tauris; and Bardanes, under the name of

Philippicus, was invested with the purple. The Imperial troops, unwilling and unable to perpetrate the revenge of Justinian, escaped his displeasure by abjuring his allegiance: the fleet, under their new sovereign, steered back a more auspicious course to the harbors of Sinope and Constantinople; and every tongue was prompt to pronounce, every hand to execute, the death of the tyrant. Destitute of friends, he was deserted by his Barbarian guards; and the stroke of the assassin was praised as an act of patriotism and Roman virtue. His son Tiberius had taken refuge in a church; his aged grandmother guarded the door; and the innocent youth, suspending round his neck the most formidable relics, embraced with one hand the altar, with the other the wood of the true cross. But the popular fury that dares to trample on superstition, is deaf to the cries of humanity; and the race of Heraclius was extinguished after a reign of one hundred years

[Footnote 1114: Of fear rather than of more generous motives. Compare Le Beau vol. xii. p. 64—M.]

Between the fall of the Heraclian and the rise of the Isaurian dynasty, a short interval of six years is divided into three reigns. Bardanes, or Philippicus, was hailed at Constantinople as a hero who had delivered his country from a tyrant; and he might taste some moments of happiness in the first transports of sincere and universal joy. Justinian had left behind him an ample treasure, the fruit of cruelty and rapine: but this useful fund was soon and idly dissipated by his successor. On the festival of his birthday, Philippicus entertained the multitude with the games of the hippodrome; from thence he paraded through the streets with a thousand banners and a thousand trumpets; refreshed himself in the baths of Zeuxippus, and returning to the palace, entertained his nobles with a sumptuous banquet. At the meridian hour he withdrew to his chamber, intoxicated with flattery and wine, and forgetful that his example had made every subject ambitious, and that every ambitious subject was his secret enemy. Some bold conspirators introduced themselves in the disorder of the feast; and the slumbering monarch was surprised, bound, blinded, and deposed, before he was sensible of his danger. Yet the traitors were deprived of their reward; and the free voice of the senate and people promoted Artemius from the office of secretary to that of emperor: he assumed the title of Anastasius the Second, and displayed in a short and troubled reign the virtues both of peace and war. But after the extinction of the Imperial line, the rule of obedience was violated, and every change diffused the seeds of new revolutions. In a mutiny of the fleet, an obscure and reluctant officer of the revenue was forcibly invested with the purple: after some months of a naval war, Anastasius resigned the sceptre; and the conqueror, Theodosius the Third, submitted in his turn to the superior ascendant of Leo, the general and emperor of the Oriental troops. His two predecessors were permitted to embrace the ecclesiastical profession: the restless impatience of Anastasius tempted him to risk and to lose his life in a treasonable enterprise; but the last days of Theodosius were honorable and secure. The single sublime word, "Health," which he inscribed on his tomb, expresses the confidence of philosophy or religion; and the fame of his miracles was long preserved among the people of Ephesus. This convenient shelter of the church might sometimes impose a lesson of clemency; but it may be questioned whether it is for the public interest to diminish the perils of unsuccessful ambition.

I have dwelt on the fall of a tyrant; I shall briefly represent the founder of a new dynasty, who is known to posterity by the invectives of his enemies, and whose public and private life is involved in the ecclesiastical story of the Iconoclasts. Yet in spite of the clamors of superstition, a favorable prejudice for the character of Leo the Isaurian may be reasonably drawn from the obscurity of his birth, and the duration of his reign—I. In an age of manly spirit, the prospect of an Imperial reward would have kindled every energy of the mind, and produced a crowd of competitors as deserving as they were desirous to reign. Even in the corruption and debility of the modern Greeks, the elevation of a plebeian from the last to the first rank of society, supposes some qualifications above the level of the multitude. He would probably be ignorant and disdainful of speculative science; and, in the pursuit of fortune, he might absolve himself from the obligations of benevolence and justice; but to his character we may ascribe the useful virtues of prudence and fortitude, the knowledge of mankind, and the important art of gaining their confidence and directing their passions. It is agreed that Leo was a native of Isauria, and that Conon was his primitive name. The writers, whose awkward satire is praise, describe him as an itinerant pedler, who drove an ass with some paltry merchandise to the country fairs; and foolishly relate that he met on the road some Jewish fortune-tellers, who promised him the Roman empire, on condition that he should abolish the worship of idols. A more probable account relates the migration of his father from Asia Minor to Thrace, where he exercised the lucrative trade of a grazier; and he must have acquired considerable wealth, since the first introduction of his son was procured by a supply of five hundred sheep to the Imperial camp. His first service was in the guards of Justinian, where he soon attracted the notice, and by degrees the jealousy, of the tyrant. His valor and dexterity were conspicuous in the Colchian war: from Anastasius he received the command of the Anatolian legions, and by the suffrage of the soldiers he was raised to the empire with the general applause of the Roman world—II. In this dangerous elevation, Leo the Third supported himself against the envy of his equals, the discontent of a powerful faction, and the assaults of his foreign and domestic enemies. The Catholics, who accuse his religious innovations, are obliged to confess that they were undertaken with temper and conducted with firmness. Their silence respects the wisdom of his administration and the purity of his manners. After a reign of twenty-four years, he peaceably expired in the palace of Constantinople; and the purple which he had acquired was transmitted by the right of inheritance to the third generation. [1115]

[Footnote 1115: During the latter part of his reign, the hostilities of the Saracens, who invested a Pergamenian, named Tiberius, with the purple, and proclaimed him as the son of Justinian, and an earthquake, which destroyed the walls of Constantinople, compelled Leo greatly to increase the burdens of taxation upon his subjects. A twelfth was exacted in addition to every aurena as a wall tax. Theophanes p. 275 Schlosser, Bilder eturmeud Kaiser, p. 197—M.]

In a long reign of thirty-four years, the son and successor of Leo, Constantine the Fifth, surnamed Copronymus, attacked with less temperate zeal the images or idols of the church. Their votaries have exhausted the bitterness of religious gall, in their portrait of this spotted panther, this antichrist, this flying dragon of the serpent's seed, who surpassed the vices of Elagabalus and Nero. His reign was a long butchery of whatever was most noble, or holy, or innocent, in his empire. In person, the emperor assisted at the execution of his victims, surveyed their agonies, listened to their groans, and indulged, without satiating, his appetite for blood: a plate of noses was accepted as a grateful offering, and his domestics were often scourged or mutilated by the royal hand. His surname was derived from his pollution of his baptismal font. The infant might be excused; but the manly pleasures of Copronymus degraded him below the level of a brute; his lust confounded the eternal distinctions of sex and species, and he seemed to extract some unnatural delight from the objects most offensive to human sense. In his religion the Iconoclast was a Heretic, a Jew, a Mahometan, a Pagan, and an Atheist; and his belief of an invisible power could be discovered only in his magic rites, human victims, and nocturnal sacrifices to Venus and the daemons of antiquity. His life was stained with the most opposite vices, and the ulcers which covered his body, anticipated before his death the sentiment of hell-tortures. Of these accusations, which I have so patiently copied, a part is refuted by its own absurdity; and in the private anecdotes of the life of the princes, the lie is more easy as the detection is more difficult. Without adopting the pernicious maxim, that where much is alleged, something must be true, I can however discern, that Constantine the Fifth was dissolute and cruel. Calumny is more prone to exaggerate than to invent; and her licentious tongue is checked in some measure by the experience of the age and country to which she appeals. Of the bishops and monks, the generals and magistrates, who are said to have suffered under his reign, the numbers are recorded, the names were conspicuous, the execution was public, the mutilation visible and permanent. [1116] The Catholics hated the person and government of Copronymus; but even their hatred is a proof of their oppression. They dissembled the provocations which might excuse or justify his rigor, but even these provocations must gradually inflame his resentment and harden his temper in the use or the abuse of despotism. Yet the character of the fifth Constantine was not devoid of merit, nor did his government always deserve the curses or the contempt of the Greeks. From the confession of his enemies, I am informed of the restoration of an ancient aqueduct, of the redemption of two thousand five hundred captives, of the uncommon plenty of the times, and of the new colonies with which he repeopled Constantinople and the Thracian cities. They reluctantly praise his activity and courage; he was on horseback in the field at the head of his legions; and, although the fortune of his arms was various, he triumphed by sea and land, on the Euphrates and the Danube, in civil and Barbarian war. Heretical praise must be cast into the scale to counterbalance the weight of orthodox invective. The Iconoclasts revered the virtues of the prince: forty years after his death they still prayed before the tomb of the saint. A miraculous vision was propagated by fanaticism or fraud: and the Christian hero appeared on a milk-white steed, brandishing his lance against the Pagans of Bulgaria: "An absurd fable," says the Catholic historian, "since Copronymus is chained with the daemons in the abyss of hell."

[Footnote 1116: *He is accused of burning the library of Constantinople, founded by Julian, with its president and twelve professors. This eastern Sorbonne had discomfited the Imperial theologians on the great question of image worship. Schlosser observes that this accidental fire took place six years after the emperor had laid the question of image-worship before the professors. Bilder sturmand Kaiser, p. 294. Compare Le Heau. vol. xl. p. 156—M.*]

Leo the Fourth, the son of the fifth and the father of the sixth Constantine, was of a feeble constitution both of mind [1117] and body, and the principal care of his reign was the settlement of the succession. The association of the young Constantine was urged by the officious zeal of his subjects; and the emperor, conscious of his decay, complied, after a prudent hesitation, with their unanimous wishes. The royal infant, at the age of five years, was crowned with his mother Irene; and the national consent was ratified by every circumstance of pomp and solemnity, that could dazzle the eyes or bind the conscience of the Greeks. An oath of fidelity was administered in the palace, the church, and the hippodrome, to the several orders of the state, who adjured the holy names of the Son, and mother of God. "Be witness, O Christ! that we will watch over the safety of Constantine the son of Leo, expose our lives in his service, and bear true allegiance to his person and posterity." They pledged their faith on the wood of the true cross, and the act of their engagement was deposited on the altar of St. Sophia. The first to swear, and the first to violate their oath, were the five sons of Copronymus by a second marriage; and the story of these princes is singular and tragic. The right of primogeniture excluded them from the throne; the injustice of their elder brother defrauded them of a legacy of about two millions sterling; some vain titles were not deemed a sufficient compensation for wealth and power; and they repeatedly conspired against their nephew, before and after the death of his father. Their first attempt was pardoned; for the second offence [1118] they were condemned to the ecclesiastical state; and for the third treason, Nicephorus, the eldest and most guilty, was deprived of his eyes, and his four brothers, Christopher, Nicetas, Anthemeus, and Eudoxas, were punished, as a milder sentence, by the amputation of their tongues. After five years' confinement, they escaped to the church of St. Sophia, and displayed a pathetic spectacle to the people. "Countrymen and Christians," cried Nicephorus for himself and his mute brethren, "behold the sons of your emperor, if you can still recognize our features in this miserable state. A life, an imperfect life, is all that the malice of our enemies has spared. It is now threatened, and we now throw ourselves on your compassion." The rising murmur might have produced a revolution, had it not been checked by the presence of a minister, who soothed the unhappy princes with flattery and hope, and gently drew them from the sanctuary to the palace. They were speedily embarked for Greece, and Athens was allotted for the place of their exile. In this calm retreat, and in their helpless condition, Nicephorus and his brothers were tormented by the thirst of power, and tempted by a Sclavonian chief, who offered to break their prison, and to lead them in arms, and in the purple, to the gates of Constantinople. But the Athenian people, ever zealous in the cause of Irene, prevented her justice or cruelty; and the five sons of Copronymus were plunged in eternal darkness and oblivion.

[Footnote 1117: Schlosser thinks more highly of Leo's mind; but his only proof of his superiority is the successes of his generals against the Saracens, Schlosser, p. 256—M.]

[Footnote 1118: The second offence was on the accession of the young Constantine—M.]

For himself, that emperor had chosen a Barbarian wife, the daughter of the khan of the Chozars; but in the marriage of his heir, he preferred an Athenian virgin, an orphan, seventeen years old, whose sole fortune must have consisted in her personal accomplishments. The nuptials of Leo and Irene were celebrated with royal pomp; she soon acquired the love and confidence of a feeble husband, and in his testament he declared the empress guardian of the Roman world, and of their son Constantine the Sixth, who was no more than ten years of age. During his childhood, Irene most ably and assiduously discharged, in her public administration, the duties of a faithful mother; and her zeal in the restoration of images has deserved the name and honors of a saint, which she still occupies in the Greek calendar. But the emperor attained the maturity of youth; the maternal yoke became more grievous; and he listened to the favorites of his own age, who shared his pleasures, and were ambitious of sharing his power. Their reasons convinced him of his right, their praises of his ability, to reign; and he consented to reward the services of Irene by a perpetual banishment to the Isle of Sicily. But her vigilance and penetration easily disconcerted their rash projects: a similar, or more severe, punishment was retaliated on themselves and their advisers; and Irene inflicted on the ungrateful prince the chastisement of a boy. After this contest, the mother and the son were at the head of two domestic factions; and instead of mild influence and voluntary obedience, she held in chains a captive and an enemy. The empress was overthrown by the abuse of victory; the oath of fidelity, which she exacted to herself alone, was pronounced with reluctant murmurs; and the bold refusal of the Armenian guards encouraged a free and general declaration, that Constantine the Sixth was the lawful emperor of the Romans. In this character he ascended his hereditary throne, and dismissed Irene to a life of solitude and repose. But her haughty spirit condescended to the arts of dissimulation: she flattered the bishops and eunuchs, revived the filial tenderness of the prince, regained his confidence, and betrayed his credulity. The character of Constantine was not destitute of sense or spirit; but his education had been studiously neglected; and the ambitious mother exposed to the public censure the vices which she had nourished, and the actions which she had secretly advised: his divorce and second marriage offended the prejudices of the clergy, and by his imprudent rigor he forfeited the attachment of the Armenian guards. A powerful conspiracy was formed for the restoration of Irene; and the secret, though widely diffused, was faithfully kept above eight months, till the emperor, suspicious of his danger, escaped from Constantinople, with the design of appealing to the provinces and armies. By this hasty flight, the empress was left on the brink of the precipice; yet before she implored the mercy of her son, Irene addressed a private epistle to the friends whom she had placed about his person, with a menace, that unless they accomplished, she would reveal, their treason. Their fear rendered them intrepid; they seized the emperor on the Asiatic shore, and he was transported to the porphyry apartment of the palace, where he had first seen the light. In the mind of Irene, ambition had stifled every sentiment of humanity and nature; and it was decreed in her bloody council, that Constantine should be rendered incapable of the throne: her emissaries assaulted the sleeping prince, and stabbed their daggers with such violence and precipitation into his eyes as if they meant to execute a mortal sentence. An ambiguous passage of Theophanes persuaded the annalist of the church that death was the immediate consequence of this barbarous execution. The Catholics have been deceived or subdued by the authority of Baronius; and Protestant zeal has reechoed the words of a cardinal, desirous, as it should seem, to favor the patroness of images. [1119] Yet the blind son of Irene survived many years, oppressed by the court and forgotten by the world; the Isaurian dynasty was silently extinguished; and the memory of Constantine was recalled only by the nuptials of his daughter Euphrosyne with the emperor Michael the Second.

[Footnote 1119: Gibbon has been attacked on account of this statement, but is successfully defended by Schlosser. B S. Kaiser p. 327. Compare Le Beau, c. xii p. 372—M.]

The most bigoted orthodoxy has justly execrated the unnatural mother, who may not easily be paralleled in the history of crimes. To her bloody deed superstition has attributed a subsequent darkness of seventeen days; during which many vessels in midday were driven from their course, as if the sun, a globe of fire so vast and so remote, could sympathize with the atoms of a revolving planet. On earth, the crime of Irene was left five years unpunished; her reign was crowned with external splendor; and if she could silence the voice of conscience, she neither heard nor regarded the reproaches of mankind. The Roman world bowed to the government of a female; and as she moved through the streets of Constantinople, the reins of four milk-white steeds were held by as many patricians, who marched on foot before the golden chariot of their queen. But these patricians were for the most part eunuchs; and their black ingratitude justified, on this occasion, the popular hatred and contempt. Raised, enriched, intrusted with the first dignities of the empire, they basely conspired against their benefactress; the great treasurer Nicephorus was secretly invested with the purple; her successor was introduced into the palace, and crowned at St. Sophia by the venal patriarch. In their first interview, she recapitulated with dignity the revolutions of her life, gently accused the perfidy of Nicephorus, insinuated that he owed his life to her unsuspicious clemency, and for the throne and treasures which she resigned, solicited a decent and honorable retreat. His avarice refused this modest compensation; and, in her exile of the Isle of Lesbos, the empress earned a scanty subsistence by the labors of her distaff.

Many tyrants have reigned undoubtedly more criminal than Nicephorus, but none perhaps have more deeply incurred the universal abhorrence of their people. His character was stained with the three odious vices of hypocrisy, ingratitude, and avarice: his want of virtue was not redeemed by any superior talents, nor his want of talents by any pleasing qualifications. Unskilful and unfortunate in war, Nicephorus was vanquished by the Saracens, and slain by the Bulgarians; and the advantage of his death overbalanced, in the public opinion, the destruction of a Roman army. [1011] His son and heir Stauracius escaped from the field with a mortal wound; yet six months of an expiring life were sufficient to refute his indecent, though popular declaration, that he would in all things avoid the example of his father. On the near prospect of his decease, Michael, the great master of the palace, and the husband of his sister Procopia, was named by every person of the palace and city, except by his envious brother. Tenacious of a sceptre now falling from his hand, he conspired against the life of his successor, and cherished the idea of changing to a democracy the Roman empire. But these rash projects served only to inflame the zeal of the people and to remove the scruples of the candidate: Michael the First accepted the purple, and before he sunk into the grave the son of Nicephorus implored the clemency of his new sovereign. Had Michael in an age of peace ascended an hereditary throne, he might have reigned and died the father of his people: but his mild virtues were adapted to the shade of private life, nor was he capable of controlling the ambition of his equals, or of resisting the arms of the victorious Bulgarians. While his want of ability and success exposed him to the contempt of the soldiers, the masculine spirit of his wife Procopia awakened their indignation. Even the Greeks of the ninth century were provoked by the insolence of a female, who, in the front of the standards, presumed to direct their discipline and animate their valor; and their licentious clamors advised the new Semiramis to reverence the majesty of a Roman camp. After an unsuccessful campaign, the emperor left, in their winter-quarters of Thrace, a disaffected army under the command of his enemies; and their artful eloquence persuaded the soldiers to break the dominion of the eunuchs, to degrade the husband of Procopia, and to assert the right of a military election. They marched towards the capital: yet the clergy, the senate, and the people of Constantinople, adhered to the cause of Michael; and the troops and treasures of Asia might have protracted the mischiefs of civil war. But his humanity (by the ambitious it will be termed his weakness) protested that not a drop of Christian blood should be shed in his quarrel, and his messengers presented the conquerors with the keys of the city and the palace. They were disarmed by his innocence and submission; his life and his eyes were spared; and the Imperial monk enjoyed the comforts of solitude and religion above thirty-two years after he had been stripped of the purple and separated from his wife.

[Footnote 1011: The Syrian historian Aboulfaradj. Chron. Syr. p. 133, 139, speaks of him as a brave, prudent, and pious prince, formidable to the Arabs. St. Martin, c. xii. p. 402. Compare Schlosser, p. 350—M.]

A rebel, in the time of Nicephorus, the famous and unfortunate Bardanes, had once the curiosity to consult an Asiatic prophet, who, after prognosticating his fall, announced the fortunes of his three principal officers, Leo the Armenian, Michael the Phrygian, and Thomas the Cappadocian, the successive reigns of the two former, the fruitless and fatal enterprise of the third. This prediction was verified, or rather was produced, by the event. Ten years afterwards, when the Thracian camp rejected the husband of Procopia, the crown was presented to the same Leo, the first in military rank and the secret author of the mutiny. As he affected to hesitate, "With this sword," said his companion Michael, "I will open the gates of Constantinople to your Imperial sway; or instantly plunge it into your bosom, if you obstinately resist the just desires of your fellow-soldiers." The compliance of the Armenian was rewarded with the empire, and he reigned seven years and a half under the name of Leo the Fifth. Educated in a camp, and ignorant both of laws and letters, he introduced into his civil government the rigor and even cruelty of military discipline; but if his severity was sometimes dangerous to the innocent, it was always formidable to the guilty. His religious inconstancy was taxed by the epithet of Chameleon, but the Catholics have acknowledged by the voice of a saint and confessors, that the life of the Iconoclast was useful to the republic. The zeal of his companion Michael was repaid with riches, honors, and military command; and his subordinate talents were beneficially employed in the public service. Yet the Phrygian was dissatisfied at receiving as a favor a scanty portion of the Imperial prize which he had bestowed on his equal; and his discontent, which sometimes evaporated in hasty discourse, at length assumed a more threatening and hostile aspect against a prince whom he represented as a cruel tyrant. That tyrant, however, repeatedly detected, warned, and dismissed the old companion of his arms, till fear and resentment prevailed over gratitude; and Michael, after a scrutiny into his actions and designs, was convicted of treason, and sentenced to be burnt alive in the furnace of the private baths. The devout humanity of the empress Theophano was fatal to her husband and family. A solemn day, the twenty-fifth of December, had been fixed for the execution: she urged, that the anniversary of the Savior's birth would be profaned by this inhuman spectacle, and Leo consented with reluctance to a decent respite. But on the vigil of the feast his sleepless anxiety prompted him to visit at the dead of night the chamber in which his enemy was confined: he beheld him released from his chain, and stretched on his jailer's bed in a profound slumber. Leo was alarmed at these signs of security and intelligence; but though he retired with silent steps, his entrance and departure were noticed by a slave who lay concealed in a corner of the prison. Under the pretence of requesting the spiritual aid of a confessor, Michael informed the conspirators, that their lives depended on his discretion, and that a few hours were left to assure their own safety, by the deliverance of their friend and country. On the great festivals, a chosen band of priests and chanters was admitted into the palace by a private gate to sing matins in the chapel; and Leo, who regulated with the same strictness the discipline of the choir and of the camp, was seldom absent from these early devotions. In the ecclesiastical habit, but with their swords under their robes, the conspirators mingled with the procession, lurked in the angles of the chapel, and expected, as the signal of murder, the intonation of the first psalm by the emperor himself. The imperfect light, and the uniformity of dress, might have favored his escape, whilst their assault was pointed against a harmless priest; but they soon discovered their mistake, and encompassed on all sides the royal victim. Without a weapon and without a friend, he grasped a weighty cross, and stood at bay against the hunters of his life; but as he asked for mercy, "This is the hour, not of mercy, but of vengeance," was the inexorable reply. The stroke of a well-aimed sword separated from his body the right arm and the cross, and Leo the Armenian was slain at the foot of the altar. A memorable reverse of fortune was displayed in Michael the Second, who from a defect in his speech was surnamed the Stammerer. He was snatched from the fiery furnace to the sovereignty of an empire; and as in the tumult a smith could not readily be found, the fetters remained on his legs several hours after he was seated on the throne of the Caesars. The royal blood which had been the price of his elevation, was unprofitably spent: in the purple he retained the ignoble vices of his origin; and Michael lost his provinces with as supine indifference as if they had been the inheritance of his fathers. His title was disputed by Thomas, the last of the military triumvirate, who transported into Europe fourscore thousand Barbarians from the banks of the Tigris and the shores of the Caspian. He formed the siege of Constantinople; but the capital was defended with spiritual and carnal weapons; a Bulgarian king assaulted the camp of the Orientals, and Thomas had the misfortune, or the weakness, to fall alive into the power of the conqueror. The hands and feet of the rebel were amputated; he was placed on an ass, and, amidst the insults of the people, was led through the streets, which he sprinkled with his blood. The depravation of manners, as savage as they were corrupt, is marked by the presence of the emperor himself. Deaf to the lamentation of a fellow-soldier, he incessantly pressed the discovery of more accomplices, till his curiosity was checked by the question of an honest or guilty minister: "Would you give credit to an enemy against the most faithful of your friends?" After the death of his first wife, the emperor, at the request of the senate, drew from her monastery Euphrosyne, the daughter of Constantine the Sixth. Her august birth might justify a stipulation in the marriage-contract, that her children should equally share the empire with their elder brother. But the nuptials of Michael and Euphrosyne were barren; and she was content with the title of mother of Theophilus, his son and successor.

The character of Theophilus is a rare example in which religious zeal has allowed, and perhaps magnified, the virtues of a heretic and a persecutor. His valor was often felt by the enemies, and his justice by the subjects, of the monarchy; but the valor of Theophilus was rash and fruitless, and his justice arbitrary and cruel. He displayed the banner of the cross against the Saracens; but his five expeditions were concluded by a signal overthrow: Amorium, the native city of his ancestors, was levelled with the ground and from his military toils he derived only the surname of the Unfortunate. The wisdom of a sovereign is comprised in the institution of laws and the choice of magistrates, and while he seems without action, his civil government revolves round his centre with the silence and order of the planetary system. But the justice of Theophilus was fashioned on the model of the Oriental despots, who, in personal and irregular acts of authority, consult the reason or passion of the moment, without measuring the sentence by the law, or the penalty by the offense. A poor woman threw herself at the emperor's feet to complain of a powerful neighbor, the brother of the empress, who had raised his palace-wall to such an inconvenient height, that her humble dwelling was excluded from light and air! On the proof of the fact, instead of granting, like an ordinary judge, sufficient or ample damages to the plaintiff, the sovereign adjudged to her use and benefit the palace and the ground. Nor was Theophilus content with this extravagant satisfaction: his zeal converted a civil trespass into a criminal act; and the unfortunate patrician was stripped and scourged in the public place of Constantinople. For some venial offenses, some defect of equity or vigilance, the principal ministers, a praefect, a quaestor, a captain of the guards, were banished or mutilated, or scalded with boiling pitch, or burnt alive in the hippodrome; and as these dreadful examples might be the effects of error or caprice, they must have alienated from his service the best and wisest of the citizens. But the pride of the monarch was flattered in the exercise of power, or, as he thought, of virtue; and the people, safe in their obscurity, applauded the danger and debasement of their superiors. This extraordinary rigor was justified, in some measure, by its salutary consequences; since, after a scrutiny of seventeen days, not a complaint or abuse could be found in the court or city; and it might be alleged that the Greeks could be ruled only with a rod of iron, and that the public interest is the motive and law of the supreme judge. Yet in the crime, or the suspicion, of treason, that judge is of all others the most credulous and partial. Theophilus might inflict a tardy vengeance on the assassins of Leo and the saviors of his father; but he enjoyed the fruits of their crime; and his jealous tyranny sacrificed a brother and a prince to the future safety of his life. A Persian of the race of the Sassanides died in poverty and exile at Constantinople, leaving an only son, the issue of a plebeian marriage. At the age of twelve years, the royal birth of Theophobus was revealed, and his merit was not unworthy of his birth. He was educated in the Byzantine palace, a Christian and a soldier; advanced with rapid steps in the career of fortune and glory; received the hand of the emperor's sister; and was promoted to the command of thirty thousand Persians, who, like his father, had fled from the Mahometan conquerors. These troops, doubly infected with mercenary and fanatic vices, were desirous of revolting against their benefactor, and erecting the standard of their native king but the loyal Theophobus rejected their offers, disconcerted their schemes, and escaped from their hands to the camp or palace of his royal brother. A generous confidence might have secured a faithful and able guardian for his wife and his infant son, to whom Theophilus, in the flower of his age, was compelled to leave the inheritance of the empire. But his jealousy was exasperated by envy and disease; he feared the dangerous virtues which might either support or oppress their infancy and weakness; and the dying emperor demanded the head of the Persian prince. With savage delight he recognized the familiar features of his brother: "Thou art no longer Theophobus," he said; and, sinking on his couch, he added, with a faltering voice, "Soon, too soon, I shall be no more Theophilus!"

PART III

The Russians, who have borrowed from the Greeks the greatest part of their civil and ecclesiastical policy, preserved, till the last century, a singular institution in the marriage of the Czar. They collected, not the virgins of every rank and of every province, a vain and romantic idea, but the daughters of the principal nobles, who awaited in the palace the choice of their sovereign. It is affirmed, that a similar method was adopted in the nuptials of Theophilus. With a golden apple in his hand, he slowly walked between two lines of contending beauties: his eye was detained by the charms of Icasia, and in the awkwardness of a first declaration, the prince could only observe, that, in this world, women had been the cause of much evil; "And surely, sir," she pertly replied, "they have likewise been the occasion of much good." This affectation of unseasonable wit displeased the Imperial lover: he turned aside in disgust; Icasia concealed her mortification in a convent; and the modest silence of Theodora was rewarded with the golden apple. She deserved the love, but did not escape the severity, of her lord. From the palace garden he beheld a vessel deeply laden, and steering into the port: on the discovery that the precious cargo of Syrian luxury was the property of his wife, he condemned the ship to the flames, with a sharp reproach, that her avarice had degraded the character of an empress into that of a merchant. Yet his last choice intrusted her with the guardianship of the empire and her son Michael, who was left an orphan in the fifth year of his age. The restoration of images, and the final extirpation of the Iconoclasts, has endeared her name to the devotion of the Greeks; but in the fervor of religious zeal, Theodora entertained a grateful regard for the memory and salvation of her husband. After thirteen years of a prudent and frugal administration, she perceived the decline of her influence; but the second Irene imitated only the virtues of her predecessor. Instead of conspiring against the life or government of her son, she retired, without a struggle, though not without a murmur, to the solitude of private life, deploring the ingratitude, the vices, and the inevitable ruin, of the worthless youth. Among the successors of Nero and Elagabalus, we have not hitherto found the imitation of their vices, the character of a Roman prince who considered pleasure as the object of life, and virtue as the enemy of pleasure. Whatever might have been the maternal care of Theodora in the education of Michael the Third, her unfortunate son was a king before he was a man. If the ambitious mother labored to check the progress of reason, she could not cool the ebullition of passion; and her selfish policy was justly repaid by the contempt and ingratitude of the headstrong youth. At the age of eighteen, he rejected her authority, without feeling his own incapacity to govern the empire and himself. With Theodora, all gravity and wisdom retired from the court; their place was supplied by the alternate dominion of vice and folly; and it was impossible, without forfeiting the public esteem, to acquire or preserve the favor of the emperor. The millions of gold and silver which had been accumulated for the service of the state, were lavished on the vilest of men, who flattered his passions and shared his pleasures; and in a reign of thirteen years, the richest of sovereigns was compelled to strip the palace and the churches of their precious furniture. Like Nero, he delighted in the amusements of the theatre, and sighed to be surpassed in the accomplishments in which he should have blushed to excel. Yet the studies of Nero in music and poetry betrayed some symptoms of a liberal taste; the more ignoble arts of the son of Theophilus were confined to the chariot-race of the hippodrome. The four factions which had agitated the peace, still amused the idleness, of the capital: for himself, the emperor assumed the blue livery; the three rival colors were distributed to his favorites, and in the vile though eager contention he forgot the dignity of his person and the safety of his dominions. He silenced the messenger of an invasion, who presumed to divert his attention in the most critical moment of the race; and by his command, the importunate beacons were extinguished, that too frequently spread the alarm from Tarsus to Constantinople. The most skilful charioteers obtained the first place in his confidence and esteem; their merit was profusely rewarded the emperor feasted in their houses, and presented their children at the baptismal font; and while he applauded his own popularity, he affected to blame the cold and stately reserve of his predecessors. The unnatural lusts which had degraded even the manhood of Nero, were banished from the world; yet the strength of Michael was consumed by the indulgence of love and intemperance. [1012] In his midnight revels, when his passions were inflamed by wine, he was provoked to issue the most sanguinary commands; and if any feelings of humanity were left, he was reduced, with the return of sense, to approve the salutary disobedience of his servants. But the most extraordinary feature in the character of Michael, is the profane mockery of the religion of his country. The superstition of the Greeks might indeed excite the smile of a philosopher; but his smile would have been rational and temperate, and he must have condemned the ignorant folly of a youth who insulted the objects of public veneration. A buffoon of the court was invested in the robes of the patriarch: his twelve metropolitans, among whom the emperor was ranked, assumed their ecclesiastical garments: they used or abused the sacred vessels of the altar; and in their bacchanalian feasts, the holy communion was administered in a nauseous compound of vinegar and mustard. Nor were these impious spectacles concealed from the eyes of the city. On the day of a solemn festival, the emperor, with his bishops or buffoons, rode on asses through the streets, encountered the true patriarch at the head of his clergy; and by their licentious shouts and obscene gestures, disordered the gravity of the Christian procession. The devotion of Michael appeared only in some offence to reason or piety: he received his theatrical crowns from the statue of the Virgin; and an Imperial tomb was violated for the sake of burning the bones of Constantine the Iconoclast. By this extravagant conduct, the son of Theophilus became as contemptible as he was odious: every citizen was impatient for the deliverance of his country; and even the favorites of the moment were apprehensive that a caprice might snatch away what a caprice had bestowed. In the thirtieth year of his age, and in the hour of intoxication and sleep, Michael the Third was murdered in his chamber by the founder of a new dynasty, whom the emperor had raised to an equality of rank and power.

[Footnote 1012: In a campaign against the Saracens, he betrayed both imbecility and cowardice. Genesius, c. iv. p. 94—M.]

The genealogy of Basil the Macedonian (if it be not the spurious offspring of pride and flattery) exhibits a genuine picture of the revolution of the most illustrious families. The Arsacides, the rivals of Rome, possessed the sceptre of the East near four hundred years: a younger branch of these Parthian kings continued to reign in Armenia; and their royal descendants survived the partition and servitude of that ancient monarchy. Two of these, Artabanus and Chlienes, escaped or retired to the court of Leo the First: his bounty seated them in a safe and hospitable exile, in the province of Macedonia: Adrianople was their final settlement. During several generations they maintained the dignity of their birth; and their Roman patriotism rejected the tempting offers of the Persian and Arabian powers, who recalled them to their native country. But their splendor was insensibly clouded by time and poverty; and the father of Basil was reduced to a small farm, which he cultivated with his own hands: yet he scorned to disgrace the blood of the Arsacides by a plebeian alliance: his wife, a widow of Adrianople, was pleased to count among her ancestors the great Constantine; and their royal infant was connected by some dark affinity of lineage or country with the Macedonian Alexander. No sooner was he born, than the cradle of Basil, his family, and his city, were swept away by an inundation of the Bulgarians: he was educated a slave in a foreign land; and in this severe discipline, he acquired the hardiness of body and flexibility of mind which promoted his future elevation. In the age of youth or manhood he shared the deliverance of the Roman captives, who generously broke their fetters, marched through Bulgaria to the shores of the Euxine, defeated two armies of Barbarians, embarked in the ships which had been stationed for their reception, and returned to Constantinople, from whence they were distributed to their respective homes. But the freedom of Basil was naked and destitute: his farm was ruined by the calamities of war: after his father's death, his manual labor, or service, could no longer support a family of orphans and he resolved to seek a more conspicuous theatre, in which every virtue and every vice may lead to the paths of greatness. The first night of his arrival at Constantinople, without friends or money, the weary pilgrim slept on the steps of the church of St. Diomede: he was fed by the casual hospitality of a monk; and was introduced to the service of a cousin and namesake of the emperor Theophilus; who, though himself of a diminutive person, was always followed by a train of tall and handsome domestics. Basil attended his patron to the government of Peloponnesus; eclipsed, by his personal merit the birth and dignity of Theophilus, and formed a useful connection with a wealthy and charitable matron of Patras. Her spiritual or carnal love embraced the young adventurer, whom she adopted as her son. Danielis presented him with thirty slaves; and the produce of her bounty was expended in the support of his brothers, and the purchase of some large estates in Macedonia. His gratitude or ambition still attached him to the service of Theophilus; and a lucky accident recommended him to the notice of the court. A famous wrestler, in the train of the Bulgarian ambassadors, had defied, at the royal banquet, the boldest and most robust of the Greeks. The strength of Basil was praised; he accepted the challenge; and the Barbarian champion was overthrown at the first onset. A beautiful but vicious horse was condemned to be hamstrung: it was subdued by the dexterity and courage of the servant of Theophilus; and his conqueror was promoted to an honorable rank in the Imperial stables. But it was impossible to obtain the confidence of Michael, without complying with his vices; and his new favorite, the great chamberlain of the palace, was raised and supported by a disgraceful marriage with a royal concubine, and the dishonor of his sister, who succeeded to her place. The public administration had been abandoned to the Caesar Bardas, the brother and enemy of Theodora; but the arts of female influence persuaded Michael to hate and to fear his uncle: he was drawn from Constantinople, under the pretence of a Cretan expedition, and stabbed in the tent of audience, by the sword of the chamberlain, and in the presence of the emperor. About a month after this execution, Basil was invested with the title of Augustus and the government of the empire. He supported this unequal association till his influence was fortified by popular esteem. His life was endangered by the caprice of the emperor; and his dignity was profaned by a second colleague, who had rowed in the galleys. Yet the murder of his benefactor must be condemned as an act of ingratitude and treason; and the churches which he dedicated to the name of St. Michael were a poor and puerile expiation of his guilt. The different ages of Basil the First may be compared with those of Augustus. The situation of the Greek did not allow him in his earliest youth to lead an army against his country; or to proscribe the nobles of her sons; but his aspiring genius stooped to the arts of a slave; he dissembled his ambition and even his virtues, and grasped, with the bloody hand of an assassin, the empire which he ruled with the wisdom and tenderness of a parent.

A private citizen may feel his interest repugnant to his duty; but it must be from a deficiency of sense or courage, that an absolute monarch can separate his happiness from his glory, or his glory from the public welfare. The life or panegyric of Basil has indeed been composed and published under the long reign of his descendants; but even their stability on the throne may be justly ascribed to the superior merit of their ancestor. In his character, his grandson Constantine has attempted to delineate a perfect image of royalty: but that feeble prince, unless he had copied a real model, could not easily have soared so high above the level of his own conduct or conceptions. But the most solid praise of Basil is drawn from the comparison of a ruined and a flourishing monarchy, that which he wrested from the dissolute Michael, and that which he bequeathed to the Mecedonian dynasty. The evils which had been sanctified by time and example, were corrected by his master-hand; and he revived, if not the national spirit, at least the order and majesty of the Roman empire. His application was indefatigable, his temper cool, his understanding vigorous and decisive; and in his practice he observed that rare and salutary moderation, which pursues each virtue, at an equal distance between the opposite vices. His military service had been confined to the palace: nor was the emperor endowed with the spirit or the talents of a warrior. Yet under his reign the Roman arms were again formidable to the Barbarians. As soon as he had formed a new army by discipline and exercise, he appeared in person on the banks of the Euphrates, curbed the pride of the Saracens, and suppressed the dangerous though just revolt of the Manichaeans. His indignation against a rebel who had long eluded his pursuit, provoked him to wish and to pray, that, by the grace of God, he might drive three arrows into the head of Chrysochir. That odious head, which had been obtained by treason rather than by valor, was suspended from a tree, and thrice exposed to the dexterity of the Imperial archer; a base revenge against the dead, more worthy of the times than of the character of Basil. But his principal merit was in the civil administration of the finances and of the laws. To replenish and exhausted treasury, it was proposed to resume the lavish and ill-placed gifts of his predecessor: his prudence abated one moiety of the restitution; and a sum of twelve hundred thousand pounds was instantly procured to answer the most pressing demands, and to allow some space for the mature operations of economy. Among the various schemes for the improvement of the revenue, a new mode was suggested of capitation, or tribute, which would have too much depended on the arbitrary discretion of the assessors. A sufficient list of honest and able agents was instantly produced by the minister; but on the more careful scrutiny of Basil himself, only two could be found, who might be safely intrusted with such dangerous powers; but they justified his esteem by declining his confidence. But the serious and successful diligence of the emperor established by degrees the equitable balance of property and payment, of receipt and expenditure; a peculiar fund was appropriated to each service; and a public method secured the interest of the prince and the property of the people. After reforming the luxury, he assigned two patrimonial estates to supply the decent plenty, of the Imperial table: the contributions of the subject were reserved for his defence; and the residue was employed in the embellishment of the capital and provinces. A taste for building, however costly, may deserve some praise and much excuse: from thence industry is fed, art is encouraged, and some object is attained of public emolument or pleasure: the use of a road, an aqueduct, or a hospital, is obvious and solid; and the hundred churches that arose by the command of Basil were consecrated to the devotion of the age. In the character of a judge he was assiduous and impartial; desirous to save, but not afraid to strike: the oppressors of the people were severely chastised; but his personal foes, whom it might be unsafe to pardon, were condemned, after the loss of their eyes, to a life of solitude and repentance. The change of language and manners demanded a revision of the obsolete jurisprudence of Justinian: the voluminous body of his Institutes, Pandects, Code, and Novels, was digested under forty titles, in the Greek idiom; and the Basilics, which were improved and completed by his son and grandson, must be referred to the original genius of the founder of their race. This glorious reign was terminated by an accident in the chase. A furious stag entangled his horns in the belt of Basil, and raised him from his horse: he was rescued by an attendant, who cut the belt and slew the animal; but the fall, or the fever, exhausted the strength of the aged monarch, and he expired in the palace amidst the tears of his family and people. If he struck off the head of the faithful servant for presuming to draw his sword against his sovereign, the pride of despotism, which had lain dormant in his life, revived in the last moments of despair, when he no longer wanted or valued the opinion of mankind.

Of the four sons of the emperor, Constantine died before his father, whose grief and credulity were amused by a flattering impostor and a vain apparition. Stephen, the youngest, was content with the honors of a patriarch and a saint; both Leo and Alexander were alike invested with the purple, but the powers of government were solely exercised by the elder brother. The name of Leo the Sixth has been dignified with the title of philosopher; and the union of the prince and the sage, of the active and speculative virtues, would indeed constitute the perfection of human nature. But the claims of Leo are far short of this ideal excellence. Did he reduce his passions and appetites under the dominion of reason? His life was spent in the pomp of the palace, in the society of his wives and concubines; and even the clemency which he showed, and the peace which he strove to preserve, must be imputed to the softness and indolence of his character. Did he subdue his prejudices, and those of his subjects? His mind was tinged with the most puerile superstition; the influence of the clergy, and the errors of the people, were consecrated by his laws; and the oracles of Leo, which reveal, in prophetic style, the fates of the empire, are founded on the arts of astrology and divination. If we still inquire the reason of his sage appellation, it can only be replied, that the son of Basil was less ignorant than the greater part of his contemporaries in church and state; that his education had been directed by the learned Photius; and that several books of profane and ecclesiastical science were composed by the pen, or in the name, of the Imperial philosopher. But the reputation of his philosophy and religion was overthrown by a domestic vice, the repetition of his nuptials. The primitive ideas of the merit and holiness of celibacy were preached by the monks and entertained by the Greeks. Marriage was allowed as a necessary means for the propagation of mankind; after the death of either party, the survivor might satisfy, by a second union, the weakness or the strength of the flesh: but a third marriage was censured as a state of legal fornication; and a fourth was a sin or scandal as yet unknown to the Christians of the East. In the beginning of his reign, Leo himself had abolished the state of concubines, and condemned, without annulling, third marriages: but his patriotism and love soon compelled him to violate his own laws, and to incur the penance, which in a similar case he had imposed on his subjects. In his three first alliances, his nuptial bed was unfruitful; the emperor required a female companion, and the empire a legitimate heir. The beautiful Zoe was introduced into the palace as a concubine; and after a trial of her fecundity, and the birth of Constantine, her lover declared his intention of legitimating the mother and the child, by the celebration of his fourth nuptials. But the patriarch Nicholas refused his blessing: the Imperial baptism of the young prince was obtained by a promise of separation; and the contumacious husband of Zoe was excluded from the communion of the faithful. Neither the fear of exile, nor the desertion of his brethren, nor the authority of the Latin church, nor the danger of failure or doubt in the succession to the empire, could bend the spirit of the inflexible monk. After the death of Leo, he was recalled from exile to the civil and ecclesiastical administration; and the edict of union which was promulgated in the name of Constantine, condemned the future scandal of fourth marriages, and left a tacit imputation on his own birth. In the Greek language, purple and porphyry are the same word: and as the colors of nature are invariable, we may learn, that a dark deep red was the Tyrian dye which stained the purple of the ancients. An apartment of the Byzantine palace was lined with porphyry: it was reserved for the use of the pregnant empresses; and the royal birth of their children was expressed by the appellation of porphyrogenite, or born in the purple. Several of the Roman princes had been blessed with an heir; but this peculiar surname was first applied to Constantine the Seventh. His life and titular reign were of equal duration; but of fifty-four years, six had elapsed before his father's death; and the son of Leo was ever the voluntary or reluctant subject of those who oppressed his weakness or abused his confidence. His uncle Alexander, who had long been invested with the title of Augustus, was the first colleague and governor of the young prince: but in a rapid career of vice and folly, the brother of Leo already emulated the reputation of Michael; and when he was extinguished by a timely death, he entertained a project of castrating his nephew, and leaving the empire to a worthless favorite. The succeeding years of the minority of Constantine were occupied by his mother Zoe, and a succession or council of seven regents, who pursued their interest, gratified their passions, abandoned the republic, supplanted each other, and finally vanished in the presence of a soldier. From an obscure origin, Romanus Lecapenus had raised himself to the command of the naval armies; and in the anarchy of the times, had deserved, or at least had obtained, the national esteem. With a victorious and affectionate fleet, he sailed from the mouth of the Danube into the harbor of Constantinople, and was hailed as the deliverer of the people, and the guardian of the prince. His supreme office was at first defined by the new appellation of father of the emperor; but Romanus soon disdained the subordinate powers of a minister, and assumed with the titles of Caesar and Augustus, the full independence of royalty, which he held near five-and-twenty years. His three sons, Christopher, Stephen, and Constantine were successively adorned with the same honors, and the lawful emperor was degraded from the first to the fifth rank in this college of princes. Yet, in the preservation of his life and crown, he might still applaud his own fortune and the clemency of the usurper. The examples of ancient and modern history would have excused the ambition of Romanus: the powers and the laws of the empire were in his hand; the spurious birth of Constantine would have justified his exclusion; and the grave or the monastery was open to receive the son of the concubine. But Lecapenus does not appear to have possessed either the virtues or the vices of a tyrant. The spirit and activity of his private life dissolved away in the sunshine of the throne; and in his licentious pleasures, he forgot the safety both of the republic and of his family. Of a mild and religious character, he respected the sanctity of oaths, the innocence of the youth, the memory of his parents, and the attachment of the people. The studious temper and retirement of Constantine disarmed the jealousy of power: his books and music, his pen and his pencil, were a constant source of amusement; and if he could improve a scanty allowance by the sale of his pictures, if their price was not enhanced by the name of the artist, he was endowed with a personal talent, which few princes could employ in the hour of adversity.

The fall of Romanus was occasioned by his own vices and those of his children. After the decease of Christopher, his eldest son, the two surviving brothers quarrelled with each other, and conspired against their father. At the hour of noon, when all strangers were regularly excluded from the palace, they entered his apartment with an armed force, and conveyed him, in the habit of a monk, to a small island in the Propontis, which was peopled by a religious community. The rumor of this domestic revolution excited a tumult in the city; but Porphyrogenitus alone, the true and lawful emperor, was the object of the public care; and the sons of Lecapenus were taught, by tardy experience, that they had achieved a guilty and perilous enterprise for the benefit of their rival. Their sister Helena, the wife of Constantine, revealed, or supposed, their treacherous design of assassinating her husband at the royal banquet. His loyal adherents were alarmed, and the two usurpers were prevented, seized, degraded from the purple, and embarked for the same island and monastery where their father had been so lately confined. Old Romanus met them on the beach with a sarcastic smile, and, after a just reproach of their folly and ingratitude, presented his Imperial colleagues with an equal share of his water and vegetable diet. In the fortieth year of his reign, Constantine the Seventh obtained the possession of the Eastern world, which he ruled or seemed to rule, near fifteen years. But he was devoid of that energy of character which could emerge into a life of action and glory; and the studies, which had amused and dignified his leisure, were incompatible with the serious duties of a sovereign. The emperor neglected the practice to instruct his son Romanus in the theory of government; while he indulged the habits of intemperance and sloth, he dropped the reins of the administration into the hands of Helena his wife; and, in the shifting scene of her favor and caprice, each minister was regretted in the promotion of a more worthless successor. Yet the birth and misfortunes of Constantine had endeared him to the Greeks; they excused his failings; they respected his learning, his innocence, and charity, his love of justice; and the ceremony of his funeral was mourned with the unfeigned tears of his subjects. The body, according to ancient custom, lay in state in the vestibule of the palace; and the civil and military officers, the patricians, the senate, and the clergy approached in due order to adore and kiss the inanimate corpse of their sovereign. Before the procession moved towards the Imperial sepulchre, a herald proclaimed this awful admonition: "Arise, O king of the world, and obey the summons of the King of kings!"

The death of Constantine was imputed to poison; and his son Romanus, who derived that name from his maternal grandfather, ascended the throne of Constantinople. A prince who, at the age of twenty, could be suspected of anticipating his inheritance, must have been already lost in the public esteem; yet Romanus was rather weak than wicked; and the largest share of the guilt was transferred to his wife, Theophano, a woman of base origin masculine spirit, and flagitious manners. The sense of personal glory and public happiness, the true pleasures of royalty, were unknown to the son of Constantine; and, while the two brothers, Nicephorus and Leo, triumphed over the Saracens, the hours which the emperor owed to his people were consumed in strenuous idleness. In the morning he visited the circus; at noon he feasted the senators; the greater part of the afternoon he spent in the sphoeristerium, or tennis-court, the only theatre of his victories; from thence he passed over to the Asiatic side of the Bosphorus, hunted and killed four wild boars of the largest size, and returned to the palace, proudly content with the labors of the day. In strength and beauty he was conspicuous above his equals: tall and straight as a young cypress, his complexion was fair and florid, his eyes sparkling, his shoulders broad, his nose long and aquiline. Yet even these perfections were insufficient to fix the love of Theophano; and, after a reign of four [1013] years, she mingled for her husband the same deadly draught which she had composed for his father.

[Footnote 1013: Three years and five months. Leo Diaconus in Niebuhr. Byz p. 50—M.]

By his marriage with this impious woman, Romanus the younger left two sons, Basil the Second and Constantine the Ninth, and two daughters, Theophano and Anne. The eldest sister was given to Otho the Second, emperor of the West; the younger became the wife of Wolodomir, great duke and apostle of russia, and by the marriage of her granddaughter with Henry the First, king of France, the blood of the Macedonians, and perhaps of the Arsacides, still flows in the veins of the Bourbon line. After the death of her husband, the empress aspired to reign in the name of her sons, the elder of whom was five, and the younger only two, years of age; but she soon felt the instability of a throne which was supported by a female who could not be esteemed, and two infants who could not be feared. Theophano looked around for a protector, and threw herself into the arms of the bravest soldier; her heart was capacious; but the deformity of the new favorite rendered it more than probable that interest was the motive and excuse of her love. Nicephorus Phocus united, in the popular opinion, the double merit of a hero and a saint. In the former character, his qualifications were genuine and splendid: the descendant of a race illustrious by their military exploits, he had displayed in every station and in every province the courage of a soldier and the conduct of a chief; and Nicephorus was crowned with recent laurels, from the important conquest of the Isle of Crete. His religion was of a more ambiguous cast; and his hair-cloth, his fasts, his pious idiom, and his wish to retire from the business of the world, were a convenient mask for his dark and dangerous ambition. Yet he imposed on a holy patriarch, by whose influence, and by a decree of the senate, he was intrusted, during the minority of the young princes, with the absolute and independent command of the Oriental armies. As soon as he had secured the leaders and the troops, he boldly marched to Constantinople, trampled on his enemies, avowed his correspondence with the empress, and without degrading her sons, assumed, with the title of Augustus, the preeminence of rank and the plenitude of power. But his marriage with Theophano was refused by the same patriarch who had placed the crown on his head: by his second nuptials he incurred a year of canonical penance; [1014] a bar of spiritual affinity was opposed to their celebration; and some evasion and perjury were required to silence the scruples of the clergy and people. The popularity of the emperor was lost in the purple: in a reign of six years he provoked the hatred of strangers and subjects: and the hypocrisy and avarice of the first Nicephorus were revived in his successor. Hypocrisy I shall never justify or palliate; but I will dare to observe, that the odious vice of avarice is of all others most hastily arraigned, and most unmercifully condemned. In a private citizen, our judgment seldom expects an accurate scrutiny into his fortune and expense; and in a steward of the public treasure, frugality is always a virtue, and the increase of taxes too often an indispensable duty. In the use of his patrimony, the generous temper of Nicephorus had been proved; and the revenue was strictly applied to the service of the state: each spring the emperor marched in person against the Saracens; and every Roman might compute the employment of his taxes in triumphs, conquests, and the security of the Eastern barrier. [1015]

[Footnote 1014: The canonical objection to the marriage was his relation of Godfather sons. Leo Diac. p. 50—M.]

[Footnote 1015: He retook Antioch, and brought home as a trophy the sword of "the most unholy and impious Mahomet." Leo Diac. p. 76—M.]

PART IV

Among the warriors who promoted his elevation, and served under his standard, a noble and valiant Armenian had deserved and obtained the most eminent rewards. The stature of John Zimisces was below the ordinary standard: but this diminutive body was endowed with strength, beauty, and the soul of a hero. By the jealousy of the emperor's brother, he was degraded from the office of general of the East, to that of director of the posts, and his murmurs were chastised with disgrace and exile. But Zimisces was ranked among the numerous lovers of the empress: on her intercession, he was permitted to reside at Chalcedon, in the neighborhood of the capital: her bounty was repaid in his clandestine and amorous visits to the palace; and Theophano consented, with alacrity, to the death of an ugly and penurious husband. Some bold and trusty conspirators were concealed in her most private chambers: in the darkness of a winter night, Zimisces, with his principal companions, embarked in a small boat, traversed the Bosphorus, landed at the palace stairs, and silently ascended a ladder of ropes, which was cast down by the female attendants. Neither his own suspicions, nor the warnings of his friends, nor the tardy aid of his brother Leo, nor the fortress which he had erected in the palace, could protect Nicephorus from a domestic foe, at whose voice every door was open to the assassins. As he slept on a bear-skin on the ground, he was roused by their noisy intrusion, and thirty daggers glittered before his eyes. It is doubtful whether Zimisces imbrued his hands in the blood of his sovereign; but he enjoyed the inhuman spectacle of revenge. [1016] The murder was protracted by insult and cruelty: and as soon as the head of Nicephorus was shown from the window, the tumult was hushed, and the Armenian was emperor of the East. On the day of his coronation, he was stopped on the threshold of St. Sophia, by the intrepid patriarch; who charged his conscience with the deed of treason and blood; and required, as a sign of repentance, that he should separate himself from his more criminal associate. This sally of apostolic zeal was not offensive to the prince, since he could neither love nor trust a woman who had repeatedly violated the most sacred obligations; and Theophano, instead of sharing his imperial fortune, was dismissed with ignominy from his bed and palace. In their last interview, she displayed a frantic and impotent rage; accused the ingratitude of her lover; assaulted, with words and blows, her son Basil, as he stood silent and submissive in the presence of a superior colleague; and avowed her own prostitution in proclaiming the illegitimacy of his birth. The public indignation was appeased by her exile, and the punishment of the meaner accomplices: the death of an unpopular prince was forgiven; and the guilt of Zimisces was forgotten in the splendor of his virtues. Perhaps his profusion was less useful to the state than the avarice of Nicephorus; but his gentle and generous behavior delighted all who approached his person; and it was only in the paths of victory that he trod in the footsteps of his predecessor. The greatest part of his reign was employed in the camp and the field: his personal valor and activity were signalized on the Danube and the Tigris, the ancient boundaries of the Roman world; and by his double triumph over the Russians and the Saracens, he deserved the titles of savior of the empire, and conqueror of the East. In his last return from Syria, he observed that the most fruitful lands of his new provinces were possessed by the eunuchs. "And is it for them," he exclaimed, with honest indignation, "that we have fought and conquered? Is it for them that we shed our blood, and exhaust the treasures of our people?" The complaint was reechoed to the palace, and the death of Zimisces is strongly marked with the suspicion of poison.

[Footnote 1016: According to Leo Diaconus, Zimisces, after ordering the wounded emperor to be dragged to his feet, and heaping him with insult, to which the miserable man only replied by invoking the name of the "mother of God," with his own hand plucked his beard, while his accomplices beat out his teeth with the hilts of their swords, and then trampling him to the ground, drove his sword into his skull. Leo Diac, in Niebuhr Byz. Hist. l vii. c. 8. p. 88—M.]

Under this usurpation, or regency, of twelve years, the two lawful emperors, Basil and Constantine, had silently grown to the age of manhood. Their tender years had been incapable of dominion: the respectful modesty of their attendance and salutation was due to the age and merit of their guardians; the childless ambition of those guardians had no temptation to violate their right of succession: their patrimony was ably and faithfully administered; and the premature death of Zimisces was a loss, rather than a benefit, to the sons of Romanus. Their want of experience detained them twelve years longer the obscure and voluntary pupils of a minister, who extended his reign by persuading them to indulge the pleasures of youth, and to disdain the labors of government. In this silken web, the weakness of Constantine was forever entangled; but his elder brother felt the impulse of genius and the desire of action; he frowned, and the minister was no more. Basil was the acknowledged sovereign of Constantinople and the provinces of Europe; but Asia was oppressed by two veteran generals, Phocas and Sclerus, who, alternately friends and enemies, subjects and rebels, maintained their independence, and labored to emulate the example of successful usurpation. Against these domestic enemies the son of Romanus first drew his sword, and they trembled in the presence of a lawful and high-spirited prince. The first, in the front of battle, was thrown from his horse, by the stroke of poison, or an arrow; the second, who had been twice loaded with chains, [1017] and twice invested with the purple, was desirous of ending in peace the small remainder of his days. As the aged suppliant approached the throne, with dim eyes and faltering steps, leaning on his two attendants, the emperor exclaimed, in the insolence of youth and power, "And is this the man who has so long been the object of our terror?" After he had confirmed his own authority, and the peace of the empire, the trophies of Nicephorus and Zimisces would not suffer their royal pupil to sleep in the palace. His long and frequent expeditions against the Saracens were rather glorious than useful to the empire; but the final destruction of the kingdom of Bulgaria appears, since the time of Belisarius, the most important triumph of the Roman arms. Yet, instead of applauding their victorious prince, his subjects detested the rapacious and rigid avarice of Basil; and in the imperfect narrative of his exploits, we can only discern the courage, patience, and ferociousness of a soldier. A vicious education, which could not subdue his spirit, had clouded his mind; he was ignorant of every science; and the remembrance of his learned and feeble grandsire might encourage his real or affected contempt of laws and lawyers, of artists and arts. Of such a character, in such an age, superstition took a firm and lasting possession; after the first license of his youth, Basil the Second devoted his life, in the palace and the camp, to the penance of a hermit, wore the monastic habit under his robes and armor, observed a vow of continence, and imposed on his appetites a perpetual abstinence from wine and flesh. In the sixty-eighth year of his age, his martial spirit urged him to embark in person for a holy war against the Saracens of Sicily; he was prevented by death, and Basil, surnamed the Slayer of the Bulgarians, was dismissed from the world with the blessings of the clergy and the curse of the people. After his decease, his brother Constantine enjoyed, about three years, the power, or rather the pleasures, of royalty; and his only care was the settlement of the succession. He had enjoyed sixty-six years the title of Augustus; and the reign of the two brothers is the longest, and most obscure, of the Byzantine history.

[Footnote 1017: Once by the caliph, once by his rival Phocas. Compare De Beau l. p. 176—M.]

A lineal succession of five emperors, in a period of one hundred and sixty years, had attached the loyalty of the Greeks to the Macedonian dynasty, which had been thrice respected by the usurpers of their power. After the death of Constantine the Ninth, the last male of the royal race, a new and broken scene presents itself, and the accumulated years of twelve emperors do not equal the space of his single reign. His elder brother had preferred his private chastity to the public interest, and Constantine himself had only three daughters; Eudocia, who took the veil, and Zoe and Theodora, who were preserved till a mature age in a state of ignorance and virginity. When their marriage was discussed in the council of their dying father, the cold or pious Theodora refused to give an heir to the empire, but her sister Zoe presented herself a willing victim at the altar. Romanus Argyrus, a patrician of a graceful person and fair reputation, was chosen for her husband, and, on his declining that honor, was informed, that blindness or death was the second alternative. The motive of his reluctance was conjugal affection but his faithful wife sacrificed her own happiness to his safety and greatness; and her entrance into a monastery removed the only bar to the Imperial nuptials. After the decease of Constantine, the sceptre devolved to Romanus the Third; but his labors at home and abroad were equally feeble and fruitless; and the mature age, the forty-eight years of Zoe, were less favorable to the hopes of pregnancy than to the indulgence of pleasure. Her favorite chamberlain was a handsome Paphlagonian of the name of Michael, whose first trade had been that of a money-changer; and Romanus, either from gratitude or equity, connived at their criminal intercourse, or accepted a slight assurance of their innocence. But Zoe soon justified the Roman maxim, that every adulteress is capable of poisoning her husband; and the death of Romanus was instantly followed by the scandalous marriage and elevation of Michael the Fourth. The expectations of Zoe were, however, disappointed: instead of a vigorous and grateful lover, she had placed in her bed a miserable wretch, whose health and reason were impaired by epileptic fits, and whose conscience was tormented by despair and remorse. The most skilful physicians of the mind and body were summoned to his aid; and his hopes were amused by frequent pilgrimages to the baths, and to the tombs of the most popular saints; the monks applauded his penance, and, except restitution, (but to whom should he have restored?) Michael sought every method of expiating his guilt. While he groaned and prayed in sackcloth and ashes, his brother, the eunuch John, smiled at his remorse, and enjoyed the harvest of a crime of which himself was the secret and most guilty author. His administration was only the art of satiating his avarice, and Zoe became a captive in the palace of her fathers, and in the hands of her slaves. When he perceived the irretrievable decline of his brother's health, he introduced his nephew, another Michael, who derived his surname of Calaphates from his father's occupation in the careening of vessels: at the command of the eunuch, Zoe adopted for her son the son of a mechanic; and this fictitious heir was invested with the title and purple of the Caesars, in the presence of the senate and clergy. So feeble was the character of Zoe, that she was oppressed by the liberty and power which she recovered by the death of the Paphlagonian; and at the end of four days, she placed the crown on the head of Michael the Fifth, who had protested, with tears and oaths, that he should ever reign the first and most obedient of her subjects.

The only act of his short reign was his base ingratitude to his benefactors, the eunuch and the empress. The disgrace of the former was pleasing to the public: but the murmurs, and at length the clamors, of Constantinople deplored the exile of Zoe, the daughter of so many emperors; her vices were forgotten, and Michael was taught, that there is a period in which the patience of the tamest slaves rises into fury and revenge. The citizens of every degree assembled in a formidable tumult which lasted three days; they besieged the palace, forced the gates, recalled their mothers, Zoe from her prison, Theodora from her monastery, and condemned the son of Calaphates to the loss of his eyes or of his life. For the first time the Greeks beheld with surprise the two royal sisters seated on the same throne, presiding in the senate, and giving audience to the ambassadors of the nations. But the singular union subsisted no more than two months; the two sovereigns, their tempers, interests, and adherents, were secretly hostile to each other; and as Theodora was still averse to marriage, the indefatigable Zoe, at the age of sixty, consented, for the public good, to sustain the embraces of a third husband, and the censures of the Greek church. His name and number were Constantine the Tenth, and the epithet of Monomachus, the single combatant, must have been expressive of his valor and victory in some public or private quarrel. But his health was broken by the tortures of the gout, and his dissolute reign was spent in the alternative of sickness and pleasure. A fair and noble widow had accompanied Constantine in his exile to the Isle of Lesbos, and Sclerena gloried in the appellation of his mistress. After his marriage and elevation, she was invested with the title and pomp of Augusta, and occupied a contiguous apartment in the palace. The lawful consort (such was the delicacy or corruption of Zoe) consented to this strange and scandalous partition; and the emperor appeared in public between his wife and his concubine. He survived them both; but the last measures of Constantine to change the order of succession were prevented by the more vigilant friends of Theodora; and after his decease, she resumed, with the general consent, the possession of her inheritance. In her name, and by the influence of four eunuchs, the Eastern world was peaceably governed about nineteen months; and as they wished to prolong their dominion, they persuaded the aged princess to nominate for her successor Michael the Sixth. The surname of Stratioticus declares his military profession; but the crazy and decrepit veteran could only see with the eyes, and execute with the hands, of his ministers. Whilst he ascended the throne, Theodora sunk into the grave; the last of the Macedonian or Basilian dynasty. I have hastily reviewed, and gladly dismiss, this shameful and destructive period of twenty-eight years, in which the Greeks, degraded below the common level of servitude, were transferred like a herd of cattle by the choice or caprice of two impotent females.

From this night of slavery, a ray of freedom, or at least of spirit, begins to emerge: the Greeks either preserved or revived the use of surnames, which perpetuate the fame of hereditary virtue: and we now discern the rise, succession, and alliances of the last dynasties of Constantinople and Trebizond. The Comneni, who upheld for a while the fate of the sinking empire, assumed the honor of a Roman origin: but the family had been long since transported from Italy to Asia. Their patrimonial estate was situate in the district of Castamona, in the neighborhood of the Euxine; and one of their chiefs, who had already entered the paths of ambition, revisited with affection, perhaps with regret, the modest though honorable dwelling of his fathers. The first of their line was the illustrious Manuel, who in the reign of the second Basil, contributed by war and treaty to appease the troubles of the East: he left, in a tender age, two sons, Isaac and John, whom, with the consciousness of desert, he bequeathed to the gratitude and favor of his sovereign. The noble youths were carefully trained in the learning of the monastery, the arts of the palace, and the exercises of the camp: and from the domestic service of the guards, they were rapidly promoted to the command of provinces and armies. Their fraternal union doubled the force and reputation of the Comneni, and their ancient nobility was illustrated by the marriage of the two brothers, with a captive princess of Bulgaria, and the daughter of a patrician, who had obtained the name of Charon from the number of enemies whom he had sent to the infernal shades. The soldiers had served with reluctant loyalty a series of effeminate masters; the elevation of Michael the Sixth was a personal insult to the more deserving generals; and their discontent was inflamed by the parsimony of the emperor and the insolence of the eunuchs. They secretly assembled in the sanctuary of St. Sophia, and the votes of the military synod would have been unanimous in favor of the old and valiant Catacalon, if the patriotism or modesty of the veteran had not suggested the importance of birth as well as merit in the choice of a sovereign. Isaac Comnenus was approved by general consent, and the associates separated without delay to meet in the plains of Phrygia at the head of their respective squadrons and detachments. The cause of Michael was defended in a single battle by the mercenaries of the Imperial guard, who were aliens to the public interest, and animated only by a principle of honor and gratitude. After their defeat, the fears of the emperor solicited a treaty, which was almost accepted by the moderation of the Comnenian. But the former was betrayed by his ambassadors, and the latter was prevented by his friends. The solitary Michael submitted to the voice of the people; the patriarch annulled their oath of allegiance; and as he shaved the head of the royal monk, congratulated his beneficial exchange of temporal royalty for the kingdom of heaven; an exchange, however, which the priest, on his own account, would probably have declined. By the hands of the same patriarch, Isaac Comnenus was solemnly crowned; the sword which he inscribed on his coins might be an offensive symbol, if it implied his title by conquest; but this sword would have been drawn against the foreign and domestic enemies of the state. The decline of his health and vigor suspended the operation of active virtue; and the prospect of approaching death determined him to interpose some moments between life and eternity. But instead of leaving the empire as the marriage portion of his daughter, his reason and inclination concurred in the preference of his brother John, a soldier, a patriot, and the father of five sons, the future pillars of an hereditary succession. His first modest reluctance might be the natural dictates of discretion and tenderness, but his obstinate and successful perseverance, however it may dazzle with the show of virtue, must be censured as a criminal desertion of his duty, and a rare offence against his family and country. The purple which he had refused was accepted by Constantine Ducas, a friend of the Comnenian house, and whose noble birth was adorned with the experience and reputation of civil policy. In the monastic habit, Isaac recovered his health, and survived two years his voluntary abdication. At the command of his abbot, he observed the rule of St. Basil, and executed the most servile offices of the convent: but his latent vanity was gratified by the frequent and respectful visits of the reigning monarch, who revered in his person the character of a benefactor and a saint. If Constantine the Eleventh were indeed the subject most worthy of empire, we must pity the debasement of the age and nation in which he was chosen. In the labor of puerile declamations he sought, without obtaining, the crown of eloquence, more precious, in his opinion, than that of Rome; and in the subordinate functions of a judge, he forgot the duties of a sovereign and a warrior. Far from imitating the patriotic indifference of the authors of his greatness, Ducas was anxious only to secure, at the expense of the republic, the power and prosperity of his children. His three sons, Michael the Seventh, Andronicus the First, and Constantine the Twelfth, were invested, in a tender age, with the equal title of Augustus; and the succession was speedily opened by their father's death. His widow, Eudocia, was intrusted with the administration; but experience had taught the jealousy of the dying monarch to protect his sons from the danger of her second nuptials; and her solemn engagement, attested by the principal senators, was deposited in the hands of the patriarch. Before the end of seven months, the wants of Eudocia, or those of the state, called aloud for the male virtues of a soldier; and her heart had already chosen Romanus Diogenes, whom she raised from the scaffold to the throne. The discovery of a treasonable attempt had exposed him to the severity of the laws: his beauty and valor absolved him in the eyes of the empress; and Romanus, from a mild exile, was recalled on the second day to the command of the Oriental armies.

Her royal choice was yet unknown to the public; and the promise which would have betrayed her falsehood and levity, was stolen by a dexterous emissary from the ambition of the patriarch. Xiphilin at first alleged the sanctity of oaths, and the sacred nature of a trust; but a whisper, that his brother was the future emperor, relaxed his scruples, and forced him to confess that the public safety was the supreme law. He resigned the important paper; and when his hopes were confounded by the nomination of Romanus, he could no longer regain his security, retract his declarations, nor oppose the second nuptials of the empress. Yet a murmur was heard in the palace; and the Barbarian guards had raised their battle-axes in the cause of the house of Lucas, till the young princes were soothed by the tears of their mother and the solemn assurances of the fidelity of their guardian, who filled the Imperial station with dignity and honor. Hereafter I shall relate his valiant, but unsuccessful, efforts to resist the progress of the Turks. His defeat and captivity inflicted a deadly wound on the Byzantine monarchy of the East; and after he was released from the chains of the sultan, he vainly sought his wife and his subjects. His wife had been thrust into a monastery, and the subjects of Romanus had embraced the rigid maxim of the civil law, that a prisoner in the hands of the enemy is deprived, as by the stroke of death, of all the public and private rights of a citizen. In the general consternation, the Caesar John asserted the indefeasible right of his three nephews: Constantinople listened to his voice: and the Turkish captive was proclaimed in the capital, and received on the frontier, as an enemy of the republic. Romanus was not more fortunate in domestic than in foreign war: the loss of two battles compelled him to yield, on the assurance of fair and honorable treatment; but his enemies were devoid of faith or humanity; and, after the cruel extinction of his sight, his wounds were left to bleed and corrupt, till in a few days he was relieved from a state of misery. Under the triple reign of the house of Ducas, the two younger brothers were reduced to the vain honors of the purple; but the eldest, the pusillanimous Michael, was incapable of sustaining the Roman sceptre; and his surname of Parapinaces denotes the reproach which he shared with an avaricious favorite, who enhanced the price, and diminished the measure, of wheat. In the school of Psellus, and after the example of his mother, the son of Eudocia made some proficiency in philosophy and rhetoric; but his character was degraded, rather than ennobled, by the virtues of a monk and the learning of a sophist. Strong in the contempt of their sovereign and their own esteem, two generals, at the head of the European and Asiatic legions, assumed the purple at Adrianople and Nice. Their revolt was in the same months; they bore the same name of Nicephorus; but the two candidates were distinguished by the surnames of Bryennius and Botaniates; the former in the maturity of wisdom and courage, the latter conspicuous only by the memory of his past exploits. While Botaniates advanced with cautious and dilatory steps, his active competitor stood in arms before the gates of Constantinople. The name of Bryennius was illustrious; his cause was popular; but his licentious troops could not be restrained from burning and pillaging a suburb; and the people, who would have hailed the rebel, rejected and repulsed the incendiary of his country. This change of the public opinion was favorable to Botaniates, who at length, with an army of Turks, approached the shores of Chalcedon. A formal invitation, in the name of the patriarch, the synod, and the senate, was circulated through the streets of Constantinople; and the general assembly, in the dome of St. Sophia, debated, with order and calmness, on the choice of their sovereign. The guards of Michael would have dispersed this unarmed multitude; but the feeble emperor, applauding his own moderation and clemency, resigned the ensigns of royalty, and was rewarded with the monastic habit, and the title of Archbishop of Ephesus. He left a son, a Constantine, born and educated in the purple; and a daughter of the house of Ducas illustrated the blood, and confirmed the succession, of the Comnenian dynasty.

John Comnenus, the brother of the emperor Isaac, survived in peace and dignity his generous refusal of the sceptre. By his wife Anne, a woman of masculine spirit and a policy, he left eight children: the three daughters multiplied the Comnenian alliance with the noblest of the Greeks: of the five sons, Manuel was stopped by a premature death; Isaac and Alexius restored the Imperial greatness of their house, which was enjoyed without toil or danger by the two younger brethren, Adrian and Nicephorus. Alexius, the third and most illustrious of the brothers was endowed by nature with the choicest gifts both of mind and body: they were cultivated by a liberal education, and exercised in the school of obedience and adversity. The youth was dismissed from the perils of the Turkish war, by the paternal care of the emperor Romanus: but the mother of the Comneni, with her aspiring face, was accused of treason, and banished, by the sons of Ducas, to an island in the Propontis. The two brothers soon emerged into favor and action, fought by each other's side against the rebels and Barbarians, and adhered to the emperor Michael, till he was deserted by the world and by himself. In his first interview with Botaniates, "Prince," said Alexius with a noble frankness, "my duty rendered me your enemy; the decrees of God and of the people have made me your subject. Judge of my future loyalty by my past opposition." The successor of Michael entertained him with esteem and confidence: his valor was employed against three rebels, who disturbed the peace of the empire, or at least of the emperors. Ursel, Bryennius, and Basilacius, were formidable by their numerous forces and military fame: they were successively vanquished in the field, and led in chains to the foot of the throne; and whatever treatment they might receive from a timid and cruel court, they applauded the clemency, as well as the courage, of their conqueror. But the loyalty of the Comneni was soon tainted by fear and suspicion; nor is it easy to settle between a subject and a despot, the debt of gratitude, which the former is tempted to claim by a revolt, and the latter to discharge by an executioner. The refusal of Alexius to march against a fourth rebel, the husband of his sister, destroyed the merit or memory of his past services: the favorites of Botaniates provoked the ambition which they apprehended and accused; and the retreat of the two brothers might be justified by the defence of their life and liberty. The women of the family were deposited in a sanctuary, respected by tyrants: the men, mounted on horseback, sallied from the city, and erected the standard of civil war. The soldiers who had been gradually assembled in the capital and the neighborhood, were devoted to the cause of a victorious and injured leader: the ties of common interest and domestic alliance secured the attachment of the house of Ducas; and the generous dispute of the Comneni was terminated by the decisive resolution of Isaac, who was the first to invest his younger brother with the name and ensigns of royalty. They returned to Constantinople, to threaten rather than besiege that impregnable fortress; but the fidelity of the guards was corrupted; a gate was surprised, and the fleet was occupied by the active courage of George Palaeologus, who fought against his father, without foreseeing that he labored for his posterity. Alexius ascended the throne; and his aged competitor disappeared in a monastery. An army of various nations was gratified with the pillage of the city; but the public disorders were expiated by the tears and fasts of the Comneni, who submitted to every penance compatible with the possession of the empire. The life of the emperor Alexius has been delineated by a favorite daughter, who was inspired by a tender regard for his person and a laudable zeal to perpetuate his virtues. Conscious of the just suspicions of her readers, the princess Anna Comnena repeatedly protests, that, besides her personal knowledge, she had searched the discourses and writings of the most respectable veterans: and after an interval of thirty years, forgotten by, and forgetful of, the world, her mournful solitude was inaccessible to hope and fear; and that truth, the naked perfect truth, was more dear and sacred than the memory of her parent. Yet, instead of the simplicity of style and narrative which wins our belief, an elaborate affectation of rhetoric and science betrays in every page the vanity of a female author. The genuine character of Alexius is lost in a vague constellation of virtues; and the perpetual strain of panegyric and apology awakens our jealousy, to question the veracity of the historian and the merit of the hero. We cannot, however, refuse her judicious and important remark, that the disorders of the times were the misfortune and the glory of Alexius; and that every calamity which can afflict a declining empire was accumulated on his reign by the justice of Heaven and the vices of his predecessors. In the East, the victorious Turks had spread, from Persia to the Hellespont, the reign of the Koran and the Crescent: the West was invaded by the adventurous valor of the Normans; and, in the moments of peace, the Danube poured forth new swarms, who had gained, in the science of war, what they had lost in the ferociousness of manners. The sea was not less hostile than the land; and while the frontiers were assaulted by an open enemy, the palace was distracted with secret treason and conspiracy. On a sudden, the banner of the Cross was displayed by the Latins; Europe was precipitated on Asia; and Constantinople had almost been swept away by this impetuous deluge. In the tempest, Alexius steered the Imperial vessel with dexterity and courage. At the head of his armies, he was bold in action, skilful in stratagem, patient of fatigue, ready to improve his advantages, and rising from his defeats with inexhaustible vigor. The discipline of the camp was revived, and a new generation of men and soldiers was created by the example and precepts of their leader. In his intercourse with the Latins, Alexius was patient and artful: his discerning eye pervaded the new system of an unknown world and I shall hereafter describe the superior policy with which he balanced the interests and passions of the champions of the first crusade. In a long reign of thirty-seven years, he subdued and pardoned the envy of his equals: the laws of public and private order were restored: the arts of wealth and science were cultivated: the limits of the empire were enlarged in Europe and Asia; and the Comnenian sceptre was transmitted to his children of the third and fourth generation. Yet the difficulties of the times betrayed some defects in his character; and have exposed his memory to some just or ungenerous reproach. The reader may possibly smile at the lavish praise which his daughter so often bestows on a flying hero: the weakness or prudence of his situation might be mistaken for a want of personal courage; and his political arts are branded by the Latins with the names of deceit and dissimulation. The increase of the male and female branches of his family adorned the throne, and secured the succession; but their princely luxury and pride offended the patricians, exhausted the revenue, and insulted the misery of the people. Anna is a faithful witness that his happiness was destroyed, and his health was broken, by the cares of a public life; the patience of Constantinople was fatigued by the length and severity of his reign; and before Alexius expired, he had lost the love and reverence of his subjects. The clergy could not forgive his application of the sacred riches to the defence of the state; but they applauded his theological learning and ardent zeal for the orthodox faith, which he defended with his tongue, his pen, and his sword. His character was degraded by the superstition of the Greeks; and the same inconsistent principle of human nature enjoined the emperor to found a hospital for the poor and infirm, and to direct the execution of a heretic, who was burned alive in the square of St. Sophia. Even the sincerity of his moral and religious virtues was suspected by the persons who had passed their lives in his familiar confidence. In his last hours, when he was pressed by his wife Irene to alter the succession, he raised his head, and breathed a pious ejaculation on the vanity of this world. The indignant reply of the empress may be inscribed as an epitaph on his tomb, "You die, as you have lived—A Hypocrite!"

It was the wish of Irene to supplant the eldest of her surviving sons, in favor of her daughter the princess Anne whose philosophy would not have refused the weight of a diadem. But the order of male succession was asserted by the friends of their country; the lawful heir drew the royal signet from the finger of his insensible or conscious father and the empire obeyed the master of the palace. Anna Comnena was stimulated by ambition and revenge to conspire against the life of her brother, and when the design was prevented by the fears or scruples of her husband, she passionately exclaimed that nature had mistaken the two sexes, and had endowed Bryennius with the soul of a woman. The two sons of Alexius, John and Isaac, maintained the fraternal concord, the hereditary virtue of their race, and the younger brother was content with the title of Sebastocrator, which approached the dignity, without sharing the power, of the emperor. In the same person the claims of primogeniture and merit were fortunately united; his swarthy complexion, harsh features, and diminutive stature, had suggested the ironical surname of Calo-Johannes, or John the Handsome, which his grateful subjects more seriously applied to the beauties of his mind. After the discovery of her treason, the life and fortune of Anne were justly forfeited to the laws. Her life was spared by the clemency of the emperor; but he visited the pomp and treasures of her palace, and bestowed the rich confiscation on the most deserving of his friends. That respectable friend Axuch, a slave of Turkish extraction, presumed to decline the gift, and to intercede for the criminal: his generous master applauded and imitated the virtue of his favorite, and the reproach or complaint of an injured brother was the only chastisement of the guilty princess. After this example of clemency, the remainder of his reign was never disturbed by conspiracy or rebellion: feared by his nobles, beloved by his people, John was never reduced to the painful necessity of punishing, or even of pardoning, his personal enemies. During his government of twenty-five years, the penalty of death was abolished in the Roman empire, a law of mercy most delightful to the humane theorist, but of which the practice, in a large and vicious community, is seldom consistent with the public safety. Severe to himself, indulgent to others, chaste, frugal, abstemious, the philosophic Marcus would not have disdained the artless virtues of his successor, derived from his heart, and not borrowed from the schools. He despised and moderated the stately magnificence of the Byzantine court, so oppressive to the people, so contemptible to the eye of reason. Under such a prince, innocence had nothing to fear, and merit had every thing to hope; and, without assuming the tyrannic office of a censor, he introduced a gradual though visible reformation in the public and private manners of Constantinople. The only defect of this accomplished character was the frailty of noble minds, the love of arms and military glory. Yet the frequent expeditions of John the Handsome may be justified, at least in their principle, by the necessity of repelling the Turks from the Hellespont and the Bosphorus. The sultan of Iconium was confined to his capital, the Barbarians were driven to the mountains, and the maritime provinces of Asia enjoyed the transient blessings of their deliverance. From Constantinople to Antioch and Aleppo, he repeatedly marched at the head of a victorious army, and in the sieges and battles of this holy war, his Latin allies were astonished by the superior spirit and prowess of a Greek. As he began to indulge the ambitious hope of restoring the ancient limits of the empire, as he revolved in his mind, the Euphrates and Tigris, the dominion of Syria, and the conquest of Jerusalem, the thread of his life and of the public felicity was broken by a singular accident. He hunted the wild boar in the valley of Anazarbus, and had fixed his javelin in the body of the furious animal; but in the struggle a poisoned arrow dropped from his quiver, and a slight wound in his hand, which produced a mortification, was fatal to the best and greatest of the Comnenian princes.

PART V

A premature death had swept away the two eldest sons of John the Handsome; of the two survivors, Isaac and Manuel, his judgment or affection preferred the younger; and the choice of their dying prince was ratified by the soldiers, who had applauded the valor of his favorite in the Turkish war The faithful Axuch hastened to the capital, secured the person of Isaac in honorable confinement, and purchased, with a gift of two hundred pounds of silver, the leading ecclesiastics of St. Sophia, who possessed a decisive voice in the consecration of an emperor. With his veteran and affectionate troops, Manuel soon visited Constantinople; his brother acquiesced in the title of Sebastocrator; his subjects admired the lofty stature and martial graces of their new sovereign, and listened with credulity to the flattering promise, that he blended the wisdom of age with the activity and vigor of youth. By the experience of his government, they were taught, that he emulated the spirit, and shared the talents, of his father whose social virtues were buried in the grave. A reign of thirty seven years is filled by a perpetual though various warfare against the Turks, the Christians, and the hordes of the wilderness beyond the Danube. The arms of Manuel were exercised on Mount Taurus, in the plains of Hungary, on the coast of Italy and Egypt, and on the seas of Sicily and Greece: the influence of his negotiations extended from Jerusalem to Rome and Russia; and the Byzantine monarchy, for a while, became an object of respect or terror to the powers of Asia and Europe. Educated in the silk and purple of the East, Manuel possessed the iron temper of a soldier, which cannot easily be paralleled, except in the lives of Richard the First of England, and of Charles the Twelfth of Sweden. Such was his strength and exercise in arms, that Raymond, surnamed the Hercules of Antioch, was incapable of wielding the lance and buckler of the Greek emperor. In a famous tournament, he entered the lists on a fiery courser, and overturned in his first career two of the stoutest of the Italian knights. The first in the charge, the last in the retreat, his friends and his enemies alike trembled, the former for his safety, and the latter for their own. After posting an ambuscade in a wood, he rode forwards in search of some perilous adventure, accompanied only by his brother and the faithful Axuch, who refused to desert their sovereign. Eighteen horsemen, after a short combat, fled before them: but the numbers of the enemy increased; the march of the reenforcement was tardy and fearful, and Manuel, without receiving a wound, cut his way through a squadron of five hundred Turks. In a battle against the Hungarians, impatient of the slowness of his troops, he snatched a standard from the head of the column, and was the first, almost alone, who passed a bridge that separated him from the enemy. In the same country, after transporting his army beyond the Save, he sent back the boats, with an order under pain of death, to their commander, that he should leave him to conquer or die on that hostile land. In the siege of Corfu, towing after him a captive galley, the emperor stood aloft on the poop, opposing against the volleys of darts and stones, a large buckler and a flowing sail; nor could he have escaped inevitable death, had not the Sicilian admiral enjoined his archers to respect the person of a hero. In one day, he is said to have slain above forty of the Barbarians with his own hand; he returned to the camp, dragging along four Turkish prisoners, whom he had tied to the rings of his saddle: he was ever the foremost to provoke or to accept a single combat; and the gigantic champions, who encountered his arm, were transpierced by the lance, or cut asunder by the sword, of the invincible Manuel. The story of his exploits, which appear as a model or a copy of the romances of chivalry, may induce a reasonable suspicion of the veracity of the Greeks: I will not, to vindicate their credit, endanger my own: yet I may observe, that, in the long series of their annals, Manuel is the only prince who has been the subject of similar exaggeration. With the valor of a soldier, he did no unite the skill or prudence of a general; his victories were not productive of any permanent or useful conquest; and his Turkish laurels were blasted in his last unfortunate campaign, in which he lost his army in the mountains of Pisidia, and owed his deliverance to the generosity of the sultan. But the most singular feature in the character of Manuel, is the contrast and vicissitude of labor and sloth, of hardiness and effeminacy. In war he seemed ignorant of peace, in peace he appeared incapable of war. In the field he slept in the sun or in the snow, tired in the longest marches the strength of his men and horses, and shared with a smile the abstinence or diet of the camp. No sooner did he return to Constantinople, than he resigned himself to the arts and pleasures of a life of luxury: the expense of his dress, his table, and his palace, surpassed the measure of his predecessors, and whole summer days were idly wasted in the delicious isles of the Propontis, in the incestuous love of his niece Theodora. The double cost of a warlike and dissolute prince exhausted the revenue, and multiplied the taxes; and Manuel, in the distress of his last Turkish campaign, endured a bitter reproach from the mouth of a desperate soldier. As he quenched his thirst, he complained that the water of a fountain was mingled with Christian blood. "It is not the first time," exclaimed a voice from the crowd, "that you have drank, O emperor, the blood of your Christian subjects." Manuel Comnenus was twice married, to the virtuous Bertha or Irene of Germany, and to the beauteous Maria, a French or Latin princess of Antioch. The only daughter of his first wife was destined for Bela, a Hungarian prince, who was educated at Constantinople under the name of Alexius; and the consummation of their nuptials might have transferred the Roman sceptre to a race of free and warlike Barbarians. But as soon as Maria of Antioch had given a son and heir to the empire, the presumptive rights of Bela were abolished, and he was deprived of his promised bride; but the Hungarian prince resumed his name and the kingdom of his fathers, and displayed such virtues as might excite the regret and envy of the Greeks. The son of Maria was named Alexius; and at the age of ten years he ascended the Byzantine throne, after his father's decease had closed the glories of the Comnenian line.

The fraternal concord of the two sons of the great Alexius had been sometimes clouded by an opposition of interest and passion. By ambition, Isaac the Sebastocrator was excited to flight and rebellion, from whence he was reclaimed by the firmness and clemency of John the Handsome. The errors of Isaac, the father of the emperors of Trebizond, were short and venial; but John, the elder of his sons, renounced forever his religion. Provoked by a real or imaginary insult of his uncle, he escaped from the Roman to the Turkish camp: his apostasy was rewarded with the sultan's daughter, the title of Chelebi, or noble, and the inheritance of a princely estate; and in the fifteenth century, Mahomet the Second boasted of his Imperial descent from the Comnenian family. Andronicus, the younger brother of John, son of Isaac, and grandson of Alexius Comnenus, is one of the most conspicuous characters of the age; and his genuine adventures might form the subject of a very singular romance. To justify the choice of three ladies of royal birth, it is incumbent on me to observe, that their fortunate lover was cast in the best proportions of strength and beauty; and that the want of the softer graces was supplied by a manly countenance, a lofty stature, athletic muscles, and the air and deportment of a soldier. The preservation, in his old age, of health and vigor, was the reward of temperance and exercise. A piece of bread and a draught of water was often his sole and evening repast; and if he tasted of a wild boar or a stag, which he had roasted with his own hands, it was the well-earned fruit of a laborious chase. Dexterous in arms, he was ignorant of fear; his persuasive eloquence could bend to every situation and character of life, his style, though not his practice, was fashioned by the example of St. Paul; and, in every deed of mischief, he had a heart to resolve, a head to contrive, and a hand to execute. In his youth, after the death of the emperor John, he followed the retreat of the Roman army; but, in the march through Asia Minor, design or accident tempted him to wander in the mountains: the hunter was encompassed by the Turkish huntsmen, and he remained some time a reluctant or willing captive in the power of the sultan. His virtues and vices recommended him to the favor of his cousin: he shared the perils and the pleasures of Manuel; and while the emperor lived in public incest with his niece Theodora, the affections of her sister Eudocia were seduced and enjoyed by Andronicus. Above the decencies of her sex and rank, she gloried in the name of his concubine; and both the palace and the camp could witness that she slept, or watched, in the arms of her lover. She accompanied him to his military command of Cilicia, the first scene of his valor and imprudence. He pressed, with active ardor, the siege of Mopsuestia: the day was employed in the boldest attacks; but the night was wasted in song and dance; and a band of Greek comedians formed the choicest part of his retinue. Andronicus was surprised by the sally of a vigilant foe; but, while his troops fled in disorder, his invincible lance transpierced the thickest ranks of the Armenians. On his return to the Imperial camp in Macedonia, he was received by Manuel with public smiles and a private reproof; but the duchies of Naissus, Braniseba, and Castoria, were the reward or consolation of the unsuccessful general. Eudocia still attended his motions: at midnight, their tent was suddenly attacked by her angry brothers, impatient to expiate her infamy in his blood: his daring spirit refused her advice, and the disguise of a female habit; and, boldly starting from his couch, he drew his sword, and cut his way through the numerous assassins. It was here that he first betrayed his ingratitude and treachery: he engaged in a treasonable correspondence with the king of Hungary and the German emperor; approached the royal tent at a suspicious hour with a drawn sword, and under the mask of a Latin soldier, avowed an intention of revenge against a mortal foe; and imprudently praised the fleetness of his horse as an instrument of flight and safety. The monarch dissembled his suspicions; but, after the close of the campaign, Andronicus was arrested and strictly confined in a tower of the palace of Constantinople.

In this prison he was left about twelve years; a most painful restraint, from which the thirst of action and pleasure perpetually urged him to escape. Alone and pensive, he perceived some broken bricks in a corner of the chamber, and gradually widened the passage, till he had explored a dark and forgotten recess. Into this hole he conveyed himself, and the remains of his provisions, replacing the bricks in their former position, and erasing with care the footsteps of his retreat. At the hour of the customary visit, his guards were amazed by the silence and solitude of the prison, and reported, with shame and fear, his incomprehensible flight. The gates of the palace and city were instantly shut: the strictest orders were despatched into the provinces, for the recovery of the fugitive; and his wife, on the suspicion of a pious act, was basely imprisoned in the same tower. At the dead of night she beheld a spectre; she recognized her husband: they shared their provisions; and a son was the fruit of these stolen interviews, which alleviated the tediousness of their confinement. In the custody of a woman, the vigilance of the keepers was insensibly relaxed; and the captive had accomplished his real escape, when he was discovered, brought back to Constantinople, and loaded with a double chain. At length he found the moment, and the means, of his deliverance. A boy, his domestic servant, intoxicated the guards, and obtained in wax the impression of the keys. By the diligence of his friends, a similar key, with a bundle of ropes, was introduced into the prison, in the bottom of a hogshead. Andronicus employed, with industry and courage, the instruments of his safety, unlocked the doors, descended from the tower, concealed himself all day among the bushes, and scaled in the night the garden-wall of the palace. A boat was stationed for his reception: he visited his own house, embraced his children, cast away his chain, mounted a fleet horse, and directed his rapid course towards the banks of the Danube. At Anchialus in Thrace, an intrepid friend supplied him with horses and money: he passed the river, traversed with speed the desert of Moldavia and the Carpathian hills, and had almost reached the town of Halicz, in the

Polish Russia, when he was intercepted by a party of Walachians, who resolved to convey their important captive to Constantinople. His presence of mind again extricated him from danger. Under the pretence of sickness, he dismounted in the night, and was allowed to step aside from the troop: he planted in the ground his long staff, clothed it with his cap and upper garment; and, stealing into the wood, left a phantom to amuse, for some time, the eyes of the Walachians. From Halicz he was honorably conducted to Kiow, the residence of the great duke: the subtle Greek soon obtained the esteem and confidence of Ieroslaus; his character could assume the manners of every climate; and the Barbarians applauded his strength and courage in the chase of the elks and bears of the forest. In this northern region he deserved the forgiveness of Manuel, who solicited the Russian prince to join his arms in the invasion of Hungary. The influence of Andronicus achieved this important service: his private treaty was signed with a promise of fidelity on one side, and of oblivion on the other; and he marched, at the head of the Russian cavalry, from the Borysthenes to the Danube. In his resentment Manuel had ever sympathized with the martial and dissolute character of his cousin; and his free pardon was sealed in the assault of Zemlin, in which he was second, and second only, to the valor of the emperor.

No sooner was the exile restored to freedom and his country, than his ambition revived, at first to his own, and at length to the public, misfortune. A daughter of Manuel was a feeble bar to the succession of the more deserving males of the Comnenian blood; her future marriage with the prince of Hungary was repugnant to the hopes or prejudices of the princes and nobles. But when an oath of allegiance was required to the presumptive heir, Andronicus alone asserted the honor of the Roman name, declined the unlawful engagement, and boldly protested against the adoption of a stranger. His patriotism was offensive to the emperor, but he spoke the sentiments of the people, and was removed from the royal presence by an honorable banishment, a second command of the Cilician frontier, with the absolute disposal of the revenues of Cyprus. In this station the Armenians again exercised his courage and exposed his negligence; and the same rebel, who baffled all his operations, was unhorsed, and almost slain by the vigor of his lance. But Andronicus soon discovered a more easy and pleasing conquest, the beautiful Philippa, sister of the empress Maria, and daughter of Raymond of Poitou, the Latin prince of Antioch. For her sake he deserted his station, and wasted the summer in balls and tournaments: to his love she sacrificed her innocence, her reputation, and the offer of an advantageous marriage. But the resentment of Manuel for this domestic affront interrupted his pleasures: Andronicus left the indiscreet princess to weep and to repent; and, with a band of desperate adventurers, undertook the pilgrimage of Jerusalem. His birth, his martial renown, and professions of zeal, announced him as the champion of the Cross: he soon captivated both the clergy and the king; and the Greek prince was invested with the lordship of Berytus, on the coast of Phoenicia.

In his neighborhood resided a young and handsome queen, of his own nation and family, great-granddaughter of the emperor Alexis, and widow of Baldwin the Third, king of Jerusalem. She visited and loved her kinsman. Theodora was the third victim of his amorous seduction; and her shame was more public and scandalous than that of her predecessors. The emperor still thirsted for revenge; and his subjects and allies of the Syrian frontier were repeatedly pressed to seize the person, and put out the eyes, of the fugitive. In Palestine he was no longer safe; but the tender Theodora revealed his danger, and accompanied his flight. The queen of Jerusalem was exposed to the East, his obsequious concubine; and two illegitimate children were the living monuments of her weakness. Damascus was his first refuge; and, in the characters of the great Noureddin and his servant Saladin, the superstitious Greek might learn to revere the virtues of the Mussulmans. As the friend of Noureddin he visited, most probably, Bagdad, and the courts of Persia; and, after a long circuit round the Caspian Sea and the mountains of Georgia, he finally settled among the Turks of Asia Minor, the hereditary enemies of his country. The sultan of Colonia afforded a hospitable retreat to Andronicus, his mistress, and his band of outlaws: the debt of gratitude was paid by frequent inroads in the Roman province of Trebizond; and he seldom returned without an ample harvest of spoil and of Christian captives. In the story of his adventures, he was fond of comparing himself to David, who escaped, by a long exile, the snares of the wicked. But the royal prophet (he presumed to add) was content to lurk on the borders of Judaea, to slay an Amalekite, and to threaten, in his miserable state, the life of the avaricious Nabal. The excursions of the Comnenian prince had a wider range; and he had spread over the Eastern world the glory of his name and religion.

By a sentence of the Greek church, the licentious rover had been separated from the faithful; but even this excommunication may prove, that he never abjured the profession of Chistianity.

His vigilance had eluded or repelled the open and secret persecution of the emperor; but he was at length insnared by the captivity of his female companion. The governor of Trebizond succeeded in his attempt to surprise the person of Theodora: the queen of Jerusalem and her two children were sent to Constantinople, and their loss imbittered the tedious solitude of banishment. The fugitive implored and obtained a final pardon, with leave to throw himself at the feet of his sovereign, who was satisfied with the submission of this haughty spirit. Prostrate on the ground, he deplored with tears and groans the guilt of his past rebellion; nor would he presume to arise, unless some faithful subject would drag him to the foot of the throne, by an iron chain with which he had secretly encircled his neck. This extraordinary penance excited the wonder and pity of the assembly; his sins were forgiven by the church and state; but the just suspicion of Manuel fixed his residence at a distance from the court, at Oenoe, a town of Pontus, surrounded with rich vineyards, and situate on the coast of the Euxine. The death of Manuel, and the disorders of the minority, soon opened the fairest field to his ambition. The emperor was a boy of twelve or fourteen years of age, without vigor, or wisdom, or experience: his mother, the empress Mary, abandoned her person and government to a favorite of the Comnenian name; and his sister, another Mary, whose husband, an Italian, was decorated with the title of Caesar, excited a conspiracy, and at length an insurrection, against her odious step-mother. The provinces were forgotten, the capital was in flames, and a century of peace and order was overthrown in the vice and weakness of a few months. A civil war was kindled in Constantinople; the two factions fought a bloody battle in the square of the palace, and the rebels sustained a regular siege in the cathedral of St. Sophia. The patriarch labored with honest zeal to heal the wounds of the republic, the most respectable patriots called aloud for a guardian and avenger, and every tongue repeated the praise of the talents and even the virtues of Andronicus. In his retirement, he affected to revolve the solemn duties of his oath: "If the safety or honor of the Imperial family be threatened, I will reveal and oppose the mischief to the utmost of my power." His correspondence with the patriarch and patricians was seasoned with apt quotations from the Psalms of David and the epistles of St. Paul; and he patiently waited till he was called to her deliverance by the voice of his country. In his march from Oenoe to Constantinople, his slender train insensibly swelled to a crowd and an army: his professions of religion and loyalty were mistaken for the language of his heart; and the simplicity of a foreign dress, which showed to advantage his majestic stature, displayed a lively image of his poverty and exile. All opposition sunk before him; he reached the straits of the Thracian Bosphorus; the Byzantine navy sailed from the harbor to receive and transport the savior of the empire: the torrent was loud and irresistible, and the insects who had basked in the sunshine of royal favor disappeared at the blast of the storm. It was the first care of Andronicus to occupy the palace, to salute the emperor, to confine his mother, to punish her minister, and to restore the public order and tranquillity. He then visited the sepulchre of Manuel: the spectators were ordered to stand aloof, but as he bowed in the attitude of prayer, they heard, or thought they heard, a murmur of triumph or revenge: "I no longer fear thee, my old enemy, who hast driven me a vagabond to every climate of the earth. Thou art safety deposited under a seven-fold dome, from whence thou canst never arise till the signal of the last trumpet. It is now my turn, and speedily will I trample on thy ashes and thy posterity." From his subsequent tyranny we may impute such feelings to the man and the moment; but it is not extremely probable that he gave an articulate sound to his secret thoughts. In the first months of his administration, his designs were veiled by a fair semblance of hypocrisy, which could delude only the eyes of the multitude; the coronation of Alexius was performed with due solemnity, and his perfidious guardian, holding in his hands the body and blood of Christ, most fervently declared that he lived, and was ready to die, for the service of his beloved pupil. But his numerous adherents were instructed to maintain, that the sinking empire must perish in the hands of a child, that the Romans could only be saved by a veteran prince, bold in arms, skilful in policy, and taught to reign by the long experience of fortune and mankind; and that it was the duty of every citizen to force the reluctant modesty of Andronicus to undertake the burden of the public care. The young emperor was himself constrained to join his voice to the general acclamation, and to solicit the association of a colleague, who instantly degraded him from the supreme rank, secluded his person, and verified the rash declaration of the patriarch, that Alexius might be considered as dead, so soon as he was committed to the custody of his guardian. But his death was preceded by the imprisonment and execution of his mother. After blackening her reputation, and inflaming against her the passions of the multitude, the tyrant accused and tried the empress for a treasonable correspondence with the king of Hungary. His own son, a youth of honor and humanity, avowed his abhorrence of this flagitious act, and three of the judges had the merit of preferring their conscience to their safety: but the obsequious tribunal, without requiring any reproof, or hearing any defence, condemned the widow of Manuel; and her unfortunate son subscribed the sentence of her death. Maria was strangled, her corpse was buried in the sea, and her memory was wounded by the insult most offensive to female vanity, a false and ugly representation of her beauteous form. The fate of her son was not long deferred: he was strangled with a bowstring; and the tyrant, insensible to pity or remorse, after surveying the body of the innocent youth, struck it rudely with his foot: "Thy father," he cried, "was a knave, thy mother a whore, and thyself a fool!"

The Roman sceptre, the reward of his crimes, was held by Andronicus about three years and a half as the guardian or sovereign of the empire. His government exhibited a singular contrast of vice and virtue. When he listened to his passions, he was the scourge; when he consulted his reason, the father, of his people. In the exercise of private justice, he was equitable and rigorous: a shameful and pernicious venality was abolished, and the offices were filled with the most deserving candidates, by a prince who had sense to choose, and severity to punish. He prohibited the inhuman practice of pillaging the goods and persons of shipwrecked mariners; the provinces, so long the objects of oppression or neglect, revived in prosperity and plenty; and millions applauded the distant blessings of his reign, while he was cursed by the witnesses of his daily cruelties. The ancient proverb, That bloodthirsty is the man who returns from banishment to power, had been applied, with too much truth, to 'Marius and Tiberius; and was now verified for the third time in the life of Andronicus. His memory was stored with a black list of the enemies and rivals, who had traduced his merit, opposed his greatness, or insulted his misfortunes; and the only comfort of his exile was the sacred hope and promise of revenge. The necessary extinction of the young emperor and his mother imposed the fatal obligation of extirpating the friends, who hated, and might punish, the assassin; and the repetition of murder rendered him less willing, and less able, to forgive. [1018] A horrid narrative of the victims whom he sacrificed by poison or the sword, by the sea or the flames, would be less expressive of his cruelty than the appellation of the halcyon days, which was applied to a rare and bloodless week of repose: the tyrant strove to transfer, on the laws and the judges, some portion of his guilt; but the mask was fallen, and his subjects could no longer mistake the true author of their calamities. The noblest of the Greeks, more especially those who, by descent or alliance, might dispute the Comnenian inheritance, escaped from the monster's den: Nice and Prusa, Sicily or Cyprus, were their places of refuge; and as their flight was already criminal, they aggravated their offence by an open revolt, and the Imperial title. Yet Andronicus resisted the daggers and swords of his most formidable enemies: Nice and Prusa were reduced and chastised: the Sicilians were content with the sack of Thessalonica; and the distance of Cyprus was not more propitious to the rebel than to the tyrant. His throne was subverted by a rival without merit, and a people without arms. Isaac Angelus, a descendant in the female line from the great Alexius, was marked as a victim by the prudence or superstition of the emperor. [1019] In a moment of despair, Angelus defended his life and liberty, slew the executioner, and fled to the church of St. Sophia. The sanctuary was insensibly filled with a curious and mournful crowd, who, in his fate, prognosticated their own. But their lamentations were soon turned to curses, and their curses to threats: they dared to ask, "Why do we fear? why do we obey? We are many, and he is one: our patience is the only bond of our slavery." With the dawn of day the city burst into a general sedition, the prisons were thrown open, the coldest and most servile were roused to the defence of their country, and Isaac, the second of the name, was raised from the sanctuary to the throne. Unconscious of his danger, the tyrant was absent; withdrawn from the toils of state, in the delicious islands of the Propontis. He had contracted an indecent marriage with Alice, or Agnes, daughter of Lewis the Seventh, of France, and relict of the unfortunate Alexius; and his society, more suitable to his temper than to his age, was composed of a young wife and a favorite concubine. On the first alarm, he rushed to Constantinople, impatient for the blood of the guilty; but he was astonished by the silence of the palace, the tumult of the city, and the general desertion of mankind. Andronicus proclaimed a free pardon to his subjects; they neither desired, nor would grant, forgiveness; he offered to resign the crown to his son Manuel; but the virtues of the son could not expiate his father's crimes. The sea was still open for his retreat; but the news of the revolution had flown along the coast; when fear had ceased, obedience was no more: the Imperial galley was pursued and taken by an armed brigantine; and the tyrant was dragged to the presence of Isaac Angelus, loaded with fetters, and a long chain round his neck. His eloquence, and the tears of his female companions, pleaded in vain for his life; but, instead of the decencies of a legal execution, the new monarch abandoned the criminal to the numerous sufferers, whom he had deprived of a father, a husband, or a friend. His teeth and hair, an eye and a hand, were torn from him, as a poor compensation for their loss: and a short respite was allowed, that he might feel the bitterness of death. Astride on a camel, without any danger of a rescue, he was carried through the city, and the basest of the populace rejoiced to trample on the fallen majesty of their prince. After a thousand blows and outrages, Andronicus was hung by the feet, between two pillars, that supported the statues of a wolf and an a sow; and every hand that could reach the public enemy, inflicted on his body some mark of ingenious or brutal cruelty, till two friendly or furious Italians, plunging their swords into his body, released him from all human punishment. In this long and painful agony, "Lord, have mercy upon me!" and "Why will you bruise a broken reed?" were the only words that escaped from his mouth. Our hatred for the tyrant is lost in pity for the man; nor can we blame his pusillanimous resignation, since a Greek Christian was no longer master of his life.

[Footnote 1018: Fallmerayer (Geschichte des Kaiserthums von Trapezunt, p. 29, 33) has highly drawn the character of Andronicus. In his view the extermination of the Byzantine factions and dissolute nobility was part of a deep-laid and splendid plan for the regeneration of the empire. It was necessary for the wise and benevolent schemes of the father of his people to lop off those limbs which were infected with irremediable pestilence— "and with necessity, The tyrant's plea, excused his devilish deeds!!"—Still the fall of Andronicus was a fatal blow to the Byzantine empire—M.]

[Footnote 1019: According to Nicetas, (p. 444,) Andronicus despised the imbecile Isaac too much to fear him; he was arrested by the officious zeal of Stephen, the instrument of the Emperor's cruelties—M.]

I have been tempted to expatiate on the extraordinary character and adventures of Andronicus; but I shall here terminate the series of the Greek emperors since the time of Heraclius. The branches that sprang from the Comnenian trunk had insensibly withered; and the male line was continued only in the posterity of Andronicus himself, who, in the public confusion, usurped the sovereignty of Trebizond, so obscure in history, and so famous in romance. A private citizen of Philadelphia, Constantine Angelus, had emerged to wealth and honors, by his marriage with a daughter of the emperor Alexius. His son Andronicus is conspicuous only by his cowardice. His grandson Isaac punished and succeeded the tyrant; but he was dethroned by his own vices, and the ambition of his brother; and their discord introduced the Latins to the conquest of Constantinople, the first great period in the fall of the Eastern empire.

If we compute the number and duration of the reigns, it will be found, that a period of six hundred years is filled by sixty emperors, including in the Augustan list some female sovereigns; and deducting some usurpers who were never acknowledged in the capital, and some princes who did not live to possess their inheritance. The average proportion will allow ten years for each emperor, far below the chronological rule of Sir Isaac Newton, who, from the experience of more recent and regular monarchies, has defined about eighteen or twenty years as the term of an ordinary reign. The Byzantine empire was most tranquil and prosperous when it could acquiesce in hereditary succession; five dynasties, the Heraclian, Isaurian, Amorian, Basilian, and Comnenian families, enjoyed and transmitted the royal patrimony during their respective series of five, four, three, six, and four generations; several princes number the years of their reign with those of their infancy; and Constantine the Seventh and his two grandsons occupy the space of an entire century. But in the intervals of the Byzantine dynasties, the succession is rapid and broken, and the name of a successful candidate is speedily erased by a more fortunate competitor. Many were the paths that led to the summit of royalty: the fabric of rebellion was overthrown by the stroke of conspiracy, or undermined by the silent arts of intrigue: the favorites of the soldiers or people, of the senate or clergy, of the women and eunuchs, were alternately clothed with the purple: the means of their elevation were base, and their end was often contemptible or tragic. A being of the nature of man, endowed with the same faculties, but with a longer measure of existence, would cast down a smile of pity and contempt on the crimes and follies of human ambition, so eager, in a narrow span, to grasp at a precarious and shortlived enjoyment. It is thus that the experience of history exalts and enlarges the horizon of our intellectual view. In a composition of some days, in a perusal of some hours, six hundred years have rolled away, and the duration of a life or reign is contracted to a fleeting moment: the grave is ever beside the throne: the success of a criminal is almost instantly followed by the loss of his prize and our immortal reason survives and disdains the sixty phantoms of kings who have passed before our eyes, and faintly dwell on our remembrance. The observation that, in every age and climate, ambition has prevailed with the same commanding energy, may abate the surprise of a philosopher: but while he condemns the vanity, he may search the motive, of this universal desire to obtain and hold the sceptre of dominion. To the greater part of the Byzantine series, we cannot reasonably ascribe the love of fame and of mankind. The virtue alone of John Comnenus was beneficent and pure: the most illustrious of the princes, who procede or follow that respectable name, have trod with some dexterity and vigor the crooked and bloody paths of a selfish policy: in scrutinizing the imperfect characters of Leo the Isaurian, Basil the First, and Alexius Comnenus, of Theophilus, the second Basil, and Manuel Comnenus, our esteem and censure are almost equally balanced; and the remainder of the Imperial crowd could only desire and expect to be forgotten by posterity. Was personal happiness the aim and object of their ambition? I shall not descant on the vulgar topics of the misery of kings; but I may surely observe, that their condition, of all others, is the most pregnant with fear, and the least susceptible of hope. For these opposite passions, a larger scope was allowed in the revolutions of antiquity, than in the smooth and solid temper of the modern world, which cannot easily repeat either the triumph of Alexander or the fall of Darius. But the peculiar infelicity of the Byzantine princes exposed them to domestic perils, without affording any lively promise of foreign conquest. From the pinnacle of greatness, Andronicus was precipitated by a death more cruel and shameful than that of the malefactor; but the most glorious of his predecessors had much more to dread from their subjects than to hope from their enemies. The army was licentious without spirit, the nation turbulent without freedom: the Barbarians of the East and West pressed on the monarchy, and the loss of the provinces was terminated by the final servitude of the capital.

The entire series of Roman emperors, from the first of the Caesars to the last of the Constantines, extends above fifteen hundred years: and the term of dominion, unbroken by foreign conquest, surpasses the measure of the ancient monarchies; the Assyrians or Medes, the successors of Cyrus, or those of Alexander.

EDWARD GIBBON – A SHORT BIOGRAPHY

Edward Gibbon was born on 8th May, 1737, the son of Edward and Judith Gibbon at Lime Grove, in the town of Putney, Surrey. He had six siblings, all of whom died in infancy. His grandfather, also named Edward, had lost everything as a result of the South Sea Bubble collapse in 1720, but eventually regained much of his wealth, so that Gibbon's father was able to inherit a substantial estate.

As a youth, Gibbon's health was under constant threat. He described himself as "a puny child, neglected by my Mother, starved by my nurse". At age nine, he was sent to Dr. Woddeson's school at Kingston-upon-Thames, shortly after which his mother died. He was then moved to the Westminster School boarding house, owned by his adored "Aunt Kitty", Catherine Porten.

By 1751, Gibbon's reading was already extensive and certainly pointed toward his future pursuits having covered such works as Laurence Echard's Roman History (1713), William Howell's An Institution of General History (1680–85), and several of the 65 volumes of the acclaimed Universal History from the Earliest Account of Time (1747–1768).

Following a stay at Bath, at age 15, in 1752 to improve his health, Gibbon was sent by his father to Magdalen College, Oxford, where he was enrolled as a gentleman-commoner (a rank of student above commoners i.e. normal students who paid the normal rate for tuition and boarding but below noblemen. They paid double the tuition fee and enjoyed more privileges). He was ill-suited, however, to the college atmosphere and later rued his 14 months there as the "most idle and unprofitable" of his life. Because of his autobiography, it used to be thought that his penchant for "theological controversy" (his aunt's influence) fully bloomed when he came under the spell of the deist or rationalist theologian Conyers Middleton, the author of Free Inquiry into the Miraculous Powers (1749). In that tract, Middleton denied the validity of such powers; Gibbon promptly objected, or so the argument used to run. The product of that disagreement, with some assistance from the work of Catholic Bishop Jacques-Bénigne Bossuet, and that of the Elizabethan Jesuit Robert Parsons, yielded the most memorable event of his time at Oxford: his conversion to Roman Catholicism on 8th June 1753. He was further 'corrupted' by the 'free thinking' deism of the playwright/poet couple David and Lucy Mallet; and finally Gibbon's father, already deeply in despair, had had enough.

However, this story has fallen somewhat into disrepute only being introduced to the final draft of Gibbon's "Memoirs" in 1792–93. There are also other accounts as to why Gibbons may have given a new 'backstory' to his conversion.

Within weeks of his conversion, the Gibbons was removed from Oxford and sent to live under the care and tutelage of Daniel Pavillard, Reformed pastor of Lausanne in Switzerland.

Here he made great friendships with Jacques Georges Deyverdun (the French-language translator of Goethe's The Sorrows of Young Werther), and John Baker Holroyd (later Lord Sheffield).

Just a year and a half later, after his father threatened to disinherit him, on Christmas Day, 1754, he reconverted to Protestantism. "The various articles of the Romish creed," he wrote, "disappeared like a dream".

He remained in Lausanne for five intellectually productive years, a period that greatly enriched Gibbon's already immense aptitude for scholarship and erudition: he read Latin literature; travelled throughout Switzerland studying its cantons' constitutions; and studied the works of Hugo Grotius, Samuel von Pufendorf, John Locke, Pierre Bayle, and Blaise Pascal.

He also met the one love in his life: the daughter of the pastor of Crassy; Suzanne Curchod. As the two developed an ever-closer relationship; Gibbon raised the question of marriage, but ultimately wedlock was out of the question, blocked both by his father's staunch disapproval and Curchod's refusal to leave Switzerland.

Gibbon returned to England in August 1758 to face his father. There was to be no refusal of his wishes. Gibbon put it rather poetically: "I sighed as a lover, I obeyed as a son." He proceeded to cut off all contact with Suzanne, even as she vowed to wait for him.

Upon his return to England, Gibbon published his first book, Essai sur l'Étude de la Littérature in 1761, which produced an initial taste of celebrity and distinguished him, in Paris at least, as a man of letters.

Interestingly to add to his interests and talents he had, from 1759 to 1770, served on active duty and then in reserve with the South Hampshire militia, his deactivation in December 1762 coinciding with the militia's dispersal after the Seven Years' War.

In 1763, he began as many men of privilege of class then did to round out and embellish their education on the Grand Tour, which included a visit to Rome. In his autobiography Gibbon vividly records his rapture when he finally neared "the great object of my pilgrimage": ...at the distance of twenty-five years I can neither forget nor express the strong emotions which agitated my mind as I first approached and entered the eternal City. After a sleepless night, I trod, with a lofty step the ruins of the Forum; each memorable spot where Romulus stood, or Tully spoke, or Caesar fell, was at once present to my eye; and several days of intoxication were lost or enjoyed before I could descend to a cool and minute investigation.

And it was here that Gibbon first conceived the idea of composing a history of the city, later extended to the entire empire, a moment known to history as the Capitoline vision: "It was at Rome, on the 15th of October 1764, as I sat musing amidst the ruins of the Capitol, while the barefooted fryars were singing

Vespers in the temple of Jupiter, that the idea of writing the decline and fall of the City first started to my mind".

In June 1765, Gibbon returned to his father's house. He would remain there for the following five years until his father's death. He always considered this span of time as the worst of his life. He busied himself with various writing projects which failed to reach fruition. His first historical narrative, the History of Switzerland, was neither published nor finished. Gibbon had become too self-critical and abandoned the work a mere 60 pages in.

His second work, Memoires Litteraires de la Grande Bretagne, in two volumes, described both the literary and the social conditions of England at the time. When published it failed to gain any traction.

With the death of his father and the settling of the estate Gibbon had enough of a legacy to be free of any financial problems. He moved to Bentinck Street in London and began to live the life that suited him. He joined a number of clubs, including Dr. Johnson's Literary Club. He succeeded Oliver Goldsmith at the Royal Academy as 'professor in ancient history' (honorary but nonetheless prestigious). And he was writing. The work for which he would gain worldwide fame was under way.

But still other interests would divert his attention.

In late 1774, he was initiated a freemason of the Premier Grand Lodge of England. That same year he was returned to Parliament for the seat of Liskeard in Cornwall through the intervention of his relative and patron, Edward Eliot. Gibbon became a typical backbencher, mute and indifferent to his responsibilities, apart from routinely voting for the Whig Administration.

After several rewrites usually brought on by self-doubt and seven years of work the first volume of The History of the Decline and Fall of the Roman Empire, was published on 17th February 1776.

It was an immediate success. Within a year it had gone through three editions and the royalties were very handsome indeed.

Further volumes followed quickly and with the same measure of success; Volumes II and III were published on 1st March 1781, and volume IV was released in June 1784. Volumes V and VI were completed during a second Lausanne sojourn (September 1783 to August 1787) where Gibbon reunited with his friend Deyverdun. By early 1787, he was "straining for the goal" and with great relief the project was finished in June. Gibbon later wrote: "It was on the day, or rather the night, of 27th June 1787, between the hours of eleven and twelve, that I wrote the last lines of the last page in a summer-house in my garden...I will not dissemble the first emotions of joy on the recovery of my freedom, and perhaps the establishment of my fame. But my pride was soon humbled, and a sober melancholy was spread over my mind by the idea that I had taken my everlasting leave of an old and agreeable companion, and that, whatsoever might be the future date of my history, the life of the historian must be short and precarious".

Volumes V, and VI finally reached the press in May 1788, their publication having been delayed since March, so it could coincide with a dinner party on the 8th celebrating Gibbon's 51st birthday.

Praise came from all directions. Leading it were such contemporary luminaries as Adam Smith, Lord Camden, and Horace Walpole. Smith remarked that Gibbon's triumph had positioned him "at the very head of Europe's literary tribe."

In November of that year, he was elected a Fellow of the Royal Society, the main proposer being his good friend Lord Sheffield.

But the high-water mark had been reached and for Gibbon the following years were of sorrow and increasing health problems.

In 1789 he returned to Lausanne only to learn of and be "deeply affected" by the death of Deyverdun, who had willed Gibbon his home, La Grotte. He resided there with little commotion, took in the local society, received a visit from Sheffield in 1791, and "shared the common abhorrence" of the French Revolution.

In a letter to Lord Sheffield on 5th February 1791, Gibbon praised Burke's Reflections on the Revolution in France: "Burke's book is a most admirable medicine against the French disease, which has made too much progress even in this happy country. I admire his eloquence, I approve his politics, I adore his chivalry, and I can even forgive his superstition...The French spread so many lyes about the sentiments of the English nation, that I wish the most considerable men of all parties and descriptions would join in some public act declaring themselves satisfied with, and resolved to support, our present constitution."

In 1793, word came of Lady Sheffield's death; Gibbon immediately left Lausanne and set sail to comfort a grieving but composed Sheffield. But for Gibbon too, time was failing. His health began to fail critically in December, and at the turn of the new year, he was in rapid decline.

Gibbon is believed to have suffered from an extreme case of scrotal swelling, probably a hydrocele testis, a condition in which the scrotum swell with fluid in a compartment overlying either testicle. In an age when close-fitting clothes were fashionable, his condition led to a chronic and disfiguring inflammation that left Gibbon a lonely figure. As his condition worsened, he underwent numerous procedures to alleviate the condition, but with no enduring success. In early January, the last of a series of three operations caused an unremitting peritonitis to set in and spread, from which he died.

Edward Gibbon, the "English giant of the Enlightenment" finally succumbed at 12:45 pm, 16 January 1794 at age 56. He was buried in the Sheffield Mausoleum attached to the north transept of the Church of St Mary and St Andrew, Fletching, East Sussex.

EDWARD GIBBON – A CONCISE BIBLIOGRAPHY

Essai sur l'Étude de la Littérature (1761)
Critical Observations on the Sixth Book of Vergil's 'The Aeneid' (1770)
The History of the Decline and Fall of the Roman Empire (Vol. I, 1776; Vols. II, III, 1781; Vols. IV, V, VI, 1788–1789)
A Vindication of some passages in the fifteenth and sixteenth chapters of the History of the Decline and Fall of the Roman Empire (1779)
Mémoire Justificatif pour servir de Réponse à l'Exposé, etc. de la Cour de France (1779)

Mémoires Littéraires de la Grande-Bretagne. co-author: Georges Deyverdun (2 vols: vol. 1, 1767; vol. 2, 1768)

Miscellaneous Works of Edward Gibbon, Esq., ed. John Lord Sheffield (2 vols., 1796; 5 vols., 1814; 3 vols., 1815) Includes Memoirs of the Life and Writings of Edward Gibbon, Esq.

Autobiographies of Edward Gibbon, ed. John Murray (1896). Edward Gibbon's complete memoirs (six drafts) from the original manuscripts.

The Private Letters of Edward Gibbon, 2 vols., ed. Rowland E. Prothero (1896)

The works of Edward Gibbon (Volume 3, 1906)

Gibbon's Journal to 28 January 1763, ed. D.M. Low (1929)

Le Journal de Gibbon à Lausanne, ed. Georges A. Bonnard (1945)

Miscellanea Gibboniana, eds. G.R. de Beer, L. Junod, G.A. Bonnard (1952)

The Letters of Edward Gibbon, 3 vols., ed. J.E. Norton (1956). vol. 1: 1750–1773; vol. 2: 1774–1784; vol. 3: 1784–1794. cited as 'Norton, Letters'

Gibbon's Journey from Geneva to Rome, ed. G.A. Bonnard (1961) Journal

Edward Gibbon: Memoirs of My Life, ed. G.A. Bonnard (1969; 1966). portions of Edward Gibbon's memoirs arranged chronologically, omitting repetition.

The English Essays of Edward Gibbon, ed. Patricia Craddock (1972)

www.ingramcontent.com/pod-product-compliance
Lightning Source LLC
Chambersburg PA
CBHW051032160426
43193CB00010B/920